T0332627

CONNECTIONISM AND THE PHILOSOPHY OF MIND

STUDIES IN COGNITIVE SYSTEMS

VOLUME 9

The titles published in this series are listed at the end of this volume.

CONNECTIONISM AND THE PHILOSOPHY OF MIND

Edited by

TERENCE HORGAN

and

JOHN TIENSON

Department of Philosophy,
Memphis State University,
Memphis, Tennessee,
U.S.A.

KLUWER ACADEMIC PUBLISHERS

DORDRECHT / BOSTON / LONDON

Library of Congress Cataloging-in-Publication Data

Connectionism and the philosophy of mind / edited by Terence Horgan
and John Tienson.
    p.   cm. -- (Studies in cognitive systems ; v. 9)
    "A third of the papers in this volume originated at the 1987
Spindel Conference ... at Memphis State University"--Pref.
    Includes bibliographical references and index.
    ISBN 0-7923-1482-4 (alk. paper)
    1. Connectionism--Congresses. 2. Philosophy of mind--Congresses.
I. Horgan, Terence. II. Tienson, John. III. Spindel Conference
(6th : 1987 : Memphis State University) IV. Series.
BD418.3.C65 1991
128'.2--dc20   91-36118

ISBN 0-7923-1482-4

Published by Kluwer Academic Publishers,
P.O. Box 17, 3300 AA Dordrecht, The Netherlands.

Kluwer Academic Publishers incorporates
the publishing programmes of
D. Reidel, Martinus Nijhoff, Dr W. Junk and MTP Press.

Sold and distributed in the U.S.A. and Canada
by Kluwer Academic Publishers,
101 Philip Drive, Norwell, MA 02061, U.S.A.

In all other countries, sold and distributed
by Kluwer Academic Publishers Group,
P.O. Box 322, 3300 AH Dordrecht, The Netherlands.

Printed on acid-free paper

Printed in the Netherlands

To
Murray Spindel

TABLE OF CONTENTS

SERIES PREFACE

This series will include monographs and collections of studies devoted to the investigation and exploration of knowledge, information and data-processing systems of all kinds, no matter whether human, (other) animal, or machine. Its scope is intended to span the full range of interests from classical problems in the philosophy of mind and philosophical psychology through issues in cognitive psychology and sociobiology (concerning the mental capabilities of other species) to ideas related to artificial intelligence and to computer science. While primary emphasis will be placed upon theoretical, conceptual and epistemological aspects of these problems and domains, empirical, experimental and methodological studies will also appear from time to time.

One of the most, if not *the* most, exciting developments within cognitive science has been the emergence of connectionism as an alternative to the computational conception of the mind that tends to dominate the discipline. In this volume, John Tienson and Terence Horgan have brought together a fine collection of stimulating studies on connectionism and its significance. As the Introduction explains, the most pressing questions concern whether or not connectionism *can* provide a new conception of the nature of mentality. By focusing on the similarities and differences between connectionism and other approaches to cognitive science, the chapters of this book supply valuable resources that advance our understanding of these difficult issues.

J.H.F.

PREFACE

A third of the papers in this volume originated at the 1987 Spindel Conference on "Connectionism and the Philosophy of Mind," at Memphis State University, and are reprinted (in some cases with revisions) from *The Southern Journal of Philosophy* 26 (1988), Spindel Conference Supplement. Several others take up issues raised at that conference and represented in its papers, some in direct response to particular papers. This conference was, we believe, the first philosophical conference on the topic of connectionism.

The Spindel Conference in Philosophy, held annually at Memphis State University, owes its existence to the generous financial support of Mr. Murray Spindel, who is a Memphis businessman, a student of philosophy, and a good friend of Memphis State's Philosophy Department. Each fall The Spindel Conference brings several top philosophers to Memphis State University to discuss a specific philosophical topic or issue. The proceedings are published as a supplementary volume of the *Southern Journal of Philosophy.*

We are grateful to Murray for his long time support, personal as well as financial, of philosophy and the Memphis State University Philosophy Department, and in particular for making possible the annual Spindel Conference, which has become one of the most popular of philosophical conferences. We also thank Murray and Chris Spindel for the gracious manner in which they have hosted the Spindel Conferences, and for making each of them a truly memorable and enjoyable event.

Connectionism has rapidly become a major movement within cognitive science, and philosophers are naturally very interested in its potential implications for philosophical questions about mentality. The original Spindel Conference papers were among the first by philosophers on the subject; they collectively articulate many of the main themes that dominate current philosophical discussion, and they also continue to represent important positions within, and contributions to, that discussion. In the meantime, further philosophical writings on connectionism have appeared, and a second generation of connectionist models has emerged. Some of the other papers in this volume carry on the philosophical discussion in light of these further developments.

Connectionist thinking has taken mental representations for granted from the beginning. So a central issue for philosophers has been the nature of representations, in connectionism and in human cognition. The papers in Sections 2, 4, and 5 represent the spectrum of current thinking on these issues. The papers in Sections 3 and 6 raise important issues that have barely even been broached elsewhere--the relationship between connectionism and classical experimental psychology, and the implications of connectionism concerning traditional philosophical problems, respectively.

We are grateful to all the participants in the conference for making the event both enjoyable and productive--in particular, those who served as commentators: Hubert Dreyfus, Mary Frances Egan, Stan Franklin, Max Garzon, Debra Long, Robert Matthews, and (the world's second strongest philosopher) Brian McLaughlin.

This volume was delivered in camera ready form to Kluwer Academic Publishers. Preparing the manuscript involved an enormous amount of effort at the Memphis State Philosophy Department. We thank Lisa Andrews, the Department's Administrative Secretary, for her active and cheerful participation in all stages of the project, and for maintaining a user-friendly environment in the Department office; Leigh Tanner, the Editorial Assistant for *The Southern Journal of Philosophy*, for her efficient work on the original Spindel Conference Supplement and for her continuing help in preparing this volume; Shari Williams, former Department Secretary, for the many hours she spent during the early stages of manuscript preparation; our colleague Denny Bradshaw, for all his time and effort in dealing with those occasionally recalcitrant physical objects, microcomputers; and our colleague John Ellis, for his own knowledgeable help with these mysterious devices. Special thanks go to Renee Arehart, Department Secretary, for the enormous amount of work she did, cheerfully and efficiently, in overseeing the later stages of manuscript preparation. All these people took charge of the day-to-day aspects of this large project, leaving us free of the headaches.

We gratefully acknowledge *The Southern Journal of Philosophy* for permission to reprint the papers that originally appeared in the Supplement to Volume 26 (those by William Bechtel; Robert Cummins and Georg Schwarz; George Graham; Terence Horgan and John Tienson; David Kirsh; Paul Smolensky; and Michael Tye); *Cognition* for permission to reprint, from Volume 35 (1990), the paper by Jerry Fodor and Brian McLaughlin; and Memphis State University for granting each of us a Developmental Leave during the period of this volume's preparation.

T.E.H. and J.L.T.

JOHN TIENSON

INTRODUCTION

Connectionism is an important new approach in the interdisciplinary field known as cognitive science, involving computer science, cognitive psychology, philosophy, linguistics, and related fields. Connectionism suggests the possibility of an alternative to the conception of mind on the model of the modern digital computer--the so-called computer metaphor--which has dominated thinking about the mind, both popular and philosophical, since the advent of artificial intelligence in the 1950's.

The most salient fact about computers is that they solve problems by virtue of being programmed with rules that refer to the problem domain. What the computer metaphor tells us, then, is that cognition is what the classical computer does, rule governed symbol manipulation. Since this is held to apply to all cognition, it involves the claim that the human mind can in principle be perfectly imitated (indeed, duplicated) by a computer program, with data structures corresponding to mental states like beliefs and desires. This picture of mind--as computer--has dominated theory and methodology in artificial intelligence and cognitive science for over a quarter century, and has deservedly been called the *classical* view in cognitive science.

By the mid-1980's, it was clear that there was a new kid on the block--connectionism. The advance sell-out of the expensive, two volume, "bible of connectionism", *Parallel Distributed Processing* (Rumelhart and McClelland 1986), attests to the rapid rise of connectionism. (Cf. Dyer, this volume, p. 383.)

Two things were clear about connectionism from the outset.[1] First, it was is a vastly different way of *doing things*. One does not write a program for a connectionist system in the familiar sense. One typically provides a training regimen from which it *learns* to solve problems. As a result, a different set of problems drew attention, with emphasis on different features of the problems. Furthermore, the mathematics was different. Connectionist mathematics is the mathematics of dynamical systems; its equations look like the equations in a physics text book. The mathematics of the classical

1

picture is discrete mathematics. Its formulae look comfortingly (to the philosopher) like the formulae of formal logic.

Second, it was, as a result, clear that connectionism was quite a different way of *thinking about* particular cognitive processes and abilities, like perceptual recognition or language learning. Furthermore, connectionism was thought of--and frequently explicitly touted as--an alternative *conception* of cognition.

Now, connectionism does offer new metaphors that feel right for certain aspects of cognition. Learning is "getting your weights changed." Deciding among alternatives is "settling", and perhaps even more appropriate, not having come to a decision is "your network not having settled yet."

Nevertheless, nothing has emerged as what could be called *a*, let alone *the*, connectionist conception of cognition. Classical cognitive science says that cognition is rule governed symbol manipulation. Connectionism has nothing as yet to offer in place of this slogan. Connectionism says that thinking is activity in a neural network--taking the human brain to be such a network. But surely not all activity in any neural network would count as mental in any sense. A network could be too small to do anything remotely resembling human cognition; a large network could have activity so uninteresting as to count at best as brain dead.

A connectionist conception of cognition would have to tell us what kind of network activity constitutes mental activity, and why. So far connectionism has not told us how to answer such questions.[2] Thus, it is unclear whether connectionism *can* provide a new conception of the nature of mind and mental activity, and if it can, what that conception would be. In part for this reason, perhaps, connectionism has attracted philosophical fans of such diverse philosophical persuasions as Paul and Patricia Churchland on one hand, and Stuart and Hubert Dreyfus on another.

Most philosophical discussion concerning connectionism to date has been concerned in one way or another with the question of whether it can replace, in whole or in part, the classical, computational conception of mind. This has involved foundational questions such as: What are, or what should be, connectionism's fundamental assumptions about the nature of mind, about the nature and structure of mental states, and about the character of mental processes? How would such assumptions differ from those of classical cognitive science? How plausible is it to give up classicism's fundamental assumptions, given the lack of success, in the history of psychology, of earlier approaches like behaviorism and associationism to which connectionism is frequently compared? Most of the papers in this volume deal with one or more aspects of these complex and multifaceted questions.

There is a deep reason for this philosophical interest in connectionism, beyond the intrinsic philosophic interest of such foundational questions. It is potentially relevant to the traditional philosophical question of the relationship between mind and body. As it appears today, the problem (for non-eliminativists, at least) is one of finding a place for the mental in the natural world, of understanding ourselves as *at once* part of the natural order studied by physics, chemistry and biology, and at the same time as intelligent agents subject to explanation and understanding in the fashion of the humanities, the social sciences, and scientific and "folk" psychology.

The computer metaphor held sway for so long in part because it seemed to be the only way to understand *how* minds could be physically embodied. Just as the events and processes in a computer can be correctly described and explained both at the level of electronic circuitry and at the level of executing a program, so, it was thought, could the events and processes in human heads be correctly described and explained in directly analogous ways. That is, the human mind could be construed as nature's program, running on neural circuitry.

Connectionism appears to offer the possibility of a dramatically different conception of how a brain could be or could embody a mind, and a comparably different account of the nature of human thinking and mentalistic explanations of human behavior. And this, in turn, could have implications for a wide variety of philosophical problems. Connectionism looks and feels different from the computer model of the mind. It looks and feels as though it should suggest alternative answers to traditional philosophical questions, not only concerning the mind per se, but also concerning such related issues as the nature of belief, knowledge, memory, understanding, explanation, perception, recognition, valuation, and consciousness. The papers in the final section of this volume begin to explore such possibilities.

Discussion of connectionism has quite naturally been shaped by the historical context in which it grew to prominence. What we have called classical cognitive science has dominated artificial intelligence and cognitive science since their beginnings as fields of research in the 1950's. Central to classical cognitive science as a research program is the idea that to make a cognizer one writes a program in terms of the problems the cognizer is to deal with, and runs that program on appropriate hardware. The assumed extension to natural cognizers is, of course, that they--we--run evolved and acquired programs on evolved hard/wetware.

A program is a explicit set of instructions for manipulating symbol strings in terms of the syntactic structure of those strings. Thus, on the classical view, an essential feature of any cognizer is its possession of syntactically structured symbols--usually referred to as "representations" in connectionist debates--the structures of which play an essential causal role in the determination of cognitive processes. When a system has syntactic structures that play such a role, we will say it has *effective* syntax. It is also part of the classical picture that the causal processes syntactically structured representations undergo are governed by precise, exceptionless rules of a sort that could constitute a program.[3]

The rise to prominence of connectionism coincides historically with an increasing perception of problems within classical cognitive science. Certain problems had essentially resisted solution for over a decade. Indeed, Horgan and Tienson (this volume) explicitly characterize the situation as a Kuhnian crisis in (classical) cognitive science, and many others have used similar language. The rise of connectionism in the mid-1980's should be seen in the light of this crisis situation. Quite simply, work in connectionism was often motivated by a desire to work on something that would yield results. Self conscious justification of this work pointed to the problems in classical cognitive science[4] and claimed a likely superiority of connectionism with respect to just those problems.[5]

Thus, evaluation of the prospects for connectionism has naturally involved comparing it with the classical paradigm. Representations in classical systems have syntactic structure automatically, by the very nature of the system. Connectionist networks, in contrast, do not require syntactically structured representations. Given the importance of syntactic structure in the classical paradigm, it was inevitable that the discussion of the merits of connectionism would focus on syntactic structure.

Practicing connectionists have characterized their systems in terms of representations from the start. But in early connectionist systems, a "representation" consisted of a node or group of nodes properly activated. With a very few possible exceptions, syntactic structure was not a feature of these systems. Their representations were analogous to general terms or to proper names, not to sentences, or even to complex noun or verb phrases. And to produce anything that can be interpreted as syntactically structured representations in a network requires some rather fancy construction and mathematics.

So two questions naturally arise: Must cognitive systems have syntactic structure? Can representations in connectionist systems have syntactic structure? For better or worse, the form of this debate has been set by Fodor and Pylyshyn's (1988) widely discussed essay, "Connectionism and Cognitive Architecture: A Critical Analysis." They argued,

(1)   Cognitive systems must have syntactic structure.

Thus, (2)   Either (a) a connectionist system does not have syntactically structured representations--in which case it is *too weak* to be an adequate model of cognition; or else (b) it is merely an unusual *implementation* of a classical system, in which case, it could not be the basis of a *new* conception of cognition.

That is, connectionism can give us either--as Fodor and Pylyshyn put it--(a) mere associationism, or (b) mere implementation. In either case, it cannot give us a viable new approach to cognition.

Fodor and Pylyshyn's most prominent argument for (1) is an argument they call the systematicity argument. Thought is systematic. You don't find creatures capable of believing that John loves Mary but not capable of believing Mary loves John. You don't find creatures capable of perceiving that the triangle is above the square, but not capable of perceiving that the square is above the triangle; nor of perceiving blue circles and red squares, but not red circles. Inference capacity is similarly systematic.

Language capacities are systematic, and that's because sentences have constituent structure. But cognitive capacities are systematic, too, and that must be because *thoughts* have constituent structure. (Fodor 1987, p. 151)

The papers in Section IV all deal in large part with the question of whether--or to what extent, or in what sense--cognitive systems must have syntactically structured representations, that is, with whether (1) is true.

Many articles in the connectionist literature purport to offer replies to Fodor and Pylyshyn. Virtually all of them, however, attempt only to show that connectionist systems are capable of supporting syntactically structured representations. That is, they deny the first disjunct of Fodor and Pylyshyn's conclusion without attempting to show that the second disjunct does not follow. There are, we agree, passages where Fodor and Pylyshyn can be construed as having simply denied the possibility of syntactic structure in connectionist networks. However, it seems clear that (2) should be taken as their official position, and hence that demonstrating connectionist syntactic structure would not in itself refute their claim.

The point of Fodor and Pylyshyn's arguments is foundational, not technical. It is that connectionism *cannot* give us a new conception of cognition because it cannot get syntactic structure right. Either it doesn't provide for syntactic structure, in which case it is too weak to be a viable conception of cognition, or it does provide for syntactic structure, in which case it offers nothing new. Several of the papers in Sections IV and V attempt to go between the horns of this dilemma. To evaluate these attempts, it is important to be clear about the nature of Fodor and Pylyshyn's challenge to connectionism.

Whether they ultimately prove to be right or not, Fodor and Pylyshyn have posed an interesting and useful challenge to anyone who contends that connectionism does or can offer a new conception of cognition. It will help to set the stage for discussion of the articles in this volume if we elaborate in light of that challenge our claim that connectionism so far *has not* offered anything new in the way of a conception of cognition.

This much seems clear. Insofar as connectionist systems engage in rule governed manipulation of syntactically structured symbols, these systems do not serve as a basis for an alternative conception of cognition. Hence the importance of the second horn of the Fodor and Pylyshyn dilemma: the threat of "mere implementation".

One thing often said in favor of connectionism is that connectionist networks are more brain-like than conventional computers. Nodes are (somewhat) like neurons, and a structure consisting of many interconnected simple processors is more like the structure of the brain than is that of a conventional computer. This could be important even if connectionism cannot give us a new picture of cognition. If classical systems can be implemented in connectionist architecture, such implementations might help show how *classical* systems could be realized in brains.

But if one is looking for a new conception of cognition, rather than merely for a new way of implementing the classical conception, it's not clear that these brain-like features matter. When a classical computer is engaged in rule governed symbol manipulation (say, running a LISP program), it does so by performing mathematical computations that are causally but not conceptually related to its data processing. And it does this number crunching by transmitting electrical impulses. But these "lower level" descriptions are not relevant to the cognitive level description of what is going on in the system. These particular numerical computations and electrical impulses constitute an implementation of the program--one possible implementation among many. For the same reason, if the brain-like features of connectionism--the individual nodes and their interactions--are far enough removed from the cognitive level, they might not figure in a cognitive level account of mental processing at all.

In some simple connectionist models, single nodes and single inter-node connection strengths are assigned their own representational contents. These tinker-toy models thereby avoid the "mere implementation" charge, but they are too simple to provide a serious model of cognition. It seems likely that connectionist systems that deserve to be taken seriously as psychological models will have representations that are fully and broadly distributed over many nodes, especially if cognitive systems must have effective syntax. No single node will represent anything by itself, just as there is no grandmother neuron or yellow Volkswagen neuron. But if all representations are distributed, then the nodes and their interaction are no more part of the cognitive level story than is the circuit diagram of a VAX part of the classical story about cognition. At least, so it would seem. It thus becomes very difficult to find anything in the connectionist literature that would count as an articulated connectionist conception of cognition.[6] And, to the extent that connectionism aspires to provide a new and different general conception of cognition, the mere implementation charge is very serious indeed.

Connectionism says that cognition is activity in a neural network. But we still lack a characterization of what kind of neural network activity counts as cognitive. For all we now know, it may turn out that only neural network activity that implements a classical system counts as cognition. And then connectionism will have given us nothing new as a story about what cognition is.

We turn now to a brief description of the several papers in this volume, and the most salient relationships among them. The grouping of the papers is somewhat arbitrary. The issues discussed here are deeply intertwined, and every paper discusses the main topic of more than one section. We have tried to group each paper on the basis of its main focus.

JOHN TIENSON

I. OVERVIEW

William Bechtel's paper, "Connectionism and the Philosophy of Mind: An Overview", was the keynote talk at the Spindel Conference on connectionism which was the origin of several of the papers in the present volume. That conference, in October, 1987, was the first philosophical conference devoted to connectionism. Bechtel's aim was to provide an introduction to some of the most prominent philosophical issues generated by connectionism. He poses a dozen questions concerning several issues, clarifying the issues by indicating the various possible answers that seem open at this point, considering how further research and argument might help adjudicate among the possibilities, and occasionally by expressing his own preference for certain answers. The issues:

1. Are there principles of design and interpretation--over and above the interaction of individual nodes--by which we can explain and understand the behavior of connectionist systems?

2. How should we characterize the differences--in representations, rules, process, etc.--between connectionist and classical systems?

3. By what criteria should we evaluate connectionist systems vis a vis classical systems?

4. Connectionist systems appear to have a clear advantage over classical systems with respect to pattern recognition; how important is pattern recognition in human cognition?

5. Is reconciliation possible? Can connectionist and classical systems be integrated to get the advantages of both, or can connectionist systems implement classical systems in ways that illuminate cognition?

6. (Since connectionist systems are said to be "*more* brain-like" than classical systems, but obviously differ from the brain in many important respects) how is connectionism related to neuro-science?

7. How is connectionism related to folk psychology?

II. CONNECTIONISM VS. CLASSICAL COGNITIVE SCIENCE: SORTING THE ISSUES

The papers in this section are concerned with the comparison of connectionism with classical cognitive science. The papers by Cummins and

Schwarz, by Hatfield, and by Rueckl each deal primarily with a specific issue: computation, rules, and levels of explanation respectively. James Garson, on the other hand, makes more global comparisons. He asks what would have to be the case (logically) for connectionism to be in a position to supplant classical cognitive science, and what are the prospects for that to occur?

Classical cognitive science is frequently characterized as computationalist. Cummins and Schwarz ask how connectionism is related to computationalism. They begin by carefully characterizing computationalism and distinguishing it from a number of theses with which it is often associated, but which are not essential to it. In summary, computationalism is the hypothesis that systems are cognitive in virtue of executing algorithms that manipulate representations of the arguments and values of cognitive functions.

Cummins and Schwarz point out that most, if not all, connectionist work so far is computationalist both in spirit and in practice. However, connectionism is not essentially computationalist, as classical cognitive science is. For connectionist research need not assume that cognitive functions are computable (i.e., recursive), because one does not need to specify an algorithm in constructing a connectionist system. What a connectionist system requires is dynamics that cause representational states to mirror the problem domain. Connectionist representational states can be states in a dynamical system whose characteristic function--defined by its dynamical equations--is not itself computable. "A network whose representational states are real-valued activation vectors and weight matrices, and whose dynamics is given by a set of differential equations, is in general, going to be just such a system" (p. 69f).

Now, Cummins and Schwarz argue, computationalism is not plausible for much of cognition, and this would seem to give a potential advantage to connectionism. For computationalism is only correct where human performance is rule describable, i.e., recursively specifiable. But it is plausible, they argue, that human performance is recursively specifiable only when the domain cognized is itself characterizable by computable functions. If the domain is not recursively characterizable, our cognizing of the domain will not be either.

It may be the case that domains that admit of a special science, e.g, thermodynamics, are recursively characterizable. But this hardly seems likely for clothing, for example. Human beings know a great deal about clothing: how to dress; what to iron, etc. But it does not form an autonomous domain of inquiry. There are many sciences that say something about clothing, but there is no science of clothing. There are no *laws* of clothing, and hence, no laws of human cognizing concerning clothing. Cummins and Schwarz speculate that this knowledge cannot be compiled into an expert system that captures human intelligence. And most areas of human knowledge seem more like clothing than thermodynamics. That is, we know a great deal about the domain, but it is not characterized by a computable function, and therefore, our cognizing of the domain cannot be either. "Perhaps human expert performance in such domains can't be rule driven because it isn't rule describable--i.e., not recursively specifiable" (p. 70).

Connectionism has been advanced as an alternative to classical cognitive science. It has also been said that connectionist explanation and analysis is at a different level than that of classical cognitive science, because connectionist systems are more "brain-like." Often both are said by the same author.[7] But prima facie, connectionism cannot be *both* an alternative explanation and an explanation at a different level.

In "Connectionism and the Notion of Levels," Jay Rueckl clarifies these matters by distinguishing levels of explanation from levels of analysis. At different levels of *explanation* the same (part of a) process is explained from different perspectives. Different levels of *analysis* focus on different sized portions of a process, from the process as a whole to its smallest steps.

Rueckl adopts David Marr's (1982) conception of three levels of psychological explanation. The *computational level* specifies what the process is, characterizing it as a mapping from one kind of information to another. The *algorithmic level* specifies the representations used to encode input information and output information, and the algorithm used to map inputs to outputs. The *implementation level* makes clear how the representations and algorithm specified at the algorithic level are instantiated in the states and processes of the underlying device.

It is natural to think of the implementation level as concerned with the physical realization of the computational process. But, as Rueckl explains, this is too simplistic. Typically, the algorithmic level will divide a process into a number of steps. And each of these steps will be susceptible to explanation at the computational, algorithmic, and implementation levels. In decently complex systems, implementation at the highest levels of analysis will describe how the computation of the algorithm is accomplished, but only in terms of the states and processes of a *virtual* machine specified in a lower but not lowest level language. At a more fine-grained level of analysis, the algorithmic level explanation will divide that step into further steps, again each susceptible of each level of explanation. Only after several such analytic steps will the physical level be reached.

Armed with the twin notions of levels of explanation and levels of analysis, Rueckl examines the structure of several connectionist models. He concludes that at the present time it is reasonable to suppose that in some domains connectionist models are best seen as explanations of how symbolic models are implemented,[8] while in other cognitive domains connectionist models are best seen as competitors that propose alternative (algorithmic level) explanations of how a cognitive task is accomplished.

Philosophers often distinguish between a system's following rules and a system merely being rule describable. The behavior of the planets is describable by physical laws. But the planets do not *follow* those laws. A cook who consults a recipe and does what it says follows those rules.

In "Representation and Rule-Instantiation in Connectionist Systems," Gary Hatfield argues that connectionist systems do not fall into either category. They do not follow rules, for no part of the system reads and interprets rules--as the CPU does in a conventional computer. Hence connectionist representations are not *symbols* in one important sense of that term, viz., in the sense in which a symbol must be a symbol *for* something--e.g., a person or CPU--that "reads" and "interprets" it.[9]

But connectionist systems are not merely rule describable, either. In Hatfield's terminology, they "instantiate" rules. A network can be configured--designed, engineered--to compute one function rather than another. Hatfield says, "It is the function computed by the configured network that I term the rule *instantiated* by the network" (p. 98). (Natural systems act in this respect *as if* they had been engineered, and so can also be said to instantiate rules. Cf. Kosslyn and Hatfield, p. 1040.)

What connectionism rejects in the symbolist paradigm is that symbol manipulation and symbolic programming can be taken as primitives from which cognitive models are to be constructed. The primitives from which connectionist models are constructed are nodes, activation levels, connections, rules of activation and learning, etc. If symbolic representations are admitted in connectionism, they are taken as something to be explained, not something to be taken as primitive. Thus, connectionism does not deny the possibility of symbolic representation, but it does not equate representations with symbols, and hence opens up the possibility that some cognitive operations are symbolic and others are not.

The rules instantiated in connectionist models may be cognitive--as in models of language processing or statistical inference--or pre- or sub-cognitive--as in models of early vision. Thus, some but not all psychological processes will be treated as inferential.

This raises a question of how the psychological is to be distinguished from physiology, since we can no longer equate psychological with inferential (as, e.g., Fodor and Pylyshyn (1981) do), and, Hatfield points out, a functionalist story will not do to delimit the psychological because many non-psychological physiological systems are functional systems. The answer, Hatfield suggests, is that psychology aims at explaining (cognitive) systems and capacities (not individual actions, as so many recent philosophical discussions would have it).

Connectionism has been put forward as an alternative to the classical paradigm in cognitive science/artificial intelligence. If it is regarded as literally an *alternative*, then to be succesful it must replace (i.e., eliminate) the old paradigm, and not merely implement classical systems. Some "wild" connectionists and fans of connectionism have claimed that it will do this. In "What Connectionism Cannot Do: The Threat to Clasical AI," James Garson attempts first to analyse the logic of this claim, and then to evaluate it.

To eliminate the classical paradigm, there would have to be a class of connectionist models that are at once *strong*--strong enough to model the mind--and also *weak*--too weak to implement classical systems. Garson interprets the latter to mean that there must be something these connectionist models can't do that they would have to do if they were to implement classical models.

First he argues that the relevant class of model will certainly involve distributed representations and recurrent processing.[10] Using the terms 'PDP model' for models that meet these conditions, Garson considers the following argument schema:

PDP models of the mind CAN'T X.

PDP models that reduce Classical AI (CAI) models of the mind MUST X.

Therefore, if PDP models are CORRECT, then CAI is eliminated.

He then considers many properties characteristic of classical systems that might serve as X in such an argument. Most are properties like constituency or causal role of representations that have been brought up in anti-connectionist arguments of the following form. Cognitive systems must X (thus, in effect, assuming the correctness of the classical paradigm). Connectionist systems can't X. Therefore,....

Though the details differ from case to case, the gist of Garson's argument in each case is that after all, there are PDP models capable of doing X, but that it is really *not* essential that they do X to reduce classical models. Thus, there is not the kind of incompatibility between connectionism and classical cognitive science that wild connectionists--and wild classicists--have claimed.

III. CONNECTIONISM AND SIMPLE LEARNING

Connectionism is often characterized as a form of associationism, presumably with the implication that it is something like a hi-tech cousin of behaviorism, suffering from the same basic limitations. Thinking of connectionism as a form a associationism is perhaps understandable, since simple causal links (associations) between nodes are the basis of connectionist processing. However, given the possibility of a huge gap between the node-level and the representational-level description of processing in a complex network, it is not at all clear at present that all connectionist systems must count as associationist at the cognitive level, nor that it is any more appropriate to call connectionism associationist than it would be to call classicism number crunching.

But connectionist architecture seems to be a natural architecture for associative processing. Surely, then, it should be able to give good accounts of simple learning--the bread and butter of behaviorism. And if it cannot even do this, it is not likely to be able to do much else well either.

In "Connectionism in Pavlovian Harness," George Graham argues that connectionism can provide a deeper understanding of simple learning--and in particular, Pavlovian conditioning--than either Behaviorism or Discrepency Theory, which is generally interpreted as giving a representational account of learning. Behaviorism, as Graham puts it, "derepresentationalizes" all learning, i.e., understands it not to involve semantic--rule governed, inferential--relations between representations and behavior. Graham interprets connectionism as doing the same for simple learning. On such a story, association or statistical correlation--not animal inference--accounts for simple learning.

Graham holds that the applicability of rules is what makes the processes the state undergoes semantic, inferential processes, rather than *merely* causal processes. Without the rules, a state would be at most a mere indicator of some external state of affairs, not a genuine representation, and would undergo at most internal causal--non-semantic, non-inferential--processes. And, he holds, such indicators are all that is required for simple learning.

Graham argues that connectionism can provide non-representational models that will account for the phenomena of Pavlovian conditioning, and given that it can, that such models should be preferred to models that incorporate representations and rules for several reasons: (i) fewer theoretical and methodological commitments, (ii) not viewing simple animals such as flatworms "in terms more befitting complex creatures," and (iii) preserving a tie between Pavlovian conditioning and non-associative learning (habituation and sensitization).

In "Connectionism and Conditioning", J. Chrisopher Maloney questions the claim that connectionism *can* account for the phenomena of simple learning. In particular, he argues that connectionist systems will not give the right results concerning the phenomena of extinction (p. 174f) and blocking (p. 177ff), at least not without ad hoc and implausible assumptions. He shows that this holds for Sutton and Barto's connectionist model that is intended to account for these phenomena, and he argues that several natural suggestions, including Graham's, for modeling these phenomena connectionistically will not work. This does not prove that it cannot be done, but it does, as Maloney says in his first paragraph, constitute a significant and interesting challenge to connectionism.

An advantage claimed for connectionism is that its systems are interestingly brain-like. All brains learn. Simple brains do only simple learning. But all brains do some simple learning. If connectionist systems are indeed interestingly brain-like, then some connectionist systems ought to be able to duplicate the phenomena of simple learning in a natural way. Hence, Graham's hints and Maloney's challenges point to a very natural connectionist research project.

IV. DOES COGNITION REQUIRE SYNTACTICALLY STRUCTURED REPRESENTATIONS?

Fodor and Pylyshyn's dilemma for connectionism raised two questions: Does cognition require syntactically structured representations? They say, yes. Can connectionism deliver syntactically structured representations? They say, no. The papers in this section are addressed to the first question, those in the following section, to the second.

Andy Clark argues that syntactic structure is *not* a requirement of cognitive systems. Clark's main and most distinctive point is his response to Fodor and Pylyshyn's systematicity argument. (He also argues that their more specific criticisms of connectionism are premature and based on a limited view of the possibilities within connectionism.) Thought *ascription*, he points out, is a holistic matter. You cannot correctly ascribe a particular thought to a creature unless you can ascribe a whole host of other, related thoughts. This is an *a priori*, conceptual constraint on thought ascription, not an empirical finding as Fodor and Pylyshyn suppose. This *a priori* constraint explains the finding of systematicity. Thus, we do not need an empirical explanation of the systematicity of thought.

Now, of course, the creature to which we holistically ascribe mental states must exhibit behavior that (holistically) warrants that ascription. But, Clark argues, what is in need of empirical explanation is this *behavior*. "But here there is no obvious pressure for a system of internal representations which *themselves* have conceptual level systematicity" (p. 204). There is a systematicity about the behavior that grounds thought ascription, and this systematicity suggests recurrent and recombinable elements. But there is no reason, Clark maintains, to suppose that these elements have conceptual level semantics, or that this in-the-head structure lines up neatly with the structure of sentences used in ascribing thoughts. Discovering this in-the-head structure is a cognitive engineering project that should be unconstrained by conceptual level semantics.

Thus, Clark supports a kind of realism about thought ascription. Thought ascribing sentences can be *true*. But they are made true holistically, not by internal states that correspond to individual sentences.

Georges Rey, on the other hand, argues for a language of thought, and indeed, for one that does line up with ordinary ascription of the attitudes. He puts forward eight kinds of phenomena (p. 230) that a cognitive theory should be able to explain, and argues that a classical, language of thought view can explain them but that they cannot be explained, or cannot be explained as well, by a connectionism--"radical" connectionism--which seeks to replace classical language of thought cognitive science, rather than supplementing or implementing it.

Rey characterizes Language of Thought theory as positing a formally specifiable language with computational relations definable over its sentences. His arguments are for constituent structure, and hence implicitly assume that connectionism will lack constituent structure.

Systematicity and productivity make up but one of Rey's eight kinds of phenomena to be explained. Thus, he does not argue this point in as much detail as Fodor and Pylyshyn, but brings many more kinds of phenomena into the picture.

Notable among them is irrational relations and errors among the attitudes. Certain mistakes to which human beings are prone are only possible for a creature with syntactically structured internal states--affirming the consequent, denying the antecedent, mistaken scope of operators, gambler's fallacy, etc. These are *formal* fallacies. In order to make sense of the fact that human beings are prone to commit the formal fallacy of, for example, affirming the consequent, we must suppose that they have propositional attitudes that *have* consequents.

All of the things Rey lists as needing explanation are characterized in common sense intentional terms. But some connectionists are eliminativists about the mental. A connectionist with eliminativist leanings might object that this list begs the question. Rey responds that non-question-begging behavioral evidence can be given for each of them by exploiting the resources of standardized tests like the SAT and GRE.

The classical view is a package deal: syntactically structured representations and rules--i.e., exceptionless, programmable rules--defined over those representations. Many authors treat the two parts of this package as inextricably bound together. The choice Rey poses, for example, is no syntax or else syntax *with programmable rules*.

There are many reasons why one might see syntactic structure as implying rules. One is simply seeing this as a package because this is the way it has been. But one might also hold, as Graham does, that rules are a necessary condition for representations. Or one might believe that syntax does not matter unless it plays a causal role in mental processes, and believe that it could not play such a causal role unless there were exceptionless rules governing those processes. Fodor and Pylyshyn (1988) argue, for example, "...if you need structure in mental representations anyway to account for the productivity and systematicity of minds, why not postulate processes that are structure sensitive to account for the coherence of mental processes? Why not be a Classicist, in short?" (p. 67)

Horgan and Tienson reject this packaging together of syntax and rules. They argue that if connectionism is to *succeed* as a new paradigm, it will have to incorporate syntactically structured representations that play a causal role in mental processes. But, they argue, it does not follow that these processes must be rule describable at the cognitive level. And if connectionism is to develop into a genuinely *new* paradigm--Garson's wild connectionism, Rey's radical connectionism--then these mental processes must *not*, in general, be rule governed or even rule describable.

They argue, first, that cognitive systems that get on in the world must have syntactically structured representational states. They must track enduring individuals in their environment, and predicate changing properties and relations to various of those individuals. And for complex, real live cognitive systems like higher animals, basketball players, and ordinary humans, they must do this on a vast scale that is only possible if complex representations are constructed as a function of simpler representations. And of course, if these representations are to help the creature get on in the world, their syntactic and semantic structure must play a role in the etiology of behavior and future states. (It does not follow from this argument that syntax must be Classical in the sense of Fodor and McLaughlin, this volume. Whether effective syntax must be Classical syntax is an open and disputed question at present. Cf. Section VI, below.)

But, second, Horgan and Tienson argue, for connectionism to become a new paradigm, it must not in general allow representations to interact in ways that are describable by exceptionless--hence programmable--rules. For if its processes were so describable, it would not constitute a genuine alternative story at the cognitive level. It would merely be a novel implementation of classical processes.

They suggest that this might be the way it really is with natural--human and higher animal--cognition. And they show that it is natural for connectionism systems--but impossible for classical systems--to have cognitive level processes that are not governed by exceptionless rules, at least with unstructured representations. Whether it is also possible with syntactically structured representations is an open question.

If Horgan and Tienson's argument for syntactically structured representations is correct, what it shows is that a cognizer must have a vast number of potential, sytematically related, syntactically structured representations. But it does not by any means follow that all the cognitive states of such a cognizer must be syntactically structured. Syntactically structured states must be function of simpler states. It is consistent with the tracking argument that there also be syntactically *un*structured representational states involving only an elementary representation. As presented, the tracking argument also suggests that there are broadly imagistic representational states, structured but not syntactically structured in any ordinary sense. (Cf. Tye, this volume.)

David Kirsh's "Putting a Price on Cognition" raises the question: *how much* of cognition involves syntactic structure? Kirsh discusses variables, not syntax in general. But variables imply syntax, and the power of syntactic operations classically comes from the power of variables. Without genuine variables, a creature could have only a very rudimentary syntax.

Variables are ubiquitous and essential to the power of classical models. On the classical view, intelligent action involves "hundreds, perhaps thousands of names and variables" (p. 262).

Kirsh's starting point is that variables are very costly to implement in connectionist systems. It takes a very large network to get the power of genuine variables--i.e., variables that (i) are logically distinct from their values (= possible substituends (as in the terminology of computer science)), (ii) are semantically connected to their values in the sense that values can be assigned to variables, and (iii) range over sets with (in general) multiple elements. And as the number of variables involved increases, the network requirements increase accordingly.

Kirsh observes that

One of the more interesting methodological premises of connectionism is that if certain psychological capacities are expensive to implement in connectionist hardware, then they are expensive to implement in neural hardware, and it is reasonable to suppose that we exercise those psychological capacities far less regularly than assumed in standard computational models. (p. 263)

Now, simple connectionist models do not use genuine variables. Complex models can be constructed that do use variables explicitly, but they pay a high price in size and complexity. So, Kirsh says, "If these complex models teach us anything about neural design, it seems to be that nature does not encourage the type of reasoning associated with explicit rules." We cannot, however, conclude that cognition is by and large not rule governed, for it may be that from an evolutionary point of view the one time set-up costs involved in building networks able to manipulate variables were worth the price.

The point is rather that connectionism forces us to reconsider whether there are alternative formulations of cognitive problems that lend themselves to solution without much variable/value pairing. So the possibility is raised that a lot less of cognition involves variable binding (and genuine syntax) than the classical picture would predict. Surely, some cognition involves variable binding. It is an empirical question how much.

Kirsh points out that we do easily use variables that range over large, frequently infinite, sets (p. 273). But it is possible that we can only bind these variables to a small number of values at one time (p. 278f).

V. CAN CONNECTIONISM PROVIDE SYNTACTICALLY STRUCTURED REPRESENTATIONS?

The authors of papers in Part V all agree that syntax--in some sense--is needed for complex cognition. The issue is whether connectionism can deliver what is needed, and that in turn raises the question of exactly what is needed. Debate on this issue has largely been structured by Fodor and Pylyshyn's critique of connectionism, which, as outlined above, poses the dilemma: either no structure sensitive processing or mere implementation.

Here Paul Smolensky argues that distributed connectionist representations, in particular, tensor product representations, let us go between the horns of the Fodor/Pylyshyn dilemma. Michael Tye shows how tensor product representations can iterate, giving us, he argues, a connectionist language of thought. Fodor and Brian McLaughlin reply that tensor products will not support constituent sensitive processing. But Timothy van Gelder suggests that it is a mistake to let the old, classical paradigm set the terms of the debate, in particular to let classical ideas fix our views about what constitutes syntactic structure. And Michael Dyer describes research directed toward developing non-classical, connectionistic, structure sensitive processing.

In "The Constituent Structure of Connectionist Mental States: A Reply to Fodor and Pylyshyn," Smolensky characterizes the dispute in terms of a "paradox of cognition":

On the one hand, cognition is *hard*: characterized by the rules of logic, by the rules of language. On the other hand, cognition is *soft*: if you write down the rules, it seems that realizing those rules in automatic formal systems (which AI programs are) gives systems that are just not sufficiently fluid, not robust enough in performance, to constitute what we want to call true intelligence. (p. 282)

The hard side is classical; it's what Fodor and Pylyshyn emphasize. The soft side is argued in some detail in Horgan and Tienson. Smolensky then considers the possible responses to this "paradox", and advocates taking the soft side as fundamental, with (the appearance of) hardness as an emergent property of sufficiently complex soft systems. "The principal justification is that if we succeed in building symbol manipulation out of 'connectoplasm' then we will have an explanation of *where symbols and symbol manipulation come from....*" And we will have "a way of explaining *why* those aspects of cognition that exhibit hardness should exhibit hardness: why the area of hardness falls where is does..." (p. 286).

Though recognizing how far we are from being able to do such things at the moment, he argues that the Fodor/Pylyshyn dilemma is a false one, because they assume that all connectionist representations are atomic. Distributed connectionist representations can give us constituent structure in two ways. In the first place, they permit us to recognize that ordinary concepts are made of "microfeatures" that are components of the concept, and that such concepts are context sensitive in that they are made up of somewhat different clusters of microfeatures in different contexts.

More important, he argues that there are techniques, such as tensor products, that can provide connectionist, non-classical constituent structure. For present purposes, what is important about tensor product representations is this. In a tensor product representation of a sentence, no spatial or temporal *parts* of the representation correspond to individual words. Tensor products have a mathematical property, physically or structurally realized in the system, which we can express intuitively like this: If you ask the representation what the subject of the sentence is, it will say 'John', and if you ask it what 'John' is in the sentence, it will say, 'the subject.' Smolensky says,

The tensor product technique provides a systematic and disciplined procedure for representing complex, structured objects....it provides a formalization that is natural for connectionist computation of the nonformal notion of constituent structure, and is a likely cadidate to play a role in connectionist cognitive science analogous to that played by constituent structure trees in symbolic cognitive science. (p. 304)

In "Representation in Pictorialism and Connectionism," Michael Tye provides an informal introduction to tensor products, and shows that they do give a genuine notion of constituency that is distinct from mere set-theoretic membership. So, for example, the tensor product representation of 'John loves Mary' is relevantly different from that of 'Mary loves John.' He also points out that tensor product operations can be iterated to yield representations of more and more complex sentences. Thus, he argues, connectionism is compatible with there being a language of thought, in a reasonable sense of 'language' that does not require that constituents be parts.

Tye begins his paper with an elucidation of Stephen Kosslyn's elusive pictorialism--the claim that some representational states are image-like (quasi-pictorial) and not sentence-like. The connection is twofold. Kosslyn's theory appears to be "constructed...with one eye on the physiology of the brain," and "in these respects...is closely allied with connectionism." (p. 315) Second, "Pictorialism really is incompatible with [a strong] language of cognition thesis, that is,...the truth of pictorialism entails the falsity of the view that mental representations are always linguistically based." (p. 316)

Smolensky's paper in this volume is a companion piece to his (Smolensky 1988) contribution to *Meaning and Mind: Fodor and his Critics* (Loewer and Rey, forthcoming). Jerry Fodor and Brian McLaughlin's "Connectionism and the Problem of Systematicity: Why Smolensky's Solution Doesn't Work" is a reply to both of these Smolensky papers.

Fodor and McLaughlin define "Classical constituents" as constituents that are tokened whenever the item of which they are constituents is tokened. Paradigm classical constituents are spatial or temporal *parts* of the items of which they are constituents. Constituent structure as formalized by tensor products is not classical in this sense. Tokening a tensor product representation does not, in general, involve tokening its syntactic constituents. This, Fodor and McLaughlin maintain, renders them incapable of explaining systematicity.

On the one hand, the cognitive architecture he endorses does not provide for representations with Classical constituents; on the other hand, he provides no suggestion as to how mental processes could be structure sensitive unless mental representations have Classical constituents; and, on the third hand (as it were) he provides no suggestion as to how minds could be systematic if mental processes aren't structure sensitive. So his reply to Fodor and Pylyshyn fails. (p. 188)

The intuition is clear: Non-classical constituents cannot be causally efficacious because they are not *there* in the system. Accordingly, Fodor and McLaughlin maintain, a connectionism that incorporated only non-classical constituents would be incapable of yielding genuine structure sensitive processing.[11]

As Fodor and Pylyshyn (1989) is more and more widely discussed, accounts of its central argument tend to get briefer and briefer. Often, now, systematicity is explained only in terms of the representational capacity of a creature: a creature is capable of being in one cognitive state only if it is capable of being in certain other, systematically related states. We might call this *representational* systematicity. Since tensor product representations are functions of their syntactic constituents, tensor products *can* explain representational systematicity. If we can have a tensor product representation with 'John' as "subject" and 'Mary' as "direct object," we can do it the other way around.

But Fodor and Pylyshyn also point to *inferential* systematicity: a creature is capable of making an inference only if it is capable of making certain other, systematically related inferences, in particular, inferences of the same form. It is inferential systematicity that tensor products cannot explain, if Fodor and McLaughlin are correct. But the more direct point seems to be that non-classical "constituents" cannot play a causal role, and hence, cannot provide *effective* syntax.

Fodor and McLaughlin also point out that microfeatures do not give a notion of syntactic constituency and do not seem to be of any help in explaining systematicity. And they point out that context dependence as Smolensky describes it requires something--microfeatures, perhaps--whose semantics are context independent.

Timothy van Gelder chides connectionists for letting classicists like Fodor and Pylyshyn set the terms of the debate. Even though "nobody yet seems altogether sure just what Connectionism *is*", there is talk of Connectionism as a new *paradigm*.

If it is new, it must be different. So, it is thought, it makes sense to consider how it is different. Not only Fodor and Pylyshyn, but friends, foes and merely interested parties have begun by trying to characterize classical cognitive science, aiming to see what connectionism must *not* have in order to be different. And, as we have seen, what comes up most often are the "twin minimal commitments" of classicism: syntactically structured representations and structure sensitive, rule-governed computational processes.

But if one takes Kuhn seriously, van Gelder observes, this should seem wrongheaded. For on Kuhn's view, a new paradigm would mean incommensurability: that the new paradigm cannot be understood in the old terms. "Insofar as we attempt to understand one paradigm in terms provided by another, we inadvertently jeopardize that very understanding" (fn. 5). (We don't characterize classical cognitive science in terms drawn from its predecessor in psychology, behaviorism.)

We should instead look at connectionism and try to understand it on its terms, though of course keeping an eye out for its differences from classicism. Furthermore, there are many features of classicism considered as scientific practice. It is not clear that there is any great value in trying to decide which features are essential.

Specifically, the notion of syntactic structure is, van Gelder suggests, so thoroughly embedded in the classical framework that we cannot use this notion effectively in considering connectionism.[12] He writes:

The concept of syntactic structure, drawn as it is from the Classical conceptual framework, is just not the right tool if we want to understand the distinctive character of Connectionist representations. (p. 372)

[Connectionist] Structure is *compositional* because the internal makeup of a representation (i.e., its location in [high-level, vector] space) is a direct function of its constituency relations; it is not however *syntactic* because tokens of those constituents are not to be found instantiated in the representation itself. (p. 372)

Far from being a tired or trivial variant on either previous dogma (e.g., "Associationism") or current orthodoxy (e.g., the Classical notion of syntactic structure), the emerging Connectionist style of structured representation is thoroughly *sui generis*, a good sign both that Connectionism really is developing a new and independent paradigm, and that some version of only functional compositionality will be an integral part of its conceptual infrastructure. (p. 373)

In "Connectionism versus Symbolism in High-Level Cognition," Michael Dyer describes his frustration with the classical paradigm as a computer scientist working on natural language processing (NLP):

Although my students and I worked diligently at designing and building such complex symbol processing systems, by 1986 I was becoming increasingly unhappy with the tremendous amount of knowledge engineering that such systems required, and unsatisfied with their resulting fragility....At the time I suspected that the inability to automatically acquire and represent the complexity of experience is a major reason for the resulting fragility of these human-engineered systems. (p. 383)

He next describes his attraction to connectionism, and almost immediate frustration with its resources for dealing with natural language processing.

As I tried to design and construct connectionist models for NLP, I began to reappreciate what nearly 40 years of computer science had built up in the way of symbol processing languages and architectures. (p. 385)

Dyer then considers possible attitudes and responses one might have to this situation, and opts for what he calls "structured connectionism": "structured connectionists are committed to ultimately realizing symbol processing in neural-like tissue, without the use of an underlying symbol processing architecture...." This is an idea also expressed by Hatfield and Smolensky in somewhat different terms: connectionism should not reject syntactically structured symbols; what it should reject is the idea that you get them *for free*, as primitives, because when you get them free, what you get is too rigid and fragile.

The bulk of Dyer's paper (the final 60%, more or less), is an overview of work he and his students at the UCLA AI lab are doing on connectionist natural language processing, involving constructing distributed, structured representations, and recirculation methods which permit representations to change so that words with similar meanings end up with similar distributed representation, as well as several connectionist methods of binding.

Dyer ends with a brief consideration of where we are in this research and where we need to go.

VI. CONNECTIONISM AND PHILOSOPHY

The papers in previous sections--like most philosophical discussion of connectionism to date--have concentrated on the issue of the viability of connectionism as an alternative to classical cognitive science, and on the foundational questions that this issue presupposes.

Connectionism is at least a different way of thinking about cognition. Whether it can lead us to an alternative conception of cognition or not, it certainly can suggest new ways of thinking about traditional philosophical concerns related to the mind. Philosophers are just beginning to think about such matters.

The papers in this final section ask what connectionism might tell us about certain traditional philosophical issues, specifically, perception and consciousness.[13] The authors are not committed to connectionism, but the papers are surely connectionist inspired.

Denny Bradshaw, in "Connectionism and the Specter of Representationalism," defends direct realism concerning perception against representational realism, understood as the epistemological doctrine that perception of external objects is epistemically--inferentially--mediated. The direct realist holds that perception of ordinary objects is not epistemically mediated.

Bradshaw argues that classical computationalism is committed to representational realism--as indeed, Fodor and Pylyshyn (1981) take themselves to be. And he argues that representational realism cannot give an adequate account of perceptual intentionality. In particular, homuncular discharge accounts are unsatisfactory.

Fodor and Pylyshyn (1981) attack J.J. Gibson's direct realist view of perception. In addition to criticisms specifically leveled at Gibson, Fodor and Pylyshyn bring up five difficulties they say direct realist theories of perception cannot handle. In Part III, Bradshaw argues that connectionism is consistent with direct realism, and that each of the difficulties is tractable from a connectionist point of view.

Gerald Glaser's paper, "Is Perception Cognitively Mediated?", is complementary to Bradshaw's. Glaser says recent theories of perception tend to divide into two types: constructive approaches that hold that perceptual processes are the result of mediating operations which construct perceptual representations from perceptual data, and Gibsonian approaches which hold that constructive operations are not necessary for perception. It is a common assumption of both approaches that if constructive operations are necessary, they must be cognitive operations. In this paper Glaser challenges that assumption. He argues that construction does not imply inference, and that connectionist models of the computational processes in perception would be constructive without being cognitive or inferential. They show the processes by which perceptual states are *caused* by sensory input without implying that they are inferred from that input. Such a view, he suggests, would explain the modularity of perception. Thus, he agrees that a connectionist theory of perception should be a direct realist theory in Bradshaw's sense, and with Hatfield that early vision is pre- or sub-cognitive.

In "Leaping to Conclusions: Connectionism, Consciousness, and the Computational Mind," Dan Lloyd makes a pregnant and intriguing suggestion: there are no non-conscious mental states. This might be seen as a complete generalization of the view advocated by Bradshaw and Glaser.

Lloyd proposes "the identity hypothesis for consciousness [which] holds that states of awareness (or states of consciousness) are identical to cognitively active states." That is, a state is a conscious state if and only if it is cognitively active. 'Active' here means causally active, which is not necessarily the same thing as connectionistically active. But it amounts to the same thing if connectionist representations remain activated only if they are *kept* activated. Add to the identity hypothesis the connectionist--but not only connectionist--idea that the only representational states of a system are *active* states--memories, etc. not being stored, but literally recreated when needed--and you get the picture that every actual representational state of a cognitive system is a conscious state.

There often are, of course, huge cognitive gaps between successive conscious states. On the classical view, these cognitive gaps are run across in many little (cognitive) steps. But connectionism offers another picture; the mind leaps these gaps in a single bound.

Connectionist models like NETtalk are striking in the complexity of the transformations on data they execute in single steps. Often these networks have no mediating layers between inputs and outputs, yet perform complex pattern matching tasks that would take a serial computer hundreds of steps. Or in other words, they cross wide cognitive gaps without intermediate cognition. (p. 452)

Whatever becomes of Lloyd's "identity hypothesis," the idea that minds leap large cognitive gaps in single or few cognitive steps is surely one of the important ways in which a connectionist picture of cognition will differ from the classical picture.

NOTES

[1] A connectionist system, or *neural network*, consists of a large number of very simple, neuron-like processors, called nodes or units, that send simple excitatory and inhibitory signals to one another. Nodes can be turned on--activated--or turned off by incoming signals, which depend upon the output of connected nodes and the strength of connection--"weight"--between them. In practice a given node may get input from just two or three other nodes, or from as many as two or three dozen. In principle, it could be thousands or millions.

The most striking difference between such networks and conventional computers is the lack of a central executive. In a conventional computer the behavior of the whole system is controlled at the central processing unit (CPU) by a stored program. In connectionist systems there is no such "executive" and no program to control the operation of the system. All connections are local, so that each node has only the information it gets from the nodes to which it is connected. And the only information that one node communicates to another is, "I'm turned on (so much)." No one in the system knows more than that. So, in particular, no one in the system knows what the system as a whole is doing. Furthermore, what goes on at one place in the system is independent of what goes on elsewhere in the system. The behavior of each node is determined only by its current state and its input. Nevertheless, connectionist systems can be interpreted to represent interesting content--analogous to the content of sentences or noun phrases--by their *patterns* of activated nodes, and as having stored (in the weights) knowledge that is not presently actively represented.

Some units--"input" units--in a connectionist system get stimuli from outside the system. Others, "output" units are thought of as sending signals outside the system. A problem is posed by activating a pattern of input nodes. Typically there is a great deal of activity, with nodes going on and off and sending and receiving signals repeatedly until the system "settles" into a stable configuration (of output units) that constitutes its solution to the problem posed.

Connectionist systems have been shown to be capable of solving interesting problems in some of the areas in which classical artificial intelligence has made little progress, such as pattern recognition, and are capable of "learning" to solve problems by systematically changing weights between nodes in response to "experience."

[2] This is not to say that we should *expect* answers to such questions at this point. It may be to early to say what the right answers are. It may turn out that simple answers are not forthcoming even if connectionism does supplant the classical picture, in whole or in part. The point is that we should understand that there is (as yet) no such thing as what the mind is like according to connectionism.

[3] The rules must be programm*able*; but there need not literally be a program. It is part of the classical picture that rules can be hardwired in, and not appear in a system as data structures.

[4] Cf. several chapters in Rumelhart and McClelland 1986, especially the first four. "The hard [i.e., classical] side has had priority for several decades now with disappointing results. It is time to give the soft side a few decades to produce disappointing results of its own" (Paul Smolensky, this volume, p. 285).

[5] So far, in fact, connectionist systems have not reached a level of sophistication where they can deal meaningfully with any of the crisis problems. They have, at best, certain properties that suggest that they could be good at dealing with certain problems.

[6] With the exception of Smolensky's (1988) "On the Proper Treatment of Connectionism."

[7] Rumelhart and McClelland 1986, Chapter 4.

[8] Rueckl bases this point on examination of extant connectionist systems. If suggestions about connectionist possibilities made in this volume by Hatfield, Horgan and Tienson, Smolensky, Tye, van Gelder, and Dyer are on the right track, then perhaps some not yet realized connectionist systems devoted to the same cognitive tasks will look less like implementation. This raises a question implicit in Kirsh's paper: how much of cognition permits only connectionist

implementation of classical systems, and how much allows or requires genuine alternatives to classicism?

[9] Pointer readings on pressure gauges are not "*symbolic* representations, because they are not mainipulated, 'read,' and 'interpreted' as symbols" (Kosslyn and Hatfield, p. 1034). "If a set of processes for manipulating, "reading," and "interpreting" symbols is imputed to a cognitive system, then it may be said to be rule following....if they are hardwired in the CPU, the CPU is not *internally* a "rule following" system [nor symbolic], but it embodies the rules of a larger rule-following [symbolic] system" (Kosslyn and Hatfield, p. 1035).

[10] In recurrent nets, the connection pattern contains loops—that is, it is possible to trace the output signal for a unit through the net until it returns as the same unit's input, and typically, such loops work in concert for large ensembles of units. As Garson points out, most discussions critical of connectionism ignore recurrent nets. But, Garson argues, "If connectionism is right, it is almost certain that some form of recurrency is required to explain language understanding and production, motor control, and even memory" (p. 118).

[11] This is quite a plausible argument.   But it is not obviously correct, for there are entities—waves, for example—that are causally efficacious but not classically present in Fodor and McLaughlin's sense. Think of the wake of a boat, superimposed upon the dominant, wind blown waves on open water, that washes out a sand castle on shore. On the other hand, it certainly has not been shown that tensor products can support effective syntax. Cf. Horgan and Tienson forthcoming 1991, Sections 4,5.

[12] In his reply to Tye's paper at the 1987 Spindel conference, Brian McLaughlin said, "The constituency relation is, of course, a part-whole relation" (McLaughlin 1987, p. 190). This is the kind of classical thinking that van Gelder opposes. He responds, in effect, "let's give them the terms 'syntax' and 'constituent', and describe connectionist processing in other terms." Note that Horgan and Tienson, this volume, (and others as well) make the same substantive point by arguing that syntactic constituency is not necessarily a part-whole relationship.

[13] Cf. also Paul Churchland's (1989) connectionist inspired discussion of explanation, and the discussion of innate structure and connectionism by psychologist Roger Shepard (1989).

REFERENCES

Churchland, P. M.: 1989, *A Neurocomputational Approach: The Nature of Mind and Structure of Science*, MIT Press, Cambridge, MA.

Fodor, J. A. and Pylyshyn, Z. W.: 1981, "How Direct is Visual Perception?: Some Reflections on Gibson's 'Ecological Approach'," *Cognition* 9, 139-196.

Fodor, J. A. and Pylyshyn, Z. W.: 1988, "Connectionism and Cognitive Architecture: A Critical Analysis," *Cognition* 28, 3-71.

Horgan, T. and Tienson, J.: (forthcoming), "Structured Representations in Connectionist Systems?" in *Connectionism: Theory and Practice*, Steven Davis (ed.), Oxford University Press, Oxford.

Kosslyn, S. M. and Hatfield, G.: 1984, "Representations without Symbol Systems," *Social Research* 51, 1019-1045.

Marr, D.: 1982, *Vision*, Freeman Press, San Francisco.

McLaughlin, B.: 1987, "Tye on Connectionism," *Southern Journal of Philosophy* 26, Supplement, 185-193.

Rumelhart, D. E. and McClelland, J. L.: 1986, *Parallel Distributed Processing*, MIT Press, Cambridge, MA.

Shepard, R.N.: 1989, "Internal Representation of Universal Regularities: A Challenge for Connectionism," in *Neural Connections, Mental Computation*, L. Nadel, L. A. Cooper, P. Culicover, and R. M. Harnish (eds.), MIT Press, Cambridge, MA.

Smolensky, P.: 1988, "On the Proper Treatment of Connectionism," *Behavioral and Brain Sciences* 11, 1-23.

Smolensky, P.: (forthcoming), "Connectionism, Constituency and the Language of Thought," in *Meaning in the Mind: Fodor and his Critics*, B. Loewer and G. Rey (eds.), Blackwell Press, Oxford.

Department of Philosophy
Memphis State University
Memphis, TN 38152

WILLIAM BECHTEL

CONNECTIONISM AND THE PHILOSOPHY OF MIND: AN OVERVIEW[1]

Connectionism has recently attracted much interest in cognitive science because it seems to promise an alternative to the now traditional rule-based approaches to modeling cognition. Philosophers have also begun to take note of connectionism. My objective in this paper is to provide a brief introduction to some of the philosophical issues generated by connectionism. I will not in this paper be defending connectionism *per se*, although I would not be undertaking a mission such as this if I did not think connectionism could offer some important contributions to our understanding of mind and mental phenomena. My goal is rather to generate and focus further discussion. Thus, in each section of this paper I will pose and briefly discuss one or more questions. In discussing these questions I will indicate some answers that I find attractive, but I will not attempt to advance definitive arguments for them on this occasion.

1. THE BASIC CHARACTER OF CONNECTIONIST MODELS OF COGNITION

Connectionist approaches to studying cognition begin with a different conception of the mechanism underlying cognition than the traditional computer model that has guided much thinking about cognition in recent decades. The alternative model is *inspired* by our understanding of brain. Although the connectionist model attempts to incorporate important features of the brain's architecture, connectionism does not advance a detailed account of neural processes. Rather, it proposes a model of the kind of processing involved in cognition. In a subsequent section I will discuss further how connectionist models relate to neural models. In this section I will present the connectionist model abstractly in the manner employed by the connectionists themselves.

30

The basic components of the connectionist architecture are simple *units* which, like neurons, are, at any given time, *activated* to some degree. Typically, this activation consists in possessing an electrical charge. These units, again like neurons, are *connected* (these connections can be of varying strengths) to other units so that, depending on their own activations, they can act to increase (excite) or decrease (inhibit) the activations of these other units. Additionally, in some connectionist systems, these connection strengths can be altered as a result of activity in the system so that the effect of one unit on another can change over time.

While this sketch covers the basic components of a connectionist system, there are a number of different ways a connectionist system can actually be set up, depending on the way a variety of parameters are set. One parameter fixes the permissible activation levels of the units: the units can be restricted to a small number of discrete states (e.g., on and off), or they can be allowed to vary over a specified range (e.g., 0 to 1). Another parameter governs how the activation of a unit is altered as a result of its previous states and the inputs it receives from other units. For example, a decay function can be included so that, without new activation, the activation of a unit drops, and a threshold can be employed such that a unit is not activated unless the input exceeds a certain quantity. A third parameter determines the output of a given unit. The output could be proportional to its own activation, or it could be governed by a threshold value. Finally, there are a variety of learning rules that can be employed to adjust the connection strengths on a given pathway. Two of the most widely employed are a Hebbian rule (which strengthens or weakens a pathway depending on whether the two units are alike or different in their level of activation) and the delta rule, which increases or decreases the strengths of each input pathway so as to increase the fit between the produced value and the target value of the unit. (For further details on the possible configurations of connection systems, see Rumelhart, Hinton, and McClelland, 1986.)

The basic processing system is an ensemble of such connected units. The activity of such an ensemble begins when an initial pattern of activation is supplied to some or all of the units. This pattern can be viewed as a problem given to the ensemble. In an interconnected network, processing ends when the system has settled into a *stable state* (e.g., one where the passing of activations through connections does not lead units to change their activation strengths). This settling occurs in accordance with thermodynamic principles: units change their activations as a result of their inputs and thereby alter their outputs, until the system settles into a state of highest entropy. The overall stable pattern, or the values on certain of the units when a stable pattern has been achieved, represents the system's answer to the problem.

In construing such a system as problem solving, we are supplying an *interpretation* to the activity of the system. In general, connectionists have employed two different types of interpretive schemes. In a *localized* interpretive scheme each unit represents some object or property. In Rumelhart and McClelland's system for word recognition, for instance, each unit represents a hypothesis about a feature, letter, or word that might be present. The degree of activation of the unit represents the degree of confidence that the corresponding item is part of the input.[2]

The alternative interpretive scheme is a *distributed* one where an interpretation is assigned to a pattern of activation over an ensemble of units. The activities of individual units way themselves have some symbolic role (e.g., representing features of an object to be recognized) but it is the overall pattern that is of primary interest, not the particular features. What makes this approach particularly interesting is that the same network can possess the capacity to settle into different activation patterns given different inputs. When one pattern is realized the others are only latently present in the sense that they could be activated with appropriate inputs. It is much more difficult for humans to follow activity in systems developed using distributed representations, but there are a variety of properties that make such systems highly attractive, such as the ability of related representations to activate units in common (which can then be interpreted as representing features of the overall objects represented by the pattern). (See Hinton, McClelland, and Rumelhart, 1986.)

While, for the most part, philosophers will not be engaged in the actual design of connectionist networks, there are some fundamental philosophical issues concerning their design. One concerns the principles which govern their operation and in terms of which we explain their capacities:

1. **Are there fundamental design principles in terms of which we can explain the behavior of connectionist systems? Or is the behavior of connectionist systems emergent (in a strong sense)?**

Some theorists have foreseen the prospect that we might build connectionist systems that simulate human cognitive performance but not be able to explain this behavior in a mechanistic fashion. The mechanistic approach to explanation is widely accepted in many disciplines where scientists have tried to explain the behavior of complex systems by *decomposing* them into components and then showing how the behavior of the system arises from the behavior of the components. In this mechanistic view, each component is viewed as making a discrete kind of contribution to the behavior of the whole system.[3]   In connectionist programs, the contributions of the components are minimized and the behavior of the system results more from the interaction of components than the behavior of the components themselves. While there are a few disciplines (e.g., thermodynamics) where explanatory models have been developed in which little explanatory function is assigned to the components and mathematical theories have been developed to show how the behavior of ensembles produces the higher-level effects, such explanations are often dissatisfying.   But a potential consequence of the development of connectionist models is that in the life sciences we may need to forego the mechanistic, decompositional approach, and accept mathematical, statistical explanations of the emergence at a higher level of a phenomenon which is not built up piecemeal from operations at the next lower level.[4]

A related issue concerns the principles researchers employ in interpreting connectionist systems:

2. Is the assignment of cognitive, intentional interpretations to activities in connectionist networks grounded on any fundamental principles?

One possibility is that researchers assign a cognitive, intentional interpretation to a connectionist network simply because the system behaves in a manner that allows it to perform the task. For example, we treat a system as recognizing a word because so interpreted, its behavior is appropriate. This is how Dennett (1978) views the attribution of intentional characterizations to any system, ourselves included, and what accounts for the instrumentalistic character of Dennett's account of intentionality. To many people, however, this is a deeply disturbing result. For them, it is a fundamental characteristic of our mental states that they are really *about* things, that is, they bear what Searle (1980) refers to as "intrinsic intentionality." If there is nothing in the actual character of states in connectionist systems that undergirds our intentional attributions, then some critics will see connectionist systems as failing to account for a basic characteristic of cognitive states. Searle makes the same objection to traditional computational accounts of mental functions such as those captured in traditional AI programs, but in at least Fodor's (1975) version of the computational theory, the syntactic operations of the program are supposed to mirror the semantics. Thus, the internal processing of the states is viewed as mirroring the kinds of semantically interpreted inferences we take the system to be making (e.g., if the system infers that it will thunder because there has been lightening, the internal processes will include an inference between the symbol we interpret as the proposition "there has been lightening" and the proposition "there will be thunder"). Connectionism rejects this sort of sentence processing model, and as a result, may seem to provide an even less-well motivated account of whatever semantic interpretation we give to the system.

There is, though, another perspective from which we might judge connectionist systems as actually faring better than traditional cognitive models with respect to intentionality. One of the objections Dreyfus (1979) raises to traditional AI programs is that they try to represent explicitly all information the system is to use. In addition to potentially rendering the endeavor of AI impossible, this attempt may also explain why such systems seem to lack intrinsic intentionality. The system's behavior is totally determined by its internal representations and hence it is not closely linked to the external objects which these representations are supposedly about. A connectionist system, however, does not rely on internal representations as its processing units. It produces internal representations as *responses* to its inputs and it is possible to develop systems that adjust the weights of their connections in such a way as to develop their own system for categorizing inputs (see Rumelhart and Zipser, 1985).[5] Moreover, it does not need to represent all relevant aspects of its environment in order to perform its cognitive operations. It must simply be able to respond to those features of the environment in the appropriate manner. This combination of tuning itself to its environment and not operating totally in terms of syntactically encoded representations may make it more reasonable to take the activities of connectionist systems as genuinely being *about* things in their environment, and hence enjoying a more intrinsic intentionality than traditional cognitive models.[6] This, however, only sketches a way in which we might motivate intentional interpretations of connectionist systems, and the potential for accounting for intentionality in these systems needs further investigation (see Bechtel, 1985a).

2. CONTRASTS BETWEEN CONNECTIONIST AND RULE-BASED ACCOUNTS OF COGNITION

Advocates of connectionist approaches often present connectionism as an alternative to and potential replacement for the now more traditional approach to explaining cognition which supposes that cognitive systems manipulate representations in accord with rules. If connectionism really is an alternative, then it will help if we can clarify precisely how the two approaches differ.

The rules-and-representations model of cognition is one that became prominent in cognitive science as a result of both Chomskyan accounts of language (according to which linguistically proper structures could be generated by application of recursive sets of rules to other linguistic structures) and the attempts to simulate cognition on the digital computer. Central to the use of the computer to simulate human cognitive performance was the assumption that both the mind and the computer are what Newell (1980) refers to as "physical symbol systems." The idea is that symbols are physically encoded in data structures which can be manipulated according to specified rules. While these rules may be directly embodied in the physics of the system (as they are in a pocket calculator), they are more typically themselves encoded in data structures, so that some elements in a data structure govern the manipulation of other components.

A basic issue arises as to how connectionist models differ from rule-based models. Since representations and rules for manipulating them are the key elements in rule-based accounts, let us examine whether there are analogues to them in connectionist models. On first appearances, connectionist systems seem to be quite unlike rule-based systems. There are no fixed representations upon which operations are performed in connectionist systems. Instead, there are activated units which function to increase or decrease the activations of other units until a stable configuration is achieved. Yet, appearances may be deceiving. The appearance of difference may be more a product of the grain of analysis we adopt with respect to the two systems. In connectionist systems we are considering activities within a single ensemble and the tasks we view such an ensemble as performing typically are basic cognitive operations (e.g., recognizing and classifying a given input). But a connectionist system that is to simulate interesting cognitive activity will require use of numerous ensembles and it may be necessary to use some ensembles to store the contents of others or to control the processing of others. When we consider ways in which collections of ensembles may be invoked to perform larger-scale cognitive tasks, we may find it much more natural to describe the activity as rule-based processing of representations.

In order to clarify the differences, if there are such, between connectionist and rule-based models, we need to look more carefully at the concepts of *representations* and *rules* for processing them. Focusing first on representations, we can ask:

3. Do representations as employed in connectionist systems differ from the representations employed in rule-based systems? [7]

Fodor and Pylyshyn (1988), in their critique of connectionism, argue that connectionists are representationalists since they supply semantic interpretations either to units (in localist interpretations) or to patterns of activation (in distributed interpretations). Is this sufficient to equate the representations used in the two systems? There remain some differences to consider. In a localized interpretation of a connectionist system, the units which are assigned representational functions are constantly present, but are turned on or off by other activity in the system. This is different from the way representations are usually handled in rule-based systems, but it is not clear how fundamental this difference is. There may be a greater difference in the case of distributed systems where it is a pattern over an ensemble of units that serves as a representation. In such systems, when a pattern is not present in the system, it is not stored, as in traditional cognitive models. Such patterns are not retrieved from memory, but are reconstructed on appropriate occasions. There are differences here, but these differences may be only matters of implementation and not such as to constitute a fundamental difference between the two types of systems. The more fundamental question is whether the representations in a connectionist system are capable of performing the same basic functions as representations in rule-based systems. This is a vexed issue, which I can only pose, not try to answer here.

There may be greater hope to contrast the two types of systems when we focus on the principles governing the operations in them. Rule-based systems operate by having specifically articulated rules direct manipulation of representations. A major objective of connectionist theorists has been to see if we cannot do away with rules by having all activity controlled by the connections that determine how activations are passed between units.[8] But this forces us to consider the question:

4. **What, precisely, are the differences (if any) between the rules that govern processing in rule-based systems and the sets of connections which govern processing in connectionist systems? Are connections the functional equivalents of rules?**

There is one sense in which connections do serve the same function as rules: They serve to transform the system from one representational state to another. The relation between sets of connections and rules is brought out even more clearly in what are called "programmable connection systems" where activity in one ensemble of units sets the connections in another ensemble, thereby determining its processing capacities (McClelland, 1986). Again, the issue of distinguishing clearly the two types of systems is vexed and I cannot resolve it here.

The attempt to differentiate connectionist from rule-based systems is made more difficult by the fact that current connectionist systems are not built directly out of hardware. Rather, they are simulated by traditional computers, where programs (consisting of rule statements) are written to determine how connectionist systems will behave. Hence, we must ask the further question:

5. **Does the use of rule-based von Neumann computers to simulate connectionist systems indicate a basic similarity between connectionist systems and rule-based systems?[9]**

This issue seems rather tricky. Some of those who have accepted the rule-based model of cognition have maintained that if we program a computer to perform the same symbol manipulations as a human being, we will have produced a real thinking entity. In a simulation of a connectionist system in a traditional computer, the computer calculates the equations governing the changes of activations of units in a connection system, and thereby determines what will be the activation strengths of all the units in a connectionist system. If the traditional computer can simulate the connectionist system, how can we maintain that the two are fundamentally different?

This way of collapsing the distinction between connectionist and rule-based systems, however, seems inadequate. The simulation of the connectionist machine in a rule-based computer is comparable to the simulation of a hurricane in a computer. In both cases what the computer does is to determine what would be the result of the causal processes that occur without actually going through those causal operations. On this view, the rule-based computer simulating the connectionist system does not instantiate the important causal properties of the connectionist system, but only tells us the result of the causal interactions in the system.

3. COMPETITION BETWEEN CONNECTIONIST AND RULE-BASED APPROACHES TO COGNITION

Although it is not clear that, in response to questions 3 and 4 above we can draw a sharp distinction between connectionist and rule-based systems, advocates of each kind of system advance relatively clear exemplars of the type of system they espouse and argue for the virtues of their type of model. Let us assume that the two types of systems are fundamentally different and turn to the question:

6. **What criteria should we employ to evaluate whether connectionist or rule-based accounts give more adequate accounts of human cognitive processes?**

This task would be easy if there were cognitive tasks which humans could perform which one, but not the other of these two types of systems could perform. Then we would have fairly strong reasons for favoring the system that could perform the tasks which humans could perform. The initial response of many rule-based theorists to connectionist models was to claim that this was the situation that actually accrued. They maintained that there are processes like recursion which humans can perform but which connectionist systems cannot and hence connectionist systems are inadequate (Fodor and Pylyshyn, 1988; and Pinker and Prince, 1988, raise objections of this sort).

This sort of outcome in which one side will show that their system can do things the other cannot is unlikely. This type of debate between rule-based and network-type models has a history that predates the current popularity of connectionism. Early generations of connectionist type models (e.g., the network models of Selfridge, 1955, and Rosenblatt, 1962) were rejected as it became clear that there were limitations to the types of models then being considered. Minsky and Papert (1969) established some important theorems showing these limitations. Current connectionists, however, have tried to show how some of these limitations can be overcome (Rumelhart and McClelland, 1986). In the early 1970s there were disputes in cognitive psychology over the relative virtues of somewhat different type of network models, semantic networks (see, e.g., Quillan, 1968), and feature set models as tools for representing concepts. Smith, Shoben, and Rips (1974) argued that their feature set model had properties that distinguished it from network models. Hollan (1975), however, challenged this distinction by showing how the model of Smith *et al.*, was isomorphic to a network model. Rips, Smith, and Shoben (1975) basically accepted Hollan's claim, but then advanced a different view of the distinction to which I will turn below. At this point, though, it seems plausible to assume that any task that can be performed by connectionist models can be accomplished through rule-based models and vice versa.

The alternative view of the distinction Rips *et al.*, advance is that "the choice of one type of representation rather than another can lead to substantive processing differences between theories, even though the representations themselves are isomorphic at some level" (p. 156). The same consideration may apply to the current dispute over connectionism. While connectionist and rule-based models may each be able to replicate the overall performance of the other, they may differ in the way they perform the task and these differences may reveal which type of model offers a better simulation of human cognition. This is, in fact, the approach many connectionists advance when they argue that their models work in ways that are more like humans than traditional rule-based models.

Connectionists argue, for example, that their models are much more biologically realistic than rule-based models. For example, they point to what is sometimes referred to as the 100 step principle (Feldman and Ballard, 1982). Given that individual neuronal processes take on the order of a few milliseconds and that many basic cognitive tasks are performed in a matter of a few hundred milliseconds, they argue that the mind/brain cannot go through more than approximately 100 serial steps. Most contemporary AI programs for carrying out these tasks, however, require many more than 100 serially executed steps, whereas connectionist machines can settle on answers well within the 100 step limit.

Connectionists also point to a number of performance features of connectionist systems which they claim show the superiority of connectionist models for human cognition. For example, it is a natural feature of a connectionist system involved in pattern recognition to be able to respond to deformed inputs or new inputs that are not precisely like those for which it has been designed or to which it has been trained to respond. It will respond to the altered input in the way it would respond to that of its previous inputs to which it most closely corresponds and it will do so without being provided special instructions telling it how to treat this new input. Moreover, the performance of a connectionist system degrades smoothly when part of the system is destroyed or when it is overloaded. For example, if some units in a connectionist system are destroyed, the system may still respond to inputs by settling into approximately the same stable states.

Put in this way, however, the connectionist argument is likely to encounter the same difficulty as the claim that one type of system can perform tasks which the other cannot. Advocates of rule-based processing models can satisfy both these biological and processing considerations. One reason, for example, that rule-based AI models seem to violate the biological constraint on the number of processing steps is that they are designed for serial processing computers. But many contemporary cognitive theories (e.g., Anderson's ACT* model) employ production system designs, and production systems would very naturally be implemented in parallel architectures. Doing so will dramatically reduce the number of sequential steps that seem to be needed for rule-based simulations of cognitive processes. Moreover, Allen Newell (1989) while adopting a rule-based approach, also invokes considerations of processing time. He uses the information about processing time as a guide to the character of the architecture and contends that his candidate architecture for a unified theory of cognition, SOAR, satisfies the data about time constraints on mental processes.

Advocates of rule-based processing can also accommodate the processing data that is advanced on behalf of connectionist models. There already exist rule-based categorization models that handle deformed or incomplete input. These systems take in information on a variety of features and employ algorithms which determine what category the object is most likely to be in on the basis of that information. To devise rule-based systems that degrade naturally, it will be necessary to build in partial redundancy to the processing procedures such systems employ. But this is not fundamentally incompatible with the idea of a rule-based model.

Behavioral data about what the two types of systems can do or about their manner of performance may be insufficient to answer question 6. The only remedy would seem to be to find some direct way of determining how the human mind works. Already within the rule-processing approach theorists like Pylyshyn (1984) have argued that we must examine the basic architecture of the mind in order to compare a cognitive simulation to a human being. He claimed that only in terms of knowledge of this architecture could we determine whether the simulation performed the same set of operations.[10] If there were a way of identifying this architecture, then we might be able to settle whether the basic operations of the human mind are those of connectionist systems or those of rule-based systems.

How, though, are we to identify the architecture of the human mind? Pylyshyn's criteria for identifying the architecture (relative reaction times for different tasks and cognitive penetrability) are behavioral and encounter the problem that we may be able to simulate with one architecture the performance of the other just as, in computers, we can compile or interpret one architecture into another. Moreover, his criterion of cognitive penetrability may already introduce a bias toward looking seeking a rule processing system since Pylyshyn seems to be focusing on penetrability of propositional sorts of information.

If it becomes so difficult to determine whether connectionist or rule-based theorists have the right account of our cognitive architecture, it may seem that the conflict between them is far less interesting than it has seemed to many. Connectionism at first seemed to offer a real contrast to rule-based processing accounts, but what I have been suggesting, both in this section and the previous one, is that the differences between the two accounts may be difficult to identify. But perhaps I am looking at the conflict in the wrong way. I have viewed it as a conflict between competing theoretical hypotheses, and have questioned how we can determine which is right. A potentially more fruitful way to approach the matter is as a conflict between two different sets of tools for building cognitive models. Here there is a fundamental difference between the two approaches. Different tasks become easier or harder to perform depending on which kind of system we adopt. Classical reasoning tasks are easier to model if we adopt a rule-based model since most models of reasoning, stemming from work in logic, are rule-based. On the other hand, there are quite different kinds of tasks, such as pattern recognition, which seem easier to handle in connectionist frameworks.

What this suggests is that we should think of the conflict not in terms of which model provides a correct account of the human cognitive system but by asking which provides a more useful framework for developing cognitive theories. In this way, we turn the conflict into one about strategies of theory development, and we can pose a new question:

7. **What are the relative advantages of developing cognitive theories within a connectionist versus a rule-processing framework?**

From this perspective, the question of what it is easy to model in a particular type of system becomes salient and the fact that we could perform many of the same processes in the competing type of system becomes far less important. The fact that a certain kind of operation is easy to perform in a particular type of system may lead those employing that type of system to take greater note of that cognitive operation than those that are difficult to realize in their system. From this perspective, the widespread introduction of connectionist models can be seen as a truly important event in cognitive science for it may lead us to take note of different sorts of cognitive phenomena. In particular, it may lead us to look beyond language processing and reasoning tasks (which seemed to lend themselves to treatment in rule-based models) to other cognitive activities, such as pattern recognition, which have proven more difficult to handle in rule-based models. To pursue this approach, let us consider pattern recognition, which has become the paradigm task studied by connectionists.

4. THE IMPORTANCE OF PATTERN RECOGNITION IN HUMAN COGNITION

The settling of a connectionist system into different stable states depending on the input it received made it natural to view such systems as performing pattern recognition or categorization. Since systems which can change their connection strengths change their response patterns over time, it became natural to view these systems as learning to classify inputs. Accordingly researchers have investigated a variety of learning procedures for such systems. As a result, connectionist systems have been designed which learn to categorize input patterns and, after this learning, proceed to categorize new inputs on the basis of similarity to previously learned patterns. (In saying that these systems judge on the basis of similarity connectionists, of course, we are not saying that connectionist systems can determine objective similarity and solve the sorts of problems regarding similarity that have been discussed in the philosophical literature. The similarity judgments of these systems is determined by the strengths of the connections in the system. Our license to speak of these systems as judging similarity depends upon the fact that they classify together patterns that we also take to be similar.) It is through their ability to make such similarity judgments that the connectionist systems demonstrate their capacity to generalize to new inputs and respond appropriately to deformed input.

The ease of performing pattern recognition tasks in connectionist systems raises an interesting question:

8. How important a cognitive task is pattern recognition?

It has been the general view of researchers in cognitive science that pattern-recognition is an important, but subordinate cognitive activity. One context where pattern recognition has been important has been in work on machine vision, where the challenge is to get machines to be able to recognize objects via sensory inputs. This is clearly a skill that machines will require before they can direct their own activities in the world (e.g., as intelligent robots). But it has not been easy to develop rule-based processing systems with good pattern recognition abilities, in part because this ability requires the machine to be able to deal with an enormous number of contextual cues, whose relevance may differ from context to context. For many purposes, however, it has been possible to overlook the problem since we can encode the information symbolically in the system and then focus directly on higher level processing that employs that information. The ability to circumvent the task of recognizing sensory inputs has given the impression that pattern recognition may only be a subordinate cognitive function that can be overlooked while addressing other cognitive tasks.

In recent years, though, there has developed a relatively large psychological literature on concepts and categorization. Categorization is a task comparable to pattern recognition in that it requires the ability to recognize similar items so as to classify them together. Within the rule-based framework it is natural to think of categorization being governed by rules that specify what characteristics something must have to belong to a category. The psychologist Eleanor Rosch (1975) challenged this perspective by arguing that categories have a prototype structure: some exemplars (e.g., robin) are judged to be better examples of the category (e.g., bird) than others (e.g., duck). This suggested that categories are not characterized in terms of necessary and sufficient conditions, as would be natural if categorization depended upon rules. Although Rosch herself did not make the prototype theory into a theory of how categories are mentally represented (see Rosch, 1978), other psychologists have. Although the adoption of a prototype theory of categories undercuts the idea that categorization is based upon simple rules specifying necessary and sufficient conditions, most psychologists who attempted to develop an account of mental representation to accommodate the prototype data still used a rule approach according to which subjects would judge the similarity of an object to a prototype on a variety of features and then apply rules to determine whether the object belonged to the category (for a review of this literature, see Smith and Medin, 1981). But there is good reason to think that this kind of process could be performed naturally by a connectionist system without using rules. As we have already noted, judging similarity is a basic capacity of connectionist models. A connectionist pattern recognition device will classify a new input pattern with the closest match of previous input patterns without requiring a specially stipulated rule. So a Roschian prototype theory of categorization might be readily and naturally implemented in a connectionist system and avoid some of the difficulties that have confronted attempts to devise rule-based categorization processes.

To those who have celebrated rule-based processing in cognitive science, though, categorization tasks may seem no more central than vision tasks (this despite the evidence that how we categorize things may critically influence how we think and reason about them). The real cognitive work, they might maintain, begins once the information is represented in the proper symbolic form or code. However, once we view these tasks as pattern recognition tasks, we may also see how pattern recognition may also figure in more central cognitive processing. Probably the most widely accepted view of higher cognitive activities like problem solving (a view due to the contributions of theorists like Simon, Newell, and Anderson) is that skilled performance in these activities depends on acquiring appropriate rules. Often these rules are thought to be learned in a fairly conscious manner, but then are made automatic so that the skilled performer can generally apply them without explicit conscious thought. Dreyfus and Dreyfus (1986), however, have recently argued that such rule learning only leads to competent performance in a domain. They maintain that expert performance depends upon being able to recognize a situation as being like certain previous ones and then responding to it in similar ways. One of the examples they consider is chess playing, an activity much studied by theorists who adopt a rule-based approach. Dreyfus and Dreyfus contend that what distinguishes expert from competent chess players is not additional rule-based knowledge but a better developed ability to recognize how a current situation resembles ones previously encountered.[11] If Dreyfus and Dreyfus are right, pattern recognition may figure in tasks that seemed to be exemplars of high-level reasoning tasks requiring rule-based reasoning. Given the ease of performing pattern recognition and comparison in a connectionist system, this would suggest that it might be worth exploiting this capacity of connectionist systems to see how much can be accomplished through pattern recognition without invoking rule-based reasoning processes.

What I have tried to do in this section is indicate some respects in which pattern recognition might be an important cognitive capacity. There are some other areas where this capacity may also be important. For example, through a pattern recognition process, a connectionist system can activate patterns associated with previous similar experiences. This provides a suggestive way of approaching the task of modeling content-addressable memory (memories activated on the basis of their content, not on the basis of knowing where they were stored). This is a form of memory that is characteristic of humans, but hard to achieve in classical architectures, where items are typically accessed on the basis of knowing in what register they were stored). We may also find a role for pattern recognition in activities that have served as exemplars of rule-processing activities such as syntax processing. We may discover that using pattern recognition systems we could devise systems that could subserve language comprehension and production without invoking complex linguistic rules. These are, of course, only suggestions, and it remains to be seen how much connectionist systems can accomplish through pattern recognition processes that do not invoke rules. It should also be recalled that in all likelihood it will prove possible to design rule-based systems that can perform the same pattern recognition tasks. The relative ease of carrying them out in connectionist systems, though, suggests that we should exploit such systems to determine how much of cognition relies on pattern recognition and does not *require* rule-based processing. If connectionist systems serve to direct our attention to such other cognitive activities as pattern recognition, which have not been focal in recent, rule-based cognitive science, they will have served an important heuristic function regardless of the final outcome of the debate over whether humans are really connectionist or rule-based processing systems.

5. POSSIBLE RECONCILIATION OF CONNECTIONIST AND RULE-AND-REPRESENTATION MODELS

Although connectionist and rule-based theorists often view themselves as competitors, I have emphasized in the last section that the two kinds of systems are naturally good at quite different types of activity. Since reasoning has often been viewed as a matter of following rules such as those articulated in systems of natural deduction, it has been relatively easy to design rule-based systems to perform complex reasoning tasks. On the other hand, connectionist systems have proven to be good at such things as pattern recognition and motor control and offer the potential for content-addressable memory. This should lead us to ask:

9. Is it possible to integrate connectionist and rule-based models so as to acquire the benefits of both in a single cognitive model?

Since connectionists view themselves as revolutionaries struggling to overcome the domination of the more traditional rule-based approach, it is not surprising that they would want to push the new approach to its limits to see just how far they can proceed with it alone. But in fact most of the work on connectionism has pursued tasks that terminate with a specific response by a system--for example, the system may identify the particular pattern with which it is confronted and then wait for its next input. But in typical human cognition the recognition of a pattern is not the end of the process. It may provide the basis for other kinds of activity. When I recognize my cat, I might consider whether I had left any food out for her or given her medicine to her today, or I might be prompted to say something to her.

There are two ways we might envisage the completion of a pattern recognition task in a connectionist system as leading to other cognitive processing. The particular pattern that is activated might spread its activation to other modules with which it is connected in a form of spreading activation. Or the recognition of a pattern might trigger further processing in which rules are applied. For example, if the pattern recognition process identified my chairperson, that might also serve to satisfy the antecedent of the currently activated rule "If I see my chairperson, ask about my travel allowance" and so fire the production.

Advocates of both approaches have allowed some room for rapprochement. Connectionists like Rumelhart and McClelland characterize their own program as one addressed to the microstructure of cognition and this seems to allow for the possibility that more traditional cognitive models might characterize the macro-structure. Rumelhart, Smolensky, McClelland, and Hinton (1986) have even tried to show how certain features of traditional rule-based cognitive systems, such as the use of schemes and frames, can be realized in connectionist systems. Touretzky (1986) has shown how to implement traditional LISP operations in a connectionist system.

On the other side, rule-based theorists such as Fodor and Pylyshyn (1988) are willing to consider the possibility that in humans rule-based processing is implemented in something like a connectionist system. What this would involve, presumably, is having the formal inference principles of a rule-based system mapped onto states of a connectionist network. Fodor and Pylyshyn, however, distinguish sharply between the mode of implementation and the actual cognitive architecture. The architecture, they maintain, must be a rule-processing system which employs (1) a combinatorial syntax and semantics and (2) structure sensitive processes. They argue for these requirements on the architecture by describing several features of cognition which they maintain require such processes: (a) the productivity of thought (i.e., we can build up complex propositions by recursive processes), (b) the systematicity of cognitive representations (which is revealed by the fact that anyone who can think the John loves Mary is also able to think that Mary loves John), and (c) the compositionality of representations (i.e., a component of a mental representation makes approximately the same semantic contribution to all mental representations in which it appears). Fodor and Pylyshyn maintain, however, not only that these features of cognition require a rule-processing system but also that all cognitive or psychological activity takes place within that architecture. The features of the system in which the architecture is implemented are *mere* matters of implementation, and so not a matter for the psychologist.

Even if we provisionally accept Fodor and Pylyshyn's claim that some features of cognition require a rule-processing type system, we can still question their negative conclusion about connectionism by asking:

10. If a rule-processing system is implemented in a connectionist system, could that have implications for the cognitive aspects of the rule-based processing system?

If in fact the human rule-processing system is implemented in a connectionist type system and this provides the system with certain capacities like pattern recognition, concept learning, and content-addressable memory, then it would seem that the mode of implementation has cognitive significance. The issue is not merely a matter of implementation but of central importance to the character of cognitive inquiry. Fodor and Pylyshyn seem to assume that investigations at lower levels, such as those at which rule-processing is implemented, do not have consequences for investigations at higher levels. They characterize psychological inquiry as basically autonomous.[12] But in other disciplines autonomy assumptions have not proven viable. For example, knowledge of structure of physical membranes has been critical for determining the form of biochemical theories and vice versa. Moreover, researchers have sometimes found it critical to bring in approaches from other disciplines (e.g., cytology) to solve problems (e.g., oxidative phosphorylation) that were thought to fall solely within the purview of one discipline (e.g., biochemistry). (For further discussion of the problems confronting the kinds of autonomy claims advanced by Fodor and Pylyshyn, see Bechtel, 1988a.) It is far from clear that implementation studies will not similarly contribute material relevant to explaining some aspects of cognitive processing within rule-based systems.

To suggest a more fruitful way of integrating rule-processing and connectionist models, I will return briefly to the topic of concepts and categorization. Concepts are a likely candidate for the units of rule-based cognitive processing. Earlier I touched upon the possibility that categorization into concepts might be implemented in a connectionist system to take advantage of the ability of such systems to recognize similarities and associate examples with prototypes. There is a further advantage to doing so. Generally, even within a Roschian perspective on concepts, concepts are taken to be relatively stable. Thus, they seem like the atoms of thought--not divisible or modifiable in themselves. But recently Barsalou (1987, 1989) has produced significant evidence for variability in our concepts. One of Rosch's measures to demonstrate the character of concepts was to ask subjects to rank the prototypicality of different members of a category. She claimed to find evidence of high between-subject correlations in such rankings. Barsalou, however, showed that her statistical measure is flawed and that when a more appropriate statistical measure is used, between-subject correlations of prototypicality judgments drop to approximately .4. Moreover, he found that even intrasubjectively, prototypicality judgments change measurably over a time interval of one month, with correlations of only .8.

From these results Barsalou draws the inference that concepts might not be stored in long-term memory as fixed units, but might be "constructed on the fly" as needed for particular reasoning tasks. It is somewhat difficult to make sense of this view within a rule-based account of cognition, since concepts would seem to be the atoms of such systems, but much easier to make sense of them from a connectionist perspective where what exist in long-term memory are only connections. These enable the subject to produce representations that play the role of concepts and may be used in solving problems for which even rules might be invoked, but the concepts need not be fixed, atomic structures as they are in most rule-based accounts. Thus, implementing concepts in a connectionist system might allow us to explain in a straight-forward manner some characteristics of concepts that might otherwise to be difficult to explain. In addition, a significant advantage of using connectionist systems to represent concepts is that we could invoke the learning capacities of connectionist system to explain how new primitive concepts are learned, a phenomenon which a rule-processing theorist like Fodor (1980) denies is possible (see Bechtel, 1985b).

I have here only sketched in broad outline how connectionist and rule-based accounts might be integrated. The basic idea is that states in connectionist systems might serve as the representations (including representations of rules) of a rule-based processing system. The advantage of such an arrangement is that some of the desirable features of connectionist systems can be utilized by the rule-processing system, and not themselves have to be performed through the invocation of rules. (I develop this sketch in a bit more detail in Bechtel, 1988b.) Clearly there are many technical problems to be solved before such an integrated system will be available, but it seems at least possible that one might be developed.

6. RELATION OF CONNECTIONIST MODELS TO NEUROSCIENCE ACCOUNTS OF COGNITION

Another philosophical issue raised by connectionism concerns the relation of connectionist theories to other theories. On the one hand, there is a question about the relation of connectionist models to those of neuroscience and, on the other, a question about the relation of connectionist models to folk psychology. Both of these questions raise the issue of whether connectionism is in some way a "reductionist" program. I shall take these topics up in turn in these last two sections.

I noted at the outset that connectionist models are neurally inspired. The degree of activation of units can be seen as comparable to the firing rate of neurons, and the passing of activations to other units is comparable to the passing of signals between neurons. But it is also clear that connectionist models are not themselves neural models since connectionists do not try to take into account all the details of neural systems, and connectionists are not, by and large, interested in making their models into more realistic neural ones. So we need to address the question:

11. **If connectionist models are not themselves neural models, what are they models of? How do the components of connectionist models relate to the components of the brain?**

Those who advocate rule-based models have a natural way of addressing the comparable question about their models: The rule-based accounts specify processes that are realized by more basic processes performed in the computer or the brain. They are accounts of real causal processes, but processes that take place at a higher level than the activities of individual neurons or even neural assemblies. But such an answer on behalf of connectionists would seem less motivated. The activities in connectionist models seem to be so like those in neural networks that it seems most natural to treat them as models of processing in those very networks.

Another way connectionists can address this issue is by maintaining that their models are abstract models of the neural processing system. As such, they overlook some of the details of real neural systems so as to characterize the features of a general class of systems (Smolensky, 1988). An analysis at such a level of abstraction in fact makes a great deal of sense when the point is to show how a certain kind of process that previously seemed miraculous might actually be carried out by a system like the brain. It proves that mechanisms of a certain kind can do certain kinds of things. Moreover, such an approach can also guide the search for understanding at the neural level. One problem neuroscience has faced is figuring out how the activities of neurons could be performing cognitive functions. Connectionist models show how they might figure in such activities, and thus prepare the way for further research to determine in detail how neural systems perform these functions.

It seems reasonable at the current time to think of connectionist models as abstract accounts of the neural system. But if this is right, then connectionist models are accounts of neural activity, not of higher levels of activity in the brain. They simply ignore some of the details of this activity. Moreover, it would seem that a plausible goal in the future would be to develop ever more accurate accounts of how neural systems actually do operate and not to maintain a distinction between connectionist theories and neural theories. The difference between neural models and connectionist models would seem to dissolve into a pragmatic difference--at this juncture in the development of our understanding of the brain and cognition it is useful to consider a broad class of connectionist models, whereas as the program develops it will be more critical to develop accounts that are more neurally accurate. This is, however, to undermine the distinction between connectionist models and neural models, which seems to be important at least to some connectionists.

This view of connectionism I have just presented may seem to give it a prominent place in a reductionist program. If connectionist models do succeed in accounting for the full range of cognitive phenomena, it would seem proper to see them as showing how to reduce traditional cognitive theorizing to neural-level theorizing. There is, however, a different perspective we might take. The distinction between cognitive research (whether connectionist or rule-based) and neural research might better be viewed more as a matter of the kinds of questions researchers ask and the concepts and research tools they employ to answer them, than as a matter of the level of organization in nature at which the research occurred (see also Abrahamsen, 1987, for a discussion of relations between research disciplines that would accommodate this view). Moreover, even if some of the basic cognitive operations are performed in simple connectionist networks, some will involve the higher level interactions between these networks and their integration. As suggested in the previous section, this is where rule-based processes might figure. The higher-level activities might be characterized in neuroscience terms, but it will also prove important to characterize them in more cognitive terms. What might emerge as a result of connectionist perspectives is a repudiation of the view that there is one unique level for cognitive theorizing but rather a view according to which cognitive theorizing (as well as neural theorizing) occurs at a variety of levels, some of which are lower than the symbolic level of traditional cognitive theorizing.

7. RELATION OF CONNECTIONIST MODELS TO FOLK PSYCHOLOGY

When philosophers have considered mental activities, they have often focused on folk psychology. This is a perspective from which we view people as having beliefs and desires and interpret them as behaving on the basis of these beliefs and desires. A major concern of philosophers is how folk psychology fares in the wake of the development of experimental inquiries in psychology and neuroscience. In folk psychology we characterize people as reasoning from their beliefs and desires to determine what to do and such folk psychology is one source of the view that cognition is a rule-based process. Insofar as rule-based models of cognition employ the model of logical reasoning that figures in folk psychological accounts and use that structure as a basis for a scientific psychology, they offer support for the claim that folk psychology is basically correct. On the other hand, if connectionists are right in their strong claims that the mind is not a rule-based system, they may seem to undercut the legitimacy of folk psychology as well as rule-based cognitive psychology. This possibility is emphasized by Eliminative Materialists like Patricia and Paul Churchland, who view connectionist and related accounts of how the brain actually performs cognitive tasks as showing the need to reject folk psychology in much the way we have learned to reject folk physics and folk medicine (see P. S. Churchland, 1986; and P. M. Churchland, 1986). A final question concerning connectionism is thus posed:

12. If connectionist models are correct, does that show that we need to eliminate folk psychology? Or is there still a place for folk psychology?

The Churchlands have maintained that psychology (including especially folk psychology) must reduce to our best theories of how the mind-brain works, or be eliminated. By reduction they seem to have in mind a reduction in the philosophical sense wherein the terms of folk psychology would be identified with terms from our scientific account of the mind-brain and then theoretical accounts of folk psychology would be derived from those of our new mind-brain theory. They doubt the likelihood of such a reduction and therefore call for the elimination of folk psychology. On the other hand, the Churchlands consider connectionist models as potentially correct accounts of the operation of the mind-brain and thus as potential replacements for folk psychology. For now I will accept assume both that folk psychology does not reduce to a correct theory about how the mind-brain operates and that connectionism may provide a basically correct account of how the mind-brain does operate. What I will question is whether we need to accept the choice of either reducing folk psychology to connectionist theories or eliminating it.

Let me briefly sketch an alternative perspective. Although some supporters of rule-based accounts of cognition have seen folk psychology as a prototype of a rule-based model of how the mind actually works, that may misrepresent the function of folk psychology. Folk psychology may better be understood as an account of people rather than of their internal mental processes. People have beliefs and desires, but these may not be internal states of people. Folk psychology may give us a way of characterizing people vis a vis their environment, but it may not be the case that people internally represent in discrete symbols all aspects of their environment. Their internal states may enable them to behave appropriately given certain aspects of their environment and accordingly we may ascribe knowledge of those aspects of their environment to them, but these beliefs and desires may not directly correspond to particular internal states. Of course, we do expect that people's behavior is due, in part, to the activities occurring within them. These internal activities may be important to how they behave and partly determine the mental states we ascribe to them via folk psychology. But the internal activities may not correspond in any direct sense to the mental states folk psychology ascribes. An analogy may make this point clearer. In terms of their capacity to produce alcohol from sugar, we characterize yeast cells as capable of carrying out fermentation. Early biochemists tried to explain fermentation as involving step-wise fermentation of the sugar molecule inside the cell. But we now know that fermentation occurs as a result of a variety of quite different operations (e.g., oxidations, reductions, phosphorylations, dephosphorylations) occurring inside the cell. Thus, in order to explain how a system has particular characteristics, such as mental states or physiological capabilities, we may appeal to quite different sorts of operations than we appeal to in describing the system itself (Bechtel, 1985a).

If the perspective just sketched is correct, then the failure of folk psychology to reduce to connectionism does not undercut the viability of folk psychology. We may continue to view folk psychology as providing a description of the behaving subject, specifying the information it has about its environment and its goals for action. As such, folk psychology (or some revised version of it) still has an important role to play. It tells us what behavioral capacities internal processing must account for. One of the dangers to which experimental theorizing has sometimes succumbed is developing theoretical models to account for behavior (like ability to memorize nonsense words) which can be elicited in laboratories, but which does not play an important role when organisms pursue their ordinary life. The way to avoid this danger is to maintain a perspective on what needs to be explained. Folk psychology gives us one perspective on what information people have about their world and the kinds of cognitive activities they perform in it. It is not the only way to gain such a perspective. Ecological approaches to psychology that emphasize real life activity of cognitive agents are another (see Neisser, 1975, 1982). My claim is only that some such perspective which characterizes people and the information they have about their environment plays a critical role for those developing any internal processing account--connectionist or rule-based. Hence, this perspective is not eliminated by internal processing accounts that employ different categories than the propositional attitudes of folk psychology. To the contrary, a successful internal processing account will explain what makes it possible for someone, when confronted with an actual environment, to satisfy the descriptions of folk psychology or ecological psychology. (See further Bechtel and Abrahamsen, 1991.)

8. CONCLUSIONS

The goal of this paper has been to indicate some of the philosophical problems to which connectionism gives rise. I have noted twelve such questions, covering such issues as how connectionist models are developed, how they can be tested against rival rule-based models, how they might be integrated with rule-based accounts, and how they relate to neuroscience theories and folk psychological accounts. The rise of connectionism constitutes a major event in the development of cognitive science, and I hope it is clear that it also poses a number of questions that are ripe for philosophical examination.

NOTES

[1] This manuscript was prepared while I was a visiting fellow at the Center for Philosophy of Science at the University of Pittsburgh. I am most grateful to the Center for its hospitality and to Georgia State University for providing me a leave of absence. Adele Abrahamsen, Larry Barsalou, David Blumenfeld, C. Grant Luckhardt, Marek Lugowski, Ulric Neisser, and Robert McCauley have each provided me with valuable comments for which I am thankful.

[2] For discussion of a variety of other connectionist simulations using this localized interpretation scheme, see Fahlman (1979); Feldman and Ballard (1982); Rumelhart and Norman (1982); and Cottrell and Small (1983).

[3] In Bechtel and Richardson (in press), we analyze how this decompositional view of nature underlies the research in a variety of disciplines of the life sciences and the kinds of research tools scientists have invoked in trying to develop explanations built on this assumption. The program of homuncular functionalism in philosophy of mind (Dennett, 1978, Lycan, 1981) represents this sort of approach to scientific explanation, for the homunculi posited each perform a significant task which is needed in order to carry out the overall activity of the system.

[4] Kauffman (1986) has proposed a model of genetic regulatory systems which, like connectionist models, construes the stability of genetic systems as an emergent phenomenon, not something performed by particular genetic units.

[5] By noting this as a feature of connectionist systems, I do not mean to imply that it cannot be found in more traditional cognitive models (e.g., Anderson, 1983). This, however, is a feature that arises naturally in connectionist systems and requires complex rule sets in rule-based systems.

[6] Neisser (personal communication) suggests that what is important for intrinsic intentionality is that the system extract the right invariants (information patterns in the sensory medium specifying features of the environment) from its sensory contact with the world. While we will be able to assess whether a system is capable of such pick up of information only when we have a full-scale system that inhabits and functions in an environment, I see no reason why connectionist devices could not subserve this extraction function.

[7] Dan Lloyd first directed me to the importance of this question.

[8] Connectionists do speak of the procedures for changing connection strengths as "learning rules." But these are quite different from the sort of rules that figure in rule-based systems. Learning rules are simply mathematical specifications of how connection strengths will change as a result of activity in the system. They are not explicitly stored rules which are formally applied to previous representations so as to create new representations.

[9] This question was initially posed to me by Max Coltheart.

[10] With traditional computer systems this idea of an architecture which specified the primitive operations is generally relative. While the machine language of a particular system ultimately specifies what primitive operations can be used in the system, most programming is done in higher level languages that are either compiled or interpreted directly, or via intermediate languages, into the machine langauge. But Pylyshyn maintains that things are not so relative in the case of the human being. There is a basic architecture that is privileged and once we identify it, we will be able to compare the operations performed in a machine simulation with those performed in us.

[11] Of course, we do not always do in the new situation precisely what we did in a similar previous situation. There are at least two situations in which we may depart from the pattern. First, if the action taken in the previous instance did not have satisfactory consequences, then we may elect not try it again. Or if we have time to be reflective, we might contemplate how we should adjust our previous response either to deal with circumstances that distinguish the current situation from the previous one or to improve upon previous performance. These might be situations where we might want to consider rules (e.g., never do A in situation B), but it is also possible that we might employ a great deal more pattern matching. For example, by activating the previous pattern we might also activate an associated recollection of the previous negative consequences of the response we tried. And one thing we might do in trying to adjust or improve on a previous response is to activate other related patterns and compare the responses we had associated with those patterns to the primary one we had just activated for the current circumstance.

[12] In fact, all Fodor and Pylyshyn actually maintain is that psychology has "autonomously stateable principles." But it is far from clear what this means. It could mean that we can discover the principles of psychology through psychological investigations alone. This would seem to be the implication required to justify the denial of any capacity of connectionism to force changes in cognitive theorizing. But it could also mean that once discovered, the principles of psychology could be states solely in psychological terms. This is more plausible, but as I discuss below, it too may be false.

REFERENCES

Abrahamsen, A. A.: 1987, 'Bridging Boundaries Versus Breaking Boundaries: Psycholinguistics in Perspective', *Synthese* **72**, 355-388.

Anderson, J. R.: 1983, *The Architecture of Cognition*, Harvard University Press, Cambridge.

Barsalou, L. W.: 1987, 'The Instability of Graded Structure: Implications for the Nature of Concepts', in U. Neisser (ed.), *Concepts Reconsidered: The Ecological and Intellectural Bases of Categories*, Cambridge University Press, Cambridge.

Barsalou, L. W.: (1989), 'Intra-concept Similarity and its Implications for Inter-concept Similarity', in S. Vosniadou and A. Ortony (eds.), *Similarity and Analogy*, (pp. 76-121), Cambridge University Press, Cambridge.

Bechtel, W.: 1985a, 'Realism, Instrumentalism, and the Intentional Stance', *Cognitive Science* **9**, 265-292.

Bechtel, W.: 1985b, 'Are the New Parallel Distributed Processing Models of Cognition Cognitivist or Associationist?', *Behaviorism* **13**, 53-61.

Bechtel, W.: 1986, 'What Happens to Accounts of the Mind-Brain Relation if We Forego an Architecture of Rules and Representations?', in A. Fine and P. Machamer (eds.), *PSA 1986* (pp. 159-171), Philosophy of Science Association, East Lansing, MI.

Bechtel, W.: 1988a, *Philosophy of Science: An Overview for Cognitive Science*, Lawrence Erlbaum Associates, Hillsdale, NJ.

Bechtel, W.: 1988b, 'Connectionism and Rules-and-Representations Systems: Are They Compatible?', *Philosophical Psychology* **1**, 5-16.

Bechtel, W. and Abrahamsen: (1991), *Connectionism and the Mind: An Introduction to Parallel Processing in Networks*, Basil Blackwell, Oxford.

Bechtel, W. and Richardson, R. C.: (in press), *A Model of Theory Development: Decomposition and Localization as a Scientific Research Strategy*, Princeton University Press, Princeton.

Churchland, P. M.: 1986, 'Some Reductive Strategies in Neurobiology', *Mind* **95**, 279-309.

Churchland, P. S.: 1986, *Neurophilosophy: Toward a Unified Science of the Mind-Brain*, MIT Press/Bradford Books, Cambridge.

Cottrell, G. W. and Small, S. L.: 1983, 'A Connectionist Scheme for Modelling Word Sense Disambiguation,' *Cognition and Brain Theory* **6**, 89-120.

Dennett, D. C.: 1978, *Brainstorms*, MIT Press/Bradford Books, Cambridge.

Dreyfus, H. L.: 1979, *What Computers Can't Do: The Limits of Artificial Intelligence*, Harper and Row, New York.

Dreyfus, H. L. and Dreyfus, S. E.: 1986, *Mind Over Machine. The Power of Human Intuition and Expertise in the Era of the Computer*, The Free Press, New York.

Fahlman, S. A.: 1979, *NETL, A System for Representing and Using Real Knowledge*, MIT Press, Cambridge.

Feldman, J. A. and Ballard, D. H.: 1982, 'Connectionist Models and Their Properties', *Cognitive Science* **6**, 205-254.

Fodor, J. A.: 1975, *The Language of Thought*, Crowell, New York.

Fodor, J. A.: 1980, *Representations*, MIT Press (Bradford Books), Cambridge.

Fodor, J. A. and Pylyshyn, Z. W.: 1988, 'Connectionism and Cognitive Architecture: A Critical Analysis', *Cognition* **28**, 3-71.

Hinton, G. E., McClelland, J. L., and Rumelhart, D. E.: 1986, 'Distributed Representations', in Rumelhart & McClelland, 1986, pp. 77-109.

Hollan, J. D.: 1975, 'Features and Semantic Memory: Set Theoretic or Network Models?', *Psychological Review* **82**, 154-155.

Kauffman, S. A.: 1986, 'A Framework to Think About Evolving Genetic Regulatory Systems', in W. Bechtel (ed.), *Integrating Scientific Disciplines*, Martinus Nijhoff, Dordrecht.

Lycan, W. G.: 1981, 'Form, Function, and Feel', *The Journal of Philosophy* **78**, 24-49.

McClelland, J. L.: 1986, 'The Programmable Blackboard Model of Reading', in McClelland & Rumelhart, 1986, pp. 122-169.

McClelland, J. L. and Rumelhart, D. E.: 1981, 'An Interactive Activation Model of Context Effects in Letter Perception. Part 1, An Account of Basic Findings', *Psychological Review* **88**, 375-407.

McClelland, J. L. and Rumelhart, D. E. and the PDP Research Group: 1986, *Parallel Distributed Processing: Explorations in the Microstructure of Cognition. Volume 2: Psychological and Biological Models*.

Minsky, A. and Papert, S.: 1969, *Perceptrons*, MIT Press, Cambridge.

Neisser, U.: 1975, *Cognition and Reality: Principles and Implications of Cognitive Psychology*, Freeman, San Francisco.

Neisser, U.: 1982, *Memory Observed*, Freeman, San Francisco.

Newell, A.: 1980, 'Physical Symbol Systems,' *Cognitive Science* **4**, 135-183.

Newell, A.: 1989, *Unified Theories of Cognition*, The William James Lectures, Harvard University Press, Cambridge.

Pinker, S. & Prince, A.: 1988, 'On Language and Connectionism: Analysis of a Parallel Distributed Processing Model of Language Acquisition', *Cognition* **28**, 73-193.

Pylyshyn, Z. W.: 1984, *Computation and Cognition. Toward a Foundation for Cognitive Science*, MIT Press (Bradford Books), Cambridge.

Quillan, M. R.: 1968, 'Semantic Memory', in M. Minsky (ed.) *Semantic Information Processing* (pp. 227-270), MIT Press, Cambridge.

Rips, L. J., Smith, E. E., and Shoben, E. J.: 1975, 'Set-Theoretic and Network Models Reconsidered: A Comment on Hollan's "Features and Semantic Memory."' *Psychological Review* **82**, 156-157.

Rosch, E. H.: 1975, 'Cognitive Representations of Semantic Categories', *Journal of Experimental Psychology: General* **104**, 192-233.

Rosch, E. H.: 1978, 'Principles of Categorization', in E. H. Rosch and B. B. Lloyd, *Cognition and Categorization* (pp. 24-48), Lawrence Erlbaum Associates, Hillsdale, NY.

Rosenblatt, F.: 1962, *Principles of Neurodynamics*, Spartan, New York.

Rumelhart, D. E., Hinton, G., and McClelland, J. L.: 1986, 'A General Framework for Parallel Distributed Processing', in Rumelhart & McClelland, 1986, pp. 45-76.

Rumelhart, D. E. and McClelland, J. L. and the PDP research group: 1986, *Parallel Distributed Processing: Explorations in the Microstructure of Cognition Volume 1: Foundations*, MIT Press (Bradford Books), Cambridge.

Rumelhart, D. E. and Norman, D. A.: 1982, 'Simulating a Skilled Typist: A Study of Skilled Cognitive-Motor Performance', *Cognitive Science* **6**, 1-36.

Rumelhart, D. E., Smolensky, P., McClelland, J. L., and Hinton, G. E.: 1986, 'Schemata and Sequential Thought Processes in PDP Models', in McClelland & Rumelhart, 1986.

Rumelhart, D. E. and Zipser, D.: 1985, 'Feature Discovery by Competitive Learning', *Cognitive Science* **9**, 75-112.

Searle, J.: 1980, 'Minds, Brains, and Programs', *Behavioral and Brain Sciences* **3**, 417-424.

Selfridge, O.: 1955, 'Pattern Recognition in Modern Computers, *Proceedings of the Western Joint Computer Conference*.

Smith, E. E., Shoben, E. J., and Rips, L. J.: 1974, 'Structure and Process in Semantic Memory: A Featural Model for Semantic Decisions', *Psychological Review* **81**, 214-241.

Smith, E. E. and Medin, D. L.: 1981, *Categories and Concepts*, Harvard University Press, Cambridge.

Smolensky, P.: 1988, 'On the Proper Treatment of Connectionism', *Behavioral and Brain Sciences* **11**, 1-74.

Touretzky, D. S.: 1986, 'BoltzCONS: Reconciling Connectionism with the Recursive Nature of Stacks and Trees', *Proceedings of the Eighth Annual Conference of the Cognitive Science Society*, Lawrence Erlbaum Associates, Hillsdale, NJ.

Department of Philosophy
Georgia State University
Atlanta, GA 30303-3083

ROBERT CUMMINS AND GEORG SCHWARZ

CONNECTIONISM, COMPUTATION, AND COGNITION

I. INTRODUCTION

Our goal in this paper is to locate connectionism in the explanatory enterprise of cognitive science. Consequently we start out by sketching the fundamentals of computationalism, which has been the dominant working hypothesis in the field. After briefly distinguishing computationalism *per se* from a number of controversial theses that are sometimes packaged with it (by friends and foes alike), we turn to our main focus: how connectionism relates to computationalism. We claim that connectionist research typically shares the defining assumptions of computationalism, though this has often been obscured by confusing computationalism with one or another special form of it (e.g., the language of thought hypothesis). Though connectionist models typically are computationalist in spirit, they needn't be. We conclude by outlining a possible connectionist position which would constitute a radical departure from basic computationalist assumptions.

II. GENERIC COMPUTATIONALISM

The working hypothesis of most of current cognitive science is that systems are cognitive in virtue of computing appropriate functions. Just how are we to understand this claim? We begin with an illustration of computationalism since it, like many things, is better understood by reference to an uncontroversial exemplar than by appeal to an abstract characterization.

Calculation

During an archeological expedition you unearth a strange looking device. Close examination reveals that the device has a lid which hides twelve buttons, each with a strange symbol etched on its face, and a small window. Curiosity leads you to experiment, and you notice that certain sequences of

60

button pushings result in certain symbols being displayed in the window, displays which consist only of symbols that also appear on the buttons. Moreover, these display states seem to be correlated with the respective buttons pushed in some non-arbitrary way. Intrigued by the device's increasingly interesting behavior, you decide to do some cryptography. The display uses only ten of the twelve little symbols found on the buttons, so you start mapping them onto the ten digits familiar from our decimal numeral system. On this interpretation your device performs operations on numbers, so you assume further that the eleventh button serves to separate the arguments, and that the remaining one is a kind of "go" button, like "=" on a standard calculator. The rest is easy, for a few test runs show that the system's output (its display state) can be consistently interpreted as the product of the numbers that interpret the antecedent sequence of button pushings. As it turns out, your ancient device is a multiplier. How does it work?

Multiplication is the familiar relation between pairs of numbers and a third one, their product. Calculators, on the other hand, are mechanical or electronic devices whose behavior is governed by the laws of physics. In virtue of what facts can calculators satisfy the product function?

What reveals the device as a multiplier is the fact that button pushings and display states can be consistently interpreted as numbers and their products. What makes such a device a multiplier, then, is that there exists (in the mathematical sense) an *interpretation function* that systematically maps physical state transitions onto the arguments and values of the product function. And it is precisely this interpretation function that reveals physical states of the system as representations of the arguments and values of the function satisfied, i.e., as numerals.

A multiplier is a device such that causing it to represent a pair of numbers causes it to represent their product. Thus, to explain how a device multiplies is (at least) to explain how representations of multiplier and multiplicand cause representations of (correct) products. One possible solution to this problem is to show that the device computes representations of products from representations of multipliers and multiplicands. According to the computationalist, systems like our multiplier compute the functions they satisfy, and it is in virtue of these computations that the relevant semantic regularities are preserved (i.e., that representations of $<n, m>$ cause representations of the product of n and m).

Computing

One way to satisfy a function is to compute it. Calculators satisfy the MULTIPLY(n1,n2) function by computing it. A falling apple, on the other hand, satisfies the function $D = (at^2)/2$ but does not compute it. What's the difference?

Most of us compute the multiplication function by executing the partial products algorithm. That algorithm, like all symbolic algorithms, is defined for a certain notation. For example, the partial products algorithm doesn't work for roman numerals. In the case of the partial products algorithm, the objects of computation--the things the algorithm manipulates--are the standard decimal numerals. While executing an algorithm always involves following rules for manipulating things--tokens, we might call them, like tokens in a game (Haugeland, 1986)--the things manipulated are not always symbols. Indeed, the objects of computation needn't be representations of any sort. An algorithm for solving Rubic's Cube requires manipulation of the cube, not of symbols for states of the cube.[1] Algorithms implemented on a computer typically manipulate symbols, but many common and useful algorithms do not. The most obvious examples are recipes and instruction manuals ("How to clean your steam iron").

The natural, familiar and, we believe, correct suggestion about computing is that computing a function f is executing an algorithm that gives o as its output on input i just in case $f(i) = o$. The problem of explaining function computation reduces to the of explaining what it is to execute an algorithm for that function. The obvious strategy is to exploit the idea that algorithm execution involves steps, and to treat each elementary step as a function that the executing system (or one of its components) simply satisfies. To execute an algorithm is to satisfy the steps, and to do so, as we say, "in the right order." So: to compute a function is to execute an algorithm, and algorithm execution is disciplined step satisfaction.

It remains to explain what it is for step satisfaction to be disciplined. This seems to be straight-forward enough in principle. The fundamental idea is that the system satisfies the steps in the right order because it is so structured that the steps are imbedded in a causal order. Steps interact causally: satisfying a step in d is an event in d, and events in d have effects in d; among those effects are the satisfaction of other steps, and so on. The discipline we are looking for is underwritten by the causal structure of the executing device. Spelling out what this comes to in detail for, e.g., a conditional branch, is a messy but conceptually straight-forward exercise. You won't go far wrong if you imagine the algorithm expressed as a flow-chart. Each box in the flow chart represents a step. To execute a step is to satisfy its characteristic function. If you think of the arrows between the boxes as causal arrows, the result is a causal network with steps--i.e., functions to be satisfied--at the nodes. A device *d* executes the algorithm if that causal network gives the (or a) causal structure of *d*.

A physical system, then, computes a function (rather than simply satisfies it) if it executes an algorithm for that function. Notice that we understand a computation as an abstract causal process--i.e., as a causal process specified abstractly as an algorithm. This is precisely what is required if computation is to play any role at all in the explanation of the behavior of physical systems. There are lots of causal processes, and only some of them are instances of function computation. It is the latter that constitute the realm of computational explanation. Moreover, there are many ways of satisfying functions, even computable functions (i.e., functions for which there are algorithms) that do not involve executing an algorithm.

Thus, a computationalist explanation of the capacity of a device to multiply will begin by attempting to identify representational states of the device and an algorithm defined over them that specifies the (abstract) causal structure of the device that disciplines transitions from one representational state to another. Our knowledge of already invented multiplication algorithms (partial products, say, or successive addition) might help, as might our familiarity with various formal schemes for representing numbers (binary, decimal, etc.). On the other hand, the system might turn out to be a very fast and very powerful look-up table. Computationalism assumes that there are right and wrong answers to this kind of question, answers that don't reduce to the realizing electronics or mechanics, or to the fact to be explained, viz., that the system satisfies the multiplication function.

Computationalism and Cognition

Systems are cognitive in virtue of satisfying cognitive functions. We think of a system as cognizing a domain rather than merely responding to an environment when that behavior essentially involves respecting epistemological constraints appropriate to some specified domain, the domain it is said to cognize. We can conceive of these epistemological constraints as determining a cognitive function, and this, in turn, allows us to think of cognitive systems as systems that satisfy cognitive functions. Computationalism is the hypothesis that systems are cognitive in virtue of computing cognitive functions. This they do in the same way that multipliers compute the multiplication function, i.e., by executing an algorithm that operates on representations of the arguments to the function to produce representations of their values.

An essential feature of this story is that the objects of semantic interpretation--the representations--are the objects of computation--the things manipulated by the algorithm. It is this extra constraint that distinguishes computationalism from a non-computational representationalism that attempts to account for representational dynamics without appealing to the idea that what disciplines changes of representational state is execution of an algorithm defined over those representations.

Summary

Computationalism, as we understand it, is the hypothesis that systems are cognitive in virtue of executing algorithms that manipulate representations of the arguments and values of cognitive functions. Thus construed, computationalism is a form of representationalism, i.e., a form of the doctrine that systems are cognitive in virtue of moving in some disciplined manner through representational states.

III. WHAT COMPUTATIONALISM IS NOT

There are several theses that are often packaged with computationalism, but which are no part of computationalism *per se*. It is worth taking some time to identify these briefly, since connectionism is sometimes spuriously distinguished from computationalism on the grounds that connectionism is incompatible with one or more of these theses. If, as we argue, connectionism in its typical forms is a species of computationalism, than any argument that one of these special theses is incompatible with connectionism is actually an argument that that thesis is incompatible with some forms of computationalism.

Symbolic vs. Sub-symbolic

Smolensky (1988) has made a good deal of the fact that connectionists need not be wedded to representations that express the sorts of concepts that are, as it were, part of the standard intellectual equipment one acquires in learning a natural language. But, of course, there is nothing known that limits, in principle, the kind or "grain" of concepts that a computational system can represent.

Distributed vs. Local Representation

Distributed representation is, in fact, commonplace in non-connectionist computational systems. In production systems, concepts are frequently represented over several rules, with the same "pool" of rules responsible for several concepts (Klahr, *et al.*, 1987). Semantic nets provide another example. A node labeled "cat" represents cats only in virtue of its place in the net. Thus, the whole net represents a number of concepts, but no single node, in isolation, represents anything.[2]   Finally, various orthodox computational models make use of spreading activation, though activation doesn't generally spread in a connectionist fashion. In models of this kind, the elements over which activation spreads can participate in either distributed or local representation or both (Anderson, 1983; Holland, *et al.*, 1986).

Serial vs. Parallel

Connectionists sometimes cite in their favor that both brains and nets process information in parallel. This, of course, does not distinguish connectionism from computationalism unless it is supposed that computationalism is committed to, and limited by, sequential processing. But this supposition is clearly mistaken.   Non-connectionist computationalism is busy exploring parallel algorithms (e.g., Lipovski and Malek, 1987), and designing parallel hardware (e.g., Hillis, 1986).[3]

The Language of Thought Hypothesis

This is the hypothesis that the representations employed by cognitive systems belong to a language-like scheme of representation that has a finite based combinatorial semantics. It is important to keep in mind that computationalism is not committed to any such view. Indeed, much productive computationalist research makes use of representational schemes that are not language like in any obvious sense, e.g., frames, semantic nets, and "images". Certainly, no combinatorial semantics has been worked out for such schemes. Arguments for or against the language of thought are thus not in themselves arguments for or against computationalism.

On the other side of the coin, it does not appear to be true, as is sometimes alleged (Fodor and Pylyshyn, 1988), that connectionism cannot avail itself of a language of thought approach. Cummins (in press) has argued that even rather simple networks can employ and exploit a representational scheme with the unbounded representational power and combinatorial semantics of propositional logic, and Smolensky (in press) has introduced techniques for representing complex hierarchies in connectionist architectures.

It is worth keeping in mind in this connection that no computational system is truly productive: all such systems are finite state automata at best. Appeal to genuine productivity is always an idealization that needs to be justified. A calculator, for example, is held to be productive because its representational (and hence computational) powers are limited only by memory and time. But it is possible to apply the same kind of argumentation to certain connectionist systems.[4] Non-connectionists have no monopoly on the competence-performance distinction.

IV: CONNECTIONISM: THE SHORT TOUR

A connectionist architecture consists of a network of connected nodes. At a given moment, a node is characterized by a variable representing its level of activation and by a constant representing its threshold. When the activation of a node exceeds its threshold, activation is propagated from that node to others along whatever links happen to exist. Links are weighted, the weights determining the (relative) quantity of activation they may carry. Connection weights may be positive or negative: that is, a given node can inhibit the nodes to which it is connected by a negatively weighted arc by subtracting from the activation. The state of the network at a time is given by the pattern of activation at that time (i.e., the activation level of each node at that time) and by the connection strengths.

An input is given to the network by providing some specified level of activation to nodes designated as input nodes. Activation then spreads throughout the network in a way determined by the antecedently existing pattern of activation and by the strengths of connecting links. The dynamics of the system is given by differential equations that determine activation spread as a function of time. The "output" of the system is the state of that portion of the network designated as the output nodes when the entire network "settles down" into a steady state. Certain processes may alter the connection strengths, thereby altering the input/output function the network satisfies. For suitable task domains, nets can thus be "trained" to compute a desired input/output function.

V: CONNECTIONISM AND COMPUTATIONALISM

Is connectionism an instance of computationalism? It is beyond question, as Fodor and Pylyshyn point out (1988) that most current connectionist research is firmly committed to representationalism. "Connectionist representation" is a flourishing topic of research (e.g., Hinton, *et al.*, 1986; Feldman, 1986; Smolensky, in press), and is clearly a species of the research in "knowledge representation" so ubiquitous in orthodox AI. Inputs and outputs to connectionist networks are standardly conceived as representations, as are patterns of activation on hidden units (Sejnowski and Rosenberg, 1987; Elman, in press), and, more recently, time trajectories over activation vectors (Elman, 1989). Moreover, transitions among representational states are typically supposed to be computationally disciplined. Articles discussing "connectionist computation" and "connectionist algorithms" appear regularly in the journals. A common procedure in building a network model is to start out by specifying the target function, to train suitable architectures on representations of argument/value pairs of that function, and then to see how well these systems generalize to novel instances. A network model is considered successful if it satisfies the target function as accurately as possible under the intended interpretation of its representational states. Much of current connectionist research, both theoretical and applied, is concerned precisely with determining what functions can be computed by what kinds of connectionist architectures.

A great deal of connectionist research, then, operates under computationalist assumptions about representation and computation and how these are to be exploited in the explanation of cognitive capacities. Competing computational theories differ in their choice of representational primitives and, as a consequence, the class of algorithms that can be used to manipulate them. What makes most connectionist models different from "classical" computational models is what kinds of representations and algorithms they employ, not whether they employ them at all.

VI: NON-COMPUTATIONAL CONNECTIONISM

While most connectionist research is straight-forwardly intended to be computationalist in spirit and practice, there is no necessary connection between the computationalist explanatory strategy and connectionism. Connectionist research needn't assume that cognitive functions are computable (i.e., recursive) functions, since a connectionist need not specify an algorithm; they need only specify connectionist dynamics that discipline representational states in a way that mirrors the way the domain disciplines whatever is represented.

There are two ways in which a connectionist architecture might discipline representational state transition non-computationally.

First, it might be that the causally relevant states of the system cross-classify the representational states of the system. While we know of no connectionist research that consciously seeks to exploit this possibility, it clearly is a possibility. The following analogy helps give a feel for what we have in mind. Imagine an academic quadrangle, with classrooms positioned all around the perimeter. Classes change on the hour. At each hour, then, each student crosses from one point on the perimeter to another, forming a pattern on the quadrangle in the process. Depending on how regular student behavior is, these patterns will be more or less regular. So: suppose that at nine, they form, like a marching band, a block "2", at ten, a "3", at eleven, a "5", a "7" at twelve, an "11" at one, and so on. The numerals are artifacts: although it is no accident that a "5" occurs at eleven, it doesn't occur because a "3" occurred at ten.[5] We can explain why the numerals occur, though not yet why they are numerals--that is just an accident so far as we know. Hence, we can't explain why we get only representations of prime numbers, or why they are in order. Yet we can explain, in terms of student schedules and the geometry of the quadrangle, the occurrence of each numeral. It is just that the availability of a systematic interpretation is, so far as we know, a coincidence.[6]

If the succession of representational states in connectionist systems were like this, then cognition would be an artifact, an astounding coincidence. No connectionists, however hot their zeal to distinguish themselves from the orthodox, take this possibility seriously. But suppose we learn that someone in the registrar's office manipulates and approves schedule requests in order to achieve this strange result. Suppose she does this by rewarding students who select schedules that fit in with her plans. Given this sort of "supervised learning", the numerals are no longer artifacts: the system is designed to produce patterns that bear a certain systematic interpretation.[7] And yet, the system does not compute these representations; there is no algorithm defined over the representations that the system executes. Indeed, the representational states of the system are not causally relevant to its dynamics: If you put on a magic pair of glasses that reveals only what is causally relevant to change over time, you won't see the numerals.[8]

So one reason why a connectionist system might discipline representational state changes non-computationally is that the semantics and the causal dynamics cross-classify states. A second reason is that the representational states, while causally significant, are states in a dynamic system whose characteristic function--the function defined by its dynamical equations--is not itself computable. This, of course, is more than a mere possibility. A network whose representational states are real-valued activation vectors and weight matrices, and whose dynamics is given by a set of differential equations, is in general, going to be just such a system.[9, 10]

Any system that is cognitive in virtue of its representational state changes, but effects those changes non-computationally, is a counter-example to computationalism. Since connectionist systems could be such systems, connectionists need not be computationalists. What reasons might there be for supposing that representational state changes are non-computationally mediated?

The Specification Problem

Let C be a cognitive function, and let R be a function on representations such that $C(x) = y$ if the value of R on a representation of x is a representation of y. If C isn't computable, then neither is R. Thus, if one had reasons to suppose that cognitive functions weren't computable, one would have a reason for studying models in which representational state transitions were effected non-computationally. Is there any reason to think that cognitive functions are not computable?

A cognitive function, recall, is a function that expresses a set of epistemic constraints satisfaction of which counts as cognizing some particular domain. Thus, computationalism implies that these constraints are always expressible as a computable function. Yet there is some reason to think that, for some domains, the relevant constraints aren't even specifiable, let alone specifiable as a computable function. Reflect for a moment on the special sciences. A special science codifies what there is to know about its proprietary domain. But you can't have a special science of any old domain: Science only works were there are natural kinds, and the like. A science of temperature per se is only possible if, as we say, thermal phenomena form an autonomous domain of inquiry. What this means is that thermodynamics is possible only to the extent that thermal phenomena are governed by laws that describe those phenomena "in their own terms," i.e., autonomously. By way of contrast, an autonomous special science of clothing is hardly possible, as Fodor has emphasized in another connection (Fodor, 1984), because there are no special laws of clothing. Clothing, of course, falls under laws, e.g., the laws of physics, chemistry and economics, so there is no question that scientific study of clothing is possible, but not scientific study of clothing *qua* clothing.

Of course, the cognitive functions that characterize a domain of human cognition need not be the same as--encode the same knowledge as--a special science of that domain (though that idea has dominated a great deal of psycholinguistic research since at least the middle sixties--see, e.g., Chomsky, 1965). But it is not implausible to suppose that the preconditions for specifiable cognitive functions and for a special science are closely related. There are, no doubt about it, "rules" in the clothing domain--how to dress for different occasions and effects, what needs ironing, what can be washed, etc. But it is doubtful whether these rules can be compiled into an expert system that captures human intelligence in the clothing domain, hence doubtful whether such a set of rules can be specified that expresses what constraints expert humans satisfy, however it is that they do it. Perhaps expert human performance in such domains can't be rule driven because it isn't rule describable--i.e., not recursively specifiable.[11] Perhaps, like the science of clothing, it is not specifiable at all, except trivially as the sum total of what some human does in that domain. Thus, it may be that we can have an autonomous specification of cognition only where we can have a special science. While we can, perhaps, have science anywhere, we surely cannot have a special science for every possible domain of intelligent human thought.

Cognition as an Ostensive and Comparative Concept

How is any cognitive science possible where there are no specifiable cognitive functions? Should the specification problem for cognition prove to be intractable, or tractable only in special cases, as seems increasingly likely, where will that leave us? We think it leaves us with biological exemplars. Cognition will simply be identified ostensively, and hence extrinsically, as what humans do when..., e.g., they solve problems, find their way home, etc. We will be left, in short, with Turing's (1950) conception: A cognitive system is just one that compares favorably with humans (or other known cognizers) in respects subject to epistemic evaluation.[12] This is, in a sense, already the status quo. One does not, for example, set out to build a computational system to play chess with a specification of a chess function (from board positions to moves, say) in hand. On the contrary, the only way we know how to specify such a function is to build a computational system to play chess.[13] When we have built a computational system to play chess, however, we have specified a chess function, for we have designed an algorithm that operates on representations of board positions to produce representations of moves. Computationalism requires an algorithm, and an algorithm is one way to specify a function. Thus, as the name implies, computationalism requires that every cognitive task must have a specifiable characteristic function that is computable (recursive). But computationalists seldom begin with a specification in hand. Instead, they proceed comparatively and ostensively, trying to build a system that compares favorably with that sort of human behavior, where "that" is a gesture toward the target, not a theoretical description of it. But: when a successful computationalist system has been built, an algorithm has been specified for computing a cognitive function. So a computationalist can succeed only if cognitive functions are computable. The difference is that non-computationalists can succeed in this game even if the target isn't computable.

NOTES

[1]   An algorithm that manipulates representations of cube states may allow us to simulate execution of a rubic's cube algorithm.

[2]   In a genuinely local representation, destruction of "neighbors" does not alter the proper interpretation. This is clearly not true of semantic nets.

[3]   There is a flip side to this point. While "orthodoxy" accommodates both serial and parallel processing, connectionists have a hard time with the former. Only the recent development of recurrent nets (e.g., Elman in press, 1989; Servan-Schreiber, D., Cleeremans, A., and McClelland, J., 1988) allows for a serious modelling of sequential processing in nets.

[4]   The simple system described in Cummins (in press) can simplify a propositional logic formula in polish notation of arbitrary length as long as it is provided with enough "delay" units. That is, for any n, there is an m such that, if the network is equipped with m delay units, it can process any formula of length n or less.

[5]   It doesn't matter that the patterns are numerals, so long as they are roughly re-identifiable and repeat with some regularity. (See Cummins, 1978, for a discussion of this kind of example in another connection.)

[6]   Even this point has to be put carefully. Given the way the system is structured, it is no accident that patterns occur that have the interpretation in question. But the patterns have no causal significance, and their meanings have no explanatory significance.

[7]   The point doesn't depend essentially on the "supervisor." What is essential is that the semantics can matter--not be artifactual--even though representational states don't matter to the dynamics, i.e., even though you need to carve up states in one way to see the causal dynamics, and another way to see the representations, and hence to see cognition. The environment of a natural system, we suppose, selects for dynamics that make for accurate and useful representation. The point of the analogy is to make it intuitively clear that this sort of selection is possible even though the representational states are not causally significant.

[8]   The kind of magic glasses we have in mind are the kind that would show you only centers of gravity and momenta when you looked at a mechanical system like a billiard table.

[9]   Essential to this point is that the set of representational states is unbounded, since any finite function is computable.

[10]   Perhaps this is what Dreyfus and Dreyfus (1985) were driving at.

[11]   It is worth recalling that there are many simple systems whose dynamics cannot be specified as a computable function--e.g., a three-body newtonian mechanical system.

[12]   Actually, a generalization of Turing's question is required so that non-linguistic behavior is covered. Still, the linguistic restriction was, in a way, on the right track. We want comparisons of behavior under interpretation, not comparisons of behavior *per se*.

[13]   Marr's (1982) now classic exposition of computationalist methodology does seem to imply that one does have to have a specification in hand before one can proceed to design a system to satisfy it. But, as the example in the text (and everyday practice) shows, this requirement is too strict.

REFERENCES

Anderson, J.: 1983, *The Architecture of Cognition*, Harvard University Press, Cambridge.

Chomsky, N.: 1965, *Aspects of the Theory of Syntax*, MIT Press, Cambridge.

Cummins, R.: 1978, 'Explanation and Subsumption', PSA 1978: *Proceedings of the Philosophy of Science Association*, v. 1, 1978, pp. 163-175.

Cummins, R.: (in press), 'The Role of Representation in Connectionist Explanations of Cognitive Capacities', in Ramsey W., S. Stich, and D. Rumelhart (in press), *Connectionism and Philosophy*, Erlbaum.

Dreyfus, H., and Dreyfus, S.: 1985, *Mind Over Machine*, Macmillan.

Elman, J.: 1989, 'Representation and Structure in Connectionist Models', *Technical Report 8903*, Center for Research in Language, University of California, San Diego.

Elman, J.: (in press), 'Finding Structure in Time', *Cognitive Science*.

Fodor, J.: (1984), 'Why Paramecia Don't Have Mental Representations', *Midwest Studies in Philosophy* 10, pp. 3-23.

Fodor, J., and Pylyshyn,Z.: 1988, 'Connectionism and Cognitive Architecture: A Critical Analysis', *Cognition* 28, pp. 3-71.

Haugeland, J.: 1986, *Artificial Intelligence: The Very Idea*, MIT Press, a Bradford Book, Cambridge.

Hillis, W.: 1985, *The Connection Machine*, MIT Press, Cambridge.

Hinton, G., McClelland, J., and Rumelhart, D.: 1986, 'Distributed Representations', in Rumelhart and McClelland (eds), *Parallel Distributed Processing*, v. 1., MIT Press, a Bradford Book, Cambridge.

Holland, J., Holyoak, K., Nisbett, R., and Thagard, P.: 1986, *Induction: Processes of Inference, Learning and Discovery*, MIT Press, a Bradford Book, Cambridge.

Klahr, D., Langley, P., and Neches, R.,(eds.): 1987, *Production System Models of Learning and Development*, MIT Press, a Bradford Book, Cambridge.

Lipovski and Malek: 1987, *Parallel Computing: Theory and Comparisons*, Riley, New York.

Marr, D.: 1982, *Vision*, W. H. Freeman, San Francisco.

Sejnowski, T., and Rosenberg, C.: 1987, 'Parallel Networks that Learn to Pronounce English Text', *Complex Systems*, v.1, pp. 145-168.

Servan-Schreiber, D., Cleeremans, A., and McClelland, J.: 1988, 'Encoding Sequential Structure in Simple Recurrent Networks', *Technical Report, CMU-CS-88-183*, Computer Science Department, Carnegie-Mellon University.

Smolensky, P.: 1988, 'On the Proper Treatment of Connectionism', *The Behavioral and Brain Sciences*, v. 11, no. 1.

Smolensky, P.: in press, 'Tensor Product Variable Binding and the Representation of Symbolic Structures in Connectionist Systems', *Artificial Intelligence*.

Turing, A.: 1950, 'Computing Machinery and Intelligence', *Mind* 59, pp. 434-460.

Robert Cummins
Department of Philosophy
University of Arizona
Tucson, AZ 85721

Georg Schwarz
Department of Philosophy
University of California, San Diego
La Jolla, CA 92093

JAY G. RUECKL

CONNECTIONISM AND THE NOTION OF LEVELS

The growing popularity of connectionism has sparked a great deal of discussion and research in the cognitive science community. To a large extent, the focus has been on the theoretical and empirical adequacy of connectionist systems as models of cognitive processes. The goal has been to determine the computational capacities of connectionist networks and to explore how such networks might be used to model the psychological processes that control behavior. Not all of the discussion about connectionism has focused on such issues, however. Indeed, a substantial literature addresses far loftier concerns about the nature of connectionism, such as whether connectionism can, in principle, provide adequate accounts of psychological phenomena, whether connectionism represents a theoretical revolution (or "paradigm shift"), and what the relationship is between connectionist and neural models on the one hand, and connectionist and symbol processing models on the other.

Much of the discussion about these issues has revolved around the notion of "levels." For its critics, the problem with connectionism is that the explanations it offers are "at the wrong level." Fodor and Pylyshyn (1988), for example, argue that connectionist models are inadequate as accounts at the psychological level and are, at best, theories about the implementation of "truly" psychological processes. Broadbent (1985) also argues for this "mere implementation" view of connectionism. But connectionism's critics are not alone in their concern with the notion of levels. Rumelhart and McClelland (1986a) state that "we do believe that in some sense PDP models are at a different level than other cognitive models." Similarly, Smolensky (1988) states that "the level of analysis adopted (by connectionist models) is lower than that of the traditional, symbolic paradigm."

Although there is fairly widespread agreement that connectionist and symbol processing models are at different levels, it is not clear that there is agreement about what those levels are. Indeed, the notion of levels can be formulated in many ways. For example, levels might be defined temporally, in terms of the time scale at which events occur (Newell, 1987).

Alternatively, levels might be defined physically, with entities at higher levels made of aggregates of entities at lower levels. For example, Sejnowski and Churchland (1988) describe the organization of the brain in relation to the following levels: molecules, synapses, neurons, local networks, layers and columns, topographic maps, and systems.

Perhaps the conception of levels that has had the greatest influence on the connectionism debate is that articulated by David Marr (1982). Marr argued that the complete account of a psychological process involved three levels of explanation. The first level of explanation is the *computational* level, where the focus is on what a process does and why it does it. At the computational level a process is characterized as a mapping from one kind of information to another, the properties of this mapping are detailed, and any environmental or teleological conditions that constrain the process are noted. The second level of explanation is the *algorithmic* level. At this level, the representations used to code the inputs and outputs are specified, as is the algorithm used to map inputs onto outputs. The third level of explanation is the *implementational* level. The purpose of this level is to make clear how the representations and algorithm specified at the algorithmic level are instantiated in the states and processes of an underlying device (hard, wet, or otherwise).

Given Marr's framework, much of the nature of the debate between the proponents and opponents of connectionism becomes clear. Here's what the proponents say: *Although connectionist networks look very much like neural systems, they're really at a more abstract level. Indeed, what they offer is a new conception of the algorithms used to carry out computational processes--one that does not rely on entities such as symbols, rules, and the like, but instead employs concepts like flow of activation, weight strength, and distributed representation. Thus, if you accept connectionist models as valid psychological theories, what you're doing is accepting new algorithmic-level explanations.*

The opponents of connectionist say this: *Look, connectionist models are simply inadequate as algorithmic level theories. We can't imagine how they could do X* (where X is usually filled in with some problem involving abstract reasoning or language use). *The only way to do X is to manipulate symbols. Now, we agree that connectionist models have many nice properties, but these properties are only important at the implementational level. Maybe connectionism will provide implementational-level accounts of symbol models. But if so, so what? The psychology is in the algorithm, not in its implementation.*

The positions seem clear. If connectionist models have any validity, they will either replace symbol models at the algorithmic level or describe the realization of symbol models at the implementational level. But things are never quite as they seem. In this case, the appeal to Marr's framework oversimplifies the issues. In particular, the distinction between the algorithmic and implementational levels is more complex than one might gather from Marr's exposition. When this distinction is examined carefully, it becomes clear that what is an algorithmic-level explanation from one perspective can be an implementational-level explanation from another. That is, although it is typical to think of the implementation of algorithmic primitives in terms of physical entities (e.g., neurons, silicon chips, or even tinker toys), such primitives are often implemented by computational processes at another level of analysis.

This algorithmic/implementational duality can be seen in Marr's own work. In his classic *Vision* (1982), Marr laid out a theory of how the human visual system derives shape information from a retinal image. Marr argued that this process involves three stages. The first step is the construction of the primal sketch, which represents information about the distribution and organization of intensity changes in the two-dimensional image. From this the 2 1/2-D sketch is constructed. At this stage information about various properties of the visible surfaces, such as orientation, distance, and reflectance, is represented in a viewer-centered coordinate system. Finally, in the third stage shapes and their spatial organization are represented in a three-dimensional, object-centered coordinate system.

Each of the three processes comprising this algorithm is itself constructed from a set of component processes. For example, the construction of the primal sketch occurs in the following way. First, intensity changes in the image ("zero-crossings") are detected. From this, edges, bars, blobs, and terminations in the image are detected and represented in the *raw primal sketch*. The tokens of the raw primal sketch are then organized according to several grouping principles, and the boundaries of these groups are determined, resulting in the *full primal sketch*. Similar stories can be told about the construction of the 2 1/2-D sketch and the 3-D model representation.

Importantly, the analysis of a process into a set of component processes does not stop at this point. For example, each of the steps taken in constructing the primal sketch (i.e., the detection of zero-crossings, the construction of the raw primal sketch, and the conversion of the raw primal sketch into a full primal sketch) is carried out by a set of subprocesses described at a lower level of analysis. In constructing the raw primal sketch, different subprocesses are responsible for detecting entities such as edges and bars. Similarly, in constructing the full primal sketch, distinct subprocesses are used to group these entities according to different organizational principles, and another set of subprocesses are used to determine the boundaries of these groups.

The point here is that a computational process can be characterized at a number of levels of analysis. At each level, one or more processes are defined, and each process is characterized at the computational, algorithmic, and implementational levels of explanation. In Marr's theory, the process under consideration at the highest level of analysis is the mapping from the retinal input to representations of the three-dimensional shapes that are present in the visual field, and the algorithm that carries out this process consists of a sequence of three subprocesses. Although these processes are in some sense implemented by neural processes, there is another sense in which they are implemented by computational processes at a lower level of analysis. At the next level of analysis the processes to be characterized are those that comprised the algorithm of the first level. Again at this level the processes under consideration are characterized at the computational, algorithmic, and implementational levels.

What this discussion illustrates is that the notion that implementational-level explanations are concerned solely with the physical realization of computational processes is too simplistic. True enough, the purpose of this level is to make clear how the representations and algorithm specified at the algorithmic level are instantiated in the states and processes of an underlying "machine." And true enough, in the simplest case these machine states correspond directly to physical states of the device (e.g., brain, silicon chip, etc.) carrying out the process. However, in many cases the representations and algorithm used to carry out a process map onto states and processes of a *virtual* machine. Virtual machine states are not defined physically, but instead are defined as the inputs and outputs of computational processes at a lower level of analysis. As noted above, these processes are themselves described at the computational, algorithmic, and implementational levels, and will themselves be instantiated on either physical or virtual machines. If the instantiation is on a virtual machine, the primitive processes of that virtual machine must in turn be analyzed, until eventually each process is given a physical instantiation.

Thus, what counts as algorithm and what counts as implementation depends on which the level of analysis chosen. From different perspectives, a "blob detection" process can be seen as (a) part of the implementation of the process that derives three-dimensional shape information from a retinal image; (b) a component of the algorithm responsible for constructing the raw primal sketch; or (c) a computational process in need of an account at each of Marr's three levels of explanation. It is crucial that this point not be lost in arguments about the relationship between connectionist and symbol processing models.

LEVELS AND CONNECTIONIST MODELS

Armed with the twin notions of levels of explanation and levels of analysis, let's now examine first the structure of connectionist models and then the potential relationships between such models and symbol manipulation systems. As an example of a connectionist model, consider the model of past tense acquisition proposed by Rumelhart and McClelland (1986b). The purpose of this model is to explain how children learn to produce past-tense verb forms. The model works in the following way. First, the phonological representation of the root form of a verb is input to the system. This input is then mapped onto a different representation of that same root form through a process of spreading activation. In this case, the root form is not represented as a set of phonemes, but instead as a set of context-dependent articulatory features. This latter representation of the root form is then mapped onto a featural representation of the past-tense form, which is in turn converted to a phonemic representation. The output of this process is then compared to the desired or "ideal" representation of the past-tense form, and an error-correction technique is used to modify connection strengths in order to improve performance. Rumelhart and McClelland have argued that this model is capable of learning to produce the past tense of both regular and irregular verbs, and that the time course of this learning mimics the time course of children's behavior in a number of respects. (But see Pinker and Prince, 1987, for a different view.)

In the present context, the past tense model has been introduced to illustrate the notions of multiple levels of explanation and multiple levels of analysis in connectionist systems. At the highest level of analysis, the computational-level characterization of the process posited by this model is a mapping from representations of present-tense verbs to representations of past-tense verbs. That the model involves other assumptions at the computational level is evidenced by the nature of many of the criticisms leveled on the model by Pinker and Prince (1987). For example, Pinker and Prince have argued that the relative frequency of regular and irregular verbs does not change over time in the way assumed by Rumelhart and McClelland's model. (Indeed, although Pinker and Prince argue strenuously that a connectionist model could never account for past tense learning, their arguments might more reasonably be taken as arguments about Rumelhart & McClelland's computational-level characterization of the process and the environment in which it operates. As such, these arguments say nothing about the potential success of a connectionist model at the algorithmic level.)

Just as it is clear that the past tense model involves a computational-level theory, it is equally clear that the model also provides an account at the algorithmic level. Consider the process that maps root forms of verbs onto their past-tense forms. In the algorithmic account, the inputs and outputs of this process are represented as sets of phonemes. The mapping between these representations is carried out by an algorithm that involves three subprocesses, one that maps the phonemic representation of the root form onto a set of context-dependent features, another that maps these features onto features representing the past-tense form, and a third that maps the latter features onto a phonemic representation of the past-tense form.

In order to describe the implementation of these component processes, we must drop down a level of analysis. At this level, the processes to be described are associative mapping functions such as the one that transforms the input from phonemic representations to featural representations. The inputs and outputs to these processes are distributed patterns of activity that represent the appropriate properties of a word's root or past-tense form. The algorithm used to map one distributed pattern onto another involves several component processes. First the net input to each output node is computed by summing the weighted signals that each node receives from the input nodes. Then the activation of each node is computed as function of its net input. Finally, each node produces an output signal that is based on its current level of activation. (It is worth noting that the implementation of these component processes is itself an unresolved issue. While it is tempting to claim that the nodes and links correspond directly to neurons and synapses, and thus that the primitive processes specified at this level of analysis correspond to events occurring within single cells and synapses, other interpretations are certainly reasonable. See, for example, Smolensky, 1988, and the commentaries that follow.)

The structure of the past tense model illustrates what may be the central premise of the connectionist framework. Namely, what connectionists propose is that in the explanation of any psychological process there is a level of analysis at which that process is described in terms of a connectionist system. The component processes of algorithms at this level (which we might call the "network" level) include processes such as the propagation and activation functions discussed above, threshold functions that determine what the output signals of a node will be as a function of its activation, learning rules that operate by modifying the strength of each connection, and feedback processes that provide measures of performance needed by certain learning rules.

As research in connectionist modeling has progressed, a picture has emerged about the nature of the algorithms carried out at the network level. Perhaps surprisingly, much can be accomplished with variations of just three basic themes: *associative mapping, relaxation,* and *incremental learning.* Associative mapping and relaxation involve changes in the pattern of activation across all or part of the system. In associative mapping functions, a pattern of activity over one set of nodes causes another pattern to occur over a different set of nodes. For example, the past tense model discussed above involves a sequence of processes of this type. Relaxation also involves a mapping from one pattern of activity to another. In this case, however, the initial and final states are not patterns of activity over two different sets of nodes, but instead are different patterns occurring at different times over the same set of nodes. The process is called "relaxation" because systems carrying out this process tend to settle, or "relax," into a stable final state (e.g., Hinton and Sejnowski, 1986; Rumelhart *et al.,* 1986). Finally, the third type of process, incremental learning, involves changes in the pattern of weights over a set of connections. The properties of various *learning* procedures of this type have been a major focus of research for many connectionists.

These processes--associative mapping, relaxation, and incremental learning--can be seen in several different lights. In one light, they are the processes that are computed at the network level. In this light, these processes are characterized at the computational level as the mapping from one pattern of activation (or connectivity) to another, and an explanation of how they are carried out is given by an algorithmic-level account that includes, for example, activation, propagation, and weight-change functions as its primitives.   In another light, associative mapping, relaxation, and incremental learning can be seen as the primitive processes that comprise algorithms at a higher level of analysis. At this level of analysis (let's call it the "pattern" level), a process is carried out by an appropriately-configured set of associative mapping, relaxation, and incremental learning processes. For example, in the past tense model the process that maps a phonological representation of a root form onto a phonological representation of its past-tense form is an example of a pattern-level process, as the algorithm that carries out this process is composed of a series of associative mapping functions.

THE RELATIONSHIP BETWEEN CONNECTIONIST AND SYMBOL PROCESSING MODELS

The twin notions of levels of explanation and levels of analysis provide a framework for understanding the relationship between connectionist and symbol processing models. The question is whether connectionist models are best seen as the competitors of symbol processing models, or if instead they are most appropriately thought of as potential explanations of how symbol models are implemented in neural wetware. Within the present explanatory framework, the implementational view would be supported if a clean and complete mapping could be found between symbol manipulation processes and processes at the pattern level. Alternatively, the implementational view would also be supported if the constructs employed by symbol processing models proved valuable as organizational principles at levels of analysis higher than the network and pattern levels.

Is it possible to directly interpret the primitive processes at the pattern level in terms of the manipulation of symbols?   One might argue, for example, that patterns of activity are simply ways of representing symbols, and that rules are stored implicitly in the pattern of connection strengths. If such a mapping were possible, then connectionist systems might best be seen as implementations of symbol manipulation systems. *Interesting* implementations, to be sure, but implementations none-the-less.

Although some progress has been made in developing symbol-level formalisms that map onto the behavior of connectionist systems (Oden, 1988; Smolensky, 1986), there are a number of potential difficulties in formulating such a mapping. One problem is that symbols are discrete entities: a symbol is either stored in memory or it is not; it is a constituent of a complex expression or it is not. Similarly, the processes that manipulate symbols typically have both discrete initiation conditions and discrete results. In contrast, whether a pattern of activity is present in a connectionist network is often a matter of degree; there is no sharp boundary determining how similar two patterns must be to count as "equivalent."

To be sure, continuousness is not completely foreign to the symbol processing approach. Indeed, several schemes have been proposed that allow symbol processing systems to take advantage of the flexibility and computational power offered by continuousness. One approach is to treat symbols as "fuzzy" propositions which can be true to various degrees (Oden, 1977; Massaro, 1987; Zadeh, 1976). Another approach has the causal efficacy of a symbol or rule depending on its degree of activation (Anderson, 1983; Collins and Loftus, 1975). Thus, one may be able to equate the degree to which a proposition is true or a symbol is activated with the degree to which a certain pattern of activity is present.

One worry about this approach is that knowing the degree to which a pattern is present is not sufficient for predicting the behavior of the system. One must also know which parts of the pattern are or aren't present. That is, two patterns of activation that are equally similar to a "prototypical" pattern may have wildly different behavioral consequences, depending on exactly how the two patterns differ. In itself, this problem may not be fatal. Smolensky (1988) has argued that even when no particular symbol is strongly activated, the behavior of a system can still be predicted if the activation of each symbol or rule is known. If so, although the spirit of the symbol approach is somewhat violated, one salvages hope of providing a mapping between the connectionist and symbol levels.

Smolensky's claim is sure to hold up in some cases (see McClelland and Rumelhart, 1981, for a suggestive example). However, in other cases connectionist systems take advantage of continuousness in ways that seem fundamentally incompatible with the symbol system approach. One such case involves learning. As the past tense model illustrates, in connectionist systems learning occurs through the modification of connection strengths, resulting in the gradual, continuous change in the structure of the system.

In symbol models, on the other hand, knowledge is stored by the set of symbols and processes stored in long-term memory, and learning results in the storage of new symbols or processes. Thus, the changes in a symbol system that occur with learning are discrete--a symbol or a process either is or is not stored in long-term memory.

It is not clear that these alternative conceptions of the learning process can be reconciled. One might attempt to use the notion of "strength" to bridge the gap between the discreteness of symbol models and the continuousness of connectionist models. That is, just as discrete symbols might be activated to various degrees to account for apparent continuousness in on-line processing, so too might rules be stored with varying strengths to account for apparent continuousness in learning. However, it does not seem likely that this move is sufficient to allow for a mapping between connectionist and symbol systems. One problem concerns the computational demands of the learning process. Learning in a symbol system requires a decision process to determine if a new symbol or process should be stored, an existing symbol or process should be modified, or nothing should be learned. It also requires a process for creating or modifying symbols accordingly. It is difficult to see how such processes would be mapped onto any known connectionist learning algorithms.

A second problem related to learning is that in symbol systems the creation or modification of one symbol or rule need not affect the storage of other symbols or rules--each symbol or rule is stored in a functionally distinct memory location. In contrast, in connectionist systems knowledge is superimposed on the same set of weights. Thus, when the weights are adjusted to learn one association, the storage of other associations is also affected. It is possible that this difference could be reconciled by supposing that learning in a symbol system involves both the creation of a new representation and the modification of all existing representations. However, it is not clear that this approach would allow for a complete specification of the transfer effects exhibited by a connectionist system. The problem is that the pattern of transfer effects that occur in a given connectionist system depends not only on the sequence of learning trials but also on the initial set of weights. Given different starting weights, two otherwise identical systems might arrive at different patterns of connectivity after the same sequence of trials, and thus exhibit different ensembles of transfer effects. In contrast, transfer effects in a symbol system are likely to be specified as a function of relationships in the content of representations involved, and these relationships will not vary as a function of starting condition. Hence, this approach would seem to underspecify the transfer effects that occur in a connectionist system.

Another problem related to the superimposition of knowledge in a connectionist system is that such systems can exhibit "virtual" knowledge, acting as if it had learned an association that in fact had never been learned. That is, the same relaxation or associative mapping process that creates the distributed representation of a familiar item is also capable of creating the pattern of activity representing a novel item, provided that the novel item is similar to some of the familiar items (a process known as "automatic generalization"; see Hinton *et al.*, 1986; and Rueckl, 1990). Within the symbol processing framework, it is reasonable to assume that in some domains the representations of both familiar and unfamiliar instances are created in the same way. For example, the representation of the syntactic structure of a sentence may be created "on-line" whether or not that sentence has been encountered before. However, in many domains symbol systems make a clear and firm distinction between old and new items. For example, the perceptual identification of a familiar object is generally thought to occur via a process that finds the best match between the perceptual input and representations stored in long-term memory. Because unfamiliar items would not be expected to match any stored representations, a second process is required to deal with these items. Although several potential solutions are known (candidates include analogy-based processes and processes that construct representations on the basis of the constituent structure of the object), the point is that in these cases the symbol systems treat familiar and unfamiliar items in fundamentally different ways.

The problem this poses for finding a direct mapping of symbol manipulation processes onto the behavior of connectionist networks is clear. If a symbol model assumes that familiar and novel inputs are processed in different ways and a connectionist model assumes that these inputs are processed in the same way, then the mapping from the symbol level to the connectionist level will be many-to-one. This would suggest that the symbol model was not "carving nature at its joints," and parsimony would demand the rejection of the symbol account in favor of the connectionist model, rather than an interpretation of the connectionist model as an implementation of the symbol processing system.

It should be noted that this problem is not restricted to the distinction between familiar and unfamiliar items. Indeed, in many cases connectionist models fail to honor the distinctions among categories of input items made by symbol models. A notable example involves domains that include both items that can be described as following a set of rules ("regular" items) and items that fail to conform to those rules ("exception" items). In English, for example, the pronunciation of most (but not all) written words can be determined by a relatively small set of orthographic-to-phonological conversion rules. Similarly, the mappings from singular to plural and from present to past tense also exhibit this "regularity plus exception" pattern. Symbol models of the processes that carry out such mappings typically honor the distinction between regular and exception items. They assume that the rules describing a mapping are explicitly represented internally, and that the transformation of regular items occurs through the application of the appropriate rules. Exceptions, on the other hand, are transformed through a second process that has access to the correct mapping for each of the exceptions. In contrast, connectionist models typically do not make these distinctions. Instead, just as a single mechanism can underlie the processing of familiar and unfamiliar items, so too can a unified account be given for the processing of regular and exception items. (See, for example, the Seidenberg and McClelland (1989) model of word naming and the Rumelhart and McClelland (1986) past tense model.)

Together, these considerations suggest that the interpretation of the pattern-level descriptions of connectionist networks in terms of symbols and symbol manipulation processes will be difficult. It may well be that the best we can hope for is an approximate mapping, in a manner similar to that in which Newtonian mechanics provides an approximation to quantum mechanics. (See Smolensky, 1988, for a discussion of this analogy.) On the other hand, as research on both connectionist and symbol models continues, advances in one paradigm may influence the development of the other, resulting in a form of co-evolution. Perhaps in the long run we will begin to think in such a way that processes such as automatic generalization and incremental learning are taken as primitives in the characterization of symbol systems.

Even if a direct symbol processing interpretation of pattern-level processes isn't forthcoming, the implementational view of connectionist models could be appropriate if pattern- and network-level processes were not sufficient as explanations of the causes of behavior. That is, it could be the case that organizational principles exist that define general classes of processes constructed from pattern-level processes such as associative mapping, relaxation, and incremental learning. If these organizational principles corresponded to representational structures or processes employed by symbol processing models, then the implementational view would be supported.

The situation can be likened to that of the relationship between high- and low-level programming languages. There is a sense in which machine language is sufficient for predicting the behavior of a computer. Given knowledge of a computer's current state and the machine language program it is running, one can predict with certainty what will happen next. Yet, in another sense, the processes and structures defined by a machine language do not provide a complete understanding of the behavior of a computer. Clearly, the data structures (e.g., lists, records, arrays) and procedures (e.g., if-then statement, loops, concatenation) of higher-level languages such as LISP or PASCAL play an important role in understanding the behavior of computers (to say nothing about actually getting them to do things). The issue, then, is whether pattern-level processes will turn out to be the largest building blocks out of which higher-level algorithms are constructed, or if instead these processes will tend to serve as the implementation of higher-level symbol structures and symbol manipulation processes, such as trees, stacks, scripts, production rules, and memory search procedures.

The present state-of-the-art suggests that both alternative may have some validity, albeit under different conditions. In recent years connectionist models have been applied to a wide variety of problem domains, ranging from classical conditioning and pattern recognition to natural language processing and problem solving. A pattern seems to be emerging from this work. In problem domains involving perceptual, motor, or associative memory processes, connectionist models tend to be offered as replacements for symbol manipulation models. That is, these models are not offered as implementations of symbol models, but instead are taken to demonstrate that symbol processing is not required to carry out these processes. For example, Rumelhart and McClelland (1986b) argue that one of the key aspects of their past tense model is that it provides an alternative to rule-based models. Similarly, Seidenberg and McClelland (1989) argue that they have provided a model that shows how words can be named without accessing stored lexical representations or making use of grapheme-to-phoneme conversion rules. In the interpretation of models of this sort, network- and pattern-level processes do the explanatory work, and any attempts to map these processes onto symbol processes are likely to be of limited heuristic value.

In contrast, connectionist models of "higher" processes, such as those involved in problem solving or syntactic parsing, often have the flavor of being implementations of symbolic models. For example, Touretzky and Hinton (1986) have developed a connectionist production system that they argue illustrates how symbolic processes can be implemented in connectionist networks. The system consists of a number of "fields" of nodes, each of which plays a distinct role in the operation of the system. One field acts as a working memory. Items are "stored" in working memory by turning on a small number (or "clique") of nodes. Typically, two to six items will be stored in working memory at any time. The second field of nodes is the *rule space*. Nodes in this field represent production rules. The antecedent for each production rule is the presence of two particular items in working memory, and the action of each rule involves the storage or deletion of items in working memory. A typical rule might be "If X and Y are present in working memory, then store A and B and delete Y." Determining whether the antecedent of a production is satisfied requires the contribution of two other fields, the *clause spaces*. Each clause space is responsible for determining if one of the two items in the antecedent of a production is present in working memory.

The system operates by cycling through a sequence of procedures. First, an associative mapping process provides the clause spaces with information about the contents of working memory. Then, a combination of associative mappings between fields and relaxation within fields allows the system to find a rule whose antecedent matches the contents of the working memory. When such a match is found, an associative mapping process alters the contents of working memory, and the search for the next match begins. Additional mechanisms provide the system with the capacity to do variable binding and to resolve conflicts when the antecedents of too few or too many productions match the contents of memory.

Touretzky and Hinton's production system provides an illustration of one way in which connectionist networks can implement symbol manipulation processes. (For other examples, see Hinton, 1981; and Pollack, 1988.) In Touretzky and Hinton's system, what can be described in terms of distributed representations and pattern-level processes at one level of analysis can also be described in terms of symbols and rules at another. In the mapping between levels, the primitive processes at the symbolic level correspond to organized structures of processes at the pattern level. For example, "matching" at the symbolic level involves a combination of relaxation and associative mapping processes at the pattern level.

The contrasting examples of Rumelhart and McClelland's past tense model and Touretzky and Hinton's production system suggest that there may be no simple story to tell about the relationship between connectionist and symbol models. It is perfectly plausible to suppose that connectionist models should sometimes be seen as the competitors of symbol models and other times be seen as explanations of how symbol models are implemented. Although this position may seem "blandly ecumenical" both to those who see connectionism as a true revolution and to those who see connectionism as a dismal and perhaps even dangerous failure, it may well be the most reasonable position to take at the present time. After all, most of the relevant evidence isn't in yet, and with the promise of future developments in both connectionist and symbol modeling (as well as the potential for mutually beneficial interactions between the two), one would surely be mistaken in thinking that we are in a position to draw definitive conclusions. This is not to say that the consideration of this issue is not of value. Indeed, by attempting to lay out alternative conceptions of the relationship between connectionism and symbol processing, one arrives at a better understanding of the structure of models of both classes, and perhaps more importantly, raises the issues that fuel further research.

AUTHOR'S NOTE

An Earlier version of this chapter was presented at the Annual Meeting of the society of Philosophy and Psychology. Thanks to Gregg Oden, Pete Sandon, and Nancy Kanwisher for helpful comments and discussion.

Correspondence can be sent to Jay G. Rueckl, Psychology Department, Harvard University, Cambridge, MA, 02138, or by electronic mail to jgr@algoma.harvard.edu.

REFERENCES

Anderson, J. R.: 1983, *The Architecture of Cognition*, Harvard University Press, Cambridge, MA.
Broadbent, D.: 1985, 'A Question of Levels: Comment on McClelland and Rumelhart,' *Journal of Experimental Psychology: General* 114, 189-192.
Collins, A. M. and Loftus, E. F.: 1975, 'A Spreading Activation Theory of Semantic Processing,' *Psychological Review* 82, 407-428.
Fodor, J. and Pylyshyn, Z.: 1988, 'Connectionism and Cognitive Architecture: A Critical Analysis," *Cognition* 28, 3-71.
Hinton, G. E.: 1981, 'Implementing Semantic Networks in Parallel Hardware,' in G. Hinton and J. A. Anderson (eds.) *Parallel Models of Associative Memory*, Lawrence Erlbaum Associates, Hillsdale, NJ.

Hinton, G. E. and Sejnowski, T. J.: 1986, 'Learning and Relearning in Boltzmann Machines,' in D. E. Rumelhart & J. L. McClelland (eds.), *Parallel Distributed Processing: Explorations in the Microstructure of Cognition, Volume I: Foundations*, MIT Press, Cambridge, MA.

Hinton, G. E., McClelland, J. L. and Rumelhart, D. E.: 1986, 'Distributed Representations,' in D. E. Rumelhart & J. L. McClelland (eds.), *Parallel Distributed Processing: Explorations in the Microstructure of Cognition, Volume I: Foundations*, MIT Press, Cambridge, MA.

Marr, D.: 1982, *Vision*, Freeman, San Francisco.

Massaro, D. W.: 1987, *Speech Perception by Ear and by Eye: A Paradigm for Psychological Inquiry*, Lawrence Erlbaum Associates, Hillsdale, NJ.

McClelland, J. L. and Rumelhart, D. E.: 1981, 'An Interactive Activation Model of Context Effects in Letter Perception: Part 1, *Psychological Review* 88, 375-407.

Newell, A.: 1987, *The Williams James Lecture Series*, presented at Harvard University, Cambridge, MA.

Oden, G. C.: 1977, 'Integration of Fuzzy Logical Information,' *Journal of Experimental Psychology: Human Perception and Performance* 3, 565-575.

Oden, G. C.: 1988, *FuzzyProp: A Symbolic Superstrate for Connectionist Models*, presented at the Second IEEE International Conference on Neural Networks, San Diego, CA.

Pinker, S. and Prince, A.: 1987, 'On Language and Connectionism: Analysis of a Parallel Distributed Processing Model of Language Acquisition,' *Cognition* 28, 73-193.

Pollack, J.: 1988, 'Recursive Auto-associative Memory: Devising Compositional Distributed Representations,' *Proceedings of the Tenth Annual Conference of the Cognitive Science Society*, Montreal.

Rueckl, J. G.: (1990), 'Similarity Effects in Word and Pseudoword Repetition Priming,' *Journal of Experimental Psychology: Learning, Memory, and Cognition* 16, 374-391.

Rumelhart, D. E. and McClelland, J. L.: 1986a, 'PDP Models and General Issues in Cognitive Science,' in D. E. Rumelhart & J. L. McClelland (eds.), *Parallel Distributed Processing, Volume 1: Foundations*, MIT Press, Cambridge, MA.

Rumelhart, D. E., Smolensky, P., McClelland, J. L. and Hinton, G. E.: 1986, 'Schemata and Sequential Thought Processes in PDP Models,' in J. McClelland and D. Rumelhart (eds.), *Parallel Distributed Processing: Explorations in the Microstructure of Cognition, Volume 2: Psychological and Biological Models*, MIT Press, Cambridge, MA.

Seidenberg, M. S. and McClelland, J. L.: 1989, 'A Distributed, Developmental Model of Visual Word Recognition,' *Psychological Review* 96, 523-568.

Sejnowski, T. and Churchland, P. S.: 1988, 'Brain and Cognition,' in M. I. Posner (ed.), *Foundations of Cognitive Science*, MIT Press, Cambridge, MA.

Smolensky, P.: 1988, 'On the Proper Treatment of Connectionism,' *The Behavioral and Brain Sciences* 11, 1-74.

Smolensky, P.: 1986, 'Neural and Conceptual Interpretations of Parallel Distributed Processing Models,' in J. McClelland and D. Rumelhart (eds.), *Parallel Distributed Processing: Explorations in the Microstructure of Cognition, Volume 2: Psychological and Biological Models*, MIT Press, Cambridge, MA.

Touretzky, D. and Hinton, G.E.: 1986, 'A Distributed Connectionist Production System,' *Technical Report*, Carnegie-Mellon University.

Zadeh, L.: 1976, 'A Fuzzy Algorithmic Approach to the Definition of Complex or Imprecise Concepts,' *International Journal of Man-Machine Studies* 8, 149-291.

Psychology Department
Harvard University
Cambridge, MA   02138

GARY HATFIELD

REPRESENTATION AND RULE-INSTANTIATION IN CONNECTIONIST SYSTEMS

Connectionist approaches to cognition afford a new opportunity for reflection on the notions of *rule* and *representation* as employed in cognitive science. For nearly a decade, from the time of Fodor (1975) to Pylyshyn (1984), representations typically were equated with symbols and were understood by analogy with the internal states of a digital computer; processing rules were equated with symbolic expressions and were understood by analogy with program instructions in a computer. Connectionist authors challenged this orthodoxy by denying that symbolic representations are needed for many cognitive tasks and by providing alternative accounts of the status of cognitive rules (Feldman & Ballard, 1982; McClelland, Rumelhart, & Hinton, 1986). I have discussed in earlier papers the grounds for denying that all cognition is symbol-based and for distinguishing representations from symbols (Hatfield, 1988b; Kosslyn & Hatfield, 1984). In this paper I examine the relationships between rules and representations in symbolist and connectionist models.

Traditional "rules and representations" accounts of cognition drew a distinction between *rule described* and *rule following* systems. The usual example of a rule *described* system is one that simply obeys natural laws, as when an object falls to earth in accordance with the law of gravity: No understanding or representation of the rule or law is imputed to the object in order to explain the fact that its motion conforms to the law. A rule *following* system conforms to the rule or law by virtue of an explicit representation of it, as when a neophyte cook follows a recipe: The cook's behavior accords with the steps in the recipe because the cook consults the recipe and follows its directions.[1] By contrast, connectionist systems *instantiate* rules without being "rule following" in the traditional sense. Nor are they merely "rule described" in the way falling objects are, for the rules they instantiate do not follow directly from natural laws (the laws of physics and chemistry), but are specific to the operation of biological systems of certain kinds.

After briefly describing traditional rules-and-representations thinking, I will explore the notion of rule instantiation that arises from reflection on connectionist models, or indeed on earlier models in physiological psychology. This particular notion of rule instantiation seems at first blush to threaten the usual distinction between physiological as opposed to psychological levels of explanation. I shall argue that the distinction should not be rejected outright, but a reformulated distinction should be substituted. According to the reformed distinction, some functions instantiated by the nervous system are physiological without being psychological, whereas other functions are psychological even if subject to neurocomputational explanation.

1. SYMBOLS, RULES, AND REPRESENTATIONS

The traditional notion of rules and representations in cognitive science derives from reflection on the architecture of Turing machines and standard digital computers. These devices provide examples of programmable symbol manipulators. They realize states that can, at an abstract level of description, be wholly characterized by their syntactic properties (Newell, 1980). Rules for responding to combinations of such states can be built into the device; in programmable devices, these rules can themselves be formulated as syntactic states (the program) that determine how the device "interprets" other syntactic states (the data). Early promoters of the field called "cognitive science" conjectured that the psychological states might be modeled by imputing to organisms an internal computational architecture similar to that of the computer (Newell & Simon, 1976). In this comparison, sensory systems are equated with input buffers and motor systems with output devices. Sensory systems provide "data" for processing in accordance with internal rules; the rules are conceived as internal symbols in a "language of thought," just as the program in a computer is conceived as expressed in a computer language (Fodor, 1975, chs. 1-2; Pylyshyn, 1984, 1989). Models of cognitive processes amount to proposals of programs for the cognitive machine (Newell, Rosenbloom, & Laird, 1989).

The so-called "computer metaphor" has in fact been taken quite literally. The intended comparison between cognitive rules and internal program statements is not equivalent to the claim that cognitive operations can be formally described in a regimented language, nor is it equivalent to the claim that cognitive processes can be simulated on the computer. Such claims might be made about a diversity of subject-matters, from classical mechanics to the sociology of poplar elections, without implying any special relation between computers and the particular subject-matter. The relation posited between cognitive rules and internal program statements, by contrast, entails that the cognitive processes of organisms are performed by internal mechanisms functionally organized in a manner similar to the processing mechanisms of computers. The envisioned similarity pertains especially to the primitive processing operations that define the elementary capacities of a given system, operations from which all other abilities or capacities must be constructed. Proponents of the symbolist paradigm maintain that symbol-manipulating capacities are primitive capacities of the cognitive system. Their arguments emphasize that many cognitive abilities require sensitivity to the constituent structure of compositionally complex representations (Fodor & Pylyshyn, 1988), and that the primitive processing operations of traditional computing devices are designed to meet this requirement (Fodor, 1975, ch. 2; Pylyshyn, 1984, ch. 3, 1989, pp. 56-62). Such primitive operations include storing arrays of symbols, "fetching" program directives from memory, and "executing" these directives on data stored elsewhere to produce a new array of data.

Serious proponents of the "rules and representations" or "symbolist" version of cognitive science do not treat the comparison between cognitive systems and standard computers as if it were merely suggestive or illustrative; they assign it real philosophical work. This point may be illustrated by considering Fodor's response to an early objection to his "language of thought." The objection charged that postulation of an internal language is the first step on the road to an infinite regress: If cognitive abilities such as reading and understanding sentences are to be explained by the postulation of internal processes occurring in an internal linguistic medium, then surely additional processes must be posited in order to explain how this internal language could be "read" and "understood"; by parity of explanation, the latter processes would themselves require postulation of another internal language, and so on. Fodor responded to this objection by explaining that the one, true *lingua mentis* might be compared to the machine language of a digital computer. The computer "uses" languages such as Fortran or Cobol by compiling them in a machine language; but it does not need to compile the machine language in a yet more primitive language in order to "use" it, since it is "built to use" the machine language.

Similarly, human beings may learn the meaning of English predicates by formulating hypotheses about their meanings expressed in the language of thought; but human beings do not need to learn the language of thought through a similar process because they are "built to understand" that language (Fodor, 1975, pp. 65-7). Fodor's response amounts to the claim that the cognitive mechanisms possessed by human beings might stand in a relation to the language of thought that parallels the relation between computers and machine language.

Symbolists assign yeoman work to yet other features of the comparison between computers and cognitive mechanisms. Pylyshyn's robustly realist interpretation of theories in cognitive science hinges on his realism about the functional architecture of cognitive systems taken as computational devices. In the abstract, any of a variety of hypothesized internal computations might account for observed relations between stimulus and response. Pylyshyn urges that models of cognitive processes should be formulated so that they impute a real-time computational architecture to the cognitive system, thereby making it possible to distinguish among candidate models by testing reaction time on tasks that are variously "easy" or "hard" depending on the primitive symbol-manipulating operations of the architecture (1984, ch. 4; 1989, pp. 70-85). More generally, Fodor and Pylyshyn (1988) have argued that "compositionality" (the sensitivity of cognitive systems to the constituent structures of representations) requires that cognitive systems have a "classical" (symbol-manipulating) computational architecture.

As these arguments illustrate, the notion that symbol manipulation is a primitive ability of cognitive systems virtually defines the symbolist position. The arguments also betray the realist commitment of the symbolist approach, which symbolists consider an advantage. The symbolist approach arose as a reaction against behaviorism (Fodor, 1975, Introduction). Postulation of an internal symbolic language provided a framework within which it made sense for cognitive scientists to be realists about internal processes and processing rules. They could neutralize the behaviorist rhetoric according to which the invocation of internal mental processes betrays a belief in ghosts or spirits (Skinner, 1963) by pointing to a ponderable machine that physically realizes internal symbolic processes: the digital computer. However, although the standard computer may once have seemed to be the only (computational) game in town (Fodor, 1975, pp. 27, 55), recently there have been some noisy new kids on the block.

2. CONNECTIONIST RULES AND REPRESENTATIONS

Connectionism is not a theory or even an ideological approach to cognitive science, but a group of theories and approaches that share an interest in computational systems that can be characterized by "connectionist" primitive operations. This point is important because connectionism sometimes is equated with positions that, although adopted by some of its adherents, are not essential to it. In particular, connectionism sometimes is equated with the position that hard rules and symbolic representations play no role in cognition. But connectionist authors have sought to model both hard rules and symbolic representations (Shastri & Ajjanagadde, 1990; Smolensky, 1987). Connectionism rejects hard rules and symbolic representations only in describing the primitive operations by which computations are performed: It rejects the symbolist claim that symbol manipulation and symbolic programming are the primitives from which models of cognitive operations must be constructed. To the extent that connectionist models admit symbolic representations such representations are conceived as something to be explained, not as explanatory primitives.

Connectionist computation lacks a formal theory delimiting its domain, equivalent to the theory of Turing computability. Connectionist models are grouped together by the computational mechanisms and primitive operations they allow. Connectionist networks consist of "nodes" connected in a pattern; the primitive operations of the network include the transmission of activation values among nodes and the subsequent instantiation of a state of activation and an output value in activated nodes. Some networks also instantiate learning rules, or rules for altering the pattern of connectivity and the rules of activation as a result of prior input or of prior input and output. The connections among nodes may be excitatory or inhibitory and may exhibit varying degrees of "gain"; the input to a node may be summed to yield a state of activation according to various summative functions, and the output value may be equal to the state of activation or may itself be subject to a function, such as a threshold function. Connectionist models postulate the network characteristics just described (and perhaps some others) as primitives which, if explained at all, are explained by appeal to a "deeper" level of explanation in terms of the physical or physiological properties of the material implementation of the system. (Classical models make corresponding assumptions about different primitive operations.)

Connectionist processing is initiated by activation of "input" nodes. Computation occurs through the passing of activation among nodes in accordance with the pattern of connectivity; this pattern constitutes the "program" of the net and determines the "rule" that relates input to output. The input nodes may be connected directly to the output nodes, or there may be "hidden layers" of nodes in between. Processing may be conceived as continuous, but is usually modeled as discrete "updatings" of network node values. (It is important to distinguish the serial nature of connectionist *simulations*, which occur on standard digital computers, from the characteristics of the modeled process: the process may involve simultaneous interactions among a host of nodes.) "Output" is typically equated with the state of activation of output nodes, although presumably the output from one network may be transmitted so as to provide input to another. The formalisms used to model network characteristics vary widely, from simple linear functions to formalisms derived from models of annealing in metals or of harmonic interactions among physical states (Hinton & Sejnowski, 1986; Rumelhart, Hinton, & McClelland, 1986; Smolensky, 1986).

Connectionist models are fundamentally *nonsymbolic* inasmuch as the values passed among nodes are simply continuously varying magnitudes of activation, as opposed to syntactically structured representations. (Of course, some parallel computing systems allow syntactic representations to be passed among "classically" structured nodes.) Although nonsymbolic in this sense, connectionism is not inherently devoid of a means for implementing cognitive *rules*, and it is not antithetical to the notion of *representation*. Connectionist networks compute one or another function, or instantiate one or another processing rule, by virtue of their connectivity; I will return to the status of such "rules" in Section 3. Connectionist models differ from classical models in that they do not, from the outset, equate representations with symbols (i.e., with syntactically defined states). While there is no agreed upon general account of representation among connectionists, two notions of representation are employed in the literature. First, knowledge or information is said to be stored or "represented" in the connection weights of a network. Thus, a pattern-recognition network "stores" the characteristics of target patterns in its pattern of connectivity; this stored information then determines the response of the network to input patterns, allowing it to accept some and to reject others (Hinton, McClelland, & Rumelhart, 1986). A suitable network could store and access a large base of knowledge (Shastri, 1988). Second, the occurrent pattern of activation of a network may be considered as a representation. Thus, in a network that stores relations among subjects and predicates in its connection weights, input may be a pattern of activation corresponding to a particular subject and the resultant pattern of activation may "represent" the predicates that apply to that subject (Shastri & Ajjanagadde, 1989). Or in network models of vision, input may be a retinal pattern, and the resultant pattern of activation a representation of the distal surface (Ballard, Hinton, & Sejnowski, 1983). In the latter case, and potentially in the others, states of the network are denominated as "representations" not because of their syntactic characteristics, but because they *stand for* a particular object or configuration of objects. Connectionist models allow the theorist to consider the possibility that although some cognitive capacities (such as language processing) require the positing of syntactic entities over which processing operations are defined, others (such as early vision) do not (see Hatfield, 1988b, in press).

Connectionists disagree over the extent to which hard rules and symbolic representations characterize cognition considered as an object of explanation. A great deal of attention has been given to the pronouncements of some connectionists (e.g., Rumelhart & McClelland, 1986a) that natural language processing, at least in its "microstructure," is better modeled probabilistically than by mechanisms operating with hard rules and symbolic representations as primitives. Such pronouncements seem to suggest that the full range of linguistic abilities can be modeled associationistically and probabilistically, a suggestion that has evoked vigorous rebuke (Pinker & Prince, 1988). Be that as it may, other connectionists would make the relation between the "soft" probabilistic operation of connection nets and the hard rules characteristic of some cognitive performance into an object of investigation in its own right. Thus, Smolensky (1987, 1988) maintains that the hard-rule governed achievements of "macro" level cognition are only approximate descriptions of actual performance. He contends that processes which are "soft" or probabilistic at the "subsymbolic" level may successfully explain both the approximation to and the deviations from such rules. Still other connectionists have argued that some hard-rule abilities, such as drawing inferences from a store of knowledge that includes multiplace predicates, can in fact be modeled connectionistically (Shastri & Ajjanagadde, 1989, 1990). One thing is clear: A variety of connectionist models, from models of visual computation to models of acquired pattern-matching, involve the realization of cognitive or perceptual rules in connectionist networks.

3. RULE INSTANTIATION

A strength of symbolist models is the ease with which they provide a realist interpretation for processing rules in psychology: Processing rules are equated with explicitly formulated statements in the internal code. Having given up the classical computational architecture with its commitment to primitive operations for manipulating symbols, connectionists are precluded from adopting the symbolist conception of rule following. But although connectionist networks are not rule following in the way symbolist models are, they nonetheless allow for a realist interpretation of processing rules. Connectionist networks do not exhibit regular behavior merely by virtue of following a basic law of nature, the way falling bodies do; nor are they merely "rule described" in the sense of exhibiting accidental or arbitrarily designated regularity (see Putnam, 1988, Appendix, for an argument that under an appropriate stipulative description, any physical object can be designated as computing any computable function). Connectionist networks are *designed* or *engineered* to instantiate a given rule, such as a rule for computing shape from shading or for pattern matching; or at least they are designed or engineered to acquire computational characteristics that will allow them to perform these tasks.[2] Let us denominate connectionist networks as *rule instantiating* in describing their relation to the rules they compute, in order to distinguish them from systems that are rule following or merely rule described.[3]

The term "rule" may be applied in several ways in descriptions of connectionist networks. There are, for instance, "rules of activation" and "rules of learning"; both sorts of rules characterize the architecture of a connectionist network, independently of the cognitive or psychological rule that the network instantiates by virtue of its architecture. These rules of the basic architecture have a status similar to the basic rules of Turing machine operation. In a Turing machine there are, for example, rules that govern the operation of the mechanism by which the head is programmed. These rules are engineered into the head so that it reads a square, performs an operation, and moves one way or the other depending on whether the head has been "set" one way or another. The settings are the "program rules" or the rules that the machine "follows." Similarly with connection nets. The rules of activation, rules of learning, and so on, are basic elements of the computational architecture that allow the network to be configured, through its pattern of connectivity and the characteristics of its rules of activation, in such a way that it computes one function rather than another. It is the function computed by the configured network that I term the rule *instantiated* by the network.

The rules instantiated by connectionist models are a diverse lot, reflecting the variety of psychological or cognitive functions for which connectionist models have been proposed. Models have been proposed for computing shape from shading (Brown, Ballard, & Kimball, 1982), separating figure from ground (Kienker, Sejnowski, Hinton, & Schumacher, 1986), recognizing patterns (see McClelland, Rumelhart, & Hinton, 1986), recognizing objects (Feldman, 1985), learning the morphology of the past tense of English verbs (Rumelhart & McClelland, 1986a), and drawing inferences from a data base (Shastri & Ajjanagadde, 1990).[4] The connection weights and network configurations in such models variously instantiate rules of inference, organized knowledge, and rules of perceptual processing. Although the principles of network operation are shared in these cases, the functions instantiated by the networks seem, from the stand point of psychological description, quite diverse. Thus, in models of stored knowledge, the network characteristics represent knowledge of the world. In the case of object recognition, connection weights instantiate conceptual representations or implicit knowledge about object characteristics. But in the case of networks that compute shape from shading or surface reflectance from retinal intensities, the rules instantiated by the network do not, intuitively, seem worthy of the designation "knowledge" or even "stored representations," anymore than do the rules of color mixture instantiated by the neurons in the human retina. In the case of early vision, the rules instantiated by the network seem intuitively to be functionally organized processes by which (visual) representations are generated, not cognitive rules that are themselves represented.

Consider a specific contrast between two models. In Shastri's model of rule-based reasoning, connection weights and node characteristics represent stored information about a domain of knowledge, say, about book ownership among a group of friends (Shastri & Ajjanagadde, 1990). This information is "in" the network characteristics in that it is by virtue of those characteristics that the network responds appropriately to queries about who owns which book. Now consider models of shape from shading, in which the connection weights instantiate rules for extracting shape by processing local difference in shading (Brown, Ballard, & Kimball, 1982). It is by virtue of the weights that the network instantiates one rule for extracting shape from shading rather than another. But does the network store knowledge or information about the rules for extracting shape from shading? Intuitively, it seems that it does not. The "rules" of processes such as those of early vision seem to be precognitive or subcognitive. Yet such "rules" are instantiated by the network, just as "knowledge" or "inference rules" may be instantiated in other cases.

The fact that various configurations of connection weights serve to instantiate a psychologically heterogeneous collection of "rules" does not by itself call into question the intuitive distinction between "stored knowledge" and subcognitively instantiated processing rules. But among those who emphasize the biological basis of computation there has in fact been a tendency to elide this distinction. The distinction can be dissolved in either direction. Some authors, such as the eliminative materialist P. S. Churchland (1986, ch. 9), predict that the vocabulary of neuroscience will some day replace the allegedly unscientific vocabulary of "inference" and "cognitive representation," thereby dissolving the distinction in the direction of neuroscientific description. Conversely, others extend the vocabulary of knowing to lower levels, including that of the computations for deriving shape from shading. Many connectionist authors and their kin describe the processes of early vision in terms of testing hypotheses or making inferences based on assumptions (e.g., Hinton & Sejnowski, 1983; see also Marr, 1982, pp. 17, 159). They would thus dissolve the distinction between cognitive and subcognitive processes by extending the domain of cognitive description to include "early" visual processing (in Marr's terminology).

For purposes of subsequent comparison it will be useful to sketch an argument for extending the vocabulary of knowing to what I have termed the "subcognitive" achievements of early vision. [5] Such an argument might begin by charging that the distinction between (a) psychological or cognitive and (b) physiological or subcognitive processes is an artifact of traditional mentalism, which distinguished merely physiological processes from the activities of a special "mind stuff." The fact that paradigmatically cognitive rules typically are accessible to consciousness, subject to the influence of conscious learning, and "cognitively penetrable" (that is, subject to the influence of beliefs and desires--Pylyshyn, 1984, 1989) leads us to distinguish such rules from "merely physiological" rules of processing because we still define the mental in terms of consciousness and belief. But, the argument might continue, subcognitive rules are the result of a type of learning that occurs through evolution. The visual system stores knowledge of the algorithms needed to extract shape from shading in environments like ours. Because the environment is stable, we do not need access to such knowledge, and the knowledge need not be cognitively penetrable. But the algorithms in question, on this view, count nonetheless as knowledge, albeit knowledge that has been gained through the "experience" of the species.

4. NEUROCOMPUTATION AND THE DISTINCTION BETWEEN PHYSIOLOGY AND PSYCHOLOGY

Although I am not prepared to accept the foregoing argument for eliminating the distinction between low-level physiological processes and psychological processes, I find that connectionist models do provide an opportunity for reflection on the relations between psychological and "merely physiological" explanations and between psychological models and their physiological realization.

The standard symbolist conception of cognition includes a particular conception of the relationship between psychology and physiology. The main idea is that psychological rules and representations constitute a distinct "level of analysis" that can be studied in its own right. Symbolists typically describe this level in robustly cognitive terms: It is the level of belief and desire and of means-ends reasoning, sometimes called the "semantic" level. As conceived by Fodor and Pylyshyn, the processes mediating the interaction of beliefs and desires are symbolic; the symbols themselves and the syntactic operations defined over them form a second level of analysis, also independent of physiology. The physiological or physical realization of the semantically and syntactically characterized processes constitutes a third level of analysis. Fodor has argued that the first two levels are not reducible to the third, from which he concludes that physiology is irrelevant to psychology (1975, p. 17). The physiological substrate is merely the medium in which cognitive functions are realized; in the absence of a strict identity between cognitive function and physiological realization (that is, in the absence of type-type identities), this medium is of no interest in formulating properly psychological theories.

The belief-desire conception of psychology paired with the symbolic conception of cognitive processing led Fodor and Pylyshyn to propose a quite odd dividing line between properly psychological and merely physiological processes. In a lengthy paper on perception (1981), they distinguish   between operation carried out by transducers and those mediated by a symbolic medium. They assign the former to physiology, the latter to psychology. According to their view, a perceptual process is either "mere transduction" or it is mediated by inference (computed in a symbolic medium).

If left unqualified this position would relegate whole fields of perceptual psychology--the psychology of space and color perception--to physiology, on the grounds that the processes involved are not obviously cognitive, at least not according to the criterion of "cognitive penetrability." The doctrine of modularity saves the day: Fodor and Pylyshyn contend that a large range of perceptual processing might indeed be mediated by inferences, but that these inferences are encapsulated within "modules" insulated from the rest of the cognitive system (see Fodor, 1983). These processes could be symbolically mediated, inferential, and belief-like, and yet insensitive to the agent's own beliefs and desires, and so "cognitively impenetrable." Fodor and Pylyshyn defend the equation of psychological processing with symbol manipulation by imputing symbol manipulation to any psychological process with processing rules of some complexity, whether the process is cognitively penetrable or not (Fodor & Pylyshyn, 1981, pp. 184-8; Pylyshyn, 1980, p. 132).

Connectionism affords a means for avoiding the extreme measure of equating the nontransduced operations in perception with symbol-mediated inferences, for it affords a way of modeling complex, rule-instantiating psychological processes without adopting a rule-following analysis of those processes. It allows one to provide a "psychologically interesting" decomposition of the processes of early vision (cf. Ullman, 1980) without describing those processes in the traditional mentalistic vocabulary of inference-mediated hypothesis formation. The products of early vision--e.g., representations of distal spatial configurations--are themselves neither inherently "belief like" nor intrinsically symbolic. In providing a nonsymbolic means for modeling computation, connectionism allows the theorist to characterize processes as psychological without appealing to symbol-mediation or belief-like representation as the criterion for this characterization. The computation of shape from shading, or of depth from

stereopsis, can be described in the vocabulary of registering and
algorithmically combining information in a computationally complex manner.
The availability of nonsymbolic computation and rule-instantiation thus
removes the chief motivation for characterizing as inferential the processes
that led to such products (see Hatfield, 1988b, for elaboration).

The symbolist program made popular a second means of demarcating the
"psychological" level of analysis: the equation of the psychological with the
functional. Under the name of "functionalism" the distinction between the
psychological and physiological came to be equated with that between
function and material realization (Fodor, 1975, Introduction). In fact,
however, the latter distinction does not provide the desired demarcation.
Physiological description itself is typically functional, even at the level of
neurons and their parts. Neurons are characterized in functional terms
when they are said to "transmit" activation. The microstructure of the
neuronal membrane is functionally characterized when one attributes to it
ion-channels that selectively "gate" the flow of various ions into the neuron,
sometimes allowing them to flow with the voltage gradient, sometimes
blocking their flow (see Kandel & Schwartz, 1985, chs. 3, 8). It seems
apparent that these functions of "transmitting" activation or "gating" ions can
be characterized abstractly, in independence of their material realization.
Indeed, functional description always affords the possibility of abstractly
characterizing a function in this manner.

What remains of the distinction between physiology and psychology? If
it can be equated neither with the horizontal distinction between
transduction and subsequent symbolic processes nor with the vertical
distinction between symbol manipulation and its material realization, won't
it simply fade away? I think not, though it may become more difficult to
state criteria for the distinction. We have already seen that in order to
avoid the position that the psychology of early vision is not properly part of
psychology, Fodor and Pylyshyn portray early vision as inferential; they in
effect impute belief-states to the visual module. This maneuver reflects their
conception that cognitive and perceptual psychology are equivalent to
"belief-desire" psychology, a conception that is widely accepted in the
philosophical literature but that shows little acquaintance with current
experimental psychology. The explanatory aims of experimental psychology
are far removed from, e.g., the effort to explain the behavior of human
beings in burning buildings through the ascription of appropriate beliefs and
desires (as in Pylyshyn, 1984, ch. 1). Perhaps we can look to the actual

practice of psychology for a conception of its subject-matter and explanatory aims that will distinguish psychology from physiology.

I have argued else where (Hatfield, in press) that experimental psychology typically takes as its object particular systems and their capacities, as opposed to the actions of freely behaving cognitive agents. Accordingly, behavior is to be seen as the chief source of evidence in psychology but not as its primary object of explanation. Thus, in the experimental investigation of visual perception, the explanandum is the visual system and its capacities, not the behavioral responses gathered during an experiment. The experimentalist's endeavor to explain observed behavioral responses arises from the use of such responses to test models of the visual system, not from an interest in "explaining behavior" for its own sake.

In my view the key to the distinction between physiology and psychology lies with functional characterization. However, it is not functional characterization per se that marks the divide between psychology and physiology, but the character of the functions ascribed. In barest terms, the vocabulary of neurophysiological analysis begins with neurons and their connections, working up toward more complex functions. As connectionism and, indeed, earlier discussions of computational nets in neurophysiology make clear, this vocabulary is capable of capturing quite complex computational abilities.[6] However, inasmuch as the vocabulary is employed in a properly neurophysiological investigation, it is tied to observations of the structure of neurons or groups of neurons and of their activity under varying internal and external conditions. In contrast, psychological description starts at a more global level of analysis: not, I have suggested, at the level of the cognitive agent, but at that of various systems or capacities, such as vision, language learning, attention, and pictorial memory. Psychology typically describes these phenomena in a vocabulary that includes no reference to neurons or to neurophysiological processes (so conceived). It studies these phenomena by using a variety of experimental techniques to measure behavioral variation under different conditions. These techniques need not, and typically do not, involve measures of physiological activity.[7]

Most neurophysiological investigation is at present quite far removed from the phenomena of psychology. Compare the topics in visual perception covered in neuroscience textbooks and in textbooks on perceptual psychology. The neuroscience book covers retinal transduction, the contribution of cones and retinal processes to color vision, the anatomy of visual pathways in the brain; it may briefly discuss how information about form and motion is received and where it is processed, and it may describe binocularly sensitive neurons (Kandel & Schwartz, 1985, chs. 27-30). Some of these topics, such as the biochemistry of phototransduction, are purely physiological; others make contact with the psychological. But properly psychological treatments of perception are differently focused; they examine the functional organization of the perceptual system itself, conceived as one system integrated with other psychological systems. Psychological treatments emphasize the function of perception in attaining information about distal states, as in the case of the so-called perceptual constancies (the various tendencies of perception to covary with the distal source of stimulation, rather than with its proximal projection--see, e.g., Epstein, 1977, and Rock, 1983). Such discussion is likely to be wholly absent in neurophysiological treatments; or if constancy is mentioned, it is as a framing conception to guide research, not as an object of explanation for the foreseeable future (Kandel & Schwartz, 1985, p. 389).

Although the gulf separating the conceptual vocabularies and experimental techniques of physiology and psychology is apparent, what it signifies is less than obvious. Two opposing attitudes toward the differences between the two disciplines have been common. The differences have been said either to reveal an ineluctable barrier between physiology and psychology, or to indicate merely the relative immaturity of the two fields. Those who believe that the theoretical notions of psychology can never be reduced to or explained by those of physiology adopt the first position (Fodor, 1975, Introduction). Those who foresee the ultimate reduction of psychology to physiology and the elimination of the vocabulary of psychology in favor of a physiological one adopt the second (Quine, 1974, pp. 10, 13-14).[8] We are thus presented with options for conceiving the relation of physiology to psychology that may, in the starkest terms, be expressed as a choice between (a) nonreduction and irrelevance or (b) reduction and elimination.

During the past decade several authors have portrayed an expanded range of possible relations between physiology and psychology. Some have sought to alter the classical conception of reduction so that reduction no longer implies an unrestricted identity between the referents of terms in the reducing and reduced theories (e.g., Richardson, 1979; also implicit in Haugeland, 1978).[9] On this view, providing a physiological explanation for a psychological function is adequate for reduction; the reduction of a functional capacity described at one level of analysis to a lower level requires merely that the lower level be used to explain the higher one. Other authors who prefer to retain the classical notion of reduction argue that the failure to achieve a reduction of psychology to physiology does not imply that the latter is irrelevant to the former. Accordingly, knowledge of the physiological structures that realize a psychological function may lead to an explanation of how the function is performed--and may suggest and explain constraints on its performance--even if a type-type identity has not been effected (Hatfield, 1988a&b; Kitcher, 1984; Kosslyn & Hatfield, 1984; Mehler, Morton, & Jusczyk, 1984).

The question of reduction notwithstanding, it clearly is possible to provide explanations cast in the language of neurons and their connections for at least some psychological phenomena. Examples of successful explanations are especially apparent in the field of sensory physiology. The explanation of Mach bands (the subjective heightening of contours at boundaries between light and dark areas of a surface) through the physiology of lateral inhibition provides one compelling example (Ratliff, 1965). Another is the discovery of three types of cone in the retina, which helped to explain certain features of color perception, especially the phenomena of color mixture and color blindness (see Kaufman, 1979, ch. 4, for a review). It is also clear that physiological investigation could help to settle theoretical disputes. Thus, various "wiring diagrams" have been proposed to explain the interaction among output from the three types of cone (contrast Boynton, 1979, pp. 211-12, with Kaufman, 1979, p. 96); although psychophysical investigation provided the basis for these diagrams, anatomical and physiological study could provide evidence for selection between rival accounts.

The connectionist program offers the vision that the most complex of psychological functions ultimately will be explicated in neurocomputational terms. The idea is that neurocomputational accounts will come to be offered for ever larger units of a given psychological system (and ultimately, some would say, for the behaving organism as a whole). Thus, one imagines building from disparity-detecting neurons to an account of global stereopsis, from intensity detectors to an account of the computation of shape from shading, and so on. One would then begin to integrate these explanations into an explanation of the perceptual system's production, through the combination of various sources of information, of stable representations of the spatial and chromatic characteristics of the distal environment. From there, one would tackle object recognition and other more cognitive perceptual abilities. In these cases, various systems-level capacities would be explained in terms of a complicated pattern of interaction among neurons that are organized into computational networks that are themselves systematically interconnected.

Most of this vision is at present sheer fantasy. I am less interested in asking whether it can ever be made real than in speculating about what it would mean for the relation between physiology and psychology if it were. By my lights, the success of the neurocomputational program would not signal the elimination or reduction of psychology, but would amount merely to the achievement of an expanded range of explanation in psychology. The matter of how to view the envisioned success may be seen as a question of who gets to claim which functions as their proper object of explanation. Since both physiology and psychology investigate functions, the neurophile may simply propose that the functions proper to neurophysiology be expanded to include those of whole systems, e.g., to include spatial perception, object recognition, and so on. But it would then be hard to see why the discipline in question should be termed "neuroscience," rather than, say, the "physiology of spatial perception." But the physiology of spatial perception is just the functional investigation of a mental capacity: it is, in other words, psychology. So while it may be granted that, in broad terms, psychology can be treated as a division of physiology (if the latter term is extended to cover all organically realized functions), that does not make psychology into a division of neurophysiology or neuroscience.

Although this last move may seem like mere wordplay, it is not. Any envisioned extension of neurocomputational explanation to spatial vision will be affected by scientific study that proceeds in both directions, that is, from neurons up and from systems-functions down. As several authors have observed, neurophysiological investigation, once it moves above the level of the single neuron, depends on a functional characterization of the systems it studies in order to proceed (Hatfield, 1988a; Mehler, Morton, & Jusczyk, 1984; see also Julesz, 1978, pp. 240-1; and Marr & Poggio, 1979, p. 324). Such functional characterizations are the subject-matter and object of explanation of psychology. If there is any wordplay here to be detected, it is on the part of those who, were it to become common for investigators of psychological phenomena to use neurophysiological concepts and findings, would simply define psychology away.

5. CONCLUSIONS

Connectionism and symbolism do not disagree over the existence of psychological rules and representations (which each can grant); rather, they differ over how rules and representations are to be construed. Symbolism equates representations with symbols in an internal code and rules with symbolic expressions in the same code. Connectionism affords an alternative conception of rules and representations. On this conception, representations may be symbolic or not (see Hatfield, in press) and rules may be directly instantiated in a connectionist network, without symbolic mediation. Connectionist systems instantiate rules without being rule following in the usual sense.

The classical conception of rules and representations invites a particular conception of the distinction between psychological and physiological processes; psychological processes are those carried out in a symbolic medium. Such processes are related to physiology as function to material realization. Because connectionism abandons the classical symbolist computational architecture, it also forsakes using instantiation in a symbolic medium as the criterion of the psychological. Connectionism would do well also to reject functional characterization as the criterion, since physiological as well as psychological processes are functionally characterized. Although the connectionist agenda does not require preservation of a distinction between physiology and psychology, I have argued that honest consideration of the empirical techniques and modes of explanation adopted by investigators who study psychological phenomena--whether these investigators be connectionists or not--indicates that the distinction should be preserved. If physiology is broadly defined to include the study of all organically realized functions, it may be appropriate to consider psychology a branch of physiology. But that would not legitimate the subsumption of psychology, which studies functionally integrated systems, under neuroscience, with its emphasis on the neural level of description and analysis. The coming of a connectionist utopia would yield neurocomputational models of vision, imagination, and memory, and so would establish a firm and widespread explanatory relation between the vocabulary of neuroscience and that of psychology. But rather than dissolving the discipline of psychology, such a development would simply add to its store of explanatory tools. And in any case, such a development could only come about with guidance provided by psychology itself. Psychology may not, like philosophy, enjoy the pleasure of burying its undertakers; but its own success in guiding neuroscience should not lead to the rumor that it has been devoured by its progeny.[10]

NOTES

[1] A distinction between systems that are merely "rule described" as opposed to "rule following" has been common for more than two decades (with some terminological variation). Dreyfus used the paths of the planets as an example of "motion according to a rule" (the law of gravity), which he contrasted with behavior causally determined by consultation of formalized rules (1972, pp. 101-2); Fodor invoked a similar distinction between planetary motion "in accordance with" rules and "rule following" on the part of organisms considered as computational systems (1975, p. 74, n. 15); Searle distinguished behavior that merely exhibits regularity that can be "described" by rules from "rule-following" or "rule-governed" behavior, that is, from behavior under the control of rules because an agent understands the content or meaning of the rules and acts on it (1980b, pp. 37-8); and Skinner distinguished "contingency-shaped" from "rule-following" behavior, explaining that in the latter case the organism behaves discriminatively toward an explicitly formulated rule or maxim, whereas in the former it responds directly to the contingencies of reinforcement without the benefit of a preconstructed discriminative stimulus (1966, pp. 241-9; I am indebted to Eckart Scheerer for this reference). All of these authors agreed on a distinction between cases in which explicitly formulated rules play a causal role in the production of behavior (because a device or organism "consults" the rules, in some sense of "consult") and cases in which motion or behavior is merely such that it can be described by a rule or law; they disagreed when applying the distinction. Dreyfus (1972, p. 68), Fodor (1975, p. 74, n. 15), and Skinner (1966, pp. 245-6) all were willing to attribute rule following to both human beings and computers. Searle, by contrast, would apply the term "rule following" only when the content of the rule (later, the "meaning"–1984, p. 46) causes the behavior in question; he thereby ruled out wholly syntactic "rule following" and hence, in his subsequent writings, rule following by standard computers (1980a; 1984, ch. 3). Although I am sympathetic with Searle's reservation about using the term "rule" univocally to refer both to ordinary human rule following and to the rules of transition between machine states in a Turing machine or standard digital computer (a usage encouraged by Turing himself–see the movement from the human computer's "following fixed rules" to the digital computer's control device seeing that "instructions are obeyed" in Turing, 1950, pp. 436-7), in this paper I employ the term "rule" according to the technical usage current in the literature of cognitive science (and related philosophical literature), while suggesting an added distinction within that usage.

[2] Connectionist models are designed or engineered by their creators. The primitive functional organization of psychological systems is not literally designed or engineered, it is evolved. However, metaphorical use of the notion of design can be helpful in analyzing natural functions, and natural functions may usefully be compared with artifactual ones in some respects (see Cummins, 1975, and Wright, 1976). On the application of the notion of natural (biological or psychological) function to connectionist models, see Hatfield, in press.

[3] Of course, the states of the mechanical or organic systems by which a classical or connectionist computational device is implemented are governed by the laws of physics and chemistry. But considered as rule following or rule instantiating,the transitions among the states of such devices are not merely law governed, for the functional organization of such devices eludes mere physical and chemical description. This may be seen by reflecting upon the fact that the state transitions of a normal as well as a broken device are each law governed, and the one no less than the other, whereas the normal device may be rule following or rule instantiating and the broken device not.

[4] Here may be the appropriate place to make a comment on the type of mental, cognitive, or perceptual rules that I consider to be likely objects of psychological explanation, whether connectionist or otherwise. As is apparent from the discussion thus far, both symbolists and connectionists have the ambitious aim of explicating "cognitive rules" in an unqualified sense: rules of inference, sophisticated rules acquired through learning (such as the rules of checkers, or those for balancing equations in chemistry), and so on. As I have indicated elsewhere (1988b, sec. 5), I consider it an open question whether cognitive psychology or cognitive science will be able to explain sophisticated cognitive achievements, and thus whether they will be able to explain thought itself; certainly current models have far to go. In particular, the normative aspects of thought have long resisted naturalistic analysis (see Hatfield, 1990, chs. 1 and 7, for elaboration), and it is unclear that the techniques made available by either standard symbolism or connectionism alter this situation. At the same time, progress has been made in the study of, e.g., early vision, imagination, attention, some aspects of language processing, and some aspects of memory.

[5] I don't consider the eliminativist position here because I find it to be decidedly implausible; my reasons for this judgment have been expressed elsewhere (Hatfield, 1988a).

[6] The notion of neural computation is commonplace in neurophysiology; see the papers in Anderson (1989) and Caianiello (1968). Recent connectionism focuses more on the abstract characteristics of computational networks than on actual neurophysiological cases (as connectionist themselves insist--Feldman & Ballard, 1982, p. 211; Smolensky, 1988, pp. 8-11). Thus, the aim of achieving connectionist neurophysiological explanations of actual psychological systems remains programmatic.

[7] I do not mean to deny the existence of physiological psychology. However, psychology proper is usually defined as the science of mental life or of behavior (e.g., Gleitman, 1986, p. 1); under either definition, neither its subject matter nor its explanatory vocabulary need include reference to physiological states and processes, so conceived.

[8] One could, of course, be a reductionist without being an eliminativist; but this qualification makes no difference to the points I will make in subsequent paragraphs. By the way, eliminativists do not deny a role to present day psychology; according to them it describes phenomena that neurophysiology cannot explain now, but which it will be able to explain one day (e.g., Quine, 1974, p. 33).

[9] The standard conception of reduction was articulated through reflection on the physical sciences; it typically portrayed reduction as consisting in type-type identities or other bridging relations between terms in the reducing and reduced theories (or their referents)--see Fodor, 1975, pp. 9-12.

[10] The final revisions of this paper took place while I was a member of the research group "Mind and Brain" at the Center for Interdisciplinary Research of the University of Bielefeld. I am grateful for the support of the Center and for its pleasant physical conditions and collegial atmosphere. I am also indebted to audiences at Brown University and the University of Wisconsin for making clear to me the need to state that while my notion of rule instantiation contrasts with rule following as understood in previous discussions in the philosophy of psychology, it need not contrast with rule following as discussed by Kripke.

REFERENCES

Anderson, J. A., and Rosenfeld, E., (eds.): 1989, *Neurocomputing: Foundations of Research*, MIT Press/Bradford Books, Cambridge, MA.

Ballard, D. H., Hinton, G. E., and Sejnowski, T.J.: 1983, 'Parallel Visual Computation', *Nature* 306, 21-26.

Boynton, R. M.: 1979, *Human Color Vision*, Holt, Rinehart, and Winston, New York.

Brown, C. M., Ballard, D. H., and Kimball, O. A.: 1982, 'Constraint Interaction in Shape-from-Shading Algorithms', *Proceedings of the DARPA Image Understanding Workshop*, pp. 1-11, National Technical Information Service, Springfield, VA.

Caianiello, E. R., (ed.): 1968, *Neural Networks*, Springer-Verlag, Berlin.

Churchland, P. S.: 1986, *Neurophilosophy: Toward a Unified Science of the Mind/Brain*, MIT Press/Bradford Books, Cambridge, MA.

Cummins, R.: 1975, 'Functional Analysis', *Journal of Philosophy* 72, 741-765.

Dreyfus, H. L.: 1972, *What Computers Can't Do: A Critique of Artificial Reason*, Harper & Row, New York.

Epstein, W., (ed.): 1977, *Stability and Constancy in Visual Perception: Mechanisms and Processes*, Wiley, New York.

Feldman, J. A.: 1985, 'Four Frames Suffice: A Provisional Model of Vision and Space', *Behavioral and Brain Sciences* 8, 265-289.

Feldman, J. A., and Ballard, D. H.: 1982, 'Connectionist Models and Their Properties', *Cognitive Science* 6, 205-254.

Fodor, J. A.: 1975, *The Language of Thought*, Crowell, New York.

Fodor, J. A.: 1980, *Representations*, MIT Press/Bradford Books, Cambridge, MA.

Fodor, J. A.: 1983, *The Modularity of Mind: An Essay on Faculty Psychology*, MIT Press/Bradford Books, Cambridge, MA.

Fodor, J. A., and Pylyshyn, Z. W.: 1981, 'How Direct Is Visual Perception?: Some Reflections on Gibson's "Ecological Approach"', *Cognition* 9, 139-196.

Fodor, J. A., and Pylyshyn, Z. W.: 1988, 'Connectionism and Cognitive Architecture: A Critical Analysis', *Cognition* 28, 3-71.

Gleitman, H.: 1986, *Psychology*, 2nd ed., Norton, New York.

Hatfield, G.: 1988a, 'Neuro-Philosophy Meets Psychology: Reduction, Autonomy, and Physiological Constraints', *Cognitive Neuropsychology* 5, 723-746.

Hatfield, G.: 1988b, 'Representation and Content in Some (Actual) Theories of Perception, *Studies in History and Philosophy of Science* 19, 175-214.

Hatfield, G.: 1990, *The Natural and the Normative: Theories of Spatial Perception from Kant to Helmholtz*, Bradford Books/MIT Press, Cambridge, MA.

Hatfield, G.: (in press), 'Representation in Perception and Cognition: Connectionist Affordances', in W. Ramsey, S. Stich, and D. Rumelhart (eds.), *Philosophy and Connectionist Theory*, Lawrence Erlbaum Associates, Hillsdale, NJ.

Haugeland, J.: 1978, 'The Nature and Plausibility of Cognitivism', *Behavioral and Brain Sciences* 1, 215-226, as reprinted in J. Haugeland, (ed.), *Mind Design*, pp. 243-281, MIT Press/Bradford Books, Cambridge, MA, 1981.

Hinton, G. E., McClelland, J. L., and Rumelhart, D. E.: 1986, 'Distributed Representations', in Rumelhart and McClelland, 1986b, pp. 77-109.

Hinton, G. E., and Sejnowski, T. J.: 1986, 'Learning and Relearning in Boltzmann Machines', in Rumelhart and McClelland, 1986b, pp. 282-317.

Julesz, B.: 1978, 'Global Stereopsis: Cooperative Phenomena in Stereoscopic Depth Perception', in R. Held, H. W. Leibofwitz, and H. L. Teuber, (eds.), *Handbook of Sensory Physiology*, Vol. 7, *Perception*, pp. 215-256, Springer-Verlag, Berlin.

Kandel, E. R., and Schwartz, J. H., (eds.): 1985, *Principles of Neural Science*, 2nd ed., Elsevier, New York.

Kaufman, L.: 1979, *Perception: The World Transformed*, Oxford University Press, New York.

Kienker, P. K., Sejnowski, T. J., Hinton, G. E., and Schumacher, L. E.: 1986, 'Separating Figure from Ground with a Parallel Network', *Perception* 15, 197-215.

Kitcher, P.: 1984, 'In Defense of Intentional Psychology', *Journal of Philosophy* **81**, 89-106.

Kosslyn, S. M., and Hatfield, G.: 1984, 'Representation without Symbol Systems', *Social Research* **51**, 1019-1045. (Reprinted in this volume.)

Marr, D.: 1982, *Vision*, Freeman, San Francisco.

Marr, D., and Poggio, T.: 1979, 'A Computational Theory of Human Stereo Vision', *Proceedings of the Royal Society of London* **B 204**, 151-180.

McClelland, J. L., and Rumelhart, D. E., (eds.): 1986, *Parallel Distributed Processing: Explorations in the Microstructure of Cognition*, Vol. 2, *Psychological and Biological Models*, MIT Press/Bradford Books, Cambridge, MA.

McClelland, J. L., Rumelhart, D. E., and Hinton, G. E.: 1986, 'The Appeal of Parallel Distributed Processing', in Rumelhart and McClelland, 1986b, pp. 3-44.

Mehler, J., Morton, J., and Jusczyk, P. W.: 1984, 'On Reducing Language to Biology', *Cognitive Neuropsychology* **1**, 83-116.

Newell, A.: 1980, 'Physical Symbol Systems', *Cognitive Science* **4**, 135-183.

Newell, A., Rosenbloom, P. S., and Laird, J. E.: 1989, 'Symbolic Architectures for Cognition', in Posner, 1989.

Newell, A., and Simon, H. A.: 1976, 'Computer Science as Empirical Inquiry: Symbols and Search', *Communications of the Association for Computing Machinery* **19**, 113-126, as reprinted in J. Haugeland, (ed.), *Mind Design*, pp. 35-66, MIT Press/Bradford Books, Cambridge, MA, 1981.

Pinker, S., and Prince, A.: 1988, 'On Language and Connectionism: Analysis of a Parallel Distributed Processing Model of Language Acquisition', *Cognition* **28**, 73-193.

Posner, M. I., (ed.): 1989, *Foundations of Cognitive Science*, MIT Press/Bradford Books, Cambridge, MA.

Putnam, H.: 1988, *Representation and Reality*, MIT Press/Bradford Books, Cambridge, MA.

Pylyshyn, Z. W.: 1984, *Computation and Cognition: Toward a Foundation for Cognitive Science*, MIT Press/Bradford Books, Cambridge, MA.

Pylyshyn, Z. W.: 1989, 'Computing in Cognitive Science', in Posner, 1989.

Quine, W. V.: 1974, *The Roots of Reference*, Open Court, LaSalle, IL.

Ratliff, F.: 1965, *Mach Bands: Quantitative Studies on Neural Networks in the Retina*, Holden-Day, San Francisco.

Richardson, R. C.: 1979, 'Functionalism and Reductionism', *Philosophy of Science* **46**, 533-558.

Rock, I.: 1983, *The Logic of Perception*, MIT Press/Bradford Books, Cambridge, MA.

Rumelhart, D. E.: 1989, 'The Architecture of Mind: A Connectionist Approach', in Posner, 1989.

Rumelhart, D. E., Hinton, G. E., and McClelland, J. L.: 1986, 'A General Framework For Parallel Distributed Processing,' in Rumelhart and McClelland, 1986b, pp. 45-76.

Rumelhart, D. E., and McClelland, J. L.: 1986a, 'On Learning the Past Tense of English Verbs,' in McClelland and Rumelhart, 1986, pp. 216-271.

Rumelhart, D. E., and McClelland, J. L., (eds.): 1986b, *Parallel Distributed Processing: Explorations in the Microstructure of Cognition*, Vol. 1., *Foundations*, MIT Press/Bradford, Books, Cambridge, MA.

Searle, J. R.: 1980a, 'Minds, Brains, and Programs', *Behavioral and Brain Sciences* **3**, 417-424.

Searle, J. R.: 1980b, 'Rules and Causation', *Behavioral and Brain Sciences*, **3**, 37-38.

Searle, J. R.: 1984, *Minds, Brains and Science*, Harvard University Press, Cambridge, MA.

Shastri, L.: 1988, 'A Connectionist Approach to Knowledge Representation and Limited Inference', *Cognitive Science* **12**, 331-392.

Shastri, L., and Ajjanagadde, V.: 1989, *A Connectionist System for Rule Based Reasoning with Multi-Place Predicates and Variables*, University of Pennsylvania Department of Computer and Information Science (Technical Report MS-CIS-89-06), Philadelphia.

Shastri, L., and Ajjanagadde, V.: 1990, *From Simple Associations to Systematic Reasoning: A Connectionist Representation of Rules, Variables and Dynamic Bindings*, University of Pennsylvania Department of Computer and Information Science (Technical Report MS-CIS-90-05), Philadelphia.

Skinner, B. F.: 1963, 'Behaviorism of Fifty', *Science* **134**, 566-602.

Skinner, B. F.: 1966, 'An Operant Analysis of Problem Solving', in B. Kleinmuntz, (ed.), *Problem Solving: Research, Method, and Theory*, pp. 225-257, Wiley, New York.
Smolensky, P.: 1986, 'Harmony Theory', in Rumelhart and McClelland, 1986b, pp. 194-281.
Smolensky, P.: 1987, *On Variable Binding and the Representation of Symbolic Structures in Connectionist Systems*, Technical Report CU-CS-355-87, University of Colorado Department of Computer Science, Boulder.
Smolensky, P.: 1988, 'On the Proper Treatment of Connectionism', *Behavioral and Brain Sciences* 11, 1-74.
Turing, A. M.: 1950, 'Computing Machinery and Intelligence', *Mind* 59, 433-460.
Ullman, S.: 'Against Direct Perception', *Behavioral and Brain Sciences* 3, 333-381.
Wright, L.: 1976, *Teleological Explanations: An Etiological Analysis of Goals and Functions*, University of California Press, Berkeley and Los Angeles.

Department of Philosophy
University of Pennsylvania
Philadelphia, PA 19104-6385

JAMES W. GARSON

WHAT CONNECTIONISTS CANNOT DO:
THE THREAT TO CLASSICAL AI

INTRODUCTION

A major battle between paradigms in cognitive science is underway. The last
thirty years have been dominated by the classical view that human cognition
is analogous to symbolic computation in digital computers. Connectionism
proposes a different picture, inspired by the neural architecture of the brain:
the mind is the result of the activity of immense numbers of simple units
(akin to neurons) connected together in complex patterns or networks. On
the classical account, information is represented by strings of symbols, just
as we represent data in computer memory or (for that matter) on pieces of
paper. The connectionist claims, on the other hand, that information is
stored non-symbolically in the weights, or connection strengths, between the
units of a neural net. The classicist believes that cognition resembles digital
processing, where strings are produced in sequence according to the
instructions of a (symbolic) program. The connectionist views mental
processing as the dynamic and graded evolution of activity in a neural net,
each unit's activation depending on the connection strengths and activity of
its neighbors, according to simple equations.

Connectionists have made significant progress recently in demonstrating
the power of neural nets. Nets can recognize patterns, retrieve information,
learn from examples, and apply that learning appropriately to novel
situations. Even more impressively, neural nets can be trained to do these
tasks, and they behave gracefully in the face of noise or partial loss of
function. This success has lead what we will call wild connectionists to think
that their new paradigm spells the death of classical artificial intelligence
(CAI). Wild connectionists claim that symbolic processing was a bad guess
about how the mind works. CAI, they complain, cannot explain graceful
degradation of function, holistic representation of data, spontaneous
generalization, appreciation of context, and many other features of human

113

intelligence which they claim are reflected in connectionist models. So wild connectionists would eliminate symbolic processing from cognitive science forever.

More conservative connectionists exhibit tolerance for the classical paradigm. The most popular tactic for working out an accommodation between the two positions is to grant the possibility that some nets that model mental abilities implement symbolic processors. On this view, the mind is a neural net; but, it is also a symbolic processor at a more abstract level of description. The role of the classical account is to describe and predict those emergent properties of nets that correspond to symbolic processes. This reductionist story has the gentlemanly feature that both models are right, but a different levels of description. The plausibility of this view depends on the mental function to be modeled. Symbolic models of low level visual processing, for example, appear to have little going for them (Marr, 1982). However, a reductionist view still appears attractive to some of those working on language and reasoning.

The purpose of this paper is to measure the threat that connectionism poses to CAI. We will explore wild connectionist arguments which claim that a reductionist rescue of CAI is impossible or unlikely. Eliminitivist arguments of this kind share a somewhat paradoxical form. Connectionism is said to threaten CAI because neural nets cannot meet some basic requirement for symbolic processing. This weakness constitutes a threat because it apparently supports an eliminitivist conditional of the form:

(EC) If connectionist models are correct then CAI is wrong.

If evidence for the correctness of connectionist models can be developed, then the mind could not be a symbolic processor at any level of description, and CAI is eliminated.

As we shall see, such eliminitivist arguments are somewhat delicate. One must first develop evidence that connectionist models of a certain kind cannot carry out some form of computation. One must then show that what these models cannot do is crucial for symbolic processing. Even if (EC) can be successfully supported in this way, the anti-classicist battle is not won. (EC) is a double-edged sword. Wild *classicists* may argue that a proper understanding of language and reasoning demands a classical account (Fodor and Pylyshyn, 1988), from which it follows from (EC) by modus tollens, that connectionist models are wrong. To thwart this classical backlash, the eliminitivist must marshall sufficient evidence for the plausibility of connectionist models to tip the balance in favor of modus ponens.

In Section 1 of this paper we will formulate the eliminitivist argument so as to maximize its likelihood of success. Our primary concern will be to locate those connectionist models which would best serve the cause of eliminitivist claims. We will also refine the argument in light of a possible reduction of classical to connectionist models. In Section 2, we will examine a number of requirements for symbolic processing which one might claim cannot be carried out by the connectionist models identified in Section 1. In each case, we will determine whether evidence from connectionist research supports the premises of the eliminitivist argument.

We will conclude that available information about connectionist models simply does not support (EC), the eliminitivist conditional. Given what we know at present, CAI is immune from eliminitivism, and wild connectionists are hasty in claiming victory over the classical paradigm. On the other side, the failure of support for (EC) also protects connectionists from wild classicist backlash.

Neural net novelty has blinded disputants on both sides to the prospects for peaceful coexistence. We will show that recent research on connectionist models supports a compatibilist rather than an eliminitivist conclusion. (See Bechtel (1988), Cummins (forthcoming), and Hawthorne (1989), for similar views.) This should help pave the way for gentler and more productive dialogue between the paradigms.

1. THE FORM OF ELIMINITIVIST ARGUMENTS

Let us begin with eliminitivist arguments of the following form:

(CAN'T) Certain connectionist models of the mind CAN'T X.

(MUST) <u>CAI models of the mind MUST X.</u>

(EC) If such connectionist models are CORRECT, then CAI is wrong. The force of such an argument will obviously depend upon the choice of X. Before we examine candidates for X, however, two other aspects of the argument must be attended to. First, we will need to identify the connectionist models mentioned by the argument, and second we will need to revise the second premise in light of the possibility that CAI models may be reduced to connectionist theories of the mind.

If an eliminitivist argument of this form is to be a convincing threat to CAI, the connectionist models at issue must meet two seemingly conflicting conditions. The first premise (CAN'T) must be true. It must be shown that the connectionist models cannot do X, and so the connectionist models must be *weak* in this respect. At the same time, the eliminitivist conditional (EC) will pose little threat to CAI unless its antecedent (CORRECT) is plausible. So we must also make sure that the connectionist models are *strong*, in the sense that they have a reasonable chance of being correct accounts of the mind. In order to maximize prospects for eliminitivist arguments, it is important to choose a class of connectionist models which have the best chance of being weak and strong in the requisite ways.

1.1 *PDP Models*

It is crucial to the eliminitivist arguments that the connectionist models mentioned be both good at modeling the mind and bad at symbolic processing. In this section we will identify connectionist models which are most likely to provide the best evidence for eliminitivist conclusions. We will call them kosher parallel distributed processing models, or PDP models, for short. They are commonly cited by connectionists in attacks against CAI. The term 'PDP model' is used fairly broadly to cover many different kinds of neural nets. In this paper, we will define it more narrowly to pick out those models that are most promising in promoting the eliminitivist argument by providing the right combination of weakness and strength.

Before we describe the defining feature of PDP models on our usage, we will briefly describe connectionist nets in general. A neural net consists of large numbers of simple units joined together in a pattern of connections. Units in a net are segregated into three classes: input units, output units, and units that have no direct connections with the external world, called hidden units. The network responds to the values at the input units by sending their signals to all connected units. Each of these receiving units gathers signals from sending units and combines them to calculate an activation value to be sent to its neighbors. The activation pattern passes from unit to unit, eventually determining the activation of the output units.

The pattern of activation set up by a net is determined by the weights, or strength of connections between the units. Weights may be both positive or negative. (A negative weight represents the inhibition of the receiving unit by the activity of a sending unit.) The activation values for the units are calculated by a simple (but possibly non-linear) activation function. The activation function determines the output of a unit by summing together the contributions of its sending units, where the contribution of a sending unit is the weight times its activation value. This sum is usually modified further, for example, by limiting the activation to a maximum value or by sending zero unless a bias or threshold level of activation is reached.

We will now describe three special features of PDP models as we define them: non-classical hardware, distributed representation and recurrency. We will examine each of these properties in turn, and explain how each helps strengthen the eliminitivist argument.

The first defining feature of PDP models is that they use non-classical hardware. It is well known that neural nets are, in general, as powerful as classical computers. Any classical computer can be built by wiring together many copies of two simple circuits: the nand gate, and the flip-flop. It is not difficult to construct small neural nets which carry out each of these two functions. It follows that any classical computer, no matter how complicated, can be simulated in a corresponding neural net that simply copies its architecture. Since the eliminitivist argument requires that the connectionist models be unable to carry out symbolic processing (CAN'T), we must exclude models that implement the structure of a classical machine. So PDP models may contain no substructures which function according to the design specifications of standard computer circuits. PDP nets must not implement nand gates, flip-flops, shift registers, addressers, multiplexers, adders, CPUs, ALUs, or any other hardware component of a digital computer.[1]

The second essential feature of PDP models is distributed representation. Information in neural nets is stored by the weights of the connections between the nodes. In PDP models, no one connection or small group of connections is responsible for recording any one piece of information. Data stored in a PDP model is reflected in the entire pattern of weights between the units.

Distributed representation is helpful to eliminitivist arguments because it appears to support (CAN'T), the view that nets cannot carry out symbolic processing. Global storage of information seems incompatible with the classical picture, where attention of the processor moves from one string to another during a computation. It is difficult to imagine how symbol strings could be represented as coherent and identifiable items if the information for each is spread throughout the net. It is even harder to see how the net could simulate the sequenced program-governed transformation of one string into another when the information represented is evolving gradually and distributed evenly.

Distributed representation also contributes to support of (CORRECT), the claim that the connectionist models are correct accounts of the mind. Global storage of information embodied in distributed representation helps explain the flexibility and resilience of human memory. Although there is evidence for some localization of memories (or perhaps localization of their evocation) in the brain, the radically local storage typically used in the hardware of classical computers is not faithful to the facts about human functioning. On the classical scheme, the loss of memory units leads to total loss of information stored in those locations, leaving other information completely untouched. If an attempt is made to store new information in a memory which is full, either the new information, or some old information will be totally lost. Distributed representation seems to parallel better the behavior of human memory. Loss of units or overloading memory results in a gradual and evenhanded degradation of all information stored.

The third feature of PDP models is recurrency. In recurrent nets, the connection pattern contains loops. A loop exists when it is possible to trace the output signal for a unit through the net until it returns back to the same unit's input. Recurrency is important because it supports (CORRECT), the claim that connectionist nets could plausibly model the mind. Without loops, a neural net settles into a single state for each setting of its inputs. Such a feed forward net has no interesting history until its pattern of inputs changes. Although feed forward nets are better understood and easier to deal with, they have limited abilities, especially when it comes to representing and generating patterns through time. If connectionism is right, it is almost certain that some form of recurrency is required to explain language understanding and production, motor control, and even memory. Although many connectionist models are feed forward nets, they are designed to handle static phenomena where interesting temporal behavior does not arise. Since the mind clearly has an interesting temporal history, it is a reasonable assumption that any net that simulates the mind is recurrent.[2]

Discussion of connectionism has tended to focus on models which are too weak. For example, Fodor and Pylyshyn (1988) assume that connectionist models use local representation, and so are unable to understand how nets can represent compositional structure in a straightforward way. Similarly, Ramsey, Stich and Garon (forthcoming) discuss non-recurrent models, and so are unable to see how connectionism can account for causal role.[3] The choice of overly weak models strengthens the first premises (CAN'T) of the eliminitivist argument, since weaker models are less capable of classical processing. There is a price to pay, however, which is often overlooked, namely that the eliminitivist conditional (EC) loses its bite.

(EC) If such connectionist models are CORRECT, then CAI is wrong. If it is unlikely that the connectionist models in question are correct accounts of the mind, (EC) is useless. If the antecedent is false, the wild connectionist cannot ponens, and a wild classicist tollens merely yields the result that the weak models chosen are inadequate, which connectionists will be happy to accept.

An interesting eliminitivist conditional must refer to models which are real contenders for modeling the mind. We believe this requires both recurrency and distributed representation. When PDP models are chosen to strengthen the antecedent of (EC), the eliminitivist argument then suffers from a different failing. As we shall argue in Section 2, PDP models have surprisingly strong symbolic processing powers. As a result, the first premise, (CAN'T), which would claim that there are things that PDP models cannot do, is no longer plausible.

1.2 *Reduction of CAI Models*

If PDP models succeed in providing a correct account of the mind, the classical account may still be correct, provided that symbolic processing emerges from the net behavior at some higher level of description. On this compatibilist scenario, CAI reduces to connectionism, and each model is correct in its own sphere. It is worth examining the nature of such a reduction more carefully, since this is the target of eliminitivist arguments.

Our account of the reduction of classical models follows the standard story concerning theoretical reduction in the sciences (see Churchland, 1979). In the reducing theory, the model is described entirely in low level vocabulary: events are explained by the activation of units, which is determined by the weights and biases. If reduction is possible, however, there is a higher level description of the same events, involving *patterns* of activation and *properties* of the weights. These emergent features of the net correspond to the symbol strings and program commands in the symbolic model. The reduction of the symbolic theory requires that there be an appropriate isomorphism which coordinates each process in the symbolic description with the corresponding emergent level event in the PDP model.

The reduction of a CAI model does not require a perfect isomorphism between the two models. A partial or approximate mapping may do, and the success of the reduction would presumably grade off with its accuracy. In case of an imperfect isomorphism, the relationship between the PDP and CAI descriptions might be something like the relationship between statistical mechanics and classical thermodynamics (Smolensky, 1988). For a wide range of conditions, emergent properties of events described at the micro-level (molecular movements) approximate quite accurately events described at the macro-level (temperature-pressure regularities), even though there are some phenomena, (for example, behavior at extremely high pressures) that cannot be accounted for by the higher level theory. A similar story might be told for (say) a symbolic natural language processor which was only approximately implemented in a PDP model. Emergent properties of the net (properties of activation levels) might approximate nicely, events described at the symbolic level (say, saving information on a stack), even though some phenomena (say, failure to parse center embeddings) could not be accounted for at the symbolic level.

1.3 A Revised Eliminitivist Argument

Eliminitivists hope to show that the classical paradigm is incompatible with PDP models. To do so effectively, they must show that compatibilist reduction of CAI models to PDP models is impossible. Our discussion of model reduction helps draw attention to a problem with our formulation of the eliminitivist argument. That argument form is invalid as it stands. Even if we locate something which PDP models can't and CAI models must do, this alone does not entail that the models are incompatible. To establish that CAI and PDP models are incompatible, it is not enough to cite their differences. One needs to show that those differences are relevant, i.e. that they rule out a reduction.

This problem may be repaired by reformulating (MUST), the second premise of the eliminitivist argument. Instead of claiming that *CAI* models must have some property, the revised premise cites a property which *PDP* models must have if they are to reduce CAI models. If a symbolic processing account is to be reduced, the isomorphism between the symbolic level description and the emergent level description of the net presumably insures that the PDP model is capable of meeting certain corresponding conditions, X, which reflect symbolic processing requirements. If PDP models cannot do X, it will follow that no classical account can be reduced to a PDP account, with the consequence that success of a PDP account of the mind eliminates CAI.

Given the revisions suggested so far, the eliminitivist argument schema (EA) takes the following form:

PDP models of the mind CAN'T X.

PDP models that reduce CAI models of the mind MUST X.

If PDP models are CORRECT then CAI is eliminated.

If the premises are true, EA yields an eliminitivist conditional which may be used in two ways. The wild connectionist hopes to establish the antecedent (PDP models are correct) and *eliminate* CAI by modus ponens. The wild classicist, on the other hand, insists that CAI is the only possible explanation for language and reasoning, so any correct model of the mind must reduce a CAI model. Given the eliminitivist conditional, the wild classicist concludes that PDP models must be wrong. Hence, success of EA amplifies the antagonism between connectionists and classicists, for its conclusion denies the possibility of peaceful coexistence. We will argue, however, that the premises of EA are not true given the likely candidates for X, and so open the doors for a compatibilist reconciliation.

2. WHAT PDP MODELS CANNOT DO

Our next project will be to search for likely candidates for X in hopes of supporting the premises of the eliminitivist argument schema. To help guide the search, let us briefly discuss basic features of the classical paradigm which promise to yield interesting constraints on reducing PDP models.

Although CAI encompasses a wide variety of approaches, two articles of faith are central to the classical picture. First, information is stored symbolically. It is represented in the form of symbol strings with constituent structure. By constituent structure we mean a form of organization which coordinates the symbols of a string into meaningful substrings. For example, a computer program is typically composed of a sequence of lines or commands. These commands may contain further substructure. For example, a conditional command may have the form: IF (condition) THEN (action1) ELSE (action2), where the items (condition) (action1) and (action2) may be complex components which contain other commands (including other conditionals).

The second article of faith in the classical paradigm is that processing is the sequential generation of symbol strings guided by their constituent structure.[4] Constituent structure provides a framework that determines how programs are to be executed. The syntactic structure of the data being processed is crucial in defining the sequence of events that comprises a computation. On the classical view, constituency has a causal role in computation, in the sense that the program commands which guide a computation are sensitive to the constituent structure of the symbolic information to which they are applied.

In the remaining sections of this paper we will discuss a number of features which seem to follow from reduction of a symbolic processing model of the mind, and to be incompatible with PDP models. In each case, however, we will show that appearances are deceiving. We will challenge both the claim PDP models are unable to generate that aspect of symbolic processing, and the claim that it is required for a successful reduction.

2.1 *Symbolic Discreteness*

If a CAI model is to be reduced to a PDP net, it appears that some emergent properties of the net must correspond to symbol strings. It would seem that to be symbolic, those properties must be stable, reproducible and distinguishable one from another. Presumably, there must be a fact of the matter as to when a given string is present in the net or not. Since a symbolic computation is sequenced production of strings, times at which one string is present in a net must be distinguishable from times at which the subsequent string is present. Of course, the evolution from one string to another may require intermediate stages where neither string appears; however, if symbolic processing is to be attributed to a PDP model, it would seem that there must be some point in time when the new string clearly emerges.

There appears to be a conflict between the local and discrete representation required in symbolic processing, and the holistic and graded representation found in PDP models. So symbolic discreteness, the requirement that net features corresponding to strings be sequentially discriminable, stable and reproducible, would appear to be an excellent choice for X in the eliminitivist argument. This suggestion works, however, only if we can show that both PDP models CAN'T, and CAI models MUST, provide for symbolic discreteness. Let us examine each of these claims in turn.

2.1.1 Can PDP Models Achieve Symbolic Discreteness?

In this section we will show that the assumption that discreteness cannot emerge in higher level properties of PDP models is mistaken. Discreteness is compatible with connectionism. Many neural nets, in fact, are designed to convert fuzzy information into a discrete representation (for example, sounds of ordinary speech, into printed text) (McClelland and Elman, 1986). Although low level net behavior may be very imprecise and/or graded, extremely accurate and fine discriminations may emerge in the higher level properties of a large ensemble.

There are two reasons why this is true. First, the dynamics of PDP models may insure that the system always settles into one of a desired set of discrete patterns (Rumelhart, McClelland et al., 1986, p. 55 and p. 71). Fuzzy, graded, and poorly discriminated processes are not only compatible with, but may help explain, accurate and fine discrimination at higher levels of description. Randomness in neural nets, for example, promotes rather than hinders convergence to an appropriate discrete state (Hinton and Sejnowski, 1986, p. 287).

Second, the use of distributed representation, which may appear at first to be incompatible with discreteness, in fact helps promote discreteness. As Hinton, McClelland and Rumelhart (1986, p. 92) point out:

> The intuitive idea that [distribution leads] to sloppier representations is entirely wrong because distributed representations hold information much more efficiently than local ones. Even though each active unit is less specific in its meaning, the combination of active units is far more specific.

By spreading the task of coding a given piece of information among many units, the system promotes in tandem two seemingly conflicting goals, namely accuracy and fine discrimination. (This "course coding" tactic is used to some extent in digital computers, which must also provide for accurate computation using inaccurate circuitry.) So symbolic discreteness is not incompatible with PDP models; it may emerge from broad and inaccurate net level discriminations.

2.1.2 *Must Reducing PDP Models Achieve Symbolic Discreteness?*

Even if it could be shown that symbolic discreteness is impossible in PDP models, one would still need to establish that discreteness is necessary for reduction of CAI models. Despite initial appearances, this is wrong. It may be appropriate to attribute symbolic processing to a net, even when none of its emergent properties is discrete.

To help establish this point, imagine a symbolic model which generates sequences of strings. Suppose there is a well established way of coordinating symbol strings with corresponding activation patterns of a net. Imagine that we have a PDP model whose behavior is so fuzzy and diffuse that none of the patterns that correspond to strings actually occur in the net. It may still be sensible to describe this net as a symbolic processor, for example, under the following conditions. Although no pattern identified with a symbol appears in the net, a measure of the degree **d** to which a symbolic pattern is present may still be defined (as, for example, the geometric distance in pattern space between the symbols pattern and the pattern of activation in the net). Suppose now that the symbolic model predicts evolution of string **t** from string **s** exactly when the net with the pattern for **s** to degree **d** subsequently displays the pattern for **t** to degree **d**. If this correspondence holds for all strings, and all degrees **d**, then one would be justified describing the net as a symbolic processor. Although no pattern of symbolic computation appears in the net to the full extent, the computation patterns (perhaps many at once) are still present in lesser degrees.

Of course it would be very lucky if things were to work out so nicely, but our purpose is to argue the logical point that the failure of a net to take on discrete states does not rule out a symbolic description. An isomorphism to a CAI model may still reveal interesting symbolic structure in the net even though it does not define a direct correspondence between symbolic processing and discrete net events.

2.2 *Causal Role*

On the classical view, computation involves the repeated generation of symbol strings from previously derived strings according to the instructions of a program. During processing, a "center of attention" moves from one symbol string to another.[5] So symbol strings in the classical picture have identifiable causal roles, in the sense that some strings are used, while others, though present, are not needed during a computation. If symbol strings correspond to activation patterns, then a string which is present in a net, but not used, corresponds to a pattern that was not active. But how can such an inactive pattern also be present in the net? The notion of present but unused strings appears to be incompatible with connectionist models, and so an ability to reflect the causal role of symbol strings may be a good choice for X in eliminitivist arguments.[6]

2.2.1 Can PDP Models Account for Causal Role?

The view that causal role is incompatible with PDP models is wrong. Present but inactive strings may be identified with dispositions of the net to have activation patterns under the appropriate circumstances.[7] Dispositional behavior of a net is defined by the weights between its units, so presence of inactive strings must amount to properties of those weights. Since symbol strings change their status from active to inactive in the course of a computation, PDP models that account for causal role must contain mechanisms for "storing" active strings in weights and reactivating stored strings in the course of a computation. In short, causal role appears to require that the reducing PDP model provide for memory.[8]

Although memory may seem at odds with the neural net paradigm, it is, in fact, one of the strong points of connectionist models (Hinton and Anderson, 1981). There are several connectionist strategies which can be used to store and retrieve activation patterns in weight properties. One of the areas of recent success in neural net research is the development of methods (for example back-propagation) for training nets to acquire and generalize information. The essence of training is to adjust the weights so as to create dispositions to take on desired activation patterns. So one way to accommodate symbolic memory in PDP nets is to use training methods to store strings during a computation. After the net settles into an activation pattern representing a symbol string just derived, it may then store away this result using training. During training, the weights of the net are adjusted so that the activation pattern will be restored when it is needed again in the computation.

The use of training is only one of several connectionist alternatives for simulating memory. Sigma-pi nets (for example) use unit equations which allow activation patterns to affect weights directly, without shifting into training mode (Rumelhart, McClelland et al., 1986, p. 73; and McClelland

and Rumelhart, 1986). Such models could easily accommodate storage of strings for later use. Similar networks show considerable promise in simulating details of the performance of human memory (Metcalf Eich, 1985). Since memory can be simulated, PDP nets have adequate resources for handling causal role in symbolic processing.

Lest we sound overly optimistic on this point, however, it should be admitted that memory in PDP nets may suffer from a human failing: namely that performance degrades when too many patterns are stored at once, especially when there are similarities among the patterns. As the net becomes overloaded, errors occur both in access and accuracy of the information retrieved. The difficulty can be overcome by adding more units, but for perfectly accurate storage one needs at least one unit for each stored pattern. The human brain, despite its billions of neurons, may very well face memory limitations that would degrade performance of complex symbolic computations. This prospect, however, need not be damaging to the classical paradigm. The presence of processing limitations does not, by itself, entail that the brain is not a symbolic processor. Every finite digital computer also exhibits processing limitations, but that is no reason for concluding that digital computers are not symbolic.

2.2.2 *Must Reducing PDP Models Account for Causal Role?*

In Section 2.1.2, we argued that symbolic processing may be attributed to a PDP net even when none of its emergent properties are symbolically discrete. The same considerations presented there entail that PDP models need not assign specific causal roles to strings in order to reduce a classical model. Given a net where symbol strings are present only partially, it makes no sense to distinguish the strings which are from those that are not involved in a given computation. Here, the participation of symbolic patterns in a computation is a matter of degree. Although a graded measure of involvement is possible in such a net, the clean identification of strings as either having or not having a causal role is impossible. The failure of a net to model precisely the "movement of attention" from one string to another may seem to argue against the existence of symbolic processing in any robust sense. On the other hand, the demonstration of a consistent correspondence between net events and partially present symbolic computations, would be hard to ignore. Classicists should be more than glad to cite such a phenomenon as a vindication of their paradigm.

2.3 Functional Discreteness

A major worry one may have concerning the adequacy of reducing PDP models is that the entire set of net weights is involved in coding each and every item of information stored in a net. So the addition of a new string to net memory consists in an adjustment to all the weights. It is hard to see how a string can be stored without disturbing information about other strings in the net. In the classical picture of computation, strings are functionally discrete.[9] They may be independently added or subtracted during computation without thereby affecting the presence or absence of other strings. Functional discreteness appears to be crucial to CAI, because symbolic processing depends on the preservation of symbolic information during a computation. Given the possibility that information in a PDP model necessarily degrades during processing, functional discreteness appears to be an excellent candidate for X in the eliminitivist argument.

2.3.1 Can PDP Models Be Functionally Discrete?

If lack of functional discreteness is to count against reduction of symbolic processing to PDP models, it must be shown that PDP models cannot preserve symbolic information while storing and retrieving strings from net memory. Smolensky (1987) provides a mathematical analysis of the prospects for functional discreteness in nets with distributed representation. There is good and bad news for both parties to the dispute. Smolensky shows that activation patterns can be perfectly stored and retrieved in net weights provided that the patterns are linearly independent. Linear independence of patterns, however, is quite costly. The number of linearly independent patterns that a net can support is no more than its number of units.

It is hard to assess the practical import of this limitation. On the gloomy side, notice that the systematicity of thought (Fodor and Pylyshyn, 1988) requires that I be able to think, (and presumably to remember) any English sentence of modest length. But the number of possible English sentences of twenty words or less exceeds the number of molecules in our galaxy. If each sentence corresponds to a separate linearly independent pattern, the number of units must be astronomical. This makes the provision for perfect storage of symbolic information appear very expensive indeed, and clearly beyond the power of the human brain.

On the other hand, there is no need for the mind to store such an immense amount of symbolic information. For example, humans remember a very small subset of the English sentences to which they are exposed. Linear independence is required only for the information patterns actually stored. The brain may very well contain mechanisms that code a modest number of symbolic structures that are to be remembered into functionally discrete activation patterns.

Unfortunately, we know very little about storage in the brain. It is true that psychological studies of conscious memory reveal information loss, cross talk, interference between similar patterns, and retrieval difficulties. However, it is possible that more accurate forms of subconscious memory are available for language understanding and problem solving. We do not have a clear enough picture of human mental functioning to determine the significance of the costs of requiring functional discreteness. It is clear, however, that functional discreteness in PDP models is not ruled out in principle, but is limited instead by practical constraints on resources.

2.3.2 Must Reducing PDP Models Be Functionally Discrete?

Even if functional discreteness is a serious problem for connectionist models, the eliminitivist must show that PDP nets which reduce CAI models must be functionally discrete. There are good reasons for believing that this is not the case. For one thing, it is possible to imagine perfectly legitimate symbolic processors which are not functionally discrete. For example, consider an expert system that maintains the integrity of its data by removing suspect information whenever an inconsistency is detected. In such a system, the addition of new information can affect the presence of other information, and so functional discreteness fails. Nevertheless, this failure does not argue against the expert system's being a symbolic processor.

Functional discreteness seems a plausible requirement when classical computation is viewed at the hardware level. A digital computer is designed to store a symbol in any memory location without disturbing symbols at other locations. However, this detail of digital hardware is not a requirement on CAI models, which are characterized at the software level. A demand that details of classical hardware be simulated in order to carry out a CAI reduction is clearly too strong; it would automatically preclude any reduction, since PDP models, by definition, do not contain classical hardware.

Obviously the demand for functional discreteness does not arise from an interest in replicating features of classical hardware. The worry is that without functional discreteness, decay in net memory would compromise symbolic processing. This is a general concern which we have already dealt with in our discussion of symbolic discreteness and causal role. It may be that classical models are only approximately implemented in the brain because of noise and error in neural processing. Nevertheless, the classical account of the mind may still be reasonable.

2.4 *Constituency*

It is a central article of faith in the classical paradigm that strings have constituent structure which guides computation. Strings are not random collections of symbols. They are recursively structured into subcomponents, and the nature of the subcomponents determines how program commands generate new strings from old ones. In recent discussion, constituency appears at the focus of debate concerning the adequacy of connectionist models. Fodor and Pylyshyn (1988), for example, argue that constituency is crucial for explaining productivity, systematicity, and learnability of language and thought. Representation of constituency looks like a sore point in the connectionist program, so it would seem to be a good choice for X in the eliminitivist argument.

2.4.1 *Can PDP Models Handle Constituency?*

Trees are an especially nice way to represent constituent structure. If a net is capable of representing constituency, then it must be able to analyze a tree into its parts, and join such structures together to form larger trees. These operations are fundamentally recursive, because each part of a tree may itself have arbitrarily complex substructure. So whether PDP models can handle constituency depends on whether they are capable of carrying out the basic operations that allow the recursive composition and decomposition of trees.

This question has been a concern throughout the history of connectionist research. Many models with abilities at recursive processing have disturbing deficiencies. Fanty's (1985) parser, for example, used local representation, and dealt with sentences of fixed length. Touretzky's BoltzCONS (1986) model used less than fully distributed representation, and needed special purpose architecture with a classical flavor (Smolensky, 1987, p. 6). The limitations in these models supports claims of Fodor and Pylyshyn (1988) that connectionists cannot properly account for constituency.

Fodor and Pylyshyn are clearly right if we restrict attention (as they do) to models with local representation of strings. However, more recent work shows that distributed models have excellent prospects for handling constituent structure. Smolensky's (1987) work on tensor product representation proves that PDP nets can, in principle, handle fully recursive tree processing. Smolensky gives a mathematical analysis which shows how trees can be stored in nets using distributed representation. He then shows that highly accurate net processes can be defined that correspond to the analysis of trees into their parts (the LISP functions CAR and CDR), and the construction of new trees from arbitrarily complex components (the LISP functions CONS).

Smolensky also shows how to view methods for representing symbolic structure that are actually used in connectionist models as special cases of tensor product representation. He discusses the practical problem of implementing tensor product operations, and suggests a simple plan for doing so with sigma-pi nets. An important strategy used here is to exploit what amounts to neural net memory to store constituent structure. This work is significant not only because it shows that no theoretical obstacles stand in the way of the development of nets that can handle recursive structuring, but also because it provides a mathematical analysis of the conditions under which accurate tree processing operations can be defined, and how they may grade off in the face of processing limitations.

One disturbing feature of these results, which we have mentioned before, is that perfection in the representation of tree structure requires linear independence of the patterns. This in turn requires as many units as there are patterns to be represented. Depending on how many strings are to be stored, the price for perfection may be too high. This explains Smolensky's belief (1988, p. 22) that the brain is a symbolic processor only to an approximation, because it is prone to the kind of degraded performance due to noise and cross-talk that is inevitable given limited resources.

Smolensky's work is somewhat abstract. He does not report the construction of working models. It is comforting, therefore, to know that Pollack (1988) and Hinton (1988) have both succeeded in producing practical models that are capable of carrying out basic tree processing operations. Again, the secret of success in handling constituency is to take advantage of neural net memory. Pollack's work on recursive auto-associative memory (RAAM) is interesting because he shows that it is possible, using standard methods, to *train* a net to carry out the basic stack functions push and pop. He exploits these structures to carry out a number of standard recursive tasks, including the famous tower of Hanoi puzzle, and the determination of the syntactic structure of simple English sentences.

Hinton (1988) models trees using a method called reduced representation. The method takes advantage of a strong point of connectionist models, namely the net's ability to retrieve a whole pattern when presented with one of its parts. To represent the sentence "the man with the golden arm snuck through the alley," for example, one trains the memory to store the general structure of the sentence in schematic form: [(NP man) + (VP ran)]. The components (NP man) and (VP ran) are partial (reduced) descriptions of the sentential structure which has been stored. When details on (say) the noun phrase are needed, the partial description (NP man) serves as a key to call up a more detailed description: [(NP the man) + (PP with arm)]. A component of this new description, say, (PP with arm), may then be used as a key again to retrieve even more detailed structure: (PP with the golden arm). Using associative memory to develop links from partial descriptions to more detailed information, chains of associations can be developed which define branches of a tree. Although reduced description may not express the whole sentence in full detail at any one time, it allows the retrieval of any part of the structure in a coordinated way, regardless of the complexity of the tree structure.

Claims that PDP models are incapable of handling constituency have little going for them. Distributed representation and neural net memory can be exploited in a number of ways to represent and help process constituent structure (van Gelder, 1990). Although practical limitations to symbolic processing may exist, there is no evidence that they pose a serious problem for classical accounts of the mind.[10]

2.4.2 *Must Reducing PDP Models Handle Constituency?*

If resource limitations of the brain severely limit the generality and power of constituent processing, one may still define a classical account of cognition. One defense simply abandons the requirement that string structure be represented by arbitrarily complex trees. Symbolic processing demands some kind of symbolic structure, but it is not clear exactly how powerful the structuring device must be. CAI models of the mind may make do with weaker devices, perhaps as little as the ordering of the symbols. More reasonably, one may restrict attention to trees that only go a few levels deep, or that forbid multiple center embeddings. Connectionists tend to view human limitations in recursive processing of natural language as evidence against a classical account of cognition (Rumelhart and McClelland, 1986, p. 119). However, even if that evidence shows fundamental weakness in the brain's ability to handle recursion, it need not cut against a classicist who chooses weaker symbolic structuring devices.

For those who demand symbolic models with unlimited recursion, there is still a second classical response to possible processing limitations, namely to take refuge in the competence-performance distinction.[11] Classicists have traditionally adopted models with unlimited resources--models which cannot therefore account for the details of human performance. Classicists may claim that while the connectionists model performance, they model competence, i.e., the behavior that could be expected if resources were unlimited. Overuse of the competence-performance distinction runs the risk of trivializing classical theories, for it may insulate them too well from the evidence. On the other hand, the claim that a classical model is a correct account of the competence of a PDP net could be tested, for example, by showing that performance of the net converges to that of the classical model as resources are made more abundant. It follows, then, that classicists may attribute symbolic processing even to PDP models which have difficulties in handling constituency.

2.5 *Representation of Rules*

If PDP models can implement recursive routines for handling constituency, it does not follow that they are powerful enough to simulate complex classical models for such tasks as language understanding and problem solving. Noise and other processing limitations may be severe enough to swamp out more complex symbolic calculations. However, connectionist research on models that carry out higher level symbolic processing gives us reasons for optimism. Touretzky and Hinton (1985) show how accurate rule-based processing is possible in nets using distributed representation. Touretzky and Geva (1988) show how to use associative memory to simulate classical data structures. Ballard (1987) shows how to simulate unification, a powerful foundation for natural language processing (Shieber, 1986) and classical programming in general. Hanson and Kegl (1987), Elman (1988, 1989), and Servan-Schreiber, Cleeremans and McClelland (1988) have shown how to train connectionist models to parse simple grammars.

The eliminitivist, however, may still feel that something is missing, no matter how effective such models may be. It is a feature of symbolic processing that symbol strings are generated by rules (program commands) which are represented in the system. The requirement that rules be represented may be exactly the property which blocks reduction of CAI models to nets. So let us examine its merits for filling in for X in the eliminitivist argument.

2.5.1 *Can PDP Models Represent Rules?*

Representation of rules in PDP models is a difficult topic. If rules are present in nets, they are presumably stored as properties of the weights. But which properties? How do we verify the presence of a rule in a net? Both Elman (1989) and Servan-Schreiber, Cleeremans, and McClelland (1988) (hereafter Servan-Schreiber) have made important progress on this question. Servan-Schreiber trained PDP models to recognize finite state grammars. After training, strings were presented to the net, and the corresponding activation patterns of the hidden units were studied. Those strings to which the same rule of the grammar would apply were found to have similar activation patterns, while strings to which different rules would apply had dissimilar patterns. Statistical analysis of the trained PDP net shows that activation patterns are classified into distinct groups--groups which can be identified with rules of the grammar. Rules are represented in these nets, in the form of a higher order statistical property of its activation, namely that exactly those situations to which the same rule applies have similar activation patterns in the PDP model.

Elman worked with an English phrase structure grammar that handled relative clauses, verb agreement, and transitive verbs. He trained a net to parse this grammar, and then looked at the *evolution* of patterns on hidden units during processing. He gives a technique for clustering temporal sequences of patterns so that they correspond fairly well to the sequence of rule firings predicted by the grammar. Since the temporal dimension is considered, Elman's analysis is more complex, and firm conclusions are harder to draw. Nevertheless, the data support the hypothesis that rule-like structures can emerge in PDP nets.[12]

Success at finding rules in nets depends, in part, on knowing what properties to look for. The development of techniques for detecting classical structure in PDP models is in its infancy, and we undoubtedly have a lot more to learn. Failure to discover symbolic structures in connectionist models "may be a description of our own failure to understand the mechanism rather than a description of the mechanism itself" (Elman 1989, p. 20). Given progress to date, there is every reason to believe that PDP models can represent rules.

2.5.2 *Must Reducing PDP Models Represent Rules?*

We should not leave the reader with the impression that rule representation in the models just cited is exact. Both Elman and Servan-Schreiber point out that classification of patterns only approximates the rules of the original grammar. Investigation of the fine structure of net pattern classification reveals distinctions which are not present in the grammar. Furthermore, as the number of hidden units increases, the net may achieve good performance without generalizing to a simple set of rules. The rule structure generated in larger nets tends to be more redundant, so that the original grammar appears as its idealized simplification.

Approximation in the emergence of classical structures in PDP models is, by now, familiar. We have pointed out already that reduction of CAI models may be legitimate even when symbolic structures appear only to a degree. So a discovery that PDP models cannot represent classical rules exactly would not weigh against a reduction.

2.5.3 *Can PDP Models Represent Rules Explicitly?*

Eliminitivists may still not be satisfied. They will complain that the rule-like features we have cited are, at best, shadows of rules. On the classical model, rules are stored *explicitly*, while the rule-like structures found in nets are only implicit. The use of training rather than explicit programming causes information entered into nets to appear elusive or even illusive. Our problems in locating and extracting information from nets strengthens this impression.

However, there is reason to believe that these difficulties will be overcome as neural nets become more familiar. Fanty (1985) has already shown how to code explicit symbolic rules into nets, and the development of more sophisticated net "compilers" looks promising. As for extracting information, a number of techniques for "disassembling" net information are available (Elman, 1989, p. 20), and more effective methods are sure to follow. Although we have nothing like the sophisticated programs available in the classical tradition for writing and reading classical structures, we must remember that it took a while for classical computer science to develop its tools. If such capabilities are developed for nets, the eliminitivist would be hard pressed to explain why net information is any less explicit than data in a classical computer.

2.5.4 *Must Reducing PDP Models Represent Rules Explicitly?*

Compatibilists have other tactics for answering the charge that rule representation is not explicit in nets. First, they may demand an account of the implicit-explicit distinction which cuts the right way. Kirsh (forthcoming) has shown how difficult it is to draw such a distinction so that classical representation is clearly explicit. (It is easy to take our access to information in classical computers for granted, and to overlook the elaborate and fragile events which make it possible.) If classical representation is no more explicit than connectionist representation, then explicitness of representation no longer poses an obstacle to reduction of CAI models.

If it can be shown that representation in connectionist models is genuinely less explicit, compatibilists may still challenge the relevance of that fact. The implicit-explicit distinction can only record differences in our ease of access to information. But why should poor *epistemic* contact with net information count against its having classical structure? Frustration with a difficult user interface in a symbolic program need not challenge our faith that its behavior has a classical model. In all fairness, poor access to information ought to leave the question of its symbolic status either open or moot.[13]

2.5.5 *Can PDP Models Represent Rules Symbolically?*

Although the issue of explicitness of representation appears to be a red herring, eliminitivists have another objection nearby. Rules in classical processing have *symbolic* form, which determines when and where they are applied. The representation of rules by net pattern classification, however, does not appear to be symbolic, for there is no sign of constituent structure in such regularities.

Whether rule structure generated in nets has constituent structure is an issue that has not been directly addressed in the literature as far as I know. However, there is no evidence that the higher order net properties that correspond to classical rules may not exhibit symbolic structure. It is certainly possible that constituent structure of rules is reflected in features of a net.

Whatever the answer to that is, the form of the argument favors the compatibilist on this point. Widely divergent formal methods may be used to generate sets of rules with identical behavior. (Think of Turing machines, the lambda calculus, Post canonical systems, and Markov algorithms, for example.) There are infinitely many equally powerful techniques, each with its different implications about the constituent structure of rules. Why should Mother Nature have hit on one of the few methods with which we are familiar? Insisting that neural nets are not symbolic unless familiar forms of constituent structure are detected is the worst form of intellectual chauvinism. It follows that the eliminitivist project must be to show that no constituent structure in net rule features exists under *any possible method for formulating rules*. This will be very difficult indeed.

2.5.6 *Must Reducing PDP Models Represent Rules Symbolically?*

Research by Elman and Servan-Schreiber shows that PDP models can develop accurate symbolic processing which is sensitive to, and hence guided by, syntactic form. Furthermore, net properties which correspond to classical rules have been detected. The classical paradigm would be amply vindicated if the same can be established for the human brain. To require as well that rule structure reflect exactly the constituent structure of some classical set of rules is too much to demand, especially if one grants the legitimacy of approximate reduction.

Detecting the constituent structure of rules amounts to deciphering the syntax of the mind's programming language. That the mind contains a programming language with a non-trivial syntax presumes a strong form of the language of thought hypothesis. Although the discovery and analysis of such a structure would be a momentous victory for CAI, it is unfair to count anything less a defeat.

Even in classical computation, the detection of program syntax is a cloudy matter. Programs are stored in computer memory in the form of machine code. Typical machine code lacks interesting constituent structure; it is a sequence of 1s and 0s arranged in multiples of 8, 16 or 32. It is true that higher level languages with complex syntactic forms are used to generate machine code. However, an analysis of machine code alone cannot determine which language was used to generate it. Since it is possible for two languages with different syntax to generate the same code, there is no fact of the matter as to which syntax it has. Given only the state of the machine to go on, little concrete can be said about program syntax. If detection of constituent structure is so difficult in classical computers, why should one demand it of PDP models?

2.5.7 *Rules and Rigidity*

We agree with Horgan and Tienson (1989) that one of the attractive features of connectionist models is their potential for overcoming the rigidity and fragility of symbolic programs. Classical description of intelligent and flexible behavior often falls short, or demands tedious (perhaps never-ending) statement of "exceptions." This difference may appear to block reduction of CAI models. If CAI models are unavoidably rigid, so that their reducing PDP models are also rigid, and if correct PDP models cannot be rigid, we would conclude that CAI models are irreducible.

This tactic for obtaining the eliminitivist conclusion faces a number of difficulties. First, it is not at all clear that CAI models are irredeemably rigid. As Fodor and Pylyshyn (1988, p. 58 ff.) point out, the classical paradigm is not committed to all-or-none decision making. (Think, for example, of expert systems based on Bayesian decision theory.) Second, when CAI models are reduced by approximation, rigidities in the classical description need not be inherited by the underlying PDP model. Finally, total rejection of CAI by this argument requires a demonstration that PDP models of the mind must be non-rigid in every respect. Even if classical rules were unable in principle to explain soft decision making used in (say) face recognition, word recognition, or everyday inference, there might still be other skills such as understanding sentences where classical constructions have explanatory value. It follows that rule rigidity, though it should cause classicists concern, does not support the eliminitivist conclusion.

3. CONCLUSION

Eliminitivists have failed to provide a convincing argument that symbolic processing can not emerge in neural nets. PDP models are clearly capable of supporting symbolic processes, if only to an approximation. Despite radical differences, there is a solid basis for a reductive alliance between the two paradigms. The conclusion that CAI models incompatible with PDP models is simply not supported by the evidence. So connectionists are protected from wild classicist backlash, since there is no warrant for arguing from the correctness of CAI models to the inadequacy of connectionism. Similarly, wild connectionists have no warrant for arguing from the correctness of *their* models to the elimination of CAI.

It could turn out, of course, that the correct account of the mind is connectionist, and allows no interesting symbolic description at any level. The structures postulated by the classical view of cognition may not be found in the brain, and CAI may find its place next to celestial spheres, phlogiston, vital essences and luminiferous ether in the gallery of scientific failures. On the other hand, the symbolic powers of PDP models show that wild connectionists are wildly premature in declaring victory over the classical paradigm. A successful refutation of the classical view will require a far better understanding of cognition.

When speculating about the future of cognitive science, there is no point in trying to project to poles of a false dichotomy (Engel, 1989). If connectionism is right, it is unlikely that the classical view will either be perfectly reduced or completely eliminated. Classical structures may emerge, but to what degree of approximation it is impossible to predict. The exploration of symbolic processing concepts has been an important methodological tactic in connectionist research. Classicists might do well to return the favor, and investigate the lessons to be learned from connectionist models. One intriguing prospect is that nets trained on a task can be used to help discover new symbolic processing principles (Cummins, 1989, p. 155). It has even been suggested that the study of connectionist models may lead to better concepts and methods in symbolic "science" (Rumelhart, McClelland et al., 1986, p. 127; Smolensky, 1988, p. 22). In any case, the classical paradigm should prepare for the likelihood that symbolic processing is only approximately present in the mind.

ACKNOWLEDGEMENTS

I owe a great debt to Steven Stich and the National Endowment for the Humanities for the opportunity to attend an inspiring seminar on the philosophical implications of cognitive science held at UCSD in the summer of 1989. This paper would have been impossible without the support and guidance of Stich, the seminar participants, and many people at UCSD, most notably Gary Cotrell and Jeff Elman. Naturally, no blame attaches to anyone but me.

NOTES

[1]   Our prohibition against classical hardware may need clarification. If, for example, a net behaves like a stack at a high level of description, it does not follow that it contains classical hardware. Classical hardware is present only when there is a *physically locatable* subcomponent of the net which simulates a classical circuit, and where the digital signals correspond directly to the activation values of the units. Also, if a net spontaneously develops subcomponents with classical functioning during training on a task, it does not necessarily violate the prohibition against classical hardware. We mean only to rule out classical structures which are wired into the net by preset and unalterable settings of certain weights.

[2]   One might argue that feed forward nets with interesting temporal histories might result from the changing patterns of their inputs. However, we believe that it is highly unlikely that the mental processing can be duplicated in feed forward nets, since they have limited abilities at detecting temporal patterns.

[3]   Actually Ramsey, Stich and Garon discuss the elimination of *folk psychology* rather than CAI. See note 6.

[4]   In describing symbolic processing as sequenced generation of symbol strings we do not mean to rule out the possibility of parallel computation. When n symbolic processes are carried out at once, we may assume the system produces strings which are n-tuples of symbol strings produced by each process.

[5]   In case of a parallel computation, many strings may be in the center of attention at once, but still the number of strings so distinguished is typically a very small fraction of all the strings.

[6]   Ramsey, Stich and Garon (forthcoming), argue that connectionism poses an eliminitivist threat to folk psychology on the grounds that an account of the causal role of beliefs is incompatible with certain connectionist models. They are right to claim that an account of causal role is not possible in the connectionist models they choose. However, the eliminitivist conditional which results from their argument poses little threat to folk psychology, since the models they cite are feed forward nets, which have little chance of modelling the mind. If they had chosen PDP models instead, the argument would have failed because it is possible to show an analogy with the reasoning of section 2.2.1 that the causal role of beliefs *can* be accounted for in PDP nets.

[7]   This suggestion is drawn from Ramsey, Stich and Garon (forthcoming).

[8]   One might object that memory is a component of classical hardware, and so incompatible with PDP models by definition. But classical memory is quite different from memory in PDP models. Classical memory uses local representation, and spatial movement of information during storage and retrieval. These processes are not carried out by PDP models and so PDP models do not simulate classical memory hardware.

[9]   Both the term and the idea are borrowed from Ramsey, Stich and Garon (forthcoming).

[10] Kirsh (1987) argues that manipulation of variables is extremely expensive in connectionist models. His discussion (p. 133) of difficulties in rapidly setting variables does not properly assess the importance of recurrency. Recurrent models such as Elman's (1989) allow one to code sequences of variable values in time rather than in space. Kirsh admits that recurrency will resolve the problem, but complains that control of iteration will require the use of classical hardware. However, recurrent nets can learn sequential patterns in general, so we can teach them to count.

[11] I owe this point to Justin Leiber.

[12] It is worth noting the importance of recurrency in these models. In feed forward nets, the prospects for training nets to learn processes that extend through time are dim.

[13] See also Fodor and Pylyshyn (1988, p. 60 ff) where it is argued that CAI does not require explicit rules.

REFERENCES

Ballard, D. H.: 1987, 'Parallel Logical Inference and Energy Minimization', *Technical Report TR142*, Computer Science Department, University of Rochester.

Bechtel, W.: 1988, 'Connectionism and Rules and Representation Systems: Are They Compatible?', *Philosophical Psychology*, 1, 5-15.

Churchland, P.: 1979, *Scientific Realism and the Plasticity of Mind*, Cambridge University Press, New York.

Cummins, R.: 1989, *Meaning and Mental Representation*, MIT Press, Cambridge, MA.

Cummins, R.: (forthcoming), 'The Role of Representation in Connectionist Explanations of Cognitive Capacities', in Ramsey, Rummelhart and Stich (forthcoming).

Elman, J.: 1988, 'Finding Structure in Time', *Technical Report CRL 8801*, Center for Research in Language, UCSD.

Elman, J.: 1989, 'Representation and Structure in Connectionist Models', *Technical Report CRL 8903*, Center for Research in Language, UCSD.

Engel, R.: 1989, 'Matters of Degree', *Journal of Philosophy*, 23-37.

Fanty, M.: 1985, 'Context-Free Parsing in Connectionist Networks', *Technical Report TR-174*, Department of Computer Science, University of Rochester.

Fodor, J. and Pylyshyn, Z.: 1988, 'Connectionism and Cognitive Architecture: A Critical Analysis', *Cognition*, 28, 3-71.

Hanson, J. and Kegl, J.: 1987, 'PARSNIP: A Connectionist Network that Learns Natural Language Grammar from Exposure to Natural Language Sentences', *Ninth Annual Conference of the Cognitive Science Society*, pp. 106-119.

Hawthorne, J.: 1989, 'On the Compatibility of Connectionist and Classical Models', *Philosophical Psychology*, 2, 5-15.

Hinton, G.: 1988, 'Representing Part-Whole Hierarchies in Connectionist Networks', *The Tenth Annual Conference of the Cognitive Science Society*, 1988, 48-54.

Hinton, G. and Anderson, J., eds.: 1981, *Parallel Models of Associative Memory*, Erlbaum, Hillsdale, NJ.

Hinton, G., McClelland, J. and Rumelhart, D.: 1986, 'Distributed Representations', Chapter 3 of Rumelhart, McClelland, *et al.*

Hinton, G. and Sejnowski, T.: 1986, 'Learning and Relearning in Boltzmann Machines', Chapter 7 of Rumelhart, McClelland, *et al.*

Horgan, T. and Tienson, J.: 1989, 'Representations without Rules', *Philosophical Topics*, 15.

Jordan, M.: 1986, 'Serial Order: A Parallel Distributed Processing Approach', *Technical Report ICS-8604*, UCSD.

Kirsh, D.: 1987, 'Putting a Price on Cognition', *The Southern Journal of Philosophy*, 26, Supplement, 119-135.

Kirsh, D.: (forthcoming), 'When is Information Explicitly Represented?', to appear in *Information Thought and Content*, P. Hanson, ed., UBC Press.

Marr, D.: 1982, *Vision*, Freeman, San Francisco.

McClelland, J. and Elman, J.: 1986, 'The TRACE Model of Speech Perception', *Cognitive Psychology*, 18, 1-86.

McClelland, J. and Rumelhart, D.: 1986, 'A Distributed Model of Human Learning and Memory', Chapter 17 of McClelland, Rumelhart, *et al.*

McClelland, J., Rumelhart, D., *et al.*: 1986, *Parallel Distributed Processing*, II, MIT Press, Cambridge, MA.

Metcalf Eich, J.: 1985, 'Levels of Processing, Encoding Specificity, Elaboration, and CHARM', *Psychological Review*, 92, 1-38.

Pollack, J.: 1988, 'Recursive Auto-Associative Memory: Devising Compositional Distributed Representation', *Technical Report MCCS-88-124*, Computing Research Laboratory, New Mexico State University.

Ramsey, W., Rumelhart, D. and Stich, S.: (forthcoming), *Philosophy and Connectionist Theory*, Erlbaum, Hillsdale, NJ.

Ramsey, W., Stich, S. and Garon, J.: (forthcoming), 'Connectionism, Eliminitivism, and the Future of Folk Psychology', to appear in Ramsey, Rumelhart and Stich (forthcoming).

Rumelhart, D., McClelland, J., and the PDP Research Group: 1986, *Parallel Distributed Processing*, I, MIT Press, Cambridge, MA.

Servan-Schreiber, D., Cleeremans, A. and McClelland, J.: 1988, 'Encoding Semantical Structure in Simple Recurrent Nets', *Technical Report CMU-CS-88-183*, Department of Computer Science, Carnegie Mellon University, also in *Advances in Neural Information Processing Systems I*, D. Touretzky, (ed.), (pp. 643-652), William Kaufmann, Inc., Los Altos, CA.

Shieber, S.: 1986, *An Introduction to Unification-Based Approaches to Grammar*, Center for the Study of Language and Information, Stanford.

Smolensky, P.: 1988, 'On the Proper Treatment of Connectionism', *Behavioral and Brain Sciences*, 11, 1-74.

Smolensky, P.: 1987, 'On Variable Binding and the Representation of Symbolic Structures in Connectionist Systems', *Technical Report CU-CS-355-87*, Department of Computer Science, University of Colorado at Boulder.

Smolensky, P.: 1986, 'Neural and Conceptual Interpretation of PDP Models', Chapter 22 of McClelland, Rumelhart, and PDP Research Group (1986).

Touretzky, D.: 1986, 'BoltzCONS: Reconciling Connectionism with the Recursive Nature of Stacks and Trees', *Eighth Annual Conference of the Cognitive Science Society*, 522-530.

Touretzky, D. and Geva, S.: 1987, 'A Distributed Connectionist Representation for Concept Structures', *Ninth Annual Conference of the Cognitive Science Society*, 155-164.

Touretzky, D. and Hinton, G.: 1985, 'Symbols Among the Neurons: Details of a Connectionist Inference Architecture,' *Proceedings of the Ninth International Joint Conference on Artificial Intelligence*.

van Gelder, T.: 1990, 'Compositionality: A Connectionist Variation on a Classical Theme', *Cognitive Science* 14, 355-384.

Department of Philosophy
University of Houston
Houston, TX 77204-3785

GEORGE GRAHAM

CONNECTIONISM IN PAVLOVIAN HARNESS

1. INTRODUCTION

1.1 *The Central Problem of This Paper*

My paper is about a single problem: whether New Connectionism can provide a deeper understanding of simple forms of learning than either Behaviorism or Discrepancy Theory.[1] It is a problem which should interest anyone inclined to wonder, as I do, about the prospects of connectionism as a basis for the psychology of human and animal learning, that is, to wonder whether learning is in general a connectionist process. What are the key issues, principles, data that lie behind the study of simple learning? What does connectionism say about these topics? How does the connectionist approach compare with alternative approaches: How may we decide whether connectionism is preferable to alternative approaches? A chief advantage of focusing on simple learning is that the insights gained may be cumulative and apply when complex forms of learning are studied, although except for some speculative remarks at the end of the paper, I shall have nothing to say about complex learning in this paper.

Now in addition to anyone concerned with connectionism as a psychology of learning, the problem of this paper should also interest anyone inclined to wonder whether simple learning involves mental representations and rule following. Is simple learning guided or driven by thoughts or mental contents? Or is it part of what John Searle usefully vaguely calls the nonrepresentational 'bedrock' on which rests representational capacities involved in certain complex learning (Searle, 1983, 153)?

To see whether simple learning is representational/rule driven we have to explore what sorts of concepts best explain the behavioral data. I want to suggest that part of what is interesting about a connectionist approach to simple learning is that it shows how the behavioral data can be explained *without* appeal to representations and rules.

Since a central question of this paper is whether simple learning involves representations and rules, before comparing behaviorism, discrepancy theory, and connectionism, I need to briefly discuss how I understand the concepts of representation, rule, and simple learning.

Let's start with the notion of representation. I shall use 'representation' so that it applies to something inner (mental) with content, perhaps a nonconscious thought or semantically interpreted symbol. A sample case is a segment (word) of mentalese in Jerry Fodor's language of thought (1975), though other examples could be given.

In speaking of representations and behavior being rule driven, I shall mean that connections between representations and between representations and behavior are *intrinsically* semantic or semantically structured. A simple example of how a connection between representations may be semantically structured may help to illustrate this idea. Consider the relation between the following two sentences:

1. The electric shock jolted the rat and the sugar tasted sweet to the philosopher.

2. The sugar tasted sweet to the philosopher.

(1) entails (2); so, of course, inferences from (1) to (2) are truth preserving. Truth is a semantic notion. I suppose that it is a crucial property of the entailment connection between (1) and (2) that the relation is semantic, in particular preserves truth. I suppose that is a crucial property *generally* of representations that they are connected semantically; that they are connected by inferential roles and relations.

If there are representations, they are semantically structured or related. Likewise, if such representations produce learned behavior, the becausal relation between representation and learned behavior is semantic. Thus, suppose lifting my finger occurs because I have learned to follow the rule "Lift finger now." What's important for present purposes is not the details of this philosophically thorny becausal relation, but the idea that the behavior occurs because it follows or conforms to the rule. Conformity to rule is a semantic relation.

In speaking of rules, two clarifications should be made. First, I am interested in the 'meaning' or 'content' of rules, not in rules which are mathematical algorithms or non-semantic mechanical procedures. Thus I wish to distinguish between acting in conformity with mechanical or mathematical procedures, and acting in conformity with rules. We can often speak illuminatingly of any creature following mechanical or mathematical procedures, falling bodies in gravitational space for example. And we can speak perhaps as if this were a matter of following rules. But in the sense in which I refer to rules in this paper, such creatures are not following rules. In the sense in which rule following involves content or thought, falling is not rule driven. The second related clarification is that I am not concerned here with the syntactical or structural form of rules or in relationships which may obtain between rule semantics and syntax. For example, I am not interested in whether the rules are map-like or sentence-like (though I express examples in terms of sentences). Rather, I am concerned only with rules as semantic (/causal) relations that representations have to each other and to behavior. Statements about behavior conforming or failing to conform to a rule reflect a semantic relation. For example, the behavior of lifting my finger conforms to the rule "Lift finger now" but fails to conform to "Step lively across the fresh cement" or "Press eyeball onto the light brown cover of this quarter's issue of *Ratio*." In referring to the meaning of rules I am saying that rules carry or are open to an *interpretation*; they mean something. They are implicitly or explicitly qualified, about the scope they have (thus affecting what may be considered to fall under or follow from them), about the weight they have (thus affecting what limits they have). For example, there is a body of rules we call 'deductive logic.' They are open to an interpretation (over scope, over weight; e.g., as for scope, can such rules provide justificational procedures for beliefs?). For another example, there are game rules, such as baseball and football rules. Following such rules is presupposed by playing the games.

In the remarks to follow I am also going to speak of *derepresentationalizing* learning. On my reading, *both* behaviorism and connectionism derepresentationalize learning, at least simple learning in the case of connectionism, though *all* learning in the case of certain forms of behaviorism. To derepresentationalize learning is to *reduce* or *eliminate* reference to representations and to semantic (rule governed, inferential) relations between representations and behavior in the description and explanation of such behavior in favor of referring to something (perhaps a causal regularity or statistical correlation) non-rule driven, non-semantic. Such a reduction or elimination, for example, is effected in talking of nonassociative habituation learning as produced by modulations of chemical transmitter. On my view, representations and rules are not required for such behavior (in simple animals). Flatworms don't follow an habituation rule; they just habituate. They don't represent; they just respond.

I will not say anything to defend my understanding of rules and representations, because I think it is shared by many theorists, and defense would deflect from the main problem of the paper. Various interpretations, in my opinion, of the nature of rules and representations are consistent with that understanding. However, for any reader who does not share my understanding, I hope the paper still holds interest by showing how complex and subtle issues can emerge from a consideration of simple learning and how connectionism may approach them.

1.2 *Simple Learning*

Simple learning may be distinguished from complex learning along a number of dimensions, for example, the species of animals paradigmatically involved, types of prototypical stimuli, and so on. There is much more to be said about the topic of simple learning than there is room to say in the present essay, in which my central concern is with connectionism and simple learning. Let me therefore bypass subtleties, and say that by 'simple learning' I mean any form of learning of which creatures with simple nervous systems, shallow memory storage, and limited stimulus sensitivities are capable. Let us call animals so described *simple animals* (also *nonadvanced*). A number of controversies within experimental psychology, which are not immediately germane to the purposes of this paper, plague the study of the phylogeny of simple learning. E.g., which species with the simplest degree of neural organization is capable of learning, specifically of Pavlovian conditioning? Land snails? Honeybees? We are unlikely, therefore, to find any uncontroversial example of 'simple animal.' But this need not be crippling, either conceptually or argumentatively. To bypass such controversies, but with the assertion that I trust readers are not unduly influenced by the species referred to in my examples, I shall usually use examples of more developed species (e.g., rats, dogs, pigeons) responding to such unsophisticated stimuli as tones and shocks.[2] Their learning performances may be deemed simple if (more) simple creatures are capable of similar performances. Further restriction and clarification in focus will be introduced as the paper proceeds.

Simple learning has traditionally been divided into two major categories: associative learning, which includes Pavlovian (classical) and operant (instrumental) conditioning, and nonassociative learning, which includes habituation and sensitization (see Hilgard & Marquis, 1940; Mackintosh,

1974). I suppose that simple nonassociative learning is nonrepresentational. Changes in behavior in simple animals classified as habituation or sensitization do not involve the animals mentally representing the environment or themselves. Rather, they are achieved by combinations of underlying cellular processes, such as modulations in the amount of chemical transmitter released by presynaptic terminals of neurons (see Hawkins & Kandel, 1984). However, the representational/nonrepresentational status of simple associative learning is, I believe, less certain. For example, Gareth Matthews has asked whether susceptibility to Pavlovian conditioning--and I shall concentrate on the Pavlovian sub-category in this paper--involves animals forming perceptual beliefs about their environment (1985). If the answer is affirmative, a central role should be given to the concept of representation in the explanation of Pavlovian conditioning, for beliefs represent.

Does Pavlovian conditioning involve representation? Consider three theories which offer answers to this question: old fashioned behaviorism, new fashioned discrepancy theory, and finally new connectionism.

Both behaviorism and connectionism contend that Pavlovian conditioning, in nonadvanced creatures, and recall we are concentrating on such subjects here, does not involve representation. The learning process is not representational, not rule driven.

Discrepancy theory is less determinate. Discrepancy theory uses the language of rules and representations in describing Pavlovian conditioning. But connectionists impressed with discrepancy theory offer a nonrepresentational extension or refinement of the theory; and, the result is that Discrepant Words counsel representation but Deep Discrepancy Theory pictures Pavlovian conditioning in nonrepresentational terms. The picture isn't simple, because a complex series of connections underlie Pavlovian conditioning. But the picture is framed without appeal to animal thought. Discrepancy theory coupled with connectionism thus supports the view that Pavlovian learning is nonrepresentational.

1.3 Why Bother Comparing Connectionism with Behaviorism?

The belief that something can be learned about simple learning and the scope of representationality by tracing from behaviorism through discrepancy theory to connectionism rests on the recognition that connectionism has affinities with behaviorist associationism. In William Bechtel's words, by not treating persons or animals as principally inference machines the new connectionism exhibits an "affinity with the associationist behaviorist tradition" (1985, 56).

Considered in crudest terms, behaviorist associationism is the doctrine that learning can and should be understood in terms of noncognitive, nonrepresentational associations or causal connections between whole animal responses and the environment. Now, although I do not wish to suggest that connectionism is behaviorism, I do suppose that both connectionism and behaviorism are committed to derepresentationalizing learning *in its simple forms.* Connectionists and behaviorists do not see the Rule Governed Representational Mind at work in the slug who learns via Pavlovian conditioning to associate one stimulus with another. The slug associates without representing or rule governing representations.

A metaphor nicely captures the derepresentational attitude towards simple learning of both connectionism and behaviorism. Traditional laboratory behaviorism frequently resorted to the Pavlovian harness in the study of animal behavior. The harness (or hammock) restricted movement so that certain features of behavior (e.g., latency, frequency) could be expressed and observed without competing features being displayed. Once restricted, it was hoped, animal behavior could be seen stark cognitively naked. As far as observers might be tempted, there would be no impulse to attribute representationality to, for example, a harnessed salivating dog. Connectionism, too, is committed to a kind of methodological harnessing in the study of simple learning (although the Pavlovian hammock itself of course is not used). Simple learning should not be characterized as a representational process. Slugs don't need an associating rule; they just associate.

2. WITHIN THE PAVLOVIAN HARNESS

2.1 *Old Fashioned Behaviorism*

If one reads of Pavlovian conditioning in warhorse introductory psychology textbooks, one reads an old fashioned behaviorist tale (e.g., McConnell, 1977, 317-318). In warhorse texts Pavlovian conditioning is described as follows:

A subject animal (e.g., rat, dog) is repeatedly presented with a neutral stimulus—a stimulus that does not cause a response other than orienting responses—followed by an unconditioned stimulus

(UCS), which reflexively causes an unconditioned response (UCR). After a number of such pairings of the neutral stimulus and the UCS-UCR, the neutral stimulus comes to elicit a response of its own, which closely resembles the UCR or some part of it. The neutral stimulus thereby becomes reclassified as a conditioned stimulus (CS). For instance, a dog is repeatedly presented with first the sound of a bell (neutral stimulus to be classified eventually as a conditioned stimulus) and then food (the UCS), which causes the dog to salivate (the UCR). In turn, the sound of the bell (CS) alone produces salivation (the CR).

For many years, behaviorists believed that for Pavlovian conditioning to occur all that was required was that the CS and UCS occur repeatedly in close temporal contiguity. There was, for example, no need to refer to the mental representations of classically conditioned creatures. Temporal associations were all that were necessary.

2.2 Discrepancy Theory

In the last twenty or so years, the understanding of Pavlovian conditioning among experimental psychologists has undergone a revision that has significantly altered description of the conditioning process. That revision was begun in Robert Rescorla's seminal papers of 1967 and 1968 which showed that conditioning involves more than temporal contiguity. Animals selectively discriminate stimuli, and selectively associate the most informative/most predictive stimuli with UCSs. For Pavlovian conditioning to occur, a stimulus must be an *informative predictor* of the UCS rather than just occurring frequently or temporally paired with the UCS. (While instrumental or operant conditioning involves learning which actions are responsible for the occurrence of a reinforcer.)

The simplest and most widely cited theory of selective response in Pavlovian conditioning is Rescorla's. It is sometimes termed, though not without potential ambiguity, as I will explain below, a mental representation theory of conditioning, and sometimes called Discrepancy Theory (e.g., Mackintosh, 1983, 189) (also Expectancy or Contingency Theory). In an article written with Wagner in 1972, he states the central idea behind his theory as follows:

Organisms only learn when events violate their expectations. Certain expectations are built up about the events following a stimulus complex; expectations initiated by the complex and its component stimuli are then only modified when consequent events disagree with the composite expectation. (p. 75)

Put less technically, an animal's behavior will change only when a stimulus is followed by an otherwise unexpected consequence; only when there is a *discrepancy* between expectation and course of events.

Blocking provides a popular example of how Pavlovian conditioning results in an "expectancy" of the UCS following presentations of the CS. In the basic blocking paradigm, a subject is exposed to a single neutral stimulus followed by an UCS. Then the subject receives training to a compound stimulus followed by the same UCS. Prior to compound training only a single stimulus signals the UCS. But during compound training both stimuli signal the UCS. Then the compound stimuli are separated and presented by themselves. Under these circumstances it has been widely shown that the first neutral/conditioned stimulus (X-CS) is more likely to evoke a response than the second neutral/conditioned stimulus (Y-CS). For example, rats are exposed to 16 trials in which a tone is followed by shock. Then, they receive 8 trials in which a compound stimulus of the tone together with a light is followed by shock. Finally, they are given the light alone to see whether it produces any conditioned response. The tone is more likely to evoke conditioned response than the light alone, despite pairing/temporal contiguity of light and shock.

How should blocking be explained? No doubt temporal relations exist between tone and shock. But temporal relations also exist between light and shock.

Rescorla argues that the stimuli in blocking experiments compete, so that other things being equal, of two stimuli both often paired with the UCS, the stimulus more frequently paired (X-CS) is favored at the expense of the other (Y-CS). Since the animal has already had several conditioning trials with X-CS, prior to compound training, and additionally X-CS precedes the UCS when paired with the second stimulus in compound training, the first stimulus (X-CS) enjoys a higher probability or frequency of occurrence with the UCS than does the second stimulus (Y-CS). So the animal neglects the second stimulus, although were the second to have been paired alone with the UCS from the start, it would produce conditioned response.

By showing that conditioning in blocking takes place to the stimulus with higher probability, Rescorla argues that an animal somehow notices or represents whether a given CS is *more* predictive of the UCS. The animal's behavior thus seems to depend on an internal process of "comparing" a representation or expectation of the UCS, given the first CS, with a representation given the second CS.[3] Conditioning to the first CS results in the expectation of the UCS on presentation of the first stimulus. The second stimulus (Y-CS) is redundant. The UCS is more likely to occur in the presence of X-CS than it is to Y-CS; so the subject is sensitive to the degree to which one stimulus predictively informs about another. To use the language of the above quotation from Rescorla and Wagner, the events of compound training do not violate the expectation that UCS follows X-CS, so conditioning to Y-CS does not occur.

The blocking result is the very opposite of what is anticipated on the basis of old fashioned behaviorism. The traditional behaviorist account supposes the properties of any given CS to rub off or stamp onto any additional stimuli that are contiguously associated with it, so that Y-CS should become a rather potent conditioned stimulus just by virtue of its pairing with X-CS. The second stimulus should elicit a more or less equally strong conditioned response.

The phenomenon of blocking is hardly the stuff of elaborate mentality or byzantine representation. Nevertheless, according to Rescorla, as a result of prior training to a single neutral/conditioned stimulus, an animal forms the representation or expectation that *one stimulus rather than another* predicts the onset of the UCS. The representation, the selective source of the subject's response, mediates behavior (in the case of tone/shock, for example, the dog withdraws).

Rescorla (1978, 16) writes:

The organism does indeed represent relations among worldly events with a richness far greater than sensitivity only to contiguity would imply.

Blocking does not constitute the only alleged evidence for representations generated by Pavlovian conditioning. Various other higher-order conditioning phenomena (such as overshadowing and postconditioning changes in the significance of the UCS) supposedly also help to confirm the model. Anything that makes it plausible to think that response depends upon *comparison* or *expectation* of stimuli encoded or registered within the animal constitutes evidence that Pavlovian conditioning is constrained by representation and not a function (directly, only) of temporal contiguity.

Consider another example. Suppose (the example comes from postconditioning studies) that a conditioning experiment is performed in which a CS (tone) is frequently followed by food, but that animals on the final trail shortly after eating it are given an injection of poison which makes them ill. How might this behavior affect their response to the original CS?

Intuition suggests that if animals find the food aversive, they will be unlikely to salivate or show other manifestations of attraction to the CS previously associated with it. This is precisely the result confirmed by Rescorla (1973) in a study of conditioned suppression in rats. Rescorla argued that if changes in the attraction value of a UCS (food), introduced only *after* conditioning was completed, can change an animal's behavior to a CS previously frequently paired with that UCS, this must mean that the stimuli are represented in the animal. Such a change in behavior requires the animal to compare two sorts of stimuli. The path from tone CS to salivary CR must be connected though some inner representation of the food, which is itself linked to the aversive effects of the poison injection in the second part of the experiment. The tone is more frequently paired with food than food with illness/injection, yet tone loses control of salivation. So, illness must act on a representation of the CS (tone) rather than on the CS/attraction response pair. To use the language of the above quotation, illness violates the animal's expectation (it does not expect to become ill), and thereby causes learning to occur.

3. CONNECTING WITH CONNECTIONISM

3.1 *With Reference to Representation*

Rescorla's discrepancy theory seems to be a representation theory in the way it overtly deploys a notion of animal expectation in the analysis of Pavlovian conditioning. However, it is my conviction that it really is *not* representational in the analysis it presupposes of how expectations or representations ought to be individuated and described and are compared or transformed. I think the theory assumes, in a manner conducive to valuable input from new connectionism, that Pavlovian conditioning--at least of the sort I have harnessed in this paper--can be understood or explained in terms of purely nonrepresentational (non-semantic) notions. In short, Pavlovian expectations are not *irreducibly* or *ineliminatably* representational or semantic. In order to test this conviction, and to mine an explanatory niche for connectionism in the analysis of simple learning, we must examine more closely Rescorla's appeal to the notion of representation in the study of Pavlovian conditioning.

Let's begin by talking about the individuation of Pavlovian representations/expectations and then move to the "internal comparison" or transformation. Note that on the issue of internal comparison we will need to learn whether comparisons are semantically structured, that is, whether the manner of transforming stimuli is inferential or rule governed. If the method is merely a means of realizing a statistical or correlational relation, Pavlovian conditioning is not genuinely rule governed or representational.

Expectations may perhaps be described and individuated in two distinct ways: in (non-circular) representation free terms, invoking nonrepresentational notions in explicating expectation, or in (circular) representational terms, assigning to representational notions an essential role in the analysis. Expectations, just to name two contrasting possibilities, might be understood in terms of type correlated and representation free bodily and environmental states, or they might be understood in terms of rule driven relations or inferences which structure expectation relations (inferring being a representational, semantic notion).

My interpretation may be controversial, but I believe that Rescorla's theory permits expectations to be described and individuated in representation free terms, without appeal to rules. In effect this means that Pavlovian expectations are not really or irreducibly representational.

On Rescorla's view, mental representations/expectations are individuated by the stimulus to which a given expectation mediates a response. (Rescorla & Wagner, 1972).[4] Meanwhile, the stimulus a representation mediates a response to is the most frequent, nonredundant, and earliest predictor of the UCS. If an expectation mediates a response to tone, for example, it represents the tone. Inference plays no necessary or essential role in the account. When a single member of a compound stimulus, such as the first CS in blocking, for example, elicits response this is not because the animal *expects that* the stimulus (X-CS) is a better predictor of the UCS. Rather, it is because X-CS *is* a better predictor. It is more reliably correlated with the UCS. The correlation relations between stimuli, expectations, and responses constitute a complex web both at a time and over time. For Rescorla, how we pick out stimulus types as represented depends on the character of those correlations, and what we take to be the stimulus responsible for conditioned response. But it does not depend--as I shall argue below--on essentially inferential or rule governed symbolic, semantic comparisons or transformations within the animal.

What about the question of inner comparison? How is one stimulus selected as the earliest predictor (etc.) or (simply) better predictor? Here again inner comparison--of one stimulus with another--may be understood in representation presupposing or free terms. Thus, if stimuli are compared inferentially, that is, if the animal *represents* one stimulus *as* a better predictor than another (i.e., it compares frequencies and infers *that* one stimulus rather than another is more frequent), then comparison is representational. Whereas if an animal "represents" or registers the better predictor but not *as the better predictor*, that is, if the better predictor controls response but this does not involve animal influence, then the method of comparison or inner transformation is not representational, not semantic. Stimuli *register* or leave traces in animals; learning requires their impact to be stored and retained. But they don't register in the form of representations, inferentially transformed or rule driven semantically interpreted symbols.

It is my conviction that the method of transformation of Pavlovian expectations or registrations in the Rescorla model is not necessarily or inevitably inferential. Notions of expectancy, representation, and inner transformation of representations are deployed at one level of analysis (the level, for instance, at which Rescorla wishes to defeat temporal contiguity or simple pairing models of conditioning), but they can be eliminated or explained away at a deeper or more extensive level (the level, for example, at which one wishes to describe frequency dependent or driven UCS/CS-UCR/CR bonds, nonredundant frequencies, and the like). Representational notions lack deep theoretical bite or explanatory force and can be dismissed.

3.2 *New Connectionism in Pavlovian Harness*

If inner transformations of stimulus registrations are not inferential, they will somehow have to be described and explained without presupposing animals infer or follow rules. Can this be done? For a true representationalist, as I have suggested, the explanation of transformation or comparison should be obvious: learning requires rule driven relations between inner representation and learned response. But for a discrepancy theorist the explanation is less clear. Both Rescorla and certain friendly expositors of his model use notions of inference and representation to describe animal conditioning (e.g., Mackintosh, 1983, 55). But, as I said above, I do not believe such language is essential to the analysis. One may agree with

Rescorla that animals are sensitive to interevent relations other than simple contiguity, and perhaps for heuristic purposes describe such sensitivity in representational terms, without ascribing representations to such creatures. And here, as far as I am concerned, is where connectionism can make an important contribution.   Connectionism offers a nonrepresentational, inference free account of (simple) animal susceptibilities and sensitivities. Connectionism can be deployed as an explanatory extension of discrepancy theory in which inner comparisons of stimulus registrations are described nonrepresentationally, noninferentially. Slugs don't expect; they associate. They don't represent; they respond.

It should be noted that Rescorla's model of Pavlovian representational transformation appeals to both friends of neurophysiological reduction (e.g., Hawkins & Kandell, 1984) and connectionists (Sutton & Barto, 1981). For example, Sutton and Barto (1981) argue that transformation of stimulus registrations involved in animal Pavlovian conditioning can be modelled by a Rescorla inspired connectionist/adaptationist network (see especially 149-150). Specifically, they argue that the readiness with which an animal may associate a CS with an UCS is a property of internal connection strengths between the two stimuli.   Internal connection strength is a complex frequency dependent variable which depends in part on the modulation of micro(neural) connections within an animal--a connectionist not an inferentialist or behaviorist notion.   Generally, the more reliably and nonredundantly two stimuli are presented the more likely will registrations of one be linked internally with registrations of the other. The result is that stimulus registrations are transformed via content free, frequency driven connections. Thoughts or inner symbols are not involved; the registrations are not representations.

To appreciate the nonrepresentational character of the connectionist approach, it may be compared with a rule driven approach. In contrast to Sutton and Barto, Holland, Holyoak, Nisbett and Thagard (1986) believe that the stimulus registrations are compared or transformed inferentially in terms of rules rather than in frequency or correlation dependent terms. Conditioning depends on rule following in response to stimuli. If two stimuli are inferred to be connected (for example, if one is inferred to predict the other, or represented as the best predictor), conditioned response occurs; otherwise not.

To illustrate the line taken by Holland *et al.*, imagine that blocking takes place because animals follow a blocking rule with content like *respond to the most frequently presented stimulus.* When then in blocking psychologists observe conditioned response to the first rather than the second conditioned stimulus, this is because animals are directed by the rule. Their behavior is rule driven. (Note: The Holland *et al.*, rule controlling Pavlovian conditioning is more complicated than this blocking rule, which I have invented for purposes of simplified illustration.) Absent the rule, conditioning would not occur.

Rule driven models like Holland's suppose that stimulus registrations are representations, which are manipulated or transformed in a semantically structured manner, via inferences made or rules followed by the animal. Inference forges connection. For this reason, rule driven models preclude reduction of representational to connectionist processes. Rules remain autonomous, perhaps implemented connectionistically or supervenient on connectionist processes but not describable in nonrepresentational terms.

3.3 *The Connectionist Contribution*

Connectionist models like Sutton and Barto's presuppose that stimulus registrations in Pavlovian conditioning are manipulated or transformed causally, correlationistically, because of regularities or event correlations within an animal when it is exposed to competing sets of stimuli. This may give the *appearance* of rules and representations driving Pavlovian learning but such learning is forged by noninferential, nonrepresentational rather than inferential, semantic forces. For example, an animal might seem to follow a blocking rule like "Respond to the most frequently presented stimulus" because it responds to the most frequently presented stimulus. Connection mimics inference without reference to inference being embedded in the connectionist explanation. Equivalently: Symbols or thoughts meaning *respond to the most frequently presented stimulus* are not inside the animal; connections effecting such a response are inside.

The following analysis of blocking derived loosely from Sutton and Barto (1981) will be used to illustrate the application of connectionism to the Pavlovian blocking case. Recall in blocking an animal is presented with a single neutral stimulus followed by a UCS, after which it receives training to a compound stimulus followed by the same UCS. Before compound training only the single stimulus signals the UCS. However, during compound training both stimuli signal the UCS. When, then, the compound stimuli are distinguished and presented independently, the first stimulus is significantly more likely to produce conditioned response than the second. A rather generic connectionist explanation is that the animal conditions to the first stimulus because internal connections become progressively strengthened during the first stage of training, attenuating or inhibiting conditioning to the second stimulus during compound training. Internal connections between the second stimulus and response are comparably weaker than those between the first stimulus and response.

This is a simplification. There are various ways in which the account might be developed. For example, one might argue that the first stimulus, since it is presented before compound training, leaves an internal registration or trace which persists and is strengthened during compound training. Such a trace might be maintained by the activation levels of some neurons, possibly by means of reverberatory circuits. In blocking, traces of the first stimulus compete with traces of the second and outweigh them, providing for deceleration of the neural activity inspired by the second stimulus. Or one might argue that the trace strength of the second stimulus autonomously decays since its presentation is sufficiently infrequent. Or one might invoke the parallel distributed processing resources of connectionism and argue that each stimulus is distinctively linked with its own inner trace, which has access to the responses of its relevant neighbor and adjusts it own responses according to how its neighbor is responding, until the whole network relaxes on the preferred conditioned response. Each of these activated trace, decay, and parallel processing speculations as well as variations of them express possibilities consistent with the connectionist account.

Which account should be preferred? Connectionism or "representationalism?" Behavior which mimics rules or which is driven by them?

A REASONABLE PREFERENCE

The basic mechanism or process behind conditioning, as Rescorla views it, is that a stimulus conditions response only when all competing candidates, or rival stimuli, are deselected. Pavlovian conditioned responses are selective; in blocking the first stimulus carries the load, in postconditioning a change in the UCS inhibits conditioned response. This main idea is neatly captured, it seems to me, by the connectionist explanation, and without reference to rules and representations. According to connectionism, internal processing units (vehicles of stimulus registrations or traces), for concreteness think of a single neuron, do not treat all inputs uniformly. Neurons receive inputs through connections, or links, and each incoming link has an associated weight. There can be continued oscillation among the contending inputs, while conditioning continues. Then rival stimuli have their internal activity levels relaxed, which means the probability of their mutual activation has declined, and the animal settles into or "selects" a response state. Conditioned response occurs.

Rule driven models do not favor selection/deselection quite so readily as the connectionist explanation. Conditioned response is anchored in rules, clues for the application of which are provided by stimulus frequencies. Stimulus frequencies apportion credit to certain rules, strengthening some, weakening others.

Rules under such circumstances are not necessarily easily applied. In the words of Holland *et al.*, "rules, new and old, compete for the right to determine action when the environment presents stimuli satisfying their conditions" (1986, 154). Does the blocking rule apply if the first stimulus occurs only once before compound training? Or must it occur two, three, four, or . . . sixteen times? Also, if the application of a rule remains indeterminate is this because one rule is competing with another rule, or because stimulus frequencies are unstable or difficult to perceive, or because the interpretative scope of the rule is ambiguous or vague? Can simple learning rules be ambiguous or vague? Are they interpreted or just followed? How does the animal brain decide which rules to treat as applicable, that is, which ones drive conditioned response? Does it rely exclusively on stimulus frequencies?

On the rule driven account a sharp distinction must be drawn between the rule which drives response and the frequencies of the stimuli presented to an animal. The former, not the latter, involves representations by which stimuli condition or fail to condition. Indeed, only such a sharp distinction--characteristic of inferential, representational models of learning--can make good sense of conditioning being governed by rules. In Holland's (*et al.*) words (154):

Conditioning. . . results only when (a certain) rule is, on average, more effective than its competitors in evoking appropriate responses in the context in which it applies.

The connectionist account is closer to the stimuli. There is no sharp distinction between the inner processes which settle on response and the frequencies of stimuli presented to an animal. In effect, inner registrations limn the structure of outer stimulus reality. Typically, the activity level associated with inner units/neurons changes with the current frequencies of stimuli; and, if the level does not settle on a threshold for conditioned response, this is not because current frequencies do not register in animals but because they may store traces of previous training or past experience with certain stimuli which compete with current conditioning. Indeed, an animal may fail altogether to condition if old traces are recalcitrant and robust.

Remember that, within connectionism, rules driving a certain response are not assumed to apply. The important question to ask, then, is whether levels of internal activation are converging on certain responses rather than others--in blocking, conditioning to the first rather than the second stimulus. There is no assumption that convergence is forged by application of a rule. Convergence, settling on a response, is driven by weightings of various interconnected strands of inner activity, which are ultimately tracked into current stimulus patterns.

This feature of connectionism, its closeness to the stimulus, as I view it, also carries with it a plausible account of preparedness or salience. Preparedness means an animal has a starting point of prepackaged correlations which tailors its susceptibility to conditioning, determined by its prior learning and ultimately selected by its evolutionary history. There are certain patterns of response which, in evolutionary time, have proven adaptive (such as avoiding sickening foods after only one exposure in postconditioning), which are built into an animal by its genetic wiring. Note that connectionism allows for an animal to be especially susceptible to certain associations, for there might be stronger or more weighty prewired connections among stimulus registrations as a result of its genetic history. When learning modifies response, it is constrained by prior connection weights. This contrasts with the rule driven approach, for which preparedness rests on prior rules, the genetic or implementational encoding or prior rules, plus the current stimulation necessary to apportion strength to a rule.

On a rule driven approach evolution must install rules before it can instill associative bias and thus survival. But when preparedness is understood connectionistically, the chores of evolution are less complex. Installed weights instill survival; connections come first and fitness follows suit.

Which account should be preferred? Each approach and model has particular attractions, but provided connectionism can fit the experimental data, which I think it does at least in the case of simple animals, I believe connectionism should be favored over a rule driven or representational account of Pavlovian conditioning. Connectionism travels light, carrying with it only internal connections and stimulus frequencies rather than also rules and the internal mechanism necessary to assign drive strength to rules. If connection weights select rules which drive behavior why can't the weights work directly on behavior? The inner connections should be able to settle on a certain response without the mediation of rules. So, as I see it, considerations of theoretical parsimony favor connectionism over a rule driven account. Also, people may learn rules to follow for complex forms of behavior, but in Pavlovian conditioning (of the nonadvanced animal sort discussed in this paper) we are interested in honeybees, slugs, and flatworms (Delthier & Stellar, 1970). Clearly, attributing rules to such non-verbal creatures endows them with cognitive resources which seem better suited to more sophisticated animals or chores. Why not just say that inside such simple creatures are networks of units or neurons that interact with each other and that, as a result of the interconnections, yield the global effect which is conditioned response? That is, one stimulus can acquire a deeper control than another over behavior by modifying the connections underlying whole animal response.

Another, third, advantage concerns the similarity between nonassociative and Pavlovian learning. Special ties exist between these two phenomena. Pavlovian learning, in nonadvanced animals, is an extension of habituation and sensitization (e.g., Thompson & Gluck, 1987). Crudely put, Pavlovian conditioning involves *differential* sensitization and habituation. For example, in blocking if X-CS is the best predictor of the UCS, then the addition of the second stimulus, Y-CS, presented simultaneously with X-CS, results in sensitization of X-CS alone and nonassociative habituation to the second stimulus.

Supposing as I do that habituation and sensitization are non-rule driven, given the ties between them and Pavlovian learning, a non-rule driven account of Pavlovian learning should be favored over a rule driven account. Connectionism is not a rule driven model, so it should be favored. Pavlovian learning should not be explained by reference to rules and representations given that habituation and sensitization can be explained without such reference--and given that Pavlovian learning involves differential sensitization and habituation.

Now I do not mean to deny that there are variations in the rule driven theme, and elements in the Holland *et al.*, account which I have neglected or perhaps fail to understand. (I use the Holland account simply as an example of a rule driven account. If Holland's rules really are not rules, in my sense, then I merely need another real or imagined example.) Also a connectionist is always facing the problem of trying to describe (within connectionist constraints) the most illuminating description of processes responsible for behavior, and many responses seem to require patterns of activation and algorithmic implementations more difficult to describe, partly because of the parallelism of connectionist architecture, than the rules they may mimic. But I do mean to claim that connectionism's (i) parsimonious methodological posture, (ii) principled reluctance to view simple animals in terms more befitting complex creatures, and (iii) prospect for preserving ties between simple nonassociative and Pavlovian learning are grounds for preferring it to a rule driven model. Such virtues are reason enough to give connectionism the overall advantage.

CONCLUSION

Human and animal learning, as I conceive it, divides into two types: nonrepresentational (non-semantic, non-rule driven) and representational (rule driven, semantic). The nature, scope, and interrelationship of these two types are matters of ongoing controversy in psychology and philosophy of mind. On one side are reductionists and eliminativists who urge wholesale application of nonrepresentational models; on the other are cognitivists who promote ascribing thoughts and rules to rats, pigeons, and even slugs. Between these two poles are ecumenists who hope for reconciliation of representational and nonrepresentational approaches. As I see it, regardless of the ultimate outcome of debates over these positions, for now Pavlovian conditioning--in the case of simple animals and stimuli such as those discussed in this paper (e.g., tones, shocks)--can and should be fitted with a methodological Pavlovian harness. We can and should account for the phenomenon without supposing that it is underlain with rules and representations. Insofar as connectionism promises a nonrepresentational, non-rule driven account, minus unwelcome allegiance to simple contiguity, we do well to exercise the connectionist account.

How far should the account be exercised? Should it be deployed generally as a model of learning processes more complicated than those involved in restricted Pavlovian learning? Above this level and outside the harness things get *very* complicated. The more complex the animal, the greater its memory capacity, the more conditioning sequences are added to its correlational store. Stimulus registrations burgeon, frequencies abound and the animal will have to backtrack: deleting past experiences to permit new associations, lest it be painted into a corner unable to profit from experience. Friends of rules and representations have not been reluctant to argue that heightened complexity strengthens the case for rules and representations and weakens the plausibility of nonrepresentational accounts (cf. Holyoak, Kuh, & Nisbett, 1989). Whose to say that Nature may not profitably plant rules into such a creature to manage the breadth, generality, and comprehensiveness of its learning? Again: the more complex the animal, the wider its range of perceptual sensitivity, the more subtle and apparently representationally enriched become the environmental events which take on stimulus properties.[5] Responsiveness to meat powder is one thing; sensitivity to the associate dean's frown is another. Whose to say that Nature may not benevolently install representations so that the untenured assistant professors may prudently respond to frowns?

Many theorists are now trying to apply connectionist ideas to complex learning phenomena involving such matters as burgeoning correlations and sophisticated stimulus sensitivities. I do not have any firm convictions about just how complicated learning must be before connectionism, at least as presented in this paper, as a *derepresentationalizing* model, may lose the plausibility behind its application. I am convinced, however, that as each research group and approach injects a variation into the growing literature, it becomes ever more important to moderate programmatic hopes with methodological temperance. For instance, some theorists think that connectionism is generally deployable as a model of learned behavior, including behavior, such as natural language acquisition, which putatively is governed by rules and representations.[6] Perhaps it is. Perhaps it is not. My own methodological disposition is to start by considering if and how connectionism can be applied in simple cases. Then I would try to apply connectionism to gradually more complex phenomena. For example, one may move from Pavlovian learning in nonadvanced animals to advanced creatures, and from there to operant conditioning and from there to, eventually, language acquisition, and so forth.

My preference for first discovering if connectionism can be deployed in simple cases is based on the following idea: If its utility is not evident in simple cases, then fans of connectionism may be prematurely hopeful about the complex cases. And my preference for then trying to apply connectionism to gradually more complicated learning phenomena and perhaps even to cases of representation is grounded on the following fear: If its utility is tested only in simple cases, then foes of connectionism may be encouraged to dogmatically dismiss connectionism's aspirations and promise. Neither naive hope nor preemptory dismissal are serviceable attitudes for the proper assessment of a new, popular, and developing theory.

NOTES

[1] This paper was originally prepared for the 1987 Spindel Philosophy Conference on Connectionism and the Philosophy of Mind, Memphis State University, October 9-11, 1987, and published in the Spindel Conference 1987 issues of *The Southern Journal of Philosophy*. It has been modestly revised for inclusion in the current collection. I have been helped by Richard Garrett, Terry Horgan, Deborah Long, and Christopher Maloney. Correspondence concerning the paper may be addressed to George Graham, Department of Philosophy, UAB, Birmingham, Alabama, 35294.

[2] See note #4.

[3] Before I go too much further in describing Rescorla's view, I want to mention one terminological point, which I trust will be obvious from the context but may not be. I describe the discrepancy model as saying that the organism somehow compares the predictive validity of alternative conditioned stimuli. This is not meant to suggest that it does so consciously or voluntarily (as when a person compares prices at the supermarket) or even that predictive power as such is what is compared (since that may suggest possessing a concept of predictive power/validity). My point is that, for Rescorla, the animal has different "expectations" for alternative conditioned stimuli, and is somehow sensitive to that difference. Response is modulated to discrepancy. It certainly is not my intention to foist various ordinary connotations of 'comparison' (conscious, voluntary, conceptually enriched) upon Rescorla. Also, let me use the occasion of this note to thank Professor Rescorla for gracious correspondence concerning the original Spindel paper. I suspect there are things he wants me to say about his view which I do not say. My only excuse is that to the topic of the Rescorla program I bring no professional disciplinary qualification, though much desire to bring his fascinating and elegant research to the attention of philosophers, especially philosophers of psychology.

[4] The notion of the stimulus a given expectation mediates a response to may involve representation, in a manner undiscussed in this paper and not directly connected with Rescorla's theory, but requiring treatment in a more systematic discussion of conditioning and representation. Let me explain, since the point is both important and occasionally neglected in discussions of conditioning in the psychological literature.

Whenever an animal learns to condition to a stimulus it does so with a degree of generalization, responding to other stimuli similarly. The similarity between stimuli often seems to have a physical basis. If we teach an animal to condition to a 1,000-cycle tone, we are likely to discover it responds to a tone of 900 or 1,000 cycles. We may find, however, that some animals seem to generalize across similarities without a physical basis. Pigeons, for example, generalize across pictures of persons, which generalizations apparently cannot be explained by nearness of physical dimensions like size or shape (e.g., Herrnstein, Loveland, & Cable, 1976). Because certain animals seem to or really do generalize across non-physical similarities, it might be argued that these creatures *mentally represent* the relevant stimuli. The argument would go something like this: Animals which respond to similarities with a physical basis need not and do not *represent* those similarities, for the similarities are in the environment. There is no work for the concept of representation to perform in describing those stimuli. However, if an animal responds to a similarity without a physical basis, mental representation is involved, for what the creature treats as similar depends on its psychology, and not (only) on its environment. Compare e.g., conditioning to tone with conditioning to the tone-of-voice-of your-broker or to the monarch's bedfellow (cf., Turkkan, 1989, p. 136).

Well, what should we make of this argument for representation in animals (such as pigeons)? I do not believe we are now in a position to know how to describe or explain the perceptual capacities of certain animals (e.g., pigeons) even in some situations of learning which otherwise are simple. I also do not believe we possess a fully adequate theoretical grasp of stimulus similarities without physical bases. So, I sidestep the issue in this paper. The stimuli I speak of animals encountering have physical rather than non-physical similarity bases (e.g., tones, shocks, etc.). This is part of what was involved back in Section 1.2 in restricting discussion to simple animals-in-simple learning. How to understand stimulus classes the very discrimination of which may presuppose mental representation (and the implications of such cases for connectionism) would introduce topics which lie well beyond the scope of the present paper. In effect, this means the present paper is about Pavlovian learning in nonadvanced creatures discriminating stimuli such as tones, not person pictures. The belts in the harness must be tightened. (Although framed not in terms of the notion of similarities without physical bases, but of stimuli with "nonnomic stimulus properties," relevant discussion of the topic of this note may be found in Fodor 1980, Loyd, 1986, and Smythe 1989. See also the concluding section of the present paper.)

[5] See note #4.

[6] An interesting question is whether connectionism is suited to explain such behavior or only suited to explain behavior (such as Pavlovian simple learning) driven by nonrepresentational registrations. Much depends on which version of connectionism is considered and on how such notions as rule, representation and related notions are understood and perhaps regimented (cf., Fodor and Pylyshyn, 1988; Horgan and Tienson, 1989).

REFERENCES

Bechtel, W.: 1985, 'Contemporary Connectionism: Are the New Parallel Distributed Processing Models Cognitive or Associationist?', *Behaviorism* 13, 53-62.
Dethier, V. G. and Stellar, E.: 1970, *Animal Behavior*, Prentice-Hall, Englewood Cliffs, NJ.
Fodor, J.: 1975, *The Language of Thought*, Crowell, Englewood Cliffs, NJ.
Fodor, J.: 'Why Paramecia Don't Have Mental Representations,' *Midwest Studies in Philosophy* 10, 3-23.
Fodor, J. and Pylyshyn, Z.: 1988, 'Connectionism and Cognitive Architecture: A Critical Analysis,' *Cognition* 28, 2-71.
Gluck, M. A. and Thompson, R. F.: 1987, 'Modeling the Neural Substrates of Associative Learning and Memory: A Computational Approach,' *Psychological Review* 94, 176-191.
Hawkins, R. D. and Kandel, E. R.: 1984, 'Is There a Cell-Biological Alphabet for Simple Forms of Learning?', *Psychological Review* 91, 375-391.
Herrnstein, R. L. Loveland, D. H. and Cable, C.: 1976, 'Natural Concepts in Pigeons,' *Journal of Experimental Psychology: Animal Behavior Processes* 2, 285-311.
Hilgard, E. R. and Marquis, D. G.: 1940, *Conditioning and Learning*, Appleton-Century-Crofts, New York.
Holland, J. H., Holyoak, K. J., Nisbett, R. E. and Thagard, P. R.: 1986, *Induction: Processes of Inference, Learning, and Discovery*, MIT Press, Cambridge, MA.
Holyoak, K. J., Kuh, K. and Nisbett, R. E.: 1989, 'A Theory of Conditioning: Inductive Learning with Rule-Based Default Hierarchies,' *Psychological Review* 96, 315-340.
Horgan, T. and Tienson, J.: 1989, 'Representations Without Rules,' *Philosophical Topics* 15.
Lloyd, D.: 1986, 'The Limits of Cognitive Liberalism,' *Behaviorism* 14, 1-14.
Mackintosh, N. J.: 1974, *The Psychology of Animal Learning*, Academic Press, New York.
Mackintosh, N. J.: 1983, *Conditioning and Associative Learning*, Oxford University Press, New York.
Matthews, G. B.: 1985, 'The Idea of a Psychological Organism,' *Behaviorism* 14, 37-52.
McConnell, J. V.: 1977, *Understanding Human Behavior*, Holt, Rinehart and Winston, New York.
Rescorla, R. A.: 1967, 'Pavlovian Conditioning and Its Proper Control Procedures,' *Psychological Review* 74, 71-80.
Rescorla, R. A.: 1968, 'Probability of Shock in the Presence and Absence of CS in Fear Conditioning,' *Journal of Comparative and Physiological Psychology* 66, 1-5.
Rescorla, R. A. and Wagner, A. R.: 1972, 'A Theory of Pavlovian Conditioning: Variations in the Effectiveness of Reinforcement and Nonreinforcement,' in A. H. Black and W. F. Prokasy (eds.), *Classical Conditioning II: Current Theory and Research*, Appleton, New York.
Rescorla, R. A.: 1973, 'Effect of US Habituation Following Conditioning,' *Journal of Comparative and Physiological Psychology* 82, 137-143.
Rescorla, R. A.: 1978, 'Some Implications of a Cognitive Perspective on Pavlovian Conditioning,' in S. H. Hulse, H. Fowler, and W. K. Honig (eds.), *Cognitive Processes in Animal Behavior*, Lawrence Erlbaum Associates, Hillsdale, NJ.
Searle, J. R.: 1983, *Intentionality*, Cambridge University Press, Cambridge.
Smythe, W. E.: 1989, 'The Case for Cognitive Conservatism: A Critique of Dan Lloyd's Approach to Mental Representation,' *Behaviorism* 17, 63-73.

Sutton, R. S. and Barto, A. G.: 1981, 'Toward a Modern Theory of Adaptive Networks: Expectation and Prediction,' *Psychological Review* **88**, 135-170.

Turkkan, J. S.: 1989, 'Classical Conditioning: The New Hegemony, *Behavioral and Brain Sciences* **12**, 121-179.

Department of Philosophy
University of Alabama
Birmingham, AL 35294

J. CHRISTOPHER MALONEY

CONNECTIONISM AND CONDITIONING

I.

First, the hook: Even if you are not a Connectionist--perhaps because you fret that Connectionism (Rumelhart and McClelland, 1986; Smolensky, 1988; Bechtel and Abrahamsen, 1989; Bechtel, 1988, 1987, 1985; and Tienson 1987) wants the conceptual resources to explain cognition generally--you may well suppose that Connectionism is sufficiently equipped gracefully and completely to explain simple learning and, certainly, conditioning. But it is not. Adequate Connectionist accounts of conditioning are not at hand, and they might be unavailable in principle. Or so I shall argue. The idea, then, that I will press is that simple learning is not so simple after all and that, as a result, it represents a serious challenge to the explanatory adequacy of Connectionism. I most assuredly do not suppose that what I have to say counts as an *a priori*, straight from the armchair, refutation of Connectionism. No, that is not how science, good science, is waged. Still, if Connectionism is finally to overcome its present and primary theoretical rival, it will need first to subdue conditioning before marching against general intelligence.

Second, the rival: It is no secret that Connectionism and the Representational Theory of the Mind are engaged in a furious competition for pride of place in psychology (Pinker, 1989; Fodor and Pylyshyn, 1988; Smolensky, 1987). Those of us who are smitten by Representationalism (Fodor, 1975, 1980, 1987; Maloney, 1989) and worried by the challenge of Connectionism, maintain that cognitive processing is, for the most part, a matter of computation defined over mental symbols or representations. These representations enjoy various semantic properties, including--among others--truth value, reference and, yes, content.[1] As representations, these vehicles of mental computation have syntactic features which determine their computational relations. Simply put, the computational connections among mental representations are syntactic relations that respect the semantic and, therefore, inferential properties of the related representations.

167

The attraction of Representationalism rests largely on the supposition that cognition is best conceived along the lines of inference disciplined by syntactically sensitive, complex and internally represented rules (Marr, 1982).[2] According to Representationalism, in order that an item within a system's cognitive economy qualify as a mental representation, it is not enough that it covary with, in some way signal, or otherwise carry the information that some particular (sort of) thing is lurking in the system's environment (Dretske, 1981; Stich, 1983). The item must also, in virtue of its computational properties, be semantically affiliated with other such items (Graham, 1987).

Not everyone who wonders about the nature of thought is cheered by the idea that thinking is just encrypted inference (Churchland, Patricia Smith, 1980; Churchland, Paul, 1981). Connectionists, in particular, typically offer explanations of cognitive achievements that seem to eschew appeal to syntactically structured representations of the sort promoted by Representationalists.[3] While certain cognitive achievements--abstract reasoning, calculation and planning--may seem to beg for accounting in terms of computationally related representations, others--simple learning and pattern recognition--appear more readily to submit to explanation within the Connectionist framework. Dogs will learn to salivate in response to a bell; people recognize faces as such and discriminate easily among them. Such feats appear to many to be independent of cognitive processing that relies on inferential or computational relations among various syntactically complex representations stored within the cognitive system. No--many Connectionists urge--better to think of these achievements as the results of networks of differentially volatile but otherwise internally homogeneous nodes settling over time into stable patterns of activation in response to recurrent patterns of stimulation. True, levels of activation of individual nodes or patterns thereof might be representations, within the system of nodes, of aspects of the system's environment. But even if such *Connectionist-representations* (which we will call "C-representations") should be deemed representations, they exhibit none of the syntactic complexity characteristic of rule governed *Representationalist-representations* (or R-representations).[4] If C-representations want syntactic complexity, they cannot possibly be, as R-representations are, computationally related. For computational relations exploit syntactic structure. Fair enough.

But not enough connectionistically to explain classical conditioning.[5] If this is so, then there is very serious reason to worry that Connectionism may lack the resources necessary successfully to compete with Representationalism. For, supposing that what I argue is correct, Connectionism fails to account for precisely that sort of rudimentary cognitive phenomenon it is widely touted as ideally positioned to explain. Should Connectionism stumble over the most elementary form of cognition, there would seem to be some reason to anticipate that it will not displace Representationalist explanations of higher order cognition.[6]

II.

Some organisms can learn some novel responses to some stimuli. Dogs will learn to salivate in response to a bell tone if the tone is regularly presented shortly before, or along with, some food. Flatworms will learn to move away from an innocuous stimulus if it is manipulated so as to covary with what might independently send them into retreat. These and similar cases are straightforward instances of classical conditioning and apparently can be explained without recourse to R-representations internal to the organisms. The movement of the worm away from the conditioned stimulus is supposedly best explained by way of reference to an acquired disposition to move in response to the stimulation. That acquiring the disposition counts as an episode of learning is taken from granted. That the learning does not require sophisticated inferential processing involving syntactically complex mental R-representations seems to be plain from the simplicity of the worm. Evidently, the worm does not move as it does because it infers, in accordance with some internally encoded and deployed rule of right reason, a description of its movement from premises encoding information about the ambient array. It is too stupid to do this. No, the worm moves simply because it has installed a disposition to move upon stimulation. Plainly, we want to know exactly how the worm manages to install this disposition, and Connectionism presents itself as the most promising explanation.

But things are not so simple as they may appear. Some time ago, Rescorla (1967, 1968, 1972, 1973, 1978)[7] reported results that suggest that the finally correct theory of classical conditioning may find it necessary to advert to constructs, such as computationally related and rule governed R-representational states, not available within Connectionism's spartan economy.[8] Animals first classically conditioned to respond to a neutral stimulus in a certain way fail similarly to respond to another neutral stimulus when, during a second learning period, the second stimulus is associated with both the first neutral stimulus and the unconditioned stimulus used in the original conditioning session. For example, a rat is conditioned to respond to a tone in some specified manner. Once the response is learned, the rat is presented with the tone in conjunction with another stimulus--say a light--during a second learning period featuring presentations of the unconditioned stimulus. The rat responds to the conjunction of the tone and light in the same way that it responds to the tone. Naive conditioning theory predicts that the rat should respond to the light in isolation from the tone just as it responds to the tone. For the light satisfies the relevant conditions satisfied by the tone: the light is reliably paired with whatever functions as the unconditioned stimulus in the same manner in which the tone is paired. In other words, the rat should be conditioned to the light for the same reason that it was conditioned to the tone. As it turns out, however, when the light is presented unaccompanied by the tone, it elicits the response at something other than the predicted rate. In short, the rat remains conditioned to the tone but has failed to learn similarly to respond to the light. The rat's conditioning to the tone has *blocked* its conditioning to the light. Why?

III.

Let's suppose without defense that since Representationalism unblushingly helps itself to internally represented rules of virtually unbounded complexity for manipulating R-representations, it enjoys sufficient resources to explain conditioning, including blocking. Still being cavalier with provocative assumptions, let's also suppose that Representationalism's presumed adequacy on this score is to be attributed to the idea that learning is likely a matter of hypothesis management of the sort that might be displayed by a system that deals in rule structured representations. Of course, the extravagance of Representationalism comes at well known costs. And so it is that we now turn to Connectionism to see how a more frugal scheme might conceive of classical conditioning.

According to Connectionism, simple conditioning is a straightforward matter of a connected system of nodes settling into a type of output state relative to a type of input state. During conditioning, the conditioned stimulus triggers a set of input nodes that serves as the system's

C-representation of the stimulus.[9] This C-representation coincides during the learning period with the activation of those other input nodes that independently signal the co-presented unconditioned stimulus. The activation of these latter nodes constitutes the system's C-representation of the unconditioned stimulus. So much is required to accommodate classical conditioning, which necessarily involves paired presentations--and hence paired C-representations--of the conditioned and unconditioned stimuli during learning.[10] Thus, and innocently, the Connectionist model allows for two types of C-representations: one represents the conditioned stimulus; the other the unconditioned stimulus. If we suppose, as is plausible, that conditioning exploits the fact that the conditioned stimulus is a good predictor of the unconditioned stimulus, that the conditioned stimulus covaries with, and therefore carries information about, the unconditioned stimulus, we may conclude that a connection between the C-representations of the conditioned and unconditioned stimuli is forged during the learning period with the result that the C-representation of the conditioned stimulus comes to control the C-representation of the unconditioned stimulus. The C-representation of the unconditioned stimulus--on every account--controls the system's response. Thus, the C-representation of the conditioned stimulus, by virtue of controlling the C-representation of the unconditioned stimulus, comes to induce the response. Figure 1 illustrates the pattern of activation under consideration.

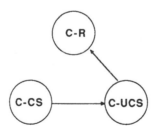

Figure 1

C-CS = The node (cluster) representing the first conditioned stimulus, i.e., the C-representation of the first conditioned stimulus.
C-UCS = The node (cluster) representing the unconditioned stimulus, i.e., the C-representation of the unconditioned stimulus.
C-R = The node (cluster) representing and controlling the response, i.e., the C-representation of the response.
The arrows represent the flow of activation.
(Recurrences of the above labels in the succeeding figures have the same meanings.)

Why does the C-representation of the conditioned stimulus take control of the C-representation of the unconditioned stimulus? Simply because of their correlation (Graham, this volume). During the learning period, the onset of the C-representation of the conditioned stimulus is a reliable predictor of the onset of the C-representation of the unconditioned stimulus. This connection is not, as Representationalism would have it, mediated by rules represented within the system that underwrite computations of the C-representation of the unconditioned stimulus from the C-representation of the conditioned stimulus. Rather, the nodes constituting the C-representation of the conditioned stimulus are variously connected to the nodes out of which the C-representation of the unconditioned stimulus is built. Nodes influence the activation level of other nodes with which they are connected as a function of their own activation levels and the transmission properties, i.e., the weights, of their connections. Thus, a node, X, implicated in the C-representation of the conditioned stimulus can influence the activation level of a connected node, Y, in the C-representation of the unconditioned stimulus. If the activation of X reaches some threshold, it will transmit activation to Y along their connection. The amount of activation that X can contribute to Y is determined by the activation value of X and the weight, either positive or negative, of the connection from X to Y. So it is, then, that the nodes comprising the C-representation of the conditioned stimulus can conspire to control the nodes jointly realizing the C-representation of the unconditioned stimulus.

Now since the conditioned stimulus is typically neutral with respect to the unconditioned stimulus, the weights of the connections running between the nodes involved in the C-representations of the conditioned and unconditioned stimulus will, at the start of conditioning, be such that the collective activation of the nodes in either of these C-representations will not tend collectively to activate the nodes in the other. However, conditioning is a process whereby the C-representation of the conditioned stimulus comes, over a period of trials to control the C-representation of the unconditioned stimulus. Thus, if Connectionism is correct, there must be a process according to which the weights of the connections running from the nodes in the C-representation of the conditioned stimulus to the nodes in the C-representation of the unconditioned stimulus are so modulated as to insure that activation of the former nodes determines the activation of the latter nodes. The natural suggestion is that our Connectionist system is dynamic and governed by a law to the effect that the weights of connected nodes that enjoy covariant activation tend to change in the direction of preserving that covariance.[11] As the conditioned and unconditioned stimuli are repeatedly paired and their respective C-representations correspondingly activated, the relevant connections weights will evolve. The result will be that when conditioning is complete, the C-representation of the conditioned stimulus will, when activated, suffice for the C-representation of the unconditioned stimulus, which, in its turn, will unleash the (now conditioned) response.

We do well to pause here to note an assumption of the immature Connectionist model now before us. We are supposing that the control that the conditioned stimulus achieves over the response is mediated by the C-representation of the conditioned stimulus gaining control over the C-representation of the unconditioned stimulus, which C-representation directly controls the C-representation of the response.[12] Alternatively and as we will soon allow, we could suppose that the conditioned stimulus C-representation enjoys a change in the weight on its connection to the C-representation of the response. On this construction, the conditioned stimulus C-representation would have direct control over the response C-representation and would not need to rely upon the C-representation of the unconditioned response, at least outside of the learning period.

In fact we are all but forced to recognize that a strong connection is bound to be forged between the C-representations of the conditioned stimulus and the response. Fluctuations in connection weights in our model are fueled by covariation. Covariation is, of course, relative to cycles of activation. An activation cycle commences when a system's input nodes are activated and concludes when the subsequent changes in activation level of the rest of the nodes in the system cease. In other words, a cycle begins with activation of the input nodes and terminates with activation of the output nodes. Nodes are correlatively activated just in case they are activated within the same cycle. This is the sense in which the C-representation of the conditioned stimulus covaries with the C-representation of the unconditioned stimulus. But if coregistration of C-representations within a cycle suffices for covariation , and covariation drives up the weights on the connections between C-representations, then the connection, supposing there is one, between the C-representation of the conditioned stimulus and the C-representation of the response should also enjoy improvement during conditioning. If this is correct, then, upon the conclusion of conditioning, the C-representation of the conditioned stimulus transmits activation to the C-representation of the response along two routes. On the one hand, it activates the C-representation of the response directly, and, on the other hand, it directly activates the C-representation of the unconditioned stimulus, which in turn directly activates the C-representation of the response. Figure 2 depicts this pattern of activation.

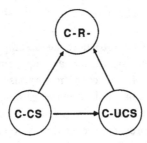

Figure 2

Once we recognize these two routes from the C-representation of the conditioned stimulus to the C-representation of the response, we should be deeply puzzled by extinction, the fact that suppression of the unconditioned stimulus after conditioning tends to depress the conditioned response to presentations of the conditioned stimulus. Extinction of a conditioned response should, presumably, draw on the fact that the suppression of the unconditioned stimulus (somehow) serves to prevent the activation of the C-representation of the unconditioned stimulus and, thereby, to prevent activation from being passed onto the C-representation of the response. But once the connection from the C-representation of the conditioned stimulus to the C-representation of the response has, because of conditioning, so improved that activation of the former suffices for activation of the latter, the conditioned response should continue unabated throughout the extinction period despite the absence of the unconditioned stimulus.

Of course, a Connectionist model can circumvent this difficulty if it lays down the postulate that activation of the C-representation of the conditioned stimulus can never come independently and directly to control or suffice for the C-representation of the response. This might be claimed because the maximum activation value of the C-representation of the conditioned stimulus is alone insufficient to send the C-representation of the response over threshold. Or perhaps the maximum weight on the connection from

the C-representation of the conditioned stimulus to the C-representation of
the response allows for the transmission of activation that is at best
insufficient independently to activate the C-representation of the response.
This might be a step toward explaining extinction, but only at the price of
being *ad hoc*. For why, in general, should we deny that activation sent
directly from the C-representation of the conditioned stimulus to the C-
representation of the response can push latter representation over threshold
while we simultaneously insist--in order to account for conditioning--that
activation sent directly from the C-representation of the conditioned
stimulus to the C-representation of the unconditioned stimulus can trip the
threshold of the C-representation of the unconditioned stimulus?

Well, perhaps our problems are predicated on the assumption
acknowledged above that, in conditioning, the C-representation of the
conditioned stimulus controls the C-representation of the unconditioned
stimulus, which representation in turn controls the C-representation of the
response. Why not suppose that the C representation of the conditioned
response is not connected to the C-representation of the unconditioned
stimulus but is connected to the C-representation of the response.
Conditioning would, then, cause the weights to grow on the connection from
the C-representation of the conditioned stimulus to the C-representation of
the response. The result would be that activation of the C-representation
of the conditioned stimulus would come to control the activation of the
C-representation of the response while having no bearing on the activation
of the C-representation of the unconditioned stimulus.

This model would explain extinction.[13] We need only suppose that just
as the conditioned system enjoys an endogenously strong connection from
its C-representation of the unconditioned stimulus to its C-representation of
the response, it also brings to conditioning a C-representation of the *absence
of the unconditioned stimulus* that has strong inhibitory connections to the
C-representations both of the unconditioned stimulus and the response. The
idea here is to posit a repressive C-representation that marks the absence
of the unconditioned stimulus and also suppresses the associated response.
The repressive C-representation is activated when and only when the
C-representation of the unconditioned stimulus is not. During extinction the
repressive C-representation is, thus, activated and tends to inhibit activation
of the C-representation of the response. This inhibition insures that during
extinction the activation level of the C-representation of the response
continually decreases and thereby decreases the weight on the connection

from the C-representation of the conditioned stimulus to the C-representation of the response. Extinction is complete when this weight atrophies to the point that activation sent along its connection from the C-representation of the conditioned stimulus is simply insufficient to activate the C-representation of the response. Such, anyway, is the point of Figure 3.

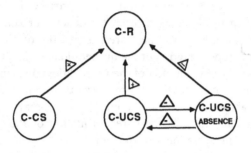

Figure 3

+   =   excitatory connection
-    =   inhibitory connection
C-UCS/ABSENCE = C-representation of the absence of the unconditioned stimulus

A near miss. First of all, it is again thoroughly *ad hoc* to assume that the C-representations of the conditioned and unconditioned stimuli are unconnected. Indeed, there is every reason to suppose that the fact that the conditioned stimulus is neutral implies that its C-representation is connected--albeit weakly--to the C-representation of the unconditioned stimulus. For notice that the neutrality of the conditioned stimulus means that, prior to conditioning, it has as little to do with the response as with the unconditioned stimulus. Yet, through conditioning it does come to control the response. That is to say that in conditioning the C-representation of the conditioned stimulus does enjoy an increase in the weight on the connection between it and the C-representation of the response. So, though the conditioned stimulus is neutral with respect both to the unconditioned stimulus and response, its C-representation must, prior to conditioning--be (weakly) connected to the response C-representation. Parallel reasoning indicates that the neutrality of the conditioned stimulus secures a weak connection between its C-representation and the C-representation of the unconditioned stimulus prior to conditioning. Once we see that the

C-representation of the conditioned stimulus must be connected to the C-representation of the unconditioned stimulus, the Connectionist model of conditioning modified so as to require no connection between conditioned and unconditioned C-representations collapses.

Still, a Connectionist might concede that the C-representations of the conditioned and unconditioned stimuli are connected and, thus, bound to have a weight on their connection that grows during conditioning. Nonetheless, the Connectionist might continue to hope that the repressive C-representation of the absence of the unconditioned stimulus will account for extinction. Simply suppose that the inhibition sent from the repressive C-representation of the absence of the unconditioned stimulus to the C-representation of the unconditioned stimulus is bound to exceed whatever activation is, after conditioning and at the beginning of the extinction period, capable of being sent from the conditioned stimulus C-representation to the unconditioned stimulus C-representation. That would prevent the unconditioned stimulus C-representation from being activated during extinction and sending its activation on to the response C-representation.[14] And that would permit extinction of the conditioned response over time. And so we consider Figure 4.

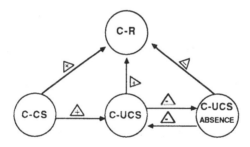

Figure 4

Missed again. This account amounts to the assumption that the conditioned system is infallible with respect to its C-representation of the unconditioned stimulus. When the Connectionist model insists that the conditioned stimulus C-representation cannot transmit enough activation along its connection with the unconditioned stimulus C-representation to activate that latter C-representation when the unconditioned stimulus is not at hand, the model supposes that the system is an infallible detector of the unconditioned stimulus. And this just is not generally true of naturally intelligent systems, systems that the model aims to explain. If systems susceptible to conditioning can mistake the presence of unconditioned stimuli--and surely they can--then this must be because their C-representations of such stimuli are connected to other C-representations which, if activated, can variously activate the C-representations of the unconditioned stimuli. Thus, there simply is every reason to reject the assumption that the conditioned stimulus C-representation cannot activate the unconditioned stimulus C-representation during extinction once it is allowed that the former can come to control the latter during conditioning.

IV.

Our worries with Connectionism presuppose that the weights on the connections between the C-representations of the conditioned and unconditioned stimuli vary in accordance with Hebbian or simple correlational principles. But, as noted above, Connectionist models of weight change typically rely on more sophisticated principles, such as the generalized delta rule (Rumelhart and McClelland, 1986; Bechtel and Abrahamsen, 1989), governing modulation of connection strengths or weights. These principles typically rely upon the propagation of an error signal, a signal that involves the system's comparing the output representation it actually produces on a trial with the target or correct representation. Once the system determines that its actual output differs from the correct output, the system's weights are selectively altered so as to reduce the degree of error between the actual and correct outputs on the next trial. When connection weights can be tuned in the light of an error signal, Connectionist systems can learn to associate astoundingly subtle patterns.

Nevertheless, Connectionist models of classical conditioning cannot legitimately exploit procedures for changing connection weights that call upon error signals. The reason is simply that the structure of classical conditioning does not allow for the possibility of erroneous response *during learning*. The response of a classically conditioned system is the response endogenously associated with representations of the unconditioned stimulus. Whenever that stimulus is represented, the unconditioned response automatically is generated. During conditioning, the unconditioned stimulus is presented along with the conditioned stimulus. Thus, throughout the learning period whenever the conditioned stimulus is presented, the system will C-represent both the conditioned stimulus and the unconditioned stimulus. The system's C-representation of the unconditioned stimulus insures that the correct response, i.e., the response naturally associated with the C-representation of the unconditioned stimulus, will occur. So, classical conditioning could not possibly rely upon an error signal to drive weight changes within the system as it learns. That would appear all but to force a Hebbian scheme back upon us.

This is not to say that the literature does not offer non-Hebbian learning rules governing weight modulation that capture conditioning in Connectionist models. But it is to say that these models help themselves to assumptions to which they are unentitled. Sutton and Barto (1981a), for example, have proposed an elegant Connectionist account of conditioning that recognizes the force of Rescorla's work and attempts to accommodate blocking.[15] Certainly, the Sutton/Barto model, as constructed, accounts for blocking, but it purchases this power by means of generating distinct C-representations of the conditioned and unconditioned responses.[16]   Once these distinct C-representations are available, the model can rely on comparisons of their values, and hence an error signal, to drive selective changes in the connection weights. Here is how.

During the learning period, presentations of conditioned and unconditioned stimuli are paired, with the former anticipating the latter. These stimuli respectively activate the C-representation of the conditioned stimulus and the C-representation of the unconditioned stimulus, which both in turn pass activation on throughout the connected system. After activation is transmitted, the distinct C-representations of the conditioned and unconditioned responses will each have some value. These values will typically differ, especially during the early portion of the learning period. This is because the connection from the C-representation of the unconditioned stimulus to the C-representation of the unconditioned response must be such as to insure that activation of the former guarantees activation of the latter. Prior to conditioning, i.e., early in the learning period, activation of the C-representation of the conditioned stimulus cannot in general be expected to activate the C-representation of the conditioned response. Accordingly, the weight on this connection must originally be such as not to insure activation of the C-representation of the conditioned response given activation of the C-representation of the conditioned stimulus. In order to push the system towards correctly responding to the conditioned stimulus, the weight on the connection from the C-representation of the conditioned stimulus to the C-representation of the conditioned response is augmented after any cycle terminating with different values assigned to the C-representations of the conditioned and unconditioned responses. If this procedure is followed, the system will tend eventually to settle into a configuration of weights that secures activation of the C-representation of the conditioned response upon activation of the C-representation of the conditioned stimulus. The system, represented in Figure 5, would then be conditioned to respond to the conditioned stimulus just as it does to the unconditioned stimulus, or so it is claimed.

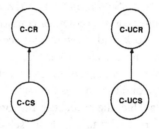

Figure 5

C-CR   = The C-representation of the conditioned response.
C-UCR = The C-representation of the unconditioned response.

Since weights are destined to change only when the C-representation of the conditioned response diverges in activation value from the C-representation of the unconditioned response, no change in the connection weights can occur during blocking, i.e., when a second conditioned stimulus is paired with the first conditioned stimulus to which the system is now conditioned. For suppose that the second conditioned stimulus is introduced and associated with the first conditioned stimulus after conditioning to the first has been achieved. The connection weight on the connection from the C-representation of the first conditioned stimulus to the C-representation of the conditioned response will have been increased well beyond its original level. Now any presentation of the first conditioned stimulus will induce, via activation of the C-representation of the first conditioned stimulus, activation in the C-representation of the conditioned response equal to the activation in the C-representation of the unconditioned response. Accordingly, the connection weight on the link from the C-representation of the second conditioned stimulus to the C-representation of the conditioned response is not altered. And so it is that when the second conditioned stimulus is finally presented in isolation from the first conditioned stimulus, the weight on the connection between the C-representation of the second conditioned stimulus and the C-representation of the conditioned response will not have been increased beyond the insignificant level it had prior to the second learning period. Hence and in conformity with blocking, the system, now depicted by Figure 6, will not have become conditioned to respond to the second conditioned stimulus.

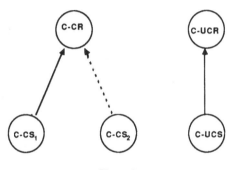

Figure 6

C-CS$_1$ = The C-representation of the first conditioned stimulus.
C-CS$_2$ = The C-representation of the second conditioned stimulus.
- - -> = A connection insufficient to insure activation in the node at the arrowhead.

Neat but not right, and this for several reasons. First, Sutton and Barto cannot legitimately employ the distinction between C-representations of the conditioned and unconditioned responses. What a classically conditioned system learns, at least in situations of the sort under examination, is to respond to a conditioned stimulus in the same way that it responds to an unconditioned stimulus.[17] This is to say that a conditioned system must learn to activate its C-representation of the unconditioned response upon activation of its C-representation of the conditioned stimulus. Otherwise, there is simply no principled reason to suppose that the system has been conditioned to respond to the conditioned stimulus as it does to the unconditioned stimulus rather than in some arbitrarily different and unrelated way.

Beyond this and supposing that Sutton and Barto can, despite what I say, claim distinct C-representations for both the conditioned and unconditioned responses, one wonders whether the account of blocking is consistent with the facts of simple conditioning. The model postulates that conditioning to the first conditioned stimulus amounts to the system's reconfiguring its connection weights so as to secure a strong connection from the C-representation of the first conditioned stimulus to a designated conditioned response C-representation, a C-representation distinct from the C-representation of the unconditioned response. Call this C-representation of the conditioned response C-CR$_1$.[18] Now, when in the second learning period, i.e., the blocking context, the second conditioned stimulus is introduced as a candidate for conditioning, a choice is forced. Conditioning to the second conditioned stimulus requires that the C-representation of the second conditioned stimulus comes to control either the same representation controlled by the C-representation of the first conditioned stimulus, i.e., C-CR$_1$, or some different C-representation. Consistency demands that C-CR$_1$ cannot be the C-representation that is the target for conditioning to the second conditioned stimulus. For notice that once the system has become conditioned to the first conditioned stimulus, the relationship between the C-representation of the first conditioned stimulus and C-CR$_1$ is precisely the same as that between the C-representation of the unconditioned stimulus and the C-representation of the unconditioned response, namely a relation of great connection strength. So, whatever reason mandates that conditioning to the first conditioned stimulus necessitates the introduction of C-CR$_1$ also urges the introduction of a different representation, C-CR$_2$, to function as the conditioning target of the second conditioned stimulus. Put differently, there is no principled reason that both sanctions the distinction between the C-representation of the unconditioned response and C-CR$_1$ and also rejects a similar distinction between C-CR$_1$ and C-CR$_2$. However, once C-CR$_2$ is on the scene, then the same procedure that, during conditioning, secured a strong weight on the connection from the C-representation of the first conditioned stimulus to C-CR$_1$ is bound also to secure a heavy weight on the connection from the C-representation of the second conditioned stimulus to C-CR$_2$. Thus, presentation of the second conditioned stimulus, even in isolation from the first, will activate the C-representation of the second conditioned stimulus. Given the now secure significant weight on the connection from the C-representation of the second conditioned stimulus to C-CR$_2$, the activation of the former will insure the activation of the latter.

But once **C-CR₂** has been activated, the system will have produced precisely the sort of response that blocking precludes. For **C-CR₂**, like **C-CR₁**, is supposed to be, for purposes of conditioning, a clone of the C-representation of the unconditioned response. And if that should be so, then the "corrected" Sutton/Barto model would violate blocking. We see, then, that it is essential to the Sutton/Barto picture that both the C-representations of the first and second conditioned stimuli take the same C-representation, **C-CR₁**, as their common target in conditioning. And yet, there appears to be no good reason to think that this should be how the picture is drawn.

V.

If Connectionist accounts of classical conditioning cannot, for reasons applicable to the Sutton/Barto model, rely on models that trade on comparisons between correct and targeted C-representations but instead require something like a Hebbian rule to transform connection weights, then blocking yet defies Connectionism. Underlying the Connectionist position is the notion that simple learning is primarily a correlational affair. A Connectionist system is a network whose nodes come selectively to resonate as a function of the correlations exemplified in the system's environment. As Graham (this volume, p. 153) puts it on behalf of the Connectionist:

> When a single member of a compound stimulus, such as the first CS (conditioned stimulus) in blocking, for example, elicits a response, this is not because the animal *expects that* the stimulus ... is a better predictor of the UCS (unconditioned stimulus) (than the second conditioned stimulus is). Rather, it is because (the first conditioned stimulus) *is* a better predictor. It is more reliably correlated with the UCS.

Nevertheless, suppose that we were to select as the first conditioned stimulus some tone familiar to the animal. The tone, we may assume, has been a more or less random feature of the animal's environment. For the second conditioned stimulus we carefully select a light of a magnitude to which the animal is sensitive but to which, as it happens, it never has been exposed. After a number of trials, the animal has been conditioned to the first stimulus. It has, then, presumably settled into a type of response to the first conditioned stimulus in virtue of picking up the correlation we have experimentally contrived between the first conditioned stimulus and some unconditioned stimulus. Although we have seen to it that the first conditioned stimulus *now* correlates nicely with the unconditioned stimulus, the correlation between the first conditioned stimulus and the unconditioned stimulus is, *over the history of the animal*, rather spotty since the first conditioned stimulus was chosen as it was.

Once we begin to pair the first and second conditioned stimuli in the second learning period and notice that the first conditioned stimulus blocks the second, we must be puzzled by the Connectionist account. For notice that during the second learning period the second conditioned stimulus is perfectly correlated with the unconditioned stimulus, and this period of exposure to the second conditioned stimulus exhausts the animal's history of acquaintance with that stimulus. So, the overall correlation between the second conditioned stimulus and the unconditioned stimulus is superior to the overall correlation between the first conditioned stimulus and the unconditioned stimulus. Thus, it cannot be that blocking is to be explained by the fact that the correlation between the first conditioned stimulus and the unconditioned stimulus is a better predictor of the unconditioned stimulus than is the correlation between the second conditioned stimulus and the unconditioned stimulus. This may well worry the Connectionist appeal to correlation as the deep explanatory construct in conditioning and blocking.

Well, our resilient Connectionist might reply that only the "short run" correlations count as far as the animal is concerned, that the animal's learning is a function only of the correlation between the various stimuli initiated when the experimenter's clock started running. No thanks. The animal has no access to the experimenter's clock and is limited to checking the correlations among stimuli by the powers of its memory. There simply is no principled reason to suppose that the limits of correlation set by the experimenter line up in any natural way with those defined by the animal's memory. If this is right, then one kind of correlation driven explanation of conditioning and blocking characteristically advanced by Connectionism cannot be adequate.

VI.

We have it, then, that if the connections among C-representations of the conditioned and unconditioned stimuli were just internal reflections of external correlations, then blocking would not occur. In order to allow for blocking within a Hebbian Connectionist model that does not exploit an error signal, it is necessary to suppose that, as the animal settles into the connection between the C-representation of the conditioned stimulus and the C-representation of the unconditioned stimulus, other possible routes to the C-representation of the unconditioned stimulus are damped, i.e., suffer reductions on their connection weights. The connection between the C-representation of the second conditioned stimulus and the C-representation of the unconditioned stimulus must remain weak despite the fact that the correlational relation between the C-representation of the second conditioned stimulus and the C-representation of the unconditioned stimulus during the second learning period might be at least as significant as the correlation that strengthened the connection between the C-representation of the first conditioned stimulus and the C-representation of the unconditioned stimulus during the first learning period. This is crucial. Figure 7 represents the model now under consideration.

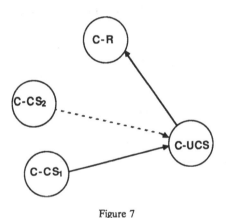

Figure 7

Generally, then, in order to accommodate blocking, a Hebbian Connectionist model might enforce the idea that the enhancement of the connection running from C-representation X to C-representation Y must weaken or otherwise damp the connections from any C-representation, Z, to Y. But, of course, if this were correct, then conditioning would wreak havoc on the connections that happen antecedently to obtain between the C-representation of the unconditioned stimulus and C-representations that appear not to be germane to the conditioning.

For example, given the present Hebbian Connectionist model of blocking, a dog conditioned to salivate to a tone ought to fail, after conditioning, to salivate when it smells food![19] To see this, just note that--according to the Connectionist theory depicted by Figure 7--the odor of food, as a distinct stimulus, causes a C-representation of the odor. This C-representation is, prior to the dog's conditioning to the tone, strongly connected to the dog's food C-representation. The C-representation of the odor, being strongly connected to the C-representation of the food, activates the food C-representation. Once this latter C-representation is engaged, it sends activation to the C-representation of the salivation response, and the dog salivates. But in order for the dog to be conditioned to salivate to the tone consistent with blocking, the forging of the connection between the C-representation of the tone and the C-representation of the food must damp the connections of other C-representations to the C-representation of the food. This, recall, is supposed to be why prior conditioning to the tone (the first conditioned stimulus) blocks subsequent conditioning to the light (the second conditioned stimulus). But, then, so much the worse for the connection between the C-representation of the odor and the C-representation of the food. Hence, as the dog learns to salivate to the tone, it would need to "forget" to salivate in response to odor if our going Connectionist account of conditioning were, as it now seems not to be, correct.

Perhaps the Connectionist reply here is that conditioning to the tone does not damp the connection between the odor and food C-representations because those connections are hardwired, innate and unlearned. But this sort of answer runs contrary to the fact of post-conditioning suppression (Graham, this volume; Rescorla, 1973). Such suppression demonstrates that reflex behavior is indeed subject to modification through learning. And that means that the implicated connections among the C-representations directing the behavior must be susceptible to fluctuation. Animals in which nausea is artificially induced soon after the presentation and ingestion of healthy, attractive food will become averse to the food that previously was naturally attractive. A dog's unconditioned salivation response to food can even be extinguished. Thus, the connections among C-representations that normally produce salivation in response to food presentations can indeed be damped, and, hence, the Connectionist explanation of blocking cannot rely on the assumption that the unlearned connections linking the likes of odor and food C-representations are beyond modification.

So, perhaps our Connectionist will rely upon a distinction between damping and "choking" a connection between a pair of C-representations.

When a connection from C-representation X to C-representation Y is damped, the probability that activation of X will activate Y is reduced from what it had been prior to damping. When activation of X chokes the spread of activation from C-representation Z to Y, the probability of Z activating Y given that X is not activated remains what it had been prior to choking. If, however, X is activated, then the probability of Z activating Y is less than what it would otherwise have been. In other words, X chokes the spread of activation from Z to Y if the probability of Y's being activated is lower when both Z and X are activated than the probability of Y being activated when Z is activated but X is not. Now, if blocking entails not that activation of X damps the spread of activation from Z to Y but rather that activation of X merely chokes the spread of activation from Z to Y, then the above objection to the Connectionist account of blocking predicated on the supposition of damping do not apply.

But this stratagem will not, after all, fortify the Connectionist position. For it is inconsistent with the empirical fact of *contextual* blocking (Balsam and Tomic, 1985). When an animal is conditioned to a specific stimulus, the environment is bound also to present other but accidental or irrelevant stimuli to the animal. A dog conditioned to a tone will see the particular colors and shapes that happen to abound in the laboratory. The dog, though presented with various stimuli, comes to be classically conditioned to one of them, the tone, and not some other, say a color. Now, if--as the prevailing suggestion would have it--blocking (*simpliciter*) involved choking rather than damping, then the dog conditioned to the tone should, in a subsequent learning session in which the color is presented as the conditioned stimulus and the tone is not sounded, find it as easy to condition to the color as it did to the tone. For if the tone is absent, its C-representation cannot choke the connection between the color C-representation and the C-representation of the common unconditioned stimulus. But this is contrary to contextual blocking. Subjects conditioned to respond to a particular conditioned stimulus in a certain way are in fact slower to condition in the same way to another conditioned stimulus if that stimulus was represented (though irrelevant) during the first conditioning session. And this just could not be so were the C-representation of the first conditioned stimulus merely to choke rather than damp spread of activation from the C-representation of the second conditioned stimulus to the common C-representation of the unconditioned stimulus.

Nevertheless, besides this and regardless of whether one conditioned C-representation damps or chokes the spread of activation from another in blocking, it is hard to understand how conditioning could occur at all consistent with Hebbian Connectionism. When a dog determines that there is food in its vicinity, it registers a food C-representation. This C-representation is contingent upon the dog's sensory system picking up certain sensuous characteristics of the detected food. The dog sees the food's color and shape and smells its odor. Thus, the dog registers a color C-representation, a shape C-representation and an odor C-representation. In other words, the sight and smell of the food lead the dog to realize that food is in the near neighborhood. The dog salivates, when it recognizes the food as such, because the food C-representation transmits activation to the salivation C-representation, which C-representation cues salivation.

Activation spreads from the C-representations of the visual and olfactory stimuli to the C-representation of food, and this spreading activation is secured by strong connections among these C-representations. Notice that the weighting of the connections among these C-representations is just the sort weighting that is supposed to be achieved in conditioning. Thus, if Connectionism were right in insisting that in a blocking context an established connection blocks an upstart connection, the connection from the C-representations of the visual and olfactory stimuli characteristic of food ought to block the connection between the C-representation of the neutral stimulus introduced in conditioning and the C-representation of food. And that would render conditioning to an original neural stimulus as unlikely as conditioning to a second neutral stimulus introduced in a blocking context!

VII.

One more objection, and then I will relent. In a blocking context the light (the blocked stimulus) and the tone (the antecedently conditioned stimulus) are presented to the dog over a significant number of trials. While the connection from the C-representation of the light to the C-representation of food may have been blocked by the prior conditioning to the tone, the connection between the C-representation of the tone and the C-representation of the light presumably has not also been blocked. Conditioning, we are assuming, is supposed to result in a blocking of the connections to the C-representation of the unconditioned stimulus but not to the C-representation of the conditioned stimulus. If so, then, since correlation between C-representations--one of which controls a response--should suffice for conditioning, the dog ought to become conditioned to respond to the light as it does to the tone.[20] This is because the connection from the C-representation of the light to the C-representation of the tone ought to be augmented during the second learning period for exactly the same reason that the connection from C-representation of tone to C-representation of food was improved during the first learning period. After all, in the blocking context the dog is regularly presented with a neutral stimulus, the light, together with a stimulus, the tone, that controls a response. So, the dog should enjoy an improvement on the connection running from its C-representation of the light to its C-representation of the tone. The light C-representation should, therefore, come to elicit the response triggered by the tone C-representation. The model ought, then, to predict--albeit incorrectly--that the dog will salivate upon presentation of the light in isolation from the tone.

Well, our intrepid Connectionist will want to say in response that the above simply fails to acknowledge that in the second learning period the presence of the food, i.e., the unconditioned stimulus, and the attendant activation of its C-representation have some--even if unspecified--roles that serve to preclude any significant improvement on the connection from the C-representation of the light to the C-representation of the tone. Yes, that much we should certainly allow. Nevertheless, Connectionists will find it very difficult to capture in their available theoretical vocabulary the suppressive effect had by C-representation of food on the connections from the C-representation of light. The reason for this is that from the Connectionist perspective it is hard to see exactly what differentiates blocking contexts from those other contexts in which a neutral stimulus is paired with two unconditioned stimuli.

Consider a dog repeatedly presented throughout a learning period with a neutral tone together with both some attractive food and a potent electric shock. We know that repeated pairings of tone and food normally serve to condition the dog to salivate to the tone. We also know that repeated pairings of tone and shock typically condition the dog to frenzied dance in response to the tone. However, when tone is paired with both food and shock together, the dog does not learn to respond to the tone by salivating while dancing. Rather one of the two unconditioned stimuli will dominate the other, and the dog will condition only to it. Given the potency of the shock, the dog will learn to dance, but not to salivate, in reaction to the tone. A natural Connectionist model of this scene will show a network in which the tone C-representation develops a strong connection to either the C-representation of the potent shock (Figure 8A) or to the C-representation of the dance (Figure 8B). No strong connection will have evolved from the tone C-representation to either the food or salivation C-representations.

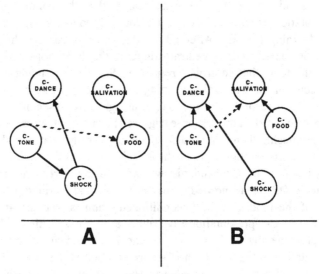

Figure 8 A/B

C-DANCE = C-representation that represents and controls the frenzied dance.
C-SALIVATION = C-representation that represents and controls salivation.
C-TONE = C-representation of tone.
C-SHOCK = C-representation of shock.
C-FOOD = C-representation of food.

Now, suppose that a neutral stimulus is paired throughout a learning period with a pair of unconditioned stimuli that both elicit the same response. Let the dog hear a tone and be shown both a pot roast and a lamb chop in each episode in the learning cycle. Guess what the dog will do when conditioning is achieved? Of course, it will salivate. For each of the unconditioned stimuli secures the same response. Regardless of which unconditioned stimuli is dominant, be it the roast or the chop, the dog will salivate since both trigger the salivation response. In modeling this a Connectionist will naturally preserve the structure of Figure 8 and simply replace the relevant C-representations. Thus, indifferently assuming the roast rather than the chop to dominate, we have Figure 9.

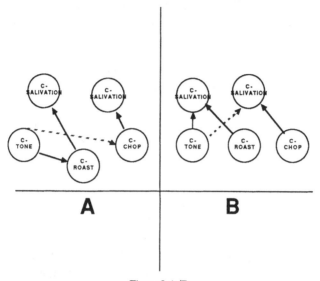

Figure 9 A/B

C-ROAST   =   C-representation of the roast.
C-CHOP   =   C-representation of the chop.

Blocking contexts are much like the case in which the dog is exposed to both the roast and the chop in the presence of a tone. For in a blocking context the subject is offered a neutral stimulus together with a pair of stimuli, both of which are antecedently determined to elicit the same response. So, it would appear that a blocking context also should have the structure depicted in Figure 9. Thus, if we take tone and food respectively to be the conditioned and unconditioned stimulus in the dog's first conditioning session, we produce a situation in which each of a pair of stimuli controls the same response. In the blocking context a neutral stimulus, the light, is then introduced in a second conditioning session and paired with the tone and the food, which both unleash salivation. We may suppose that one of these two latter stimuli dominates the other but leave it undetermined which dominates which. For regardless of which dominates, the light should, given the model in Figure 9, come to control salivation. But, of course, in fact it does not. The point, then, is that Connectionism blurs the difference between stimulus dominance and blocking, and thereby loses its grip on blocking.

Alright, alright, there is a difference between blocking and stimulus dominance that the above does not acknowledge. In stimulus dominance, both the dominant and dominated stimuli are unconditioned stimuli. In blocking contexts, this is not the case. Only one of the stimuli, the food, is unconditioned. The other two, the tone and the light, are neutral stimuli subject to conditioning. So, if Connectionism is to make something of this fact, it will want to say something in way of distinguishing unconditioned and neutral stimuli. Neutral stimuli presumably differ from unconditioned stimuli with respect to their abilities to induce behavior in an animal prior to learning. In Connectionist jargon, this is to say that unconditioned stimuli are those whose C-representations enjoy strong connections to other C-representations prior to learning. Neutral stimuli are those whose C-representations do not have weighty connections to other C-representations prior to learning. Learning, of course is nothing but weight fluctuation, and strong or weighty connections are just those that guarantee activation in the node or C-representation to which activation is being transmitted. Given this, the Connectionist will urge that stimulus dominance is distinguished from blocking by way of differences in unconditioned and neutral stimuli.

This may sound right but it is just hopeless for two reasons. First, so what? So what that prior to learning, i.e., prior to any fluctuations of connection weights in the animal, some C-representations have weighty connections and others do not? How exactly is that supposed to be a determinant of the distinctive character of blocking? What we need in addition to this commotion about primordial connection weights is some clear mechanism that, in virtue of the aboriginal distribution of connection weights, distinguishes in the mature animal--the animal subsequent to successive alterations in its weights--between situations that amount to stimulus dominance and those that require blocking. Without the specification of this mechanism all we have from our Connectionist friend is a pretty tune whistled in the dark.

Second, the animal does not have a way of keeping track of its history of connection weight fluctuation. The animal, *qua learning system*, is--just a system of connected nodes and a set of weights on the connections. Period. Maybe we manipulators of the animal can keep track of which of its connections were originally significant and which were not. But the animal doesn't because it can't. And if you say that it can so long as it is blessed with a subsystem of nodes that C-represents its history of weight fluctuations, just remember that we're talking about simple animals here--flatworms, rats, dogs, nobel laureates--animals that just do not maintain an ever constantly updated autobiography of their cognitive exploits and achievements. The attraction of Connectionism is supposed to be that it does not rely on stored information of the sort we are now entertaining. So, toss this red herring back, and remember, Connectionism isn't the only fish in the sea.

NOTES

* I am grateful to George Graham for his instructive, critical comments on an earlier draft of this paper. A steady e-mail exchange with Bill Bechtel on Connectionism was also very useful to me. Thanks too to my colleague, Rob Cummins, for his ready ear and sharp objections to my evolving complaints with Connectionism. Terry Horgan and John Tienson both and individually lodged their objections in some very useful correspondence. None of these fine philosophers should be construed as endorsing what I have tried to do here. But, with time and luck, they'll come around.

[1] Both narrow and broad. See Putnam (1975), Fodor (1980; 1987), Burge (1979), Baker (1987) and Maloney (forthcoming).

[2] See Horgan and Tienson (1989) for the view that cognition should be viewed as a process defined over syntactically structured representations within systems that do not encode rules governing the relations among the representations.

[3] Unless Fodor and Pylyshyn (1988) are right in maintaining that Connectionism is merely a story about how certain cognitive systems manage to implement computationally related representations.

[4] At least according to the sort of Connectionism I have in mind here. Certainly there are some prominent Connectionists who think of patterns of nodes as syntactically structured representations (Smolensky, 1988; Horgan and Tienson, 1989). But all Connectionists seem to coalesce in the idea that mental representations are not, as C-representations, subject to operations defined across their syntax. Rather, the only theoretically sanctioned processes open to C-representations are activation excitation, inhibition and transmission. (Modulation of connection weights is, strictly, not a process of node activation but rather effected through procedures extrinsic to the system of nodes [Cummins, forthcoming]). If beauty is in simplicity, that's the beauty of Connectionism.

[5] See Rescorla (1988) and Turkkan (1989) for comprehensive reviews of recent developments in conditioning theory.

[6] Of course, I am *assuming*, contentiously and without defense, that Representationalism neatly accommodates conditioning. But nothing here trades essentially on this assumption since I am content to contend that, regardless of the success of Representationalist explanations of conditioning, Connectionist accounts of the same are open to serious question.

[7] These works are all cited in Graham (this volume). A good deal of what I have to say here is by way of reaction to Graham's thoughtfully developed case in support of Connectionist accounts of simple learning.

[8] This is not to say that Rescorla maintains that classical conditioning is a computational process.

[9] Alternatively, we can think of the input nodes, activated as they are by the conditioned stimulus, individually as representing elementary features of the conditioned stimulus. In this case, we might allow that the activation of the input nodes by the elementary features of the conditioned stimulus eventuates in the activation of some distinct cluster of hidden nodes—nodes sandwiched between the input and output layers of nodes—that represents the conditioned stimulus. Nothing here will trade on the distinction between local and distributed representation (Rumelhart and McClelland, 1986), which we may ignore.

[10] This pairing of conditioned and unconditioned stimuli typically involves the presentation of the unconditioned stimulus on the heels of the presentation of the conditioned stimulus, but nothing important hangs on this fact here.

[11] This is a sort of Hebbian rule since it does not trade on the propagation of an error signal. Such simple rules are not popular in Connectionist literature and are typically replaced by more sophisticated alternatives, but they do suffice for simple pattern association, which is what is at stake here. Later we'll attend to descendants of Hebbian rules (Sutton and Barto, 1981a; Rumelhart and McClelland, 1986, pp. 36-37; Bechtel and Abrahamsen, 1989).

[12] It is a troubling consequence of this assumption that a conditioned response trades on hallucination in a quite precise sense. Hallucination is the occurrence under abnormal conditions, including the absence of a designated stimulus, of a representation of the sort that would normally occur as a result of the presentation of that stimulus. This is precisely what happens in the Connectionist model when a conditioned system responds to the conditioned stimulus in the absence of the unconditioned stimulus. The conditioned stimulus activates its conditioned stimulus C-representation which, in turn, activates the C-representation of the unconditioned stimulus. The unconditioned stimulus C-representation is (a token of) the very (type of) representation that would occur were the unconditioned stimulus to have been present. So, the C-representation of the unconditioned stimulus is an hallucination. For similar reasons it also follows from the model now before us that a conditioned subject should respond to a presentation of the unconditioned stimulus in the absence of the conditioned stimulus with an hallucination of the conditioned stimulus.

[13] And it would also handle the problem of hallucination mentioned in note 12. Since we are now supposing that the conditioned and unconditioned stimuli C-representations are not connected, activation of the one would have no effect on the other after conditioning.

[14] No need, then, to fret about hallucination of the unconditioned stimulus during the extinction period.

[15] This model predates Rumelhart and McClelland (1986) and thus is not rendered in what, since Rumelhart and McClelland, counts as canonical Connectionist terminology. So, my presentation of Sutton and Barto departs from their own but not in any way, I think, that misrepresents their central idea. Besides putting their model into the terminology of this paper, I also ignore the fact that Sutton and Barto rely on representations of "traces" of stimuli and responses in addition to representations of stimuli and responses. I also suppress details of their rule for connection weight modulation since my remarks are directed to that aspect of their model that exploits the general features of an error signal. See also Sutton and Barto (1989a and b, 1987, 1981b). *Lector caveat!*

[16] Up to this point, we have assumed that conditioning requires that the activation of the C-representation of the conditioned stimulus eventuates in the activation of the very response C-representation natively connected to the C-representation of the unconditioned stimulus. Sutton and Barto relax this condition, supposing that in conditioning the conditioned stimulus C-representation comes to activate some response C-representation distinct from, but in certain ways similar to, the response C-representation naturally tied to the unconditioned stimulus C-representation.

[17] Things are not really so simple. In some situations a classically conditioned system does indeed learn to respond to a conditioned stimulus in the same way that it responds to an unconditioned stimulus. The dog's salivation in response to the bell mimics its response to food. Here we naturally say that the conditioned response is the same as the unconditioned response. However, consider the rat placed on the electric grid. Here the unconditioned stimulus is a shock to which the rat responds with some frenzied dance. The rat is conditioned to a tone. But when, after conditioning, the tone is sounded in isolation from the shock, the rat will not dance. Rather, it freezes in anticipation to the shock it predicts. Thus, we would seem to have a case in which conditioning does not involve the conditioned stimulus eliciting the unconditioned response (Rescorla, 1988).

Of course, one might well say that the example of the rat trades on a lack of precision regarding the individuation of responses. That is, the rat's freezing in response to the tone might well be a token of the same behavioral type as is the rat's dance in reaction to the shock. Both the freezing and dancing are, the argument goes, embodiments of fear, horror or who-knows-what, but something behaviorally common anyway.

But this aside, so long as *some* conditioning episodes involve the system's generating a conditioned response the same as its unconditioned response, a model of conditioning cannot, as Sutton's and Barto's model does, entail that all conditioned responses differ from unconditioned responses.

[18] How, by the way, is the system to know that, of all the C-representations to which it is connected prior to conditioning, it is $C\text{-}CR_1$ which is to have its activation value compared to that of $C\text{-}CR$?

[19] More precisely, the dog, after being conditioned to salivate to a tone, ought to be less likely to salivate upon smelling food than it was prior to conditioning.

[20] The literature on second order conditioning is relevant here. For starters, see Turkkan (1989).

REFERENCES

Baker, Lynne Rudder: 1987, *Saving Belief*, Princeton University Press, Princeton.
Balsam, P. D., and Tomic, P.: 1987, *Context and Learning*, Erlbaum, Hillsdale.
Bechtel, W., and Abrahamsen, Adele A.: 1989, *Connectionism and the Mind: An Introduction to Parallel Processing in Networks*, Basil Blackwell, Oxford.
Bechtel, W.: 1988, 'Connectionism and Rules-and-Representations Systems: Are they Compatible,' *Philosophical Psychology*, 1.
Bechtel, W.: 1987, 'Connectionism and the Philosophy of Mind: An Overview,' *The Southern Journal of Philosophy*, XXVI (Supplement), 17-41. (Reprinted in this volume, pp. 30-59.)
Bechtel, W.: 1985, 'Are the New Parallel Distributed Processing Models of Cognition Cognitivist or Associationist?', *Behaviorism*, 13, 53-61.
Burge, Tyler: 1979, 'Individualism and the Mental,' in P. A. French, T. E Uehling and H. K. Wettstein (eds.), *Midwest Studies in Philosophy: Studies in Metaphysics* 4, University of Minnesota Press, Minneapolis, 73-122.
Churchland, Patricia Smith: 1980, 'Language Thought and Information Processing,' *Nous* 14, 147-170.
Churchland, Paul: 1981, 'Eliminative Materialism and the Propositional Attitudes,' *Journal of Philosophy*, LXXVIII, 67-90.
Cummins, Robert: (forthcoming), 'The Role of Representation in Connectionist Explanations of Cognitive Capacities,' (typescript).
Fodor, Jerry: 1987, *Psychosemantics*, MIT Press, Cambridge, MA.
Fodor, Jerry: 1986, 'Why Paramecia Don't Have Mental Representations,' in P. A. French, T. E. Uehling and H. K. Wettstein (eds.), *Midwest Studies in Philosophy*, X, University of Minnesota Press, Minneapolis, 3-24.
Fodor, Jerry: 1983, *Modularity of Mind*, MIT Press, Cambridge, MA.
Fodor, Jerry: 1980, 'Methodological Solipsism Considered as a Research Strategy in Cognitive Psychology,' *The Behavioral and Brain Sciences* 3, 63-109 (including peer review).
Fodor, Jerry: 1975, *The Language of Thought*, Thomas Y. Crowell, New York.
Fodor, J. A. and Pylyshyn, Z: 1988, 'Connectionism and Cognitive Architecture: A Critical Analysis,' *Cognition* 28, 3-71.
Graham, George: 1987, 'Connectionism in Pavlovian Harness,' *Southern Journal of Philosophy*, XXVI (Supplement), 73-91. (Reprinted in this volume, pp. 143-166.)
Holland, J. H., Holyoak, K. J., Nisbett, R. E. and Thagard, P. R.: 1986, *Induction: Processes of Inference, Learning, and Discovery*, MIT Press, Cambridge, MA.
Horgan, T. and Tienson, J.: 1989, 'Representations without Rules,' *Philosophical Topics*, XVII, 147-174.
Long, Debra L.: 1987, 'Commentary: Connectionism in Pavlovian Harness,' *Southern Journal of Philosophy*, XXVI, 93-96.
Maloney, J. Christopher: 1989, *The Mundane Matter of the Mental Language*, Cambridge University Press, Cambridge, MA.
Maloney, J. Christopher: (forthcoming), 'Saving Psychological Solipsism,' *Philosophical Studies*.
Marr, D.: 1982, *Vision*, Freeman, San Francisco.
Pinker, Steven: 1988, 'On Language and Cognitive Architecture: A Critical Analysis,' reprinted in *Connections and Symbols*, Steven Pinker and Jacques Mehler, (eds.), MIT Press/Bradford Books, Cambridge, MA, 77-193.
Putnam, Hilary: 1988, *Representation and Reality*, MIT Press, Cambridge, MA.
Putnam, Hilary: 1975, 'The Meaning of "Meaning",' in Putnam's *Mind, Language and Reality, Philosophical Papers* 2, Cambridge University Press, Cambridge, MA, 215-271.
Rescorla, R. A.: 1988, 'Pavlovian Conditioning: It's Not What you Think,' *American Psychologist* 43, 151-160.
Rescorla, R. A.: 1978, 'Some Implications of a Cognitive Perspective on Pavlovian Conditioning,' in Hulse, S. H., Fowler, H., and Honig, W. K. (eds.) *Cognitive Processes in Animal Behavior*, Erlbaum, Hillsdale, NJ.

Rescorla, R. A.: 1973, 'Effect of US Habituation Following Conditioning,' *Journal of Comparative and Physiological Psychology* **82**, 1371-43.

Rescorla, R. A.: 1968, 'Probability of Shock in the Presence and Absence of CS in Fear Conditioning,' *Journal of Comparative and Physiological Psychology* **66**, 1-5.

Rescorla, R. A.: 1967, 'Pavlovian Conditioning and its Proper Control Procedures,' *Psychological Review* **74**, 71-80.

Rescorla, R. A. and Durlach, P.: 1987, 'The Role of Context in Intertrial Interval Effects in Autoshaping,' *The Quarterly Journal of Experimental Psychology* **39B**, 35-48.

Rescorla, R. A. and Wagner, A. R.: 1972, 'A Theory of Pavlovian Conditioning: Variations in the Effectiveness of Reinforcement and Nonreinforcement,' in Black, A. H. and Prokasy, W. F. (eds.), *Classical Conditioning II: Current Theory and Research*, Appleton, New York.

Rumelhart, David E. and McClelland, James L.: 1986, *Parallel Distributed Processing*, **I-II**, MIT Press, Cambridge, MA.

Smolensky, Paul: 1988, 'On the Proper Treatment of Connectionism,' *Behavioral and Brain Sciences* **11**, 1-74 (including peer review author's replies).

Smolensky, Paul: 1987, The Constituent Structure of Mental States: A Reply to Fodor and Pylyshyn," *The Southern Journal of Philosophy*, **XXVI**, 137-162. (Reprinted in this volume, pp. 282-309.)

Sutton, R. S. and Barto, A. G.: 1989a, 'A Temporal Model of Classical Conditioning," *Proceedings of the Ninth Annual Conference of the Cognitive Science Society*, 335-378.

Sutton, R. S. and Barto, A. G.: 1989b, 'Tim-Derivative Models of Pavlovian Reinforcement,' forthcoming in Moore, J. W. and Gabriel, M. (eds.), *Learning and Computational Neuroscience*, MIT Press, Cambridge, MA.

Sutton, R. S. and Barto, A. G.: 1987, 'A Temporal-Difference Model of Classical Conditioning,' *Proceedings of the Ninth Conference of the Cognitive Science Society*, 355-378.

Sutton, R. S. and Barto, A. G.: 1981a, 'Toward a Modern Theory of Adaptive Networks: Expectation and Prediction,' *Psychological Review* **88**, 135-170.

Sutton, R. S. and Barto, A. G.: 1981b, 'An Adaptive Network That Constructs and Uses an Internal Model of its Environment,' *Cognition and Brain Theory Quarterly* **4**, 217-246.

Tienson, John: 1987, 'An Introduction to Connectionism,' *The Southern Journal of Philosophy*, **XXVI**, 1-16.

Turkkan, J. S.: 1989, 'Classical Conditioning: The New Hegemony,' *Behavioral and Brain Sciences* **12**, 121-179 (including peer commentary and author's responses).

Department of Philosophy
University of Arizona
Tucson, AZ 85721

ANDY CLARK

SYSTEMATICITY, STRUCTURED REPRESENTATIONS AND COGNITIVE ARCHITECTURE: A REPLY TO FODOR AND PYLYSHYN*

INTRODUCTION

The connectionist backlash is under way. In a recent edition of *Cognition*, J. Fodor and Z. Pylyshyn launch a powerful and provocative critique aimed at the very foundations of the connectionist programme. In effect, they offer the friend of connectionism an apparently fatal dilemma. Either connectionism constitutes a *distinctive but inadequate* cognitive model, or, if it constitutes an adequate cognitive model, it must do so by specifying an *implementation* of *distinctively classical* processing strategies and data-structures. (A similar dilemma is urged on connectionists by Pinker and Prince in the same issue.) In this Reply I argue that the Fodor and Pylyshyn critique is based on a mixture of philosophical confusion and empirical shortsightedness. The structure of the Reply is as follows. I begin (Section 1) by contesting, on purely philosophical grounds, a certain picture of the nature of thought ascription. Once thought-ascription is seen for the *holistic* enterprise it is, the facts concerning the *systematicity* of thought (the mainstay of Fodor's and Pylyshyn's argument) are revealed as *conceptual inevitabilities*. The power of the Fodor and Pylyshyn critique depends, by contrast, on seeing those facts as a contingent empirical regularity to be explained by a certain model of in-the-head processing. I go on (Section 2) to consider a variety of more specific worries concerning the need for structured, in-the-head representations. Here it seems that Fodor and Pylyshyn simply fail to see the wide spectrum of possibilities which exist *within* a distinctively connectionist research program. By way of illustration I sketch some recent speculations. Section 3 considers the general issue of *levels of explanation*. Fodor and Pylyshyn seem to believe in a neatly delineated level of *cognitive* psychological interest, nicely divorced from questions at a level of so-called implementation detail. Whilst accepting (and wholeheartedly endorsing) their demand for clarity and their insistence on a clear understanding of the notion of a virtual machine, I nonetheless contest this idea of a neat and uniform separation of a cognitive from an implementation level.

1. SYSTEMATICITY

One day, a famous group of AI workers announced the unveiling of the world's first genuine, *thinking* robot. This robot, it was claimed, *really had* beliefs. The great day arrived when the robot was put on public trial. Disappointment! All the robot could do, it seemed, was output a single sentence: "The cat is on the mat." (Certainly, it was a sophisticated machine since it generally responded with the sentence when and only when it was in the presence of a bematted cat.) Here is an extract from a subsequent interchange between the robot's designers and some influential members of the mildly outraged academic community.

Designers: Perhaps we exaggerated a little. But it really *is* a thinking robot. It really does have at least the *single* belief that the cat is on the mat.

Scoffers: How can you say that? Imagine if you had a child and it could produce the sentence "The cat is on the mat" but could not use the words 'cat', 'on' and 'mat' in *any* other ways. Surely you would conclude that the child had not yet learned the meaning of the words involved.

Designers: Yes, but the child could still *think* that the cat is on the mat, even if she has not yet learned the meanings of the words.

Scoffers: Agreed, but the case of your robot is even worse. The child would at least be capable of appropriate perceptual and behavioral responses to other situations like the mat being on the cat. Your robot exhibits no such responses.

Designers: Now you are just being a behaviorist--we thought all that stuff was discredited years ago. Our robot, we can assure you, has a data-structure in its memory, and that structure comprises a set of distinct physical tokens. One token stands for 'the', one for 'cat', one for 'is', one for 'on' and one for 'mat'. Unless you're a behaviorist, why ask more of a thought than that?

Scoffers: Behaviorist or not, we can't agree. To us, it is *constitutive* of having the thought that P is Q to be able to have other thoughts involving

P and Q, e.g., S is Q , P is S, P is not Q and so on. To have a thought is to be in a state properly described by the ascription of a set of concepts and relations. And you *can't have a concept in a semantic vacuum*. You can't know what addition is if *all* you can do is output '2 + 2 = 4'. Possession of a concept involves a large and structured set of abilities to *do* things, either internally or externally. This is not any kind of peripheralist behaviorism; it's just a reflection on the actual nature of the project of thought ascription. As a matter of fact, we think that's what the business of thought ascription is all about. It's a way of making global sense of a *whole set* of dispositions to behave.

The moral of the story is just this. You *can't get away* with ascribing the thought that P is Q to a system unless you can *also* get away (in actual *or* counterfactual circumstances) with ascribing *other* P and Q involving thoughts to it. (This observation pervades much recent philosophy of language. The general 'global, holistic' nature of belief ascription is well described in various works by D. Davidson (see the collection, Davidson (1985)). And the point about the need to be capable of entertaining *many* P and Q involving thoughts to be capable of entertaining any is made explicit as the *generality constraint* in Evans (1982) pp. 100-105.

Consider now the mainstay of Fodor and Pylyshyn's (1988-henceforth *CCA*) assault on connectionism--the requirement of *systematicity*. The argument goes like this:

Observation: Normal (native speaker) linguistic competence is *systematic*.
    Speakers who know how to say 'John loves the girl' generally *also* know how to say 'The girl loves John'.
Explanation: Linguistic competence involves grasp of compositional semantics. The speaker learns to construct meaningful sentences by combining meaningful atomic parts in a particular way. Thus competence with 'John', 'loves', 'the' and 'girl', alongside competence with subject-verb-object constructions, immediately yields a capacity to produce 'The girl loves John'.

Sentences have genuine constituent and constructive structure, and this fact *explains* the phenomenon of systematicity. Fodor and Pylyshyn then propose an exactly analogous argument for *thought*. It goes like this:

Observation: Normal (human and animal) cognitive competence is systematic. You *don't find* creatures with punctate minds, e.g., creatures whose cognitive capacities 'consist of the ability to think seventy-four unrelated thoughts' (*CCA*, p. 40). Creatures who can *think* that John loves the girl can typically also think that the girl loves John.

Explanation: Thoughts, like sentences, have constituent structure. Thinking that John loves the girl involves being in some relation to an internal representational structure with proper parts standing for 'John', 'loves', 'the' and 'girl' and with some kind of combinatorial syntactic structuring.

In sum, there will be two mental representations, one corresponding to the thought that John loves the girl and one corresponding to the thought that the girl loves John. And there will be some systematic relation between them such that 'the two mental representations, like the two sentences, must be made of the same parts' (*CCA*, p. 39). Fodor and Pylyshyn conclude:

> If this explanation is right (and there don't seem to be any others on offer), then mental representations have internal structure and there is a language of thought. So the architecture of the mind is not a connectionist network. (*CCA*, p. 40)

The anti-connectionist conclusion is, of course, not yet compelling. It depends on a lemma to the effect that connectionist work, by contrast, posits *unstructured* mental representations. Fodor and Pylyshyn certainly endorse such a lemma. They write:

> Connectionists propose to design systems that can exhibit intelligent behavior without storing, retrieving or otherwise operating on structured symbolic expressions. (*CCA*, p. 5)

(Call this the *lemma of unstructured representations.*)

The overall form of argument is now visible.
1. Thought is systematic
2. So internal representations are structured
3. Connectionist models posit unstructured representations
so: 4. Connectionist accounts are inadequate (as distinctive cognitive models.

Classical accounts, by contrast, are said to posit internal representations with rich syntactic and semantic structure. They thus refresh the cognitive parts that connectionists cannot reach. This argument is deeply flawed in at least two places. First, it misconceives the *nature* of thought-ascription, and with it the significance of systematicity. Second, it mistakenly infers lack of compositional, generative structure from lack of what I shall call *conceptual level compositional structure*. These two mistakes turn out to be quite interestingly related.

Regarding the nature of thought ascription, the point to notice is that systematicity, as far as Fodor and Pylyshyn are concerned, is a *contingent, empirical* fact. This is quite clear from their discussion of the systematicity of infraverbal, animal thought. Animals that can think aRb, they claim, can generally think bRa also. But they allow that this *need not* be so. "It is," they write, "an empirical question whether the cognitive capacities of infraverbal organisms are often structured that way" (*CCA*, p. 41).[1] Now it is certainly true that an animal might be able to respond to aRb and not to bRa. But my claim is that in such a case we should (ceteris paribus) conclude *not* that it has, say, the thought '*a* is taller than *b*' but cannot have the thought '*b* is taller than *a*'. Rather, its patent incapacity to have a *spectrum* of thoughts involving *a*'s, *b*'s and the taller-than relation should defeat the attempt to ascribe to it the thought that *a* is taller than *b* in the first place! Perhaps it has a thought we might try to describe as the thought that-*a*-is-taller-than-*b*. But it does *not* have the thought reported using the ordinary sentential apparatus of our language. For grasp of the thought requires grasp of its component concepts, and *that* requires satisfying the generality constraint.

In short, Fodor and Pylyshyn's 'empirical' observation that you don't find creatures whose mental life consists of seventy-four unrelated thoughts, is no *empirical* fact at all. It is a *conceptual* fact just as the 'thinking' robot's failure to have a *single*, isolated thought is a conceptual fact. Indeed, the one is just a limiting case of the other. A radically punctate mind is no mind at all.

These observations should begin to give us a handle on the *actual* nature of thought ascription. Thought ascription, I suggest, is a means of making sense of a *whole body* of behavior (actual and counterfactual). We ascribe a *network* of thoughts, to account for/describe a rich variety of behavioral responses. This picture of thought ascription echoes the claims made in Dennett (1981). The 'folk-psychological' (I don't like the term but I suppose we are stuck with it) practice of thought ascription, he suggests:

might best be viewed as a rationalistic calculus of interpretation and prediction—an idealizing, abstract, instrumentalistic interpretation method that has evolved because it works.... (Dennett, 1981, p. 48)

Putting aside the irrealistic overtones of the term 'instrumentalism' (a move Dennett himself now approves of--see Dennett (1987, pp. 69-81), the general idea is that thought ascription is an 'abstract, idealizing holistic' process which therefore need not correspond, in any simple way, to the details of any in-the-head processing story. The latter story is to be told by what Dennett (1981) calls 'sub-personal cognitive psychology'. In short (see Clark (1989) for an extended defence of this position) there need be no neat and tidy quasi-reductive arrow linking in-the-head processing to the sentential ascriptions of belief and thought made in daily language. Instead, a subtle story about in-the-head processing must explain the rich body of behavior (actual and counterfactual, external and internal) which we *then* make holistic sense of via the ascription of a systematic network of abstract thoughts.

But now it may seem that we have merely succeeded in *re-locating* the very systematicity which Fodor and Pylyshyn require. For although it is a conceptual fact, and hence as unmysterious to a connectionist as to a classicist, that *thoughts* are systematic, it is a plain old *empirical* fact that the behavior (which holistically warrants the thought-ascriptions) is generally as systematic as it is. If it wasn't systematic the upshot wouldn't be punctate minds, so much as no minds. But that it *is* systematic is an empirical fact in need of explanation. That explanation, according to Fodor and Pylyshyn, will involve wheeling out the symbolic combinatorial apparatus of classical AI. So doesn't the classicist win, but one level down so to speak? No. At least, not without an *independent* argument for what I called *conceptual level compositional structure*. It's time to say what that means.

One pivotal difference between accounts which are *classical* and those which are genuinely and distinctively *connectionist* lies, according to Fodor and Pylyshyn, in the nature of the internal representations they posit. Very briefly, classicists posit internal representations which have a similar semantic and syntactic structure to the sentences of a natural language. This is often put as the claim that 'classical theories--but not connectionist theories--postulate a "language of thought"' (*CCA*, p. 12). And what *that* amounts to is at least the following: that the internal representation, like a sentence of natural language, be composed of *parts* which, in conjunction with syntactic rules, determine the meanings of the complex strings in which they figure. It is further presumed that these parts will line up with the very items which figure in the sentences which *report* the thoughts. Thus to have the thought that John loves the girl is to stand in some relation to a complex internal tokening whose proper parts have the (context-independent) meanings of 'John', 'loves' and so on. This is what it is to have a *conceptual level compositional semantics* for internal representations. Connectionists, by contrast, do not posit recurrent internal items which line up with the parts of conceptual level descriptions. An internal state with a conceptual level description which reads 'The coffee is in the cup' will, to be sure, have a sub-pattern which stands for 'coffee'. But that sub-pattern will be heavily context-dependent and will involve microfeatures which are specific to the in-cup context. I shall not dwell on the details of this difference here (see e.g., Smolensky (1988); Clark (1989) for more discussion). For our purpose, the point is simply this: *there is no independent argument for conceptual level compositionality of internal representations. And without one, systematicity does not count against connectionism.*

Let's see how this works. Fodor and Pylyshyn require a kind of systematicity which argues for a language of thought, i.e., for a system of internal representations with conceptual level compositionality. One approximation to such an argument in the text is the following:

it is...only insofar as 'the' 'girl' 'loves' and 'John' make the same semantic contribution to 'John loves the girl' that they make to 'The girl loves John' that understanding the one sentence implies understanding the other. (*CCA*, p. 42)

If the locus of systematicity in need of explanation lay in thought-ascribing *sentences*, then this would indeed constitute the required argument. But the systematicity of the thought ascribing sentences is, we saw, a *conceptual* matter. It is a requirement of finding thoughts there at all that the ascriptive sentences form a semantically structured network. What is *not* a conceptual matter is the systematicity of the *behavior* which holistically *warrants* the ascriptions. But here there is no obvious pressure for a system of internal representations which *themselves* have conceptual level systematicity. All we need is to be shown an internal organization which explains why it is that a being able interestingly to respond to, for example, blue square inside a yellow triangle, should *also* be able interestingly to respond to a yellow square in a blue triangle and so on. And connectionist models, invoking e.g., various geometric microfeatures as a means of identifying squares and triangles, may do just this. And they may do so *even if* the resultant system has no single internal state which constitutes a recurrent and context-independent representation of 'square' 'triangle' and so on. Likewise in the rooms example (McClelland, Rumelhart and the PDP Research Group (1986) Vol. II, Chapter 14) we are shown a model which could represent bedrooms and living rooms as sets of microfeatures. And it is no mysterious coincidence that the model was thereby enabled to represent a large fancy bedroom (i.e., one with a sofa in it). It could do so because of the recurrence of microfeatures across all three cases. Highly distributed microfeatural systems will surely thus exhibit all kinds of systematic behavioral competence *without* that competence requiring explanation in terms of conceptual level compositionality.[2]

In sum:

> The systematicity of thoughts, as ascribed using ordinary sentence structures, is a conceptual requirement if we are to be justified in finding any thoughts at all.
>
> What stands in need of empirical explanation is not the systematicity of *thoughts* but the systematicity of the behavior which grounds thought ascription.
>
> Such systematicity indeed suggests recurrent and recombinable elements. But there is no reason to suppose these have to have a conceptual level semantics. (Indeed, given the holistic nature of the thought ascriptions from which conceptual level entities are drawn, this looks unlikely.)

The lemma of unstructured representations, upon which the anti-connectionist force of the systematicity considerations depends, is thus unsupported. All that is supported is, if you like, a lemma of 'non-conceptual level structure'. But once we cease to be blinded by the glare of sentential thought ascriptions, any lack of conceptual level structure ceases to be a problem and begins to look suspiciously like an advantage.

2. STRUCTURED REPRESENTATIONS

Apart from the global critique of connectionism examined in Section 1, CAA contains a number of subsidiary arguments and observations. None of these, so far as I can see, constitutes the powerful independent argument for conceptual level compositionality which Fodor and Pylyshyn require. But they succeed in raising several interesting problems which, at present, have only partial and suggestive solutions.

The first subsidiary argument concerns what Fodor and Pylyshyn call 'real constituency'. Real constituency, they insist, has to do with parts and wholes; 'the symbol "Mary" is literally a part of the symbol "John loves Mary" (*CCA*, p. 22). Likewise:

In (a) classical machine, the objects to which the content *A* and *B* is ascribed (viz. tokens of the expression '*A* and *B*') literally contain, as proper parts, objects to which the content *A* is ascribed. (*CCA*, p. 16)

The contrast is with an imaginary connectionist machine in which a node representing 'A and B' is excitatorily linked to a node representing A and a node representing B. The 'A and B' node does not have the others as its proper parts. In fact, it has no semantically interpreted parts at all (*CCA*, p. 17). Hence the inevitability of 'A and B's linkage to 'A' and 'B' is an illusion fostered by the use of labels which, in the case of the connectionist machine, are not any part of the actual causal structure of the processing (*CCA*, p. 17).

With these observations, Fodor and Pylyshyn commence an extended discussion of the demerits of systems which depend on internal representations which lack semantically interpreted parts. The natural response would be to insist that connectionist internal representations *do* have semantically interpreted parts which *do* figure in the actual causal structure of the processing--only those parts do not line up with the concepts and relations visible at the conceptual level. Connectionist machines, we might say, have a compositional *microsemantics* involving whatever physical and functional properties are coded for by units (nodes) or groups of units having some recurrent integrity (stable sub-patterns). Not only would it be natural to say this, I am inclined to think it would be correct. But Fodor and Pylyshyn consider and reject such a response. It is, they say:

> among the major misfortunes of the connectionist literature that the issue about whether common sense concepts should be represented by sets of microfeatures has gotten thoroughly mixed up with the issue about combinatorial structure in mental representations. (*CCA*, p. 21)

But just what *is* the mix-up here? Fodor and Pylyshyn go on to say that:

> A moment's consideration will make it clear, however, that even on the assumption that concepts are distributed over microfeatures, '+ has-a-handle' [this is their example of a microfeature] is not a constituent of cup in anything like the sense that 'Mary' (the word) is a constituent of (the sentence) 'John loves Mary'. (*CCA*, p. 21)

But this, as far as I can see, is simply to beg all the important questions. It is of course *right* to say that connectionist microfeatures are not literal constituents of the *conceptual level expression* CUP. But the connectionist claim is that there is *no* in-the-head structure which neatly and recurrently lines up with the conceptual level expression CUP. Rather, there is a state of activation defined across microfeature encoding units (or groups of units) which, in a given case, grounds our thought of a cup. In another thinking about a cup, a somewhat different set of units may ground the thought. The sub-pattern for cup is thus context-variable. If (see Section 1) we are not impressed by any need to find in-head analogues to the context-independent parts of sentences (i.e., words like 'cup') this variability won't bother us. The only notion of 'real constituency' we will need is the notion of possibly overlapping sets of microfeature encoding units capable of grounding systematic behavior, e.g., of enabling cup-recognition in both the context of seeing a cup and saucer, and seeing a cup and plate. There can, I'm sure, be real constituency and compositionality here; but it needn't have much, if anything, to do with the constituency and compositionality of the conceptual level apparatus of the expressions of ordinary language.

Following these somewhat confusing comments about 'real Constituency' Fodor and Pylyshyn go on to criticize the capacity of a microfeatural analysis to capture *role relations*--a problem which they regard as a 'symptom of a more pervasive difficulty' concerning the capacity to group concepts into propositions. Here the issues are clear and real though the connectionist position is not as desperate as they presume.

Role-relations concern facts such as the following. John is the subject of the belief 'John loves Mary', Mary is the object of the same belief and so on. Fodor and Pylyshyn propose to consider the question of how connectionists can encode such facts--facts which are given by the syntactic structure of the classical representation corresponding to the expression 'John loves Mary'. The problem, as they see it, is that the only apparatus the connectionist has available is that of simultaneous feature activation. And on pain of an enormous proliferation of features (see below) this simply won't do the work.

The second subsidiary argument thus goes like this: suppose we (qua connectionists) want to represent 'John loves Mary'. We need some way of representing not just 'John' 'loves' and 'Mary' but *also* (it seems) the role relations--John is the subject and Mary is the object of the loving. But we can't introduce these as straightforward syntactic relations among the constituents (the classical option). Suppose, then, that we try to introduce them as microfeatures. The obvious move is to introduce microfeatures like 'John-subject' and 'Mary-object'. But this opens the floodgates for an explosion of such microfeatures. For consider the expression 'John loves Mary and Bill hates Sally'. If all we have available to fix the role relation of Mary is the micro-feature 'Mary-object', this leaves it open whether it is the loving or the hating of which she is the object. So what do we do? We could introduce a microfeature 'John-subject-hates-Mary-object'. But now it looks as if we need to have special purposes microfeatures for just about every complex sentence! The recourse to microfeatures such as 'John-subject' thus looks like a dead end. But the only other picture of how to capture role relations is the classical theorists' notion of a symbol system with syntactic structure (*CCA*, pp. 23-24).

There is no doubt that Fodor and Pylyshyn are here probing a difficult and sensitive topic. I suspect, however, that things are not quite as bleak as they suppose. One feature of the *CCA* account which may make the situation look unrealistically bleak is their use of conceptual level terms such as 'John' and 'subject' in the construction of the cases. This blinds the reader to a more promising part which truly microfeatural analysis may play in resolving the role relation difficulty. What I have in mind is that there need be no microfeatures which consist of strictly *grammatical* properties at all; instead, this work may be done by systematic variation in the microfeatures which (at the conceptual level, in a given case) we say stand for 'John'.

This possibility (and it is no more than a possibility) is best illustrated by an analogy with real world physical systems, of which John and Mary are convenient examples. Suppose (perish the thought) that Mary hits John. In a range of clear and central cases, we will have no need of labels such as 'Mary-hitter' and 'John-hitter' in order to get the roles right. For John will look different as a result of being hit. And Mary may show signs (anger, remorse, hand-rubbing) of being the aggressor. In other words, we can *see* who did what, since *the very objects* (John and Mary) *bear the signs of their roles on their persons*. (Of course, the signs are, as it were, already *attached* to the right individuals, and this may seem to give an unfair advantage over the connectionist case--but I'll come to that in a moment.)

The proposal, as is by now obvious, is that something analogous takes place in the microfeatural *representation* of John and Mary, allowing the representations to wear their role relations on their sleeve. If Mary hit John, the representation of John may include e.g., 'unwilled damage' microfeatures. If John hit Mary, these would be associated with a different sub-pattern (see below)--i.e., the one associated with Mary. But grammatical labels (subject, object etc.) are, on this account, artifacts of the conceptual level, needed to differentiate 'John' in 'John loves Mary' from 'John' in 'Mary loves John'. Since, at that level, the *same* symbol does the work in each case, such labels are needed in classical machines. This need not be the case in a connectionist machine in which role relations are reflected *inside* the representations of 'John' 'Mary' and so on.

It may seem, however, as if we have merely glossed over a crucial difficulty. For suppose we have the following microfeatures active; a bunch of Mary-microfeatures, a bunch of John-microfeatures and, let's suppose, an 'unwilled damage' microfeature. What determines that the latter attach to *John* rather than *Mary*? Here we must appeal to the notion of a stable sub-pattern. The "unwilled damage" microfeature must be activated in a way that associates it more strongly with the clearly John-relating microfeatures than with the clearly Mary-relating ones. This fact would be visible across contexts. Thus given two consecutive sentences

(1) Mary hit John

(2) John went to the bathroom,

we'd want to set it up so that the 'unwilled damage' microfeature recurred in the new context provided by (2).

This is not mere hand waving. The notion of a stable sub-pattern is one that is quite well worked out in the connectionist literature. A simple example is found in the rooms model mentioned earlier. Here a stable sub-pattern around sofa exists *within* a standard lounge pattern. It is this stable sub-pattern which recurs when the system is asked to represent a non-standard room with a bed and a sofa. The authors of the model refer to this process as embedding and call the stable sub-patterns sub-schemata. They write:

> Subschemata correspond to small configurations of units which cohere and which may be a part of many different stable patterns. [Thus] large schemata...can be conceptualized as consisting, in part, of a configuration of subschemata which may or may not be present as wholes. (Rumelhart, Smolensky, McClelland and Hinton, 1986, pp. 35-36)

Perhaps, then, this notion of a stable sub-pattern can be extended to underwrite the co-association of microfeatures needed to ensure the correct assignment of role-indicating microfeatures such as 'unwilled damage'. If it can, then we would have made progress towards a solution to the more general problem which Fodor and Pylyshyn see as underlying the specific difficulties about role relations viz. finding a way to capture, within a connectionist setting, something of the way concepts group into propositions. Thus they note that:

> When representations express concepts that belong to the same proposition, they are not merely simultaneously active but also *in construction with each other. (CCA,* p. 23 (their emphasis))

The general question then, is how can a connectionist model capture the facts about what is in construction with what? And the basic form of our answer is now obvious. Those microfeatures which are to count as grouped together, in semantically significant ways, will be distinguished as *temporarily stable sub-patterns*.

Now, it might be argued, in response to this, that schemata constitute a special case. The idea might be that it makes sense to speak of a finite set of stable sub-patterns being the *constituents* of a given schema, but that it would be hopeless to seek a similar, *fixed* set of constituents within a representation of John. That's to say, there may be some tension between on the one hand the idea of extreme *context-variability* of representation, and on the other, the idea of *stable sub-patterns*. Certainly there is an extra problem in our proposed account since what it requires is a *temporarily* stable sub-pattern linking e.g., 'unwilled damage' to the microfeatural representation of John. It would be fair to object that I have so far described no mechanism capable of effecting such a temporary linkage. But some connectionist work is now beginning to address this very issue. Thus Hinton and Plaut's recent work on fast weights described later on in this section provides, as we shall see, a means of effecting the temporary binding of features into coherent wholes.

First, however, a note of caution. In all this, Fodor and Pylyshyn are continually pushing the connectionist to account directly for what are really conceptual level phenomena. Thus they insist that *the thought that* John loves Fido must be the *same* whether or not it is entertained along with e.g., a blue sky microfeature. So the activity of blue-sky microfeatures must be neatly divided off for the activity of 'John' 'loving' and 'Fido' ones (*CCA*, p. 25). But given our (Section 1) picture of thought ascription, this context-independent identity of thoughts *need not* have any in-the-head analogue. Of course, we find it useful to construct, in our dealings with one another, an abstract notion of thought which depends on the ascription of context-independent propositional attitudes. But the connectionist, in explaining the systematic behavioral tendencies which make such ascription fruitful, need not posit any such hard and fast commonality. She may allow that Fred's thought that John loves Fido *involves* blue-sky microfeatures, while Mary's does not. The *same* thought, on this account, may be arbitrarily different in respect of a microfeatural analysis of the in-head processing going on at the time.

And a second note of caution. The identification of microfeatures is *itself* parasitic on the conceptual level apparatus. And it may turn out that no such talk (i.e., no genuinely *semantic* talk) properly captures the role of individual nodes or of sub-groupings of nodes.

We cannot help but try to understand the operation of connectionist machines in such terms; but at the end of the day this could turn out to be a heuristic crutch rather than an accurate reflection of the precise contribution of parts of a network. This would not be surprising. Microfeature description is carried out using strictly conceptual level resources, tailored in novel (non daily language) ways. But these resources (e.g., the words 'unwilled' and 'damage' in 'unwilled-damage') are just tools adapted for carrying out the different, abstract task of capturing commonalities in behavior (*however* caused) in an inter-personal calculus. (This, I think, is the very radical option embraced by Dennett.[3])

Returning to the mainflow of our discussion, the last subsidiary argument I want to consider concerns the idea of a functional distinction between memory and program. Fodor and Pylyshyn assert that program and memory are inextricably interwoven in connectionist machines with the result that such architectures 'cannot by their very nature, support an expandable memory' (*CCA*, p. 35). The unwelcome upshot of which, they argue, is the connectionists inability to make sense of any kind of competence/performance distinction. This criticism is instructively false; instructively, because it illustrates the danger of pronouncing too soon on the question of what is and is not possible within the bounds of a distinctively connectionist research programme.

Very simply, the idea of a competence/performance distinction amounts to the thought that our linguistic cognitive capacities, say, are *in themselves* capable of supporting the solution of a large or unbounded set of linguistic (parsing) puzzles. But *other* limitations (e.g., attention and short-term memory) intervene so as to produce a more finite *actual* capacity (performance). Part of Fodor and Pylyshyn's criticism[4] depends on the thought that, in a classical machine, you have a program/memory distinction which makes sense of the idea of adding memory (hence improving the performance) while leaving the program (competence) unchanged. 'By contrast', they insist,

in a...connectionist machine, adding to the memory (e.g., by adding units to a network) alters the connectivity relations among nodes and thus does affect the machine's computational structure. (*CCA*, p. 35)

But now consider (very briefly) the following proposal (Hinton and Plaut (1987)). Instead of having just a single weight on each connection, why not have two.[5] One of these is the usual ('slow') weight, which encodes the long-term knowledge of the network. The other--the new 'fast' weight--has two special properties. First, it changes very rapidly in response to inputs. But second, it *decays* quite rapidly back to zero. Thus:

At any instant we can think of the system's knowledge as consisting of the slow weights with a temporary overlay of fast weights. The overlay gives a temporary context--a temporary associative memory that allows networks to do more flexible information processing. (Hinton and Plaut, 1987, p. 177)

For our purposes, it will suffice to note two properties claimed for such an architecture.

1. It provides for rapid temporary learning (even one trial learning).
2. It allows the *temporary binding* of features into a coherent whole. (adapted from Hinton and Plaut (1987, p. 177))

Notice immediately that this second property is exactly what we required earlier to complete the discussion of role relations and the binding of features into semantically related packages. (Hinton and Plaut also cite work by Von der Malsburg (1981) and Feldman (1982) in this context.) Notice also that by providing an increased range of fast and medium-fast weights, you could augment a system's performance *without* changing its basic computational structure (the 'program' stored in the slow weights). Distinctively connectionist architectures, I conclude, *can* provide for some kind of competence/performance distinction, and *can* provide for the temporary binding of features into coherent wholes. What Fodor and Pylyshyn have fixed on are not essential limitations of connectionist architectures so much as temporary artifacts of the early stages of development of such approaches. Much of what looks, to Fodor and Pylyshyn, like irremediable, fundamental deficiencies in the very idea of connectionism, may turn out to be just such temporary artifacts. Fodor, as a philosopher, should be more sensitive than most to the dangers of confusing lack of imagination with a priori impossibility.

To sum up, none of the subsidiary arguments in *CCA* seem capable of lending support to the conclusion that classical, conceptual level compositionality is an essential ingredient of an account of in-the-head processing. The arguments depend, for the most part, on a rather blinkered view of the range of possibilities which may exist within a distinctively connectionist paradigm. In the next section, I consider the common charge, repeated in *CCA*, that connectionists are simply confused about levels of explanation.

3. COGNITIVE ARCHITECTURE

Fodor and Pylyshyn criticize connectionists for confusing the level of *psychological explanation* and the level of *implementation*. Of course, they insist, the brain is a connectionist machine at one level. But that level may not be identical with the level of description which should occupy anyone interested in our *cognitive architecture*. For the latter may be best described in the terms appropriate to some virtual machine (a classical one, they believe) *implemented* in the connectionist sub-structure.

A cognitive architecture, we are told;

consists of the set of basic operations, resources, functions, principles etc....whose domain and range are the *representational states* of the organism. (*CCA*, p. 10)

Fodor and Pylyshyn's claim is that such operations, resources etc. are fundamentally *classical*; they consist of structure-sensitive processes defined over classical, conceptual level, internal representations. Thus *if* we were convinced (say by the systematicity argument reviewed in Section 1) of the need for classical representations and processes, the mere fact that the brain is a kind of connectionist network ought not to impress us. Connectionist architectures can be implemented in classical machines and *vice versa*.

This argument, in its pure form, need not concern us if we totally reject Fodor and Pylyshyn's reasons for believing in classical representations and processes. But it is, I think, worth pausing to notice the possibility of an intermediate position. Suppose we accepted that, for some purpose at least, the brain simulates (using a connectionist sub-structure) a *classical* machine. Even then, I want to suggest, it need not follow that the connectionist sub-structure constitutes psychologically irrelevant implementation detail. For one benefit of connectionist research has surely been to show how psychologically interesting properties can emerge out of what, from a classical perspective, looks to be mere implementation detail.

To take an example, consider the idea (Smolensky (1988)) of a 'subconceptually implemented rule-interpreter'. This is, in effect, a classical symbol processor implemented using a connectionist machine. Now consider the task of generating mathematical proofs. Implementing the classical rule interpreter in a larger connectionist sub-structure, Smolensky suggests, might permit it to access and use some characteristic PDP-style operations. For example, it may generate the rule to apply by using a flexible, context-sensitive best-match procedure. Once generated, however, the rules could be applied rigidly and in serial by the classical virtual machine. Thus:

> The serial search through the space of possible steps that is necessary in a purely symbolic approach is replaced by intuitive generation of possibilities. Yet the precise adherence to strict inference rules that is demanded by the task can be enforced by the rule interpreter; the creativity of intuition can be exploited while its unreliability can be controlled. (Smolensky, 1988, p. 13)

It seems, then, that a connectionist implementation of a classical machine (the rule-interpreter) may exhibit representation-involving properties which, if they are to be explained at all, require reference to the details of connectionist modes of storage and recall. It is, of course, open to Fodor and Pylyshyn to deny that the explanation of such properties is a matter of proper psychological interest. But this surely does not ring true. To take just a single case, Warrington and McCarthy (1987) propose an explanation of semantically specific deficits (roughly, aphasias in which *classes* of knowledge are differentially impaired--e.g., loss of names of indoor objects, or of fruits and vegetables) which is both connectionist in spirit and depends on factors which, to a classicist, would look remarkably like 'mere implementation detail'. Roughly, they suggest that a connectionist model of the *development* and *storage* of semantic knowledge may account for the fractionations observed.[6]

At the very least it must surely be a mistake to think (as Fodor and Pylyshyn appear to do) in terms of 'one task, one cognitive model'. For our performance of any one top-level task (e.g., mathematical proof) *may* require computational explanation in terms of a number of (possibly interacting) virtual machines, some classical, some connectionist and some God (as yet) knows what. And this multiplicity will be mirrored in the explanation of various task-related pathologies aphasias and so forth. What is implementation detail relative to one aspect of (or interest in) our performance of a particular task may be highly relevant (psychological, representation-involving) detail relative to other aspects of the same task.

What this opens up is the possibility of a partial reconciliation between the friends of classical AI and the connectionists. For *some* aspects of our performance of *some* tasks, it may well be entirely correct (i.e., non-approximate) and obligatory to couch a psychological explanation in classical terms.   Perhaps some of Fodor and Pylyshyn's arguments (e.g., their comments on the difficulties which beset certain kinds of logical inference if we use context-relative representations (*CCA*, p. 46)) serve to pick out those aspects of human performance which involve the use of a virtual classical machine. But first, given that their completely *general* argument for the systematicity of thought fails, these cases all constitute a much smaller part of human cognition than they expect. And second, even when a classical virtual machine is somehow implicated in our processing, its operation may be deeply and inextricably interwoven with the operation of various connectionist machines. In a recent talk,[7] G. Hinton hints at a picture of high-level cognition which would facilitate just such a reconciliation.   The idea is to give a system *two* different internal representations of everything.   One of these would be a single feature standing for e.g., Mary--Hinton calls this the reduced description. The other would be a fully articulated microfeatural representation of Mary--the so-called 'expanded' description. And it would be possible to go on from one of these to the other in some non-arbitrary fashion.   The idea is not elaborated and I shall not risk too much speculation here. But it is worth just noticing that such a model would seem to provide (in the reduced descriptions) the kind of data-structure upon which any virtual classical machine would need to operate. But it provides such structures *within* the context of an overall system in which the existence and availability of the expanded ('connectionist') representation is presumably crucial to many aspects of performance.

4. CONCLUSIONS

CCA is a serious and compelling critique of the major assumptions behind the current wave of interest in connectionist cognitive architectures. But its pessimism sweeps far beyond the persuasiveness of its argument. This is because (1) Fodor and Pylyshyn seek to base a perfectly *general* argument against connectionism in facts concerning the systematicity of thought. But such systematicity is, in the first instance, an artifact of the project of thought ascription. What stands in need of computational explanation is not the systematicity of *thought* per se, but the systematicity of the behavior which holistically warrants the ascription of the thoughts. And this latter systematicity seems tractable within a connectionist framework. And (2), the many subsidiary arguments and observations, although serving to highlight genuine difficulties in the connectionist approach, are nevertheless insensitive to the kinds of extension and refinement already conceivable from *within* the connectionist paradigm (e.g., Hinton's work on fast weights and the attendant possibility of temporary feature binding as a solution to the general difficulty of seeing what features are 'in construction' with each other at a given time). Finally, Fodor and Pylyshyn's underlying conception of a cognitive architecture seems suspiciously binary. There is no reason, as far as I can see, to endorse any picture of 'one task, one cognitive architecture'. Different facets of task performance (including pathologies and breakdowns) may require psychological explanations which advert to different virtual machines. Understanding the mind will surely require understanding a multiplicity of such machines and the complex interplay between them.

At the end of the day, Fodor and Pylyshyn see the cognitive world through glasses which are classical through and through. They see heads full of *thoughts*, with the internal articulation of the language we use to express them; and they see computational processes designed to be sensitive to that very articulation. If the project is indeed to explain how we have those kinds of thought in our heads, it may well be that connectionism is congenitally unable to come up with the goods. But the project of re-creating truly intelligent behavior by thrusting classical thoughts into the machine has not been notably successful. Perhaps, then, some theorists should indeed be trying a different tack. Put aside the classical glasses, and don't worry about getting *those* thoughts[8] back inside the head. It may take time for the eyes to adjust; but it is hardly wise to wear philosophical blindfolds from the start.

NOTES

* This is a greatly expanded version of part of chapter 8 of my book *Microcognition: Philosophy, Cognitive Science and Parallel Distributed Processing*, (MIT/Bradford, 1989). Thanks to the publisher for permission to re-use some of this material here.

[1] For the contingency made explicit regarding human systematic thought, see Fodor (1987), p. 152.

[2] This point, I think, is essentially analogous to one made by Dennett in the discussion of what he calls 'core beliefs'--the allegedly explicitly stored beliefs out of which the infinite number of implicit beliefs can be generated. Facts about generativity, he notes, do indeed bespeak some kind of compositional operations on recurrent core elements. But, he adds:

> No reason at all has thereby been given to suppose that any of the core elements will be beliefs rather than some ... neural data structures of vastly different properties. (Dennett, 1987, p. 70.)

[3] Thus: The rigorous computational theory ... will be at a lower level, where only semantics is internal and somewhat strained as semantics. (Dennett, 1986, p. 70)

[4] I am not concerned here with the question of *infinite* productivity per se, but only with the availability of *some* connectionist analogue to a competence/performance distinction.

[5] Or three, or four ... the use of just two weights, however, keeps the exposition simple.

[6] Such deficits are pictured as arising out of the differential weighting of various 'channels of sensory/motor evidence' for the comprehension of different classes of word. Thus the differentiation of two animals may depend heavily on information associated with a visual channel, whereas the differentiation of two foods (e.g., butter and cheese) may depend more strongly on taste information than on visual information. The idea (which they view as a return to a classical concept of associative agnosia) is that recognising and 'understanding' an object requires associating its various properties into a complex whole. But some channels of sensory/motor evidence are more important to the understanding of some classes of objects than others. So impairment of channel-specific skills will result in the selective impairment of classes of knowledge. Assuming some kind of topographical or otherwise systematic storage of such kinds of knowledge (e.g., sub-networks specialised for taste, or sight) damage resulting in, say, the partial isolation of such a sub-network will naturally have the greatest effect on knowledge of those classes of object for which that kind of information is heavily weighted.

Warrington and McCarthy are thus proposing an account of semantically specific deficits which is both associationist in spirit, and depends on the 'topographical or physiological organisation of neural systems that are involved in knowledge processing'. They note that their overall approach 'has much in common with ... connectionist models of knowledge processing in which representations are computed on the basis of weighted entries in parallel processing systems'. (Warrington and McCarthy, 1987, p. 1292)

[7] Talk given to the Experimental Psychology Seminar, University of Sussex, Autumn, 1987.

[8] Classical thoughts, if they are internally represented at all, may after all be just a recent and messy overlay on much more evolutionarily basic strategies of pattern-recognition and sensori-motor control (see Clark, 1987). Classical representations, minus such a sub-structure, threaten to be brittle and contentless shells.

REFERENCES

Clark, A.: 1987, 'The Kludge in the Machine', *Mind and Language* vol. 2, no. 4, p. 277-300.
Clark, A.: 1989, *Microcognition; Philosophy, Cognitive Science and Parallel Distributed Processing,* MIT/Bradford, Cambridge, MA.
Davidson, D.: 1985, *Inquiries Into Truth Interpretation,* Clarendon Press, Oxford.
Dennett, D.: 1981, 'Three Kinds of Intentional Psychology', reprinted in Dennett, D., *The Intentional Stance,* MIT/Bradford, Cambridge, MA, 1987.
Dennett, D.: 1986, 'The Logical Geography of Computational Approaches: A View from the East Pole', in M. Brand and R. Harnish (eds.), *The Representation of Knowledge and Belief,* University of Arizona Press, Tucson, 1986, pp. 59-80.
Dennett, D.: 1987, *The Intentional Stance,* MIT/Bradford, Cambridge, MA.
Evans, G.: 1982, *The Varieties of Reference,* Clarendon Press, Oxford.
Feldman, J.: 1982, 'Dynamic Connections in Neural Networks', *Biological Cybernetics* 46, pp. 27-39.
Fodor, J.: 1987, *Psychosemantics: The Problem of Meaning in the Philosophy of Mind,* MIT Press, Cambridge, MA.
Fodor, J. and Pylyshyn, Z.: 1988, 'Connectionism and Cognitive Architecture' *Cognition* 28, pp. 3-71.
Hinton, G. and Plaut, D.: 1987, 'Using Fast Weights to Deblur Old Memories, *Proceedings of the Annual Conference of the Cognitive Science Society,* Seattle, July, 1987, pp. 177-186.
Rumelhart, D., Smolensky, P., McClelland, J., and Hinton, G.: 1986, 'Schemata and Sequential Thought Processes in PDP Models', in Rumelhart, McClelland and the PDP Research Group, *Parallel Distributed Processing: Explorations in the Microstructure of Cognition* vol II, MIT/Bradford, Cambridge, MA., 1986, pp. 7-58.
Smolensky, P.: 1988, 'On the Proper Treatment of Connectionism', in *Behavioral and Brain Sciences* 11, pp. 1-74.
Von der Malsburg, C.: 1981, 'The Correlation Theory of Brain Function', *Internal Report* 81-2, Department of Neurobiology, Max-Plank Institute for Biophysical Chemistry, P.O. Box 2841, Gottingen, F.R.G.
Warrington, C. and McCarthy, R.: 1987, 'Categories of Knowledge: Further Fractionations and an Attempted Integration, *Brain* 110, pp. 1273-1296.

School of Cognitive Sciences
University of Sussex
Brighton, U.K.

GEORGES REY

AN EXPLANATORY BUDGET FOR
CONNECTIONISM AND ELIMINATIVISM[1]

I. RADICAL VS. LIBERAL CONNECTIONISM

Particularly since the Sixties and Kuhn's *Structure of Scientific Revolutions*, new theories in a field are often presented as overthrowing an existing "paradigm," replacing it with another that is supposed to address the anomalies with which the old one was unable to contend. Presumably the new one is also supposed to handle the old one's successes; but this is a point that is seldom stressed among revolutionaries, political or scientific.

Radical Connectionism (RCON) is frequently presented in just such terms.[2] It is supposed to overthrow the Classical "Symbolic" Paradigm--what I will call "Language of Thought Theory" (LOTT)--replacing it with a theory of a "softer," more flexible system of excitation nodes that seem better able to match the speed and efficiency that human intelligence seems to exhibit. For some (e.g., Ramsey, Stich and Garon 1990), it further invites the complete elimination of most traditional, "folk" mentalistic ways of explaining human behavior. In these ways it is to be contrasted with what might be called *Liberal Connectionism* (LCON), according to which connectionist networks provide a novel implementation or supplementation of classical (LOTT) processes, a view that I have no wish to contest.

Choosing between competing theories standardly consists in isolating consequences of one that are not consequences of the other and determining independently which of the consequences obtain. When a theory fails (*ceteris paribus*) to predict a given datum, then assessments need to be made of the prospects of revisions, what ancillary hypotheses might be needed, and whether the cost for saving the theory is less than for saving its rival. In this paper I want to present just such an explanatory budget, considering not only the differential explanatory costs of (LOTT) and (RCON), but also of the mentalistic vs. the eliminativist approaches to which they are plausibly linked.

219

Specifically, at the risk of seeming a reactionary defender of the *ancien regime* (the trouble is that regimes become *ancien* so quickly these days!), what I want to do in this paper is indicate the explanatory disasters an (RCON) revolution would wreak. I want to indicate some of the important desiderata of any psychological explanation and show how mentalism and particularly (LOTT)--warts, inefficiencies and all--promises to meet them, where eliminativism and (RCON) don't seem to stand a chance. Consequently, defenders of eliminativism and (RCON) must either show how their models could in principle meet these desiderata or show on independent grounds that these desiderata are somehow mistaken. This presents (RCON) with a dilemma: if it doesn't either meet or reject these desiderata, it fails to be explanatorily adequate; on the other hand, if it does devise a way to satisfy the desiderata, it risks being a "mere implementation." I shall end by discussing some kinder, gentler radical positions Smolensky (1988, 1990) has proposed, and why they seem unlikely as well.

II. ESSENTIAL MENTALISM

Eliminativists are the present time's village atheists. Indeed, it seems to have become as fashionable in the late 20th century to deny the existence of the mind as it was in the late 19th to deny the existence of God.[3] To my mind, this is a large part of the interest of the connectionist debate, even if the analogy ends there: while it is not hard to imagine the present world without God, the present world without minds is virtually unintelligible.[4] Nevertheless, many defenders of (RCON) seem disposed to embrace this "eliminativism" should (RCON) otherwise succeed. In order to become clear about just what eliminativism would involve--so as to judge, in the phrase of Ramsey, Stich and Garon (1990:502), whether connectionism is "ontologically conservative" or "radical"--it is worth demarcating what is essential to the mental, and therefore what an (RCON) model will have to explain if it is provide any *mentalistic* explanations, and what it will have to *explain away* if it is to be joined to an eliminativist alternative.

By way of specification of general functionalist proposals that have been made by a number of writers,[5] I take the heart of mentalistic ascription--or "essential mentalism," (EM)--to consist in a certain structure of explanation involving at least two kinds of attitude states: "informational" ones, such as *believing, noticing, expecting*, which involve representing the world as being with a certain probability one way or another, and "directional" ones, such as *preference, desire, thinking it morally right that,* which direct the agent towards or away from the world being one way or another. What seems to be essential to these states is that they combine in certain systematic, "content" sensitive ways that are responsible for much behavior: stimuli cause informational states (perception), some of which get somehow retained (memory) and combine both among themselves (thinking) and with directional states (practical reasoning) to produce action.

There are at least three interesting properties such states exhibit in these processes, *intentionality, rationality,* and *logical combination*: the states are "about" things--properties, states of affairs, possibilities--and, in their being about these things, the ways they combine are sometimes truth-preserving and goal-satisfying; moreover, it is by logical combination and processes of reasoning that the sensitivities of the organism are indefinitely expanded so that they come by rational means to discriminate arbitrary phenomena in the world: cats, dogs, sentences, microbes, molecules, galaxies, Bach fugues, Dead Sea scolls. What is at issue in defenses of "folk psychology" is, I submit, merely this explanatory structure. All else is inessential.[6]

A perennial complaint about (EM) style explanations is that they seem too easy: one can (and many people do) apply them anywhere. Thus, one often hears that it could as easily be said of water, as a of a person, that it runs downhill "because it wants to." Some, indeed, are inclined to treat mentality purely instrumentally, as a mere "dramatic idiom," (Quine 1960), or a mere "stance" (Dennett 1971), reflecting more on the lack of intelligence of the ascriber than on any genuine intelligence in the ascribee. Others (Bealer 1984; Searle 1990) think that the distinctions on which (EM) depends can be drawn only "subjectively."

Against these charges, there is this to be said: (EM) explanation involves genuine propositional attitudes insofar as it involves the agent's relation to *genuine propositional structures.* What is it to regard a structure as genuine? A crystal genuinely has a certain molecular structure insofar as that structure is *causally responsible* for how it behaves; the stars do not genuinely have the structure of the constellations ("Scorpio" does not really have the structure of a scorpion), since there is presumably no behavior at all for which that supposed structure is responsible. Similarly, what makes it genuinely true of Mary that she runs downhill because she *wants* to is that a desire to run is causally responsible for her running. The ordinary desire ascription indicates--indirectly and perhaps a little loosely--a propositional structure, as it might be, [I run downhill], that plays a specific causal role in the production of her behavior. It's the sort of structure that, were it to interact with another such structure, [If I'm to run downhill, I'd better get my shoes on], would cause her to go get her shoes; and, were it to interact with [If I'm to run downhill, I'd better say my prayers], would cause her to say her prayers; and so forth, for innumerable other attitudes.

Moreover, just as having causally efficacious parts is what makes it the *structure* of a molecule that is responsible for what the crystal does, so is it the having of casually efficacious, semantically valuable parts that makes *the propositional structure* responsible for what Mary does. Thus, the constituents, [I], [run] and [downhill] each can combine in standard syntactic ways with other constituents to form other propositional structures in Mary that produce still further behaviors: for example, she runs uphill when she wants to run back; walks downhill when she thinks running unseemly; and stays put if she thinks [I ought to stop and watch you run instead].

There is, of course, much controversy about what makes these propositional structures intentional (or *about* specific phenomena in the world). Remaining here as neutral as possible to those controversies, I will assume merely that intentionality depends upon at least three kinds of facts:[7]

  (i)   causal co-variance
  (ii)   actual causal history
  (iii) internal inferential (or conceptual) role.

Each of these properties arguably play some role in a complete theory of meaning: (i), for example, seems to provide a basis for at least the primitive concepts of a system; (ii) a basis for concepts of individuals; and (iii) a basis for the indefinitely rich multitude of complex concepts that human beings seem capable of formulating, which enable them to think about the non-existent, the impossible, and the real in an indefinite variety of different ways. For purposes here, it will be enough to assume that these three conditions (particularly the third) are at least *necessary* for any adequate account of how propositional attitudes have the range of specific semantic contents they do.

It is this commitment to states having causally efficacious semantically valuable constituents that distinguishes genuine from metaphorical, "as if" intentionality. Mary plausibly has such states; water does not. It is this commitment that is central to standard mentalistic explanations of human and higher animal behavior, and that I want to defend in the controversy between (LOTT) and (RCON) approaches to psychology.

III. (LOTT) VS. (RCON) APPROACHES

(LOTT) takes the above considerations to recommend a specific hypothesis about the structure of the brain. There is a formally specifiable language, meaningful tokens of which are encoded in the nervous systems (or other hardware) of intelligent creatures; for any genuine propositional attitude, there is some computationally definable operation such that the system bears that relation to that sentence if it enjoys that attitude. Thus, in the above example, it is because Mary would bear different computational relations to sentences that encode [I run downhill], [If I'm to run downhill, I'd better get my shoes on], etc., that she acts as she does. As Fodor (1975: ch. 2) has emphasized, such a model seems to be presupposed by most hypotheses in cognitive psychology, in particular in theories of decision making, concept learning, and perception.

Against these latter reasons for (LOTT), there are the well-known problems that Smolensky (1988) cites regarding how "brittle" and "impractical" (LOTT) structures are, their failure to capture the extraordinary swiftness of perception and thought, their awkwardness in dealing with "family resemblances," their failure to perform "gracefully" in degraded circumstances. Connectionist approaches do appear in these respects to be better off. They involve networks of excitation nodes connecting input and output, the excitation of any particular node depending upon the excitation of surrounding nodes and the values assigned to the connections between them. These values are gradually changed as a result of the system's history in a fashion that is supposed to cause the system to adapt to its environment and exhibit what psychological regularities are to be observed. Such systems seem well suited to perform the kinds of massively parallel, rapid statistical analyses that characterize human pattern recognition and feature detection, and they suggest a way of handling the confirmation "holism" and "isotropy" that Quine (1953) and Fodor (1983) argue characterize central cognitive processing in general.[8]

Of course, so characterized, it is not clear that there is any real conflict between the two approaches. After all, a connectionist network could simply *supplement* (LOTT). Or it could provide one way that an (LOTT) could be *realized*: both descriptions would be true of people, but simply at different levels of generality, much as neurophysiology, chemistry, and physics would provide still greater levels of generality and description than either of them. In a fashion familiar from discussions of functional organization,[9] each level would be important to capturing generalizations lost at another. Such would be the plea of (LCON). But of course such a claim is not particularly interesting philosophically--it foments fewer Kuhnian revolutions (although for all that it might of course be true and important).

What distinguishes (RCON) from (LCON), and raises significant theoretical issues, is an assumed incompatibility with (LOTT). (RCON) models are regarded as competing at the same level for the same generalizations, and it is claimed that the explanations they provide are superior and so ought to replace them. Given the intimacy between (RCON) and eliminativism, this then raises the possibility of a serious argument against (EM). Such a claim needs to be assessed by considering crucial psychological data and considering the prospects of the one approach over the other, to which I now turn.

IV. COMPARATIVE PROSPECTS

An issue of some concern to philosophers of at least a generation ago was whether non-question begging data could be provided for the supposed mental "theory" on which the folk were supposed to be relying in their use of mental terms.[10] Indeed, casting (EM) into doubt is so unusual that it is very difficult to describe the evidence for any psychological hypothesis without using mentalistic terms, e.g., terms involving thought and deliberate action. And for the nonce I won't try. Data is dispute relative and I want to take the disputes at hand one at a time. I will therefore first compare (RCON) with (LOTT) *on the assumption of (EM)*: I will consider eight consequences of a reasonable version of (EM), consequences that I will describe in the standard attitude terms of (EM). As will be seen, I am skeptical that (RCON) can deal with those consequences as well as (LOTT). However, should a defender of (RCON) then attempt to take refuge in eliminativism, rejecting (EM) and these consequences as spurious, I'll then suggest a way in which those consequences could be established in non-question-begging, non-mentalistic terms.

The eight phenomena are:

(1) the propositional structure of attitudes
(2) the productivity and systematicity of attitudes
(3) rational relations among the attitudes
(4) irrational relations and errors among the attitudes
(5) conceptual stability
(6) the fine-grainedness of attitudes
(7) the multiple roles of attitudes
(8) the causal efficacy of attitudes

I will discuss each in turn.

(1) *The Propositional Structure of Attitudes*: As noted above, the notion of a propositional structure is crucial to a realist conception of the attitudes. What is it to be such a structure? This question is so often overlooked, but is of such fundamental importance, that it is worth lingering for a moment on its history. Russell (1903:Sec. 54) wrestled valiantly over it when he worried about what he called "the unity of the proposition," or how to distinguish a proposition from a mere list, for example, how to distinguish between the sentence 'Socrates is bald' and the *co-referential list* 'Socrates, being, baldness'; or 'Romeo, love, Juliet' and 'Romeo *loves* Juliet' and 'Juliet *loves* Romeo'; or between thinking "someone, love, everyone" and *the thought that* someone loves everyone or *that* everyone is loved by someone or other. Frege (1966:31, 54-55) struggles with much the same problem with his notoriously awkward theory of concepts and objects and the resulting "Kerry paradox." The difference between lists and propositions is essential to the function of a proposition or mental state expressing some judgment or representing some possible state of affairs, a function that cannot be performed by mere sets of associations.[11]

Wittgenstein (1921/1961) directly addresses Russell's and Frege's quandary. Arguably, the metaphysics of "facts" with which the *Tractatus* begins is the result of a transcendental argument from the possibility of representation, which he recognizes must allow for names and objects standing in various relations:

Only facts can express a sense, a set of names cannot. ... Instead of, "The complex sign '*aRb*' says that *a* stands to *b* in the relation *R*" we ought to put, "*That* '*a*' stands to '*b*' in a certain relation says *that aRb*."   —#3.142, 3.1432

What distinguishes 'aRb' from 'bRa' is obviously not that their constituents name different things, but that these constituents enter into *different relations* with each other. In atomic sentences the predicate and (in English) the order of the terms perform the function of actually creating that relation;[12] in molecular and general ones it is the placement of the quantifiers. Putting metaphysics to one side, at least this can be said: any vehicle for the expression of thought, judgment, or the representation of the world must involve diverse constituent relations.

(LOTT) captures these diverse relations by defining different *computational* roles for different sorts of symbols--predicates, singular terms, variables, quantifiers--to play.   Thus, 'aRb' is subject to different computations than 'bRa', as is 'Someone loves everyone' vs. 'everyone loves someone.'[13] As in the *Tractatus*, it is the *relations* among there symbols that constitute the sentential facts capable of representing the possible facts to which thought has access.[14]

Since all the nodes in a connectionist network play an identical type of role, (RCON) approaches have a serious *prima facie* difficulty with any such distinction. There would seem to be little room for the *different kinds of relations* provided by the different kinds of symbols, and so no basis for the requisite propositional structure.   Lists or associations like 'Socrates, baldness' and 'Romeo, love, Juliet' would seem to be all that a network could ground. *Pace* Tienson (1987:11), we have no basis for saying of merely a system that has states that co-vary with being Penelope and being English that it "believes *Penelope is English*" (emphasis reversed).

(2) *The Productivity and Systematicity of Attitudes*: People seem to be able to think a potential infinitude of thoughts, and in ways that are systematically related: e.g., if someone can think that [Romeo loves Juliet], she can also think that [Juliet loves Romeo], that [Romeo loves Juliet and Juliet loves Romeo], that [if Romeo loves Juliet then Juliet loves Romeo], and so forth in most of the usual patterns of logical construction.[15]

Symbolic approaches capture these kinds of differences by supposing the agent stands in sufficiently rich computational relations to a productive language system: since the constituents of the language are available to the system in order for it to think one thought, they are available to think of logical permutations of those constituents. Insofar as (RCON) models do not make the constituents of thoughts available, it would be entirely *accidental* that a system that could think one thought could similarly think the related logical permutations.

I have heard it suggested[16] that systematicity could simply be a collection of separate capacities, one for each particular systematic concept and that the apparent general systematicity of human beings could be explained by natural selection serving as a filter on any non-systematicities. The claim seems immensely improbable: n.b., the class of systematicities involves not only every n-place relation people can conceive, but also every combination of logical operator they can construct. What an extraordinary achievement of natural selection to have picked all and only them! But such an account also undermines what would seem to be perfectly good laws, such as that people can be trained to detect properties and relations *among* properties and relations (e.g., being n-place, being transitive, symmetric). That is, the systematicities are themselves systematic, forming a natural kind of natural kinds to which the agent is also sensitive.

(3) *Rational Relations Among Attitudes*: Many of peoples' attitudes seem at least *sometimes* related in rational ways: e.g., there's a deductive relation between a person's belief that there is an infinitude of primes and her belief in the steps of Euclid's proof; some kind of inductive relation between her belief that smoking causes cancer, and her belief in various statistical studies and theories of cancer; some kind of "practical syllogism" involved in her belief that smoking causes cancer, her desire not to die, and her deciding not to smoke. These relations typically involve relations among constituents of different attitudes: practical reasoning works by beliefs about means having constituents that *overlap* desires for certain ends. Thus, my thinking there's water to the left combines with my desire for water crucially through the constituent [water]; my ducking as a consequence of the thought that a madman is likely to kill *me*, and the thought that *I* could duck, depends crucially upon the marked co-referential role of the constituents [I] and [me].

(LOTT) captures these relations by postulating not only logically complex objects, but logically constructive abilities among the computational abilities of the brain. In this, it benefits from the substantial achievements of modern logic (as well as from work in confirmation and decision theory). (RCON) by sharp contrast would seem to be committed to creating an entirely new system of logic that somehow captured logical relations *without exploiting any notion of logical form*!   Mssrs Frege and Russell would have been most intrigued.

(4) *Irrational Relations and Errors Among Attitudes*: It is frequently thought that the possession of attitudes depends upon an agent's display of rationality (see Dennett 1971; and Cummins and Schwarz, this volume). Although there is some truth in this, it can be seriously misleading. Much irrationality is just as attitudinal, just as dependent upon a constituent syntax and semantics. Introductory logic texts are full of typical fallacies in reasoning that turn entirely on matters of structure and content. Thus, *antecedents* of conditionals are reversed with their *consequents*, sufficient with necessary conditions (affirming the consequent, denying the antecedent); *the cause* of a view is confused with its *justification* (genetic fallacy); what's true of *the parts* of a thing is confused with what's true of *the whole* (composition, division); what's true of an *infinite series* is taken to be true of *finite* subsets of it (the gambler); *scopes of operators* are notoriously confused (e.g., quantifier reversal). In order to characterize the generalizations about human beings that underlie these foibles, we need to suppose that they have attitudes sensitive to the issues of form and content that these italicized expressions express.

(LOTT) captures these relations by supplying appropriate objects and plausible computational errors for explaining such mistakes: e.g., computing errors in dealing with repeated symbols and syntactically similar forms; mis-representing reasons and causes, parts and wholes, finite and infinite. It would seem entirely fortuitous for a connectionist model to predict e.g., reversals of conditionals, or scope ambiguities that, per (1), it would even have trouble *expressing*.

Interestingly, connectionist networks do offer a promise for accounting for some forms of irrationality. As Wason and Johnson-Laird (1972) and Kahneman and Tversky (1982) have shown, people are biased towards positive instances in confirming hypotheses and ignore background frequencies in assessing probabilities. Tversky (1977) argues that this is due to the primacy of prototypical forms of reasoning. Considered for a moment as a phenomenon in isolation from the other issues, such mistakes lend themselves to treatment by a connectionist network. A node for a particular concept would activate and be activated by the activation of nodes for the prototypes and their typical features, so that reasonings involving the concept would be biased by reasonings involving the prototypes.

The trouble is, however, that such models of reasoning prove too much. Many people--e.g., Kahnemann and Tversky themselves, and surely all the readers of this volume--*can see the error of their ways*, and free themselves (at least temporarily) from such biases. It is hard to resist the suggestion that, at least in many cases, stereotypical reasoning forms a "quick and dirty" performance routine that can mask underlying rational competencies, of a sort standardly captured by (LOTT). Indeed, the prototype literature (e.g., Rosch (1973) and Smith and Medin (1981)) generally disregards the evidence for:

(5) *The Stability of Concepts*:   Against the supposed ubiquity of "proto-typicality" and "family resemblance" structures across concepts, I have argued elsewhere (Rey 1983, 1985, 1990a) that at least in the case of most adult human beings, subjects' grasp of concepts is not particularly tied to the exemplars or prototypes of them that they may have encountered. Concepts are more stable than that, both across people and within a given person. People typically are able to *transcend* the stereotypes and resemblances that they may nevertheless exploit in accessing the concepts for which such stereotypes are merely *addresses*. Thus, people with very different stereotypes are able to reason with each other about the *same* constituent concepts; they readily recognize the possibility of non-typical cases (penguins are perfectly good birds), fradulent cases (decoy ducks are not), certain possibilities and not others (paralyzed birds but not inanimate ones), and engage in classical conceptual combination (a tropical bird is a bird that lives in the tropics, not one that somehow combines what is typical of bird with what is typical of tropical); all of which phenomena are contrary to the usual predictions of prototype theory (see esp., Rey 1985).

(LOTT) can capture this stability by supposing concepts are represented by discrete symbols that can function *independently of their ties to most typical properties and any particular instance*. [Penguins are birds] and [decoy ducks are not] can be firmly believed by a (LOTT) system, even if it hesitates slightly in assenting to the former and is sometimes taken in by examples of the latter, since the computational roles of the constituent symbols are not *confined* to the statistical similarity relations to typical evidence. By con-trast, the activation of a node for a concept in (RCON) is linked to the activation of the nodes for associated features. The more (statistically) typical a particular feature turns out to be, the more it should swamp any untypical features. For example, in people regularly exposed to sparrows and ducks but no penguins, the node for bird would presumably be acti-vated more readily by the node for sparrow than by the node for penguin. Such people would consequently be saddled with the belief that penguins are less genuine birds than are sparrows; and that well-painted decoy ducks are ducks.

(6) *The Fine-Grainedness of Attitudes*: There is a difference between thinking that Mark is fat, Sam is fat, that man is fat, and the funniest American writer is fat, even where Mark=Sam=that man=the funniest American writer. There is a difference between thinking London is beautiful and that Loundres is. There's even a difference between thinking that a square lies in a circle and that a square lies in a locus of co-planar points equidistant from a given point.[17] Minds exceed the abilities of mere detectors: a mind can piece together constituents to form a complex concept for a property that might also be detected by a logically simple state. This is presumably the way in which we gain theoretical insight into the phenomena we otherwise detect with simple concepts, e.g., geometrical shapes, colors, species, substances.

Now both (LOTT) and (RCON) can avail themselves of co-variational and causal relations to properties, and so capture even nomological co-extension. But the distinctions of the mind notoriously outrun the distinctions the world provides: the world doesn't distinguish the triangles from the trilaterals, the circles from the point-equidistant loci of points, the groups of 27 from the groups that are the cube of 3. Only the mind does.

(LOTT) captures these further fine distinctions by distinguishing between different, logically equivalent and even co-intentional symbolic structures to which an agent can be related. By contrast, (RCON) seems confined to merely casual and associative semantics. All the problems raised in (1)-(3) would seem to be compounded: lacking structure and logic, (RCON) would seem to lack the means of forming most logically complex concepts. Ignoring for a moment the structural problems of (1), it could arguably deal with *conjunctive* concepts by mere associations; but what about *disjunctive* and *recursive* ones? Or ones involving quantification, as in Ramsey(-Lewis) sentences that seem to afford a main entry for theoretic terms (see Lewis 1970)?

Even in the case of conjunctive associations, there is the problem of isolating the *common core*. Smolensky (1990) blithely allows that [coffee] extracted from [coffee cup] would differ from [coffee] extracted from [coffee tree] and [coffee can]: but how then is it we are able to think that *what grows on the coffee tree is what is ground up and stored in the coffee can and used to brew what is poured into the coffee cup*? How does one form the notion of a *common* substance with different complex aspects?

(7) *The Multiple Roles of Attitudes*: It is a crucial part of (EM) that different attitudes can be directed upon the same thoughts. People often *wish* for the *very same thing* that they *believe* does not presently obtain; they often come to *think* what they previously only *feared* e.g., that Sam (but not Mark) might come to dinner. (LOTT) captures this commonality by positing different computational relations (to a first approximation, one for each attitude) to the same internal representation. (RCON) would seem to be committed to positing different nets of excitation for each attitude (indeed, it isn't at all clear how it is to distinguish between the attitude *state* and the *object* of that state, between, e.g., the *believing* and *what is believed*).

Without these multiple roles, it's utterly unclear why one should regard a system as genuinely having attitudes at all. Again, why think with Tienson (1987:11) that, just because a connectionist system has networks whose activation co-varies with being Penelope and being English, that it *believes* anything? Belief is ordinarily supposed to be a state that interacts with e.g., desires, fears, hopes in ways involving overlapping constituents. How is (RCON) to capture different kinds of accessibility relations to the *same representations*?

(8) *The Causal Efficacy of Attitudes*: The above rational, irrational, and fine-grained patterns of thought seem sometimes to involve *causal* relations among attitudes, not only "(ir)rationalizing," but also *causally explaining* changes of state and behavior. That is to say, there is a *non-accidental* relation between the antecedent and consequent states.

(LOTT) permits this possibility by supposing that tokens of sentences that are (partial) objects of attitudes are physically entokened in the nervous systems of the agents, and that, moreover, there are laws connecting the various states *by virtue of their syntactic and semantic constituents*. Thus, there are both laws relating states by virtue of their *content* (e.g., "People who think they're getting tender, loving care release more endorphins") and laws relating states by virtue of their *constituent form* (e.g., "For any thoughts P and Q, reasonings involving '[P&Q]' are easier than reasonings involving '-[-P v -Q]'"). Lack of constituent causality is, of course, how Smolensky (1990) proudly distinguishes (RCON) from (LOTT).

As I mentioned, an (RCON) theorist can be--and often is--also an eliminativist, and could protest that the above eight phenomena all beg the question, couched as they obviously are in mentalistic terms. Non-question-begging evidence for each of them could be provided, however, simply by exploiting the resources of "standardized" tests like the SAT or GRE: one need only tailor appropriate questions and then present them in such a form that the "questions" and "answers" are physically specifiable, e.g., as strings of shapes on the "Question" page, and patterns of graphite on the "Answer" sheet. Questions could then be framed that would reveal subjects' sensitivities to propositional structure, systematicities, simple rational relations, co-intensional distinctions, and conceptual stabilities; and their liabilities to structure and content dependent fallacies and errors (cf. the "bait" questions typically included on aptitude tests). Moreover, by altering the introductory stimuli on the tests to include indications of the rewards or penalties of right or wrong answers, we could systematically alter any of the patterns of graphite responses established by the other means.

The causal role of attitudes could be established by showing by standard statistical analysis that the resulting inter- and intra-test correlations are "non-accidental." They could, of course, be no more interesting than rolling six sixes in dice; the null hypothesis is a possible hypothesis here as elsewhere. I take it that this is simply unlikely in the extreme. We could acquire (indeed, with existing SAT and GRE scores we actually possess!) as good evidence here as anywhere that it is *no coincidence* that the pattern of graphite responses would converge. As with any science, the task of any psychological theory is either to explain these apparently nomological regularities or show them to be illusory.

(EM) provides a plausible sketch of how these regularities could be explained: the subjects understand the input as questions, are motivated to answer them, and have certain minimal knowledge and reasoning abilities that enable them to do so.[18] The challenge to any eliminativist is to do so well. Behaviorists tried, but notoriously failed. As Horgan and Graham (forthcoming) quote Quayle as observing, "A mind is a terrible thing to lose, or not to have at all." As far as any one knows, (EM) is the best explanation of the above and other regularities anyone has conceived. Insofar as (LOTT) provides a way of capturing most of the basic features of (EM) and (RCON) does not, this is a reason to suppose that it is explanatorily better off.

I am not claiming that it is *impossible* for (RCON) to find ways to explain (1)-(8); only that it is a responsibility it must assume if it is to be taken seriously. As in the case of any "paradigm" shift, it's not enough that a new theory like (RCON) is able to explain *some* things; it needs to explain *crucial* things that the old one didn't, in addition to most of the things it *did*. Einstein didn't replace Newton by predicting the perihelion of Mercury, but getting the periodicity of pendulums completely wrong! Just so, (RCON) won't replace (LOTT) if it gains some efficiencies only at the expense of (1)-(8).

Nor am I claiming that (EM) doesn't run into problems. The point is that there is no reason to think the problems might be in principle intractable: we know the kinds of processes that are plausibly involved; what we don't know is how to specify them in detail. Budgets can be met in a variety of ways. The question is whether there's more reason to risk credit with (LOTT) than (RCON). It's hard to see why one shouldn't prefer a rich system of representation that merely needs supplementing with efficient methods of access to an utterly impoverished system of representation that needs to be enriched in as yet unimagined ways.

V. TOWARDS A LIBERAL CONNECTIONISM

Smolensky (1988, 1990) has been one of the most articulate defenders of (RCON). He is careful to admit the limitations of present connectionist results, and to avoid dismissing (LOTT) out of hand. However, he also wants to avoid the "genuine defeat" of regarding connectionist models as "mere implementations" of (LOTT). Where between explaining (1)-(9) and avoiding being a mere implementation is there room for a view?

Smolensky (1988) anticipates this issue, arguing that the advantages of (LOTT) can be captured by regarding those models as special cases of connectionist ones. (LOTT) structures are, for example, to be identified with "patterns of activation" in connectionist systems. These special cases, however, are "crude" ones: (RCON) in the end ought to replace approximate (LOTT), just as quantum mechanics ought in the end to replace Classical Physics.

Suppose that patterns of activation can be shown to play the role of (LOTT) structures. Why think that these latter structures are only crude approximations, that non-conscious processing is not tractable at the

(LOTT), but "only" at the sub-symbolic level? Smolensky's pessimism in this regard is no doubt based in part upon the aforementioned problems of symbolic models in AI. But, notoriously, AI has been largely concerned with emulating human behavior.[19] Someone might claim we should look instead for laws of a system's competencies. Why shouldn't we expect there to be symbolic laws capturing the competencies underlying e.g., (1) and (3)?

Smolensky (1988) worries about this issue as well. He acknowledges the competence/performance distinction, but reverses the usual understanding of it: where the (LOTT) approach presumes that the laws will characterize competencies, performance being explained as the result of interactions, Smolensky expects the reverse: that the laws will lie with *performance*, competencies being explained as special cases. But this reversal alone can't be a problem, since a special case may still be a perfectly exact one. Where this difference in perspective makes a theoretical difference is in the way the specialty arises: (LOTT) presumes competence laws will concern the *internal* states of the system, while Smolensky claims that competence laws will emerge only out of specific *environmental* conditions. The internal system by itself has no sharp conceptual order: from a conceptual point of view it is a hodgepodge of associations governed by non-symbolic "thermodynamic" laws. Competencies are "harmony maxima" arising out of a general network of chaos ("If in the midst of life we are in death, so in sanity are we surrounded by madness" observed the later Wittgenstein (1956) in the midst of remarks on mathematics).[20]

This is an ingenious, to my mind improbable claim, additional to the general (RCON) approach. There are the general, quite powerful arguments Chomsky (1959) raised against Skinner (1957) in this regard: the cognitive competencies of human beings seem far to outrun the sensory regularities to which they are exposed. To meet this challenge, Smolensky needs to show not only that (RCON) can accommodate (1)-(8), but also that it will do so in essentially the same way that his system learned Ohm's Law, without internal symbolic laws emerging. I don't, however, see how the example generalizes. For example, the reasoning patterns adumbrated in (2)-(4) seem to be quite general and non-graduated: once you see the forms you (can) apply them to an indefinite variety of cases; they do not seem to be stimulus-driven in the way that Smolensky's view commits them to be. Similarly, for our grasp of many concepts: we regularly are able to transcend the particular examples that are salient in our experience and fasten on the underlying kinds in a fashion that seems substantially *independent* of our particular experience.

In a later paper, Smolensky (1991) argues that the constituent structure needed to meet some of the above desiderata can be met by organizing connectionist networks into tensor products. These are essentially a way of trying to capture at least one distinction crucial to constituent structure, between roles and items that fill those roles (e.g., between 'xRy' and 'John loves Mary'). The only trouble is that, by Smolensky's own admission, the vector components are *not in the least genuine*: they are simply mathematical constructs, completely lacking in causal efficacy. They may be there for the entertainment of the theorist; they certainly are not available to *explain* any of (1)-(8). Such networks can be analyzed "as if" they had genuine propositional structures,[21] but they don't genuinely have them, any more than water does, or than the stars genuinely realize the constellations. And so they certainly aren't available to explain rational and fallacious patterns of thought, differences among co-referential thoughts, or the causal efficacy of the attitudes.

Whether or not this tensor product proposal will be adequate even for the purposes for which it is intended, it is striking that, in distinguishing it from a "mere implementation," Smolensky mentions four possible points of discrepancy (uniqueness of roles and fillers, boundedness of depth, memory confusability, and processing dependence). However, he *nowhere considers whether these discrepancies correspond to testable psychological fact.* Indeed, this seems to me symptomatic of the general problem Smolensky and any connectionist approach faces: if their accounts are to avoid being implementations of (LOTT) then *the ways in which they depart from (LOTT) need to be supported by independent psychological data.* To some extent, this is provided by the usual advantages of connectionist models--their massive parallelism, the ease of statistical inference and learning, graceful degradation, and the like. But these are not phenomena that (LOTT) couldn't in principle explain.[22] What is needed are *crucial* experiments, experiments over which (LOTT) and (RCON) seem genuinely in principle to *differ*, for example, the data I have summarized in (1)-(8). But on that score (LOTT) would seem clearly to have the edge.

But why think that Liberal Connectionism (LCON), i.e., being a connectionist implementation or supplementation of an (LOTT) system, would be a "defeat" for the connectionist? Should it turn out that there are (LOTT) structures that can in fact be encoded gracefully only as patterns of activation, this would be of considerable significance for both connectionism and (LOTT). It might well turn out, for example, that an (LOTT) system has access to connectionist sub-systems: much of memory, particularly the lexicon, seems to be organized along lines of a "spreading activation" network for which a connectionist network seems a natural model (see e.g., Morton 1969; Collins and Loftus 1975; Meyer and Schwanveldt 1971). And perhaps there is a way of integrating a connectionist sub-system so as to achieve the holism and isotropy noted earlier. Connectionist networks might still be interesting even if the more Classical picture of competence and performance survived: performance might often be the result of a network, for which an (LOTT) system is a fall-back. Each approach could then benefit from the strengths of the other. As the history of the FBI shows, one doesn't have to be a revolutionary, or even the only president you've got, to pique the interest of the investigators.

NOTES

[1] This paper is a very much expanded version of my commentary (Rey 1988a) on Smolensky (1988). I am grateful to Steven Harnad for permission to use that material here. I also want to thank Micheal Devitt, Jerry Fodor, and especially Ken Taylor for noticing a number of problems in earlier drafts.

[2] See for example Tienson (1987), Smolensky (1988), Ramsey, Stich and Garon (1990), and Cummins and Schwarz (this volume).

[3] For various statements of eliminativism, see Feyerabend (1963), Rorty (1963, 1979), P.M. Churchland (1981), P.S. Churchland (1986), and Stich (1983). Note that in this paper, 'psychological' is being used in a fashion neutral to mentality.

[4] This is meant to come as close to suggesting a transcendental argument for the existence of minds as it's possible to come without endorsing one. Indeed, I'm quite opposed to those that have been suggested by such philosophers as Malcolm (1968), to a limited extent by Baker (1987), and in full flower by Boghossian (1990)); see Devitt and Rey (forthcoming) for discussion.

[5] E.g., Putnam (1960), Lewis (1963), Fodor (1968).

[6] Some writers—e.g., Davidson (1980:86), Stich (1983:231)—also insist upon including dispositions to express introspectible attitudes in an external language; others—e.g., Searle (1990)—upon "consciousness." I see no reason to include such stipulations—plenty of perfectly clear mentalistic explanations could proceed without them (see Freud, 1915/1959; Nisbett and Wilson, 1977; and Rey: 1988a, 1988b for further discussion). But this issue is inessential to the concerns here.

[7] I omit proposals that I think are inadequate to the task on independent grounds, e.g., introspectionist proposals of Bealer (1984) and Searle (1990), and "telefunctional" proposals of Millikan (1984) and Papineau (1986). Nothing in the present discussion seems to me to turn on this omission.

[8] Some readers may well detect a tension between Fodor's (1984:ch 4) despair of a theory of central processing and his opposition to (RCON): after all, if (LOTT) can't explain a holistic and isotropic system, why not give a network a chance? Although for reasons sketched in Rey (1984) I don't share in Fodor's despair, I agree with what I would take to be his insistence that (LOTT) is a *necessary* condition on any solution to the problem. He just doesn't think it--or anything else we're likely to think of--will be *sufficient*.

[9] See e.g., Fodor (1975) and Lycan (1981).

[10] This was a favorite theme of both Rogers Albritton and of Burton Dreben in their seminars at Harvard in the early 1970s.

[11] Fodor and Pylyshyn (1988:27) cite Kant (1787/1968:B142) as a source of the point, but the passage is, I think, equivocal, and confounded with Kant's more interesting preoccupation with the distinction between objective and subjective judgment.

[12] This is, I think, the central point of his unjustly maligned "picture theory of language": pictures simply present us with cases in which the relation between the names is (roughly) *identical* to R. It can be lost in an excessively referential semantics of the sort Fodor and McLaughlin (1990:4-5) inadvertently deploy against Smolensky (1990).

[13] Cf. Fodor and Pylyshyn's (1988:23ff) discussion of the distinction between 'John loves Sally and Bill hates Mary' and 'John hates Mary and Bill loves Sally'.

[14] Just for the sake of the record, it is worth noting that (the early) Wittgenstein also proposed a *language* of thought. In a letter (19 Aug 1919) to Russell he writes, 'I don't know *what* the constituents of a thought are but I know *that* it must have such constituents which correspond to the words of language. Again the kind of relation the constituents of the thought and of the pictured fact is irrelevant. It would be a matter of psychology to find out" (Wittgenstein [1961:129]).

[15] See Fodor (1987), Fodor & Pylyshyn (1988) and Fodor and McLaughlin (1990) for rich discussion of this issue.

[16] By David Israel and Kim Sterelny in conversation.

[17] For rich discussion of these examples, see Church (1946), Mates (1951), Quine (1956), Kaplan (1969), Burge (1978), Kripke (1979), Loar (1987), Bealer (1982), Perry (1979) and Salmon (1986:121-123). Chisholm (1956:510) and Searle (1990) can be taken as suggesting that the phenomena of non-substitutability are constitutive of the mental (and/or the ascription thereof).

[18] Of course (EM) might not explain *everything*: in particular, it may well be inadequate to explain what bothers Churchland (1981): sleep, neuroses, pathologies. It does not cure wooden legs either.

[19] Indeed, it has for too long been associated with the "Turing Test" for machine intelligence, an essentially behavioristic test that is implausible even by behavioristic standards and which makes it vulnerable to the otherwise confused objections of Searle (1980). See Rey (1986) for discussion.

[20] Smolensky in this way adds a new perspective to an old debate, siding here not only with the later as against the early Wittgenstein (with regard to which see also Wittgenstein [1967:##608-611] and Kripke [1980]), but with Hume against Kant, Skinner against Chomsky, and, most recently, Burge (1986) and Barwise (1986) against Fodor (1986, 1987).

[21] Smolensky here is playing right into Searle's (1990) hands: such networks can at best provide a basis for "as-if" intentionality. In my reply to Searle (Rey 1990b), I argue that constituent causal structure is a natural way to distinguish literal from such metaphorical intentionality.

[22] Fodor and Pylyshyn (1988:54-55) discuss a number of ways that (LOTT) could accommodate these problems.

REFERENCES

Baker, L.: 1987, *Saving Belief: a Critique of Physicalism*, Princeton University Press, Princeton.
Baker, L.: (forthcoming), "Cognitive Suicide," in R.H. Grimm and D.D. Merrill (eds.), *Contents of Thought: Proceedings of the 1985 Oberlin Colloquium in Philosophy*.
Barwise, J.: 1986, "Information and Circumstance," *Notre Dame Journal of Formal Logic* 27, #3 (July), 324-38.
Barwise, J. and Perry, J.: 1981, *Situations and Attitudes*.
Bealer, G.: 1982, *Quality and Concept*, Clarendon Press, Oxford.
Bealer, G.: 1984, "Mind and Anti-Mind," in *Midwest Studies in Philosophy*, vol. IX, pp. 283-328, University of Minnesota Press, Minneapolis.
Block, N.: 1986, "Advertisement for a Semantics for Psychology," in P. French, T. Euhling, and H. Wettstein (eds.), *Studies in the Philosophy of Mind*, vol. 10, *Midwest Studies in Philosophy*, University of Minnesota Press, Minneapolis.
Boghossian, P.: 1990, "The Status of Content," *Philosophical Review* XCIX #2, 57-184.
Burge, T.: 1978, "Belief and Synonymy," *Journal of Philosophy* 75, 119-38.
Burge, T.: 1979, "Individualism and the Mental," *Midwest Studies in Philosophy* IV, 73-121.
Burge, T.: 1986, "Individualism and Psychology," *Philosophical Review* XCV, #1, 3-46.
Burge, T.: (in preparation), "Individualism and Causation in Psychology."
Carnap, R.: 1937, *The Logical Syntax of Language*, Harcourt Brace, New York.
Casteneda, H.: 1966, "'He': A Study in the Logic of Self-Consciousness," *Ratio* 8, 130-57.
Chisholm, R.: 1956, "Sentences About Believing," H. Feigl, M. Scriven, and G. Maxwell, (eds.), *Minnesota Studies in the Philosophy of Science*, vol. II, pp. 510-520.
Church, A.: 1946, Review of Morton White's 'A Note on the "Paradox of Analysis"', Max Black's 'The "Paradox of Analysis"; Again: A Reply', Morton White's 'Analysis and Identity: A Rejoinder', and Max Black's 'How Can Analysis Be Informative?'; in *Journal of Symbolic Logic* 11, 132-133.
Churchland, P.M.: 1981, "Eliminative Materialism and Propositional Attitudes," *Journal of Philosophy* LXXVIII #2, 67-89.
Churchland, P.S.: 1986, *Neurophilosophy: Toward a Unified Science of the Mind-Brain*, MIT (Bradford), Cambridge.
Collins, A. and Loftus, E.: 1975, "A Spreading-Activation Theory of Semantic Processing," *Psychological Review* 82 407-428.
Cummins, R.: 1989, *Meaning and Mental Representation*, MIT (Bradford), Cambridge.
Dennett, D.: 1971, "Intentional Systems," *Journal of Philosophy* LXVIII 4, 87-106.
Devitt, M.: 1981, *Designation*, Columbia University Press, New York.
Devitt, M. and Rey, G.: (forthcoming), "Transcending Transcendentalism: A Response to Boghossian," *Pacific Philosophical Quarterly*.
Dretske, F.: 1981, *Knowledge and the Flow of Information*, MIT Press (Bradford Books), Cambridge.
Dretske, F.: 1988, *Explaining Behavior: Reasons in a World of Causes*, MIT (Bradford), Cambridge.
Feyerabend, P.: 1983, "Mental Events and the Brain," *Journal of Philosophy* LX, 11 295-296.
Field, H.: 1977, "Logic, Meaning, and Conceptual Role," *Journal of Philosophy* LXXIV (July), 379-408.
Field, H.: 1978, "Mental Representation," in N. Block, (ed.), *Readings in Philosophy of Psychology*, vol. II, pp. 78-114, Harvard University Press, Cambridge, MA.
Fodor, J.: 1975, *The Language of Thought*, Crowell, New York. (Paperback, Harvard University Press.)
Fodor, J.: 1983, *The Modularity of Mind, an Essay on Faculty Psychology*, MIT (Bradford) Press, Cambridge.
Fodor, J.: 1987, *Psychosemantics*, MIT (Bradford), Cambridge.
Fodor, J.: 1986, "Information and Association," *Notre Dame Journal of Formal Logic* 27, #3 (July), 307-23.

Fodor, J.: 1990, "Psychosemantics, or Where Do Truth Conditions Come From?" in W. Lycan, (ed.), *Mind and Cognition*.

Fodor, J. and McLaughlin, B.: 1990, "Connectionism and the Problem of Systematicity: Why Smolensky's Solution Doesn't Work," this volume.

Fodor, J. and Pylyshyn, Z.: 1988, "Connectionism and Cognitive Architecture", *Cognition* **28**, Nos. 1-2, pp.3-71.

Frege, G.: 1966, *Translations from the Philosophical Writings of Gottlob Frege*, trans by Peter Geach and Max Black, Blackwell, Oxford.

Freud, S.: 1915/1959, "The Unconscious," in *Collected Papers* **4**, pp. 98-136, Basic Books, New York.

Horgan, T. and Graham, G.: (forthcoming), "In Defense of Southern Fundamentalism," *Philosophical Studies*.

Kaplan, D.: 1969, "Quantifying In," in Davidson and Hintikaa (1968).

Kripke, S.: 1979, "A Puzzle About Belief," in *Meaning and Use*, A. Margalit, (ed.), Reidel, Dordrecht.

Kripke, S.: 1980, *Wittgenstein on Following a Rule*, Harvard University Press, Cambridge.

Lewis, D.: 1970, "How to Define Theoretical Terms," *Journal of Philosophy* **67**, 427-44.

Lycan, W.: 1981, "Form, Function, and Feel," *Journal of Philosophy* **78**, 24-50.

Malcolm, N.: 1968, "The Conceivability of Mechanism," *Philosophical Review*, 45-77.

Meyer, D. and Schvanerveldt, R.: 1971, "Facilitation in Recognizing Pairs of Words: Evidence of a Dependence between Retrieval Operations," *Journal of Experimental Psychology* **90**, 227-234.

Millikan, R.: 1984, *Language, Thought, and Other Biological Categories*, MIT (Bradford), Cambridge.

Morton, J.: 1969, "The Interaction of Information in Word Recognition," *Psychological Review* **76**, 165-178.

Nisbett, R. and Wilson, T.: 1977, "On Saying More than We Can Know," *Psychological Review* **84**(3), 231-259.

Papineau, D.: 1987, *Reality and Representation*, Blackwell, Oxford.

Perry, J.: 1979, "The Problem of the Essential Indexical," *Nous* **13**, 3-21.

Quine, W.V.: 1953, "Two Dogmas of Empiricism," in *From a Logical Point of View and Other Essays*, Harper & Row, New York.

Quine, W.: 1956, "Carnap and Logical Truth," in *Ways of Para-dox and Other Essays*, pp. 107-132 (2nd ed: 1976), Harvard University Press, Cambridge.

Quine, W.: 1960, *Word & Object*, MIT, Cambridge.

Ramsey, W., Stich, S. and Garon, J.: 1990, "Connectionism, Eliminativism and the Future of Folk Psychology," in J. Tomberlin (ed.) *Philosophical Perspectives* **4**, 499-534.

Rey, G.: 1983, "Concepts and Stereotypes," *Cognition* **15**, 237-262.

Rey, G.: 1988a, "A Question About Consciousness," in *Perspectives on Mind*, H. Otto and J. Tuedio, (eds.), Reidel, Dordrecht.

Rey, G.: 1988b, "Towards a Computational Theory of Akrasia and Self-Deception," in B. MacLaughlin and A. Rorty, *Essays in Self-Deception*, University of California Press, Berkeley.

Rey, G.: 1985, "Concepts and Conceptions," *Cognition* **19**, 297-303.

Rey, G.: 1986, "What's Really Going On In Searle's "Chinese Room," *Philosophical Studies* **50**, 169-185.

Rey, G.: 1990a, "Transcending Transcendentalism," *Metaphilosophy*, Sept.

Rey, G.: 1990b, "Constituent Causation and the Reality of Mind," commentary on Searle (1990), *Behavioral and Brain Sciences*.

Rorty, R.: 1965, "Mind-Body Identity, Physicalism, and Categories," *Review of Metaphysics* **XIX**, 1, 24-54.

Rorty, R.: 1979, *Philosophy and the Mirror of Nature*, Princeton University Press, Princeton.

Rosch, E.: 1973, "On the Internal Structure of Perceptual and Semantic Categories," in T.E. Moore, (ed.), *Cognitive Development and Acquisition of Language*, pp. 111-144, Academic Press, New York.

Rosenthal, D. (ed.): 1971, *Materialism and the Mind-Body Problem*, Prentice Hall, Englewood Cliffs (NJ).

Russell, B.: 1904/1938, *Principles of Mathematics*, Norton, New York.

Searle, J.: 1990, "Consciousness, Explanatory Inversion, and Cognitive Science," *Behavioral and Brain Sciences* (forthcoming).

Smith, E. and Medin, D.: 1981, *Categories and Concepts*, Harvard University Press, Cambridge.

Smolensky, P.: 1988, "On the Proper Treatment of Connectionism," *The Behavioral and Brain Sciences* 11, 1-23.

Smolensky, P.: 1990, "The Constituent Structure of Connectionist Mental States: A Reply to Fodor and Pylyshyn," this volume.

Stampe, D.: 1977, "Towards a Causal Theory of Linguistic Representation," *Midwest Studies in Philosophy*, pp. 42-63, University of Minnesota Press, Minneapolis.

Tienson, J.: 1987, "Introduction to Connectionism," *Southern Journal of Philosophy* XXVI (supplement), pp. 1-16.

Tversky, A.: 1977, "Features of Similarity," *Psychological Review* 84 #4, 327-352.

Wason, P.V. and Johnson-Laird, P.: 1972, *Psychology of Reasoning Structure and Content*, Batsford, London.

Wittgenstein, L.: 1921/1961, *Tractatus Logico-Philosophicus*, trans. by D.F. Pears and B.F. McGuinness, Routledge and Kegan Paul, London.

Wittgenstein, L.: 1961, G.H. von Wright and G.E.M. Anscombe (eds.), *Notebooks 1914-1916*, Basil Blackwell, Oxford.

Wittgenstein, L.: 1953, *Philosophical Investigations*, Macmillan, New York.

Wittgenstein, L.: 1956, *Remarks on the Foundations of Mathematics*, Blackwell, Oxford.

Wittgenstein, L.: 1965, *Zettel*, Blackwell, Oxford.

Department of Philosophy
University of Maryland
College Park, MD 20742

TERENCE HORGAN AND JOHN TIENSON*

SETTLING INTO A NEW PARADIGM

There is a Kuhnian crisis in cognitive science. This is one reason for the enormous increase in connectionist research in the last five years. Reflecting on the problems that have provoked the crisis, and the reasons why connectionism is attractive as a response to those problems, has led us to a view of cognition and cognitive processing that we think deserves serious consideration whatever one may think of connectionism. Our main purpose in this paper is to draw attention to this neglected region in the logical space of views about cognition.

To lay our cards on the table, we believe that an adequate model of cognition requires complex representations with syntactic structure--just as standard cognitive science says--and that cognitive processing is sensitive to that structure. But, we believe, cognitive processes are not driven by or describable by exceptionless rules as required by the standard paradigm. Standard cognitive science goes wrong in its *programmable* computer metaphor for the mind. We will attempt to characterize this region of logical space more fully in Section 2. To our knowledge, none of the work done to date in the connectionist framework falls squarely within this region (Section 3). But we believe there is reason to hope that a version of connectionism can occupy this region. In Section 4 we will examine certain plausible but fallacious arguments that might be taken to show that it cannot do so.

1.) We begin by trying to motivate our view in terms of an extended example. Let us think seriously about what is involved in a highly developed cognitive capacity, say, that underlying the skills of a good passer in the game of basketball. Larry Bird and Ervin Johnson come first to mind, but what we have to say applies to dozens of professional, college, and even high school players. Take a concrete example of the exercise of their skills, say, a bounce pass that hits the floor between two running opponents and reaches a running teammate at waist level just in time for him to go in for the dunk.

You might reflect on the complexity of the computation that determined the precise force and direction needed to deliver the ball on a bounce to a moving target from a source moving with a different direction and velocity. But that isn't what we want to talk about.

When he made the pass, the player had a number of options. He could have passed the ball to two or three other players. He could have made a lob instead of a bounce pass. He could have pulled up and taken a jump shot, or continued driving for the basket. But he could not, of course, do just anything. He could not, for example, pick up the ball and walk over to talk to the announcers. And he would not intentionally throw the ball to an opponent. The game situation determined a limited number of possible courses of action, and he chose one of them. Change the situation slightly, and he would have chosen a different one. Skilled players do not make the best decision all the time. But they do make good decisions the vast majority of the time.

A decision like this is made in the light of a certain goal, roughly, in this case, to get the ball in the other team's basket, literally to score a goal. Various things had to be taken into account in coming to this decision: the position of the goal and the player's own position and motion relative to the goal, the position and motion of each of his teammates, and the position and potential activity of five aggressive, mobil obstacles. It is not just their positions at the moment of decision or at the moment of release of the ball that must be taken into account, but the predicted positions at the time the ball arrives at various points, and for some time thereafter. (Will he be in a position to get a good shot off?) So what is taken into account is the future positions of teammates, and the positions and possible responses of opponents.[1]

If you cannot do a fair job of taking into account all these factors at once, you won't be much good at basketball. But good passers routinely take into account much more. They have to know who has good hands to catch the tough pass; they have to have a good idea of the height, strength, speed, quickness, and jumping ability of teammates and opponents; and they have to know the shooting range and ability of each of their teammates.

In addition, the score, time clock, and time left in the game often help determine what pass is made. Good passers also take into account more subtle game (and season) factors: who has the hot hand, who is not having a good game and needs a couple of easy baskets to get going, who has, and who has not, been getting the number of shots he needs to keep him happy, and so forth.

Many, perhaps sometimes all, of these factors go into determining whether to pass and where, and indeed into the decisions of each player, not just the one with the ball, virtually continuously throughout the course of the game.

Since we are in the process of admiring basketball players, let us also take note of how rapidly many of these decisions are made in response to sudden changes in the evolving scene.

Basketball skills nicely illustrate at least one of the two clusters of problems that have produced the crisis in classical cognitive science. The core of this cluster of problems is the need to deal simultaneously with numerous constraints and the resultant threat of computation explosion. There is no definite limit on the factors that may properly influence a decision on a basketball court. Anything having to do with basketball might appropriately be a factor, and it is at least a practical impossibility to list all of these factors.

Often these are soft constraints, that is, constraints that can be violated when the system is functioning properly, a particularly difficult problem for classical cognitive science. Sometimes it is necessary to make the difficult pass to the guy with stone fingers and hope for the best, or to take a desperation shot at the end of the game.[2] We think it is crazy to think that anything like representations and rules can model the system that decides what to do on the basketball court. That is, we believe, no program could model the cognitive system of a basketball player, which deals smoothly with multiple simultaneous, soft constraints. And the problem is not just in the constraint structure. How do you specify in advance the set of options from which the choice must be made? The options are determined by the situation, and in any two situations the options differ in a number of specifiable ways.[3]

Connectionist systems, on the other hand, are by their very nature good at dealing with multiple simultaneous constraints, and with soft and optional constraints. It seems more plausible to us to think of the basketball cognitive system as settling into a decision configuration--an output or near output configuration--on the basis of a goal or goals and several constraints, some determined by the evolving scene, some more long term and hence, internal but changeable. The cognitive processing underlying skillful physical activity has a connectionist feel about it.

But the purpose of the basketball story is not to attack classical cognitive science. The point is that the system that drives decisions on the basketball court is a rich, highly structured representational system, and it is typical in this respect. Any successful development of connectionism, we believe, must incorporate a representational system of this kind. Let us mention just some of this representational complexity. At the heart of it is a representation of an evolving scene. Individual players must be tracked in this evolving scene. This information might be in some sense imagistic. But, remember, it is not just a perceptual representation of the passing show. It always involves a representation of the (potential) short term future(s) for at least a good many of the players on the court, and of the court configuration. So at any particular time there must be representations of distinct individuals, each with spatio/temporal properties and relations extended over a span of time and possibilities.[4]

On the other hand, some of the information that goes into court decisions is of a sort that would normally be thought of as propositional, that is, as having a propositional, sentence-like structure. Some of this information concerns the game as a whole, the score, time on the shot clock, etc. Some of it is about particular players--good shooter, hot hand, bad knee. Some relevant predicates--playing point guard, in foul trouble, shooting well--apply to different players at different times in the game, and to a player at one time in the game, but not at another. We need co-reference and co-predication to encode this information. That is, we need repeatable predicates applied to repeatable subjects. We need syntactic structure.

Furthermore, this propositional information must be related to in the right way to the more imagistic representation of the evolving scene. This cannot be done by mere association of two representational substructures. There are many, relevantly different, ways in which parts of all of this information are related. Smith is near Jones, who he is guarding. That is one relationship. White is not near his teammate Jones, but they are closely related in another way. Many different ways of being related must be distinguished, and mere association--which varies on only one dimension--cannot do that.

In fact, there must, to start with, be a connection of all the players in the game as being in the game. Various people in the total perceptual scene are related in different ways to players in the game, as a group and individually. If you know the center is dating the head cheerleader, center and head cheerleader are related in your mind. That may affect how you play. But it does not make the cheerleader someone you can pass to. That person is related to players, maybe to all of them, but not in the in-the-game way. In thirty odd years of observing basketball, I've only seen a ball passed to a cheerleader once.

Thus, part of what one acquires in becoming a skilled basketball player is a specialized cognitive system, which generates appropriate representations that are different from those of the unskilled in the same circumstances. These representations are interrelated in a variety of ways, and some, at least, are syntactically structured. And in part they are generated anew in response to each situation, not recalled from memory, since court situations repeat themselves only in general ways, not in detail. In this, and other cognitive systems, the situation that determines what is generated includes both perceptual input and propositionally encoded background information.

To this one might object that what the skilled player has acquired is a system that issues, not in representations, but in behavior. The only relevant representations are perceptual, and there is nothing cognitive that has to do specifically with basketball skills. This, we think, is a mistake in at least two ways. First, the system can function without issuing in behavior, and even when not employed in the service of basketball behavior.

We can drive a temporal wedge to distinguish the decision from the action. A sudden injury may prevent the action. But the player knows just what he was going to do. And one can consciously stop an action, in response, for example, to a coach's whistle in practice, and again, know what was coming next.

Also, the same system can issue not in decisions, but in judgments, when the player is watching a game film, or watching from the bench, or retired and doing color commentary. Many players are good at seeing that the wrong decision was made. A few are good at articulating the reasons why the decision was wrong. But none can give exceptionless explanations for that.

Second, and more important, on the court the system acquired by the basketball player does not issue merely in behavior. For players can make novel responses to the same stimuli. Thus, an essential part of the process that leads to a behavioral response is the production of representations, both particularly neat-for-the-purpose perceptual representations and representations of the expected and potential near future. We will mention two kinds of novelty that seem to us to require this.

There is a temptation to think of practicing a physical skill as learning a system of appropriate responses to stimuli. This is at best misleading. No situation on a basketball court is exactly like any other. You have never practiced the situation you are in. But of course, players repeat similar situations in practice. One might suppose that one acquires a system of responses which in effect extrapolates from experienced situations to new situations. It is not clear what this might mean, however, since small changes in the situation can lead to large changes in what is clearly the best response. It is not correct in any event, for players do not always respond to similar situations in similar ways. Players intentionally use different moves in similar situations for tactical reasons. Sometimes they make up a new move on the spot. (As Bill Russell said, "Great offensive players have imagination.") It is hard to see how this could be possible without a representation of the situation to be responded to.

There is, for our purposes, a more important way in which responses can be novel. A skilled basketball player can shave points or throw a game. His response to a given physical stimulus (plus information about game and players) will be subtly different from what it would normally have been. He does not have to practice doing these things.[5] He can do them the first time, without learning anything new. A player can also do such things as adopt a new style, to see how it works or to imitate an upcoming opponent in practice. It is, of course, the same system of skills and abilities that is put to use to produce all these different responses. The basketball player can do these things; we can not. From long experience, what he sees tells him where people are, where they are going, and what they can do. And he knows what he wants to do and acts accordingly. So the basketball player cannot properly be thought of as having a system that merely generates responses to stimuli. It generates representations that can be put to use to produce responses, either typical or atypical, depending on other factors.

Thus a skilled basketball player has a specialized cognitive system which generates percepts and expectations about the short term future, and on this basis, (judgments and) decisions. It does this very quickly, on the basis of several different types of information. Some of our acquaintances talk about "dumb jocks." Most basketball players may not be very good at the sort of thing philosophers do, but their brains are marvelous cognitive engines. We suspect it would be a good deal easier to model the cognitive system of the average professional philosopher.

Basketball skills are not unique in this respect. All sports require interesting, highly developed cognitive systems, and many require the full a mix of features we have found in basketball. Furthermore, all of us have physical skills, such as driving an automobile, that require cognitive systems with these features, though in most of us they are not as efficient or highly developed.

We have expressed two beliefs about such systems. First, they function by some kind of process like settling, with something like best fit and winner take all, and not by rules or programs. And second, the input and output and possibly intermediate states of the settling process include highly and variously structured representations that are interconnected in a variety of ways. That is, it is *connectionist*-like processing that is sensitive to the structure and interconnections of representations. If connectionism or some development of connectionism is to succeed, this is the direction it must take.

We do not mean that connectionists should be trying to model the cognitive systems of basketball players, or even of color commentators. Our purpose thus far has been to point to a certain region of logical space, which embodies a conception of cognition that is significantly different from the standard conception in cognitive science. We maintain that if a new connectionist paradigm is to develop as a viable alternative to standard cognitive science, it must lie in this hitherto unexplored region.

2.) We shall now attempt to characterize this region of logical space more fully by explicitly contrasting it with the standard conception. The traditional paradigm in cognitive science is sometimes dubbed the "rules and representations" paradigm (henceforth, the RR paradigm). As the label suggests, both representations and rules are centrally important.

According to the RR paradigm, representations have complex internal structure. In particular, there are sentence-like representations, which encode propositional information by means of their compositional syntax.[6] Representations are processed in accordance with programmable rules. This implies that the rules have the following five important features.

First, they are *obligatory*, rather than optional. That is, they determine what the cognitive system *shall* do when it is in any particular global representational state, not merely what it may do. (By contrast, the inference rules of formal logic are optional rules.)

Second, the rules are *hard*, rather than soft. That is, they are fully precise, and they are never violated when the system is working properly. (If they are violated, that indicates a malfunction.) Soft descriptive generalizations, on the other hand, either (i) are fully precise but subject to exceptions even when the system is working as it should, or (ii) are inherently vague, perhaps by virtue of containing (implicitly or explicitly) a built in, ineliminable, '*ceteris paribus*' qualifier.

Third, the rules are *representation-level.* That is, the cognitive system's processing of its representations conforms with rules statable over the representations. Often, of course, the rules are also contained in the system as data structures, i.e., as a program, but that is not necessary. Although the processing may also conform with rules statable at one or more lower levels (e.g., at the level of machine language), such lower level rules are not the kind that count.

Fourth, the rules are *formal.* That is, they advert to the structural features of the representations. Thus, the cognitive system is a "syntactic engine," since its processing is driven by the syntactic, (i.e., formal) features of those representations, independent of what their content happens to be. So, to the extent that its processing is sensitive to, or appropriate to, the content of its representations, this is because the formal rules mirror significant relations among entities and properties in the content-domain of the representations.

Fifth, the rules are *tractable.* The rules must be general and systematic enough, and interrelated in such a way that they could constitute a program. Though it is hard to say exactly what this amounts to, the intuitive idea seems clear enough. A mere list of all possible inputs with the resulting output for each, for instance, would not qualify as a set of tractable rules.

Henceforth, unless we say otherwise, when we speak of *rules* we will mean rules with at least the first four of these five features. (Tractability will play but a small role in our discussion.)

If a new paradigm for cognitive science is to emerge as a viable alternative to the RR paradigm, we contend, it must crucially involve structured representations, but it must *not* involve rules in the sense just described. That is, it must include:

(A) Representations with complex internal structure that can be related in various ways that go beyond mere association.

(B) Processing that depends on this structure and these relations.

(C) But (for large and significant areas of cognition) no rules adverting to representational structure or content. (The model is not to contain or *be describable by* such rules.)

We shall use the phrase "representations without rules" (RWR) to describe this alternative picture. More specifically, RWR means representations without obligatory, hard, representation-level rules. Points (A) and (B) are shared in common by both the RR and RWR conceptions. Thus, the crucial novelty in the RWR approach is point (C), which eschews cognitive level rules, both formal and contentful.

Numerous real-life cognitive tasks, including the demands of skilled basketball play, require a cognitive system that satisfies (A) and (B). The crisis in cognitive science, on the other hand, suggests that human cognition also satisfies (C). These two points together give us the RWR conception, (A)-(C).

The view that the crisis in classical RR cognitive science is genuine, and that the classical paradigm cannot solve the recalcitrant problems it faces, has become increasingly common. That this view has the consequence expressed in (C) has not, we believe, been sufficiently appreciated, *viz.*, that models capable of solving these problems will not even be *describable* by cognitive level rules. For if the system underlying, say, basketball skills could be described by such rules, then a classical RR model of the same system could be produced in which these rules (or purely formal isomorphic ones) are explicitly represented as a stored program.[7] Then the problem of modeling cognitive systems underlying complex physical skills would be solvable in the classical paradigm. And if it is, then it seems likely that the other presently recalcitrant problems of cognitive science would be solvable as well. It is an important feature of RWR, therefore, that cognitive processing not be rule describable.

The denial of cognitive rules does not mean cognitive anarchy. As (B) says, processing must be *sensitive* to representational content and structure, a fact that will reveal itself through the existence of many true *ceteris paribus* representation-level generalizations about the cognitive system. Indeed, our belief (strong suspicion at least) is that a fairly extensive range of such soft generalizations must be true of a system in order for attributions of representational content to its inner states to be appropriate at all, and hence in order for theorizing and explanation to be possible at the cognitive level. We also believe that being describable by soft generalizations but not hard rules is characteristic of virtually all of human cognition.

We realize that at this point the reader may wonder *how* there *can be* content sensitive processing, and soft generalizations, without hard rules. In Section 4 we will describe several ways in which this can happen in connectionist systems.

3.) If a new paradigm is to develop out of connectionism, we think that it must lie in the RWR region. However, even if (as we believe) the truth about cognition lies in this region, it does not follow that connectionism can occupy this area. For one thing, one of the defining characteristics of connectionism is that the only *primitive* relation within a system is (causal) association, a relation that can vary along one dimension only (weight). It is not yet clear whether connectionism will allow construction of the rich variety of relations among representations that RWR requires.

Furthermore, certain natural connectionist representations--nodes or sets of nodes--are not sententially structured. Indeed, most current connectionist models employ such unstructured representations. Some models rely on "local coding," where contents (even entire propositional contents) are assigned to individual nodes by the modeler's decree. You do not get structure-sensitive processing out of this sort of representation scheme, since the representations do not even have structure. The content-sensitive processing in these models is evidently entirely associative, or statistical. This sort of analog-style associative/statistical processing may prove very useful for modeling some cognitive or semi-cognitive processes, such as those subserving the transduction of incoming information from the system's sensory periphery. But such models will not scale up into serious models of real life cognition in general.

Many connectionist models employ some form of "coarse coding," with many nodes combining to constitute a representation, and each node contributing to many representations. In addition, such "distributed representations" are often combined with nodes or pools of nodes that have no assigned representational interpretation and which intervene between interpreted nodes. Typically, such coarse coded distributed representations amount to little more than the representation of an entity by a pool of nodes, each of which represents a "micro-feature" of that entity. Thus, the micro-features are locally represented. And the operative role of intervening nodes is typically to record Boolean combinations of local micro-feature representations. So the distributed representations in these models still have very little structure, and the global settling process is still associative processing over locally coded representations of low level features and combinations of features. Hence, these models also do not employ richly structured representations, processed in richly structure-sensitive ways. Accordingly, they will surely not scale up into serious general accounts of complex cognitive processing.

These scale-up problems underscore how large the gap is between current models and any future connectionist paradigm for cognitive science. Now, there is wide agreement that it is possible to use a connectionist network to simulate a Turing machine, hence, to simulate a von Neumann machine, hence to simulate any RR model of cognition.[8] Thus it is possible to construct structured representations within a connectionist network, and indeed, connectionists have given us some models with structurally complex representations. But where they have done so it has been for the purpose of implementing what can be done (more easily) on a von Neumann computer. That is, the structured representations have served as a basis for implementing standard RR framework hard rules.[9]

Connectionist implementation architectures of this sort might well prove interesting at the level of cognitive theory, and not merely at the level of implementation *per se*. For they might lead to new forms of structurally complex representations and/or new kinds of hard rules for the processing of structured representations. But such connectionist inspired innovations *could not* lead to a new paradigm in cognitive science. Insofar as they resort to rule-describable processing of structured representations, they still fall within the classical paradigm.

Thus, very little extant connectionist research seems to us to be on the road to a new paradigm. It has merely implemented processing that falls within the old paradigm, or employed representations that are too simple to scale up to serious models of cognition. It would be a mistake, however, to conclude that connectionism cannot provide a model of cognition of the sort that we think is necessary. We think recent work of Paul Smolensky begins to show how connectionism might be developed to satisfy the RWR conception.[10] Moreover, connectionist models employing relatively simple representational structures have had some success in dealing with features of cognition that are especially problematic under the traditional RR approach. So perhaps these successes can be extended to the RWR region. We think it is worth a try, especially in the milieu of Kuhnian crisis. Thus, we would like to see connectionist research directed toward structure-sensitive, non-rule-driven, non-sequential processing of structurally rich representations.

4.) However, there are certain lines of thought in the air, and perhaps in the literature, which could be construed as arguments to the effect that what we are asking for, connectionist RWR models, is impossible. In this section we will discuss two interrelated such arguments, which we will call the syntactic and semantic arguments. Our discussion will in fact suggest a plausibility argument to the opposite effect, that a suitable version of connectionism can occupy the RWR region.

We suspect that the initial plausibility of these arguments may help explain why the RWR option for connectionism has been so widely overlooked; for these arguments may reflect widely held, though largely tacit, assumptions which tend to prevent a clear perception of the full range of possibilities in logical space.[11]

The syntactic argument goes as follows. It is indisputable that a connectionist network is rule-characterizable at *some* level of description, *viz.*, at the level of the individual nodes, whose computations and interactions conform to precise mathematical algorithms. Call these *node-level* rules (NL rules). And if there are structured representations in a connectionist model, there must be precise rules specifying how both the atomic constituents of these representations and their combinatorial syntax are realized in the system.[12] Call these *representation instantiation* rules (RI rules).

But if there are hard NL rules describing the behavior of the nodes, and hard RI rules determining the representational structure of the system from its node level description, then it would seem that it must *follow* that the system will be describable by hard rules that advert entirely to the compositional structure of the representations. That is, it appears, representation level rules will simply follow from the NL and RI rules. Hence, an RWR version of connectionism is impossible.

This is a plausible sounding aggregation argument. It is also badly fallacious. Suppose you have a simple connectionist network trained up so that if it is given input A alone, it goes into output state C. And if it is given input B alone, it goes into state D. But states C and D are incompatible.[13] This system is then correctly describable by the *ceteris paribus* (CP) generalizations, "If A, then CP, C", and "If B, then CP, D".

What if we now give the system input A and B together? We do not know, of course. We do not have enough information. But the interesting fact is, given only that the input is A + B, the system could be such that there is no determinate fact of the matter about what output state it will settle into. When given input A + B, it might sometimes settle into state C, sometimes into state D, perhaps with equal likelihood. It might sometimes refuse to settle at all (as happens to all of us occasionally). And if it were a bit more sophisticated, it might sometimes find a compromise output (as we frequently must).

Here are a few of the simpler reasons why this can happen.

(1) Suppose, for example, identical networks have been trained up from different small random weights (as is normal), so that both obey the simple generalizations, if A, then CP, C and if B, then CP, D. Having started training from different weights, they will have different final weights.[14] Because of this, it might happen that when given input A + B one settles in C and the other settles in D.

Of course, the *state* of the system (including input) determines output. The point is, many different states of the system are compatible with the same representational description.

(2) Weights can change over time in a network, for example, if weights are allowed to decay on unused connections. Because of this, a system might consistently obey the simple generalizations, but vary over time between going to C and to D when given A + B.

(3) Level of activation of nodes can vary. It might be that the activization of a representation consists in each of its component nodes being active to a certain degree, say, .8. Then A and B both being activated is consistent with a considerable range of possible states of the system. It could be that from some of these states it goes into C, for others it goes into D. So, even at one time, there will be no way of knowing what it will do just from knowing its representational state.

(4) With coarse coding, it is also possible to have different nodes on to activate a particular representation. A representation could correspond to a certain set of nodes, and activation of the representation consist of activation of a sufficient percentage, say 95%, of those nodes. The activating percentage, of course, could be realized by different sets of nodes, which could affect the outcome of processing.

Thus, the same representation level description is consistent with differences in weights, in degree of activation of nodes, and in what nodes are active. All of these factors can affect the (representational) outcome of processing, and of course, all can be involved at once.

But it is important to notice that, although processing is not determined by content, it is sensitive to content. In the simple case we have imagined, you can think of each input representation fighting for its output. No representation level description determines the outcome of the fight.

We have described the simplest case to make the point. However, we think this might well be the way human cognition works in general.[15] Imagine this possibility in a complex representational state containing numerous component representations analogous to states A and B, compounding indeterminacy exponentially. Here you have our connectionist inspired vision of the cognitive situation of a skilled basketball player on the verge of deciding where to pass. Whatever decision the player reaches will be an appropriate and reasonable one, but will not be the product of processing describable by rules. Instead it will be the product of "massively non-serial soft constraint satisfaction," involving a process something like settling.[16]

Put in general terms, the syntactic argument is fallacious because it is characteristic of connectionist representations that they permit multiple realizations in ways that can affect the outcome of processing.[17] The RI rules are what we might call "upward obligatory." Given a node level description of the system, the RI rules determine a representation level description. But in general, connectionist RI rules are not "downward obligatory." Given a representation level description, the RI rules place constraints on permissible node level descriptions, but they may be compatible with many, perhaps even infinitely many, node level descriptions. We have mentioned several different reasons for this. All of them can affect processing in such a way that processing from two different node level realizations of the same total representation level description might lead to node level states that are realizations of different representational states.

We turn now to the semantic argument against the possibility of an RWR version of connectionism. The reasoning runs as follows. In a connectionist network, the only primitive relation among the computational units (the nodes) is causal association, as determined by the inter-node weights. Thus a network's processing is thoroughly associative. Each individual unit updates its activation level on the basis of immediate associative relations consisting of weighted excitatory and inhibitory inputs from the units connected to it (plus perhaps, direct excitatory or inhibitory input from outside the system in the case of input units). So unless a network is being employed as a mere implementation architecture for an RR model, it can only perform associative processing. But, as Fodor and Pylyshyn remark (note 12), association is not a structure sensitive relation. Hence, an RWR version of connectionism, in which representations are processed in a structure sensitive but non-rule-governed way, is impossible.[18]

There is surely *something* wrong with this argument. If it worked at all, it would prove too much, *viz.*, that connectionist networks cannot even serve as implementation architectures for RR models. The observation that a network's processing is thoroughly associative applies to all connectionist systems, including those that are employed to implement rule governed processing of syntactically structured representations. So if a network's being association-driven in this way were really incompatible with structure sensitive processing of complex representations, then connectionist systems could not be used to implement the RR approach. But they can be; hence the semantic argument must be fallacious.

Let us consider why the reasoning would fail in the case of a network employed as an implementation architecture for some RR model. For such a system, there will be two distinct levels at which processing can be described. First is the *representational* level, at which complex representations and their constituents are cited. At this level, the network's processing will be non-associative, since it will be correctly describable by programmable formal rules, the rules of the RR model that is being implemented. Second, at the *subrepresentational* level, the system will be correctly describable as operating entirely associatively. In such a network, processing that is associative at the subrepresentational level is nonetheless decidedly non-associative at the representational level. Non-associative processing is, one might say, an emergent property of the system. Thus, it is a mistake to infer from the fact that a connectionist network is subrepresentationally associative, that it cannot do structure sensitive processing of complex representations.[19]

But of course, the semantic argument purports to show that an RWR version of connectionism is impossible, not that connectionist implementations of RR models are impossible. Nevertheless, the fallacy of the argument has been exposed. It assumes, incorrectly, that higher level non-associative computational properties cannot emerge in an associative network.[20] Hence, the semantic argument does not prove the impossibility of connectionist systems with structure sensitive, but non-rule governed processing. It does not follow, of course, that such an RWR version of connectionism is possible.

Associative relations between nodes are a kind of causal connection. The trick of making a conventional (RR, von Neumann) computer is to get the causal structure of the machine to mirror the syntactic structure of the language in which data is processed. The problem is the same in implementing an RR system in a network. The trick is to get the causal (= associative) structure of the network to mirror the syntactic structure of the language of the RR system. (Of course, the trick is immensely more difficult in a neural network, since that is not what they are good at.) However, the causal connections in a network are themselves soft. The activation level of any given node is normally the result of conspiracy of the causal input from several nodes. No single causal link determines what happens. For this reason, the sort of soft generalizations that we discussed in response to the syntactic argument are to be expected. Thus, it seems reasonable to expect that, since structure sensitive hard rules can be implemented in a connectionist network, it would also be possible to implement structure sensitive processes that could be countermanded by further activity in the network.[21]

We have, then, a simple plausibility argument. We know that connectionist networks can have *content* sensitive processing that obey only *ceteris paribus* generalizations. And we know that we can have structure sensitive processing in connectionist networks. Put these together, and we will have structure sensitive processing that obeys soft generalizations only.[22]

Imagine a cognitive system faced with a problem. The total representational state of the system involves many component representations[23], including representations of the task and pertinent constraints and data. The system evolves until it reaches a stable state that constitutes its decision or solution. Along the way, it generates relevant representations that are part of the process of reaching a solution but are not contained in the solution state itself. Some of these intervening representations may be memories, not because they are dredged up from some place called "memory", but because they, along with their present etiology, satisfy certain prior existence conditions. Others are new to the system.

Often, particular intervening component representations will be traceable to prior component representations in the system. In the context of this system, it will be true that some small set of representations caused the activation of a subsequent representation. But it is not the case that this same set of representations would have had the same outcome in any context. Furthermore, there may be no tractable set of rules that describes the possible sequences of evolution of this system from global representational state to global representational state. Indeed, as we showed in response to the syntactic argument, given only the representational state S of the system, its succeeding representational state may not be determined, since this may depend upon the subrepresentational realization of S. Hence, processing is by and large locally relevant and globally effective. It produces representations that are pertinent to the problem and appropriately related to preceding representations, and it results in representational states that constitute reasonable (though not necessarily correct) solutions to the original problem. But it does not conform to hard rules.

We think many different kinds of human cognitive activity--conscious or unconscious, rapid or deliberate--fit this general pattern. We suspect that this pattern underlies not only physical skills, but also a much wider range of activities, including: normal local navigation, complex recognition and understanding, many kinds of expert problem solving, moral reasoning, practical reasoning, and inductive reasoning. Connectionism just might show us *how* a physical system can embody processing of this kind.

Such processing could conceivably be only part of the story; it might turn out that some but not all structure sensitive processing is describable by hard rules. We think, however, that the available evidence strongly suggests that all human cognition satisfies the RWR conception, that is, structure/content sensitive mental processes without hard rules.[24] We find this an enticing vision of human cognition, with ramifications for our understanding of practical reason, the science of psychology, folk psychology, and much more.[25]

NOTES

* This paper is thoroughly collaborative; order of authorship is alphabetical.

[1]   Let us add that basketball is a continuous activity. It is natural to say, "at any moment" a player must choose among a number of options. But this does not mean you make a decision, move to the next frame ("moment"), update information, and make the next decision. There is a continuously changing scene, hence a continuously updated representation of the scene, its future, and range of choices.

[2]   Much is made of the phenomenon of graceful degradation in the connectionist literature. As limits are approached, performance gradually declines. Natural systems do not perform normally up to a point and then collapse. So too, basketball players' cognitive systems degrade gracefully, although usually they do not gracefully degrade gracefully. When players are overmatched, they often make poor court decisions; they seldom sit down and cry.

[3] The other cluster of problems precipitating the crisis in cognitive science concerns understanding and behavior that depend selectively on the whole vast store of common sense knowledge. This includes the problems of representing common sense knowledge, of recognizing the relevance of bits of it, and of finding the relevant bit, hence, of content addressable memory, and as a special case, the so-called frame problem. This is not irrelevant to the basketball story. Practically anything of interest to human beings might influence a decision on the basketball court. For an easy example, the center is dating the head cheerleader, and the passer is jealous.

[4] Phenomenological evidence that the representations are temporally extended and not just perceptual: sometimes you are surprised because what you expected did not happen. Sometimes you imagine what will happen before it does—or does not. Of course, this does not happen all the time, because it is a truism that successful athletic decision making cannot depend on a conscious process.

[5] This is not to say that one would not improve with practice at this nefarious activity, nor that one's performance would be as smooth as normal.

[6] Some versions of the standard conception also posit structured representations that are image-like rather than sentential. Others construe imagistic representation as a species of sentential representation.

[7] Thus the question of whether rules are explicitly represented (as a stored program), is very much a side issue.

[8] At the Spindel conference, everyone agreed to this, but no one could point to a proof. Our colleagues in the mathematics department at Memphis State University, Stan Franklin and Max Garzon, have recently shown how to simulate a Turing machine in a non-trivial way (cf. Garson, this volume p.7 of type script) in a neural network. "Neural Network Implementation of Turing Machines," forthcoming. The question of what constitutes an acceptable simulation turns out to be quite tricky.

[9] Cf. for example, D. Touretzky and G. Hinton, "Symbols among the Neurons: Details of a Connectionist Inference Architecture, *Proceedings of the Ninth International Conference on Artificial Intelligence*, 1985.

[10] This is not the place to pursue this point, but one thing we have in mind is tensor product representations. See the paper by Michael Tye in this Volume for discussion. Tensor products provide a rich and robust notion of constituent structure on which the constituents are *not* spatial parts. To our knowledge, very little work has been done on *processing* involving tensor product representations. One intriguing possibility is a system that takes input from one system of tensor products and yields a tensor product from another system, under various constraints.

[11] This conceptual blindspot concerning RWR permeates a recent influential critique of connectionism by Jerry A. Fodor and Zenon Pylyshyn, "Connectionism and Cognitive Architecture: A Critical Analysis," *Cognition* 28, 3-71. The bulk of their paper is devoted to arguing the need for language-like mental representations (and structure sensitive processing). (Their arguments, which appeal to attributes of cognition they call "productivity" and "systematicity," are somewhat different from, but complementary to, our arguments in section 1 above.) They appear to take themselves to have proven the need for rules and representations, RR. The only hope they hold out for connectionism with structured representations is "To opt for structured mental *representations* but insist upon an Associationist account of mental *processes*. This...has a problem that we don't believe can be solved: Although mental representations are, on the present assumption, structured objects, *association is not a structure-sensitive relation*. The problem is thus how to reconstruct the semantical coherence of thought without postulating psychological processes that are sensitive to the structure of mental representations...[or] Treat connectionism as an implementation theory."

[12] Actually, once one sees why the syntactic argument fails, it is apparent that this may not be strictly true; vagueness is possible in the RI rules. But it may as well be true for present purposes.

[13] Here is a simple example we use with our underpaid graduate students. If you are offered tickets to the sold out basketball game (A), and nothing else is on for that night, you will go to the game (C). If you are offered a chance to earn some extra money (B), all else equal, you will take it (D). Since the extra work and the game are at the same time, you cannot do both. What do you do?

People are not as simple as the network described in the text. There are many factors that affect the decision: how much money; who you would work with, or go to the game with; who the opponent is; who you least want to offend, and so on without practical limit. But, we submit, in the end it comes to the same thing; there are plenty of situations in which, from as complete a representation level (belief/desire, etc.) description of the situation as you please, it is impossible to determine what decision you will make. (Of course, in the end we will *say* that one desire was stronger, but that is an after the fact description, not determinable before the decision.) This is not cognitive anarchy. You will almost always do something relevant. We suspect this sort of indeterminacy is endemic in human cognition.

[14] Quine says, "Different persons growing up in the same language are like different bushes trimmed and trained to take the shape of identical elephants. The anatomical details of twigs and branches will fulfill the elephantine form differently from bush to bush, but the overall results are alike.", *Word and Object*, p. 8. Differences in connection strengths are a simple way in which different networks can fulfill the elephantine form differently. Networks can fulfill the elephantine form differently in more radical ways; they can differ in internal structure, of nodes, or connections or both, and yet be input/output equivalent on simple, CP cases.

Consider, that when we grow up in our language, it is by and large simple cases on which we are trimmed and trained. The different anatomical details of twigs and branches may yet result in surprising differences in new cases.

[15] It is not hard to imagine neural analogues to the factors we have mentioned.

[16] There is a rather different, and more sophisticated, source of indeterminacy that has an interesting bearing on rapid paced activities like basketball. Various kinds of networks, like Smolensky's harmony theory, handle settling non-algorithmically. They can settle into any of various final activation states which constitute a "local harmony maximum" in multidimensional activation space but not the "global harmony maximum." They are "decent guesses" but not the best or right answer. Which location in activation-space the system settles into will depend largely on just the kinds of subrepresentational details that make the syntactic argument fallacious.

The tendency to settle into a non-optimal location can be diminished, indeed, removed, by introducing gradually diminishing "computational temperature" (roughly, random jogging to kick it out of local maxima) into the processing. But this slows down processing. Settling on a decent solution quickly is often more important than settling on an ideal solution, especially in cognitive tasks like basketball.

[17] This is not true of classical computers, of course. The syntactic argument applies, *mutatis mutandis*, to them.

[18] The appeal of this argument is no doubt enhanced by the fact that familiar non-implementation connectionist models are thoroughly associative at the representational level.

[19] The semantic argument is somewhat analogous to inferring that since at one level of description all operations in a von Neumann computer are numerical operations, it cannot do data processing.

[20] Cf. the emergence of sequential decision making in Paul Smolensky's harmony theory electricity problem solving model, pp. 240-250 of "Information Processing in Dynamical Systems: Foundations of Harmony Theory," Chapter 6 of *Parallel Distributed Processing* Volume 1, Ed. by David E. Rumelhart and James L. McClelland, New York: MIT press, 1986.

[21] And which might be such that from only a representation level description of that further activity, we could not determine whether it would be countermanded.

[22] One of the most striking features of connectionist architecture is that there is no clear distinction between memory and central processing. The only representations literally present in a system at any given time are the active ones. Memories, and all representations, are literally (re-) created on the spot.

Thus, the soft generalizations we envision will describe the *representational dispositions* of the system to construct new representations from currently active ones. For each of a vast range of *representational* states that might occur, the system's subrepresentational structure would dispose it to generate a new total representational state that is highly sensitive to the structure and content of the initial state (but, as we said in response to the syntactic argument, not necessarily determined by the preceding representational state).

In some cases, the basis for these dispositions might be fairly direct, as in simple inductive reasoning, in which associative/statistical relations could be encoded in weights. But in general, we suppose that the relation between the subrepresentational basis and the representational level will be both complex and remote, so that, for example, knowledge will be in weights only of the system as a whole. There will be no single weight, or small set of weights, that encodes any particular item of knowledge.

[23] These components need not be *spatially* distinct; there are useful non-spatial ways of defining *component* connectionistically. See Note 11.

[24] Simple rules of logic are sometimes cited as examples of hard rules in human cognition. But if you believe P and you believe if P, then Q, and you put them together, it does not follow that you will believe Q. You might be unwilling to accept Q, and hence give up P (or the conditional) instead, or simply not know what to believe. Modus ponens is not a rule of mental *processing*.

[25] See our "Representations without Rules," *Philosophical Topics* 17 (1989), 147-174; "Soft Laws," *Midwest Studies in Philosophy* 15 (1990), 256-279; and *Connectionism and the Philosophy of Psychology*, Cambridge, MA: MIT Press, forthcoming.

Department of Philosophy
Memphis State University
Memphis, TN 38152

DAVID KIRSH

PUTTING A PRICE ON COGNITION

INTRODUCTION

In this essay I shall consider a certain methodological claim gaining currency in connectionist quarters: The claim that variables are costly to implement in PDP systems and hence are not likely to be as important in cognitive processing as orthodox theories of cognition assume.

It is widely argued, as a consequence of connectionist accounts, that an adequate theory of human activity must explain how we can act intelligently without much formal reasoning, even at an unconscious level. Formal inference, whether mathematical or purely logical, is something ordinary people do poorly in their heads. To prove theorems, we generally need the help of pencil and paper to keep track of our progress. The same holds for generating proofs in grade school algebra, or in searching a network of possibilities. Humans do not find it easy to recall dozens of freshly generated premises. It is easier to write down intermediate results and then act responsively to those scribblings.

What applies at a conscious level may also apply at an unconscious level due to the nature of the human processor. From a computational viewpoint, an agent places the same demands on memory and processing power whether he reasons consciously or unconsciously. Inference is inference. Whatever makes it difficult for us to reason at a conscious level in a logical manner may also make it difficult for us to reason logically at an unconscious level. In each case, our memory is required to store the values of a large number of variables. If our memories are not appropriately designed for this task, this will be difficult.

According to the classical theory of Artificial Intelligence, (hereafter AI), most intelligent actions presuppose a sizable amount of internal search, which in turn presupposes a sizeable amount of variable binding. Unconscious inference is rampant. For instance, AI dogma holds that rational agents decide what to do next by running through in their heads the consequences of performing chains of actions. They plan. They weigh

261

alternative courses of action, simulating the consequences of selecting one over another, and choose the best.

Variables enter this picture because actions are defined in AI theories in a sufficiently general way to be applied in many situations. Thus an action, such as **MOVE X**, will standardly be defined by a set of pre and postconditions, which state that IF **X** satisfies properties $P_1 , P_2 ...$ such as X *is-liftable*, X *is-graspable*, X *is-freely-movable* THEN **X** will satisfy certain other properties such as X *occupy-newposition*, X *is-freely-movable*... Accordingly, to decide whether it is wise to move a certain book, an AI system will first bind **X** to the particular object in question, say **book-9107**, then determine whether **book-9107** satisfies **MOVE**'s preconditions, then update **book-9107**'s properties and relations in accordance with **MOVE**'s postconditions in order to determine whether the changes in the world as a whole bring the agent closer to its goals.

Variables, and the process of binding variables to specific values are an essential part of the standard AI model of reasoning. Indeed, the standard model does not bind variables every now and then; variables are continually being bound. To return to the planning example, a plan itself is represented in an AI planner as a variable that takes a sequence of actions as a value. As a plan is built up, more actions are added to the sequence. The plan is lengthened, hence the variable **plan** is given new values. But old bindings are not dropped away. In many planning contexts we will have to *backtrack*: we will have to delete members in our action sequence, because we discover that certain sequences lead to a dead end, or paint us into a corner, or cause looping. In those cases, we want to be able to unwind the action sequence, and pick up our simulation of the effects of the plan at an earlier choice point where we believe we first chose unwisely. If actions are not totally reversible, the only way we can pick up our simulation at an earlier point without having to start all over again from world state zero, is if we have stored a trace of the world state at each choice point in our plan.

The upshot is that intelligent action, on the received view, involves reasoning with hundreds, perhaps thousands of variables and names. To cope with this complicated assignment of values to variables, standard computers maintain a large address space where they can keep track of the connections between variables and their values, and between variables and other variables. As changes occur the memory cells assigned to store the current value of a variable change. Similarly, as new connections are made between variables, such as that $K = X$, or that G belongs to the same family as H, additional pointers are introduced to ensure that the relevant inferences about inherited properties etc. can be made.

Now, if it is true that intelligent action requires much unconscious inference, and if it is true that variables are involved in inference, then nature must have found a method of implementing variables neurally. One of the more interesting methodological premises of connectionism is that if certain psychological capacities are expensive to implement in connectionist hardware, then they are expensive to implement in neural hardware, and it is reasonable to suppose that we exercise those psychological capacities far less regularly than assumed in standard computational modes. Accordingly, if we wish to have psychologically realistic models of cognition, we should construct computational models that are less profligate in their use of these 'expensive' capacities. In particular, we should construct computational models of, say, intelligent action, or skillful activity, which do not require much reasoning in a rule governed, or algebraic style. We are advised, that is, to rethink cognitive problems with an eye to finding computational solutions that do not rely on manipulation many explicit variables or names.

If this methodological directive can be made to work, it will be of great import. At present, we conceive of cognitive tasks in algebraic terms, wherever possible. Much of cognition is modelled on problem solving, and our understanding of problem solving is biased by the few explicit algebraic models we have. Who is to say that we are not being narrow minded in our conceptualization of these problems? According to the way we understand cognition now, most higher forms of cognition make essential use of variables, quantifiers, and search control knowledge. Might this not be a bald mistake? Might it not be possible to rethink cognition in a way that does not require those mechanisms?

In what follows I shall make a first pass at appraising this argument. How believable is it? Why couldn't evolution build brains that paid the full cortical price of variables? Do the benefits of having variables as basic psychological capacities outweigh their costs? How should we measure cost? And what exactly is the problem of building PDP networks with variables?

The paper itself is divided in three parts. In the first part, I discuss what a variable is and what powers it confers upon its users. I then consider why standard PDP systems have trouble learning variables and why specially designed PDP systems that support variable binding must pay a high price for that ability. I conclude with a brief discussion of alternative theories of cognition that try to accommodate constraints on variable binding.

What Do Variables Buy Us?

In algebra, variables serve two basic functions: as placeholders for unknowns, and as simplifying descriptions for more complex structures or expressions.

First, as placeholders for unknowns, variables serve to mark a subject that we have yet to identify, as in x is whatever satisfies the following conditions:

$x > 3$
x is odd
$x < 7$

That is, x serves the same function as the impersonal pronoun 'it' in

It transports about 7 people spacebound.
It is covered with heat resistant tiles.
It weighs more than 10 tons.

To decide what *it* refers to, or to determine the value of x, we treat each condition as imposing a constraint on the set of entities that might be possible objects of reference. We then *analyze* the interaction of these conditions to single out the referent that satisfies all the constraints. That is, if a given system of equations determines a unique answer, we can often discover that answer analytically, rather than by plugging in separate values for the equations in order to decide empirically by trial and error what the solution is.

Moreover, once we have variables around, we can often exploit them for higher forms of analysis too. For instance, if we can describe the behavior of a system by a set of n linear equations in n variables, we can determine without calculation that there is a unique answer. Similarly, we can determine whether the behavior of a system is under-determined, and hence indeterminate with respect to our knowledge. The power of analysis should not be underestimated.

Related to analysis, but worth distinguishing, is the power of generalization or abstraction. This is the second major function of variables. It sometimes happens that we know the referent of a variable, or we know a description that uniquely specifies it, but we need a way of referring to that referent compendiously.   In these cases, variables let us simplify descriptions; they let us abstract from complexity.

For instance, to state that when we add two numbers together it does not matter which number we take first (the commutative property of addition), we write down the simple expression $a + b = b + a$.

Variables, here, provide us with a way of *explicitly specifying* constraints or invariant relations that hold over a class of entities. There is no doubt about what the variables refer to: numbers. But variables provide us with the needed mechanism for stating what the generalization is. Without variables to range over all numbers we would have to specify the relation in extension, showing for each number pair that it sums identically whatever its order.

The full power of this descriptive feature of algebra only becomes evident if we consider just how complex the regularities are that we can describe simply. This is the celebrated virtue of notation.

In the case of the set $[(1,1)(2,4)(3,9) ..., (x,x^2)]$ it is easy to notice that $y + x^2$ expresses the invariant relation that holds among the members. As with the commutative property, variables here let us state a general relation compendiously, though it is less clear that we need variables themselves to find the invariant relation in the first place.

But consider recursion. A sequence such as $[1, 2, 6, 24, 120, 720 ...]$ may have no obvious structure to it until we think to compare each member with the member preceding it. Even then, the structure is not transparent, for we must note that if we divide every number by the number preceding it, we get a factor that is equal to n, the position in the sequence. Clearly, the invariant here is much harder to discover. And for a good reason. The position a number has in a sequence is not explicitly represented as an element in the sequence itself. The invariant here is not a relation between members, but a relation between members and their position in the sequence. How can we be expected to notice that?

We need a perspicuous notation. Owing to the creative nature of algebra, we can create whatever notation we need. In this case, a notation using variabilized names, as in R_n and R_{n-1}, where the variable n explicitly designates the position in the sequence and R_n designates the number at that position, nicely exposes both position and number. With this notation we can state the relevant invariance. Without such notation it is extremely hard to describe and recognize such regularities. We cannot keep track of their structure.

It is one of the singular virtues of algebra, then, that it makes it easy to generate increasingly abstract functions, abstract names for relations. This power, too, should not be underestimated.

To distinguish the two powers discussed, let us call the first, *the power of analysis*, and the second, *the power of abstraction*.

In order to be able to achieve these two powers a variable must satisfy at least three conditions:

1. Variables must be logically distinct from their values. Thus tokens of x must be logically distinct from tokens of the value of x. This means we can create tokens of a variable on the fly, erase and duplicate those tokens, (i.e., physically pass them around), while not physically touching or creating tokens of its value.

2. Variables and their values must be semantically connected in the interesting sense that values can be explicitly assigned to variables, as in the statement *Therefore x = 3 and y = 1*; or in the statement *Let x = 5* where x is assigned a value in order to test certain conjectures by substituting 5 for x. In physical systems this semantic relation must be enforced by a process which can *access x's* assigned values and use that value in place of x. Thus, characteristically, x will be physically connected to its values. And x will hold that value stably until some process alters it.

3. Variables, unlike names, must range over a set with more than one element. Thus a variable is something with a suppressed quantifier. This is the feature which allows them to encode generalizations so simply, as in '$a + b = c$', where a, b, and c are all universally quantified; and also to serve as logical subjects of predicates, as in x weighs more than 10 tons, where the logical form displays an implicit existential quantifier: 'There exists an x, such that ....'

Variables behave in a related manner in programming languages. In LISP, for instance, great power is achieved by relying on simple names and variables to refer to the results of performing complex computations. We can call on a variable, or pass it around, without triggering the process that would determine its value. The two entities: variable and value are logically distinct. Thus we can use a variable to refer to the result of performing arbitrarily complex operations. In this way computational objects of increasing complexity can be built up step by step. For once we have a name for a function, we can use it as an argument in a higher order function, and so incrementally increase the complexity of the functions we can define.

For example, we may define (square x) to be the result of multiplying x by itself, as in:

$$(\text{define (square x) (* x x))}$$

Once defined, however, we can use **square** as a building block in defining other procedures. For example, $x^2 + y^2$ can be expressed as:

$$(+ \text{ (square x) (square y))}$$

and we can define a new procedure **sum-of-squares** that, given any two numbers as arguments, produces the sum of their squares:

$$(\text{define (sum-of-squares x y) (+ (square x)(square y)))}$$

And so on.

Moreover, analytic power is exploited in programming languages because the value sought after need not be known. We may wish to introduce a variable to hold the place of the value we are trying to discover. As more is known, constraints are added to the description of x. At some point it may be possible to show that a unique answer exists, or that no answer exists; or it may be possible to simply solve for x.

The power of a variable, then, whether in algebra or in programming, comes from having something *explicit* in a system which can serve as a proxy for a value (or a procedure if the value of the variable is a procedure). Because the two entities, variable and value, are logically distinct we can perform operations on variables without actually performing operations on the values they designate.

We must now consider why it is hard for PDP systems to learn and implement variables.

Systems Which Use Variables Do More Than Just Pass Values

The simplest explanation of why standard PDP systems have trouble learning
and implementing variables is that PDP systems do not have separate tokens
for variables and their values. Hence, unless they are specially designed,
they cannot distinguish variables and values. Input enters a system as
activations on input nodes, it gets transformed by weights and nodal
functions, and finally it emerges as activations on output nodes. The whole
system works simply by modifying and passing activations from input to
output. The system simply propagates values. Hence standard PDP systems
crunch values, not variables.

Now of course at one level of analysis familiar variable manipulating
computers simply work by modifying and passing activations from input to
output as well. All physical systems crunch values. But at another level of
analysis it is essential to the performance of digital computers that they
explicitly represent variables and rules. This difference in explicitness marks
a real difference in possible performance.

To see this difference, imagine that we have an electrical circuit which
obeys the constraints $x + y = 4$ and $2x - y = 5$ without explicitly representing
those constraints. See Figure 1a. This circuit performs as an activity passer.
Input enters the system as activations on certain wires, it gets transformed
at certain modules in accordance with certain functions, and finally it
emerges as activations on output wires. It is immaterial to our general point
that the modules are labelled and that it is easy for us to interpret the
'meaning' of the signals flowing across wires. For whether *we* can interpret
what is happening in the system is irrelevant to whether the system itself is
merely an activity propagator. If at a certain point in its processing the
system passes a signal with the value of 6, we may interpret that signal, in
light of its function in the whole network, to mean something like 'the value
of $2x$ is 6 right now'. But *our* ability to so interpret the signal should not be
confused with that signal being treated by the system as a token of the
variable $2x$. The system has no way of referring to $2x$ in general. It behaves
exactly like a localist connectionist device, passing values around without
having a means of independently labelling those values.

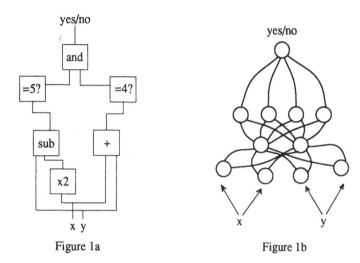

Figure 1a   Figure 1b

Figure 1. A non-connectionist circuit which acts *in accordance* with the rules $x + y = 4$ and $2x - y = 5$. Because wires flow between labelled modules, it is easy to interpret the meanings of the signals that flow through the system. Nonetheless, this system does not have variables represented explicitly. At each point in the process there are only values. There is no logical distinction between a token of a value and a token of a variable. The system is a value propagator rather than a variable manipulator. Figure 1b is a connectionist version that implements the same constraint system. Exactly how the constraints are embedded in the network constraints is more complex.

Such a circuit was designed to behave in a predictable matter. If we put in any values for (x, y) other than $(3,1)$ the system outputs (0). For $(3,1)$, the system outputs (1). What ensures that this system is a value propagator, and nothing more, is that the only way it has of deciding whether a given pair is acceptable--that is, of deciding whether the pair satisfies the constraints--is to have the pair presented as input. It can decide only by trial and error. It cannot determine analytically that $(3,1)$ is the only answer because analysis requires explicit representation of the constraints.

Thus the system acts as a recognizer; it decides only by being presented with input. It can never make any global judgments about possible inputs. For systems that can pass only values of variables can reason only with single values.

By contrast, systems that use variables as entities distinct from their values can achieve the effect of reasoning over sets of values in single transformations, as when x is assumed to refer to the odd integers. There is no way this extra power can be recouped by a system lacking explicit variables. Even if a system used some clever way of coding lists of numbers instead of singletons in order to operate over lists, this clever coding could never encode infinite lists. In any event, the type of circuits that would operate over lists of numbers would be different in design than those designed to act in accordance with the rules $x + y = 4$ and $2x - y = 5$ as defined earlier. The list processing circuit would, in effect, be processing the rules $x + y = 4$ and $2x - y + 5$, where x, y, 4 and 5 refer to lists or matrices of the same cardinality, as in $[x_1, x_2, ..., x_n + y_1, y_2, ..., y_n = 4, 4, ..., 4]$. These are different constraints entirely than the simple $x + y = 4$ and $2x - y = 5$ constraints where x and y refer to single values.

The upshot is that systems that act in accordance with constraints (rules) are not as powerful as systems which explicitly represent the constraints they use. Explicit representation buys analytic power.

The Cost Of Implementing Genuine Variables

Suppose, now, that a connectionist wishes to instill his system with the power to use explicit variables. This means that whatever implements the variable must in principle be able to be bound to any value in the variable's range, and to be usable in more ways than just as the object of a 'retrieve value' call--i.e., to be manipulable. How might this be done?

In ordinary computers, to achieve this flexibility, and to permit the variable to be bound as many times as is needed for reasoning, the standard digital design is to append a binary pointer to the variable to indicate the address of the memory cell containing its current value. If the same variable is multiply instantiated, as when Px is instantiated by Pa, and Pb, and Pc, and all these bindings are held in memory, there is some contextual marker used to distinguish when x is bound to a, b, or c. In both cases, though, each memory cell is free to accept any value, including a pointer to other memory cells, for it often happens that the value bound to one variable is itself a variable which in turn has a value bound to it.

Such a system satisfies the three conditions of genuine variablehood mentioned above. It logically (and physically) separates variable tokens from value tokens; it permits explicit assignment of values; and because of the freedom, in principle, to write any value in a memory cell it treats variables as ranging over many possibilities.

Pointers are an elegant, even if obvious, solution to the variable binding problem. But they have their cost. They work only if a system can read addresses, write values and new addresses in memory cells, and follow the address named in a pointer to the relevant memory location. Connectionist systems do not operate like that. They are not designed to create and exploit pointers on the fly.

How Do Connectionists Bind Variables?

One obvious way connectionists bind variables is shown in Figure 2. Here the fact that A can range over the values 1 to 4 means that we must be able to distinguish A with value 1, from A with value 2, and so on. As A's value changes, its effect on the computation performed by the network must change. Thus A with the value 2 must effect the network as a whole differently than A with the value 3.

To do this, a network is constructed with enough nodes to represent every variable value pair. Thus, if we have n variables and m values, we will have n times m nodes. The greater the number of values each variable can range over, the greater the number of nodes that will be required. This model is a purely localist representation, for each node has a unique representational function in the system. Nodes are dedicated; the same node can never participate in the representation of other variable value pairs.

As Smolensky[1] has pointed out, purely local representations of variable value pairs suffer from three problems:

(1) n times m units are required, most of which are inactive and do no work at any given time;
(2) the number of units and hence the number of possible pairings has a fixed, rigid upper limit;
(3) the fact that different variables may take the same or similar values is not exploited; thus every pairing is distinct, displaying no common structure.

Each of these problems, in effect, emphasizes that a localist representation of pairings is not space efficient.

Smolensky's own solution diverges from the localist answer in using wholly distributed representations. Accordingly, the same units may be used to represent many different variable value pairs. This has the effect of answering his three objections because 1) almost all units will be involved in representing variable value pairs, hence units will rarely be inactive; 2) the number of units will not set a rigid upper limit on possible pairings because a set of units can always be trained to accept another distributed representation defined over it, as long as all representations remain linearly separable; and 3) similar pairings will be represented by similar representations because that is a natural feature of distributed representations.[2]

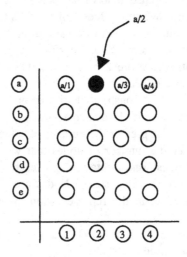

Figure 2. A localist method of binding variables. Neither the variables along the left edge of the matrix, or the values along the bottom, are actually present. Rather the network consists of the central units, which represent variable value pairs. Thus when A has the value 2 the unit in the second column at the top comes on. All the other values for A are inhibited. The system has the capacity to simultaneously represent one value for every variable; for each variable is independent. But it is impossible in this design to assign more than one value to a variable.

Yet this is still not good enough. A tensor product approach also suffers from inefficiency when we consider large value sets. Although we can bind more variables to their values by superposition, we cannot bind more values to a variable without increasing the vector field.

Furthermore, a tensor product approach does not distinguish a token of a variable from a token of a value. This is not an intrinsic limitation, for it is likely that if we added real nodes for the left column and bottom row, the matrix would now have distinct representations of variables and distinct representations of values, but the cost will again be greater nodal size.

Other connectionists, such as, Touretzky and Hinton,[3] Touretzky,[4] have developed elaborately structured models which explicitly represent tokens of variables and tokens of values. These support variable binding, and even some measure of recursion. But, as Pollack has argued[5]

(1) A large amount of human effort was involved in the design of these systems; and
(2) They require expensive and complex access mechanisms, such as pullout networks or clause spaces.

In short, the various elaborate solutions seem both *ad hoc*, and more importantly, inefficient. A high price is paid to be able to bind a small number of variables to a small number of possible values. Once again, as we increase the number of values the variables can be bound to, the size of the network must be expanded by a multiple. This might not be a problem if we never use variables that range over large sets, but *prima facie* that is just false. It is natural and easy to entertain thoughts about arbitrary people we have met, even though that number easily exceeds a thousand. The same applies to numbers, books, houses, friends, countrymen and Romans. *Prima facie*, we often think thoughts whose logical form quantifies over variables with large ranges. There seems no ready way of escaping the fact that a static network has to pay a high price for duplicating the powers of a dynamically reconfigurable network.

Static vs. Reconfigurable Networks

To see what, at bottom, is the real problem of variable binding let us consider in the simplest manner how both dynamically reconfigurable and static networks might bind variables.

To make the problem concrete, let us suppose we are a telephone company hired to build a network which will link salesmen in Building A with possible buyers in Building B. Each salesman wants to be able to talk to each potential buyer. We may think of this association as follows: A_1 wishes to bind with $B_1, B_2, ..., B_m$, A_2 wishes the same thing, and so on up to A_n.[6]

Now, the simplest case is where each salesman has a direct line to each buyer. In Figure 3, we see what this looks like for the retrograde case where there is only one salesman, and then in the complete case where there are A_n salesmen. Networks like 3b are called totally connected. The localist network described earlier formally resembles this case. Perceptron models are also examples of totally connected networks, as are the layers in PDP networks, though characteristically these other systems use non-localist representations.

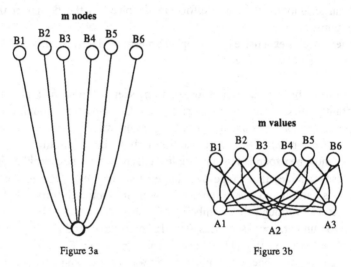

Figure 3a

Figure 3b

Figure 3. In 3a and 3b we see examples of totally connected networks. 3a shows the retrograde case where there is only one node (one variable) connected by dedicated lines to m nodes (values). 3b shows the standard graph, where n variables are connected with m values. As the number of values rises by j the number of connections increases by nj.

A reconfigurable network, by contrast, will be more like a telephone system, where any salesman can reach any buyer by dialing his location. It is a further characteristic of such systems that buyers too can reach any other buyer.

Reconfigurable networks have switches which translate addresses into paths that lead to the physical unit residing at that address. In Figure 4 we see a simple switching network. It takes addresses as input, and locks open the relevant path from origin to address.

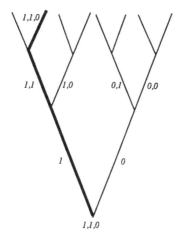

Figure 4. A switching network, such as a telephone system, is designed to open paths to named destinations. In a simple system, each numeral in the destination address corresponds to a position of a switch. As the address courses through the system, local switches mechanically check the relevant digit and respond appropriately. In this figure we can see the system opening the path (1,1,0).

Now, let us consider how the two networks fair on two cases: 1) where x may designate a list of arbitrary length; and 2) where we stipulate that $x \quad x + 1$, as part of an iteration, or a recursive call.

To cope with a *list* of arbitrary length, where x may be$[n_1]$ or$[n_1, n_2]$ or $[n_1, n_2, ..., n_m]$, a static network of the sort just shown must be large enough to have direct lines not only to the n possible values that can occupy every position, but n^m nodes, for each list structure is a distinct possible value.

Put in terms of buyers and sellers, if a certain seller wishes to canvass the opinions of buyer 1, and buyer 2, first separately, then sequentially, where the sequence could matter, he will have to have set up his lines specially for each possibility. He cannot alter the set up once the lines are laid down, so he cannot alter, on the fly, whom he speaks with. If he wishes to speak with buyer 1, the system will be set up so that he speaks to buyer 1 and no one else. If he wishes to speak to several buyers simultaneously, the same network can be rewired to permit that too. But if he wishes to speak to several buyers simultaneously where sequence matters--a type of conference call where he hears from each buyer in predetermined order--the network will have to be extended, for his lines cannot mark order.

By contrast, in reconfigurable networks we can handle sequences and changes in values simply by binding the new values with pointers. Thus, to handle extensions to a list, we can begin by pointing to [1] as the value of x, and then if we discover that x now is [1,2], we cancel the left parenthesis marker and add a pointer to a new memory cell which shows that the value of the second position in the list is 2. Unlike static networks, longer lists do not require larger memory capacities, for we can introduce pointers that pick out existing memory cells, providing they contain the appropriate values. Moreover, we are not obliged to destroy our first entry; we simply add to it by creating pointers as we need it.   So the process is conservative, monotonic. Whereas in static systems if the new values range beyond the set of values the network was designed for, a new network would have to be built by adding more units to the old one and then be retrained. Often the new training is more like training from scratch, for the old learned connections do not carry over.[7]

Smolensky maintains that totally distributed representations allow him to reuse some of the same units over again when representing extensions of a set such as the extension from the set [1] to the set [1,2]. This is accomplished by seeing [1,2] as a superposition of [1] and [2].

This is a significant improvement as far as it goes. But as Smolensky emphasizes, this technique applies only if the two values are linearly separable. That means that a network will have trouble distinguishing the sequence [1,2] from the sequence [2,1] unless it has further nodes to represent position.

However, even with nodes for position the system falls short of a pointer system. Suppose we wish to use the same network to represent $x = [n_{1,2},...n_m]$ and $y = [j_1, j_2,...,j_m]$. It is reasonable to want to make use of large networks to store bindings of more than one variable if they have the same or overlapping ranges. Yet, how can we do this in a static distributed network? The values of y must be superimposed on the network in the same way that [1,--] as a value for x is superimposed on [--,2] as a value for x to yield [1,2] as the composite value for x. But if we superimpose yet another [1,--], this time as a value for y, we will have altered the vector field that is supposed to represent x's value as well. Thus we cannot make use of large networks to store bindings of more than one variable if they have the same or overlapping ranges.

The second task exposes the same difficulty. It is one of the great virtues of a reconfigurable network that portions can be used again and again. Thus, if we have designed a network to perform the procedure $x \rightarrow x + 1$, we can reuse the same network as many times as we like just by resetting the value of x and starting over again. Naturally, the process which makes this possible involves pointers. For on each iteration we must quickly set the new value of x before calling up x's value at the new start of the procedure.

In a static feed-forward network, though, we have to know in advance how many times the procedure in question will be reapplied. We then string out in space as many duplicates of the procedure as will be needed.

To be sure this conversion of iteration to space can be surmounted by having a static network feedback on itself, mediated by a counter which checks that the system does not cycle past a certain value. But this style of network violates the spirit of connectionism. It presupposes that part of the network--the counter--is *insulated* from the other processes--the procedure. A mechanism had to be introduced to let each iteration rapidly set a new value for the variable *number-of-times-iterated-so-far*. Yet this rapid setting of a value is precisely one of the issues that makes variable binding so different in connectionism. Arbitrary iteration then, is another problem for static networks.

Some Consequences

I have been at pains to show that simple connectionist models do not make use of variables in the full and proper sense. More complex models can be constructed which do use variables explicitly, but they pay a high price in size and complexity. If these complex models teach us anything about neural design, it seems to be that nature does not encourage the type of reasoning associated with explicit rules.

This is not a strong argument against rule-governed thought, however. For a sequence of information states may be rule-governed even if there is no rule explicitly represented in a system to structure the process. Such a sequence is correctly called rule-governed, as opposed to rule-obeying, if it supports the appropriate counterfactuals. For instance, if a certain bit of information had not entered the system then the resulting information trajectory would have to change exactly as predicted by the rule set. Similarly, if the process were to be interrupted, or pushed to an extreme, the state of the system at the halt point or at the point of system deviation would make sense with respect to the rule set.

Nor does the argument establish that the adaptive benefits of reasoning do not outweigh the adaptive costs of using up much of our cortex for explicit variable binding. From an evolutionary standpoint, the one time set-up costs involved in building networks able to manipulate variables may have been well worth the price. Only neurophysiologists can tell us whether the brain has a design that accommodates variable binding to a considerable degree.

Nonetheless, I think connectionism justly forces us to reconsider whether there are alternative formulations of the problems the cognitive system solves, formulations that lend themselves to solution without much variable value pairing either explicitly or implicitly.

It is patent that static networks run into trouble as soon as they must represent large numbers of variables or small numbers of variables with large ranges of values. But static networks may be quite adequate in accommodating a reasonable number of variables with small ranges. The trick of rethinking cognition, then, becomes that of finding a way to solve problems with variables that have a restricted value set.

One suggestion[8] is to use indexicals in place of constants. This may allow us to cope with complex situations, by using and reusing a small number of binding slots. The fact that in many situations we do not care whether the object we are dealing with is object-25 or object-26 as long as it 'does the job,' means that we may only have to keep in our minds a small set of variable value pairings.

For example, in setting the table, I am usually indifferent to the token identity of cutlery. I care whether I have laid a fork and knife, but not whether I laid salad-fork-10. This generalization of instances may extend in all directions. Accordingly, on this view the hard part of acquiring a skill is to discover the general properties of the environment that matter in performing the task. These general properties may well be non-standard, and quite unintelligible outside the context of the task. Hence they must be discovered through practice. Once they are learned, however, they have the consequence of simplifying the complexity of the task with respect to the number of variables and values that may be active at any one time.

To take another example, when driving a car, we seldom worry about the token identity of other cars as they approach us. What matters is their relative position, velocity, and so on. It is reasonable to expect a connectionist system to learn the appropriate relations between these n-tuples. And it is reasonable to expect the system to be able to make appropriate responses. Whether these responses are readily codified by a set of rules is irrelevant to the basic issue. For the real problem was to learn which properties of the world partition the task environment in a tractable manner. That is, what properties simplify the task of driving? These may be arbitrarily task specific. Once we have discovered these specialized properties, it may not be necessary to bind them to many different values. Thus, from the vantage point of driving, it may not be important to be able to identify and reidentify objects in any more satisfying way than as 'the-car-now-coming-at-me-from-the-right.'9 At times there may be more than one car filling the description. On those occasions the system will have to be able to bind the predicate to separate entities, separate values. Even under such conditions, though, the number of such bindings can be expected to remain small.

It is an empirical matter how far the indexicalization of our knowledge can be pushed. Some tasks lend themselves to this reduction, others resist it. It is one of the virtues of the connectionist approach that it encourages us to explore this problem.

ACKNOWLEDGEMENTS. I would like to thank Phil Agre, David Chapman and Eric Saund for many hours of helpful discussions.

NOTES

[1] "A Method for Connectionist Variable Binding," Proceedings of the American Association of the Artificial Intelligence, 1987.

[2] *Ibid.*

[3] "Symbols Among the Neurons: Details of Connectionist Inference Architecture," in Proceedings of the Ninth International Joint Conference on Artificial Intelligence, Los Angeles, CA.

[4] "BoltzCONS: Reconciling Connectionism with the Recursive Nature of Stacks and Trees," in Proceedings of the Eighth Annual Conference of the Cognitive Science Society, Amherst, MA, 522-530.

[5] "Recursive Auto-Associative Memory: Devising Compositional Distributed Representations." Computing Research Laboratory, New Mexico State University, Las Cruces, MCCS-88-124.

[6] This does not quite duplicate the binding problem in connectionism because the point of binding in PDP is to turn on nodes which have the right overall effect on the system. This may be achieved without actually representing the variable and its value in distinct nodes, as the localist and Smolensky do. Nonetheless, it seems reasonable to assume that if two nodes are on at the same time their joint effect on a network will be different than their separate effects. If this joint effect does not duplicate the overall effect of a variable value binding, we can introduce more nodes, which are appropriately related to the rest of the network and which co-vary with a variable value pairing.

[7] Although it is an open empirical question just how much new training is required to teach an old network to respond appropriately with its new nodes, it is clear that as more new nodes are added the amount of new training required rises non-linearly.

[8] For an interesting first try at explaining a skill as a controlled response to 'indexical-functional' properties, see P. Agre, and D. Chapman, Pengi: "Implementing a Theory of Activity," in Proceedings of the American Association for Artificial Intelligence, 1987.

[9] Cf. ibid.

Cognitive Science
Room D-015
University of California
La Jolla, CA 92093

PAUL SMOLENSKY

THE CONSTITUENT STRUCTURE OF
CONNECTIONIST MENTAL STATES:
A REPLY TO FODOR AND PYLYSHYN

The primary purpose of this article is to reply to the central point of Fodor and Pylyshyn's (1988) critique of connectionism. The direct reply to their critique comprises Section 2 of this paper. In short, I argue that Fodor and Pylyshyn are simply mistaken in their claim that connectionist mental states lack the necessary constituent structure, and that the basis of this mistake is a failure to appreciate the significance of distributed representations in connectionist models. Section 3 is a broader response to the bottom line of their critique, which is that connectionists should re-orient their work towards *implementation* of the classical symbolic cognitive architecture. I argue instead that connectionist research should develop *new formalizations* of the fundamental computational notions that have been given one particular formal shape in the traditional symbolic paradigm.

My response to Fodor and Pylyshyn's critique presumes a certain meta-theoretical context that is laid out in Section 1. In this first section I argue that any discussion of the choice of some framework for cognitive modeling (e.g., the connectionist framework) must admit that such a choice embodies a response to a fundamental cognitive paradox, and that this response shapes the entire scientific enterprise surrounding research within that framework. Fodor and Pylyshyn are implicitly advocating one class of response to the paradox over another, and I wish to analyze their critique in this light.

1. THE PARADOX AND SEVERAL RESPONSES

In this section, I want to consider the question of what factors go into the decision about what cognitive modeling formalism to adopt, given the choice between the symbolic formalism and the connectionist formalism. I want to argue that the crucial move in deciding this question is to take a stance on the issue that I will refer to as "the Paradox of Cognition," or more simply, "the Paradox."

The Paradox is simple enough to identify. On the one hand, cognition is *hard*: characterized by the rules of logic, by the rules of language. On the other hand, cognition is *soft*: if you write down the rules, it seems that realizing those rules in automatic formal systems (which AI programs are) gives systems that are just not sufficiently fluid, not robust enough in performance, to constitute what we want to call true intelligence. That, quite simply, is the Paradox. In attempting to characterize the laws of cognition, we are pulled in two different directions: when we focus on the rules governing high-level cognitive competence, we are pulled towards structured, symbolic representations and processes; when we focus on the variance and complex detail of real intelligent performance, we are pulled towards statistical, numerical descriptions. The Paradox could be called, somewhat more precisely, The Structure/Statistics Dilemma.[1] The stance one adopts towards the Paradox strongly influences the role that can be played by symbolic and connectionist modeling formalisms. At least five noteworthy stances have been taken on the Paradox, and I will now quickly review them. I will consider each in its purest form; these extreme stances can be viewed as caricatures of the more subtle positions actually taken by cognitive scientists.

The first stance one should always consider when confronted with a paradox is *denial*. In fact, that is probably the most popular choice. The denial option comes in two forms. The first is to *deny the soft*. A more reputable name for this might be *rationalism*. In this response to the Paradox one insists that the essence of intelligence is logic and following rules--everything else is inessential. This can be identified as the motivation behind the notion of ideal competence in linguistics (Chomsky, 1965), where soft behavior and performance variability are regarded as mere noise. The fact that there is tremendous regularity in this noise is to be ignored--at least in the purest version of this stance.

The other denial stance is obviously to *deny the hard*. According to this view, rule following is really characteristic of *novice*, not expert, behavior; the essence of real intelligence is its *evasion* of rule-following (Dreyfus & Dreyfus, 1986). Indeed, some of the strongest advocates of this position are connectionists who claim "there are no rules" in cognition.

If one rejects the denial options, one can go for the opposite extreme, which I will call *the split brain*.[2] On this view, the head contains both a soft machine and hard machine, and they sit right next to each other. This response to the Paradox is embodied in talk about systems that have "connectionist modules" and "rule-based modules" and some sort of communication between them. There is the right, connectionist brain doing soft, squishy processing, and the left, von Neumann brain doing the hard rule-based processing. Rather than "the split brain," this scene of a house divided--right and left working side-by-side despite their profound difference--might better be called by its French name: *cohabitation*.

Advocates of this response presumably feel they are giving both sides of the Paradox equal weight. But does this response really grapple with the full force of the Paradox? In the split brain, there is a *hard line* that surrounds and isolates the softness, and there is no soft line that demarks the hardness. The softness is neatly tucked away in an overall architecture characterized by a hard distinction between hard and soft processing. The full force of the Paradox insists that the soft and hard aspects of cognition are so intimately intertwined that such a hard distinction is not viable. Not to mention the serious problem of getting the two kinds of systems to intimately cooperate when they speak such different languages.

The third approach to the Paradox is *the fuzzy approach* (Gupta, Ragade, & Yager, 1979). Here the basic idea is take a hard machine and coat its parts with softness. One takes a rule-based system for doing medical diagnosis and attaches a number to every rule that says how certain the inference is (Shortliffe, 1976; Zadeh, 1975, 1983); or one takes a set,.and for every member in the set attaches a number which says how much of member of the set it is (Zadeh, 1965). In this response to the Paradox, softness is defined to be degrees of hardness. One takes the ontology of the problem that comes out of the hard approach, and one affixes numbers to all the elements of this ontology rather than reconceptualizing the ontology in a new way that intrinsically reflects the softness of the system.

On such ontological grounds, the fourth approach is starting to get rather more sophisticated. On this view, the cognitive machine is at bottom a hard machine; fundamentally, everything works on rules--but the machine is so complex that it *appears soft* when you look at it on a higher level. *Softness emerges from hardness.* This response to the Paradox is implicit in a comment such as

o.k., maybe my expert system *is* brittle, but that is because it is just a toy system with only 10,000 rules. . .if I had the resources, I would build the *real* system with 10^{10} rules, and it would just be as intelligent as the human expert.

In other words, if there are enough hard rules sloshing around in the system, fluid behavior will be an emergent property.

In terms of levels of description, here is the picture. There is a level of description at which the cognitive system is hard: the lower level. And there is a level of description at which it is soft: the higher level. That is the sense in which this approach is getting more sophisticated: it uses *levels of analysis* to reconcile the hard and soft sides of the Paradox.

The question here is whether this approach will ever work. The effort to liberate systems built of large numbers of hard rules from the brittleness that is intrinsic to such rules has been underway for some time now. Whether the partial successes constitute a basis for optimism or pessimism is clearly a difficult judgment call.

The fifth and final approach I want to consider is the one that I have argued (Smolensky, 1988a) forms the basis of the proper treatment of connectionism. On this view, which I have called the *subsymbolic* approach, the cognitive system is fundamentally a soft machine that is so complex that it sometimes appears hard when viewed at higher levels. As in the previous approach, the Paradox is addressed through two levels of analysis--but now it is the lower level that is soft and the upper level that is hard: now *hardness emerges from softness*.

Having reviewed these five responses to the Paradox, we can now see why the decision of whether to adopt a symbolic computational formalism or a connectionist one is rooted in a stance on the Paradox. The issue is whether to assume a formalism that *gives for free* the characteristics of the hard side of the Paradox, or one that gives for free the characteristics of the soft side. If you decide not to go for combining both formalisms (*cohabitation*), but to take one as fundamental, then whichever way you go, you have got to either *ignore* the other side, or *build it* in the formalism you have chosen.

So what are the possible motivations for taking the soft side as the fundamental substrate on which to build the hard--whatever hard aspects of cognition need to be built? Here are some reasons for giving the soft side priority in that sense.

*   A fundamentally soft approach is appealing if you view *perception*, rather than *logical inference*, as the underpinning of intelligence. In

the subsymbolic approach, the fundamental basis of cognition is viewed as categorization and other perceptual processes of that sort.

* In overall cognitive performance, hardness seems more the exception than the rule. That cuts both ways, of course. The denial option is always open to say it is only the 3% that is not soft that really characterizes intelligence, and that is what we should worry about.

* An evolutionary argument says that the hard side of the cognitive paradox evolved later, on top of the soft side, and that your theoretical ontogeny should recapitulate phylogeny.

* Compared to the symbolic rule-based approaches, it is much easier to see how the kind of soft systems that connectionist models represent could be implemented in the nervous system.

* If you are going to base your whole solution to the Paradox on the emergence of one kind of computation from the other, then it becomes crucially important to be able to analyze the higher level properties of the lower level system. That the mathematics governing connectionist networks can be analyzed for emergent properties seems a considerably better bet than extremely complex rule-based systems being analyzable for their emergent properties. The enterprise of analyzing the emergent properties of connectionist systems is rather closely related to traditional kinds of analysis of dynamical systems in physics; it has already shown signs that it may ultimately be as successful.

* Finally, the hard side has had priority for several decades now with disappointing results. It is time to give the soft side a few decades to produce disappointing results of its own.

The choice of adopting a fundamentally soft approach and building a hard level on top of that has serious costs--as pointed out in some detail by Kirsh in his paper in this volume. The power of symbols and symbolic computation is not given to you for free; you have to construct them out of soft stuff, and this is really very difficult. At this point, we do not know how to pull it off. As Kirsh points out, if you do not have symbols in the usual sense, it is not clear that you can cope with a number of problems. Fodor and Pylyshyn's critique is basically a statement of the same general sort: that the price one has to pay for going connectionist is the failure to account for certain regularities of the hard side, regularities that the symbolic formalism gives you essentially for free.

If the force of such critiques is taken to be that connectionism does not *yet* come close enough to providing the capabilities of symbolic computation to do justice to the hard side of the Paradox, then I personally think that they are quite correct. Adopting the subsymbolic stance on the Paradox amounts to taking out an enormous loan--a loan that has barely begun to be paid off.

If, on the other hand, the force of such critiques is taken to be that connectionism can *never* come close enough to providing the capabilities of symbolic computation without merely implementing the symbolic approach, then, as I will argue in the remainder of this article, I believe such critiques must be rejected.

Where are the benefits of going with the subsymbolic approach to the Paradox? Why is this large loan worth taking out? In my view, the principal justification is that if we succeed in building symbols and symbol manipulation out of "connectoplasm" then we will have an explanation of *where symbols and symbol manipulation come from*--and that is worth the risk and the effort; very much so. With any luck we will even have an explanation how the *brain* builds symbolic computation. But even if we do not get that directly, it will be the first theory of how to get symbols out of anything that remotely resembles the brain--and that certainly will be helpful (indeed, I would argue, crucial) in figuring out how the brain actually does it.

Another potential payback is a way of explaining *why* those aspects of cognition that exhibit hardness should exhibit hardness: why the area of hardness falls where it does; why it is limited as it is; why the symbolic approach succeeds where it succeeds and fails where it fails.

Finally, of course, if the subsymbolic approach succeeds, we will have a truly unified solution to the Paradox: no denial of one half of the problem, and no profoundly split brain.

We can already see contributions leading towards these ultimate results. The connectionist approach is producing new concepts and techniques for capturing the regularities in cognitive performance both at the lower level where the connectionist framework naturally applies and at the higher level where the symbolic accounts are important. (For recent surveys, see McClelland, Rumelhart, & the PDP Research Group, 1986; Rumelhart, McClelland, & the PDP Research Group, 1986; Smolensky, forthcoming). The theoretical repertoire of cognitive and computer science are being enriched by new conceptions of how computation can be done.

As far as where we actually stand on achieving the ultimate goals, in my opinion, what we have are interesting techniques and promising suggestions. Our current position in the intellectual history of connectionist computation, in my view, can be expressed by this analogy:

$$\frac{\text{current understanding of connectionist computation}}{\text{current understanding of symbolic computation}} \quad \frac{\text{Aristotle}}{\text{Turing}}$$

We are somewhere approximating Aristotle's position in the intellectual development of this new computational approach. If there are any connectionist enthusiasts who think that we can really model cognition from such a position, they are, I fear, sadly mistaken. And if we cannot get from Aristotle to (at least) Turing in our understanding of subsymbolic computation, we are not going to get much closer to real cognition than we are now.

One final comment before proceeding to Fodor and Pylyshyn's critique. The account given here relating the choice of a connectionist framework to the hard/soft paradox sheds some light on the question, often asked by observers of the sociology of connectionism: "Why does the connectionist fan club include such a strange assortment of people?" At least in the polite reading of this question, "strange assortment" refers to a philosophically quite heterogenous group of cognitive scientists whose views have little more in common than a rejection of the mainstream symbolic paradigm. My answer to this question is that the priority of the hard has made a lot of people very unhappy for a long time. The failure of mainstream formal accounts of cognitive processes to do justice to the soft side of the paradox has made people from a lot of different perspectives feel alienated from the endeavor. By assigning to the soft the position of priority, by making it the basis of the formalism, connectionism has given a lot of people who have not had a formal leg to stand on a formal leg to stand on. And they *should* be happy about that.

At this point, "connectionism" refers more to a formalism than a theory. So it is not appropriate to paraphrase the question of the previous paragraph as "What kind of theory would have as it adherents such a disparate group of people?" It is not really a question of a *theory* at all--it is really a question of what kind of *formalism* allows people with different theories to say what they need to say.

Having made my case that understanding the choice of a connectionist
formalism involves considering alternative stances towards the Paradox of
Cognition, I now proceed to consider Fodor and Pylyshyn's critique in this
light.

2. FODOR AND PYLYSHYN ON THE CONSTITUENT
STRUCTURE OF MENTAL STATES

Here is a quick summary of the central argument of Fodor and Pylyshyn
(1988).

(1) Thoughts have composite structure.

By this they mean things like: the thought that *John loves the girl* is not
atomic; it is a composite mental state built out of thoughts about *John, loves,*
and *the girl*.

(2) Mental processes are sensitive to this composite structure.

For example, from any thought of the form p & q--regardless of what p and
q are--we can deduce p.
  Fodor and Pylyshyn elevate (1) and (2) to the status of defining the
Classical View of Cognition, and they want to say that this is what is being
challenged by the connectionists. I will later argue that they are wrong, but
now we continue with their argument.
  Having identified claims (1) and (2) as definitive of the Classical View,
Fodor and Pylyshyn go on to argue that there are compelling arguments for
these claims. [They admit up front that these arguments are a rerun
updated for the 80's, a colorized version of a film that was shown in black
and white some time ago--with the word "behaviorism" replaced throughout
by "connectionism."] Mental states have, according to these arguments, the
properties of productivity, systematicity, compositionality, and inferential
coherence. Without going into all these arguments, let me simply state that
for present purposes I am willing to accept that they are convincing enough
to justify the conclusion that (1) and (2) must be taken quite seriously.
Whatever the inclinations of other connectionists, these and related
arguments convince me that denying the hard is a mistake. They do not

convince me that I should deny the soft--nor, presumably, are they intended to.

Now for Fodor and Pylyshyn's analysis of connectionism. They assert that in (standard) connectionism, *all representations are atomic*; mental states have no composite structure, violating (1). Furthermore, they assert, (standard) *connectionist processing is association* which is sensitive only to *statistics*, not to *structure*--in violation of (2). Therefore, they conclude, (standard) connectionism is maximally non-Classical; it violates both the defining principles. Therefore connectionism is defeated by the compelling arguments in favor of the Classical View.

What makes Fodor and Pylyshyn say that connectionist representations are atomic? The second figure of their paper (p. 16) says it all--it is rendered here as Figure 1. This network is supposed to illustrate the standard connectionist account of the inference from *A & B* to *A* and to *B*. It is true that Ballard and Hayes wrote a paper (Ballard & Hayes, 1984) about using connectionist networks to do resolution theorem proving in which networks like this appear. However, it is a serious mistake to view this as a paradigmatic connectionist account for anything like human inferences of this sort. This kind of *ultra-local* connectionist representation, in which entire propositions are represented by individual nodes, is far from typical of connectionist models, and certainly not to be taken as *definitive* of the connectionist approach.

Figure 1: Fodor & Pylyshyn's network

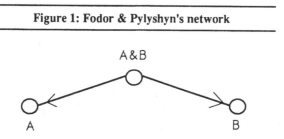

My central counter-argument to Fodor and Pylyshyn starts with the claim that any critique of the connectionist approach must consider the consequences of using *distributed representations*, in which the representations of high level conceptual entities such as propositions are distributed over many nodes, and the same nodes simultaneously participate in the representation of many entities. Their response, in Section 2.1.3 (p. 19), is as follows. The distributed/local representation issue concerns (they assume) whether each of the nodes in Figure 1 refers to something complicated and lower level (the distributed case) or not (the local case). But, they claim, this issue is irrelevant, because it pertains to a *between level* issue, and the compositionality of mental states is a *within level* issue.

My response is that they are correct that compositionality is a within level issue, and correct that the distributed/local distinction is a between level issue. Their argument presumes that because of this difference, one issue cannot influence the other. But this is a fallacy. It assumes that the between-level relation in distributed representations cannot have any consequences on the *within level* structure of the relationships between the representations of *A & B* and the representation of *A*. And that is simply false. There are implications of distributed representations for compositionality, which I am going to bring out in the rest of this section through an extended example. In particular it will turn out that Figure 1 is no more relevant to a distributed connectionist account of inference than it is to a symbolic account. In the hyper-local case, Figure 1 is relevant and their critique stands; in the distributed case, Figure 1 is a bogus characterization of the connectionist account and their critique completely misses its target. It will further turn out that a valid analysis of the actual distributed case, based on suggestions of Pylyshyn himself, leads to quite the opposite conclusion: connectionist models using distributed representations describe mental states with a relevant kind of (within level) constituent structure.

Before developing this counter-argument, let me summarize the bottom line of the Fodor and Pylyshyn paper. Since they believe *standard* connectionism to be fatally flawed, they advocate that connectionists pursue instead a *nonstandard* connectionism. Connectionists should embrace principles (1) & (2); they should accept the classical view and should design their nets to be implementations of classical architectures. The logic implicit here is that connectionist models that respect (1) and (2) must necessarily be implementations of a classical architecture; this is their second major fallacy, which I will return to in Section 3. Fodor and Pylyshyn claim that connectionism should be used to implement classical architectures, and that having done this, connectionism will provide not a new cognitive architecture but an implementation for the old cognitive architecture--that what connectionism can provide therefore is not a new paradigm for cognitive science but rather some new information about "implementation science" or possibly, neuroscience.

If connectionists were to follow the implementation strategy that Fodor and Pylyshyn advocate, I do believe these consequences concerning cognitive architecture *would* indeed follow. But I do not believe that it follows from accepting (1) and (2) that connectionist networks must be implementations. In Section 3, I argue that connectionists can consistently accept (1) and (2) while rejecting the implementationalist approach Fodor and Pylyshyn advocate.

For now, the goal is to show that connectionist models using *distributed* representations ascribe to mental states the kind of compositional structure demanded by (1), contrary to Fodor and Pylyshyn's conclusion based on the network of Figure 1 embodying a hyper-local representation.

Figure 2: Representation of *cup with coffee*

Units	Microfeatures
●	upright container
●	hot liquid
○	glass contacting wood
●	porcelain curved surface
●	burnt odor
●	brown liquid contacting porcelain
●	porcelain curved surface
○	oblong silver object
●	finger-sized handle
●	brown liquid with curved sides and bottom

My argument consists primarily in carrying out an analysis that was suggested by Zenon Pylyshyn himself at the 1984 Cognitive Science Meeting in Boulder. A sort of debate about connectionism was held between Geoffrey Hinton and David Rumelhart on the one hand, and Zenon Pylyshyn and Kurt VanLehn on the other. While pursuing the nature of connectionist representations, Pylyshyn asked Rumelhart: "Look, can you guys represent a copy of coffee in these networks?" Rumelhart's reply was "Sure" so Pylyshyn continued: "And can you represent a cup without coffee in it?" Waiting for the trap to close, Rumelhart said "Yes" at which point Pylyshyn pounced: "Ah-hah, well, the difference between the two is just the representation of *coffee* and you have just built a representation of *cup with coffee* by combining a representation of *cup* and with a representation of *coffee*."

So, let's carry out exactly the construction suggested by Pylyshyn, and see what conclusion it leads us to. We will take a *distributed* representation of *cup with coffee* and subtract from it a distributed representation of *cup without coffee* and we will call what is left "the connectionist representation of *coffee*."

To generate these distributed representations I will use a set of "microfeatures" (Hinton, McClelland, & Rumelhart, 1986) that are not very micro--but that is always what happens when you try to create examples that can be intuitively understood in a nontechnical exposition. These microfeatures are shown in Figure 2.

Figure 2 shows a distributed representation of *cup with coffee*: a pattern of activity in which those units that are active (black) are those that correspond to microfeatures present in the description of a cup containing coffee. Obviously, this is a crude, nearly sensory-level representation, but again that helps make the example more intuitive--it is not essential.

Given the representation of *cup with coffee* displayed in Figure 2, Pylyshyn suggests we subtract the representation of *cup without coffee*. The representation of *cup without coffee* is shown in Figure 3, and Figure 4 shows the result of subtracting it from the representation of *cup with coffee*.

Figure 3: Representation of *cup without coffee*

Units	Microfeatures
●	upright container
○	hot liquid
○	glass contacting wood
●	porcelain curved surface
○	burnt odor
○	brown liquid contacting porcelain
●	porcelain curved surface
○	oblong silver object
●	finger-sized handle
○	brown liquid with curved sides and bottom

Figure 4: Representation of *coffee*	
Units	**Microfeatures**
○	upright container
●	hot liquid
○	glass contacting wood
○	porcelain curved surface
●	burnt odor
●	brown liquid contacting porcelain
○	porcelain curved surface
○	oblong silver object
○	finger-sized handle
●	brown liquid with curved sides and bottom

So what does this procedure produce as "the connectionist representation of *coffee?*" Reading off from Figure 4, we have a burnt odor and hot brown liquid with curved sides and bottom surfaces contacting porcelain. This is indeed a representation of *coffee*, but in a very particular context: the context provided by *cup*.

What does this mean for Pylyshyn's conclusion that "the connectionist representation of *cup with coffee* is just the representation of *cup without coffee* combined with the representation of *coffee?*" What is involved in combining the representations of Figures 3 and 4 back together to form Figure 2? We assemble the representation of *cup with coffee* from a representation of a *cup*, and a representation of *coffee*, but it is a rather strange combination. It has also got a representation of the *interaction* of the cup with coffee--like *brown liquid contacting porcelain*. Thus the composite representation is built from a representation of *cup* together with a representation of *coffee extracted* from the situation *cup with coffee*, together with their interaction.

So the compositional structure is there, but it is there in an *approximate* sense. It is *not* equivalent to taking a context-independent representation of *coffee* and a context-independent representation of *cup*--and certainly not equivalent to taking a context-independent representation of the relationship *in* or *with*--and sticking them all together in a symbolic structure, concatenating them together to form the kinds of syntactic compositional structures that Fodor and Pylyshyn think connectionist nets should implement.

To draw this point out further, let's consider the representation of *coffee* once the cup has been subtracted off. This, suggests Pylyshyn, is the connectionist representation of *coffee*. But as we have already observed, this is really a representation of *coffee* in the particular context of being inside a cup. According to Pylyshyn's formula, to get the connectionist representation of *coffee* it should have been in principle possible to take the connectionist representation of *can with coffee* and subtract from it the connectionist representation of *can without coffee*. What would happen if we actually did this? We would get a representation of ground brown burnt smelling granules stacked in a cylindrical shape, together with granules contacting tin. This is the connectionist representation of *coffee* we get by starting with *can with coffee* instead of *cup with coffee*. Or we could start with the representation of *tree with coffee* and subtract off *tree without coffee*. We would get a connectionist representation for *coffee* which would be a representation of brown beans in a funny shape hanging suspended in mid air. Or again we could start with *man with coffee* and get still another connectionist representation of *coffee*: one quite similar to the entire representation of *cup with coffee* from which we extracted our first representation of *coffee*.

The point is that the representation of *coffee* that we get out of the construction starting with *cup with coffee* leads to a different representation of *coffee* than we get out of constructions that have equivalent status a priori. That means if you want to talk about the connectionist representation of *coffee* in this distributed scheme, you have to talk about a *family of distributed activity patterns*. What knits together all these particular representations of *coffee* is nothing other than a *family resemblance*.

The first moral I want to draw out of this *coffee* story is this: unlike the hyper-local case of Figure 1, with distributed representations, complex representations *are* composed of representations of constituents. The constituency relation here is a *within level* relation, as Fodor and Pylyshyn require: the pattern or *vector* representing *cup with coffee* is composed of a *vector* that can be identified as a distributed representation of *cup without coffee* together with a *vector* that can be identified as a particular distributed representation of *coffee*. In characterizing the constituent vectors of the vector representing the composite, we are *not* concerned with the fact that the vector representing *cup with coffee* is a vector comprised of the activity of individual microfeature units. The *between level* relation between the vector and its individual numerical elements is *not* the constituency relation, and so Section 2.1.4 (pp. 19-28) of Fodor & Pylyshyn (1988) is irrelevant--there they address a mistake that is not being made.

The second moral is that the constituency relation among distributed representations is one that is important for the analysis of connectionist models, and for explaining their behavior, but it is *not* a part of the causal mechanism within the model. In order to process the vector representing *cup with coffee*, the network does not have to decompose it into constituents. For processing, it is the *between level* relation, not the within level relation, that matters. The processing of the vector representing *cup with coffee* is determined by the individual numerical activities that make up the vector: it is over these lower-level activities that the processes are defined. Thus the fact that there is considerable arbitrariness in the way the constituents of *cup with coffee* are defined introduces no ambiguities in the way the network processes that representation--the ambiguities exist only for us who analyze the model and try to explain its behavior. Any particular definition of constituency that gives us explanatory leverage is a valid definition of constituency; lack of uniqueness is not a problem.

This leads directly to the third moral, that the decomposition of composite states into their constituents is not precise and uniquely defined. The notion of constituency is important but attempts to formalize it are likely to crucially involve *approximation*. As discussed at some length in Smolensky (1988a), this is the typical case: notions from symbolic computation provide important tools for constructing higher-level accounts of the behavior of connectionist models using distributed representation--but these notions provide approximate, not precise, accounts.

Which leads to the fourth moral, that while connectionist networks using distributed representations *do* describe mental states with the type of constituency required by (1), they do *not* provide a literal implementation of a syntactic language of thought. The context dependency of the constituents, the interactions that must be accommodated when they are combined, the inability to uniquely, precisely identify constituents, the need to take seriously the notion that the representation of *coffee* is a collection of vectors knit together by family resemblance--all these entail that the relation between connectionist constituency and syntactic constituency is *not* one of literal implementation. In particular, it would be absurd to claim that even if the connectionist story is correct then that would have no implications for the cognitive architecture, that it would merely fill in lower level details without important implications for the higher level account.

These conclusions all address (1) without explicitly addressing (2). Addressing (2) properly is far beyond the scope of this paper. To a considerable extent, it is beyond the scope of current connectionism. Let me simply point out that the Structure/Statistics Dilemma has an attractive possible solution that the connectionist approach is perfectly situated to pursue: *the mind is a statistics-sensitive engine operating on structure-sensitive numerical representations*. The previous arguments have shown that distributed representations do possess constituency relations, and that, properly analyzed, these representations can be seen to encode structure. Extending this to grapple with the full complexity of the kinds of rich structures implicated in complex cognitive processes is a research problem that has been attacked with some success but which remains to be definitively concluded (see Smolensky, 1987, and Section 3 below). Once we have complex structured information represented in distributed numerical patterns, statistics-sensitive processes can proceed to analyze the statistical regularities in a fully structure-sensitive way. Whether such processes can cope with the full force of the Structure/Statistics Dilemma is apt to remain an open question for some time yet.

The conclusion, then, is that distributed models *can* satisfy both (1) and (2). Whether (1) and (2) can be satisfied to the point of providing an account adequate to cover the *full demands of cognitive modeling* is of course an open empirical question--just as it is for the symbolic approach to satisfying (1) and (2). Just the same, distributed connectionist models do *not* amount to an implementation of the symbolic instantiations of (1) and (2) that Fodor and Pylyshyn are committed to.

Before summing up, I would like to return to Figure 1. In what sense can Figure 1 be said to describe the relation between the distributed representation of *A & B* and the distributed representations of *A* and *B*? It was the intent of the *coffee* example to show that the distributed representations of the constituents are, in an approximate but explanation-relevant sense, part of the representation of the composite. Thus, in the distributed case, the relation between the node of Figure 1 labelled *A & B* and the others is a sort of whole/part relation. An inference mechanism that takes as input the vector representing *A & B* and produces as output the vector representing *A* is a mechanism that extracts a part from a whole. And in this sense it is no different from a symbolic inference mechanism that takes the syntactic structure **A & B** and extracts from it the syntactic constituent **A**. The connectionist mechanisms for doing this are of course quite different than the symbolic mechanisms, and the approximate nature of the whole/part relation gives the connectionist computation different overall characteristics: we do not have simply a new implementation of the old computation.

It is clear that, just as Figure 1 offers a crude summary of the symbolic process of passing from **A & B** to **A**, a summary that uses the labels to encode hidden internal structures within the nodes, *exactly the same is true of the distributed connectionist case*. In the distributed case, just as in the symbolic case, the links in Figure 1 are crude summaries of complex processes and not simple-minded causal channels that pass activity from the top node to the lower nodes. Such a causal story applies only to the hyper-local connectionist case, which here serves as the proverbial straw man.

Let me be clear: there is no distributed connectionist model, as far as I know, of the kind of formal inference Fodor and Pylyshyn have in mind here. Such formal inference is located at the far extreme of the hard side of the Paradox, and is not at this point a cognitive process (or abstraction thereof) that the connectionist formalism can be said to have built upon its soft substrate. But at root the Fodor and Pylyshyn critique revolves around the constituent structure of mental states--formal inference is just one setting in which to see the importance of that constituent structure. So the preceding discussion of the constituent structure of distributed representations does address the heart of their critique, even if a well-developed connectionist account of formal inference remains unavailable.

So, let's summarize the overall picture at this point. We have got principles (1) and (2), and we have got a symbolic instantiation of these in a language of thought using syntactic constituency. According to Fodor and Pylyshyn, what connectionists should do is take that symbolic language of thought as a higher level description and then produce a connectionist implementation in a literal sense. The syntactic operations of the symbolic language of thought then provide an exact formal higher level account.

By contrast, I argue that the distributed view of connectionist compositionality allows us to instantiate the same basic principles of (1) and (2) *without* going through a symbolic language of thought. By going straight to distributed connectionist models we get *new instantiations of compositionality principles*.

I happen to believe that the symbolic descriptions *do* provide useful approximate higher level accounts of how these connectionist models compute--but in no sense do these distributed connectionist models provide a literal implementation of a symbolic language of thought. The approximations require a willingness to accept context sensitive symbols and interactional components present in compositional structures, and the other funny business that came out in the *coffee* example. If you are willing to live with all those degrees of approximation then you can usefully view these symbolic level descriptions as approximate higher level accounts of the processing in a connectionist network.

The overall conclusion, then, is that *the classical and connectionist approaches differ not in whether they accept principles (1) and (2), but in how they formally instantiate them*. To confront the real classical/connectionist dispute, one has to be willing to descend to the level of the particular formal instantiations they give to these nonformal principles. To fail to descend to this level of detail is to miss the issue. In the classical approach, principles (1) and (2) are formalized using syntactic structures for thoughts and symbol manipulation for mental processes. In the connectionist view (1) and (2) are formalized using distributed vectorial representations for mental states, and the corresponding notion of compositionality, together with association-based mental processes that derive their structure sensitivity from the structure sensitivity of the vectorial representations engaging in those processes.

In terms of research methodology, this means that the agenda for connectionism should not be to develop a connectionist implementation of the symbolic language of thought but rather to develop formal analysis of vectorial representations of complex structures and operations on those structures that are sufficiently structure-sensitive to do the required work.

In summary: distributed representations provide a description of mental states with semantically interpretable constituents, but there is no precise formal account of the construction of composites from context-independent semantically interpretable constituents. On this account, there *is* a language of thought--but only approximately; the language of thought does not provide a basis for an exact formal account of mental structure or processes--it cannot provide a precise formal account of the cognitive architecture.[3]

3. CONNECTIONISM AND IMPLEMENTATION

In Section 2 I argued that connectionist research should be directed toward structure-sensitive representations and processes but not toward the implementation of a symbolic language of thought. In this section I want to consider this middle ground between implementing symbolic computation and ignoring structure. Many critics of connectionism do not seem to understand that this middle ground exists. (For further discussion of this point, and a map that explicitly locates this middle ground, see Smolensky, 1988b.)

A rather specific conclusion of Section 2 was that connectionists need to develop the analysis of distributed (vectorial) representations of composite structures and the kinds of processes that operate on them with the necessary structure sensitivity. More generally, my characterization of the goal of connectionist modeling is to develop formal models of cognitive processes that are based on the mathematics of dynamical systems continuously evolving in time: complex systems of numerical variables governed by differential equations. These formal accounts live in the category of continuous mathematics rather than relying on the discrete mathematics that underlies the traditional symbolic formalism. This characterization of the goal of connectionism is far from universal: it is quite inconsistent with the definitive characterization of Feldman & Ballard (1982), for example. In Smolensky (1988a) I argue at some length that my characterization, called *PTC*, constitutes a Proper Treatment of Connectionism.

A central component of PTC is the relation hypothesized between connectionist models based on continuous mathematics and classical models based on discrete, symbolic computation. That relationship, which entered briefly in the Fodor and Pylyshyn argument of Section 2, might be called the *cognitive correspondence principle*: When connectionist computational systems are analyzed at higher levels, elements of symbolic computation appear as emergent properties.

Figure 5 illustrates the cognitive correspondence principle. At the top we have nonformal notions: the central hypotheses that the principles of cognition consist in principles of memory, of inference, of compositionality and constituent structure, etc. In the Fodor and Pylyshyn argument, the relevant nonformal principles were their compositionality principles (1) and (2).

The nonformal principles at the top of Figure 5 have certain formalizations in the discrete category, which are shown one level down on the right branch. For example, memory is formalized as standard location-addressed memory or some appropriately more sophisticated related notion.

Inference gets formalized in the discrete category as logical inference, a particular form of symbol manipulation. And so on.

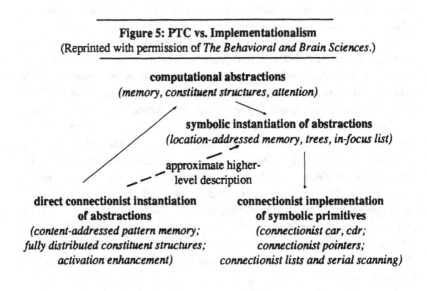

Figure 5: PTC vs. Implementationalism
(Reprinted with permission of *The Behavioral and Brain Sciences*.)

computational abstractions
(memory, constituent structures, attention)

symbolic instantiation of abstractions
(location-addressed memory, trees, in-focus list)

approximate higher-
level description

direct connectionist instantiation   **connectionist implementation**
of abstractions   **of symbolic primitives**
(content-addressed pattern memory;   *(connectionist car, cdr;*
fully distributed constituent structures;   *connectionist pointers;*
activation enhancement)   *connectionist lists and serial scanning)*

The PTC agenda consists in taking these kinds of cognitive principles and finding new ways to instantiate them in formal principles based on the mathematics of dynamical systems; these are shown in Figure 5 at the lowest level on the left branch. The concept of memory retrieval is reformalized in terms of the continuous evolution of a dynamical system towards a point attractor whose position in the state space is the memory; you naturally get content-addressed memory instead of location-addressed memory. (Memory storage becomes modification of the dynamics of the system so that its attractors are located where the memories are supposed to be; thus the principles of memory storage are even more unlike their symbolic counterparts than those of memory retrieval.) When reformalizing inference principles, the continuous formalism leads naturally to principles of statistical inference rather than logical inference. And so on.

The cognitive correspondence principle states that the general relationship between the connectionist formal principles and the symbolic formal principles--given that they are both instantiations of common nonformal notions--is that if you take a higher level analysis of what is going on in the connectionist systems you find that it matches, to some kind of approximation, what is going on in the symbolic formalism. This relation is indicated in Figure 5 by the dotted arrow.

This is to be contrasted with an implementational view of connectionism which Fodor and Pylyshyn advocate. As portrayed in Figure 5, the implementational methodology is to proceed from the top to the bottom not directly, via the left branch, but indirectly, via the right branch; connectionists should take the symbolic instantiations of the nonformal principles and should find ways of implementing *them* in connectionist networks.

The PTC methodology is contrasted not just with the implementational approach, but also with the eliminitivist one. In terms of these methodological considerations, eliminitivism has a strong and a weak form. The weak form advocates taking the left branch of Figure 5 but ignoring altogether the symbolic formalizations, on the belief that the symbolic notions will confuse rather than enlighten us in our attempts to understand connectionist computation. The strong eliminitivist position states that even viewing the nonformal principles at the top of Figure 5 as a starting point for thinking about cognition is a mistake; e.g., that it is better to pursue a blind bottom-up strategy in which low-level connectionist principles are taken from neuroscience and we see where they lead us without being prejudiced by archaic prescientific notions such as those at the top of Figure 5.

In rejecting both the implementationalist and eliminitivist positions, PTC views connectionist accounts as reducing and explaining symbolic accounts. Connectionist accounts serve to refine symbolic accounts, to reduce the degree of approximation required, to enrich the computational notions from the symbolic and discrete world, to fill them out with notions of continuous computation. Primarily that is done by descending to a lower level of analysis, by focusing on the microstructure implicit in these kinds of symbolic operations.

I call this the cognitive correspondence principle because I believe it has a role to play in the developing microtheory of cognition that is analogous to the role that the quantum correspondence principle played in the development of microtheory in physics. The case from physics embodies the structure of Figure 5 quite directly. There are certain physical principles that arch over both the classical and quantum formalisms: the notions of space and time and associated invariance principles, the principles of energy and momentum conservation, force laws, and so on. These principles at the top of Figure 5 are instantiated in particular ways in the classical formalism, corresponding to the point one level down on the right branch. To go to a lower level of physical analysis requires the development of a new formalism. In this quantum formalism, the fundamental principles are reinstantiated: they occupy the bottom of the left branch. The classical formalism can be looked at as a higher level description of the same principles operating at the lower quantum level: the dotted line of Figure 5. Of course, quantum mechanics does not *implement* classical mechanics: the accounts are intimately related, but classical mechanics provides an approximate, not an exact, higher-level account.[4] In a deep sense, the quantum and classical theories are quite incompatible: according to the ontology of quantum mechanics, the ontology of classical mechanics is quite impossible to realize in this world. But there is no denying that the classical ontology and the accompanying principles are theoretically essential, for at least two reasons: (a) to provide explanations (in a literal sense, approximate ones) of an enormous range of classical phenomena for which direct explanation from quantum principles is hopelessly infeasible, and (b), historically, to provide the guidance necessary to discover the quantum principles in the first place. To try to develop lower level principles without looking at the higher level principles for guidance, given the insights we have gained from those principles, would seem, to put it mildly, inadvisable. It is basically this pragmatic consideration that motivates the cognitive correspondence principle and the PTC position it leads to.

In the PTC methodology, it is essential to be able to analyze the higher level properties of connectionist computation in order to relate them to properties of symbolic computation, e.g., to see whether they have the necessary computational power. I now want to summarize what I take to be the state of the art in the mathematical analysis of computation in connectionist systems, and how it relates to Fodor and Pylyshyn's critique. This summary is presented in Figure 6.

Figure 6 shows the pieces of a connectionist model and elements of their analysis. The connectionist model basically has four parts. There is the task that the model is supposed to perform--for example, to take some set of inputs into a set of outputs described in the terms characteristic of the problem domain. Then there is an actual connectionist network which will perform that mapping from input to output; but between the original task and the model we need methods for encoding and decoding. The encoding must take the problem domain characterization of an input and code it into a form that the network can process, namely, activities of certain input processors. Similarly, the activity of the output processors has to be decoded into some problem domain statement which can be construed as the output of the network. The input-to-output mapping inside the network is the computational algorithm embodied in the network and, more often than not, in addition, there is a learning algorithm which modifies the parameters in the computational algorithm in order to get it to converge on the correct input/output behavior of the correct computation.

In terms of analyzing these four elements of connectionist modeling, things get progressively worse as we move from right to left. In the area of connectionist learning, there are lots of analyses: algorithms for tweaking lower-level connection strengths which will produce reasonable higher level convergence towards the correct input/output mapping. The figure shows as many as would fit conveniently and there are many more.[5]

So, if you think that the problem with connectionism is that a particular learning algorithm has some characteristic you do not like, then chances are there is another learning algorithm that will make you happy. Relative to the rest, the learning theory is in good shape, even though when it comes to theorems about what functions can be learned by a given algorithm, there is very little.

With respect to analyzing the higher-level properties of the algorithms for computing outputs from inputs, there is considerably less theory. The technique of analyzing convergence using a function that measures the "energy" or "harmony" of network states (Ackley, Hinton, & Sejnowski, 1985; Cohen & Grossberg, 1983; Geman & Geman, 1984; Hinton & Sejnowski, 1983; Hopfield, 1982; Smolensky, 1983, 1986a) gets us somewhere, as do a few other techniques[6] but it seems rather clear that the state of analysis of connectionist computation is considerably less developed than that of connectionist learning.

After this, things get *very* thin. What about the theory behind encoding and decoding, the theory of how to take the kinds of inputs and outputs that have to be represented for cognitive processes and turn them into actual patterns of activity? By and large, it is a black art: there is not much in the way of analysis. People have been getting their hands dirty exploring the representations in hidden units (e.g., Hinton, 1986; Rosenberg, 1987), but so far I see little reason to believe our understanding of these representations will go further than understanding an occasional node or a few statistical properties. There are a few other simple analyses[7] but they do not take us very far.

At the far left of Figure 6 is the theory of the task environment that comes out of a connectionist perspective. This is essentially nonexistent. To many, I believe, that is really the ultimate goal: the theory of the domain in connectionist terms.

As Figure 6 makes clear, there is a very important weak leg here: the connectionist theory of representation. In particular, until recently we have not had any systematic ideas about how to represent complex structures. In fact, it was Fodor and Pylyshyn who really got me thinking about this, and ultimately convinced me. The result was the tensor product technique for generating fully distributed representations of complex structures (Smolensky, 1987). For this reason the tensor product representation is dedicated to Fodor and Pylyshyn. This representational scheme is a formalization and generalization of representational techniques that have been used piecemeal in connectionist models. As others have discussed in this volume, the tensor product technique provides a systematic and disciplined procedure for representing complex, structured objects. One can prove that the tensor product representation has a number of nice computational properties from the standpoint of connectionist processing. In this sense, it is appropriate to view the tensor product representation as occupying the lower level corner of Figure 5: it provides a formalization that is natural for connectionist computation of the nonformal notion of constituent structure, and is a likely candidate to play a role in connectionist cognitive science analogous to that played by constituent structure trees in symbolic cognitive science.

The tensor product representation rests on the use of the tensor product operation to perform in the vectorial world the analog of binding together a variable and its value. Figure 6 shows where tensor product variable binding and tensor product representations of structures fit into the overall problem of analyzing connectionist cognitive models.

I hope this last section has made more plausible my working hypothesis that between the connectionist view that Fodor and Pylyshyn attack--denying the importance of structured representations and structure-sensitive processes--and the connectionist methodology they advocate--implementation of the classical symbolic cognitive architecture--there is a promising middle ground on which productive and exciting research can be pursued.

Figure 6: Theory of Connectionist Models

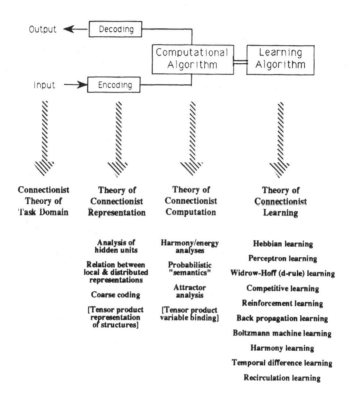

ACKNOWLEDGEMENTS

This work has been supported by NSF grants IRI-8609599 and ECE-8617947 to the author, and by a grant to the author from the Sloan Foundation's computational neuroscience program.

NOTES

[1] For related discussions, see, e.g., Gerken & Bever, 1986; Greeno, 1987.

[2] For some somewhat spooky empirical results directly bearing on this issue, see Bever, Carrithers, & Townsend, 1987.

[3]   An important open question is whether the kind of story I have given on *cup of coffee* using these hokey microfeatures will carry over to the kind of distributed representations that real connectionist networks create for themselves in their hidden units—if you make the analysis appropriately sophisticated. The resolution of this issue depends on the (as yet inscrutable) nature of these representations for realistic problems. The nature of the problem is important, for it is perfectly likely that connectionist networks will develop compositional representations in their hidden units only when this is advantageous for the problem they are trying to solve. As Fodor and Pylyshyn, and the entire Classical paradigm, argue, such compositional representations are in fact immensely useful for a broad spectrum of cognitive problems. But until such problems—which tend to be considerably more sophisticated than those usually given to connectionist networks—have been explored in some detail with connectionist models, we will not really know if hidden units will develop compositional representations (in the approximate sense discussed in this paper) when they "should."

[4]   Many cases analogous to "implementation" *are* found in physics. Newton's laws provide an "implementation" of Kepler's laws; Maxwell's theory "implements" Coulomb's law; the quantum principles of the hydrogen atom "implement" Balmer's formula.

[5]   Here are a smattering of references to these learning rules; rather than giving historically primary references I have cited recent easily accessible expositions that include the original citations. (In fact I have chosen papers in Rumelhart, McClelland, and the PDP Group, 1986, when possible.) For an exposition of Hebbian, perceptron, and Widrow-Hoff or delta-rule learning, see Rumelhart, Hinton, & McClelland, 1986, and Stone, 1986. For competitive learning see Grossberg, 1987, and Rumelhart & Zipser, 1986. For reinforcement learning, see Barto, Sutton, & Anderson, 1983, and Sutton, 1987. For back propagation learning see Rumelhart, Hinton, & Williams, 1986. For Boltzmann machine learning, see Hinton & Sejnowski, 1986. For harmony learning, see Smolensky, 1986a. Temporal difference learning is reported in Sutton, 1987. A simple recirculation learning algorithm is discussed in Smolensky, 1987; the idea has been under exploration by Hinton & McClelland for several years, and their first paper should appear in 1988.

[6]   On giving the computation in connectionist networks semantics based on statistical inference, see Shastri & Feldman, 1985; Smolensky, 1986a; Golden, 1988.

[7]   For some simple explorations of the relation between local and distributed representations, see Smolensky, 1986b. For some observations about the power of the distributed representational technique called "coarse coding," see Hinton, McClelland, & Rumelhart, 1986.

REFERENCES

Ackley, D. H., Hinton, G. E., and Sejnowski, T. J.: 1985, 'A Learning Algorithm for Boltzmann Machines', *Cognitive Science* 9, 147-169.
Ballard, D. and Hayes, P. J.: 1984, 'Parallel Logical Inference', *Proceedings of the Sixth Annual Conference of the Cognitive Science Society*, Rochester, NY, June.
Barto, A. G, Sutton, R. S., and Anderson, C. W.: 1983, 'Neuronlike Elements That Can Solve Difficult Learning Control Problems', *IEEE Transactions on Systems, Man, and Cybernetics* SMC-13, 834-846.
Bever, T. G., Carrithers, C., and Townsend, D. J.: 1987, 'A Tale of Two Brains: The Sinistral Quasimodularity of Language', *Proceedings of the Ninth Annual Conference of the Cognitive Science Society*, Seattle, WA, July, 764-773.
Chomsky, N.: 1965, *Aspects of the Theory of Syntax*, MIT Press, Cambridge, MA.
Cohen, M. A. and Grossberg, S.: 1983, 'Absolute Stability of Global Pattern Formation and Parallel Memory Storage by Competitive Neural Networks', *IEEE Transactions on Systems, Man, and Cybernetics* SMC-13, 815-826.
Dreyfus, S. E. and Dreyfus, H. L.: 1986, *Mind Over Machine: The Power of Human Intuition and Expertise in the Era of the Computer*, Free Press, New York.
Fodor, J. A. and Pylyshyn, Z. W.: 1988, 'Connectionism and Cognitive Architecture: A Critical Analysis', *Cognition* 28, 2-71.
Feldman, J. A. and Ballard, D. H.: 1982, 'Connectionist Models and Their Properties', *Cognitive Science* 6, 205-254.
Geman, S. and Geman, D.: 1984, 'Stochastic Relaxation, Gibbs Distributions, and the Bayesian Restoration of Images', *IEEE Transactions on Pattern Analysis and Machine Intelligence* 6, 721-741.
Gerken, L. and Bever, T. G.: 1986, 'Linguistic Intuitions are the Result of Interactions between Perceptual Processes and Linguistic Universals', *Cognitive Science* 10, 457-476.
Golden, R.: 1988, 'A Unified Framework for Connectionist Systems', *Biological Cybernetics*, in press.
Greeno, J. G.: 1987, 'The Cognition Connection', *The New York Times*, Jan. 4, p. 28.
Grossberg, S.: 1987, 'Competitive Learning: From Interactive Activation to Adaptive Resonance', *Cognitive Science* 11, 23-63.
Gupta, M., Ragade, R., and Yager, R. (eds.): 1979, *Advances in Fuzzy Set Theory and Applications*, North-Holland, Amsterdam.
Hinton, G. E.: 1987, 'Learning Distributed Representations of Concepts', *Proceedings of the Eighth Annual Meeting of the Cognitive Science Society*, 1-12.
Hinton, G. E., McClelland, J. L. and Rumelhart, D. E.: 1986, 'Distributed Representations', in J. L. McClelland, D. E. Rumelhart, and the PDP Research Group, *Parallel Distributed Processing: Explorations in the Microstructure of Cognition. Volume 2: Psychological and Biological Models*, MIT Press/Bradford Books, Cambridge, MA.
Hinton, G. E. and Sejnowski, T. J.: 1983a, 'Analyzing Cooperative Computation', *Proceedings of the Fifth Annual Conference of the Cognitive Science Society*, Rochester, NY.
Hopfield, J. J.: 1982, 'Neural Networks and Physical Systems with Emergent Collective Computational Abilities', *Proceedings of the National Academy of Sciences, USA* 79, 2554-2558.
McClelland, J. L., Rumelhart, D. E., and the PDP Research Group: 1986, *Parallel Distributed Processing: Explorations in the Microstructure of Cognition. Volume 2: Psychological and Biological Models*, MIT Press/Bradford Books, Cambridge, MA.
Rosenberg, C. R.: 1987, 'Revealing the Structure of NETtalk's Internal Representations,' *Proceedings of the Ninth Annual Meeting of the Cognitive Science Society*, Seattle, WA, July, 537-554.
Rumelhart, D. E., Hinton, G. E., and Williams, R. J.: 1986, 'Learning Internal Representations by Error Propogation', in D. E. Rumelhart, J. L. McClelland, and the PDP Research Group, *Parallel Distributed Processing: Explorations in the Microstructure of Cognition. Volume 1: Foundations*, MIT Press/Bradford Books, Cambridge, MA.

Rumelhart, D. E., Hinton, G. E., and McClelland, J. L.: 1986, 'A General Framework for Parallel Distributed Processing', in D. E. Rumelhart, J. L. McClelland, and the PDP Research Group, *Parallel Distributed Processing: Explorations in the Microstructure of Cognition. Volume 1: Foundations*, MIT Press/Bradford Books, Cambridge, MA.

Rumelhart, D. E., McClelland, J. L., and the PDP Research Group: 1986, *Parallel Distributed Processing: Explorations in the Microstructure of Cognition. Volume 1: Foundations*, MIT Press/Bradford Books, Cambridge, MA.

Rumelhart, D. E. and Zipser, D.: 1986, 'Feature Discovery by Competitive Learning', in D. E. Rumelhart, J. L. McClelland, and the PDP Research Group, *Parallel Distributed Processing: Explorations in the Microstructure of Cognition. Volume 1: Foundations*, MIT Press/Bradford Books, Cambridge, MA.

Shastri, L. and Feldman, J. A.: 1985, 'Evidential Reasoning in Semantic Networks: A Formal Theory', *Proceedings of the International Joint Conference on Artificial Intelligence*, Los Angeles, CA.

Shortliffe, E. H.: 1976, *Computer-based Medical Consultations: MYCIN*, American Elsevier, New York.

Smolensky, P.: 1983, 'Schema Selection and Stochastic Inference in Modular Environments', *Proceedings of the National Conference on Artificial Intelligence*, Washington, D. C.

Smolensky, P.: 1986a, 'Information Processing in Dynamical Systems: Foundations of Harmony Theory', in D. E. Rumelhart, J. L. McClelland and the PDP Research Group, *Parallel Distributed Processing: Explorations in the Microstructure of Cognition. Volume 1: Foundations*, MIT Press/Bradford Books, Cambridge, MA.

Smolensky, P.: 1986b, 'Neural and Conceptual Interpretations of Parallel Distributed Processing Models', in J. L. McClelland, D. E. Rumelhart, and the PDP Research Group, *Parallel Distributed Processing: Explorations in the Microstructure of Cognition. Volume 2: Psychological and Biological Models*, MIT Press/Bradford Books, Cambridge, MA.

Smolensky, P.: 1987, 'On Variable Binding and the Representation of Symbolic Structures in Connectionist Systems', Technical Report CU-CS-355-87, Department of Computer Science, University of Colorado at Boulder, February. (Revised version to appear in *Artificial Intelligence*).

Smolensky, P.: 1988a, 'On the Proper Treatment of Connectionism', *The Behavioral and Brain Sciences* 11(1), in press.

Smolensky, P.: 1988b, 'Putting Together Connectionism–Again', *The Behavioral and Brain Sciences* 11(1), in press.

Smolensky, P.: (forthcoming), *Lectures on Connectionist Cognitive Modeling*, Lawrence Erlbaum, Hillsdale, N. J.

Stone, G. O.: 1986, 'An Analysis of the Delta Rule and Learning Statistical Associations', in D. E. Rumelhart, J. L. McClelland, and the PDP Research Group, *Parallel Distributed Processing: Explorations in the Microstructure of Cognition. Volume 1: Foundations*, MIT Press/Bradford Books, Cambridge, MA.

Sutton, R. S.: 1987, 'Learning to Predict by the Methods of Temporal Differences', Technical Report 87-509.1, GTE Laboratories, Waltham, MA.

Zadeh, L. A.: 1965, 'Fuzzy Sets', *Information and Control* 8, 338-353.

Zadeh, L. A.: 1975, 'Fuzzy Logic and Approximate Reasoning', *Synthese* 30, 407-428.

Zadeh, L. A.: 1983, 'Role of Fuzzy Logic in the Management of Uncertainty in Expert Systems', *Fuzzy Sets and Systems* 11, 199-227.

Computer Science Department
University of Colorado
Boulder, CO 80309

MICHAEL TYE

REPRESENTATION IN PICTORIALISM
AND CONNECTIONISM

Pictorialism is the thesis that mental images represent in the manner of pictures. Connectionism, or "parallel distributed processing," as it is sometimes called, is a much more general thesis about the mind. Central to this thesis are the following claims: the mind is a huge structure of simple units linked together in a uniform, largely parallel network; units interact by exciting or inhibiting activity in one another; information processing takes place through the interactions between units; mental representations are typically patterns of activation involving many units.[1] On the face of it, then, pictorialism and connectionism have little in common. Under the surface, however, there are certain similarities. Both views introduce concepts of representation which are not easy to grasp. Both views, although couched in information processing terms, have a definite physiological flavor. Admittedly, in the case of pictorialism, this flavor is not immediately discernible. But, it comes to the fore, as we shall see later, once the pictorialist thesis is fully stated. And both views seem opposed to the dominant idea in cognitive psychology over the past twenty-five years that the exercise of our cognitive capacities always involves the computational manipulation of linguistic or quasi-linguistic representations.

My primary interest, in this paper, is with certain aspects of this opposition to the dominant linguistic view. In particular, I wish to discuss whether there is really any *incompatibility*, at the representational level, between the hypothesis that there is an inner "language" within which mental representation is confined (hereafter the language of cognition thesis) and either pictorialism or various connectionist theses. Obviously this issue cannot be properly addressed unless the relevant concepts of representation are clearly understood. So, I also present an elucidation of pictorialist and connectionist concepts of representation.

The paper is divided into three sections. In Section I, I present an analysis of the concept of quasi-pictorial representation. I explain what role this concept plays in pictorialism. And I argue that the truth of pictorialism entails the falsity of the language of cognition thesis. In Section II, I elucidate various connectionist concepts of representation. In Section III, I take up the issue of compatibility, at the representational level, between connectionism and the language of cognition thesis. I argue that in two of the three cases I distinguish there is no easily discernible incompatibility, and I explain why the question of compatibility is one that might be supposed to be of concern to connectionists.

I.

Some cognitive psychologists, notably Stephen Kosslyn,[2] have argued that the best explanation of a variety of experiments on imagery is that mental images are pictorial. Although Kosslyn has valiantly tried to explain just what the basic thesis of the pictorial approach to imagery, as he accepts it, amount to, his position remains difficult to comprehend. As a result, I believe, it has been badly misinterpreted both by prominent philosophers and by prominent cognitive scientists. In this section I shall attempt to clarify Kosslyn's position.

Kosslyn's initial proposal is that mental images are to be conceived of on the model of displays on a cathode ray tube screen attached to a computer. Such displays are generated on the screen by the computer from information that is stored in the computer's memory.

This model, primitive though it is, is superior to certain other pictorialist models. For example, consider the suggestion that mental images are like slides or photographs which are stored in memory and which are taken out whenever the experience of imagery occurs. This model cannot explain our ability to imagine entirely novel scenes (as, for example, when an image is formed of a frog leaping over a rhinoceros) or our ability to add to or alter features of images (as, for example, when a hat is imaginatively added to an imaged man).

Neither of the above abilities is problematic if we think of images as being like displays on a computer monitor screen, since such displays are *generated* rather than retrieved and they can easily be added to or altered by manipulating the information stored in the computer's memory. But there are obvious differences between mental images and screen displays.

So just what are the respects in which the former are supposed to be like the latter?

Kosslyn suggests that before we answer this question, we reflect upon how a picture is formed on a monitor screen and what makes it pictorial. We may think of the screen itself as being covered by a matrix in which there are a large number of tiny squares or cells. The pattern formed by placing dots in these cells is pictorial, Kosslyn asserts, because it has spatial features which correspond to spatial features of the represented object.[3] In particular, dots in the matrix represent points on the surface of the object and relative distance and geometrical relations among dots match the same relations among object points. Thus, if dots A, B, and C in the matrix stand respectively for points P_1, P_2, and P_3 on the object surface then if P_1 is below P_2 and to P_3's left (as the object is seen from a particular point of view) then likewise A is below B and to C's left (as the screen is seen from a corresponding point of view). Similarly, if P_1 is further from P_2 than from P_3 then A is further from B than from C.

It is perhaps worth noting that this last claim needs qualification if it is to be generally applicable. For P_1 may be further from P_2 than from P_3 on the object surface and yet appear to be closer to P_2 within the context of the relevant point of view. It would be more accurate to say, then, that if P_1 appears further from P_2 than from P_3 (relative to the relevant point of view), then A is further from B than from C. A qualification of this sort is also needed, I might add, in Kosslyn's claim concerning geometrical relations.[4]

Kosslyn's reasoning now becomes more opaque. The main strand of thought which is to be found in Kosslyn's writings seems to be that although mental images lack the above spatial characteristics, they nonetheless function *as if* they had those characteristics. Thus, in Kosslyn's view, it is not literally true that mental images are pictures. Rather the truth is that mental images are *functional* pictures.

But just what is involved in something's being a functional picture (or a "quasi-picture" as Kosslyn sometimes says)? Kosslyn's discussion of this pressing question is not easy to follow. In *Ghosts in the Minds Machine*, Kosslyn presents an example, the aim of which is to illuminate what he has in mind. Here is the example (with minor modifications). Suppose a cross figure is drawn in a 7 x 7 matrix as in diagram A:

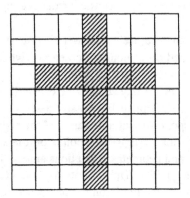

Diagram A

Suppose now that forty-nine different people are each shown diagram A and are each told to memorize whether a given square is filled, different squares being assigned to different people. The information that is in A is now also stored in the group of forty nine people. If you later meet this group of people and ask if square (1,1) is filled, if square (1,2) is filled, and so on through the whole matrix, you can reconstruct from their responses--either the single word "filled" or silence--what is pictured in diagram A. This group of people--or more precisely their collective positive responses--form a functional picture, according to Kosslyn. He says:

Even though the people may be standing anywhere, they [can] function to represent points that are close together in the matrix, diagonal, and so on. All the information in the picture is available, even though there is no actual picture.[5]

It is, I think, evident that this example does *not* really clarify what makes something a functional picture and hence that Kosslyn's picture theory remains obscure. I want now to try to remove this obscurity. Later I shall return to Kosslyn's example and I shall show why the positive replies of the group of people form a functional picture, as Kosslyn asserts.

We saw earlier that, according to Kosslyn, spatial structure plays a central role in pictorial representation. What Kosslyn needs to arrive at a significant thesis, I suggest, is some way of exploiting this view without thereby being forced into the extreme position that mental images are genuine, realistic pictures.

It seems to me that one possible model in this context is presented by the retinotopic representations found on the visual cortex in visual perception. These retinotopic representations reconstruct the retinal image in the cortex. However, the retinal surface is not reconstructed in a linear manner. Rather the image is distorted as if it had been printed on a sheet of rubber, which had then been irregularly stretched. Consider, then, the case of a pictorial pattern of a single object O imprinted on rubber. After the rubber has been stretched in all directions in varying degrees, many of the pattern's internal spatial relations (for example, its components' relative distance relations) will change dramatically, and the pattern as a whole will no longer be a realistic picture. Nonetheless, any path drawn on the rubber prior to stretching and divided into segments retains the same number of segments after stretching even though their lengths change. Moreover, both before and after stretching, every part of the rubber that represents anything represents a part of the represented object O.

Reflection upon these facts suggests to me a general analysis of quasi-picturing along the following lines:

A representation R is a quasi-picture of an object O as seen from point of view V if, and only if, (i) every part of R that represents anything represents a part of O visible from V; (ii) a sufficient number of apparent relative surface distance relationships among parts of O visible from V is represented in R; (iii) for any three O parts, X, Y, and Z, if X appears at a greater surface distance from Y than from Z, then this fact is represented in R if, and only if, there are more R parts representing apparently adjacent O parts which are connected by the shortest apparent path on the surface of O between X and Y and which are each of the same apparent length L as measured along that path than there are R parts representing the corresponding O parts of apparent length L between X and Z.

Some comments are necessary on this proposal: (1) Insofar as an analysis is being offered, it is an analysis of what makes a given representation a *quasi-picture* (of O) and not an analysis of what makes something a *quasi-pictorial representation* (of O). In this paper, I shall have nothing to say about the concept of representation in general. (2) Condition (i) is included in the analysis on the assumption that R is a quasi-picture of O and no other object that is not an undetached part of O.[6] If R is a quasi-picture of O together with certain other objects (that are not parts of O), condition (i) will be too strong and should be replaced by the following condition: the part of R that represents O has representational parts, each of which represents a part of O visible from V. (3) In those cases where a representation R meets the three stated conditions without the restrictions on point of view and appearance, R may be said to be a quasi-picture of O without adding the qualification "as seen from point of view V." (4) If we want to say that quasi-picturing admits of degrees so that some representations are very minimal quasi-pictures whereas others are strongly quasi-pictorial, we will need to replace the phrase "a sufficient number" in (ii) by some such term as "few" or "numerous," whichever is appropriate to the given degree of quasi-picturing. (5) The stated analysis applies to the case of quasi-pictorial representation of one given object.[7] It is not intended to cover what it is for a representation to be a quasi-picture of an object of type F (though no one object of that type in particular).

Now the proposal we have arrived at not only has some continuity with Kosslyn's view of the way in which a display on a monitor screen is genuinely pictorial but it also unifies and sharpens various other statements that Kosslyn makes, statements such as the following:

The primary characteristic of representations in this format [i.e., quasi-pictures] is that every portion of the representation must correspond to a portion of the object such that the relative interportion distances on the object are preserved by the distances among the corresponding portions of the representation.[8]

Importantly distance in the medium [of quasi-pictorial representation] can be defined without reference to actual physical distance but merely in terms of the number of locations intervening between any two locations.[9]

Furthermore we can understand why Kosslyn holds that the positive answers of the forty nine people in the example cited earlier form a functional picture of the cross figure in diagram A. Give the context provided by the questions, Kosslyn takes each token of the term "filled" to represent a cross figure part. These tokens are themselves representationally simple. Hence the scattered entity--call it "S"--composed of these tokens has no representational parts that do not represent parts of the cross figure. Hence S meets condition (i).[10] S also meets both (ii) and (iii) without the qualifications about point of view and appearance, assuming we agree that a sufficient number of relative surface distance relations among parts of the cross figure is represented in S, as (ii) requires. Hence S is a functional picture of the cross figure. By contrast, a description such as "the cross shaped figure in diagram A" or "the figure composed of eleven darkened squares located within the central column and the third row from the top in the diagram on an earlier page of this paper" would not be a functional picture of the cross figure, since none of the conditions (i)-(iii) are met.

Nor even would a list which expressed in written sentences of the form "Square *(n, k)* is filled" the information that is conveyed by all the positive responses of the people qualify as a functional picture of the cross figure. This is because such a list does not meet condition (i): there are representationally complex parts of the list, e.g., "Square (3,2) is filled," whose component representational parts, e.g., "2," "3," "is filled," do not represent parts of the cross figure. Hence, although quasi-pictures are not full-fledged realistic pictures they nonetheless represent in a different way than either sentences or descriptions. Hence, Kosslyn cannot be charged with taking a view of mental imagery which does not provide a significant *alternative* to the view of Pylyshyn and other descriptionalists.

There is one further aspect to Kosslyn's conception of the basic thesis of the picture theory which must still be introduced. Consider again a cathode ray tube screen on which a picture is displayed. The screen may be thought of as the medium in which the picture is presented. This medium is spatial and it is made up of a large number of basic units or cells, some of which are illuminated to form a picture. Analogously, according to Kosslyn, there are various functional spatial media, each made up of a number of basic units or cells.[11] These units or cells may be active or not. For example, in the case of the represented cross figure, the functional spatial medium is made up of the forty nine responses. Those responses that are positive, i.e., those that token the word "filled" in answer to a question, are the active units in the functional medium. Those responses that are silent are the inactive units. Each of the former responses, by virtue of being active, represents the presence of a filled square at a particular spatial location in diagram A. Each of the latter responses, by virtue of being inactive, represents the absence of a filled square at a particular spatial location.

We are now ready to state the basic thesis of the only picture theory of imagery that has been worked out in any real detail: mental images exist in a medium that functions as a space; they are themselves functional pictures in this medium.[12] Given the above account of what makes something a functional picture in a functional space, this basic thesis of the picture theory has a straightforward physiological interpretation.[13] Moreover, reading Kosslyn's work one cannot help but come away with the impression that Kosslyn constructed his theory with one eye on the physiology of the brain. In these respects, as I noted at the beginning of the paper, pictorialism is closely allied with connectionism.

We have seen that pictorialism really is incompatible with the language of cognition thesis, that is, that the truth of pictorialism entails the falsity of the view that mental representations are always linguistically based. Let us now move on to the connectionist accounts of representation.

II.

The simplest concept of representation to be found in the connectionist literature is that of local representation. Perhaps the easiest way for me to introduce this concept is by a very brief illustration. McClelland and Rumelhart have proposed a connectionist model of visual four letter word recognition.[14] The model assumes that there are units that detect four letter words, units that detect visual features which distinguish letters in each of the four letter positions in the presented words, and units that detect the letters themselves in each of the four positions. These units are separated into three levels--feature, letter, and word--with the first two containing four times as many units as the third. In the model each unit has an activation value that corresponds to how strongly it represents that its detected feature, letter, or word is present in the visual input. Moreover, each unit is connected to many others both within its own level and between levels. If two units function as representations the contents of which are mutually consistent (e.g., the unit for the letter T in the first position and the unit for the word THEN), then the connection between the two units is such that they tend to excite one another. However, if two units function as mutually inconsistent representations (e.g., the unit for the letter T in the first position and the unit for the word BLOW), then the connection is inhibitory and the activity in each of the two connected units is reduced. Below is a diagram[15] showing a fragment of the connections between units for the letter T in the first position of a four letter array:

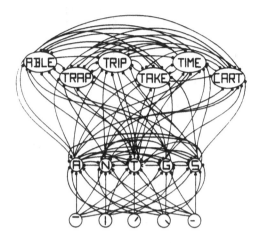

Diagram B
(Arrow connections are excitatory, dot connections are inhibitory)

Just how four letter word recognition takes place within this network, given the presentation of the appropriate visual stimulus, need not concern us.   The salient point for our purposes is that within the model representation is always local.   What this means is that every entity represented in the network is represented by the activity in a *single* unit dedicated to such a purpose.

Imagine now that the network is modified so that letters in each of the four letter positions are no longer represented by isolated active units. Rather, letters in positions 1, 2, 3, and 4 are detected via appropriate activation levels in the groups of units detecting visual features in each of the four positions. For example, when a word beginning with A is presented, there is a whole pattern of activated units representing the letter A in position 1. Such a pattern is a distributed representation, since it is spread out over a number of different active units.

Although this network contains distributed representations of letters in specific letter positions, there is a sense in which these distributed representations are still local, however. For they are always to be found within localized pools or groups of units, each of which consists of units that, when active, detect features within a single letter position.   Thus, the representation of A in position 1 will take place within the group of units dedicated to position 1; the representation of A in position 2 will take place within the group of units dedicated to position 2, and so on. Let us call such representations locally distributed, where a locally distributed representation is defined as follows:

R is a locally distributed representation with respect to a network N of units if, and only if, (i) N has as a part a pool P of units, alternative patterns of activation within which represent things of the same type T, where T is a type to which the item that R represents belongs; (ii) R is a pattern of activation within P.[16]

Now not all distributed representations have to be locally distributed.[17] To see this, consider the following three figures pertaining to the representation of letters and letter positions in four letter words:

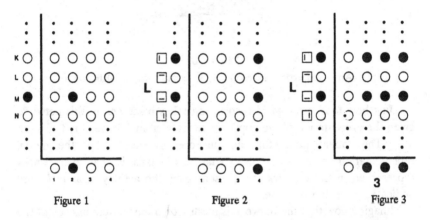

Figure 1   Figure 2   Figure 3

In Figure 1, each unit on the left edge, when active (as indicated by blackening), represents a letter. Since within any four letter word each letter fills a position, we may call the units dedicated to representing letters "filler" units. Each unit on the bottom edge of Figure 1, when active (again as indicated by blackening), represents a letter position. If we think of letter positions as roles occupied by letters, it makes sense for us to call units dedicated to representing such positions "role" units. The rest of the units in Figure 1 are the ones used to represent letters in specific positions (the "binding" units, as Smolensky calls them: each one represents a filler bound to a role[18]). Figure 1, then, gives us a purely local representation of the letter M in position 2.[19] In Figure 2, the units on the left edge are filler units representing, when active, visual features of letters. The remaining units are as before. In the situation indicated, the letter L in position 4 is represented by the pattern of activation in the units above the horizontal line in the far right hand column. Here it is evident that the representation of L in position 4 is *locally* distributed. In Figure 3, the units on the left edge are as in Figure 2. The units on the bottom edge are now role units that *together* represent position. In the case shown position 3 is represented via activity to varying degrees in three of the four units.[20] Other positions would be represented by different combinations of activity. The units to the right of the vertical line and above the horizontal line are again the ones in the network used to represent letters in positions. What is displayed in Figure 3, thus, is the pattern of active units representing L in position 3. This pattern is a fully distributed representation. For not only is there no one unit representing L in position 3 (as in local representation), there is no one pool of units within the network dedicated to representing letters in position 3 and no other positions (as in locally distributed representation).

In all three of the above cases, the activity of each binding unit is the product of the activities of the associated letter and position units. In the first two cases the latter activities are always zero except for a single activity of 1. In the last case, the latter activities vary from 0 to 1 (with higher activities indicated by darker coloring). We may view the activities on the left edge in each figure as forming one activity vector and the activities on the bottom as forming another. Once we do so, we may hold that the tensor product of these vectors represents the relevant letter in the relevant position. From this perspective, which is due to Paul Smolensky,[21] the above local, locally distributed, and fully distributed representations are all tensor product representations.

This perspective generalizes further. Suppose that in our network we wish to have distributed representations not just of letters in given positions in four letter words but also of the four letter words themselves. Then we simply sum the tensor products of the vectors associated with each letter in each position.

In the fully distributed case, this procedure is appropriate, since each letter in each position in any given four letter word is represented by a pattern of activity that extends across the whole network and the simplest way of combining these patterns is to add them up (i.e., to superimpose them on top of one another).[22] One way of implementing this proposal is to activate the filler and role units so that they initially represent the first letter and the first letter position respectively. The activities in the filler and role units may then be simultaneously inputted to the appropriate junctions at which they are multiplied and the resultant activities may be transmitted to the binding units in the network. The activities in the filler and role units may then be eliminated and replaced with activity patterns representing the second letter and the second letter position. These activities may be inputted in like fashion and the whole procedure repeated for the third and fourth letters and letter positions. So long as the binding units retain their activation as each input activity pattern is eliminated and replaced by another, at the end of the process each binding unit will have an activity which is the sum of the activities fed into it.

Turning now to the locally distributed case, the summing of tensor products is appropriate, since there are separate pools for each letter position and superimposing the relevant patterns of activity generates a representation in each pool of a specific letter in one of the four letter positions.

If we extend the usage of the description "tensor product representation" to vectors that are sums of tensor products of activity vectors such as those above, we arrive at a concept of representation which is applicable whenever the represented entity consists of other entities that fill roles within it. I hope that I have said enough to give the reader a reasonably clear sense of what this concept involves. For a precise general definition of the concept together with a formal treatment of various associated topics the reader should consult Smolensky.

III.

In this section, I want to take up the issue of compatibility at the representational level between the language of cognition hypothesis and various connectionist theses. Consider first the view that all mental representations are local. In this case it is obvious that there is a direct conflict. For the language of cognition thesis introduces quasi-linguistically structured representations composed of word-like representations. And local representations have no representational parts at all. This case is not very interesting, however, for two reasons. First, connectionists generally have argued that theories that invoke distributed representations not only make more efficient use of the processing abilities of networks of simple units but also handle a variety of problems more easily than theories that are restricted to local representations.[23] Secondly, to my knowledge, there are no connectionists who hold that mental representations are *always* local.

Consider next the view that mental representations are either local or locally distributed. In this case, the issue of compatibility with the language of cognition hypothesis is not so easy to settle. Consider, e.g., the sentential representation of the state of affairs of John's hitting Mary. How could this representation be produced, given only local and locally distributed representations? Well, we can imagine a connectionist network of units containing a pool dedicated to states of affairs. The representation of John's hitting Mary might, then, be identified with a distributed activity pattern within this pool. But this proposal does not clearly yield anything like a sentential representation. For it has not been shown how the given representation is representationally complex nor relatedly how it differs from the representation of Mary's hitting John.

In a recent paper, Hinton, McClelland, and Rumelhart make some suggestions about locally distributed representation.[24] These suggestions are interesting in their own right. But they may also appear relevant in the present context. Let us, then, briefly examine their views.

Suppose that we wish to construct a locally distributed representation of John in the role of agent. One way of doing this is to generate a pattern in a module dedicated to representing agents from two other separate locally distributed patterns lying outside the agent module, one of which represents John and the other the role as in Figure 4:

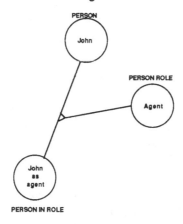

Figure 4

A procedure of this sort can be used to generate combined representations from patterns for other identities and roles. For example, we can construct a representation of Mary as patient in a module dedicated to representing patients. We can also construct in another module a representation of hitting as the relationship between the person (whomever it may be) represented in the agent module and the person (whomever it may be) represented in the patient module. The overall scheme is shown as follows:

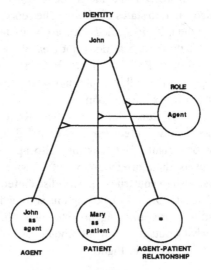

*Hitting as relationship between the person represented in the agent module and the person represented in the patient module.

Figure 5

In the scheme sketched here, we can represent the state of affairs of John's hitting Mary by inducing appropriate activity patterns in each of the three modules shown at the bottom.[25] The representation whose content is that John hits Mary--call it "R"--is then spatially composed of these three locally distributed activity patterns. R itself is also a locally distributed representation, since it is spread out over modules which together are dedicated to representing relational agent/ patient states of affairs.

The general idea is that representations can be structured so as to capture the relationship between wholes and parts by introducing subrepresentations that represent part identity/role combinations. Hinton, McClelland, and Rumelhart note:

> This proposal differs from the simple idea that the representation of the whole is the sum of the representations of its parts because the subpatterns used to represent identity/role combinations are quite different from the patterns used to represent the identities alone. They do not, for example, contain these patterns as parts.[26]

So, the representation, R, does not have the patterns for John, Mary, and hitting, whatever their roles, as parts, on the above view. Rather there are access paths connecting the appropriate patterns. Given these access paths, there is easy movement from R to the representation of John (or Mary or hitting) alone. Now the fact that R lacks a part representing John, a part representing Mary, and a part representing the relation of hitting, whatever their roles, suggests that R is *not* sentential. For any ordinary sentence which represents that John hits Mary certainly has such parts. It appears, then, that the scheme we have considered does not show us how a locally distributed representation could be sentential.

Is R *really* a non-sentential representation? Well, it might be argued that R does not really lack a part representing John, whatever his role, since the activity pattern in the agent module can be taken to function in the manner of a description in which the name "John" is embedded, namely "John in the role of agent." This argument is unsuccessful, however. For while "John in the role of agent" has a part representing John alone, it also has a part representing the role of agent. And the activity pattern in the agent module, *ex hypothesi*, has no part that represents any role. So R cannot be viewed on the model of a sentence which includes a name-involving *description* of John.

Still, R might be viewed on the model of a sentence which includes a special name for John applicable to him only when he occupies the role of agent. This name will abbreviate the description "John in the role of agent" but, unlike the description, it will have no part that represents the role of agent. The same points apply *mutatis mutandis* to the part of R pertaining to Mary. However, they do not extend in any straightforward way to the part pertaining to hitting. So again R is not easily classified as sentential.

An alternative strategy might be to argue that although the patterns representing John, Mary, and hitting, whatever their roles, are not spatial parts of R, they are nonetheless functional parts of R. Were such a strategy successful, R could be classified as sentence-like after all. The crucial question here is whether a clear, usable concept of functional part can be elucidated. I shall not explore this question in the context of the present proposal. But I shall return to it shortly in the context of another approach which combines McClelland, Rumelhart, and Hinton's suggestions with those of Smolensky. This latter approach, I suggest, is overall much more promising than the one sketched above.

Suppose that we have alternative patterns of activity in a module dedicated to representing persons. Suppose also that we have another module dedicated to person roles and that different roles are each locally represented by the activity in a single unit. We may then design a network in which the units in the person module and the units in the person role module are input *filler* units and input *role* units respectively. The binding units in the network are located in a third module dedicated to representing persons engaged in roles as shown below:

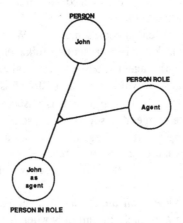

Figure 6

Given this network we begin the task of generating a sentence-like representation by constructing a locally distributed representation of John as agent within the person-role module. We then superimpose upon this representation another representation of Mary as patient so that a complex representation of John as agent and Mary as patient results. The units in which this representation is realized now become input filler units to a further module. The input role units which go with these filler units make up a module dedicated to actions, e.g., hitting, with different actions each locally represented by the activity in a single unit. Role units of this sort are chosen, since the filler units here represent pairs of persons as agent and patient and such pairs fill or occupy actions. The final binding units will now represent relational agent/patient states of affairs as shown in the following figure:

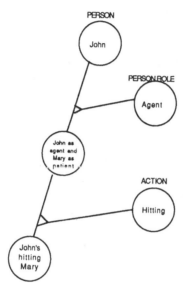

Figure 7

In this scheme, the representation of John's hitting Mary is a locally distributed representation within the bottom module. Now, it seems to me, there is no obvious difficulty in classifying this representation as quasi-sentential.[27] Let me explain. The representations of John and Mary, whatever their roles, may be viewed as activity vectors Vj and Vm respectively in the space of the person filler units in the top module. Similarly the representations of the roles of agent and patient may be viewed as vectors Va and Vp respectively in the space of the (person role) role units. The representation of John-as-agent may then be identified with the tensor product Tj of Vj and Va, and the representation of Mary-as-patient with the tensor product Tm of Vm and Vp. Thus the complex representation of John as agent and Mary as patient is the sum S of Tj and

Tm. Now in an abstract functional sense of the term "part," Vj and Vm are both parts of the vector S. This is because both Vj and Vm are recoverable from S by an operation of unbinding. This operation, in application to a tensor product representation, generates, for any given role in the structure represented, the very vector that represents the filler to which that role is bound in the structure.[28]

Turning to the action module, we find that the representation of hitting may be viewed as an activity vector Vh with respect to the units in the module, units which function as input action role units in the scheme diagrammed. Since the units in which S is realized are not only binding units for the initial person and person role units, but also input agent/patient pair filler units for the bottom module in Figure 7, the final representation of the state of affairs of John's hitting Mary may be identified with the tensor product T of S and Vh. T has S as a part. So, by the transitivity of parthood, T has Vj and Vm as parts. Vj, Vm, and Vh, then, are all parts of T. So, in this scheme, it seems to me that the locally distributed representation whose content is that John hits Mary can reasonably be categorized as sentence-like.

Of course, if the claim that an item is a quasi-sentence is interpreted as requiring that all the (representational) parts of the item be spatial parts just as the (representational) parts of real, public sentences are, then the final representation T cannot be classified as a quasi-sentence. Such an interpretation seems unduly restrictive, however. After all, quasi-sentences are not exactly like real, public sentences any more than quasi-pictures are exactly like real, public pictures.

It is not difficult to see how connectionist schemes which utilize higher order tensor product representations (schemes such as the one shown in Figure 7) can generate further more complex quasi-linguistic representations. Consider, for example, the quasi-sentential representation whose content is that John hits Mary or Jane hits Paul. In this case, we superimpose the representation of Jane's hitting Paul on the representation of John's hitting Mary in the bottom module in figure 7. We then make the units in this module input filler units for representations of agent/patient states of affairs. The corresponding role units are now units in a new module dedicated to certain logical "relations," e.g., the disjunctive "relation," with different "relations" each locally represented there. Give the appropriate input from this module, the final binding units, located in a further module, will contain an activity pattern representing that John hits Mary or Jane hits Paul.[29]

I do not know whether the view that all mental representations are either local or locally distributed can be developed along the general lines sketched above so that no conflicts whatsoever arise, at the representational level, with the language of cognition hypothesis. But it does seem to me that the introduction of higher order tensor product representations can generate considerable representational complexity and that there is no obvious reason to suppose that the representational complexity required by the language of cognition hypothesis cannot be captured (provided, of course, that the notion of parthood relevant to the hypothesis is permitted to cover abstract functional parts).

The final connectionist view I want to mention is the view that there are complex mental representations all of which are fully distributed. In this case, no new discussion is required. This is because the examples presented above can easily be modified so as to yield fully distributed representations. It suffices merely to change the representations in the various role modules from local to distributed. So, if there is no incompatibility at the representational level between the previous connectionist view and the language of cognition hypothesis then there is no incompatibility here either.

Why should connectionists care whether their views on representation are compatible with those of advocates of the language of cognition hypothesis? After all, if mental images are quasi-pictorial, as pictorialists assert, then that hypothesis is false anyway. The answer, I think, has three parts. First, it is not generally agreed that mental images are quasi-pictorial. Secondly, even if the pictorialist view of imagistic representation is true, this would not show that quasi-linguistic representations are not required in memory, language understanding, and other areas of cognition. Finally, there is a powerful traditional argument for the conclusion that the mental representations involved in the propositional attitudes *must* be linguistically structured. The argument I am referring to goes very briefly as follows: The ability to think certain thoughts seems intrinsically connected with the ability to think certain others. For example, the ability to think that John hits Mary goes hand in hand with the ability to think that Mary hits John, but not with the ability to think that English butlers are polite. Why is this? Well, the ability to produce or understand certain sentences is intrinsically connected with the ability to produce or understand certain others. For example, there are no native speakers of English who know how to say "John hits Mary" but who do not know how to say "Mary hits John." Similarly, there are no native speakers who understand the former sentence but not the latter. These facts are easily explained if sentences have a syntactic and semantic structure. But if sentences are taken to be atomic, these facts are a complete mystery. What is true for sentences is true also for thoughts. Thinking thoughts involves manipulating mental representations. If mental representations with a propositional content have a semantic and syntactic structure like that of sentences then it is no accident that one who is able to think that John hits Mary is thereby also able to think that Mary hits John. Furthermore, it is no accident that one who can think these thoughts need not thereby be able to think thoughts having different components, e.g., the thought that English butlers are polite.[30]

One might respond that this argument shows only that propositional thought is representationally complex, not that it is representationally complex in the manner of sentences. For the ability to produce certain *pictures* (e.g., a picture of John hitting Mary) is intrinsically connected with the ability to produce certain others (e.g., a picture of Mary hitting John). So, the hypothesis that thoughts are picture-like will explain the relevant data just as well as the hypothesis that thoughts are sentence-like.

However, the complexity imposed upon the mental representations of propositional thought by a pictorialist model does not begin to explain the breadth of such thought.[31] Once facts about breadth are included, I think it is clear that the traditional argument for a sententialist model has substantial force. Still it does not clearly refute those connectionists who avail themselves of the tensor product approach. For my claim has been that once higher order tensor product representations are introduced, various representations *will* be intrinsically connected. Of course, it might be charged that if the connectionist view is elaborated along the lines I have sketched, then there is nothing new or interesting about the connectionist's position. This is just not so, however, since the tensor product approach may be seen as providing a more basic "subsymbolic" model of representation out of which complex quasi-symbolic and non-symbolic (e.g., quasi-pictorial) representations can be constructed.[32]

NOTES

[1]   I ignore here interactions that generate local representations. For a discussion of the difference between local and distributed representations, see Section II below.

[2]   For a summary of Kosslyn's work, see his *Image and Mind* (Cambridge, Mass.: Harvard, 1980); also his *Ghosts in the Mind's Machine* (New York: W. W. Norton, 1983).

[3]   See, for example, *Ghosts in the Mind's Machine, op. cit.*, p. 22.

[4]   Actually even this claim is too strong. For some apparent relative distance relations among represented points on the object surface (relative to the relevant point of view) need not be directly represented in the picture at all. This fact may be accommodated by weakening the stated requirement so that it obtains only in a sufficient number of cases and only when P_1, P_2, and P_3 do not appear to be at different distances away.

[5]   See Kosslyn, *ibid.*, p. 23.

[6]   This assumption is not the same as the assumption that R is a quasi-picture of O and only of O. The latter assumption is too strong, since a quasi-picture of O, like a real picture of O, must represent other objects that are undetached parts of O. I owe this point to Brian McLaughlin.

[7]   More precisely, one given physical object.

[8]   See "The Medium and the Message in Mental Imagery," in *Imagery, op. cit.*, p. 217.

[9]   *Ibid.*, p. 215. The parenthetical phrases in the two quoted passages are mine.

[10]   This conclusion rests on the assumption that the representational parts of a representation lie spatially within that representation. Without this assumption it could be denied that the tokens of "filled" are representationally simple. I should perhaps add here that the proposed general account of quasi-pictorial representation does not have to be tied to a spatial interpretation of the term "R part" in conditions (i) and (iii). For some comment on non-spatial parthood, see Section III below.

[11]   See, for example, *ibid.*, pp. 213-214.

[12]   I should perhaps add here that the claim that mental images are functional pictures in a functional spatial medium is *only* the basic thesis of Kosslyn's picture theory. His view has many other interesting associated theses which I cannot take up here. For a more detailed discussion of Kosslyn's position, see my "The Picture Theory of Mental Images," *Philosophical Review*, 97 (1988), pp. 497-520; also my *The Imagery Debate*, (MIT Press, Cambridge, MA, 1991).

[13]   Of course, there is no *requirement* that the picture theory be given this interpretation.

[14]   J. L. McClelland and D. E. Rumelhart, "An Interactive Activation Model of Contexts Effects in Letter Perception: Part I. An Account of Basic Findings," *Psychological Review*, 88 (1981).

[15]   *Ibid.*, p. 380.

[16]   Three points of clarification: (1) I am elucidating "locally distributed" not "locally distributed representation," so the proposed definition is not circular; (2) "Part" in the definition (and elsewhere) means proper part; (3) "Pattern of activation," as I use it here, cannot apply to the activation in a single unit.

[17]   The remainder of this section draws heavily on Paul Smolensky's recent work. See his "A Method for Connectionist Variable Binding," forthcoming; also "On Variable Binding and the Representation of Symbolic Structures in Connectionist Systems," forthcoming.

[18]   Paul Smolensky, *ibid*. Following Smolensky, I assume that there is one binding unit for each pair of filler and role units.

[19]   In the McClelland-Rumelhart network described earlier there are no actual filler and role units over and above the units representing individual letters in specific positions. So, the present model seems not to apply to that network. Still, Smolensky *seems* to want to say that in that case the filler and role units are imaginary. See his "A Method for Connectionist Variable Binding," *op. cit.*, p. 2.

[20]   There does not have to be activity in all four units for a given letter position to be represented. What is crucial is that the activity be spread out over two or more units.

[21] See Smolensky, *op. cit.*

[22] If the separate bindings are not to be confused, the patterns in the role units must not be too similar. For more on this issue, see Smolensky, *ibid.*

[23] For a summary of the virtues of distributed representations, see G. E. Hinton, J. L. McClelland, and D. E. Rumelhart, "Distributed Representation," *Parallel Distributed Processing*, Volume I, by McClelland, Rumelhart, and the PDP Research Group (Cambridge, Mass.: MIT Press, 1986), pp. 77-109.

[24] *Ibid.*

[25] We cannot simultaneously represent that John hits Mary and that Paul kisses Jane, say, in this scheme. For multiple such representations, we will need multiple copies of the entire arrangement. See here Hinton, McClelland, and Rumelhart, "Distributed Representations," *op. cit.*

[26] "Distributed Representations," *op. cit.*, p. 106.

[27] There is also no danger of conflating the representation of John's hitting Mary with the representation of Mary's hitting John.

[28] Given certain restrictions on the role vectors. For a statement of these restrictions together with a discussion of how the tensor product unbinding operation works, see Smolensky, *op. cit.*

[29] The scheme I have sketched does not distinguish between the tensor product representation whose content is that John hits Mary or Jane hits Paul and the representation whose content is that Jane hits Paul or John hits Mary. However, it is a simple enough matter to extend the scheme so as to keep these representations distinct. We first construct the representation of John's hitting Mary in the bottom module in figure 7. We then bind this (*qua* filler) to a "left component" role. We do likewise with the "right component" role. The representation formed by this second binding is superimposed on the first and the whole resultant representation is bound finally to a disjunctive "relation" role. This will give us a representation with the content that John hits Mary or Jane hits Paul. If we want the commuted version we proceed as above except that we reverse the representations bound to the "left component" and "right component" roles. A similar procedure may be adopted in the case of representations having a conjunctive or conditional quasi-sentential structure.

[30] The above argument is developed at length by Jerry Fodor and Zenon Pylyshyn in their "Connectionism and Cognitive Architecture: A Critical Analysis," *Cognition*, 28 (1988), pp. 3-71.

[31] Moreover, if thinking that John is bald, say, is merely a matter of producing an inner picture of a bald John, then contrary to fact, thinking that John is bald must go hand in hand with thinking that he has various other unrelated visual properties. For a picture of a bald John is necessarily a picture of John with certain further properties (e.g., standing, facing left, frowning, being tall, being fat). Cf. Jerry Fodor, "Imagistic Representation," in *Imagery*, ed. by Ned Block (Cambridge, Mass.: MIT Press, 1981).

[32] The term "sub-symbolic" is Smolensky's. See his "On the Proper Treatment of Connectionism," *Behavioral and Brain Sciences* 11 (1988).

Department of Philosophy
Temple University
Philadelphia, PA 19122

JERRY FODOR AND BRIAN P. MCLAUGHLIN

CONNECTIONISM AND THE PROBLEM OF SYSTEMATICITY: WHY SMOLENSKY'S SOLUTION DOESN'T WORK

INTRODUCTION

In two recent papers, Paul Smolensky (1987, 1988b) responds to a challenge Jerry Fodor and Zenon Pylyshyn (Fodor and Pylyshyn, 1988) have posed for connectionist theories of cognition: to explain the existence of systematic relations among cognitive capacities without assuming that cognitive processes are causally sensitive to the constituent structure of mental representations. This challenge implies a dilemma: if connectionism can't account for systematicity, it thereby fails to provide an adequate basis for a theory of cognition; but if its account of systematicity requires mental processes that are sensitive to the constituent structure of mental representations, then the theory of cognition it offers will be, at best, an implementation architecture for a "classical" (language of thought) model. Smolensky thinks connectionists can steer between the horns of this dilemma if they avail themselves of certain kinds of distributed mental representation. In what follows, we will examine this proposal.

Our discussion has three parts. In Section I, we briefly outline the phenomenon of systematicity and its Classical explanation. As we will see, Smolensky actually offers two alternatives to this Classical treatment, corresponding to two ways in which complex mental representations can be distributed; the first kind of distribution yields complex mental representations with "weak compositional structure", the second yields complex mental representations with "strong compositional structure". We will consider these two notions of distribution in turn: in Section II, we argue that Smolensky's proposal that complex mental representations have weak compositional structure should be rejected both as inadequate to explain systematicity and on internal grounds; in Section III, we argue that postulating mental representations with strong compositional structure also fails to provide for an explanation of systematicity. The upshot will be that

Smolensky avoids only one horn of the dilemma that Fodor and Pylyshyn proposed. We shall see that his architecture is genuinely non-Classical since the representations he postulates are not "distributed over" constituents in the sense that Classical representations are; and we shall see that for that very reason Smolensky's architecture leaves systematicity unexplained.

I. THE SYSTEMATICITY PROBLEM AND ITS CLASSICAL SOLUTION

The systematicity problem is that cognitive capacities come in clumps. For example, it appears that there are families of semantically related mental states such that, as a matter of psychological law, an organism is able to be in one of the states belonging to the family only if it is able to be in many of the others. Thus, you don't find organisms that can learn to prefer the green triangle to the red square but can't learn to prefer the red triangle to the green square. You don't find organisms that can think the thought that the girl loves John but can't think the thought that John loves the girl. You don't find organisms that can infer P from P&Q&R but can't infer P from P&Q. And so on over a very wide range of cases. For the purposes of this paper, we assume without argument:

(i) that cognitive capacities are generally systematic in this sense, both in humans and in many infrahuman organisms;

(ii) that it is nomologically necessary (hence counterfactual supporting) that this is so;

(iii) that there must therefore be some psychological mechanism in virtue of the functioning of which cognitive capacities are systematic;

(iv) and that an adequate theory of cognitive architecture should exhibit this mechanism.

Any of i-iv may be viewed as tendentious; but, so far as we can tell, all four are accepted by Smolensky. So we will take them to be common ground in what follows.[1]

Classical syntax and Classical constituents

The Classical view holds that the syntax of mental representations is like the syntax of natural language sentences in the following respect: both include complex symbols (bracketing trees) which are constructed out of what we will call *Classical constituents*. Thus, for example, the English sentence "John loves the girl" is a complex symbol whose decomposition into Classical constituents is exhibited by some such bracketing tree as:

```
                Sentence
        •  •  •  •  •  •
        •              •
    Subject        Predicate
                          •
        •          •          Object
        •          •              •
        •          •              •
      John       loves         the girl
```

Correspondingly, it is assumed that the mental representation that is entertained when one thinks the thought that John loves the girl is a complex symbol of which the Classical constituents include representations of John, the girl, and loving.

It will become clear in Section III that it is a major issue whether the sort of complex mental representations that are postulated in Smolensky's theory have constituent structure. We do not wish to see this issue degenerate into a terminological wrangle. We therefore stipulate that, for a pair of expression types E1, E2, the first is a *Classical* constituent of the second *only if* the first is tokened whenever the second is tokened. For example, the English word "John" is a Classical constituent of the English sentence "John loves the girl" and every tokening of the latter implies a tokening of the former (specifically, every token of the latter *contains* a token of the former; you can't say "John loves the girl" without saying "John").[2] Likewise, it is assumed that a mentalese symbol which names John is a Classical constituent of the mentalese symbol that means that John loves the girl. So again tokenings of the one symbol require tokenings of the other.

It is precisely because Classical constituents have this property that they are always accessible to operations that are defined over the complex symbols that contain them; in particular, it is precisely because Classical mental representations have Classical constituents that they provide domains for structure-sensitive mental processes. We shall see presently that what Smolensky offers as the "constituents" of connectionist mental representations are non-Classical in this respect, and that is why his theory provides no account of systematicity.

Classical semantics

It is part of the Classical picture, both for mental representation and for representation in natural languages, that generally when a complex formula (e.g., a sentence) S expresses the proposition P, S's constituents express (or refer to) the elements of P.[3] For example, the proposition that John loves the girl contains as its elements the individuals John and the girl, and the two-place relation "loving". Correspondingly, the formula "John loves the girl", which English uses to express this proposition, contains as constituents the expressions "John", "loves" and "the girl". The sentence "John left and the girl wept", whose constituents include the formulas "John left" and "the girl wept", expresses the proposition that John left and the girl wept, whose elements include the proposition that John left and the proposition that the girl wept. And so on.

These assumptions about the syntax and semantics of mental representations are summarized by condition C:

C: If a proposition P can be expressed in a system of mental representation M, then M contains some complex mental representation (a "mental sentence") S, such that S expresses P and the (Classical) constituents of S express (or refer to) the elements of P.

Systematicity

The Classical explanation of systematicity assumes that C holds by nomological necessity; it expresses a *psychological law* that subsumes all systematic minds. It should be fairly clear why systematicity is readily explicable on the assumptions, first, that mental representations satisfy C, and, second, that mental processes have access to the constituent structure of mental representations. Thus, for example, since C implies that anyone who can represent a proposition can, ipso facto, represent its elements, it implies, in particular, that anyone who can represent the proposition that John loves the girl can, ipso facto, represent John, the girl and the two-place relation *loving*. Notice, however, that the proposition that the *girl loves John* is *also* constituted by these same individuals/relations. So, then, assuming that the processes that integrate the mental representations that express propositions have access to their constituents, it follows that anyone who can represent John's loving the girl can also represent the girl's loving John. Similarly, suppose that the constituents of the mental representation that gets tokened when one thinks that P&Q&R and the constituents of the mental representation that gets tokened when one thinks that P&Q both include the mental representation that gets tokened when one thinks that P. And suppose that the mental processes that mediate the drawing of inferences have access to the constituent structure of mental representations. Then it should be no surprise that anyone who can infer P from P&Q&R can likewise infer P from P&Q.

To summarize: the Classical solution to the systematicity problem entails that (i) systems of mental representation satisfy C (a fortiori, complex mental representations have Classical constituents); and (ii) mental processes are sensitive to the constituent structure of mental representations. We can now say quite succinctly what our claim against Smolensky will be: on the one hand, the cognitive architecture he endorses does not provide for mental representations with Classical constituents; on the other hand, he provides no suggestion as to how mental processes could be structure sensitive unless mental representations have Classical constituents; and, on the third hand (as it were) he provides no suggestion as to how minds could be systematic if mental processes aren't structure sensitive. So his reply to Fodor and Pylyshyn fails.

Most of the rest of the paper will be devoted to making this analysis stick.

II. WEAK COMPOSITIONALITY

Smolensky's views about "weak" compositional structure are largely inexplicit and must be extrapolated from his "coffee story", which he tells in both of the papers under discussion (and also in 1988a). We turn now to considering this story.

Smolensky begins by asking how we are to understand the relation between the mental representation COFFEE and the mental representation

CUP WITH COFFEE.[4] His answer to this question has four aspects that are of present interest:

(i) COFFEE and CUP WITH COFFEE are activity vectors (according to Smolensky's weak compositional account, this is true of the mental representations corresponding to all commonsense concepts; whether it also holds for, for example, technical concepts won't matter for what follows). A vector is, of course, a magnitude with a certain direction. A pattern of activity over a group of "units" is a state consisting of the members of the group each having an activation value of 1 or 0.[5] Activity vectors are representations of such patterns of activity.

(ii) CUP WITH COFFEE representations contain COFFEE representations as (non-Classical)[6] constituents in the following sense: they contain them as *component* vectors. By stipulation, **a** is a component vector of **b**, if there is a vector **x** such that **a** + **x** = **b** (where "+" is the operation of vector addition). More generally, according to Smolensky, the relation between vectors and their non-Classical constituents is that the former are derivable from the latter by operations of vector analysis.

(iii) COFFEE representations and CUP WITH COFFEE representations are activity vectors over units which represent microfeatures (units like BROWN, LIQUID, MADE OF PORCELAIN, etc.).

(iv) COFFEE (and, presumably, any other representation vector) is *context dependent*. In particular, the activity vector that is the COFFEE representation in CUP WITH COFFEE *is distinct from* the activity vector that is the COFFEE representation in, as it might be, GLASS WITH COFFEE or CAN WITH COFFEE. Presumably this means that the vector in question, with no context specified, does not give necessary conditions for being *coffee*. (We shall see later that Smolensky apparently holds that it doesn't specify sufficient conditions for being *coffee* either).

Claims i and ii introduce the ideas that mental representations are activity vectors and that they have (non-Classical) constituents. These ideas are neutral with respect to the distinction between strong and weak compositionality so we propose to postpone discussing them until Section III. Claim iii, is, in our view, a red herring. The idea that there are microfeatures is orthogonal both to the question of systematicity and to the issues about compositionality. We therefore propose to discuss it only very briefly. It is claim iv that distinguishes the strong from the weak notion of compositional structure: a representation has weak compositional structure if it contains context-dependent constituents. We propose to take up the question of context-dependent representation here.

We commence by reciting the coffee story (in a slightly condensed form).

Since, following Smolensky, we are assuming heuristically that units have bivalent activity levels, vectors can be represented by ordered sets of zeros (indicating that a unit is "off") and ones (indicating that a unit is "on"). Thus, Smolensky says, the CUP WITH COFFEE representation might be the following activity vector over microfeatures:

1-UPRIGHT CONTAINER
1-HOT LIQUID
0-GLASS CONTACTING WOOD[7]
1-PORCELAIN CURVED SURFACE
1-BURNT ODOR
1-BROWN LIQUID CONTACTING PORCELAIN
1-PORCELAIN CURVED SURFACE
0-OBLONG SILVER OBJECT
1-FINGER-SIZED HANDLE
1-BROWN LIQUID WITH CURVED SIDES AND BOTTOM[8]

This vector, according to Smolensky, contains a COFFEE representation as a constituent. This constituent can, he claims, be derived from CUP WITH COFFEE by subtracting CUP WITHOUT COFFEE from CUP WITH COFFEE. The vector that is the remainder of this subtraction will be COFFEE.

The reader will object that this treatment presupposes that CUP WITHOUT COFFEE is a constituent of CUP WITH COFFEE. Quite so. Smolensky is explicit in claiming that "the pattern or vector representing *cup with coffee* is composed of a vector that can be identified as a particular distributed representation of *cup without coffee* with a representation with the content *coffee*" (1988b, p. 10).

One is inclined to think that this must surely be wrong. If you combine a representation with the content *cup without coffee* with a representation with the content *coffee*, you get not a representation with the content *cup with coffee* but rather a representation with the self-contradictory content *cup without coffee with coffee*. Smolensky's subtraction procedure appears to confuse the representation of *cup without coffee* (viz., CUP WITHOUT

COFFEE) with the representation of *cup* without the representation of *coffee* (viz., CUP). CUP WITHOUT COFFEE expresses the content *cup without coffee*; CUP combines consistently with COFFEE. But nothing does both.

On the other hand, it must be remembered that Smolensky's mental representations are advertised as context dependent, hence noncompositional. Indeed, we are given *no clue at all* about what sorts of relations between the semantic properties of complex symbols and the semantic properties of their constituents his theory acknowledges. Perhaps in a semantics where constituents don't contribute their contents to the symbols they belong to, it's all right after all if CUP WITH COFFEE has CUP WITHOUT COFFEE (or, for that matter, PRIME NUMBER, or GRANDMOTHER, or FLYING SAUCER or THE LAST OF THE MOHICANS) among its constituents.

In any event, to complete the story, Smolensky gives the following features for CUP WITHOUT COFFEE:

1-UPRIGHT CONTAINER
0-HOT LIQUID
0-GLASS CONTACTING WOOD
1-PORCELAIN CURVED SURFACE
0-BURNT ODOR
0-BROWN LIQUID CONTACTING PORCELAIN
1-PORCELAIN CURVED SURFACE
0-OBLONG SILVER OBJECT
1-FINGER-SIZED HANDLE
0-BROWN LIQUID WITH CURVED SIDES AND BOTTOM etc.

Subtracting this vector from CUP WITH COFFEE, we get the following COFFEE representation:

0-UPRIGHT CONTAINER
1-HOT LIQUID
0-GLASS CONTACTING WOOD
0-PORCELAIN CURVED SURFACE
1-BURNT ODOR
1-BROWN LIQUID CONTACTING PORCELAIN
0-PORCELAIN CURVED SURFACE

0-OBLONG SILVER OBJECT
0-FINGER-SIZED HANDLE
1-BROWN LIQUID WITH CURVED SIDES AND BOTTOM

That, then, is Smolensky's "coffee story".

Comments

(i) Microfeatures

It's common ground in this discussion that the explanation of systematicity must somehow appeal to relations between complex mental representations and their constituents (on Smolensky's view, to combinatorial relations among vectors). The issue about whether there are microfeatures is entirely orthogonal; it concerns only the question *which properties the activation states of individual units express*. (To put it in more Classical terms, it concerns the question which symbols constitute the *primitive vocabulary* of the system of mental representations.) If there are microfeatures, then the activation states of individual units are constrained to express only (as it might be) "sensory" properties (this volume, p. 293). If there aren't, then activation states of individual units can express not only such properties as *being brown* and *being hot*, but also such properties as *being coffee*. It should be evident upon even casual reflection that, whichever way this issue is settled, the constituency question--viz., the question how the representation COFFEE relates to the representation CUP WITH COFFEE--remains wide open. We therefore propose to drop the discussion of microfeatures in what follows.

(iv) Context-dependent representation

As far as we can tell, Smolensky holds that the representation of *coffee* that he derives by subtraction from CUP WITH COFFEE is context dependent in the sense that it need bear no more than a "family resemblance" to the vector that represents *coffee* in CAN WITH COFFEE, GLASS WITH COFFEE, etc. There is thus no single vector that counts as *the* COFFEE representation, hence no single vector that is a component of all the representations which, in a Classical system, would have COFFEE as a Classical constituent.

Smolensky himself apparently agrees that this is the wrong sort of constituency to account for systematicity and related phenomena. As he remarks, "a true constituent can move around and fill any of a number of different roles in different structures" (1988b, p. 11) and the connection between constituency and systematicity would appear to turn on this. For example, the solution to the systematicity problem mooted in Section I depends exactly on the assumption that tokens of the representation type JOHN express the same content in the context LOVES THE GIRL that they do in the context THE GIRL LOVES; (viz., that they pick out *John*, who is an element both of the proposition *John loves the girl* and of the proposition *the girl loves John*). It thus appears, prima facie, that the explanation of systematicity requires context-independent constituents.

How, then, does Smolensky suppose that the assumption that mental representations have weak compositional structure, that is, that mental representation is context dependent, bear on the explanation of systematicity? He simply doesn't say. And we don't have a clue. In fact, having introduced the notion of weak compositional structure, Smolensky to all intents and purposes drops it in favor of the notion of strong compositional structure, and the discussion of systematicity is carried out entirely in terms of the latter. What, then, he takes the relation between weak and strong compositional structure to be,--and, for that matter, which kind of structure he actually thinks that mental representations have[9]--is thoroughly unclear.

In fact, quite independent of its bearing on systematicity, the notion of weak compositional structure as Smolensky presents it is of very dubious coherence. We close this Section with a remark or two about this point.

It looks as though Smolensky holds that the COFFEE vector that you get by subtraction from CUP WITH COFFEE is not a COFFEE representation when it stands alone. "This representation is indeed a representation of coffee, but [only?] in a very particular context: the context provided by *cup* [i.e., CUP]" (this volume, p. 294). If this is the view, it has bizarre consequences. Take a liquid that has the properties specified by the microfeatures that comprise COFFEE in isolation, but that isn't coffee. Pour it into a cup, et voila! it *becomes* coffee by semantical magic.

Smolensky explicitly doesn't think that the vector COFFEE that you get from CUP WITH COFFEE gives necessary conditions for being coffee, since you'd get a different COFFEE vector by subtraction from, say, GLASS WITH COFFEE. And the passage just quoted suggests that he thinks it doesn't give sufficient conditions either. But, then, if the microfeatures associated with COFFEE are neither necessary nor sufficient for being *coffee*[10] the question arises what, according to this story, *does* make a vector a COFFEE representation; when does a vector have the content *coffee*?

As far as we can tell, Smolensky holds that what makes the COFFEE component of CUP WITH COFFEE a representation with the content *coffee* is that it is distributed over units representing certain microfeatures *and* that it figures as a component vector of a vector which is a CUP WITH COFFEE representation. As remarked above, we are given no details at all about this reverse compositionality according to which the embedding vector determines the contents of its constituents; how it is supposed to work isn't even discussed in Smolensky's papers. But, in any event, a regress threatens since the question now arises: if being a component of a CUP OF COFFEE representation is required to make a vector a *coffee* representation, what is required to make a vector a *cup of coffee* representation? Well, presumably CUP OF COFFEE represents *cup of coffee* because it involves the microfeatures it does *and* because it is a component of still another vector; perhaps one that is a THERE IS A CUP OF COFFEE ON THE TABLE representation. Does this go on forever? If it doesn't, then presumably there are some vectors which aren't constituents of any others. But now, what determines *their* contents? Not the contents of their constituents because, by assumption, Smolensky's semantics isn't compositional (CUP WITHOUT COFFEE is a constituent of CUP WITH COFFEE, etc.). And not the vectors that they are constituents of, because, by assumption, there aren't any of those.

We think it is unclear whether Smolensky has a coherent story about how a system of representations could have weak compositional structure.

What, in light of all this, leads Smolensky to embrace his account of weak compositionality? Here's one suggestion: perhaps Smolensky confuses being a representation of a cup with coffee with being a CUP WITH COFFEE representation. Espying some cup with coffee on a particular occasion, in a particular context, one might come to be in a mental state that represents it as having roughly the microfeatures that Smolensky lists. That mental state would then be a representation of a cup with coffee in this sense: there is a cup of coffee that it's a mental representation of. But it wouldn't, of course, follow, that it's a CUP WITH COFFEE representation; and the mental representation of that cup with coffee might be quite different from the mental representation of the cup with coffee that you espied on some other occasion or in some other context. So *which mental representation a cup of coffee gets is context dependent*, just as Smolensky says. But that doesn't give Smolensky what he needs to make mental representations themselves context dependent. In particular, from the fact that cups with coffee get different representations in different contexts, it patently doesn't follow that the mental symbol that represents something as *being* a cup of coffee in one context might represent something as being something else (a giraffe say, or The Last of The Mohicans) in some other context. We doubt that anything will give Smolensky that, since we know of no reason to suppose that it is true.

In short, it is natural to confuse the true but uninteresting thought that how you mentally represent some coffee depends on the context, with the much more tendentious thought that the mental representation COFFEE is context dependent. Assuming that he is a victim of this confusion makes sense of many of the puzzling things that Smolensky says in the coffee story. Notice, for example, that all the microfeatures in his examples express more or less perceptual properties (cf., Smolensky's own remark that his microfeatures yield a "nearly sensory level representation"). Notice, too, the peculiarity that the microfeature "porcelain curved surface" occurs *twice* in the vector for CUP WITH COFFEE, COFFEE, CUP WITHOUT COFFEE and the like. Presumably, what Smolensky has in mind is that, when you look at a cup, you get to see two curved surfaces, one going off to the left and the other going off to the right.

Though we suspect this really is what's going on, we won't pursue this interpretation further since, if it's correct, then the coffee story is completely irrelevant to the question of what kind of constituency relation a COFFEE representation bears to a CUP WITH COFFEE; and that, remember, is the question that bears on the issues about systematicity.

III. STRONG COMPOSITIONAL STRUCTURE

So much, then, for "weak" compositional structure. Let us turn to Smolensky's account of "strong" compositional structure. Smolensky says that:

A true constituent can move around and fill any of a number of different roles in different structures. Can *this* be done with vectors encoding distributed representations, and be done in a way that doesn't amount to simply implementing symbolic syntactic constituency? The purpose of this section is to describe research showing that the answer is affirmative. (1988b, p. 11)

The idea that mental representations are activity vectors over units, and the idea that some mental representations have other mental representations as components, is common to the treatment of both weak and strong compositional structure.   However, Smolensky's discussion of the latter differs in several respects from his discussion of the former. First, units are explicitly supposed to have continuous activation levels between 0 and 1; second, he does not invoke the idea of microfeatures when discussing strong compositional structure; third, he introduces a new vector operation (multiplication) to the two previously mentioned (addition and subtraction); fourth, and most important, strong compositional structure does not invoke--indeed, would appear to be incompatible with--the notion, that mental representations are context dependent.   So strong compositional structure does not exhibit the incoherences of Smolensky's theory of context-dependent representation.

We will proceed as follows. First we briefly present the notion of strong compositional structure. Then we turn to criticism.

Smolensky explains the notion of strong compositional structure, in part, by appeal to the ideas of a tensor product representation and a superposition representation.   To illustrate these ideas, consider how a connectionist machine might represent four-letter English words. Words can be decomposed into roles (viz., ordinal positions that letters can occupy) and things that can fill these roles (viz., letters). Correspondingly, the machine might contain activity vectors over units which represent the relevant roles (i.e., over the *role units*) and activity vectors over units which represent the fillers (i.e., over the *filler units*). Finally, it might contain activity vectors over units which represent roles (i.e., letters in letter positions); these are the *binding units*. The key idea is that the activity vectors over the binding units might be tensor products of activity vectors over the role units and the filler units. The representation of a word would then be a superposition vector over the binding units; that is, a vector that is arrived at by superimposing the tensor product vectors.

The two operations used here to derive complex vectors from component vectors are vector multiplication in the case of tensor product vectors and vector addition in the case of superposition vectors. These are iterative operations in the sense that activity vectors that result from the multiplication of role vectors and filler vectors might themselves represent the fillers of roles in more complex structures. Thus, a tensor product which represents the word "John" as "J" *in first position, "o" in second position...etc.*

might itself be bound to the representation of a syntactical function to indicate, for example, that "John" has the role subject-of in "John loves the girl". Such tensor product representations could themselves be superimposed over yet another group of binding units to yield a superposition vector which represents the bracketing tree (John) (loves (the girl)).

It is, in fact, unclear whether this sort of apparatus is adequate to represent all the semantically relevant syntactic relations that Classical theories express by using bracketing trees with Classical constituents. (There are, for example, problems about long-distance binding relations, as between quantifiers and bound variables.) But we do not wish to press this point. For present polemical purposes, we propose simply to assume that each Classical bracketing tree can be coded into a complex vector in such fashion that the constituents of the tree correspond in some regular way to components of the vector.

But this is not, of course, to grant that either tensor product or superposition vectors *have* Classical constituent structure. In particular, from the assumptions that bracketing trees have Classical constituents and that bracketing trees can be coded by activity vectors, it does *not* follow that activity vectors have Classical constituents. On the contrary, a point about which Smolensky is himself explicit is vital in this regard: the components of a complex vector need not even correspond to patterns of activity over units actually in the machine. As Smolensky puts it, the activity states of the filler and role units can be "imaginary" even though the ultimate activity vectors--the ones which do not themselves serve as filler or role components of more complex structures--must be actual activity patterns over units in the machine. Consider again our machine for representing four-letter words. The superposition pattern that represents, say, the word "John" will be an activity vector actually realized in the machine. However, the activity vector representing "J" will be merely imaginary, as will the activity vector representing *the first letter position*. Similarly for the tensor product activity vector representing *"J" in the first letter position*. The only pattern of activity that will be *actually tokened* in the machine is the superposition vector representing "John".

These considerations are of central importance for the following reason. Smolensky's main strategy is, in effect, to invite us to consider the components of tensor product and superposition vectors to be analogous to the Classical constituents of a complex symbol; hence to view them as providing a means by which connectionist architectures can capture the causal and semantic consequences of Classical constituency in mental representations.   However, the components of tensor product and superposition vectors differ from Classical constituents in the following way: when a complex Classical symbol is tokened, its constituents are tokened. When a tensor product vector or superposition vector is tokened, its components are not (except per accidens).   The implication of this difference, from the point of view of the theory of mental processes, is that whereas the Classical constituents of a complex symbol are, ipso facto, available to contribute to the causal consequences of its tokenings--in particular, they are available to provide domains for mental processes--the components of tensor product and superposition vectors can have no causal status as such. What is merely imaginary can't make things happen, to put this point in a nutshell.

We will return presently to what all this implies for the treatment of the systematicity problem. There is, however, a preliminary issue that needs to be discussed.

We have seen that the components of tensor product/superposition vectors, unlike Classical constituents, are not, in general, tokened whenever the activity vector of which they are the components is tokened. It is worth emphasizing, in addition, the familiar point that there is, in general, no *unique* decomposition of a tensor product or superposition vector into components. Indeed, given that units are assumed to have continuous levels of activation, there will be *infinitely* many decompositions of a given activity vector. One might wonder, therefore, what sense there is in talk of *the* decomposition of a mental representation into significant constituents given the notion of constituency that Smolensky's theory provides.[11]

Smolensky replies to this point as follows. Cognitive systems will be dynamical systems; there will be dynamic equations over the activation values of individual units, and these will determine certain regularities over activity vectors.   Given the dynamical equations of the system, certain decompositions can be especially useful for "explaining and understanding" its behavior. In this sense, the dynamics of a system may determine "normal modes" of decomposition into components, So, for example, though a given superposition vector can, in principle, be taken to be the sum of many different sets of vectors, yet it may turn out that we get a small group of sets--even a unique set--when we decompose in the direction of normal modes; and likewise for decomposing tensor product vectors. The long and short is that *it could, in principle, turn out* that, given the (thus far undefined) normal modes of a dynamical cognitive system, complex superposition vectors will have it in common with Classical complex symbols that they have a unique decomposition into semantically significant parts. Of course, it also could turn out that they don't, and no ground for optimism on this point has thus far been supplied.

Having noted this problem, however, we propose simply to ignore it. So here is where we now stand: by assumption (though quite possibly contrary to fact), tensor product vectors and superposition vectors can code constituent structure in a way that makes them adequate vehicles for the expression of propositional content; and, by assumption (though again quite possibly contrary to fact), the superposition vectors that cognitive theories acknowledge have a unique decomposition into semantically interpretable tensor product vectors which, in turn, have a unique decomposition into semantically interpretable filler vectors and role vectors; so it's determinate which proposition a given complex activity vector represents.

Now, assuming all this, what about the systematicity problem?

The first point to make is this: if tensor product/superposition vector representation solves the systematicity problem, the solution must be quite different from the Classical proposal sketched in Section I. True tensor product vectors and superposition vectors "have constituents" in some suitably extended sense: tensor product vectors have semantically evaluable components, and superposition vectors are decomposable into semantically evaluable tensor product vectors. But the Classical solution to the systematicity problem assumes that *the constituents of mental representations have causal roles*; that they provide domains for mental processes. The Classical constituents of a complex symbol thus contribute to determining the causal consequences of the tokening of that symbol, and it seems clear that the "extended" constituents of a tensor product/superposition representation can't do that. On the contrary, the components of a complex vector are typically not even tokened when the complex vector itself is tokened; they are simply constituents into which the complex vector *could be* resolved consonant with decomposition in the direction of normal modes. But, to put it crudely, the fact that six *could be* represented as "3 x 2" cannot, in and of itself, affect the causal processes in a computer (or a brain) in which six *is* represented as "6". Merely counterfactual representations have no causal consequences; only actually tokened representations do.

Smolensky is, of course, sensitive to the question whether activity vectors really do have constituent structure. He defends at length the claim that he has not contorted the notion of constituency in claiming that they do. Part of this defense adverts to the role that tensor products and superpositions play in physical theory:

The state of the atom, like the states of all systems in quantum theory, is represented by a vector in an abstract vector space. Each electron has an internal state (its "spin"); it also has a role it plays in the atom as a whole: it occupies some "orbital", essentially a cloud of probability for finding it at particular places in the atom. The internal state of an electron is represented by a "spin vector"; the orbital or role of the electron (part) in the atom (whole) is represented by another vector, which describes the probability cloud. The vector representing the electron as situated in the atom is the tensor product of the vector representing the internal state of the electron and the vector representing its orbital. The atom as a whole is represented by a vector that is the sum or superposition of vectors, each of which represents a particular electron in its orbital.... (1988b, pp. 19-20)

"So", Smolensky adds, "someone who claims that the tensor product representational scheme distorts the notion of constituency has some explaining to do" (1988b, p. 20).

The physics lesson is greatly appreciated; but it is important to be clear on just what it is supposed to show. It's not, at least for present purposes, in doubt that tensor products *can represent* constituent structure. The relevant question is whether tensor product representations *have* constituent structure; or, since we have agreed that they may be said to have constituent structure "in an extended sense", it's whether they have the kind of constituent structure to which causal processes can be sensitive, hence the kind of constituent structure to which an explanation of systematicity might appeal.[12] But we have already seen the answer to *this* question: the constituents of complex activity vectors typically aren't "there", so if the causal consequences of tokening a complex vector are sensitive to its constituent structure, that's a miracle.

We conclude that assuming that mental representations are activation vectors does not allow Smolensky to endorse the Classical solution of the systematicity problem. And, indeed, we think Smolensky would grant this since he admits up front that mental processes will not be causally sensitive to the strong compositional structure of mental representations. That is, he acknowledges that the constituents of complex mental representations play no causal role in determining what happens when the representations get tokened.   "...Causal efficacy was not my goal in developing the tensor product representation..." (1988b, p. 21).   What are causally efficacious according to connectionists are the activation values of individual units; the dynamical equations that govern the evolution of the system will be defined over these.   It would thus appear that Smolensky must have some *non-*

Classical solution to the systematicity problem up his sleeve; some solution that does *not* depend on assuming mental processes that are causally sensitive to constituent structure. So then, after all this, what *is* Smolensky's solution to the systematicity problem?

Remarkably enough, *Smolensky doesn't say.* All he does say is that he

hypothesizes...that...the systematic effects observed in the processing of mental representations arise because the evolution of vectors can be (at least partially and approximately) explained in terms of the evolution of their components, even though the precise dynamical equations apply [only] to the individual numbers comprising the vectors and [not] at the level of [their] constituents--i.e., even though the constituents are not causally efficacious. (1988b, p. 21)

It is left unclear how the constituents ("components") of complex vectors are to explain their evolution (even partially and approximately) when they are, by assumption, at best causally inert and, at worst, merely imaginary. In any event, what Smolensky clearly does think is causally responsible for the "evolution of vectors" (and hence for the systematicity of cognition) are unspecified processes that affect the states of activation of the individual units (the neuron analogs) out of which the vectors are composed. So, then, as far as we can tell, the proposed connectionist explanation of systematicity (and related features of cognition) comes down to this: Smolensky "hypothesizes" that systematicity is somehow a consequence of underlying neural processes.[13] Needless to say, if that *is* Smolensky's theory, it is, on the one hand, certainly true, and, on the other hand, not intimately dependent upon his long story about fillers, binders, tensor products, superposition vectors and the rest.

By way of rounding out the argument, we want to reply to a question raised by an anonymous *Cognition* reviewer, who asks

...couldn't Smolensky easily build in mechanisms to accomplish the matrix algebra operations that would make the necessary vector explicit (or better yet, from his point of view,...mechanisms that are sensitive to the imaginary components without literally making them explicit in some string of units)?[14]

But this misses the point of the problem that systematicity poses for connectionists, which is not to show that systematic cognitive capacities are *possible* given the assumptions of a connectionist architecture, but to explain how systematicity could be *necessary*--how it could be a *law* that cognitive capacities are systematic--given those assumptions.[15]

No doubt it is possible for Smolensky to wire a network so that it supports a vector that represents aRb if and only if it supports a vector that represents bRa; and perhaps it is possible for him to do that without making the imaginary units explicit[16] (though there is, so far, no proposal about how to ensure this for *arbitrary* a, R and b). The trouble is that, although the architecture permits this, it equally permits Smolensky to wire a network so that it supports a vector that represents aRb if and only if it supports a vector that represents zSq; or, for that matter, if and only if it supports a vector that represents The Last of The Mohicans. The architecture would appear to be absolutely indifferent as among these options.

Whereas, as we keep saying, in the Classical architecture, if you meet the conditions for being able to represent aRb, YOU CANNOT BUT MEET THE CONDITIONS FOR BEING ABLE TO REPRESENT *bRa*; the architecture won't let you do so because (i) the representation of a, R and b are constituents of the representation of aRb, and (ii) you have to token the constituents of the representations that you token, so Classical constituents can't be just imaginary. So then: it is *built into* the Classical picture that you can't think aRb unless you are able to think bRa, but the Connectionist picture is *neutral* on whether you can think aRb even if you can't think bRa. But it is a law of nature that you can't think aRb if you can't think bRa. So the Classical picture explains systematicity and the Connectionist picture doesn't. So the Classical picture wins.

CONCLUSION

At one point in his discussion, Smolensky makes some remarks that we find quite revealing: he says that, even in cases that are paradigms of Classical architectures (LISP machines and the like), "...we normally think of the 'real' causes as physical and far below the symbolic level..." Hence, even in Classical machines, the sense in which operations at the symbol level are real causes is just that "...there is...a complete and precise algorithmic (temporal) story to tell about the states of the machine described..." at that level (1988b: p. 20). Smolensky, of course, denies that there is a

...comparable story at the symbolic level in the human cognitive architecture...that is a difference with the Classical view that I have made much of. *It may be that a good way to characterize the difference is in terms of whether the constituents in mental structure are causally efficacious in mental processing.* (1988b, p. 20 (our emphasis))

We say that this is revealing because it suggests a diagnosis: it would seem that Smolensky has succumbed to a sort of generalized epiphenomenalism. The idea is that even Classical constituents participate in causal processes solely by virtue of their physical microstructure, so even on the Classical story it's what happens at the neural level that *really* counts. Though the evolution of vectors can perhaps be explained in a predictively adequate sort of way by appeal to macroprocesses like operations on constituents, still if you want to know what's *really* going on--if you want the *causal* explanation--you need to go down to the "precise dynamical equations" that apply to activation states of units. That intentional generalizations can only approximate these precise dynamical equations is among Smolensky's recurrent themes. By conflating the issue about "precision" with the issue about causal efficacy, Smolensky makes it seem that to the extent that macrolevel generalizations are imprecise, to that extent macrolevel processes are epiphenomenal.

It would need a philosophy lesson to say all of what's wrong with this. Suffice it for present purposes that the argument iterates in a way that Smolensky ought to find embarrassing. No doubt, we do get greater precision when we go from generalizations about operations on constituents to generalizations about operations on units. But if that shows that symbol-level processes aren't really causal, then it must be that unit-level processes aren't really causal either. After all, we get *still more* precision when we go down from unit-sensitive operations to molecule-sensitive operations, and more precision yet when we go down from molecule-sensitive operations to quark-sensitive operations. The moral is not, however, that the causal laws of psychology should be stated in terms of the behavior of quarks. Rather, the moral is that whether you have a level of causal explanation is a question, not just of how much precision you are able to achieve, but also of *what generalizations you are able to express*. The price you pay for doing psychology at the level of units is that you lose causal generalizations that symbol-level theories are able to state. Smolensky's problems with capturing the generalizations about systematicity provide a graphic illustration of these truths.

It turns out, at any event, that there is a crucial caveat to Smolensky's repeated claim that connectionist mechanisms can reconstruct everything that's interesting about the notion of constituency. Strictly speaking, he claims only to reconstruct whatever is interesting about constituents *except their causes and effects*. The explanation of systematicity turns on the causal role of the constituents of mental representations and is therefore among the casualties. Hilary Putnam, back in the days when he was still a Metaphysical Realist, used to tell a joke about a physicist who actually managed to build a perpetual motion machine; all except for a part that goes back and forth, back and forth, back and forth, forever. Smolensky's explanation of systematicity has very much the character of this machine.

We conclude that Fodor and Pylyshyn's challenge to connectionists has yet to be met. We still don't have *even a suggestion* of how to account for systematicity within the assumptions of connectionist cognitive architecture.

NOTES

[1] Since the two are often confused, we wish to emphasize that taking *systematicity* for granted leaves the question of *compositionality* wide open. The systematicity of cognition consists of, for example, the fact that organisms that can think aRb can think bRa and vice versa. *Compositionality* proposes a certain explanation of systematicity: viz., that the content of thoughts is determined, in a uniform way, by the content of the context-independent concepts that are their constituents; and that the thought that bRa is constituted of the same concepts as the thought that aRb. So the polemical situation is as follows. If you are a Connectionist who accepts systematicity, then you must argue either that systematicity can be explained without compositionality, or that connectionist architecture accommodates compositional representation. So far as we can tell, Smolensky vacillates between these options: what he calls "weak compositionality" favors the former and what he calls "strong compositionality" favors the latter.

We emphasize this distinction between systematicity and compositionality in light of some remarks by an anonymous *Cognition* reviewer: "By berating the [connectionist] modelers for their inability to represent the common-sense [uncontextualized] notion of 'coffee'...Fodor and McLaughlin are missing a key point--the models are not supposed to do so. If you buy the...massive context-sensitivity...that connectionists believe in." Our strategy is *not*, however, to argue that there is something wrong with connectionism because it fails to offer an uncontextualized notion of mental (or, mutatis mutandis, linguistic) representation. Our argument is that if connectionists assume that mental representations are context sensitive, they will need to offer some explanation of systematicity that does not entail compositionality *and they do not have one*.

We do not, therefore, offer direct arguments for context-insensitive concepts in what follows; we are quite prepared that "coffee" should have a meaning only in context. Only, we argue, *if* it does, then some non-compositional account of the systematicity of coffee-thoughts will have to be provided.

[2] Though we shall generally consider examples where complex symbols literally *contain* their Classical constituents, the present condition means to leave it open that symbols may have Classical constituents that are not among their (spatio-temporal) parts. (For example, so far as this condition is concerned, it might be that the Classical constituents of a symbol include the values of a "fetch" operation that takes the symbol as an argument.)

[3] We assume that the elements of propositions can include, for example, individuals, properties, relations and other propositions. Other metaphysical assumptions are, of course, possible. For example, it is arguable that the constituents of propositions include *individual concepts* (in the Fregian sense) rather than individuals themselves; and so on. Fortunately, it is not necessary to enter into these abstruse issues to make the points that are relevant to the systematicity problem. All we really need is that propositions have internal structure, and that, characteristically, the internal structures of complex mental representations correspond, in the appropriate way, to the internal structure of the propositions that they express.

[4] The following notational conventions will facilitate the discussion: we will follow standard practice and use capitalized English words and sentences as canonical names for mental representations. (Smolensky uses italicized English expressions instead.) We stipulate that the semantic value of a mental representation so named is the semantic value of the corresponding English word or sentence, and we will italicize words or sentences that denote semantic values. So, for example, COFFEE is a mental representation that expresses (the property of being) *coffee* (as does the English work "coffee"); JOHN LOVES THE GIRL is a mental representation that expresses the proposition that *John loves the girl;* and so forth. It is important to notice that our notation allows that the mental representation JOHN LOVES THE GIRL can be atomic and the mental representation COFFEE can be a complex symbol. That is, capitalized expressions should be read as the names of mental representations rather than as structural descriptions.

[5] Smolensky apparently allows that units may have continuous levels of activation from 0 to 1. In telling the coffee story, however, he generally assumes bivalence for ease of exposition.

[6] As we shall see below, when an activity vector is tokened, its component vectors typically are not. So the constituents of a complex vector are, ipso facto, non-Classical.

[7] Notice that this microfeature is "off" in CUP WITH COFFEE, so it might be wondered why Smolensky mentions it at all. The explanation may be this: operations of vector combination apply only to vectors of the same dimensionality. In the context of the weak constituency story, this means that you can only combine vectors that are activity patterns *over the same units*. It follows that a component vector must contain the same units (though, possibly at different levels of activation) as the vectors with which it combines. Thus if GRANNY combines with COFFEE to yield GRANNY'S COFFEE, GRANNY must contain activation levels for all the units in COFFEE and vice versa. In the present example, it may be that CUP WITH COFFEE is required to contain a 0-activation level for GLASS CONTACTING WOOD to accommodate cases where it is a component of some other vector. Similarly with OBLONG SILVER OBJECT (below) since cups with coffee often have spoons in them.

[8] Presumably Smolensky does not take this list to be exhaustive, but we don't know how to continue it. Beyond the remark that although the microfeatures in his examples correspond to "...nearly sensory-level representation[s]..." that is "not essential", Smolensky provides no account at all of what determines which contents are expressed by microfeatures. The question thus arises why Smolensky assumes that COFFEE is not itself a microfeature. In any event, Smolensky repeatedly warns the reader not to take his examples of microfeatures very seriously, and we don't.

[9] They can't have both; either the content of a representation is context dependent or it's not. So, if Smolensky does think that you need strong compositional structure to explain systematicity, and that weak compositional structure is the kind that Connectionist representations have, then it would seem that he *thereby* grants Fodor and Pylyshyn's claim that Connectionist representations can't explain systematicity. We find this all very mysterious.

[10] If they were necessary and sufficient, COFFEE wouldn't be context dependent.

[11] The function of the brackets in a Classical bracketing tree is precisely to exhibit its decomposition into constituents; and when the tree is well formed this decomposition will be unique. Thus, the bracketing of "(John) (loves) (the girl)" implies, for example, both that "the girl" is a constituent and that "loves the" is not.

[12] It's a difference between psychology and physics that whereas psychology is about the casual laws that govern tokenings *of (mental) representations,* physics is about the causal laws that govern (not mental representations but) atoms, electrons and the like. Since *being a representation* isn't a property in the domain of physical theory, the question whether mental representations have constituent structure has no analog in physics.

[13] More precisely: we take Smolensky to be claiming that there is some property D, such that if a dynamical system has D its behavior is systematic, and such that human behavior (for example) is caused by a dynamical system that has D. The trouble is that this is a platitude since it is untendentious that human behavior is systematic, that its causation by the nervous system is lawful, and that the nervous system is dynamical. The least that has to happen if we are to have a substantive connectionist account of systematicity is: first, it must be made clear what property D is, and second it must be shown that D is a property that connectionist systems can have by law. Smolensky's theory does nothing to meet either of these requirements.

[14] Actually, Smolensky is forced to choose the second option. To choose the first would, in effect, be to endorse the Classical requirement that tokening a symbol implies tokening its constituents; in which case, the question arises once again why such a network isn't an implementation of a language of thought machine. Just as Smolensky mustn't allow the representations of roles, fillers and binding units to be subvectors of superposition vectors if he is to avoid the "implementation" horn of the Fodor/Pylyshyn dilemma, so too he must avoid postulating mechanisms that make role, filler and binding units explicit (specifically, accessible to mental operations) whenever the superposition vectors are tokened. Otherwise he again has symbols with Classical constituents and raises the question why the proposed device isn't a language of thought machine. Smolensky's problem is that the very feature of his representations that make them wrong for explaining systematicity (viz., that their constituents are allowed to be imaginary) is the one that they have to have to assure that they aren't Classical.

[15] Fodor and Pylyshyn were very explicit about this. See, for example, 1988, p. 48.

[16] Terence Horgan remarks (personal communication) "...often there are two mathematically equivalent ways to calculate the time-evolution of a dynamical system. One is to apply the relevant equations directly to the numbers that are elements of a single total vector describing the initial state of the system. Another way is to mathematically decompose that vector into component normal-mode vector, then compute the time-evolution of each [of these]...and then take the later state of the system to be described by a vector that is the superposition of the resulting normal-mode vectors". Computations of the former sort are supposed to be the model for operations that are "sensitive" to the components of a mental representation vector without recovering them. (Even in the second case, it's the theorist who recovers them in the course of the computations by which he makes his predictions. This does not, of course, imply that the constituents thus "recovered" participate in causal processes in the system under analysis.)

REFERENCES

Fodor, J., and Pylyshyn, P.: 1988, 'Connectionism and Cognitive Architecture: A critical analysis', *Cognition* **28**, 3-71.

Smolensky, P.: 1987, 'The Constituent Structure of Mental States: A Reply to Fodor and Pylyshyn, *Southern Journal of Philosophy* **26**, 137-160.

Smolensky, P.: 1988a, 'On the Proper Treatment of Connectionism', *Behavioral and Brain Sciences* **11**, 1-23.

Smolensky, P.: 1988b, 'Connectionism, Constituency and the Language of Thought', University of Colorado Technical Report; also forthcoming in B. Loewer, and G. Rey, (eds.), *Meaning in Mind: Fodor and His Critics*, Oxford, Blackwell.

Jerry Fodor
Department of Philosophy
City University of New York
New York, NY 10031, U.S.A.

Brian P. McLaughlin
Department of Philosophy
Rutgers University
New Brunswick, NJ 08903, U.S.A.

TIMOTHY VAN GELDER

CLASSICAL QUESTIONS, RADICAL ANSWERS:
CONNECTIONISM AND THE STRUCTURE
OF MENTAL REPRESENTATIONS

Communication across the revolutionary divide is inevitably partial.

- Kuhn (1962) p. 149.

The many and obvious contrasts between Connectionism and (something like) "most other work in Cognitive Science" often give rise to rather grandiose talk of scientific upheaval. Thus it is common to hear the proposal that Connectionism represents (or is the beginning of, or at least points in the general direction of) a whole new approach and perhaps even a whole new *paradigm* in the study of cognition, an approach which directly contests and may even be displacing (something like) the dominant symbolic view. This is an exciting prospect, especially for those philosophers and others who prefer to view such topics as artificial intelligence and cognitive psychology in terms of the grand sweep of intellectual history. Unfortunately, despite the endless tabloid observations, nobody yet seems altogether sure just what Connectionism *is*, in any sense going beyond the standard fare of dull details and techno-truisms about the nature of typical Connectionist networks. Indeed, in discussion to date there is very little agreement even over how the phenomenon itself is best described: some regard Connectionism as nothing less than a whole new *paradigm*, while others--using progressively more vague terminology--have described it as a radically new *architecture, theory, framework, model, approach*, and simply as a new *view*.

This general situation is more than a little embarrassing for the philosophy of psychology. As philosophy of mind, it conspicuously failed to anticipate the Connectionist upheaval with anything like a theory of mind that Connectionism might instantiate; while as a branch of cognitive science, it appears derelict in its primary responsibility, that of fretting about the foundational assumptions of the enterprise while others get on with some

355

real work. Fathoming the Connectionist beast, however, is no easy task. There is already an impressive proliferation of Connectionist theories, models and mechanisms, and many different areas in which they have been applied. Which features of this work (if any) are deep, conceptually significant and theoretically revolutionary? Which, by contrast, are merely incidental, transient distractions, just a superficial veneer laid over familiar old ideas (or perhaps radical new ones)? Given the sometimes bewildering diversity of particular proposals, it is hard to tell. Compounding the difficulty is the fact that Connectionism seems to thrive in a conceptually and historically rarified atmosphere, in which there are few obvious investigative guidelines available.

Short of despair, it has seemed plausible to many that we should approach this difficult problem in a somewhat circuitous fashion. The mainstream symbolic or "Classical"[1] paradigm, which has allegedly dominated research in the study of cognition for the last 20 to 30 years, is more familiar conceptual territory. The general lay of the land is by now relatively well known, thanks to the pioneering surveying work of authors such as Fodor, Simon, Newell, Pylyshyn and Haugeland. If Connectionism really is a genuine alternative to the mainstream symbolic approach, its conceptual landscape must surely differ in some concretely specifiable ways. This conveniently provides a general methodology for comprehending Connectionism: let the conceptual framework of the old approach be our guide. Having articulated the central theoretical commitments of the previous paradigm, the real nature of Connectionism should spill out fairly swiftly: it must be the only remotely plausible stance denying one or more commitments of the old view. Of course, we should also bear in mind that the theoretical stance deduced in this way ought to be somehow related to what we know of various extant attempts to model cognitive processes using neural networks, but this is a defeasible or "soft" constraint because Connectionism may be yet to fully blossom, or at least consolidate; it may well not have fully realized all its own deep theoretical commitments. Insofar as practicing connectionists do not yet conform to the deduced stance, they cannot be True Connectionists.

In short, to arrive at the nature of Connectionism we simply describe the Central Tenets of the Current Paradigm, and then deduce what the new paradigm *must* be like if it is really going to amount to something significantly different to *that*. The well-known Fodor and Pylyshyn critique of Connectionism (Fodor and Pylyshyn, 1988) is an obvious example of this strategy, and the extent to which that critique has dominated subsequent philosophical discussion testifies to the initial plausibility of the general approach. But many other authors have, independently and in their own way, adopted some variant of the same path: see, for example, Cummins and Schwarz (1987), Horgan and Tienson (1987, 1989), Dennett (1986), Tye (1987); Bechtel (1985, 1986); and even Cussins (1988).[2] An especially remarkable feature of this group is the diversity of perspectives and sympathies represented. Those traveling this route rarely fail to notice two of the most unavoidable landmarks of Classical terrain, the use of (something like) syntactically structured, semantically interpretable representations on the one hand, and the use of (something like) structure-sensitive, rule-governed computational processes on the other: features that, in what follows, will be referred to as the *twin minimal commitments*. Between them, they dominate the Classical vista, and the most plausible suggestion for Connectionism--which must presumably stand to the Classical approach as Swaziland to Switzerland--is that it must deny, or at the very least significantly vary, at least one of them.

This general approach holds out a comforting promise of methodological rigor, and usually seems to result in swift progress. But what are its chances of eventual success? Put another way, how likely are we to reach an understanding of a new paradigm when the very possibilities afforded to that paradigm are drawn, quite directly and explicitly, from the old? On what grounds do we suppose that the vocabulary and general conceptual framework of one currently dominant view will be sufficient for the task of describing (even in negative terms) its competitor? Certainly Kuhn himself gives little reason for optimism on this score. A pervasive theme of his work on paradigm shift is that competing paradigms are *incommensurable*. While incommensurability takes many forms, of particular importance here is the fact that a major new scientific theory is never simply a reshuffling of the conceptual framework of the old; rather, it inevitably introduces a comprehensive *new* framework which displaces the previous one as a whole. Though the new theory often takes over many terms, it only does so in a way that significantly alters the meanings of those terms: Einsteinian space, in one of Kuhn's examples, is just not the same thing as Euclidean space, and so the term "space" itself has undergone shifts in meaning. As a consequence, there are rarely (if ever) tidy logical relationships between one paradigm and its competitor; their respective proponents, talking from within their favored conceptual frameworks, typically misunderstand and "talk past" each other.   For these reasons a new paradigm cannot be properly comprehended on the basis of the resources provided by the old; rather, the scientist must undergo a wholesale conversion, a kind of comprehensive "gestalt shift" which leads to an understanding of the new paradigm in its *own* terms.

This rather sweeping line of thought is of course familiar old stuff, but when applied to the current situation it has a surprising consequence. It suggests that, insofar as one takes seriously the idea that Connectionist work is heralding a genuine paradigm shift, attempting to *develop* an understanding of Connectionism by deducing what it must be like if it is to differ interestingly from the Classical paradigm is to risk failing to understand it at all. (Conversely, and somewhat ironically, the attempt to fathom Connectionism in terms of the rejection of some clearly characterizable aspect of the Classical approach really amounts to an implicit denial--from the very outset--that Connectionist work is heralding a genuine paradigm shift.[3]) In what follows I will be arguing that this risk is in fact a very real one; that, to a significant extent, philosophical attempts at understanding Connectionism (and related topics) tend to suffer when they take the conceptual detour in question. In particular, I will argue that certain kinds of questions that follow naturally from the Classical perspective are demonstrably inappropriate if our aim is to develop a sympathetic understanding of the Connectionist enterprise.

What we really need, prior to contrasting Connectionism with the Classical approach, is an *independent* conception of the nature of that enterprise, involving a thorough elaboration of its computational mechanisms,[4] general architectural constraints, learning principles, and so forth. This elaboration should not be constantly looking over its shoulder at Classical theories of cognition. Attention should be concentrated primarily on the distinctive and original aspects of Connectionism itself, rather than on what it must *not* be if it is genuinely different from Classicalism. Assuming we can provide such an independent elaboration, we should then be able to compare and contrast the two conceptions, much as we can now juxtapose, say, Newtonian and Einsteinian mechanics. Indeed, it would be difficult if not impossible to gain a proper perspective on the supposed new alternative unless such a comparison were eventually drawn out. Nevertheless, the crucial point is that we are unlikely to *arrive* at the required independent theory by *setting out* contrasting Connectionism with the Classical approach. Major competing scientific theories typically do not stand in some structured "logical space," such that the essential commitments of one can be derived, by relatively simple logical transformations, from those of another.

For comparisons' sake, it is interesting to note that *none* of the canonical characterizations of the nature of the computational theory of cognitive processes are framed in terms that make essential reference to the preceding paradigm in psychological theorizing. Insofar as they look over their shoulders at all, standard characterizations of the Classical approach typically reach back not to the Behaviorism of previous decades but to such apparently remote concerns as logic and the theory of computation, and before that to philosophers such as Hobbes and Descartes. There is, to be sure, a recurrent emphasis on the need to posit internal representations, and mental processes operating on those representations, but such emphasis hardly springs in any very direct way from a statement of the Central Tenets of Behaviorism conjoined with the requirement that the new paradigm deny some such tenets. In fact, it is a rather telling exercise to see if one can gain *any coherent idea at all* of the kind of paradigm dominating "pre-Classical" research by looking only at the canonical characterizations of the Classical approach.[5] There is a marked contrast here with current attempts at articulating Connectionism, which are almost invariably constructed, step by step, around a primer on the computational theory of mind.

Now, I am certainly *not* claiming that any adverting to mainstream symbolic theorizing automatically renders one incapable of arriving at an adequate understanding of Connectionism. The work of Smolensky is an obvious example of the progressive development of at least one independent conception of Connectionism, and yet that development evolves in constant counterpoint with detailed consideration of the Classical approach.[6] Crucially, however, Smolensky does not *begin* with the Classical paradigm on the way to understanding Connectionism; rather, he places his independently formulated views on Connectionism in constant and useful *juxtaposition* with Classical theory, such that both theories can be seen as only *approximately* related under the terms of their common obeisance to some rather wider and more general "computational abstractions." Even those embarking more directly on the kind of detour in question can do so in a way that is sufficiently sophisticated to avoid the conceptual quagmire. Setting out by acknowledging the nature of the current Classical paradigm can be useful in fixing one's bearings, and by no means precludes one from eventually arriving at the intended goal. The point that needs to be stressed, however, is that there are certain very real dangers that present themselves automatically as soon as one takes this path, conceptual trolls lurking under apparently logical bridges. These trolls not only threaten our further progress, they exact a heavy toll even on understanding that was thought to have been securely established.

For example, the drive to define Connectionism in relation to Classicalism demands that we have a succinct, point-by-point characterization of the Classical approach itself. Thus, as mentioned above, those taking the conceptual detour usually boil the Classical approach down to just two fundamental commitments, to syntactically structured representations and structure-sensitive rule-governed operations. Though clean and neat, this distillation of Classical theorizing lands one directly in the midst of bickering and ultimately rather pointless debates over what is, and what is not, essential to the Classical approach. That approach has very often been taken to have many more--and rather more specific--commitments than just these two very general points: it has often been supposed, for example, that Classical architectures must exhibit such features as serial processing, explicit rules, a distinction between CPU and memory, localized (and hence fragile) storage, and so forth. When a Classical theorist disavows any and all such further commitments, there is always a lingering sense that this is somehow unfair; after all, standard Classical *practice* has generally been such as to justify their attribution.

This sense can be sharpened by recognizing that, as Kuhn stressed, there is always much more to a scientific research paradigm than just its central, explicitly formulated and acknowledged doctrines. A paradigm includes a whole network of shared commitments (explicit *and* implicit), practices, investigative techniques, issues, and questions. Which subset of these are so theoretically embedded that they can appropriately be regarded as somehow of the essence of the Classical approach is an important but sometimes rather murky question, one that inevitably leads to squabbling over details. Those inclined to reject the overall Classical approach naturally favor saddling it with more of the stronger and less plausible features, while those anxious to defend it prefer to limit their liabilities, withdrawing to the relative safety of the most theoretically entrenched and apparently incontestable principles. It is possible to argue at length over the extent to which this kind of withdrawal is legitimate, but it should be borne in mind that there is no real necessity to adjudicate this issue strictly--*unless*, that is, we find ourselves forced to provide some crisp statement of the Central

Tenets of the Classical Approach for some further purpose, such as delimiting the nature of Connectionism. Otherwise, we can be content to recognize that the mainstream symbolic approach to the study of cognition is currently characterized by a broad cluster of commitments of varying strengths, some which are incidental, relatively shallow, and theoretically severable, and others which run rather more deeply and are likely to be carried over to future theoretical developments. *Exactly* which minimal features strictly define a Classical architecture can be an interesting question, but one in which (for the purposes of the current enquiry at least) we would be wise not to get too bogged down.

Another and more serious danger in taking the indirect route to Connectionism is that we end up with a distorted understanding of research in *cognitive psychology* as that has proceeded in the last few decades. As noted, taking the indirect route automatically creates the obligation that we provide some reasonably succinct statement of the nature of some extant theoretical framework to which Connectionism, *qua* psychological research endeavor, can be contrasted. This obligation is then often discharged by claiming that cognitive psychology itself has been dominated by something like the mainstream symbolic tradition, which is boiled down in turn to some version of the twin minimal commitments. But this can be really rather misleading. Many cognitive psychologists are mystified at the claim that their dominant concern has always been determining the syntax of the Language of Thought and the algorithms governing transformations of formulae of that Language. Casual perusal of any standard textbook on cognitive psychology makes it obvious that much of the canonical research in that discipline has, at least on the surface of it, very *little* to do with the rule-governed transformation of syntactically structured representations: consider, for example, the mental imagery experiments of Shepard, Cooper, Kosslyn and others; Rosch's prototype theory of concepts; the Shiffrin and Schneider results on controlled versus automatic processing; and the Tulving work on types of memory (to name but a few of the most well known lines of investigation).

What *is* true is that there is a certain impressive tradition of research at the computer modeling end of cognitive psychology, an end dominated by artificial intelligence, which takes the computational theory of mind as its guiding inspiration and *does* tend explicitly to postulate symbolic representations and algorithms for processing them. Research in this tradition meshes naturally with the rest of cognitive psychology, since it is concerned with many of the same phenomena; and the empirical results found in the wider discipline must eventually be brought to bear in constraining the computational models. This tradition also has a certain obvious appeal to philosophers since it can be related relatively straightforwardly to more familiar topics such as mainstream philosophy of mind, theory of computation, and proof theory. But to take its central tenets as forming the crux of a paradigm which has dominated cognitive psychology in general is to mistake part (or aspect) for whole in an egregious fashion. It is akin to the economist supposing that the broad philosophical discipline of ethics is dominated by gross utility calculations and rules of choice for maximizing the result. A more responsible attitude is to insist that there is something like "the mainstream symbolic or Classical approach to the *computational modeling* of cognitive processes," an approach essentially characterized by the twin minimal commitments. This more conservative description doesn't have quite the same sweeping drama, and still faces the above problem of sorting out which features really are essential, but at least it has the virtue of not distorting cognitive psychology before we even begin describing Connectionism.

Third, and most seriously of all, taking the indirect route can distort our interest in and perception of Connectionist work itself, thereby hindering the development of an appropriately independent overall conception of the emerging Connectionist alternative. The vocabulary, theoretical commitments, issues and questions characteristic of the old approach will tend to be carried over to the investigation of the new, defining the terms of the enquiry and setting standards to which the new paradigm is most unlikely to conform.[7] In particular, if our investigative horizons have been largely fixed by the framework and issues of the Classical approach, it will seem perfectly natural to ask such questions as whether cognitive processes must be based on syntactically structured representations, and whether Connectionist representations are syntactically structured; and it will seem reasonable to suppose that such questions should be more or less straightforwardly answerable. After all, the distilled Classical paradigm is partially defined in terms of a notion of syntactically structured representations, a notion which is generally taken as primitive or unexplained within that paradigm;[8] and since the Classical approach purports to explain cognitive behavior in terms of operations defined over such representations, it is natural enough to demand of any competing framework that it tell us where it stands on precisely these general issues.

This is the challenge that was placed before Connectionism, in a strategically brilliant counterattack, by Fodor and Pylyshyn, those most ardent defenders of the old approach. In doing so they effectively (and quite literally) set the terms of the debate, thereby casting much philosophical consideration of Connectionism into a mold taken directly from the paradigm it is supposedly trying to displace. We would, however, be unwise to engage with them on their home ground at this very early stage. Before venturing into such a dangerous forum we need a healthy *independent* conception of Connectionism, a conception that has not been stunted by growing in the shade of the Classical conceptual framework. Developing this conception will be difficult if we focus from the beginning on these two particular questions, since the notion of *syntactic structure* in play--a notion that is drawn directly from theoretical framework of the Classical paradigm--is, it turns out, too crude an exploratory instrument. Just as the Euclidean conception of space must be rejected if we want an adequate understanding of a relativistic universe, so the Classical concept of syntactic structure is not suited to the task of characterizing the kind of representations Connectionism is in the process of developing.

To see this it will be helpful initially to move away from the notion of syntactic structure itself, and consider instead the closely related but nevertheless significantly different notion of *compositionality*. I have urged in another paper[9] that it is appropriate to understand a given representation as having a compositional structure insofar as it belongs to a scheme in which representations stand in certain abstract *constituency relations* to each other (i.e., insofar as there are in the scheme types of compound representation which can be said to have other representations as constituents). The constituency relations among representations are fixed by a set of abstract general rules defining representation types in terms of their constituency relations, rules which are usually known as the *grammar*, and sometimes also known as the *syntax*, for that particular scheme. Now, in virtually all cases with which we are familiar, the constituency relations among representations are themselves mirrored directly in (or, more accurately, are instantiated by) quite literal part-whole relations: tokens of compound representations actually contain tokens of their constituents, just as the particular logic expression *((P&Q)&R)* contains, in a very concrete sense, a token of type "(P&Q)". In such cases complex representations are constructed by *concatenation*, a very general means of combining constituents according to the grammatical rules to obtain expressions in such a way as to preserve, in any instance of a complex expression, instances of its constituents.

It is however possible to have compositional schemes of representation in which compound representations are *not* constructed by concatenation. In such cases, representations are appropriately said to stand in constituency relations, but this is not by virtue of the presence of internal constituent tokens; rather, it is due to the presence of general and reliable combination and decomposition processes. These are processes that can construct tokens of a given compound type from tokens of its constituents, and deconstruct the compound into instances of its constituents once again. Crucially, it is possible to implement ways of performing these operations which do not rely on the simple concatenation of constituents in constructing compound expressions.

To obtain an intuitive feeling for such a scheme, suppose we have set up a correspondence between all expressions of a given compositional scheme (sentences of English, for example) and elements in some vector space. Since there is an infinite number of elements in the space, such a mapping is always possible, and indeed there will always be any number of such mappings. Imagine now that we also have two black boxes. These boxes are ordinary mechanical devices; to say that they are "black" boxes means only that for the moment we don't care exactly how it is they work, not that they are oracles or magical in any way. One of these boxes is a grammatical *composition* device; given at one end the vectors corresponding to the constituents of an expression, it will spit the vector for that expression out the other. (The grammatical composition box might, for example, take the *tensor products* of pairs of constituent vectors and hand us the sum of the results.[10]) The other box is a grammatical decomposition device, performing the converse operations: given a "compound" vector in one end, it grinds away and eventually spits sets of constituents out the other. If we now consider elements of the vector space as representations of the complex expression types to which they correspond, then--as long as we have the black boxes handy--we have a scheme of representations that in an obvious sense have *constituents*, but where these constituents are merely *functional* parts, rather than the kind of literal parts found in concatenative schemes. We have a compositional scheme, but it is *not* one where the constituency relations among representations are instantiated in strict part-whole relations among tokens.

This distinction between strictly concatenative and merely functional compositionality can be used to illuminate the difference between Classical and Connectionist architectures. It is possible to demonstrate that the Classical approach is deeply committed to representations having concatenative compositionality. In fact, this is typically just what a Classical theorist *means* when she claims that a representation is "syntactically structured," and this use is quite appropriate, since when expressions are constructed by concatenation their particular "syntax" is instantiated in their internal formal structure in a very direct way. This commitment to concatenative structure can be demonstrated in many ways: by appeal to *authority* (i.e., by reference to the canonical statements of the Classical approach); in *theory* (i.e., by showing the crucial theoretical role that concrete constituency relations play in the Classical explanation of cognitive processes); and by simply pointing to Classical *practice*, which has always been such as to utilize concatenatively structured representations.[11]

By contrast, careful consideration of many and diverse recent developments in Connectionist research reveals an increasing tendency to utilize schemes of representation with a merely functional compositionality. These Connectionist schemes take *exactly* the form outlined in the fictional black-box example given just above. That is, representations in the scheme are vectors in a certain space, vectors which describe levels of activity over a certain set of units; and the black boxes are simply appropriately configured networks, networks which have been trained or otherwise developed so as to be able systematically to construct the appropriate vector for a compound given the vectors corresponding to the constituents, and to decompose the compounds again when necessary. Examples abound, but some of the more well-known cases include Hinton's proposals for representing hierarchical structures, Pollack's RAAM methods, the St John and McClelland sentence processing model, Elman's Simple Recurrent Networks, and--particularly prominent in the current debate--Smolensky's tensor product formalism.[12]

Now, returning to the main line of argument: it was pointed out above that if we take the broad conceptual detour in understanding Connectionism, a perfectly natural questions to ask is *are its representations syntactically structured or not?* With the above discussion in mind, however, we can show that *both* alternatives provided here are really very awkward. Insofar as Connectionist representations have a merely functional compositionality, it is at best inappropriate and at worst positively misleading to say either that they are, or that they are not, syntactically structured. It is a prime example of the conceptual framework of one approach simply failing to do justice to the nature of another.

Thus, suppose one is tempted by the obvious compositional nature of these representations to maintain that they are in fact syntactically structured--though being careful to acknowledge, of course that constituents are merely *functional* and are not literal (e.g., are not strictly spatial).[13] One immediately apparent difficulty in taking this line is that it instantly creates the problem of explaining in what way Connectionism amounts to anything more than simply a way of neurally *implementing* the Classical approach, a problem which is particularly pronounced if you accept that approach can be distilled down to the two minimal commitments.[14] However, not everyone will be convinced that this really is a difficulty; after all, it may turn out that we were mistaken all along in assuming that Connectionism is in the business of developing a whole alternative explanatory paradigm for cognition. Thus it is important to realize that there is a much more serious problem if one takes this approach.

The problem arises because, in the context of this debate at least, the notion of syntactic structure is theoretically embedded in the overall Classical conceptual framework, from which it gains whatever theoretical significance it has. Thus, among other things, a syntactically structured representation just is the kind of thing that can figure in the Classical explanation of cognitive processes, and that style of explanation makes essential appeal to the presence of the constituents of a complex representation. The nature of this appeal is described in detail in Pylyshyn (1984) and Fodor and Pylyshyn (1988), and will only be summarized here. Briefly, the causal role of a representation in the cognitive economy of an intelligent system must be systematically appropriate to the nature of the item or situation that it is representing. Thus a representation of John's loving Mary must be such as to be able to causally influence the overall system to draw certain kinds of inferences rather than others.   Those inferences differ systematically, as John probably realizes, from the inferences that can be drawn from knowledge that Mary loves John; hence the *causal* properties of the latter representation must also differ systematically. A crucial explanatory task is to show how there can be a scheme of representations, and a system in which they are processed, that can exhibit these systematically appropriate causal effects. The Classical proposal is that we recognize the structured nature of the represented situations, and have that structure reflected in the structure of the representations themselves. This is achieved by systematically constructing representations of a given complex situation out of representations of its parts. It is then possible to design processes that transform representations in a way that is causally sensitive to, or in other words driven by, the presence of these constituent representations. The result is that the overall causal role of a complex representation is a direct function of the causal effects of its constituents, with the consequence that (if the processes have been designed correctly) the required systematic causal appropriateness of representations to their contents will be guaranteed.

In short, the Classical explanation of cognitive processes depends crucially on the causal role of constituents of a representation, and guarantees that constituents *have* such causal roles *by* constructing complex representations directly from tokens of their constituents; by requiring, in other words, that representations be syntactically structured. Now (to rephrase and generalize a point made in McLaughlin (1987)) representations whose compositionality is *only* functional do not--by definition--have tokens of their constituents as parts. Consequently the causal role of a compound representation cannot be construed as a direct function of the causal roles of its constituents; and so Connectionist representations, though they are compositional, are simply not capable of playing a Classical role in the explanation of cognitive processes. Putting it bluntly, you can't explain the causal role of a whole by reference to the causal roles of its parts if it doesn't actually have those parts. Moreover, it's of no help at all to suggest that, since Connectionist representations are functionally compositional, all we need do is first extract constituent tokens and let *them* causally govern the processes in the system. By relying on the causal role of the extracted constituent tokens, this is simply reverting to a trivial variant of the Classical picture, except that in order to see the Classical, syntactically structured representations we now have to take a little loftier perspective and look at states of the system over certain time periods.

Connectionist representations with only functional compositionality are therefore not the kinds of things that can figure in Classical-style explanations of cognitive processes. For this reason, if we insist on describing Connectionist representations as syntactically structured, we will be *distorting* the nature of Connectionist representations by misassimilating them to their Classical, concatenatively constructed counterparts. Alternatively, we must be wrenching the term "syntactic structure" from its previous relatively well-defined framework and using it in such a loose and vague way as to encompass *both* representations with a strictly concatenative internal structure and representations with only functional compositionality. Since these kinds of representations are very different, and do not have anything like the same explanatory properties, such usage would simply be muddying the whole debate.

It might seem, then, that it is preferable to choose the other option--i.e., to claim that Connectionist representations are *not* syntactically structured. Now, while there is a certain trivial sense in which this is probably true, there are severe drawbacks in making this assessment as well. To see this, we first have to be clear about the conditions under which a representation is appropriately described as having any kind of significant internal structure (i.e., as being "Structured"). Virtually all representations have *some* kind of internal structure, in the sense that they usually have a distinctive internal makeup or configuration. This is true not only of complex symbolic expressions but also of most primitive symbolic constituents (such as words or even letters); it is certainly true of any vector-based Connectionist representations. If nothing else, this internal makeup plays the crucial role of permitting the reidentification of the token as being of a given type. However, merely possessing a discernible internal makeup is typically not enough for a representation to count as Structured. For this to be the case the internal makeup must be such as to have a certain systematic semantic or computational significance, a significance that is only acquired if the internal makeup exhibits some kind of further regularities that occur across many different representations of different situations.

Thus, in the Classical case, we have a Structured representation just in case the internal makeup can be analyzed as *constituent* structure. The internal physical configuration of the representation must do more than simply permit reidentification; it must be such that it instantiates the various constituents of the representation, right down to its primitive symbolic constituents. Complex representations can then stand in structural relations to each other according to how (and where) they contain such constituents. Since primitive (or "Unstructured") symbolic constituents can be assigned basic semantic significances, and we can have rules for interpreting the whole in terms of its parts, the constituent structure of a complex representation has a systematic *semantic* significance. Since, moreover, we can design and implement ways of processing these representations that are causally sensitive to the presence of constituents, and thereby appropriate to their semantic properties, the internal structure has a systematic *computational* significance.[15]

Now, a great danger in describing Connectionist representations as "not syntactically structured" is that one will assume that they must, for that reason, be literally Unstructured (i.e., such that their internal makeup has no systematic semantic or computational significance at all.) An excellent example of the assimilation of lack of *syntactic* Structure to lack of Structure *per se* is the Fodor and Pylyshyn discussion of Connectionism. They argue at length for an understanding of all Connectionist representations--even so-called "distributed" representations, and representations of complex items--as structurally unrelated primitive nodes, on the grounds that such representations are without the Classical variety of combinatorial syntactic and semantic Structure. Reasoning along these lines, they conclude that--since the internal structure of Connectionists representations is of no systematic causal significance at all--Connectionist mental processes must be simply "Associationist," where an Associationist process is a matter of statistical correlation that is "not sensitive to features of the content or the structure of representations per se."

This assimilation is quite a natural one, since we do have rather few models for understanding the way in which representations can count as significantly Structured other than the Classical notion of constituent structure. There is, of course, at least *one* other familiar way in which representations can count, by virtue of their particular internal configuration, as Structured--namely, by virtue of the general principles of pictorial or imagistic representation. But nobody seriously supposes that Connectionist representations in general are imagistic, and most people would agree that Connectionism would be a rather hopeless enterprise if they were. The only available alternative, it seems, is that Connectionist representations are Unstructured.

This is however precisely the point at which it becomes essential to pay close attention to the nature of Connectionist work itself, for there is an important sense in which representations in the functionally compositional schemes under development are Structured, yet the principles by virtue of which they *count* as Structured are *not* those of Classical constituency (and not those of imagery either). A functionally compositional representation, such as a tensor product, is a vector, and as such is often fruitfully conceived as corresponding to a point in a certain high-dimensional space. Just where in the space that point actually lies is, of course, determined by the particular values that vector has in each of its places; it is determined, in other words, by its particular internal structure (little "s"). Once we consider representations as points in a space, moreover, it is a natural move to think of how these points are related to each other, or in other words what the "distance" between them is. This can be assessed using any of a variety of vector comparison measures. In short, on this way of looking at things, the fact that Connectionist representations have a certain kind of internal makeup is important in that it provides us with a basis for understanding how they stand to each other; and the *particular* internal makeup of a *given* representation determines how it stands to other representations.

Now, all this counts for nothing unless these relationships somehow *matter*; unless, in other words, the location of a given representation in the space is such as to be of some kind of systematic semantic and computational significance. Interestingly enough, however, it can be shown that these locations can, under the right circumstances, have such significance. First we should notice that there is a purely *formal* sense in which there are systematic relationships among representations in a functionally compositional scheme. The internal makeup of such a representation, which determines where it is located in relation to others, is determined in turn by two factors: (1) the nature of its constituents (in other words, their location in vector space[16]); and (2) the nature of the combination process (i.e., the internal mechanics of the grammatical composition box). These factors operate to determine the location of a given representation in a completely regular and systematic way: given the combination process, the location of a compound representation is fixed by its constituency relations, or in other words by its grammatical structure. As a consequence, *grammatically* related representations end up in systematically related *positions* in the space; or, to rephrase the point very roughly, representations with similar sets of constituency relations end up as "neighboring" points in the space. The systematic nature of these spatial relationships can be discerned using sophisticated techniques for the comparison of large groups of vectors such as cluster analysis.

Since the position of a representation varies systematically as a function of its constituency relations, and since its basic constituents can be assigned primitive semantic significances, the *position* of a representation in the vector space can be seen as corresponding systematically to its *content*, i.e., to what it is a representation *of*.[17] Thus, in the tensor product case, basic role and filler vectors can be interpreted as representing features of the world, and the meaning of a complex tensor product representation can be systematically determined as a function of the interpretations of its basic role and filler vector constituents.   Thus, under the terms of the non-concatenative scheme in question, the position of a representation in the space has a semantic significance; vary its position in that space, and you automatically vary the interpretation that is appropriate for it. Moreover, as a consequence, *relationships* among points in the space have a systematic semantic significance; again, to put it roughly, representations with similar *meanings* will be found grouped in neighboring points in the space.

Finally, the position of a representation in the space plays a crucial role in determining how that representation will be processed. Its position is determined by the value it has in each place, and these values correspond to levels of activity in particular processing units in a network. Since the primary causal mechanism in a Connectionist network is the mediated transfer of activation between units, the precise position of a representation in the space has a direct *causal* effect on how that representation will be processed. Now, as was just noted, the position of a representation is a systematic function of its grammatical structure. Consequently, the way a representation is processed by the network is going to depend crucially on its grammatical structure, i.e., on its functional constituency relations. And since the position of a representation in the space also systematically corresponds to its meaning, the way it is processed by the network will depend indirectly on its semantic properties; hence the internal structure of the representation (which defines its position in space) has a wider computational relevance.

In short, the internal makeup of a functionally compositional Connectionist representation has a wider significance in formal, semantic and computational terms. It determines the representation's constituency relations, its interpretation, and how it will be processed by the system, and it does so in a completely regular way. Thus, to think of Connectionist representations as essentially Unstructured--as on a par with primitive vocabulary items in a normal symbolic scheme--is to miss out on much (if not all) that is interesting and important about them. Connectionist representations belonging to a functionally compositional scheme are in fact Structured, but in a novel and highly distinctive way. To properly perceive this Structure (as opposed to internal structure) we should not be looking inward for constituent tokens; rather, we need to take a more "externalist" perspective, looking outward to location in vector space. To understand its systematic *causal* significance, we have to look not to the Classical theory of computation but rather to distinctive Connectionist styles of processing. This Structure is *compositional* because the internal makeup of a representation (i.e., its location in space) is a direct function of its constituency relations; it is not however *syntactic* because tokens of those constituents are not to be found instantiated in the representation itself.

The real problem in claiming that Connectionist representations are *not* syntactically structured, then, is not that it is false. The real problem is not even that it tends to *mislead* one into supposing that such representations are completely Unstructured, thereby misconceiving them; this mistake is avoidable if one accepts that there can be other ways that internal structure becomes significant than by instantiating constituent structure. Rather, the deep problem is that the concept of a representation's being *not syntactically structured* is much too coarse; it simply cannot be used effectively in describing what is really interesting and distinctive about certain kinds of Connectionist representations. It is as if we were trying to describe the color *red* using just the concepts *blue* and *not blue*. Certainly it is an important fact about a color whether it is blue or not, but there is a whole range of further interesting differences in the color spectrum that this distinction alone cannot comprehend. Likewise, the concept of syntactic structure, drawn as it is from the Classical conceptual framework, is just not the right tool if we want to understand the distinctive character of Connectionist representations. For these reasons, the best answer to the received question about Connectionist representations is that they are *neither* syntactically structured *nor* not syntactically structured. Neither answer characterizes them acceptably. We need to set aside that particular vocabulary, which is embedded in and effectively limited to the Classical framework, and develop a new set of conceptual tools which will be sufficient to comprehend the emerging Connectionist alternative.

We should naturally expect that this will be a difficult and long-term task, one at which progress can only be made in slow tandem with the actual development of Connectionist work itself. At this early stage, however, there are a number of reasons to suppose that the idea of representations having only functional compositionality, together with the corresponding "externalist" perspective on the structural significance of such representations, will be an important piece of the picture. For one thing, the very idea of utilizing representations with only functional compositionality is thoroughly novel and unanticipated, a possibility that has only really emerged with the recent resurgence of Connectionist work. With the benefit of hindsight we can point to earlier schemes of representation having this property (Gödel numbering might, for example, be construed this way); and it is possible to find, in certain quite independent philosophical investigations, the true groundwork that needs to be laid in order to adequately articulate and defend the very idea of such a scheme.[18] Nevertheless, it has only been with Connectionism that both the need and the ability to develop practical schemes of this kind for psychological purposes has arisen, and it is only in the attempt to understand these Connectionist schemes that the concept itself is being articulated. Far from being a tired or trivial variant on either previous dogma (e.g., "Associationism") or current orthodoxy (e.g., the Classical notion of syntactic structure), the emerging Connectionist style of structured representation is thoroughly *sui generis*, a good sign both that Connectionism really is developing a new and independent paradigm, and that some version of only functional compositionality will be an integral part of its conceptual infrastructure.

In fact, there is a wider perspective from which the conceptual independence of only functional compositionality can be seen as running even deeper than this. The schemes of representation being devised by Connectionists such as Pollack, Smolensky, Hinton, Elman *et al.*, are special cases of *distributed* representation. By this I do not mean simply that they are spread over many processing units, or that they are, or would be, realized over a large area in any sense (whether spatially, or neurally, or whatever). Despite rather widespread acceptance--especially among philosophical commentators--this is a relatively shallow conception of what it is for a representation to be distributed. Rather, I mean that they belong to schemes whose primary feature is the super(im)position of semantic responsibility; or in other words the effective representing of many items or parts over the same space, whether that space is "spread out" or not. Though there is not room here, it can be demonstrated that distributed representations form a whole independent genus in exactly the way in which, for example, symbolic representations form a distinctive genus. In particular, it can be shown that distributed representations are formally, semantically and computationally *incompatible* with symbolic representations in just the same way that, for example, symbolic representations are incompatible with imagery.[19] Consequently, insofar as Connectionism is constructing models of cognitive processes that are based on genuinely distributed representations, it is striking out in a radically new direction, developing computational architectures that are based on principles unlike any we have been familiar with before. The use of the specific kind (species or "sub-genus") of non-concatenative compositional representations is simply one form that this radical new development is taking. In short, distribution is just the kind of original and quite general principle which might play a key role in a whole new paradigm, and this gives powerful reason to believe that the more specific notion of only functionally compositional representation is just the kind of conceptual tool we would need in adequately characterizing that paradigm.

However, leaving such broad speculation aside, there are other ways to show the centrality of a concept such as this: namely, by showing the extent to which it is theoretically embedded among other distinctive Connectionist commitments. It was just pointed out that the vector-based functionally compositional representations under development are a special case of distributed representation. In fact, they can also be seen as occurring at the natural intersection of three, more specific theoretical principles typically accepted by Connectionists. The first is the general recognition that to achieve any kind of sophisticated cognitive performance, a system must be able to effectively represent complex structured items or situations. This requires representing the internal structure of those items in a way that is accessible to and hence usable by the system. The second principle is perhaps the most characteristic Connectionist step of all--a commitment to using large networks of simple neural units as the basic processing mechanism. This commitment immediately entails that at least some representations in the system will take the form of *vectors*, (alternatively, as points in a space) describing activity levels in sets of neural processing units. The third principle is the widespread, generally implicit, and decidedly non-Classical practice of using network architectures with strictly limited resources (e.g., fixed network size). If you want to be able to represent items with arbitrarily complex structure, and you only have a strictly limited number of units with which to do it, then you simply cannot assign a distinct set of those units to form a discrete symbol for each part of a given structure, for sooner or later you will run up against an item that is so complex you do not have enough units to do the job. The general solution, as Connectionists have discovered, is to use a different pattern over the whole group to represent each structure, no matter how complex (which requires, of course, clever recursive techniques for determining what that pattern should be).[20] The result is a vectorial representation of a complex structure, but not one in which you can find the constituents of that representation instantiated in the internal formal structure; rather, the vector manages to represent the whole structure by virtue of its *functional* constituency relations, which systematically determine exactly where in the space the corresponding point lies. Incidentally, it is this third commitment which really has the effect of forcing Connectionists to develop specifically *distributed* schemes of representations in the above strong sense. Since, in standard ways of generating a unique pattern for each complex structure, each part of that pattern varies as a function of each part of that structure, the automatic result is that each part of the structure is effectively represented over the whole pattern; we have, in other words, genuinely distributed representations.

In short, the use of schemes of representation with only functional compositionality is not some contingent and theoretically severable feature of particular Connectionist models; rather is intimately embedded in a wider network of characteristically Connectionist commitments such as the use of neural network mechanisms, fixed resources, and distribution. This is the deep reason we find the same style of representation emerging simultaneously in many relatively independent lines of Connectionist investigation, a fact that would otherwise be rather surprising. It also provides good *prima facie* reason to think that we are on the right track in attributing to Connectionism a deep commitment to this style of representation. *Confirming* its key status is a matter of continuing the lengthy process of tracing the intricate maze of conceptual ties among various features of Connectionist work. More needs to be said, for example, about how functionally compositional representations are integrated with Connectionist processes for transforming such representations, and in particular how it is possible for network processes to transform them in a way that is systematically *appropriate* to their grammatical structure and hence indirectly to their semantic properties. Together, these characteristic representations and processes give rise to an as yet largely unexplored but distinctively Connectionist style of explanation of cognitive capabilities (including in particular what Fodor and Pylyshyn have called the *productivity, systematicity,* and *compositionality* of those capabilities). This style of explanation does not refer, as Classical explanation does, to the causal role of the constituents of representations given Classical structure-sensitive mental processes. Rather, it makes reference to the causal import of the "external" structure (i.e., the position in space) of a functionally compositional vectorial representation given the specific complex differential equation governing the evolution of activation in the network as a whole. The key idea, in other words, is that constituency relations govern the direction of processing not through the direct causal role of constituent tokens but rather by determining the position of a representation in the space and consequently how it will influence activity levels in the network. Looking in another direction again, it will have to be shown how functionally compositional representations and the corresponding "structure-sensitive" network processes are related to Connectionist learning mechanisms. How it is possible for a system to develop such representations, and the dynamical structure for transforming them appropriately, simply from exposure to "experience" in the form of training regimes?

Questions such as these, and no doubt a host of others, will have to be addressed thoroughly before we will be conclusively entitled to assert that Connectionists are committed to non-concatenative compositional representations in much the same deep way that Classical theorists are committed to syntactic structured representations. Nevertheless, at this stage all the evidence points in this direction, making possible a confident dismissal (rather than denial) of the idea that genuinely Connectionist representations are, or even are not, syntactically structured. More generally, until the process of developing a sympathetic, independent conception of the nature of Connectionism is relatively advanced, it will be impossible to address which of the paradigms is more likely to succeed in accounting for cognition, and in particular whether the employment of syntactically structured representations is a necessary condition for any sophisticated cognitive capabilities. It is futile to compare the relative merits of two competing approaches until we have a deep understanding of each of those approaches; and it is *doubly* futile to compare the relative merits of two competing approaches when we have allowed the conceptual framework of one to define the very terms of evaluation. The boxer will always beat the chess player in the ring, but that's not a very interesting contest.

NOTES

[1] "Classical" is the term that was adopted by Fodor and Pylyshyn to denote a framework for understanding cognition that has variously been described as the *Language of Thought Hypothesis* (Fodor 1975), the *Physical Symbol System Hypothesis* (Newell and Simon 1976), *Cognitivism* (Haugeland 1981), *GOFAI* (Haugeland 1985), *High Church Computationalism* (Dennett 1986),

the *Rules and Representations Approach* (Horgan and Tienson 1987); and is often more causally known as, among other things, *the symbolic approach* or *the computational theory of mind*. Since "Classical" is succinct, elegant, and is sufficiently vague to keep the peace, I will follow their usage, stopping only to note that preferring some alternative framework does not thereby make one *non-Classical* or *anti-Classical,* any more than being *pro-choice* makes one *anti-life.*

[2] As its title clearly suggests, my own "Compositionality: A Connectionist Variation on a Classical Theme: (1990) certainly appears to fall squarely within this tradition.

[3] Quite often, in fact, those predisposed to debunk Connectionism do quite openly deny that Connectionism amounts to a new paradigm in psychology. Since the Classical framework has been progressively refined, over a long period, to be as strong and plausible as possible (i.e., so as to reach a kind of local maximum in the plausibility landscape), any theoretical framework that is straightforwardly deducible from that framework will inevitably be rather obviously implausible. Consequently, these theorists usually end up claiming that the most profitable way to view neural network research is as an investigation of how the mechanisms required under the terms of their own conceptual framework might be implemented in real brains. Insofar as their attempts to understand Connectionism begin by detouring through their own familiar paradigm, however, it probably shouldn't be altogether surprising that they often end up making this kind of assessment; from the Kuhnian perspective just outlined, this kind of deflationary conclusion is virtually guaranteed the moment the detour is taken.

[4] If we consider *computation* solely in the strict sense in which it is defined in the general theory of computability as worked out by Turing *et al.,* and perhaps in the Classical framework more widely, then it will appear rather nonsensical to talk of Connectionism's *computational* mechanisms while at the same time urging that Connectionism be considered a radical alternative to the Classical approach. Here and below, however, I use "computational" more in a more general sense. Thus, in this context, "computational mechanisms" refers to the combination of representations and processes which together make possible the transformation of representations in semantically appropriate ways within a system, whether that system is Classical, Connectionist, or something else altogether. Consequently, one important part of the challenge in understanding the Connectionist enterprise will be articulating a novel theory of computation.

[5] By "canonical characterization" here I mean those characterizations which actually *succeeded* in articulating the fundamental theoretical assumptions of the Classical paradigm. Some early formulations, such as that of Neisser (1967), do place much emphasis on the need to posit internal representations and information processing mechanisms as a way of overcoming inherent limitations of the previous paradigm. With over twenty years of hindsight, however, it can be seen that this formulation was only a rough initial stab in the direction of a genuine computational theory of mind; the deep ramifications of the computer metaphor were not properly understood until quite a bit later. This merely underlines my point: insofar as we attempt to understand one paradigm in the terms provided by another, we inadvertently jeopardize that very understanding.

[6] See Smolensky (1988).

[7] Kuhn points out that this kind of move is a standard strategy of entrenched defenders of an old paradigm. When the new paradigm is found wanting, as it almost inevitably will be, this is taken as confirmation of their favored viewpoint.

[8] That is, it is a quite remarkable fact that within the whole corpus of Classical theory there are almost no attempts to explain, in any reasonably detailed and thorough way, exactly what syntactic structure actually consists in (i.e., what it is for a formal feature of a representation to count as a syntactic feature); and this despite the fact that a variety of authors make the concept the centerpiece of their proposals. It is usually presumed to be understood, and is in effect *implicitly* defined via the use that is made of "syntactic," "syntax," and other related terms. For this reason it is hardly surprising that confusion results when we attempt to apply the concept in analyzing a wholly novel phenomenon.

[9] van Gelder (1990); see also (1989a).

[10] Simply to *specify* a mapping from the unbounded expressions of a recursive scheme such as English to elements of a vector space we would have to use recursive techniques. All the grammatical black box has to do is implement the mathematics of this recursive specification.

[11] These points are elaborated in van Gelder (1990) sec.2.1.

[12] See Hinton, 1988; Pollack, 1988, 1989; St. John and McClelland, 1988; Elman, 1989. Actually, although going into this issue in any detail here would greatly complicate the paper, there is a certain difficulty in describing a given tensor product representation as compositional. The basic problem is that such a representation, as a sum of tensor products of role and filler vectors, has any number of decompositions into sets of role and filler constituents. Given the entirely neutral nature of the decomposition processes, none of these have any *a priori* privilege as *the* set of constituents of the overall representation. Of course, if we combine a tensor product representation with a given series of role vectors, then we can obtain a determinate answer about the fillers of those roles, and vice versa. But in such a case, the tensor product only has a determinate decomposition *in the context of* this further set of determinate role (or filler) vectors; in which case the effective representation is the collection of all the vectors needed to determine a given decomposition. This way we obtain a determinate decomposition, but only at the cost of rendering the effective representation decidedly Classical in appearance, in its *de facto* preservation of constituent tokens. This difficult issue was broached in my unpublished manuscript, *The State of Connectionist Constituents* (1988) and is in need of further exploration. Meanwhile, for the purposes of the current debate, in which tensor products are often invoked as a paradigm of novel and interesting connectionist representations, I will continue to discuss tensor product representations as if they were unproblematic.

[13] This kind of position (though not in exactly these words) is taken up by Michael Tye, who argues that when Connectionists make use of "distributed" representations formed according to, say, Smolensky's tensor product methods, they are employing representations which have "functional parts" and hence can be appropriately classified as "quasi-sentential" in a way that is perfectly compatible with the Classical "language of cognition" hypothesis. The inherent difficulty in this position was noted by McLaughlin (1987) and is brought out below.

[14] Smolensky tackles this difficulty by pointing out that although tensor product representations stand, just like their Classical counterparts, in constituency relations, such representations do not merely implement a "language of thought" because, for a number of reasons, the constituency relations of tensor product representations are only *approximate*.

[15] Ultimately, it is by virtue of their relation to these kinds of wider significances that the internal formal structure of tokens will *count* as genuine syntactic structure (Brandom, 1987). Another way of putting this point is that our entitlement to describe a physical feature as syntactic comes from our being able to show how occurrences of that feature make systematic semantic (and eventually computational or pragmatic) differences.

[16] This space may or may not be the same as the space in which the complex vector resides; though usually it can be regarded as a sub-space.

[17] Here, to say that position corresponds systematically to content is to say that position varies, in a way that is fixed in a determinate and regular fashion by the particular non-concatenative scheme employed, with the content of that representation. There is no guarantee that this systematic correspondence will be preserved under change of scheme, dimensionality, and so forth.

[18] See Brandom (1987).

[19] For detailed elaboration of this controversial series of claims, see van Gelder (1989b).

[20] At least in principle, there is no difficulty in the fact that there are arbitrarily many structures to be represented, since any vector space contains an infinite number of vectors. The practical problem is one of keeping individual representations distinct, since, given arbitrarily many structures to represent, the vectors must become arbitrarily close together as the recursive

assignment gradually fills the space. In short, unbounded resources and concatenation pretty much guarantee the digital separability of all representations. Connectionists, who reject this approach, have to bet that *sufficiently* many representations will be *sufficiently* distinct to account for the complexity of human cognitive processing.

REFERENCES

Bechtel, W.: 1985, 'Contemporary Connectionism: Are the New Parallel Distributed Processing Models Cognitive or Associationist?' *Behaviorism* 13, 53-61.

Bechtel, W.: 1986, 'What Happens to Accounts of Mind-Brain Relations If We Forego an Architecture of Rules and Representations?' *Philosophy of Science Association* 1, 159-171.

Brandom, R.: 1987, 'Singular Terms and Sentential Sign Designs.' *Philosophical Topics* 15, 125-167.

Cummins, R. and Schwarz G.: 1987, 'Radical Connectionism,' *Southern Journal of Philosophy* 26, Supplement, 43-61.

Cussins, A.: 1988?, 'The Connectionist Construction of Concepts.' *Behavioral and Brain Sciences*.

Cussins, A.: 1990, 'Connectionist Construction of Concepts', in M.A. Boden (ed), *The Philosophy of Artificial Intelligence* (Oxford Readings in Philosophy), (pp. 368-440), Osford University Press, Oxford.

Dennett, D.C.: 1986, 'The Logical Geography of Computational Approaches: A View from the East Pole,' in M. Brand and R. M. Harnish, *The Representation of Knowledge and Belief*, University of Arizona Press, Tucson.

Elman, J. L.: 1989, 'Representation and Structure in Connectionist Models,' *Technical Report 8903*, Center for Research in Language, University of California, San Diego.

Fodor, J. A. and McLaughlin, B. P.: (this volume), 'Connectionism and the Problem of Systematicity: Why Smolensky's Solution Doesn't Work.'

Fodor, J.A. and Pylyshyn, Z. W.: 1988, 'Connectionism and Cognitive Architecture: A Critical Analysis,' *Cognition* 28, 3-71.

Fodor, J. A.: 1975, *The Language of Thought*, Harvard University Press, Cambridge, MA.

Haugeland, J.: 1978, 'The Nature and Plausibility of Cognitivism,' *Behavioral and Brain Sciences* 1, 215-226.

Haugeland, J.: 1985, *Artificial Intelligence: The Very Idea*, Bradford/MIT Press, Cambridge, MA.

Hinton, G. E.: 1988, 'Representing Part-Whole Hierarchies in Connectionist Networks,' *Proceedings of the Tenth Annual Conference of the Cognitive Science Society*, pp. 48-54, Montreal, Quebec, Canada.

Horgan, T. and Tienson, J.: 1987, 'Settling Into a New Paradigm,' *Southern Journal of Philosophy* 26, Supplement, 97-113.

Horgan, T. and Tienson, J.: 1989, 'Representations Without Rules,' *Philosophical Topics* 15.

Kuhn, T.S.: 1962, *The Structure of Scientific Revolutions*, University of Chicago Press, Chicago.

McLaughlin, B.: 1987, 'Tye on Connectionism,' *Southern Journal of Philosophy* 26, Supplement, 185-193.

Neisser, 1967, *Cognitive Psychology*, Appleton-Century-Croft, New York.

Newell, A. and Simon, H.: 1976, 'Computer Science as an Empirical Inquiry,' *Communications of the Association for Computing Machinery* 19, 113-126.

Pollack, J.: 1988, 'Recursive Auto-Associative Memory: Devising Compositional Distributed Representations,' *Proceedings of the Tenth Annual Conference of the Cognitive Science Society*, Montreal, Quebec, Canada.

Pollack, J.: (forthcoming), 'Recursive Distributed Representations,' *Artificial Intelligence*.

Pylyshyn, Z. W.: 1984, *Computation and Cognition: Toward a Foundation for Cognitive Science*, MIT Press, Cambridge, MA.

Smolensky, P.: 1987, 'On Variable Binding and the Representation of Symbolic Structures in Connectionist Systems,' *CU-CS-355-87*.

Smolensky, P.: 1988, 'The Proper Treatment of Connectionism,' *Behavioral and Brain Sciences* 11(1), 1-23.

St. John, M. F. and McClelland, J. L.: 1988, 'Applying Contextual Constraints in Sentence Comprehension,' *Proceedings of the Tenth Annual Conference of the Cognitive Science Society*, (August 1988), pp. 26-32, Montreal, Quebec, Canada.

Tye, M.: 1987, 'Representation in Pictorialism and Connectionism,' *Southern Journal of Philosophy* 26, Supplement, 163-184.

van Gelder, T.: 1989a, 'Compositionality and the Explanation of Cognitive Processes,' *Proceedings of the Eleventh Annual Meeting of the Cognitive Science Society*, Ann Arbor Michigan.

van Gelder, T.: 1989b, 'Distributed Representation,' Ph.D Thesis, University of Pittsburgh.

van Gelder, T.: (1990), 'Compositionality: A Connectionist Variation on a Classical Theme,' *Cognitive Science* **14**, 355-384.

Department of Philosophy
Indiana University
Bloomington, IN 47405

MICHAEL G. DYER

CONNECTIONISM VERSUS SYMBOLISM
IN HIGH-LEVEL COGNITION*

1. INTRODUCTION

Symbolic processing rests on a computational technology that includes dynamic memory management, virtual pointers to created structured objects, and the use of variables to propagate bindings. Connectionist models have lacked these features, but create distributed representations that are "rich," i.e., that encode numerous statistically based expectations, acquired from experience. It is argued here that a synthesis of both symbolic and connectionist features will make important contributions to our understanding of high-level cognition. In what follows, a motivation is given for the need of such a synthesis, along with several, novel techniques used in connectionist systems designed to perform high-level, language-related processing tasks.

1.1 *A Personal Odyssey*

I completed my dissertation research in Computer Science at Yale University, in 1982, studying natural language processing (NLP) under W. Lehnert and R. Schank. For my Ph.D. I had constructed a rather complex, symbol processing system, called BORIS (Dyer, 1983), that read three small narrative texts in depth (each 4-5 paragraphs in length). The processes of comprehension in BORIS involved: (a) instantiating symbolic structures (representing narrative themes, scripts, settings, physical objects and character goals, plans, emotions, actions, and interpersonal relationships), (b) interconnecting these conceptual objects with causal/intentional links, along with indexing structures to organize and access them, through the use of delayed procedures ("demons"), and (c) then comprehending and answering questions concerning these structures, by accessing and traversing the relevant indices and causal/intentional links. After completing my dissertation, I joined Schank's company, Cognitive Systems, Inc. and put BORIS-related theory and technology to work by building NLP systems for commercial use.

In 1983 I took a faculty position at UCLA and established an Artificial Intelligence (AI) lab for NLP research. I started several Ph.D. research projects, all involving symbol processing extensions to address NLP issues that had arisen during the construction of the BORIS system. These issues included: (a) automatic acquisition of the syntax and semantics of phrases in context (Zernik and Dyer, 1987), (b) recognition of thematic structures (Dolan and Dyer, 1986) in narratives, (c) analysis of goal/plan misconceptions (Quilici *et al.*, 1988) during advice giving, (d) argument comprehension in non-narrative texts, such as editorials, through tracking beliefs and their attack/support relationships (Alvarado *et al.*, 1989), (e) analysis of reasoning in legal texts (Goldman *et al.*, 1988), (f) comprehension of mechanical device descriptions in technical texts (Dyer *et al.*, in press, b), and (g) explanation-based learning from multiple examples (Pazzani and Dyer, 1989).

Although my students and I worked diligently at designing and building such complex symbol processing systems, by 1986 I was becoming increasingly unhappy with the tremendous amount of knowledge engineering that such systems required, and unsatisfied with their resulting fragility. I began to question whether symbol processing (based on hand-coded knowledge constructs and processing strategies, such as logical predicates, frames, scripts, demons, unification, discrimination trees, and so on) was the only available research path to modeling the mind. While symbol processing technology allows one to build sophisticated architectures, capable of exhibiting complex behavior in limited task/domains, it seems very difficult to theorize as to how such complex structures and processes could have arisen in the first place in such systems, through learning and experience. In addition, hand-coded structures seemed to lack an inherent "richness" in representation. At the time I suspected that the inability to automatically acquire and represent the complexity of experience is a major reason for the resulting fragility of these human-engineered systems.

Around that time, the two volume PDP books came out (Rumelhart and McClelland, 1986). Like many, I had preordered these books and upon their arrival "devoured" them with great excitement, seeing in them the potential solution to all of my problems. Here was an alternative paradigm and technology, holding the promise of automatic acquisition of knowledge, where knowledge consists of distributed representations, and where processing involves spreading activation (versus the unification-based symbol processing mechanisms I had been using).

1.2 *Attractive Features of Connectionism*

The connectionist paradigm excited me (and many other cognitive scientists) because of the attractive features that many connectionist models exhibit, namely:

(a) *Automatic learning and generalization:* Learning is so fundamental to these models that they are not really programmed (in the algorithmic sense) but modify their behavior as the result of supervised training or reinforcement. Instead of induction over a preexisting symbol vocabulary, connectionist models learn through incremental adaptation in the face of repeated interaction with a set of input/output mappings. By local modification of connection weights, such models categorize the data such that novel inputs can be handled, based on a generalization of the statistical structure that has been extracted from the training set.

(b) *Associative memory, massive parallelism and fault tolerance:* Complete memory patterns can be generated from fragmentary and noisy cues in the input. In contrast, in symbolic models one must explicitly decide how a symbolic structure will be indexed for retrieval. Connectionist models also exhibit smooth degradation in the face of 'lesions' (removal of processing units and alteration of connection weights).

(c) *Smooth parallel constraint satisfaction:* The expectations generated by connectionist models are statistical in nature, and the model finds a memory based on satisfying a large number of soft constraints in parallel. The process is one of settling into a minimal energy state, rather than generating a proof path through the chaining of rules. Rather than viewing "soft" behavior as arising through the interaction of a great number of "hard" rules, connectionists predict that "hard" behavior will emerge through the interaction of a great number of "soft" constraints (Smolensky, 1988a).

(d) *Reconstructive memory:* Since all long-term memories are encoded in the connection weights, memories are shared over the same hardware. Thus, retrieval is more a matter of reconstructing a memory than going to a discrete location to find it. As new memories are added to connectionist models, they can exhibit retroactive interference, but repetition of the original data will reestablish the older memories. If the same amount of repetition were required, then such models would not be so interesting. However, a recent study (Hetherington and Seidenberg, 1989) indicates that less repetition is required during relearning. Thus, the most effective learning strategy in such models (i.e., train via repetition; learn something new; then briefly retrain on the earlier material) seems to parallel similar aspects of learning in children. In contrast, phenomena of forgetting and memory confusions (Bower *et al.*, 1979) have only been explained in symbolic models through the loss of pointers or the reorganization of other indexing structures (Schank, 1982). Connectionist models, however, explain forgetting and confusions in a very natural way, through interference over shared hardware.

(e) *Distributed representations and neural plausibility:* Representations are distributed over many simple processing elements and properties of the model are "emergent phenomena" from the interaction of a great many elements. It is the distributed nature of these representations that allows the models to exhibit their adaptive learning, generalization, and fault tolerant properties. In addition, connectionist models are loosely inspired by what is known about real nervous systems, and thus hold out the potential of linking mind to brain at some future date.

Consequently, I decided to immediately apply this new technology to my current problems (e.g., of argument and narrative comprehension, generalization from multiple story input, theme analysis, question comprehension and retrieval, etc.) but rapidly hit a major barrier. It turned out that the new technology, while offering adaptive learning and statistical generalization features, did not supply me with the constructive operations I required for building long-term, episodic memories from natural language input. As I tried to design and construct connectionist models for NLP, I began to reappreciate what nearly 40 years of computer science had built up in the way of symbol processing languages and architectures.

1.3 *Attractive Features of Symbolism*

Symbol processing (until recently) has been the only viable approach to modeling high-level cognitive functions, namely because of the following attractive features:

(a) *Tokens and types:* In symbolic systems, one can dynamically create instances (e.g., HUMAN13) that can be kept distinct from the general type (HUMAN). In connectionist systems, it is easy to form types, but difficult to keep instances straight, e.g., connectionist models suffer from "cross-talk" (Feldman, 1989).

(b) *Inheritance:* Given types and tokens, one can update a type (e.g., learn that HUMAN--ISA--> MORTAL) and immediately this fact is deducible for all relevant tokens that are instances of that type.

(c) *Virtual reference:* One symbol structure can point to another structure that resides at a distant location in physical memory, thus supporting the creation of complex virtual memories without having to reorganize physical memory. In fact, it is this virtual memory capability that allows current von Neumann machines to simulate any connectionist model. In contrast, it is unclear how a pattern in one region of a connectionist memory could refer to patterns in physically distant regions. Suppose one region of memory contains the schema instance (BELIEVES (ACTOR JOHN) (ROBBED (ACTOR FRED) (OBJECT CAR) (FROM JOHN)), we would like to have the system build a representation (ANGRY (ACTOR JOHN) (AT FRED)). In a symbol model, we can simply bind the ACTOR of an instance of the ANGRY schema with a pointer to JOHN. In connectionist models, the propagation of such dynamic bindings is problematic.

(d) *Structure and compositionality:* Given pointers, complex recursive structures can be built "on the fly" and used to represent the recursive and constituent structures exhibited by the embedded syntax and semantics of NL grammar and concepts (e.g., "John told Mary that Bill promised Fred that he would mow the lawn."). Symbolic systems are also able to take separate facts and rules and then combine them to produce a potentially infinite number of new structures, through repeated composition of structure. In contrast, connectionist systems cannot combine two distinct sources of knowledge to perform novel tasks, e.g., see discussion by Touretzky (1989).

(e) *Variables and structure sensitive operations:* With variables and structure, one can specify, for an infinite number of possible instances, how knowledge is to be propagated and instantiated from one structure to another; e.g., one can specify that ((x SELLS obj TO y FOR-COST z)--results--> (AND (OWNS y obj) (OWNS x (MONEY AMOUNT (PREVIOUS MINUS z))))). In connectionist models, one can only approximate such rules, by giving the network a large number of instances of the rule. These instances will influence subsequent generalizations, but logical inferences are able to function independently of the statistical structure inherent in any particular training set.

(f) *Communication and control:* In structure manipulating languages, such as LISP, what one function produces can be interpreted by any other function. This is the case because every LISP function has access to, and uses, the same structure-building and structure-traversing primitive operations (e.g., CONS, CAR, CDR). Such operations allow one function to communicate its results to other functions, thus supporting parallelism and communication at the structural level. In contrast, it is unclear how the connection weights developed through learning in one network can be used by another network. Current connectionist models have only primitive communication and control architectures.

(g) *Memory management:* In symbolic systems there is always a function that will supply "raw" memories on request, for the run-time construction of episodes. Such functions (e.g., GENSYM and MAKSYM in LISP) allow one to build new memories from old memories and new input. In connectionist models, however, the number of processing units is fixed at the onset. For example, if there are too few hidden units, then the network will not be able to learn the training data. But if there are too many hidden units, then the network will simply memorize the training data without forming the shared representations that support generalizations to new inputs. Connectionist systems need to incorporate a theory of how weakly active "neurons" become "recruited" as the need for new memories grow or as new tasks are learned.

It is difficult to handle the counterplanning strategies of agents in narrative text or the argument and belief structures in editorial text when one is lacking recursive data structures, pointers, variables, instantiation, unification, rules, inheritance, etc. When I first started out to reimplement NLP in connectionist networks, I quickly discovered that I could not even encode my (variable length) natural language input properly on the (fixed width) input layers of connectionist networks.

1.4 *Reactions to Connectionism*

Upon first encountering connectionism, I thought that all of my problems were solved and that perhaps, as an "old time symbol pusher" I was obsolete and would have to abandon symbols, logic, frames, etc. and replace it all with sigmoidal thresholding functions and backpropagation. But then I began to realize how impoverished were the representational and processing constructs supplied by connectionism. I began to realize that making connectionist technology actually useful for high-level cognitive processing might require completely reimplementing the last 40 years of computer science, NLP and computational linguistic theories and technologies. In any case, I decided that there were four possible reactions I might have to connectionism:

(1) *The big hype:* I had been lied to. I should ignore/abandon connectionist theory/technology and stick to the symbolic level where one can get things done.

(2) *Old mental baggage:* My problem stemmed from trying to get a new technology to do old things in the same old way (like using a refrigerator just to make ice to put into old ice boxes, or using television just to show old stage shows). Instead, I needed to abandon my old ways of thinking because I did not really need symbols or symbol processing (I just thought I did). I should first learn what simple connectionist models can really do and then work my way upward, toward symbol-like behavior, with the hope that the resulting models would somehow perform high-level cognitive tasks, but without encoding anything like classical symbols.

(3) *Pragmatic engineering:* Some problems need symbols and symbol processing while others need connectionist approaches. So I should build hybrid models, with some modules being symbolic and others being connectionist, or attach markers (i.e., symbolic pointers) to spreading activation networks, and not worry about how symbols might be implemented in neural tissue or what effects distributed representations might have on symbol processing *per se*.

(4) *New synthesis:* I needed both connectionism and symbolism, but symbol processing needs to be embedded, in a fundamental way, within connectionist architectures. The result would be systems with symbolic capabilities, but with learnable symbol representations. Such systems would merge the attractive features of both paradigms.

After a reexamination of the current capabilities and weaknesses of both the symbolic and connectionist models (Dyer, in press) I decided that the "new synthesis" approach was the most appealing.

2. A SPECTRUM OF POSITIONS

There is a game that philosophers like to play; i.e., they invent broad philosophical categories, give these categories labels (e.g., "nativists," "dualists," "functionalists") and then caricaturize the subtle and complex positions of their colleagues by attaching these labels to them. Since this paper is to appear in a philosophically oriented book, I have decided that it is okay for me to play the same game. Below are four labels, which caricaturize the major philosophical positions of cognitive scientists toward connectionism. These positions correspond roughly to the reactions I considered above. Smolensky (1988a) also describes a similar set of reactions.

(1) The *radical connectionists* (Churchland, 1986; Churchland, and Sejnowski, 1989) hold that the symbolic level is "merely a weak approximation" of what is really going on. They use the metaphor of the relation of quantum mechanics to classical Newtonian mechanics. At gross levels of observation, the quantum level acts as if it is Newtonian, but a more careful examination reveals a radically different level of behavior. The discovery of the quantum level has allowed scientists to generate fundamentally new predictions, while retaining Newtonian mechanics as a kind of approximate characterization. The radical connectionists believe that most of the language of cognition, such as symbols, symbol structures, and the language of goals, plans and beliefs are merely folk psychological constructs (Stich, 1983), and will either be eliminated entirely, or remain as loose, everyday characterizations of high-level cognitive phenomena. It is not clear what will replace symbols, but it will be in the direction of something like the "energy landscape" metaphor of connectionist models.

Researchers with radical connectionist leanings tend to work in a bottom-up fashion, sticking to very simple connectionist architectures that support learning, e.g., a single network with 3 feed-forward layers and one recurrent layer (Ellman, 1988, 1989; Servan-Schreiber *et al.*, 1989). They tend to avoid postulating many modules, heterogeneity of structure, or higher-order connections for gating, process control and communication.

(2) The *radical symbolists* (Fodor and Pylyshyn, 1988; Pinker and Prince, 1988) take the position that all interesting cognitive processing resides at the symbolic level. They believe that current connectionist models cannot perform symbol processing and therefore are currently inadequate to compete with symbolism as a language for describing thought. Furthermore, if/once connectionist models can perform symbol processing, they will constitute "merely an implementation" for classical symbol processing. Just as the semantics of high-level programming languages (e.g., PASCAL, LISP, PROLOG) are largely independent of the semantics of the underlying implementational languages and/or architectures; in the same way, the implementational level of symbols in the mind will, for the most part, be only

loosely coupled to the symbolic level. The symbolic level, therefore, is still "where the action is" and the mind can still be "cut off" above the brain and successfully studied solely in terms of symbol processing.

Researchers whose leanings are toward radical symbolism tend to ignore connectionist models and continue with their symbolist agenda, but with the need for increasing rear-guard actions to defend their position, as more and more researchers join the connectionist bandwagon.

(3) The *hybrid symbolists* (Charniak, 1986; Hendler, 1988; Lehnert, in press; Sumida *et al.*, 1988), take the position that what connectionism supplies is the convenience of numbers attached to symbols, since numbers can be added, multiplied, negated, and thresholded, while symbols can be passed around to implement the propagation of bindings. Pure symbols are either all or nothing, while attaching a number to a symbol allows the representation of a varying amount of commitment to a given symbol or relationship. Hybrid symbolists can build models that remain preeminently symbolic but possess the smooth, parallel constraint satisfaction features of connectionist models.

(4) The *structured connectionists*, e.g., (Dyer, in press; Feldman and Ballard, 1982; Pollack, 1987; Shastri, 1988; Touretzky and Hinton, 1988, Touretzky, 1989), recognize that high-level cognition requires symbol processing capabilities and are willing to postulate and design complex connectionist architectures that support symbol processing. Unlike hybrid symbolists, structured connectionists are committed to ultimately realizing symbol processing in neural-like tissue, without the use of an underlying symbol processing architecture (as in marker passing systems). The structured connectionists believe that a complete reexamination of what is a reasonable symbol is in order and that the resulting reimplementation of symbol processing with distributed representations will explain many of heretofore unexplained or ignored phenomena of human high-level cognition (Smolensky, 1988b).

There is a slippery slope, however, from hybrid symbolism to structured connectionism and many "symbol pushers" start out as hybrid symbolists, only to end up as structured connectionists. For instance, Sumida *et al.*, (1988) proposed a marker-passing system, only to later discover that a multitude of markers could be abandoned once they were replaced by propagation of distributed representations (Sumida and Dyer, 1989). Hendler (1988a) also began with symbolic marker passing for planning, but has since incorporated distributed representations into his model (Hendler, 1988b). Lehnert's recent NLP model (Wermter and Lehnert, in press) also incorporates distributed representations. Structured connectionists emphasize the need to have a great deal of structure in their networks, to support communication (Feldman, 1989), composition (Touretzky, 1989), propagation of bindings without symbolic pointers (Ajjanagadde and Shastri, 1989; Lange and Dyer, 1989a,b), and knowledge-level parallelism (Sumida and Dyer, 1989).

It is probably a good sign that the bulk of cognitive science researchers working on high-level cognition are neither radical connectionists nor radical symbolists, since it is in the middle ground where the most promising developments lie. Meanwhile, those who take extreme positions are useful for those who are working in the middle ground, since the radical positions make the issues stand out more starkly and indicate what obstacles have to be overcome to satisfy both radical symbolists and connectionists.

3. TWO TYPES OF KNOWLEDGE?

Consider task domains such as music, art, law, etc. Each appears to require both "hard" and "soft" forms of knowledge (see Table 1).

Hard	Soft
articulable	ineffable
deliberate	automatic
plan based	skill based
symbolic	perceptual
compositional	holistic
logical, inductive leaps	statistical, gradual, adaptive
critical features	family resemblances
supports invention	supports recognition
preeminently human	exhibited by animals

Table 1: Forms of Knowledge

For example, many people become very good at recognizing different styles of music, without having ever taken any music instruction. Without knowing what are octaves, scales, harmonies, quarter notes, arpeggios, etc. they can still learn to discriminate jazz from rock from blues from classical music.

They can form a varying number of discriminations within a given genre (e.g., waltzes vs mazurkas within classical music). They can even learn to recognize the work of a given composer and predict who is the composer or performer of pieces they have never heard. They can learn to do all of this simply through interaction with the data, i.e., through hearing examples of music. On the other hand, it is difficult to be musically inventive without some knowledge of basic musical elements and the ways in which these elements can be combined. One cannot elaborate a musical composition by varying the tempo, altering the meter, inserting harmonies, transposing chords, or adding grace notes, etc. if one does not know something about these elements.

But the task of composition also seems to rely on "soft" knowledge. Intermixed with articulable decisions to "add an arpeggio here for romantic effect" there is an ineffable response to each chord and note sequence being generated, that causes the composer to either like or dislike the ongoing results of his labor. This response seems to involve an application of the composer's entire musical background and is largely unarticulable. The composer either likes it or not and usually cannot explain why a given choice is better or worse than alternatives being considered. Recurrent connectionist networks, e.g., (Todd, 1989), can learn to recognize musical sequences after being trained on examples and capture some aspects of this kind of "soft" musical knowledge.

The domain of law also has hard and soft elements, e.g., the "I know it when I see it" problem and the problem of open predicates (Gardner, 1987) cannot be handled by logical rules. Likewise, in the domain of art, we can learn to recognize the style of Picasso or Dali without knowing anything about how such art was produced.

Other researchers have also noted the intermix of hard and soft forms of knowledge in a wide variety of domains. For example, Horgan and Tienson (1988) have considered sports domains and describe in detail how a basketball player makes use of both forms of knowledge simultaneously. Dreyfus and Dreyfus (1986) describe a chess grandmaster who is able to beat a master-level layer player even while being forced to maintain a running sum from a stream of numbers. Such phenomena suggest that even strategic-level thinking can be turned into a pattern recognition process as the result of years of experience. Smolensky (1988b) has argued that the brain is continuously attempting to compile explicit knowledge into a form so that it can be manipulated like a perceptual/motor skill. If this is the case, then learning to relate concepts, e.g., the OWN schema to the BUY schema, may require the same kind of practice (mentally) that learning to shoot a basket requires (physically). At the same time, relating BUY to OWN requires generalizing these schemas and their relationship so that an infinite number of novel owners, buyers and objects can be related to one another. Without the ability to propagate representations that refer to distinct entities and concepts having constituent structure, no amount of practice will result in the infinite generative capacity exhibited by humans (Pollack, 1987).

3.1 *Logical Inference vs. Connectionist Inference*

A major problem with connectionist networks is the inability to create dynamic bindings. In symbolic systems, this capability is achieved through the use of pointers, which create virtual references between elements of conceptual memory that reside at distant sites in physical memory. Dynamic bindings are essential for implementing logical rules and propagating information. Consider the following simple rule:

R1: (TELL (ACTOR x) (MSG y) (TO z))
$= = = >$ (KNOW (ACTOR z) (MSG y))

To implement R1, a network must be able to propagate, without alteration, the bindings in the TELL schema to the corresponding binding sites in the KNOW schema. As a result, R1 will work for *any* recursive structures bound to x and y.

A very different type of inference is one that is statistically based. For instance, in PDP networks (Rumelhart and McClelland, 1986), one can train the input layer of the network with instances of the left-hand side of the above rule and the output layer with the corresponding right-hand side. Suppose the majority of the training pairs have an implicit statistical structure, say, that whenever females tell males something the message tends to be that the females are hungry. If this is (statistically) the case, then the network will infer (i.e., generalize) for a new instance (e.g., Mary telling John) that Mary is hungry. This kind of statistically based inference is very nice to have, since it adds a richness (what Elman (1989) calls "context sensitivity") to the representation of each telling experience. However, statistically based techniques appear to be incapable of handling totally novel inputs, such as Mary telling John that her bicycle has a flat tire. With logical inferential capability, a system can conclude immediately that John now knows that Mary's bicycle has a flat tire, independent of the number and/or content of past telling (or bicycle) experiences.

3.2 *Von Neumann Symbols vs. Connectionist Symbols*

While propagation of bindings is a critical feature of symbolism, the symbols in von Neumann architectures have no intrinsic *microsemantics* of their own; e.g., symbols are formed by concatenating ASCII codes that are static, human engineered, and arbitrary. To gain a *macrosemantics*, these arbitrary and static bit vectors are placed into structured relationships with other arbitrary symbols, via pointers. In contrast, symbols in connectionist systems can be represented as patterns of activity over a set of processing units and these patterns can directly have semantic significance. For example, when these patterns are place onto the input layer of a connectionist network, they cause the reconstruction of patterns in the output layer(s) where the kind of output produced depends critically on the nature of the input patterns.

In the brain it is probably not the case that symbols are static or arbitrary. It is likely that the symbol for, say, DOG, is dynamically formed through interaction with dogs and when placed into a perceptual network in a given context, DOG causes the reconstruction of visual and other sensory experiences of a given dog. Thus the symbol DOG is *grounded* (Harnad, 1987, 1990) in perceptual experience. Placing this symbol into a network that encodes more abstract knowledge (e.g., relating ownership of dogs to responsibility for their typical actions) causes abstract inferences to be made (e.g., as when you realize that your neighbors do not like it when your dog barks at night, so you bring him inside).

4. CONNECTIONIST METHODS FOR AUTOMATIC SYMBOL FORMATION

What we want is a method by which each symbol dynamically forms its own microsemantics, while at the same time entering into structured, recursive relationships with other symbols. The general technique for accomplishing this goal we call *symbol recirculation*. Symbols are maintained in a separate connectionist network that acts as a *global symbol lexicon* (GSL), where each symbol is composed of a distributed pattern of activation. Symbol representations start with random patterns of activation. Over time they are "recirculated" through the symbolic tasks being demanded of them, and as a result, gradually form distributed representations that aid in the performance of these tasks. Symbol representations arise as a result of teaching the system to form associative mappings among other symbols, where these mappings capture structured relationships.

The basic technique of symbol recirculation involves: (1) starting with an arbitrary representation for each symbol, (2) loading these symbols into the input/output layers of one or more networks, where each network is performing a given mapping task, (3) forming a distributed symbol representation that aids in the performance of the task, by modifying the connection weights (via some adaptive learning method) of both the task network and of the symbol representations being used to train the network, (4) storing the modified symbol representations back into a global symbol memory as patterns of activation, and (5) iterating over all symbols and tasks until all symbol representations have stabilized for all tasks.

In previous connectionist networks, the connection weights change, but the encoding of representations on the input and output layers, which represent the training set, remain unchanged. With symbol recirculation, however, the representations of the training set are undergoing modification while the task (which involves forming mappings between those representations) is being learned.

At the UCLA AI lab we have been exploring three methods of symbol recirculation: FGREP, DUAL, and XRAAM. All three methods involve the use of a GSL that is separate from the architecture being used to learn a given task. Symbols are taken from the GSL and loaded into the input and output layers of the architecture to represent the I/O pairs the architecture is learning to associate.

4.1 *Extending Backpropagation into Symbols with FGREP*

In the FGREP method, each symbol is represented as a pattern of weights in a GSL. The values of these weights are placed in both the input and output layers. To modify the representations of the symbols as they are used, back-error propagation (Rumelhart *et al.*, 1986) is extended into the weights representing the symbols being used. These new symbol representations are then used to represent other I/O mappings in the training data. The basic architecture is shown in Figure 1.

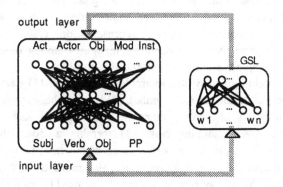

Figure 1: FGREP Method applied to task of mapping NL syntax to semantics. Symbols (w1...wn) in GSL are placed into syntactic segments (Subj., etc.) of input layer and into semantic segments (Act, Actor, etc.) of semantic (output) layer. Weight changes (for each symbol used) are backpropagated into the GSL, thus modifying the (initially random) representations of each symbol in GSL.

The FGREP method has been used to map syntactic structures to semantic representations and as a result, word representations are formed in which words with similar semantics form similar distributed patterns of activation in the GSL. For more description of FGREP, see (Miikkulainen and Dyer, 1988, 1989a).

4.2 *Manipulating Weights as Activations in DUAL*

In this method, the architecture consists of a short-term memory (STM) and a long-term memory (LTM), along with a GSL. See Figure 2 for an overview of the DUAL architecture. A set of slot/value pairs (representing a given frame/schema) are learned by the STM (via backpropagation). The representations of each STM filler are initially random. The resulting STM weights (from the input to hidden layer and from the hidden to output layer) are loaded into the input (bottom) layer of the LTM, where they are autoassociated with the LTM's output layer. The pattern formed over the LTM hidden layer is a compressed representation of an entire schema of slot/filler pairs and is placed in the GSL. When the slot of one frame F1 points to another frame F2 as its value, then the pattern of activation representing F2 is taken from the GSL and placed in the output layer of STM and the weights in STM are modified to learn that slot/value association. These modified weights are then placed back into LTM and the new representation for F1 is placed back into the GSL. To reconstruct the slot/value properties associated with, say, frame F1, the F1 distributed symbol is taken from the GSL and placed into the hidden layer of LTM, which causes LTM to reconstruct a pattern on its output layer. This pattern can then be used to modify all of the weights in STM. STM will now represent frame F1. For a more detailed description of DUAL, see (Dyer *et al.*, in press, a).

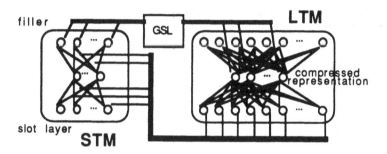

Figure 2: DUAL Method. STM is trained to associate a slot name (property) on the input layer with a filler (value) on the output layer. LTM is an autoassociative memory. The number of STM weights equals the number of input/output units in LTM. The number of hidden units in LTM equals the number of input/output units in STM. GSL holds symbols representations that were formed in the hidden layer of LTM.

4.3 *Using Recursive Autoassociation to Form Distributed Semantic Representations*

This method makes use of the extended recursive autoassociative PDP networks (XRAAM) and was originally developed by Pollack (1988) under the term "RAAM," where RAAMs functioned without the use of a global symbol lexicon. In the XRAAM method, a PDP network is trained to autoassociate a [predicate slot value] pattern on the input and output layers. The resulting pattern of activation on the hidden layer is then placed in a

GSL and represents the predicate. See Figure 3 for an overview of the architecture.

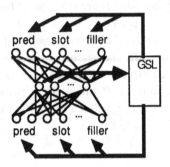

Figure 3: XRAAM Method, based on extending Pollack's RAAMs with a GSL. Compressed representation in the hidden layer of units is placed in GSL and later fed back into one of the roles in the input/output layers.

For example, suppose we want to form a distributed symbol for MILK. We load the following patterns into the XRAAM network:

MILK	HAS-COLOR	WHITE
MILK	CLASS	LIQUID
MILK	PRODUCED-BY	COW
	...	...

As each autoassociation is learned, we place the compressed pattern (from the hidden layer) into the GSL. Then we reuse this pattern to represent MILK in the subsequent [predicate slot value] tuples being learned. As a result, a distributed representation for MILK is slowly formed and will serve to reconstruct information associated with it. For example, given the partial pattern [MILK PRODUCED-BY xxxx], a decoding XRAAM network can reconstruct the pattern COW. Of course, COW itself is a symbol that has also been dynamically formed by tuples such as:

COW	#-LEGS	FOUR
COW	PRODUCES	MILK
COW	SOUND	MOO

Based on the XRAAM method, a system, DYNASTY (Lee *et al.*, 1989), has been built that was trained to learn script-based symbols and lexical entries. DYNASTY can generate paraphrases of script-based stories (Lee *et al.*, 1990) and infer plans and subgoals in plan-based stories (Lee, 1991).

4.4 *Forming Symbols with Microsemantics*

As a result of these symbol recirculation methods, the symbols formed have their own "microsemantics." For example, in natural language understanding tasks, *words with similar semantics* (as defined by word usage) *end up forming similar distributed representations in the lexicon* (Miikkulainen and Dyer, 1989a,b).

Figure 4 shows the initial and final states of distributed representations for four words. Initially, their patterns are random and unrelated. After many iterations, words used identically have identical representations and words used nearly identically have formed very similar representations. The resulting theory of semantics in distributed connectionist models is very different from that of traditional NLP, in which word meanings are represented in terms of explicit inference rules, e.g., (Dyer, 1983). In symbol recirculation, word representations are automatically formed through use. As a result of learning, *the representation of each word carries a memory trace of all the contexts of use that serve to define it.*

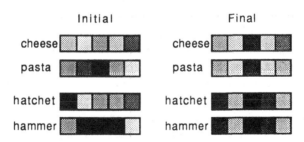

Figure 4: Each word is represented as a distributed pattern of continuous values.

If two words are used identically, their representations will converge. However, as their uses diverge, so also will their representations. Ambiguous words end up producing composite representations, sharing activity profiles with both classes/uses from which their meanings are drawn.

5. CONNECTIONIST METHODS FOR CREATING
AND PROPAGATING BINDINGS

One method of solving the problem of dynamic binding propagation is to augment connectionist networks with propagation of markers, e.g., (Charniak, 1986; Hendler, 1988; Sumida *et al.*, 1988), where markers contain symbolic pointers. However, a symbolic pointer implies that there is an underlying symbol processing architecture (e.g., von Neumann machine) available at every node in the connectionist network. This approach thus undermines one of the major goals of connectionism, which is to implement cognitive processes in networks of simple processing units that, although perhaps highly abstracted, are still functionally related to the known properties (and limitations) of real neurons. Thus, a major task facing connectionism is the creation and propagation of virtual pointers. Currently, there are three methods we are exploring, each capable creating bindings. These methods make use of tensors, ID+Content representations, and signature activations.

5.1 *Tensor Manipulation Networks*

In (Rumelhart and McClelland, 1986), one page (Hinton *et al.*, 1986, p. 90) is devoted to *conjunctive coding*, a method in which an association between two binary vectors, X and Y (say, each of size n) are stored by allocating n^2 processing units (i.e., a 2-dimensional plane) of memory. The pattern for X is placed across one dimension of the plane and then that pattern is repeated in the other dimension wherever the vector Y has a nonzero value. Hinton *et al.* point out that, while this method is expensive in the number of units required, it does solve the binding problem, since, given X, one can extract Y and vice versa. We did a number of experiments using conjunctive coding (Dolan and Dyer, 1987, 1989) to represent bindings for natural language processing tasks. During that time, we discovered that Smolensky (1987) had generalized conjunctive coding to the use of tensors, which allow nonbinary values and the use of memories of arbitrary dimension. Recently, Dolan has applied Smolensky's tensor approach to build CRAM, a hybrid connectionist/symbolic natural language understanding system. CRAM reads and extracts novel planning advice from Aesop's Fables (Dolan, 1989). In the tensor method, bindings between vectors X and Y are represented as the tensor outer product of two vectors and bindings can be extracted through the use of inner product operations. CRAM uses 3-dimensional tensors to represent [frame slot value] structures and employs 5-dimensional tensors to represent bindings across frames. However, as many mappings are overlaid into the same tensor, cross-talk occurs (Feldman, 1989). Dolan has had to create specialized circuits in order to extract bindings in the face of cross-talk. One interesting result is that cross-talk is eliminated more efficiently in CRAM as more knowledge is added to discriminate frames encoded within CRAM's memory. As a result, CRAM's accuracy of recall can actually improve as it acquires more knowledge (Dolan, 1989).

5.2 ID+Content Representations

Symbolic systems supply architectures so that symbols can be propagated without alteration. The result is that novel symbols can be propagated, but the symbols lack a microsemantics. Connectionist architectures can dynamically form symbols with a microsemantics, but have difficulty propagating patterns without alteration. One solution is to break up each symbol into two parts: (1) the *ID-part* contains a pattern of activation that uniquely identifies a given symbol as a unique instance of a more general class and (2) the *content-part* contains a pattern of activation that can be modified via symbol recirculation to carry a trace of the training tasks in which that symbol has been involved (see Figure 5).

Figure 5: ID+Content symbol representation. Each network is trained to pass on the ID-part without alteration while the content-part develops into a prototype (i.e., similar words develop content-parts with similar distributed representations).

For the ID+Content scheme to work, each network must be trained to pass the ID representation along without alteration. In order to support a large number of new IDs, the networks can be trained to autoassociate a large number of random ID patterns as each content-part is being formed. After such training, the network will accept distributed representations with different IDs and propagate these IDs without alteration. This technique is used to propagate script-based role bindings in DISPAR (Miikkulainen and

Dyer, 1989b), a connectionist script application and acquisition system (see, in press, Section 6.2.2.).

5.3 *Signature Activations*

At the UCLA AI Lab, we have implemented virtual pointers in a connectionist network system designed to comprehend natural language input involving ambiguous words that require dynamic reinterpretation in subsequent contexts. The resulting system, ROBIN (Lange and Dyer, 1989a,b,c), accomplishes its task while relying on only simple processing units (i.e., summation, summation with thresholding, and maximization). ROBIN makes use of two forms of activation.

(1) *Evidential activation* spreads across processing units and weighted (excitory and inhibitory) links as in other connectionist models. As in other localist models, each unit represents a semantic (or syntactic) node and the amount of evidential activation on a node represents the amount of evidence or support for that node.

(2) *Signature activation* is used in ROBIN to create and propagate dynamic, virtual bindings. Each instance node (e.g., JOHN) generates a unique activation value. A schema-slot node (e.g., TELL:ACTOR, which is the ACTOR slot of the TELL schema in rule R1) is bound to an instance node when its unique, signature activation value is propagated to the corresponding schema-slot node. For instance, if the signature activation for JOHN is 3.4, then the TELL:ACTOR node is considered bound to JOHN upon receiving an activation value of 3.4.

In ROBIN's localist networks there are special pathways along which signature activation is spread. These pathways connect role nodes to related frames (e.g., from TELL:TO to KNOW:ACTOR in R1). These pathways have unit-valued weights and intervening processing units along the path act only to maximize the activations they receive as inputs. These two features serve to preserve activation values as they are propagated from a slot in one frame to another. As an example of how ROBIN processes its input, consider the following two phrases:

P1: John put the pot inside the dishwasher...
P2: because the police were coming

When ROBIN first encounters P1, it initially interprets "pot" as a COOKING-POT (versus FLOWER-POT or MARIJUANA), based on greater evidential activation spreading from "dishwasher." However, a subsequent goal/plan analysis causes ROBIN to reinterpret "pot" as MARIJUANA. This analysis is achieved through the propagation of signatures across knowledge frames, where each frame is represented in terms of nodes and weighted links between them. Just some of the bindings that must be propagated are (informally) stated as follows:

If police see actor X with illegal object O = = > then police will arrest X

If actor Z is near object O = = > then Z can see O

If actor X places O inside object Y and Y is opaque
= = > then actor Z cannot see O

If actor X thinks X will be arrested by police seeing object O
= = > then X will do act A to block police seeing O

This knowledge, combined with various facts (e.g., that dishwashers are opaque), leads ROBIN to conclude, via the spread of signature and evidential activation, that John has placed marijuana in the dishwasher in order to block the police seeing the marijuana, and thus achieve John's plan of avoiding arrest. As spread of activation stabilizes, the MARIJUANA interpretation of "pot" is finally selected over the other candidates, due to the higher evidential activation on MARIJUANA. Meanwhile, the representation of JOHN as the one to place the MARIJUANA inside the DISHWASHER is created through the propagation of signature activations on the slot nodes of the relevant frames in the network.

At first, it may seem that there is not enough resolution to maintain a large number of unique signatures. However, signatures need not be represented as a single value; instead, a signature can be implemented as a pattern of activation over a set of processing units. Nodes can be represented as ensembles of processing units and links between semantic nodes as full (or nearly full) connectivity between units in one ensemble with those in another.

6. STRUCTURED CONNECTIONIST SYSTEMS
FOR HIGH-LEVEL COGNITION

Given the symbol formation and binding propagation techniques mentioned above, we can now begin to reimplement NLP systems.   This reimplementation must lead to new insights at the "knowledge level" (Newell, 1981), otherwise the position of the radical symbolists will be essentially correct. Below are examples of two connectionist architectures, DCAIN and DISPAR. In DCAIN, the structure of semantic networks is maintained, but the distinction between separate token and type symbols is eliminated. In DISPAR, scripts are automatically formed, so that the script representations that are formed have a much greater richness than symbolic scripts, while maintaining the capability of propagating script role bindings.

6.1 *Representing Schemas in PDS Networks*

A major problem in distributed connectionist (PDP) models is that of representing structured objects, while a major problem in strictly localist connectionist networks is that of representing multiple instances (Feldman, 1989). Both of these problems can be resolved by combining the structural properties of localist networks with the distributed properties of PDP networks (Rumelhart *et al.*, 1986). The result we call *parallel distributed semantic (PDS) networks.*

At a macroscopic level, semantic nodes are joined by semantic links to form the standard semantic networks used to represent everyday world knowledge, as is done in AI systems. At a microscopic level, however, each semantic node actually consists of an ensemble of PDP units. For example, the frame-node INGEST would be represented as an ensemble of PDP units and a semantic-level connection between two semantic nodes actually consists of every PDP processing unit in one ensemble being connected to every PDP unit in the other ensemble. These connection weights are then set by an adaptive learning algorithm, such as back-error propagation.

Instances are represented very differently in a PDS network. In a semantic network, the instance "John ate a pizza" would be represented by creating new symbols, say, JOHN13 and PIZZA4, and linking them into a new frame instance, e.g., INGEST8 with its own ACTOR and OBJECT slots, that inherit properties from the general INGEST, HUMAN, and FOOD frames. This approach to representing instances creates memories that are too accurate (do you remember every single meal that you have ever eaten?) and results in severe storage problems for very large episodic memories. In contrast, instances are stored in PDS networks much as in PDP networks, i.e., as a pattern of activation over the PDP units in a given ensemble. Instead of creating JOHN13, a pattern of activation is created over an ensemble that is connected to another ensemble over which INGEST8 will emerge as a pattern of activation. The connection weights between ensembles are modified (e.g., via backpropagation) so that the JOHN13 pattern in one ensemble causes the reconstruction of the INGEST8 pattern in the other ensemble (see Figure 6).

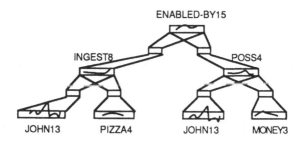

Figure 6: A PDS network representing the knowledge that John's eating a pizza was enabled by his having money. The wavy lines are suggestive of the particular patterns of action that are currently active over the ensembles (rectangles). Each pattern of activation has been given a mnemonic name (e.g., ENABLED-BY15) for convenience. The full bidirectional connectivity between ensembles is represented by the projections to/from the hidden units (small rectangles). After the networks are trained on the given instance, the pattern ENABLED-BY15 will cause the pattern POSS4 to be reconstructed, which will then cause the patterns JOHN13 and MONEY3 to appear in the bottom right-hand ensembles.

Unlike many PDP architectures, which usually consist of 3 ensembles connected in a feedforward (or simple recurrent) manner, our current PDS networks (Sumida and Dyer, 1989) consist of many ensembles, connected macroscopically in a semantic network fashion. As a result, we get the structural representation capabilities of semantic networks, while retaining the generalization and reconstructive capabilities of PDP networks.

6.2 Reconstructing Scripts within the Connectionist Framework

A *script* (Schank and Abelson, 1977) is a stereotypic action sequence in a given cultural setting. Scripts have been an important theoretical construct in NLP systems, supplying a context for disambiguating word senses, resolving pronoun references, and inferring unstated events (Dyer *et al.*, 1987). Until recently, the only implementations of script representations and script application have been symbolic in nature. An action sequence realized as a sequence of symbolic structures, where each hand-coded structure represents a conceptual event (e.g., the diner ingesting the food).

6.2.1. *Symbolic Scripts Reviewed*

Symbolic scripts work very well for certain tasks, but poorly for others. For instance, Cullingford's (1981) SAM system could handle a class of pronominal references and script-based inferences extremely well. SAM could read stories of the sort:

> John went to Leone's. The waiter seated him. The waiter brought him the menu. He ordered lobster. He left him a big tip.

When SAM read "John went to Leone's" it activated $RESTAURANT and bound John to the DINER role in the script $RESTAURANT. In this script there are symbolic structures representing events, somewhat like the following:

```
(MTRANS (ACTOR DINER)
        (TO WAITER)
        (C-CAUSE ANTE  (PTRANS
                               (ACTOR WAITER)
                               (OBJECT FOOD)
                               (TO DINER)))
               (CONSE  (STATE-CHANGE
                               (ACTOR DINER)
                               (TO POSITIVE-STATE)))))
```

This symbol structure represents the diner telling (MTRANS) the waiter that if the waiter brings the food to the diner, the diner will be happy. In the lexicon, there are several patterns for "order," one of them being (informally) that [x MTRANS to y that if y DO-ACT then x will be happy.] This pattern will match the scriptal pattern above and lobster will then be bound to the FOOD role in $RESTAURANT. Once all of the script roles are bound, SAM can infer that John ate the lobster, even though the story does not explicitly state this fact. The inference is easy to make, since FOOD is already bound to lobster and DINER to John, and there is another pattern in $RESTAURANT indicating that it is the DINER (not the WAITER) who eats the FOOD. Notice that pronouns can be handled in much the same way. The sentence "he left him a big tip" produces a representation of the sort:

```
(ATRANS     (ACTOR (ANIMATE (INSTANCE ANIMATE3)
                            (GENDER MALE)))
            (OBJECT (MONEY (TYPE TIP)))
            (TO   (ANIMATE  (INSTANCE ANIMATE4)
                            (GENDER MALE))))
```

which represents the abstract transfer of possession of money from one male to another. This pattern is matched against the other patterns in $RESTAURANT, one of which is:

```
(ATRANS     (ACTOR DINER)
            (OBJECT (MONEY (TYPE TIP)))
            (TO WAITER))
```

with the bindings:

```
DINER   <---(HUMAN
                (GENDER MALE)
                (NAME JOHN))

WAITER  <---(HUMAN
                (GENDER MALE))
```

The pattern matcher will successfully match these two ATRANS patterns, since HUMAN is a member of the class ANIMATE and since the other symbols match in content and structure.

In the SAM system, there were several script *paths* to represent different alternative actions (e.g., not paying if the food is burnt) and several script *tracks* to represent different types of the same general script (e.g., fast food restaurants versus fancy restaurants). To recognize a given script required matching inputs against key portions of each script, called *script headers*. In the FRUMP system (Dejong, 1982), for example, script headers were organized into a discrimination tree for efficient access.

These hand-coded script representations and accessing schemes never really captured the richness of even a single class of scripts. Consider the variability and context sensitivity of just the restaurant script. There are seafood restaurants, chinese restaurants, hole-in-the-wall diners, bars that serve meals, bar-b-q restaurants, different kinds of fast food restaurants, including fast food chinese restaurants, drive-thru restaurants, airport restaurants (where people often stand when they eat) and so on. As we experience more and more restaurants, we automatically form new restaurant categories and make predictions based on these categorizations. While it is relatively easy for a knowledge engineer to build a symbol-processing system that can bind an input character in a story to the diner role, it is very difficult for that same engineer to anticipate the richness and variability that will be encountered in even such highly stereotypic experiences as scripts. The knowledge engineer cannot be expected to write rules of the sort:

If x eats at a seafood restaurant in the Malibu area
Then the meal will be more costly and have a more impressive salad bar.

Instead, we want learning systems in which these kinds of rich, statistically based associations are formed automatically, and in which all these associations interact in a smooth manner to lead to an overall impression and to a set of expectations concerning experiences to follow in that context.

6.2.2   Script Acquisition and Application in DISPAR: A Distributed Connectionist Architecture

DISPAR (Miikkulainen and Dyer, 1989b, in press) reads script-based stories and acquires distributed representations of scripts. In addition, given novel stories (involving similar scripts) as input, DISPAR performs role bindings to generate causally completed paraphrases. For example, given the story:

John went to Lenoe's. John asked the waiter for lobster. John gave a large tip.

DISPAR generates the paraphrase:

> John went to Leone's. The waiter seated John. John asked the waiter for lobster. The waiter brought John the lobster. John ate the lobster. The lobster tasted good. John paid the waiter. John gave a large tip. John left Leone's.

DISPAR maintains a global symbol lexicon (GSL), where lexical entries are stored as distributed patterns of activation. These patterns are modified via the FGREP method, where each FGREP module (see Section 4.1.) also contains a recurrent hidden layer (Elman, 1988), in order to handle sequences on input and output. The GSL is connected to four recurrent FGREP modules (see figure 7).

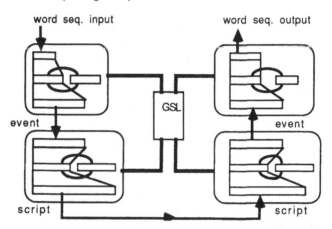

Figure 7: DISPAR Architecture. Word sequences enter the word parser and are trained to form distributed event representations, which enter the event parser to form a distributed script representation. On the right-hand side, the process occurs in reverse; i.e., event sequences are generated from a script representation and word sequences are generated from an event representation. During both training and performance, words are taken from GSL. During training, words in GSL are modified via FGREP. The arcs in each module represent recurrent connectivity between the hidden layer and the context layer.

(1) The *word parser* receives word sequences as input (i.e., one word at a time, taken from the GSL) and is trained (via backpropagation) to produce a *case-frame representation* (i.e., patterns of activation for the actor, object, act, location, etc.) in its output layer. For example, given the input sequence "John went to Leone's," the output layer is trained to place the

pattern of activation for "John" in the ACTOR slot and "Leone's" in the LOCATION slot in the output layer. At the same time, using the recurrent FGREP method, the patterns of activation representing "John" and "Leone's" are altered by this training and new representations for these lexical symbols are placed back into the GSL.

(2) The *event parser* takes a sequence of case-role representations as input (from the word parser) and is trained to produce a script representation in its output layer. This script representation consists of a set of patterns of activation over a set of script roles. For instance, here the pattern of activation for "John" would reside in the DINER slot in the output layer. Again, the learning of this mapping task causes the representation for the lexical symbol "John" to be modified via the FGREP method (see Section 4.1.) and thus the representations in GSL are repeatedly updated during training.

(3) The *event generator* is trained to take a script representation as input and produce, in sequence on the output layer, a set of event representations (i.e., case-role associations for each event). Again, each lexical entry (e.g., "John," "the," "Leone's," etc.) is modified as a result.

(4) The *word generator* produces a sequence of words, one at a time, on its output layer, given a case-role representation as input. For example, given the case-role associations: [LOCATION = Leone's, ACT = went, ACTOR = John], the word generator will produce the word sequence: "John went to Leone's."

When trained on a number of scripts, DISPAR automatically extracts statistical structure inherent in the data. In one experiment, for example, whenever DISPAR read about going to a fancy-restaurant, the customer left a large tip, but whenever the story involved a coffee-shop track, the tip was small. For fast-food stories, no tip was left. As a result, DISPAR automatically made these inferences when reading new stories, based on the type of script events encountered. To keep DISPAR from confusing role bindings, ID+Content representations are used. The use of ID+Content representations allows one portion of a representation to become similar, while retaining a unique, unchanged portion (see Section 5.2). Thus DISPAR can be trained on stories about John, but when asked to generate a paraphrase of a portion of a story concerning Mary, DISPAR will still correctly bind the script roles with Mary. Thus, DISPAR maintains rich representations, that are sensitive to past experience, while at the same time correctly propagating script-role bindings.

7. FUTURE DIRECTIONS

How close are we to discovering how knowledge is represented and manipulated in human brains? One way to address such a difficult question is to briefly describe two major weaknesses in current high-level connectionist models, and mention approaches that look promising in addressing these weaknesses.

(1) *Static representations.* Current connectionist models for high-level cognition suffer from having overly static distributed representations. In most connectionist models, a single activation value represents the average firing rate of some idealized neuron. Real neurons, however, generate actual pulses, which can encode complex timing patterns and whose frequencies can change over time. Recent evidence indicates that the brain is a chaotic system (Skarda and Freeman, 1987) and this form of analysis suggests that memories may be stored as strange attractor states (Pollack, 1989). Recently, Lange et al., (in press) and (Ajjanagadde and Shastri, 1989) have proposed a method by which propagation of signature activations (Section 5.3) can be realized as phase locking of non-linear artificial neural oscillators. Tomabechi and Kitano (1989) have proposed "frequency modulation networks" in which symbols are represented and propagated as frequency modulated pulses that are oscillated by groups of neurons. As larger models are built, based on such ideas, the resulting memories should circle around strange attractors, never passing through identical positions in state space. The knowledge that is encoded in such nonlinear, dynamical systems will be distributed both spatially and temporally.

(2) *Formation of structure through self-organization.* The models that the structured connectionists postulate have a great deal of complexity, in order to implement the propagation of bindings and to allow the knowledge acquired by one network to be made accessible to other networks. In symbolic systems, new structures are built by "grabbing" new memory cells from a "heap" (e.g., LISP). An open question concerns the kinds of innate, neurally plausible structures and processes that are needed to support the creation of virtual memories. Work, for example, by Kohonen (1988) and Edelman (1987) represents some initial steps in this direction.

8. CONCLUSIONS

Symbols do not consist of arbitrary codes (such as ASCII) but are dynamically discovered by the organism, such that their representations are intimately involved in the operations being demanded of them. Symbols are grounded in perception while capturing what is invariant across multiple sensory modalities and many experiences. This invariance is structural in nature, i.e., in terms of how symbols relate to one another. Symbol processing bestows on an organism the capability of making an infinite number of novel inferences, independent of the statistical structure used initially to construct the symbols. Symbol processing involves the dynamic linkage of symbols to one another, at great physical distances, through virtual reference and dynamic memory management. But the position that the symbolic level is independent of the implementational level is no longer a viable position. Changing the way knowledge is represented causes a great many changes in the way it is going to be processed.

Symbolism and connectionism each have an important, complementary role to play. Connectionist systems exhibit features of fault tolerance, adaptive learning, category formation, and reconstructive associative retrieval, while symbolic systems support logical reasoning in structural and combinatorial domains. In this paper we have briefly examined the positions of the radical connectionists and radical symbolists and found neither fully satisfying, leading to a middle ground in which symbolic models are taking on many of the neurally inspired features of weighted links, thresholds, and spreading activation, while distributed connectionist models are taking on the structural and symbol-binding features of the symbolic models. Human high-level reasoning exhibits both of these capabilities. Thus a synthesis is in order. Several techniques, for both symbol formation and propagation of bindings, have been presented here as an initial step toward such a synthesis.

---

*The research reported here was supported in part by grants from the JTF Program of the DoD (monitored by JPL), the ITA Foundation, the Office of Naval Research, the W. M. Keck Foundation and the Hughes Artificial Intelligence Center. Hardware grants in support of this research were supplied by Apollo Computer, Hewlett-Packard, the W. M. Keck Foundation and the National Science Foundation.

REFERENCES

Ajjanagadde, V. and Shastri, L.: 1989, 'Efficient Inference with Multi-Place Predicates and Variables in a Connectionist System', *Proceedings of the 11th Annual Conference of the Cognitive Science Society*, Lawrence Erlbaum Associates, Hillsdale, NJ.

Alvarado, S. J., Dyer, M. G. and Flowers, M.: 1990, 'Natural Language Processing: Computer Comprehension of Editorial Text', in H. Adeli (ed.), *Knowledge Engineering: Volume 1, Fundamentals*, (pp. 286-344), McGraw-Hill, New York.

Bower, G. H., Black, J.B. and Turner, T.J.: 1979, 'Scripts in Memory for Text', *Cognitive Psychology* 11, 177-220.

Charniak, E.: 1986, 'A Neat Theory of Marker Passing', *Proceedings of the Fifth National Conference on Artificial Intelligence*, (pp. 584-588), Morgan Kaufmann, San Mateo, CA.

Churchland, P. S.: 1986, *Neurophilosophy: Toward a Unified Science of Mind-Brain*, MIT Press, Cambridge.

Churchland, P. S. and Sejnowski, T. J.: 1989, 'Neural Representation and Neural Computation', in L. Nadel, L. A. Cooper, P. Culicover and R. M. Harnish (eds.), *Neural Connections, Mental Computation*, Bradford Book, MIT Press, Cambridge.

Cullingford, R. E.: 1981,'SAM', in R. C. Schank and C. K. Reisbeck (eds.), *Inside Computer Understanding: Five Programs Plus Miniatures*, (pp. 75-119), Lawrence Erlbaum Associates, Hillsdale, NJ.

Dolan, C. and Dyer, M. G.: 1986, 'Encoding Planning Knowledge for Recognition, Construction, and Learning', *Proceedings of the Annual Conference of the Cognitive Science Society (CogSci-86)*, Amherst, MA.

Dolan, C. and Dyer, M.G.: 1987, 'Symbolic Schemata, Role Binding and the Evolution of Structure in Connectionist Memories', *Proceedings of the IEEE First Annual International Conference on Neural Networks*, San Diego, CA.

Dolan, C. P. and Dyer, M. G.: 1989, 'Parallel Retrieval and Application of Conceptual Knowledge', in Touretzky, Hinton and Sejnowski (eds.), *Proceedings of the 1988 Connectionist Models Summerschool*, Morgan Kaufmann, San Mateo, CA.

Dolan, C. P.: 1989, *Tensor Manipulation Networks: Connectionist and Symbolic Approaches to Comprehension, Learning, and Planning*, Ph.D. Computer Science Department, UCLA.

DeJong II, G. F.: 1982, 'An Overview of the FRUMP System', in W. G. Lehnert and M. H. Ringle (eds.), *Strategies for Natural Language Understanding*, (pp. 149-176), Lawrence Erlbaum Associates, Hillsdale, NJ.

Dreyfus, H. and Dreyfus, S.: 1986, *Mind Over Machine*, Macmillan, NY.

Dyer, M. G.: 1983, *In-Depth Understanding: A Computer Model of Integrated Processing for Narrative Comprehension*, MIT Press, Cambridge, MA.

Dyer, M. G.: (in press), 'Symbolic NeuroEngineering for Natural Language Processing: A Multilevel Research Approach', in J. Barnden and J. Pollack (eds.), *Advances in Connectionist and Neural Computation Theory 1*, Ablex, Norwood, NJ.

Dyer, M. G., Cullingford, R. and Alvarado, S. J.: 1987, 'SCRIPTS', in Shapiro (ed.), *Encyclopedia of Artificial Intelligence*, John Wiley and Sons, NY.

Dyer, M., Flowers, M. and Wang, Y. A.: (in press), 'Distributed Symbol Discovery through Symbol Recirculation: Toward Natural Language Processing in Distributed Connectionist Networks', in Reilly and Sharkey (eds.), *Connectionist Approaches to Natural Language Understanding*, Lawrence Erlbaum Associates, Hillsdale, NJ.

Dyer, M., Hodges, J. and Flowers, M.: (in press), 'Computer Comprehension of Mechanical Device Descriptions', in J. Gero (ed.), *Knowledge-Based Systems in Engineering and Architecture*, Addison-Wesley, Reading, MA.

Edelman, G. M.: 1987, *Neural Darwinism: The Theory of Neuronal Group Selection*, Basic Books, NY.

Elman, J. L.: 1988, 'Finding Structure in Time', *Technical Report 8801*, Center for Research in Language, UCSD, San Diego.

Elman, J. L.: 1989, 'Structured Representations and Connectionist Models', *Proceedings of the 11th Annual Conference of the Cognitive Science Society*, (pp. 17-25), Lawrence Erlbaum Associates, Hillsdale, NJ.

Feldman, J. A.: 1989, 'Neural Representation of Conceptual Knowledge', in Nadel, Cooper, Culicover and Harnish (eds.), *Neural Connections, Mental Computation*, MIT Press, Cambridge.

Feldman, J. A. and Ballard, D. H.: 1982, 'Connectionist Models and Their Properties', *Cognitive Science* 6.

Fodor, J. A. and Pylyshyn, Z. W.: 1988, 'Connectionism and Cognitive Architecture: A Critical Analysis', in Pinker and Mehler (eds.), *Connections and Symbols*, Bradford Books/MIT Press, Cambridge.

Goldman, S., Dyer, M. G. and Flowers, M.: 1988, 'Representing Contractual Situations', in C. Walter (ed.), *Computer Power and Legal Language: The Use of Computational Linguistics, Artificial Intelligence, and Expert Systems in Law*, (pp.99-118), Quorum Books, NY.

Harnad, S. (ed.): 1987, *Categorial Perception: The Groundwork of Cognition*, Cambridge University Press, NY.

Harnad, S.: 1990, 'The Symbol Grounding Problem', *Physica D*.

Hendler, J. A.: 1988a, *Integrated Marker-Passing and Problem-Solving: A Spreading Activation Approach to Improved Choice in Planning*, Lawrence Erlbaum Associates, Hillsdale, NY.

Hendler, J. A.: 1988a, 'Problem Solving and Reasoning: A Connectionist Perspective', *Technical Report CS-TR-2161*, Computer Science Department, University of Maryland.

Hetherington, P. A. and Seidenberg, M. S.: 1989, 'Is There "Catastrophic Interference" in Connectionist Networks?', *Proceedings of the 11th Annual Conference of The Cognitive Science Society*, (pp. 26-33), Lawrence Erlbaum Associates, Hillsdale, NJ.

Hinton, G. E., McClelland, J. L. and Rumelhart, D. E.: 1986, 'Distributed Representations', in Rumelhart and McClelland, *Parallel Distributed Processing* 1, Bradford Book/MIT Press.

Horgan, T., and Tienson, J.: 1988, 'Settling into a New Paradigm', in T. Horgan and J. Tienson (eds.), *Spindel Conference 1987: Connectionism and the Philosophy of Mind*, XXVI, (pp. 97-113), Supplement of *The Southern Journal of Philosophy*, Department of Philosophy, Memphis State University.

Kohonen, T.: 1988, *Self-Organization and Associative Memory*, (2nd ed.), Springer-Verlag, Secaucus, NJ.

Lange, T. E. and Dyer, M. G.: 1989a, 'Dynamic, Non-Local Role Bindings and Inferencing in a Localist Network for Natural Language Understanding', in D. Touretzky (ed.), *Advances in Neural Information Processing Systems 1*, Morgan Kaufmann, San Mateo, CA.

Lange, T. E. and Dyer, M. G.: 1989b, 'Frame Selection in a Connectionist Model of High-Level Inferencing', *Proceedings of the Eleventh Annual Conference of the Cognitive Science Society (Cog-Sci-89)*, Ann Arbor, MI.

Lange, T. E. and Dyer, M. G.: 1989c, 'High-Level Inferencing in a Connectionist Network', *Connection Science* 1(2).

Lange, T. E., Vidal, J. J. and Dyer, M. G.: (in press), 'Phase Locking of Artificial Neural Oscillators Can Perform Dynamic Role-Bindings and Inferencing', *Neurocomputers and Attention: Proceedings in Nonlinear Science*, Manchester University Press, UK.

Lee, G.: 1991, 'Learning Distributed Representations of Conceptual Knowledge and Their Application to Script/Goal/Plan-Based Story Processing'. Computer Science Department, Ph.D., UCLA.

Lee, G., Flowers, M. and Dyer, M. G.: 1990, 'Learning Distributed Representations For Conceptual Knowledge and Their Application to Script-Based Story Processing', *Connection Science* 2(4), 313-345.

Lehnert, W. G.: (in press), 'Symbolic/Subsymbolic Sentence Analysis: Exploiting the Best of Two Worlds', in J. Barnden and J. Pollack, *Advances in Connectionist and Neural Computation Theory 1*, Ablex, Norwood, NJ.

Miikkulainen, R. and Dyer, M. G.: 1988, 'Forming Global Representations with Extended Backpropagation', *Proceedings of the IEEE Second Annual International Conference on Neural Networks (ICNN-88)*, San Diego, CA.

Miikkulainen, R. and Dyer, M. G.: 1989a, 'Encoding Input/Output Representations in Connectionist Cognitive Systems', in Touretzky, Hinton and Sejnowski (eds.), *Proceedings of the 1988 Connectionist Models Summerschool*, Morgan Kaufmann, San Mateo, CA.

Miikkulainen, R. and Dyer, M. G.: 1989b, 'A Modular Neural Network Architecture for Sequential Paraphrasing of Script-Based Stories', *Proceedings of the International Joint Conference on Neural Networks (IJCNN-89)*, Washington D. C.

Miikkulainen, R. and Dyer, M. G.: (in press), 'Natural Language Processing with Modular PDP Networks and Distributed Lexicon, *Cognitive Science*.

Newell, A: 1981, 'The Knowledge Level', *AI Magazine* 2(2), 1-20.

Pazzani, M. J. and Dyer, M. G.: 1989, 'Memory Organization and Explanation-Based Learning', *Expert Systems: Research and Applications* 2(3), 331-358.

Pinker, S. and Prince, A.: 1988, 'On Language and Connectionism: Analysis of a Parallel Distributed Processing Model of Language Acquisition', in Pinker and Mehler (eds), *Connections and Symbols*, Bradford Books/MIT Press, Cambridge, MA.

Pollack, J.: 1987, *Connectionist Models of Natural Language Processing*, Ph.D University of Illinois (Computing Research Laboratory, Technical Report MCCS-87-100 New Mexico State University).

Pollack, J.: 1988, 'Recursive Auto-Associative Memory: Devising Compositional Distributed Representations', in *Proceedings of the Tenth Annual Conference of the Cognitive Science Society*, Lawrence Erlbaum Associates, Hillsdale, NJ.

Pollack, J.: 1989, 'Implications of Recursive Distributed Representations', in D. S. Touretzky (ed.), *Advances in Neural Information Processing 1*, (pp. 527-536), Morgan Kaufmann, San Mateo, CA.

Quilici, A., Dyer, M. G., and Flowers, M.: 1988, 'Recognizing and Responding to Plan-Oriented Misconceptions', in *Computational Linguistics* 14(3), 38-51.

Rumelhart, D. E., and McClelland, J. L. (eds.): 1986a, *Parallel Distributed Processing: Explorations Into the Microstructure of Cognition*, (Vols. 1 and 2), Bradford Books/MIT Press, Cambridge, MA.

Rumelhart, D., Hinton, G. and Williams, R.: 1986, 'Learning Internal Representations by Error Propagation', in Rumelhart and McClelland, *Parallel Distributed Processing*.

Schank, R. C. and Abelson, R.: 1977, *Scripts, Plans, Goals and Understanding*, LEA Press, Hillsdale, NJ.

Schank, R. C.: 1982, *Dynamic Memory: A Theory of Reminding and Learning in Computers and People*, Cambridge University Press, NY.

Servan-Schreiber, D., Cleermans, A. and McClelland, J. L.: 1989, 'Learning Sequential Behavior in Simple Recurrent Networks', in D. S. Touretzky (ed.), *Advances in Neural Information Processing Systems 1*, (pp. 643-652), Morgan Kaufmann, San Mateo, CA.

Shastri, L.: 1988, *Semantic Networks: An Evidential Formalization and its Connectionist Realization*, Morgan Kaufmann, San Mateo, CA.

Skarda, A. and Freeman, W. J.: 1987, 'How Brains Make Chaos In Order To Make Sense of the World', in *Behavioral and Brain Sciences* 10 (2), 161-173.

Smolensky, P.: 1987, 'A Method for Connectionist Variable Binding', *Technical Report CU-CS-356-87*, Department of Computer Science and Institute of Cognitive Science, University of Colorado, Boulder, CO.

Smolensky, P.: 1988a, 'The Constituent Structure of Connectionist Mental States: A Reply to Fodor and Pylyshyn', in T. Horgan and J. Tienson (eds.), *Spindel Conference 1987: Connectionism and the Philosophy of Mind* XXVI, Supplement of *The Southern Journal of Philosophy*, Department of Philosophy, Memphis State University, Memphis, TN.

Smolensky, P.: 1988b, 'On the Proper Treatment of Connectionism', in *The Behavioral and Brain Sciences* 11 (1).

Stich, S.: 1983, *From Folk Psychology to Cognitive Science: The Case Against Belief*, Bradford Books/MIT Press, MA.

Sumida, R. A., and Dyer, M. G.: 1989, 'Storing and Generalizing Multiple Instances While Maintaining Knowledge-Level Parallelism', in *Proceedings of the Eleventh International Joint Conference on Artificial Intelligence (IJCAI-89)*, (pp.1426-1431), Detroit, MI.

Sumida, R. A., Dyer, M. G., and Flowers, M.: 1988, 'Integrating Marker Passing and Connectionism for Handling Conceptual and Structural Ambiguities', in *Proceedings of the Tenth Annual Conference of the Cognitive Science Society*, Montreal, Canada.

Todd, P.: 1989, 'A Sequential Network for Musical Applications', in D. Touretzky, G. Hinton and T. Sejnowski (eds.), *Proceedings of the 1988 Connectionist Models Summerschool*, (pp. 76-84), Morgan Kaufmann, San Mateo, CA.

Tomabechi, H. and Kitano, H.: 1989, 'Beyond PDP: The Frequency Modulation Neural Network Architecture', in *Proceedings of the Eleventh International Joint Conference on Artificial Intelligence*, (pp. 186-192), Morgan Kaufmann, San Mateo CA.

Touretzky, D. S.: 1989, 'Connectionism and PP Attachment', in Touretzky, Hinton and Sejnowski (eds.), *Proceedings of the 1988 Connectionist Models Summerschool*, (pp. 325-332), Morgan Kaufmann, San Mateo, CA.

Touretzky, D. S. and Hinton, G. E.: 1988, 'A Distributed Connectionist Production System', in *Cognitive Science* 12 (3), 423-466.

von der Gardner, L. A.: 1987, *An Artificial Intelligence Approach to Legal Reasoning*, Bradford Books/MIT Press, Cambridge, MA.

Werter, S. and Lehnert, W. G.: (in press), 'Noun Phrase Analysis with Connectionist Networks', in N. Sharkey and R. Reilly (eds.), *Connectionist Approaches to Language Processing*, North Holland, Amsterdam.

Zernik, U. and Dyer, M. G.: 1987, 'The Self-Extending Phrasal Lexicon', in *Computational Linguistics* 13 (3-4), 308-327.

Computer Science Department
University of California
Los Angeles, CA 90024

D. E. BRADSHAW

CONNECTIONISM AND THE SPECTER
OF REPRESENTATIONALISM*

Conscious, deliberate thinking is both exhausting and infrequent, a last resort to be appealed to only when all habitual capacities have failed.
— Anthony Quinton
"The Problem of Perception"

As one acquires a certain skill [including a perceptual skill], one does not internalize the conscious inferences and make them faster, but rather the rules underlying the skill become embodied in the agent's physiological and cognitive structures—thus one conserves mental effort.
— Aaron Ben-Zeev
"Can Non-pure Perception Be Direct?"

INTRODUCTION

Jerry Fodor and Zenon Pylyshyn's 1988 attack on connectionism is both well known and widely discussed.[1] It is meant to shore up support for the classical computationalist view of cognition, in the face of recent connectionist challenges. Less well known is their 1981 attack on the direct realism of J. J. Gibson.[2] It is meant to provide a similar sort of support, by sustaining the representational realism to which the classical computationalist view is committed.

I shall argue that, in fact, holding the classical computationalist view, with its inherent representationalism, precludes one from giving a successful account of perceptual intentionality. Connectionism, on the other hand, offers the hope of giving a direct-realist account of such intentionality as an emergent characteristic of perceivers. Furthermore, connectionism shows how to answer the criticisms of direct realism raised by Fodor and Pylyshyn.

I take it that this interplay between positions in the epistemology of perception and positions in the philosophy of mind is significant. There would seem to be two metaphilosophical morals to be drawn. The first moral is that, in general, one needs to consider one's position in the philosophy of mind when articulating a position in epistemology. This is perhaps the less controversial of the two morals.

417

For example, upon reflection, most philosophers would acknowledge that knowing presupposes understanding: knowing that p presupposes understanding p. Hence, an adequate theory of knowledge would benefit from an antecedent consideration of the cognitive skills required for this type of understanding. And, indeed, some philosophers do now seem to be concerning themselves with issues in the philosophy of mind in providing their accounts in epistemology.[3]

What is perhaps more controversial is the second moral, namely, that one would do well to consider one's position in epistemology when articulating a position in the philosophy of mind. Thus, the discussion in Part II of this paper may be taken to illustrate how a position in epistemology can influence one's position in the philosophy of mind. It is also worth noting, here, that this kind of influence is itself at least gaining a toehold in the recent philosophical literature.[4]

The structure of the paper is as follows: In Part I, I lay the conceptual groundwork. I sketch two epistemic positions in the philosophy of (visual) perception, representationalism and direct realism. I also sketch two positions in the philosophy of mind with regard to the nature of cognition, the computationalist approach and the connectionist approach. I argue that the computationalist account of mind requires a representationalist account of perception; whereas, the connectionist account appears to avoid any such commitment and to be at least *prima facie* compatible with direct realism.

In Part II, I discuss how direct realism informs our work in the philosophy of mind. I argue that the computationalist account of intentional, particularly perceptual, phenomena is inadequate and unilluminating. I claim that an intentional level of discourse vis-à-vis the functioning of a cognitive system should be introduced into one's theory of mind in a direct-realist fashion. I suggest that connectionist models of mind seem better suited to such an introduction.

In Part III, I discuss how connectionism informs our epistemological theories of perception. I consider the objections, put forward by Fodor and Pylyshyn, that are purported to show that perception cannot be direct. I argue that a connectionist account of cognition can help to make plausible a direct-realist account of perception by providing replies to the sorts of objections suggested by Fodor and Pylyshyn.

PART I

My task here is to lay the conceptual foundations for the rest of the paper. I fear that some will think I am traveling ground which has already been sufficiently trodden. But, bear with me: Much turns on our being clear about the relevant positions.

I take representationalism within a philosophical account of perception to be the view that, with regard to a certain type of object, we perceive those objects only mediately, by first being aware of some *other* type of object immediately (the latter of which are then said to *represent* the former) and then inferring the nature of the initial type of object. A number of points need to be made explicit here: First, representationalism as an account of perception is always to be relativized to a class of objects. Typically, the view of interest is representationalism with regard to our perception of medium-sized physical objects (and it is this version of representationalism that will be the focus of our interest, here). Philosophers of perception are usually concerned with the mediacy or immediacy of our perceptual awareness of table, chairs, and other objects that common sense tells us we perceive.

Secondly, even the representationalist must hold that there is something that we are aware of immediately. For mediate awareness and inference presuppose immediate awareness, on pain of regress.[5] There is, however, less agreement among the representationalists concerning how the representation of which we are immediately aware is to be construed--whether as a sensory state of the perceiver (one sense of sensation), as a particular kind of *thing* (a sense-datum), etc.

In any case, the key component of the representationalist view is the inferential component. The view is not just that we are aware, for example, of certain sensory phenomena in being aware of external physical objects. Even the direct realist may hold that some type of awareness of our sensory states *causally* mediates our awareness of physical objects. But, in addition to this, the representationalist holds that our awareness of those sensory states *epistemically* or cognitively mediates our awareness of physical objects via inference.

I take direct realism within a philosophical account of perception to be the view that, with regard to a certain type of object, we perceive those objects immediately, that is, *without* having first to be aware of some other type of object which cognitively mediates our awareness of the former type of object via inference. Again, the view is always relativized to a class of objects. But, here, the key component is the absence of epistemic mediation, the absence of any inferential component.[6]

It should be noted that, as I have construed it, direct realism is wholly an epistemic position. In this regard, my statement of the position differs from that of some others. H. H. Price, for example, sees the position in a significantly metaphysical light. In an early article[7] he says, the direct realist holds that perception "makes no difference" to what is perceived, that is, he or she holds that the objects of perception are mind independent, are not dependent upon the perceptual act for their existence or for their character.[8] As I construe it, direct realism is neutral with respect to the ontological status of perceptual objects.

Now, to the positions in the philosophy of mind. Practically everyone who is keeping up with the work being done in cognitive science and artificial intelligence is claiming to have a "computational theory" of mind.[9] Thus, in order to be able to contrast it with the connectionist account, I shall mean something more specific by 'computationalist account' of cognition. I shall mean by 'computationalist account' what others have called Good Old Fashioned Artificial Intelligence (GOFAI)[10], High Church Computationalism (HCC)[11], and the "rules and representations" theory of mind.[12]

On the computationalist account, intelligent thought is understood to involve computations--that is, rule-governed symbol manipulation. The symbols are syntactically-structured representations. The rules operate over these representations; they are formal rules that advert to the syntactic structure of the representations.[13]

But rule-governed symbol manipulation is just what the standard computer does. Hence, on the computationalist account, capacities for intelligent thought, involving intentional states (i.e., thoughts *about* things), are held to be capable of being instantiated in information-processing systems. On this model, capacities for thought can be instantiated as capacities of a computer to execute information-processing programs; in effect, "intentionally characterized capacities are computationally instantiated."[14]

William Bechtel further notes,

Central to the use of the computer to simulate human cognitive performance was the assumption that both the mind and the computer are what Newell refers to as 'physical symbol systems.' The idea is that symbols are physically encoded in data structures which can be manipulated according to specified rules.[15]

This is, then, at least approximating the view that John Searle calls Strong AI, the view that "the brain is a digital computer and the mind is just a computer program."[16]

The connectionist picture of intelligent thought is quite different. A connection machine is fundamentally composed of nodes and connections between nodes. Each node, operating in parallel, receives input signals from its neighbors; this input, together with the node's own prior value determines its current activation level. When its activation level exceeds a certain threshold, it transmits an output signal to other, surrounding nodes.[17]

How does the picture of intelligent thought presented by this model differ from that presented by the computationalist model? On the connectionist model, all computational interactions are local. There is no central processing unit controlling the overall behavior of the whole system, as is the case with a computationalist system, instantiated in a traditional computer architecture. And information is not stored in a connection machine in the form of discrete data-structures, but rather is contained globally in the weights that, in part, constitute the processing system itself.

There is no "program running" in a connectionist network in the sense in which the computationalist model involves a program running. Paul Smolensky suggests that notions from symbolic computation may provide important tools in constructing higher-level accounts of the behavior of connectionist systems, but says that these notions will provide, at best, approximate generalizations of what is going on in such systems, not precise accounts.[18] On this view, intentional characteristics are *emergent*, more or less global, characteristics of connectionist networks.[19]

This brings us to the issue of interest. To what extent do the computationalist and connectionist models make use of representations? And to what extent do either of the models suggest a representationalist account of perception?

It would appear that the computationalist account, at least as traditionally conceived, tends toward representationalism. John Haugeland notes that, on this account, our capacity to think about things basically amounts to a faculty for internal, automatic symbol manipulation--and this commitment to *internal* symbol manipulation commits the computationalist to understanding intelligent systems as containing computational sub-systems which carry out the manipulations.[20] Computationalism is thus fundamentally homuncular, at least at one level of analysis--namely, at the level of problem-domain intentional descriptions, at the level of program execution.[21] But this is precisely the level at which the computationalist wishes to delineate his or her account of intelligent thought.

For the computationalist, perception involves inference. Computations--including perceptual computations--operate over problem-level representations. In terms of the intentional descriptions that the computationalist uses in expressing the position, it is the representations of which the system is directly aware; the objects of perception (i.e., the physical objects) are known only mediately via inference. This is the crucial element of the information-processing views of perception that are part and parcel of the general computationalist approach.[22]

The connectionist account, on the other hand, is not *prima facie*, representationalist. The intentional characteristics of connection machines--to the extent that they can be characterized intentionally--are emergent, macro-level characteristics. How exactly such emergence is to be understood is a difficult issue.[23] But there does not seem to be any reason why such intentional characteristics could not be expressed in a direct-realist way, for example, in terms of the system (as a whole) seeing or recognizing some physical object.

Since the operations of a connectionist network are typically not describable in terms of its components' executing some problem-level program, the intentional descriptions (if any) that are true of the system need not imply an awareness of representations which are manipulated by and traded between system components. The sense in which connectionists talk about *distributed representations* is wholly different from the sense in which computationalists conceive of representations. As was noted, most "information" in a connectionist network is stored globally, in the connection weights. There are no discretely stored data-structures to be altered according to formal rules.

From the beginning, connectionists have talked about representations. In the face of Fodor and Pylyshyn's recent criticisms,[24] they have discussed the need for syntactically structured representations in a connectionist model--to account, for example, for the compositional nature of intelligent thought.[25] But what they seem to have in mind in using the term 'representation' is really just a *thought* and not the *object* of a thought, not what the thought is about.[26] In the perceptual case, it would be the relevant state of awareness, not that of which one is (immediately) aware.

Connectionists' use of the term 'representation' is probably here to stay. But it is worth keeping in mind that this use of 'representation' is misleading with respect to the philosophical tradition. For within the epistemological tradition (including Descartes and Locke, among others) which gives rise to representationalism as a theory of perception, representations are usually taken to be the objects of intentional acts of awareness and not the acts themselves. (In any case, I shall continue to mean by 'representation' an object of awareness and not the act or state of being aware.)

PART II

How are we to account for--to make sense of--the intentionality of perceptual states of awareness in intelligent, intentional systems? This is the issue that lies at the heart of the area of overlap between epistemic theories of perception and theories of intentionality in the philosophy of mind. And it is here that the direct-realist approach may suggest to us the more appropriate model of cognition.

I want to begin by claiming that the computationalist account of intentionality is inadequate. We shall consider a central problem that plagues any computationalist account of intentionality.[27] It will be seen to be due, in effect, to the representationalism inherent in the computationalist position.

The computationalist account of perception is homuncular (cf. Part I).[28] As a number of writers have noted, computationalist accounts are themselves accounts in terms of intentional processes and, if taken literally, presuppose intelligent homunculi (with intentional states) who do the computing.[29] The computationalist understands perception as involving manipulations carried out on internal representations (some of which would be incoming sensory representations and some of which would be stored, previously acquired representations). In engaging in such computations, it is the internal representations of which the system--or its homuncular components--is directly aware.

As an account of perceptual intentionality this is, of course, inadequate. The regress is obvious: In accounting for the intentionality of the perceptual states of awareness of a system, appeal is made to computational processes that involve further intentional states of awareness (this time of the relevant representations).

Daniel Dennett and William Lycan have attempted to avoid the viciousness of this regress by analyzing the relevant intentional states or capacities of a system in terms of the states or capacities of *simpler and simpler* homunculi. The idea is that there is nothing wrong with invoking homunculi, so long as the homunculi invoked at any given level do not--each one of them--presuppose exactly those capacities that they are to account for.[30] For both Dennett and Lycan, the intentionality involved is ultimately cashed out when the analysis proceeds down to a level where we can see how the intentional capacities of the system are realized physically. Dennett says,

If we then look closer at the individual boxes [of a flow chart] we see that the function of each is accomplished by subdividing it via another flow chart into still smaller, more stupid homunculi. Eventually this nesting of boxes within boxes lands you with homunculi so stupid (all they have to do is remember whether to say yes or no when asked) that they can be, as one says, "replaced by a machine."[31]

Yet, this method of appealing to stupider and stupider levels of homunculi is unable to account for the intentionality of the perceptual states of the overall system. The homuncular analysis faces a serious difficulty. The analysis must result in an intentional characterization, a program, so simple as to be unproblematically seen as describing the behavior of a physical system (a system whose behavior may also be characterized in a non-intentional way). That is, the resulting program must clearly be realizable in the relevant physical system.

In general, it is not too difficult to design a program that in some sense describes the functioning of a simple physical system. For the behavior of any simple physical system can be characterized using intentional terminology. Indeed, even my top desk drawer can be described as "instantiating" a rather simple program:

First, check to see whether you are open or closed.
If you are open, check to see whether anyone is pushing on your handle.
If you are open and someone is pushing on your handle, close.
If you are closed, check to see whether anyone is pulling on your handle.
If you are closed and someone is pulling on your handle, open.

Similar programs and flow charts can be given to describe the behavior of coffee makers, thermostats, etc.[32]

But the fact that any simple physical system can be so characterized hardly helps the proponent of homuncular analysis. For now saying that a system is able to instantiate a program, that its behavior can be described using a program, does little to suggest that it is really an intentional system.[33]

Rather than its resulting in an understanding of how an intentional system can be realized physically, the homuncular analysis merely yields an intentional description that can be applied to the behavior of a physical system--though not taken literally.

But why not take it literally? Because simple physical systems--the kind whose behavior can be unproblematically described by a program--are too simple to have literally the sorts of *concepts* employed in any real intentional system. Virtually all of the concepts used by real cognizers get their meaning, at least in part, from their interconnections with other concepts, that is, from their employment in the context of the potential employment of other concepts.[34]

Concepts are holistically linked to other concepts in ways that cannot be realized in simple physical systems of the sort to which Dennett appeals at the lowest level of his homuncular analysis. For the functional complexity of simple physical systems is too simple to mirror the functional complexity of any intentional system, the states of which involve the activity of such holistically interconnected concepts. Yet, the functional complexity of the simple physical systems would have to mirror the functional complexity of the intentional systems for those physical systems to be capable of literally being seen as having the relevant concepts and realizing or instantiating the relevant programs.

Consider the program describing the behavior of my desk drawer. Understood literally, my drawer would have to have concepts such as 'open,' 'closed,' 'pull,' 'push,' and 'handle.' But it does not have such concepts. Even these relatively simple concepts are still quite sophisticated. Imagine the range of skills (some physical, some linguistic perhaps) that a child would have to have in order for us to consider him or her to have the concept of something's being open.

(Of course, Dennett's homunculi are *really* stupid. All they have to do is to remember to say, "Yes," or, "No," when asked. But, asked what? Understood as (stupid) intentional systems, they are to be asked whether they are on or off, whether their voltage is positive or negative, etc. And whatever concepts would be operative in answering these questions are, again, not atomistically independent of other concepts.)

The holistic interconnectedness of virtually all concepts is easily illustrated using cases of the sort in which we are here interested, namely, cases of perceptual recognition. In such cases, taking oneself to be presented with an X, seeing the relevant object as an X, presupposes a number of concepts in addition to one's concept of X's. For example, in order to recognize an object as an open door, I must at least be able to be aware of the surrounding objects as walls, of the door frame, of the threshold, etc. It is plausible to hold that I would also need to know what it would be (how it would look) for the door to be closed and perhaps to know how at least some other doors, walls, open things, etc. would look.

Conceptual holism can be illustrated by appealing to cases of linguistically expressible beliefs, as well. Stephen Stich's example of Mrs. T. is a case in point.[35] One cannot have the concept of assassination as a constituent of a belief state without having a number of other concepts (in addition to the concepts making up the rest of the belief), for example, the concept of death.

Now, the computationalist could try to avoid such difficulties by adopting a different account of meaning. Rather than taking intentional content to be largely determined by functional role, one could, for example, hold a causal, denotational theory of content. Fodor holds such a theory.[36] He claims that some concepts--such as one's concept of redness--are, in effect, tied to the world in ways that can be specified in non-semantic, non-teleological, non-intentional terms.

Psychophysics is precisely in the business of telling us how much of the wall has to be painted red..., and how red it has to be painted, and how close to the wall one has to be, and how bright the lights have to be, and so forth...such that if it's that much red, and that bright, and you're that close...then you'll think 'red' if your eyes are pointed toward the wall and your visual system is intact...And it does so in nonintentional, nonsemantical vocabulary: in the vocabulary of wavelengths, candlepowers, retinal irradiations, and the like.[37]

It is unclear whether the computationalist can really make good on such promises. For it would seem that even our lowest-level concepts are irreducibly holistic. We cannot specify the conditions under which one will come to be aware of something's being red independently of one's other beliefs. Whether one takes an object to be red depends upon what one takes the object to be, one's beliefs about the normality of the ambient lighting conditions, etc. One is more likely to take an object to be red, for example, if one believes that that object is an apple rather than a pear.

Perhaps the computationalist would rather shift to phenomenal terminology and try to specify the conditions under which a thing at least looks or appears to be red. But this is also unworkable. As Wilfrid Sellars points out, the concept of appearing red itself seems to presuppose the concept of being red. The sense in which a thing looks red is the same as the sense in which things are red.[38] He continues, likewise, regarding the concepts of looking green and being green:

The point I wish to stress at this time, however, is that the concept of *looking green*, the ability to recognize that something *looks green*, presupposes the concept of *being green*, and that the latter concept involves the ability to tell what colours objects have by looking at them--which, in turn, involves knowing in what circumstances to place an object if one wishes to ascertain its colour by looking at it...And while this does not imply that one must have concepts before one has them, it does imply that one can have the concept of green only by having a whole battery of concepts of which it is one element.[39]

Here, then, is a summary of the argument against the computationalist account of perceptual intentionality: The classical computationalist is a representationalist and understands perceptual awareness to be mediated awareness, involving immediate awareness of representations plus inference. The computationalist account is homuncular: sub-system components are aware of the representations over which the relevant computations take place. (The computations would have to include comparisons of sensory representations with previously stored representations, for example, as in the case of recognizing a thing or type of thing with which one is already familiar.) Such computations are themselves characterized intentionally. A regress ensues with regard to understanding the intentionality found in perception. And this intentional burden cannot be discharged by appealing to stupider and stupider levels of homunculi, given the relative simplicity of the physical systems in which the lowest-level homunculi are to be realized and the relative complexity of the holistically interconnected concepts that would constitute the intentional states of these lowest-level homunculi.

The alternative "account" of perceptual intentionality, inspired by direct realism, is, in effect, to forgo giving an account--at least, to forgo giving the sort of homuncular analysis involving the manipulation and awareness of representations that characterizes the computationalist's position. The alternative account takes the intentionality of a cognitive system at the point of perceptual interface with its environment to be an emergent characteristic of the system, unanalyzable in terms of further, problem-level computational notions. As Aaron Ben-Zeev says, according to such an account, the product (i.e., the emergent perceptual state) is not taken to be distinct from some prior (cognitive) producing process; rather, the perceptual state is taken to be constituted by (realized in) the on-going (physical) processes of the system.[40]

This alternative is seemingly more compatible with the connectionist paradigm of cognition. For, as I noted in Part I, at least some connectionists hold intentional descriptions to be true of connectionist networks only globally. And they hold that the intentional characteristics of such networks are emergent and not further analyzable in intentional terms.[41]

The alternative account is inspired by direct realism in that the cognitive system's perceptual awareness is not taken to be cognitively mediated by any further states of awareness--specifically, it is not taken to be mediated by the awareness of any problem-level representations. Representationalism is avoided. Indeed, it must be avoided, if one is to avert the regress of states of awareness that threatens the computationalist account.

(It is worth noting that there may be a way out for the cagey computationalist. If one has a very sparse notion of representation, such that, in manipulating representations (even understood as discrete data-structures), the computational sub-systems are not thereby seen as themselves exhibiting intentionality,[42] then one may still be able to hold a computationalist account. Such a cagey computationalist might even go on to claim that intentionality is an emergent characteristic, true of (the right kind of) computationalist systems only globally. The point to notice, here, is that the cagey computationalist is no classical computationalist. For, as I have sketched it, cagey computationalism is at least *prima facie* compatible with direct realism and classical computationalism is not. And it is the classical computationalist's representationalism that I am concerned to argue against.)

The main difficulty with our direct-realist solution to the problem of making sense of the place of perceptual intentionality in the philosophy of mind is that direct realism has itself come to be thought of as fraught with problems. In Part III, we shall examine some of these problems. There, we shall see that the connectionist paradigm can help us to resolve many of the difficulties that appear to face the direct-realist account of perception.

PART III

Fodor and Pylyshyn provide an extensive critique of J. J. Gibson's ecological approach to perception.[43] We shall by and large ignore the criticisms that are concerned with specific features of Gibson's view. Instead, we shall focus upon those criticisms that can be construed as general criticisms of any direct-realist account of perception. In each case, we shall see that the difficulties become more tractable from a connectionist perspective or that they really go beyond the epistemic/psychological concerns which we (and Fodor and Pylyshyn (p. 156)) have taken to be at issue.

Fodor and Pylyshyn can be seen to present five general problems for any direct-realist account of perception: (1) the underdetermination of the object of perception, (2) the cognitive penetrability of perception, (3) the apparent lack of a processing mechanism, (4) the problem of intentionality, and (5) the problem of misperception. They claim that only a computationalist/representationalist account of perception can deal with these problems. And such an account, depending as it does upon inference, holds perception to be indirect or epistemically mediated.

Supporters of inferential, information-processing, computationalist accounts of perception typically claim that perception requires more than mere sensation, more than just the sensory stimulus. For, as Fodor and Pylyshyn note, the causally effective stimulus for perception very often underdetermines what is seen (pp. 142, 171, 185). One could say that there is an informational gap between the physical stimulus and the content of the perceptual state.[44] The computationalists then conclude that the only way to utilize the other relevant knowledge that the system might have is by means of inference.

In a similar vein, the computationalists note that perception (unlike mere transducer output) is cognitively penetrable--that is, perceptual states can be influenced by the beliefs, desires, etc. of the overall system (pp. 182-183). It is a commonplace in the psychology of perception that an organism's expectations selectively affect what it sees.[45] Again, the computationalists conclude that other cognitive states could influence perception only if perception involved inference, rule-governed computations that operate over such states and their constituent representations.

Next, Fodor and Pylyshyn argue that, on the one hand, there must be some processing of the incoming sensory data occurring, while, on the other, any such processing would seem to be incompatible with the directness of perception. The relevant type of processing for them is clearly inference:

[H]ow, if not by inference, do you get from what you pick up about the light to what you perceive about the environmental object that the light is coming from (p. 143)?
Finally, we are going to need a *mechanism* for the direct perception of phenomenological properties...(p. 150).
Some process *must* be postulated to account for the transition from one of these states of mind to the other, and it certainly looks as though the appropriate mechanism is inference (p. 166).

They think that this is most evident with regard to certain types of recognition:

In short, cases where perceptual recognition depends upon analysis of internal structure are cases where the direct perception model fails to apply (p. 181).
Gibson appears to recognize the importance of the issue of internal structure in percepts, since he frequently refers to the perceptual objects in the environment as being "nested." However, he denies that the detection of such nested units is cascaded in the sense that the identification of the higher units is dependent upon the prior identification of the lower ones. He *must* deny this because the mechanisms in virtue of which the identification of the former is contingent upon the identification of the latter could only be inferential (pp. 181-182).

In reply to (i) the underdetermination and (ii) the cognitive penetrability problems, note that these two problems are intimately connected. Both problems are concerned with how a perceptual system is able to make use of information in addition to that contained in the sensory stimulus. Specifically, then, the question at issue in each case is whether a connectionist system can utilize such information without relying on inference. The answer is that it can.

Prior learning, other cognitive states of belief, etc. would be able to influence the perceptual states of a connectionist system. For the overall state (of activation) of such a system at a given time is in part a function of the relevant connection weights; and, most of the effects of prior learning, other cognitive states, etc., to the extent that they remain in the system, remain in the form of altered connection weights. No inference needs to be involved in the transitions between the states of such a system. Indeed, since the residual knowledge is embedded in the system *in potentia* (in the connection weights, as dispositions of the connections to transmit states of activation between nodes to a certain degree) rather than *in actu* (as actual, discrete data-structures, stored in the system), the notion of inference, computations operating over explicit representations, makes no sense here.

In reply to (iii) the processing-mechanism problem, note that there is, of course, a processing mechanism operating within a connectionist system in a sense. But the processes involved are not inferential--there are no state transitions to account for *qua states of mind*. For there are no problem-level rules or program that describe the behavior of such a system. There is *causal* mediation of perception, to be sure, but there need be no *epistemic* mediation; it is this that the connectionist model illustrates.

Nor is the processing of "internal structure" a special problem. The relevant structural characteristics are input into the system at the point of perceptual interface, affecting the states of activation of the input nodes and the subsequent overall states of the system. But this, of course, does not involve their being themselves recognized and then becoming the data for further computations.

Fodor and Pylyshyn, however, seem to think that there is another facet of recognition that must involve mental representation--namely, cases of "recognizing as" or "seeing as." It is the problem of accounting for such cases that they call the "problem of intentionality" (pp. 188 ff.). (This problem is especially important given that they also hold that every case of seeing or recognizing a thing probably involves seeing it *as* something or other (p. 195 note 19).[46]) Their argument runs as follows:

To see the Pole Star as the Pole Star is (a) to see it; and (b) to take what one sees to satisfy some such representation as, for example, the open sentence "is the Pole Star" (p. 190).

(Reply to (iv) the intentionality problem:)   In virtue of what does something satisfy such a representation? The most straightforward answer is that it satisfies such a representation in virtue of being the Pole Star! Thus, the non-question-begging way of describing this type of seeing or recognition would be, for example, in terms of our "taking the thing to be the Pole Star" (or, perhaps, "our taking it to have the property of being the Pole Star" (cf. p. 191)).

The question is then how this type of seeing is to be understood. Fodor and Pylyshyn think that this kind of intentionality can only be accounted for by appealing to representations. But, now the homuncularity objection from Part II is seen to re-arise in a slightly altered form. For, presumably, seeing or recognizing as would have to involve a comparison of the sensory representations with certain stored representations.   Yet, the stored representations which are relevant to the current calculations would themselves have to be recognized as such and a regress ensues.[47] Fodor and Pylyshyn hope, ultimately, to be able to discharge this intentional burden.

The hope is...that theoretical appeals to the semantic content of mental representations will ultimately prove dispensable; in particular, that identities and differences among the semantic contents of mental representations will be reconstructible in terms of identities and differences among their functional (e.g., causal) roles.   Such a functionalist account of the semantic properties of mental representations would then round out the Establishment theory of intentionality (pp. 190-191).

But this project is just a version of the overall computationalist project that we considered, and found to be wanting, in Part II.

Finally, Fodor and Pylyshyn note that direct-realist views of perception appear to encounter difficulties in accounting for perceptual error. In effect, they present the direct realist with a dilemma.

If "directly perceive that" is taken to be factive, then by stipulation "x directly perceives that y is edible" will entail that y is edible. It follows that what goes on when one misperceives something as edible cannot be the direct perception of edibility. If, on the other hand, "directly perceives that" is *not* taken to be factive, then it is logically possible to, as it were, directly *misperceive* that something is edible. But Gibson will then need an account of what has gone wrong when misperception is direct. Notice, in particular, that he *cannot* account for such cases by saying that what you pick up when you directly misperceive the edibility of a thing is *apparent* edibility. For, things that are misperceived to be edible *do* have the property of being *apparently* edible, and the problem for a theory of misperception is to explain how things could be taken to have properties that in fact they do *not* have. (A way out would be to say that you pick up the apparent edibility and *infer* the edibility from that; but this just *is* the Establishment way out and, of course, it is closed to Gibson.) (p. 153)

It becomes clear, later, that the alternative which they want to avoid is Meinong's.

For one thing, if merely intentional (including non-actual) objects can be perceived, we will have to give up the enormously plausible principle that perception is mediated by causal transactions between the perceiver and perceivee. Non-actual objects cannot, of course, be actual causes. (p. 193 note 18).

In reply to (v) the misperception problem, just a couple of comments will have to suffice, here. First, this is, in effect, a *metaphysical* difficulty. Our concern and Fodor and Pylyshyn's is with whether perception is epistemically mediated. The claims in Part II were intended to show that it cannot be. The appeals to the connectionist paradigm, here, in Part III, are meant to resolve some of the apparent difficulties confronting the view that perception is epistemically *un*mediated.

To resolve fully the difficulties having to do with cases of perceptual error, we would have to consider issues of overall ontology that are subjects for another paper. It is worth noting, however, that a Meinongian position (accepting non-actual objects of misperception) is not wholly anathema to the view that perception is causally mediated. Indeed, on this point, the indirect realist and the Meinongian direct realist can say the same things: Perception is a process that is mediated causally. In veridical perception, the object that plays the central causal role is the intentional object. In misperception, this is not the case.

Fodor and Pylyshyn conclude their 1981 article as follows:

According to the Establishment theory...the mind is a mechanism for the manipulation of representations, and how what you see affects what you know is primarily a matter of how you represent what you know and see. This is what modern cognitive theory has inherited from the classical tradition in epistemology, and, as we remarked, it may be wrong. But there will be no successful anti-Establishment [i.e., anti-computationalist] revolution in cognitive psychology until some alternative to this account is provided (p. 195).

My intention in Part III has been to suggest that connectionism may provide such an alternative account.

NOTES

*   I would like to thank Panayot Butchvarov, David K. Henderson, and John Tienson for their helpful comments on an earlier draft of this paper.

[1]   Jerry A. Fodor and Zenon W. Pylyshyn, "Connectionism and Cognitive Architecture: A Critical Analysis," *Cognition, 28* (1988), pp. 3-71.

[2]   J. A. Fodor and Z. W. Pylyshyn, "How Direct is Visual Perception?: Some Reflections on Gibson's 'Ecological Approach'," *Cognition, 9* (1981), pp. 139-196.

[3]   See, for example, William G. Lycan, *Judgement and Justification* (Cambridge: Cambridge University Press, 1988).

[4]   See Michael Tye, *The Metaphysics of Mind* (Cambridge: Cambridge University Press, 1989).

[5]   Fodor and Pylyshyn, "How Direct is Visual Perception?" p. 155.

[6]   Cf., *ibid.*, p. 140.

[7]   H. H. Price, "Reality and Sensible Appearance," *Mind, 33* (1924), pp. 26 ff.

[8]   Although it still has a metaphysical twist, his view of direct or naive realism in *Perception* differs from this earlier view. In *Perception* he says that, in the case of visual or tactile sensing, the direct realist holds that the relevant sense-data are parts of the surfaces of physical objects (*Perception*, second edition (Westport, Connecticut: Greenwood Press, 1981 reprint of the 1950 Methuen edition), p. 26).

[9]   See Margaret A. Boden, "What is Computational Psychology?" *Proceedings of the Aristotelian Society, 58* (1984), pp. 17-18; also, Daniel C. Dennett, "The Logical Geography of Computational Approaches: A View from the East Pole," in Myles Brand and Robert M. Harnish (eds.), *The Representation of Knowledge and Belief* (Tucson: University of Arizona Press, 1986), p. 59.

[10]   John Haugeland, *Artificial Intelligence: The Very Idea* (Cambridge, Massachusetts: Bradford/M.I.T. Press, 1985), pp. 112 ff.

[11]   Dennett, *op. cit.*, pp. 60 ff.

[12]   John Tienson, "Introduction to Connectionism," *Southern Journal of Philosophy, 26* (1987) (Spindel Supplement), p. 2.

[13]   *Ibid.*

[14]   Robert Cummins, *The Nature of Psychological Explanation* (Cambridge, Massachusetts: Bradford/M.I.T. Press, 1983), p. 90.

[15]   William Bechtel, "Connectionism and the Philosophy of Mind: An Overview," *Southern Journal of Philosophy, 26* (1987) (Spindel Supplement), p. 21.

[16]   John Searle, *Minds, Brains, and Science* (Cambridge, Massachusetts: Harvard University Press, 1984), p. 43.

[17]   The connections between nodes, in effect, instantiate weighting functions which can vary in strength (both between different connections and within a given connection at different times). Thus, the input signal to a given node is a function of both the output signal from the neighboring nodes and the weights of the connections between the given node and its neighbors. The overall state of activation of the connectionist network is then given by specifying both the activation levels of the nodes and the weights of the connections.

A key feature of a connectionist network is that the initial values of the nodes and the initial weights of the connections need have no specific, pre-designed organization. Unlike traditional computational systems, connection machines are not *programmed* to do a specific task. At most, a connectionist network is designed in a general way to "learn" to do more specific tasks, for which one would try to write a program on the computationalist approach.

During the training period, the connection machine is presented with inputs and generates more or less random outputs, at least initially. (I am here sketching what I take to be the most intuitively understandable example of training a connectionist net, namely, back propagation of error in a simple, feed-forward network. Cf. D. E. Rumelhart, G. E. Hinton, and R. J. Williams, "Learning Internal Representations by Error Propagation," in David E. Rumelhart, James L. McClelland, and the PDP Research Group, *Parallel Distributed Processing: Explorations in the Microstructure of Cognition*, volume 1 (Cambridge, Massachusetts: Bradford/M.I.T. Press, 1986), pp. 322 ff.) The extent of the errors, the differences between the actual output values and the desired or correct output values (given the task for which the network is being trained), are calculated. In each case, for each training trial, the connections that contributed to a given error are adjusted: the values of their weights are changed. Those connections that contributed more to the error on a given trial are adjusted to a greater extent; those that contributed less are adjusted to a lesser extent.

For a more extended introductory discussion of connectionism, see Tienson, *op. cit.*, and Bechtel, *op. cit.* For more detailed, technical descriptions of the characteristics of connectionist models, see J. A. Feldman and D. H. Ballard, "Connectionist Models and Their Properties," *Cognitive Science*, 6 (1982), pp. 205-254; and Rumelhart, *et al.*, *op. cit.*, Chapters 1-4.

[18]   Paul Smolensky, "The Constituent Structure of Connectionist Mental States: A Reply to Fodor and Pylyshyn," *Southern Journal of Philosophy*, 26 (1987) (Spindel Supplement), p. 147; see, also, "On the Proper Treatment of Connectionism," *Behavioral and Brain Sciences*, 11 (1988), pp. 1-23.

[19]   Smolensky, "The Constituent Structure of Connectionist Mental States," p. 152; cf. Terence Horgan and John Tienson, "Settling into a New Paradigm," *Southern Journal of Philosophy*, 26 (1987) (Spindel Supplement), p. 109.

[20]   Haugeland, *op. cit.*, p. 113.

[21]   Daniel C. Dennett, "Intentional Systems," reprinted in *Brainstorms* (Cambridge, Massachusetts: Bradford/M.I.T. Press, 1978), p. 12.

[22]   Fodor and Pylyshyn, "How Direct is Visual Perception?" p. 139.

[23]   For a detailed discussion of the concept of emergence (and its compatibility with various forms of reductionism), see William C. Wimsatt, "Reductionism, Levels of Organization, and the Mind-Body Problem," in Gordon G. Globus, *et al.* (eds.), *Consciousness and the Brain* (New York: Plenum Press, 1976).

[24]   See Fodor and Pylyshyn, "Connectionism and Cognitive Architecture," pp. 41 ff.

[25]   Compositionality is perhaps most easily explicated in terms of the compositional nature of natural languages: Roughly, the idea is that complex expressions are made up of simpler semantic units which are able to play similar roles in different contexts—i.e., in different complex expressions.

[26] It is the same sense in which Gilbert Harman suggests that all mental states might be said to be mental representations ("Is There Mental Representation?" in C. Wade Savage (ed.), *Perception and Cognition, Minnesota Studies in the Philosophy of Science*, volume 9 (Minneapolis: University of Minnesota Press, 1978), p. 57).

[27] For a more extended treatment of the inadequacies of the computationalist account, see Aaron Ben-Zeev, "A Critique of the Inferential Paradigm in Perception," *Journal for the Theory of Social Behavior, 17* (September, 1987), pp. 250 ff.

[28] See Irvin Rock, *The Logic of Perception* (Cambridge, Massachusetts: Bradford/M.I.T. Press, 1983), p. 39.

[29] Cummins, *op. cit.*, pp. 45 ff.

[30] Daniel C. Dennett, "Artificial Intelligence as Philosophy and Psychology," reprinted in *Brainstorms*, pp. 123 ff.; and William G. Lycan, "Form, Function, and Feel," *Journal of Philosophy, 78* (January, 1981), pp. 27 ff.

[31] Dennett, "Artificial Intelligence as Philosophy and Psychology," p. 124. Cf. Lycan, "Form, Function, and Feel," p. 33; also, Dennett, "Why the Law of Effect Will Not Go Away," reprinted in *Brainstorms*, pp. 80-81.

[32] Cf. John McCarthy, "Ascribing Mental Qualities to Machines," in Martin Ringle (ed.), *Philosophical Perspectives in Artificial Intelligence* (Sussex: Harvester Press, 1979), pp. 173-175.

[33] Such a system would be what Robert Cummins calls *cognitive without being cognitive (*op. cit.*, pp. 54 ff., 82 ff.).

[34] Cf. Paul Churchland's discussion of the computational functionalist's view of meaning (*Matter and Consciousness*, revised edition (Cambridge, Massachusetts: Bradford/M.I.T. Press, 1988), pp. 31, 36, 56 ff.).

[35] Stephen Stich, *From Folk Psychology to Cognitive Science* (Cambridge, Massachusetts: Bradford/M.I.T. Press, 1983), pp. 54 ff.

[36] Jerry A. Fodor, *Psychosemantics: The Problem of Meaning in the Philosophy of Mind* (Cambridge, Massachusetts: Bradford/M.I.T. Press, 1987), pp. 72 ff.

[37] *Ibid.*, pp. 112-113.

[38] Wilfrid Sellars, "Empiricism and the Philosophy of Mind," in *Science, Perception, and Reality* (London: Routledge & Kegan Paul, 1963), p. 141.

[39] *Ibid.*, pp. 146, 148.

[40] Ben-Zeev, *op. cit.*, pp. 256-257; cf., also, "The Schema Paradigm in Perception," *Journal of Mind and Behavior, 9* (Autumn, 1988), pp. 490 ff.

[41] Smolensky, "The Constituent Structure of Connectionist Mental States."

[42] See Robert Cummins, *Meaning and Mental Representation* (Cambridge, Massachusetts: Bradford/M.I.T. Press, 1989), Chapter 8.

[43] Fodor and Pylyshyn, "How Direct is Visual Perception?" (Hereafter, the parenthetical citations will refer to this work.)

[44] Aaron Ben-Zeev, "Can Non-pure Perception Be Direct?" *Philosophical Quarterly, 38* (1988), p. 316.

[45] See, for example, Julian Hochberg, "In the Mind's Eye," in Ralph Norman Haber (ed.), *Contemporary Theory and Research in Visual Perception* (New York: Holt, Rinehart, and Winston, 1968).

[46] Cf. Noel Fleming, "Recognition and Seeing As," *Philosophical Review, 66* (April, 1957), pp. 161-179.

D. E. BRADSHAW

[47] I discuss this point at greater length in, "The Nature of Concepts" (unpublished manuscript).

Department of Philosophy
Memphis State University
Memphis, TN 38152

GERALD W. GLASER

IS PERCEPTION COGNITIVELY MEDIATED?

Recent theories of perception tend to divide into two rather broad theoretical orientations. The constructivist approach holds that perceptual processes are the result of mediating operations which construct the perceptual representation from sensory data, and that such operations are cognitive and inferential in nature. A second approach, the Gibsonian theory, holds that such constructive operations are not necessary in order to account for perceptual processes. A common assumption of *both* approaches is that *if* constructive operations are needed, then these must be cognitive operations which are similar to those which characterize thinking, reasoning, inference, and problem-solving.

In this paper I challenge the assumption that mediating processes in perception must be cognitive in nature. Instead, I develop an alternative analysis of perceptual processing which I characterize as non-cognitive computation.

The constructivist theory makes the following basic claims about the perceptual process. First, the information in retinal stimulation must be supplemented by information from other sources in order to account for various perceptual phenomena. For example, consider the case of perceptual *constancy*. It is well known that the size of the retinal image of an object is inversely proportional to the distance of the object to the eye. Thus, with every doubling of the distance to the distal stimulus the retinal image is reduced to half its size. Yet, over a relatively wide range of distances, the *perceived* sizes of objects are quite constant. Clearly, it is argued, some *supplementary process* must intervene between the proximal stimulus (retinal image) and the percept: the perceptual system must "take distance into account" in computing the perceived sizes of objects.

Second, constructivists argue that the processes which supplement the sensory data are *cognitive* operations. According to Irvin Rock, there is an inherent "logic" of perception, in which "perception makes use of assumptions and of internalized rules" (1983, p. 15). Rock maintains that perception is cognitive because the percept is a description which is propositional and conceptual in nature. In terms of Fodor's view of

437

representation (Fodor, 1975), such computations are symbolic and must occur in a "language of thought". Zenon Pylyshyn (1984) also argues that perception is symbolic and knowledge-based, involving inferential cognitive processes.

Third, the cognitive processes which account for perception are essentially the same sort as those which occur in thinking, reasoning, and problem-solving. Richard Gregory argues that "perception is not determined simply by the stimulus patterns; rather, it is a dynamic searching for the best interpretation of the available data...Indeed, we may say that the perception is an hypothesis, suggested and tested by the sensory data." (Gregory, 1978, p. 12) Likewise, Irvin Rock has argued that "perception is intelligent in that it is based on operations similar to those that characterize thought" (Rock, 1983, p. 1). In short, according to this approach, the sort of processing which goes on in perception is not different in kind from that which occurs in reasoning, inference and problem-solving.

This cognitivist account of perception has been challenged by James J. Gibson (1966, 1979) and his proponents (Turvey, et al., 1981). The Gibsonian view is that cognition is required only if there is insufficient information in stimulation. Gibson argued that theorists have been led to the conclusion that there was insufficient information due to a very narrowly conceived view of the stimulus for perception. One of Gibson's central achievements was his demonstration that stimuli can be constituted by highly complex gradients, ratios, and rates of change. He believed that such higher-order stimuli stand in lawful relationships to distal properties and that the visual system need only "pick up" or "resonate" to such invariants in order to perceive such properties. A useful way to conceive of Gibson's concept of resonance is in terms of the notion of *transduction*, in which a process can be explained simply in terms of the *physical* properties of the system, without bringing in *mentalistic* explanations.

Unfortunately, Gibson offers little explanation of *how* such higher-order information is extracted from the optic array, and his account of information pickup remains obscure. Even if there is sufficient information in proximal stimulation to specify distal properties, this does not preclude some mediational account of how such information is utilized by the visual system.

Nevertheless, I believe that Gibson is correct in calling attention to the problematic notion of cognitive mediation in the constructivist approach. It may indeed be the case that there is a need for mediating processes in perception, but what entitles us to call these *cognitive*? Could such talk of unconscious inference and hypothesis formation simply be a mentalistic overlay for an essentially *non-cognitive* mechanism, or do these processes *really* involve cognitive structures such as concepts and beliefs, and processes such as reasoning and hypothesis-testing? Cognitive theorists typically argue for the theory on the basis of an *analogy* between perceptual processes and ordinary inference and problem-solving.   They argue that proximal stimulation stands to the percept as the premises in an inference stand to its conclusion, or as the data stands to the hypothesis that best explains it. One of the central problems here is that the notions of inference and hypothesis formation are *themselves* rather vague concepts which require more explicit formulation.   Unless and until this is achieved, the basis of the cognitive theorist's analogy remains unclear.

Moreover, there are some rather troublesome *disanalogies* between perceptual processes and those such as hypothesis formation and problem-solving. For example, some theorists (Fodor, 1983, 1984) have noted that many perceptual processes occur in a manner which is largely *independent* of what the perceiver knows or believes about the distal state of affairs. As a case in point, consider the fact that knowledge of geometrical illusions, such as the Muller-Lyer display, has no effect whatsoever on the nature of the percept. Thus, it would appear that in at least *this* sense perceptual processes are remarkably *unintelligent*, insofar as one requirement of intelligence is the ability to bring to bear all that one knows in solving a problem.

A common assumption in this debate is that if there *are* mediating psychological processes in perception, these must be *cognitive*. Gibsonians claim that the *only* viable alternative to cognitive mediation is transduction. But is there a kind of information processing which is *neither* transductive nor cognitive?

In response to such perplexities, Fodor (1983, 1984) has argued that perception involves processes of a quite *different* sort than those which characterize ordinary hypothesis-testing and problem-solving. He maintains that perceptual processes are *modular* insofar as they are domain specific, mandatory, limited in terms of central access, and informationally encapsulated from other cognitive processes. Fodor concludes that the constructivist theory is wrong *not* because it argues that perceptual processes essentially involve cognitive processes (hence, his disagreement with Gibson) but because it classifies these cognitive operations with those having to do with reasoning, problem-solving, and hypothesis-testing. These types of cognitive operations are not modular on Fodor's view and are functions of what he calls the "central systems".

Fodor's analysis is intriguing, but it raises some interesting problems of its own. One is that at least *some* types of problem-solving and inference are *also* modular in their operation. Studies of the psychology of inference by Nisbett and Ross (1980) as well as Kahneman, Slovic and Tversky (1982) suggest that there are various kinds of fallacies of reasoning which are extremely recalcitrant with respect to new knowledge. Another problem is that Fodor offers little explanation of *why* one class of cognitive processes should become informationally isolated from the rest of the cognitive system.

The concept of modularity in perception is significant in that it suggests an important distinction *between* perceptual and cognitive processes. Nevertheless, Fodor (like the cognitive theorists he criticizes) chooses to view perceptual processes as a specific *class* of cognitive operations. However, as I shall argue, there are good reasons for holding that at least *some* significant perceptual processes are not cognitive at all. I maintain that it is quite plausible to view such processes as cases of *non-cognitive computation*: computations which are do not employ symbolic/propositional representations.

In order to illustrate how such a process might work, consider the phenomenon of visual orientation constancy. It is quite clear that the visual system utilizes information about body and head tilt in computing the perceived orientation of objects, for unless it did so the visual scene would appear to rotate every time the optical image becomes tilted on the retina (Ebenholtz, 1977). Now suppose that we want to build a device which is able to compute the actual orientation of objects, given only the optical projection of the object on a photosensitive screen. In addition, suppose that the device has a built-in algorithm for computing object orientation from information about the object's optical projection together with information about the tilt of the device itself relative to gravity. Such an algorithm could be expressed in the following manner:

$$CO = A + OD$$

where "CO" refers to the computed object orientation, "A" refers to the angle of the optical image relative to the coordinates of the photosensitive screen, and "OD" refers to the orientation of the device relative to the force of gravity. Thus, when OD signals a (+)20 degree clockwise tilt and A indicates a (-)20 degree counterclockwise tilt, then the computed angular tilt is zero, corresponding to an upright object orientation.

Such a device could be constructed from a photosensitive screen with a mechanism to measure angular displacement of the image, a weight on a freely moving arm which can indicate the direction of the force of gravity and the angle of the arm relative to the device, and an adding mechanism which computes the object orientation by combining information about optical projection with information about the orientation of the device. Notice that once we understand how such a device works we can even "fool" the system by immobilizing the arm used to measure gravitational direction. We have here an analogue of a visual illusion.

Now it is clear that while it may be illuminating to *describe* the operations of this device in terms of "selecting hypotheses" and "performing inferences" about object orientation on the basis of "known rules", such mentalistic language may easily mislead one into attributing genuine cognitive capabilities to such a device. In point of fact it is obvious that the internal operation of this device can be completely explained *without* any attribution of cognitive states and processes.

The important point here is that there is nothing in such a process which requires, or even warrants the claim that such an algorithm is a cognitive mode of information processing. Instead, what we have is an example of process whereby certain *registered* magnitudes enter into a computational relationship to determine object orientation. To suppose that a "cognitive agent" is performing any inferences or framing any hypotheses concerning such registered magnitudes is both superfluous and misleading. It is superfluous because such a process can be accounted for without the assumption of cognitive agency, and it is misleading because it falsely suggests that there is some kind of inference of the cognitive system occurring by means of rules represented in a symbolic medium or a language of thought. Perhaps such a mechanism as I have described behaves *as though* it knew certain rules. However, such "knowledge" is embodied in the mechanism without any process of inference from the registration of information to the symbolic representation of this information in some internal language.

There is empirical evidence for the view that non-cognitive computational processes can account for phenomena which might appear at first sight to be explicable only by the supposition of cognitive inferential operations. The notion of a non-cognitive algorithm can be explicated by considering the process of lateral inhibition as applied to brightness perception (Ratliff, 1972). The cognitive explanation of brightness constancy holds that the perceiver must "take illumination into account" in arriving at the perception of brightness. However, it has been shown that many phenomena of brightness perception can be explained by the interactive processes among retinal receptors, without top-down processes from the cognitive systems. Likewise, the phenomenon of "subjective contours" (Kanizsa, 1976) might appear to provide convincing evidence for the role of conceptually-driven processing. But in contrast to the cognitive accounts offered by Gregory and Rock, there are those by Ginsburg (1975), Becker and Knopp (1978), and Frisby (1980) which attribute such effects to the working of relatively low-level sensory processes such as lateral inhibition. Although the precise explanation of subjective contours is a matter of some dispute, it cannot be denied that there *are* non-cognitive explanations of such phenomena, and under such circumstances it would seem preferable to push the low level data-driven theories as far as possible to see what their limits are before bringing in the cognitive explanations.

Some recent connectionist models of mind may lend support to this mode of information processing. Connectionist theories view the computational processes in perception in a quite different way from that proposed by the constructivists.   Connectionist models have been designed in which computations are performed through the interaction of a large number of small units in a network, without the postulation of a symbolic medium of representation (Rumelhart and McClelland, 1986). In addition, much of the work of Marr (1982) was intended to show how one can account for many types of visual processing without bringing high level background knowledge to bear on the processing involved. I do not wish to imply that Marr's theories are free from problems, but they do provide a way to understand how relatively complex computational processing can occur without the intervention of knowledge and belief, at least at the level of the perception of surface properties. Recent studies by Poggio and Koch (1987) also provide evidence for the role of non-symbolic connectionist processes in visual perception. On their view, the detection of visual motion, and even the perception of velocity, occur by means of the interaction of retinal receptors without any symbolic, discursive, level of representation.

This non-cognitive computational account of perceptual processes provides a basis for making a distinction between perceptual and cognitive processes, and helps to explain *why* perceptual processes are typically modular in nature, something which is quite mysterious in the cognitive theory. They are modular perhaps because they are not cognitive operations *at all*, but rather comprise a mode of information processing quite distinct from that advocated in cognitive accounts.

REFERENCES

Becker, M. F. and Knopp, J.: 1978, 'Processing of Visual Illusions in the Frequency and Spatial Domains', *Perception and Psychophysics* **23**, 521-526.
Ebenholtz, S.: 1977, 'The Constancies in Object Orientation: An Algorithm-Processing Approach, in W. Epstein (ed.), *Stability and Constancy in Visual Perception*, Wiley, New York.
Fodor, J. A.: 1975, *The Language of Thought*, Thomas Crowell, New York.
Fodor, J. A.: 1983, *The Modularity of Mind*, MIT Press, Cambridge, MA.
Fodor, J. A.: 1984, 'Observation Reconsidered', *Philosophy of Science* **51**, 23-43.
Frisby, J. P.: 1980, *Seeing: Illusion, Brain, and Mind*, Oxford University Press, Oxford.
Gibson, J. J.: 1966, *The Senses Considered as Perceptual Systems*, Houghton-Mifflin, Boston.
Gibson, J. J.: 1979, *The Ecological Approach to Visual Perception*, Houghton-Mifflin, Boston.
Ginsburg, A. P.: 1975, 'Is the Illusory Triangle Physical or Imaginary'?, *Nature* **257**, 219-220.
Gregory, R. L.: 1970, *The Intelligent Eye*, McGraw-Hill, New York.
Gregory, R. L.: 1978, *Eye and Brain*, 3rd ed., McGraw-Hill, New York.
Kahneman, D., Slovic, P., and Tversky, A., (eds.): 1982, *Judgment Under Uncertainty: Heuristics and Blases*, Cambridge University Press, Cambridge.
Marr, D.: 1982, *Vision: A Computational Investigation into the Human Representation and Processing of Visual Information*, W.H. Freeman, San Francisco.
Nisbett, R. E., and Ross, L.: 1980, *Human Inference: Strategies and Shortcomings of Social Judgment*, Prentice-Hall, Englewood Cliffs, NJ.
Poggio, T. and Koch, C.: 1987, 'Synapses that Compute Motion', *Scientific American* **256**, 42-48.
Pylyshyn, Z.: 1984, *Computation and Cognition*, MIT Press, Cambridge, MA.
Ratliff, F.: 1972, 'Contour and Contrast', *Scientific American* **226**, 90-101.
Rock, I.: 1983, *The Logic of Perception*, MIT Press, Cambridge, MA.
Rumelhart, D., and McClelland, J., (eds.): 1986, *Parallel Distributed Processing: Explorations in the Microstructure of Cognition: Vol. I. Foundations*, MIT Press, Cambridge, MA.
Turvey, M. T., Shaw, R. E., Reed, E. S., and Mace, W. M.: 1981, 'Ecological Laws of Perceiving and Acting: In Reply to Fodor and Pylyshyn', *Cognition* **9**, 237-304.

Department of Philosophy
Wheaton College
Norton, MA 02766

DAN LLOYD

LEAPING TO CONCLUSIONS: CONNECTIONISM, CONSCIOUSNESS, AND THE COMPUTATIONAL MIND

These are strange times for consciousness. Considered subjectively, and as the reader may confirm for herself, we are as thoroughly aware of our inner and outer world as ever. The light of consciousness falls on these words and their meanings, leaps nimbly to the noises in the background, attends to a slight pang of thirst and frames a private plan to allay it, then settles back once more, with an inner sigh, to the unfolding text of this paper. It is for us as it was for Descartes, and presumably as it is, was, and will continue to be for all humanity.

But there's trouble brewing. Cognitive scientists, studying our same conscious minds from the outside, find perplexity in the obvious givens of conscious experience. It is not only that consciousness is an elusive subject of study, though it is certainly that. Rather, consciousness seems to have no role in cognitive models of mind. These models explain cognition through the computational interaction of inner rules and representations. Some of these rules and representations are conscious, but it is widely assumed that many are not. Cognitive science is generally silent on the distinction between conscious and unconscious representation, but this omission is inconsequential, since these inner rules and representations do their work quite independently of whether they are conscious or not. One is tempted to say that consciousness is *immaterial* to cognitive science. Daniel Dennett expresses the conundrum as follows:

...Now we are losing our grip on the very idea of *conscious* mentality. What is consciousness *for*, if perfectly unconscious, indeed subject-less, information processing is in principle capable of achieving all the ends for which conscious minds were supposed to exist? If theories of cognitive psychology can be true of us, they could also be true of zombies, or robots, and the theories seem to have no way of distinguishing us. How could any amount of mere subject-less information processing (of the sort we have recently discovered to go on in us) add up to or create that special feature with which it is so vividly contrasted? (Dennett 1987)

As Dennett suggests, the twin problems of scientific elusiveness and seeming irrelevance magnify each other. Though it is the inescapable center of our

444

subjective lives, consciousness nonetheless finds itself squeezed into the mysterious margins of the objective, scientific picture of mind.

The plight of consciousness is familiar. A generation ago a similar squeeze threatened the mind altogether: The intricate machine of the body left no gaps to harbor a ghostly mind. The problem dissolved when a thoughtful materialism saw both the ghost and the machine as matter under different descriptions. Cognitive science rests on a reconception of the problem of mind and body, demanding that two wildly different sorts of thing be seen as one identity (in some sense of the term). The identification of the sparkling tracery of the mind with the lumping mortality of the body is still one of the most outrageous of human proposals, and would be scorned--except that it works. The mind-body identity hypothesis offers science an approach to the mind and, more important, provides an intuitively coherent picture of the relation between humans and the natural world.

The grand unification of mind and body suggests an analogous project, the reconciliation of consciousness and representation. This paper is a preamble to this more modest reconciliation, exploring the hypothesis that (one type of) representation and (a corresponding type of) consciousness are identical. Thus, while mind-body identity theory proposes an intertheoretic bridge between psychology and brain science, the consciousness-representation identity theory proposes an *intra*theoretic bridge between two concepts in psychology. Even so, the identification is prima facie outrageous, not something to be proven in a spare afternoon. This paper merely sketches the hypothesis, considers a few of the more conspicuous objections, and outlines part of a possible empirical exploration of consciousness.

I. AN IDENTITY THEORY OF CONSCIOUSNESS

The identity hypothesis for consciousness holds that states of awareness (or states of consciousness) are identical to cognitively active representations. A representation is active at a given time if it is coming into being (via the appropriate causal mechanisms) at that time, or if it is causing other representations to come into being, or causing some behavior (again, via the appropriate mechanisms) at that time. In short, an active representation is party to an occurrent casual process, occupying either the position of effect in the causal chain, or the position of cause.[1]

A theory of consciousness should elucidate not only consciousness in general, but the many distinctions among types of consciousness found in ordinary conscious experience. From the basic statement of the identity hypothesis one can outline a partial theory of consciousness which explains one familiar distinction of phenomenology. Philosophers traditionally distinguish between "primary awareness" and "reflective awareness." Ray Jackendoff, whose terminology I've just borrowed, illustrates the distinction through a series of contrasting statements:

"Hey, there's a dog!" vs. "I see a dog!"

"Train's coming!" vs. "I hear/see a train coming!"

"That smells terrible!" vs. "That smells terrible to me!"

"You're awful!" vs. "I hate you!" (1987, 4)

Primary awareness, exemplified by the first member of each pair, is just our immediate awareness of the world around us, a world which includes our bodies. The statements of reflective awareness, in contrast, "inject the experiencer into the picture" (Jackendoff 1987, 4). How is reflective awareness different from primary awareness? The paired statements above seem very similar in content, but all share a shift in logical form. The monadic predicates of primary awareness reports become relations in the reflective reports--reports of *what is* turn into reports of *what seems to me*. The shift could be called an increase in inferential sophistication: Each statement is the conclusion of a (short) chain of reasoning, but the reflective statements take more of the total situation of the experiencer into account. The commonsense concept of reflection also suggests inferential elaboration, insofar as the reflective person is one who thinks more (reasons longer). In sum, primary awareness and reflective awareness could be regarded as falling on a continuum, from relatively immediate perceptual states to relatively deliberated inferential conclusions.[2]

The identity hypothesis suggests straightforward claims about both primary and reflective awareness. Let us call a representation that is currently in the process of formation a nascent representation. (Though I will talk primarily of representations, for the present purposes beliefs and desires might be substituted.) The identity hypothesis suggests the following subhypothesis about primary awareness:

PRIMARY AWARENESS: A nascent representation of x = a state of primary awareness of x.

If you open your desk drawer, you will quickly form a perceptual representation--a belief--about its contents. The identity just suggested asserts that as the belief is forming, it is a state of awareness of the contents of the drawer, and you are aware of exactly what is captured in the nascent belief. The content of awareness is the content of the belief, and both vary widely depending on your purposes and the state of your desk.

The hypothesis of primary awareness identifies one kind of consciousness with active representations as the effects of causal processes. Representations can also be active as occurrent causes of other representations, and this suggests a subhypothesis of the identity theory to encompass reflective awareness. Let us call representations that have been caused by other representations "secondary representations." A secondary representation, then, is nascent while another representation causes it to form. The identity hypothesis suggests the following view of reflective awareness:

REFLECTIVE AWARENESS: A nascent secondary representation of a representation R = the reflective awareness of R.

The import of this subhypothesis is not only in its claim that the nascent representation is a state of reflective awareness. It also asserts that the first representation, R, is an *object* of awareness. When we are reflectively aware, we are aware of it. The statements of opposition listed above provide several examples of the turn from the primary awareness of the world to the distinct representation of oneself as the perceiver of the world. Your drawer provides another example, illustrating the continuum from primary to reflective states: If you rifle through it, and discover on the basis of a series of perceptual beliefs about rubber bands, old photographs, and the like, that you have run out of stamps, then the nascent belief about stamps is, among other things, a reflective awareness of the initial beliefs about the drawer. (The conclusion, however, constitutes a state of awareness of its premises only as it is forming.)[3]

These two applications of the identity theory, as hypotheses about primary and reflective awareness, will need considerable explication and defense as conceptual theories. I think that they are resilient to philosophical objections, and invite some interesting revisions of the concept of consciousness. But my primary intent in this position paper is to consider the identity theory as an empirical hypothesis, and suggest some reasons to take it seriously as such. The approach will be indirect.

II. UNCONSCIOUS REPRESENTATIONS: SOMETHING IS HAPPENING BUT YOU DON'T KNOW WHAT IT IS

The identity hypothesis has several explanatory virtues, but one's appreciation of it is blunted by its collision with another doctrine, the widespread assumption that there are unconscious representations. This the identity theory denies by equating representation with consciousness. Thus, a good place to begin in the defense of the identity theory is with the concept of the unconscious. My target is a doctrine I will call "the hypothesis of the unconscious (HU)." Here is one form of the hypothesis:

> HU: There exist a special class of representations, unconscious representations, with the following properties:

   i) Like ordinary representations, they enter into causal processes leading to other representations and behavior.
   ii) Even as they are "in play," entering into causal processes, they are not conscious.

Before elaborating HU, we should note that many sorts of unconscious phenomena are not covered by the hypothesis. For example, there are processes occurring right now on the far side of the moon of which I am not aware. To me these are "unconscious processes," but the hypothesis of the unconscious (and my challenging of it) does not concern these. Similarly, many biological processes are occurring right now in my pancreas, but I am not aware of them. Neither pancreatic nor lunar events fall under the hypothesis of the unconscious because neither concern representations. Like events in my pancreas, some brain events are likewise unconscious, merely biological. HU has nothing to do with them. Finally, there are many beliefs which I hold right now of which I am not conscious. For example, I have beliefs about my zip code and other vital numbers. Most of the time, I am not aware of these representations. But HU doesn't concern them either: HU posits a group of representations that are simultaneously unconscious *and* involved in the causal processes of inference and behavior, and the zip code representations do not meet both conditions at the same time. Most of the time, when I am oblivious to these representations, they are inferentially inert. When they actively guide my behavior (as I address a letter to you), then I am aware of them.

In sum, the hypothesis of the unconscious exactly denies the identity hypothesis: HU makes a specific claim about a class of representations that are simultaneously active (involved in inference and behavior) and unconscious (to the believer). The hypothesis of the unconscious is not an a priori or philosophical theory. Rather, it is an empirical hypothesis, offered to explain and unify diverse observations. As an empirical hypothesis, it invites our assent only if it is the best explanation of the data of cognition. Perhaps there is some other way to explain things--or so I will suggest, drawing on connectionism as a platform for challenging the assumption of the unconscious.

What evidence supports the hypothesis of the unconscious? The observations that compel the appeal to unconscious processing might be collected under the heading of "cognitive gaps." A cognitive gap is a leap from one observed state to another, where the latter (or both) are complex cognitive states. The pioneering neurobiologist Karl Lashley has provided an apt description of these gaps, as they are experienced subjectively:

No activity of mind is ever conscious. This sounds like a paradox, but it is nonetheless true. There are order and arrangement, but there is no experience of the creation of that order. I could give numberless examples, for there is no exception to that rule. A couple of illustrations should suffice. Look at a complicated scene. It consists of a number of objects standing out against an indistinct background: desk, chairs, faces. Each consists of a number of lesser sensations combined in the object, but there is no experience of putting them together. The objects are immediately present. When we think in words, the thoughts come in grammatical form with subject, verb, object, and modifying clauses falling into place without our having the slightest perception of how the sentence structure is produced....Experience clearly gives no clues as to the means by which it is organized. (Lashley 1956, 4)

The first piece of evidence, then, is the phenomenal leap from some state A to another state B. A and B are both complicated and cognitive (that is, representational). The leap is neither arbitrary nor random. To get from A to B the mind must be working through many complex intermediate states. But these are not accessible to consciousness. An old Bob Dylan lyric can be pressed into service here: Something is happening but you don't know what it is. Since you don't know what it is, the "something" is unconscious. That's a cognitive gap.

But this is not yet evidence for a *cognitive* unconscious. HU, recall, posits the existence of *representations* that are simultaneously dynamic and unconscious. The leaps Lashley described certainly involve complex processes of the brain, but we go beyond Lashley if we maintain that these cognitive leaps involve intervening representational processes. Yet Lashley's two examples, visual perception and the production of grammatical sentences, are particularly compelling. It seems hard to imagine these processes occurring without some sort of cognitive intermediaries, and any theory of either process will need to posit cognitive states in abundance.

But why are these examples so compelling? I have a hunch, and in presenting it I will begin to work toward an alternate conception of cognitive processing, one that renders the identity hypothesis more plausible. If it is hard to resist the magnetism of the cognitive unconscious, I suspect that, lately at least, we are observing the tacit pull of the computer metaphor of the mind. Computers influence our thinking about the mind not only by providing opportunities for formal models of psychological processes, but also in more mundane ways by shaping our expectations about how physical systems can meet cognitive ends. The latter, informal, understanding of computers and computations is more influential, I think, than most of us realize. There are two familiar features of computers which I think are working here. I'll describe these, then explain their role in the appeal to the unconscious.

First, computers operate with very simple basic operations. The central processing unit is the heart of any digital computer, and its function is largely confined to binary addition and the loading and unloading of registers. The moving bits can be interpreted as computations in a machine language, but the machine language remains very limited in its vocabulary, and so offers at best very cumbersome descriptions of anything beyond the most basic computations. But computers do perform amazingly complicated tasks. They perform their computational feats via a second main feature, namely, by means of the repeated application of explicit rules to explicit (stored) representations. This is the familiar idea of programming. A computer's memory holds not only data but rules to apply to the data, and the CPU successively accesses both data and instructions. This enables the dumb CPU to do smart things, including complex operations which can be interpreted as basic operations in a high level computer language, which in turn can be chained to execute even more complex computations. The relevant moral is that when a computer does anything complex, it does so by passing through many simpler intermediate steps, which steps are representational in two ways: one sort of representation (a rule) is applied to another sort (a piece of data).

If that's how computers do it, why not minds as well? For many reasons, the analogy between human minds and human-made computers is an attractive one. It suggests that minds cross cognitive gaps in much the same way computers do, by passing through many rule-governed intermediate steps. Those states must be there, the analogy suggests. But even when we "introspect" with furrowed brows, we cannot accurately report most of the intermediate steps. Therefore, we are unconscious cognizers.

III. CONNECTIONISM AND THE COGNITIVE UNCONSCIOUS

If I am right that the digital computer shapes our intuitions about the mind, then shaking the influence of the computer could remove the intuitive support for the hypothesis of the unconscious. Until recently, digital computers were the only physical systems offering concrete models of cognition. But now that is beginning to change. Recent advances in the use of neural network models, based in large part on our nascent understanding of the brain, offer new hardware to inspire new intuitions. In particular, these network models offer examples of complex cognition which occurs *without* explicit rule-governed intermediate cognition. I will survey the importance of these network models in two steps.

First, as a preliminary, we should remember that some cognitive operations must be *immediate*, running from start to finish without any intermediate cognition (Fodor 1975, Dennett 1978). Fodor (1981, 63) tells a parable of How We Tie Our Shoes as an illustration of the orthodox cognitive science view of cognition (inspired by the computer metaphor). We tie our shoes, he imagines, when a little homunculus runs to the mind's library to check out the pamphlet entitled "How to Tie Shoes." In that pamphlet are instructions like "Grasp the left lace and pull it to the right," which send the homunculus (or other homunculi) scurrying to borrow "How to Grasp," "How to Pull," and similar self-help titles. The point here is that this decomposition comes to an end somewhere--there are some operations (like muscle contractions) which the homunculus already knows how to do. It executes these basic commands without consulting the library. When we ask, concerning these basic operations, "How did I do it?" we find no introspectable answer, since there is no representation, no cognition, involved. We just did it, without any mediating beliefs. Thus, the absence of introspectable beliefs or representations is not the symptom of *unconscious* cognition. Rather, it is the symptom of *no* cognition. The process at this basic level is exclusively physiological, like digestion. In sum, there are cognitive gaps without cognitive bridges, neither conscious nor unconscious.

How complex can immediate cognition be? The computer metaphor suggests that immediate cognition is no more complex than the basic operations of a digital computer. But network models tell another story. They suggest that immediate cognition can be complex indeed. I will give just one example of the suggestive results of network modelling, one among many.

NETtalk is a computer network that, in the words of its creators, "learns to read aloud" (Sejnowski and Rosenberg 1987, Churchland and Sejnowski 1989). That is, NETtalk takes input in the form of English language text and translates that input into descriptions of phonemes. These in turn can drive a synthesizer to produce generally accurate pronunciations of the input text. The interest in NETtalk is not, however, what it does but how it does it. The network consists of 309 neuron-like basic processing units, each receiving input from many units and sending output to many other units. The behavior of the network as a whole depends on the operations of these units in concert--the computation is distributed or spread out throughout the network. NETtalk is not programmed. Rather, it "learns" to process text through a series of trials where the behavior of the network is incrementally adjusted to more closely mirror the target performance. This brief description only sketches the deep differences in architecture between NETtalk and standard digital computer. A standard computer (running a program like DECtalk, which also "reads aloud") would process input text with the sequential application of hundreds of rules. (DECtalk uses a lexicon of several thousand whole words and their pronunciations, together with a set of rules for words not found in the lexicon.) Furthermore, a standard computer would have a separate memory to store the various rules and intermediate stages of processing. NETtalk lacks both the separate memory and the rules to put there. Many who work in network modelling argue that their models perform cognitive tasks *without* any explicitly represented rules at all (for example, McClelland, Rumelhart, and Hinton 1986; Nadel, Cooper, Harnish, and Culicover 1989; for discussion see

Horgan and Tienson 1989). I have argued elsewhere that they are correct (Lloyd 1989, Chapter 4). Moreover, connectionist models like NETtalk are striking in the complexity of the transformations on data they execute in single steps. Often these networks have no mediating layers between inputs and outputs, yet perform complex pattern matching tasks that would take a serial computer hundreds of steps. Or in other words, they cross wide cognitive gaps without intermediate cognition.

Why does this matter? It's exciting and important, I think, because NETtalk and other neural networks are deliberately modelled on the hardware of brains. If we want to know how the mind works, we get our ultimate answer, of course, by looking at the brain. Network models are therefore suggestive of the psychology we might discover in that golden age when we understand ourselves from the bottom up. The cognitive gap crossed by NETtalk is relatively modest, but then, so is the network: Its 309 units give it only about three percent of the brain power of a garden snail. The human brain, with around 10^{11} neurons, is a neural network with great cognitive ability, and perhaps the ability to leap large cognitive gaps in a single bound, with one step of immediate cognition.

One consequence for consciousness is straightforward. The neural networks provide an alternative to the standard digital computer, and at least undermine the plausibility of the intuitive empirical argument for unconscious mental processing. If the brain can cross complex cognitive gaps without passing through intermediate representational states, then we are no longer compelled to posit unconscious representational processing to explain the data. The question of the existence of the unconscious is thrown open. It is possible that the reason we can't report the mental representations that bridge cognitive gaps may be less because those representations are unconscious, and more because they simply don't exist. This is not to say that nothing bridges the cognitive gaps of consciousness. The leaps of perception and thought are not *absolute* leaps. The processes that transform written inputs into phonemic outputs in NETtalk are complex--the 309 units are linked via about 18,000 separate connections. But those complex processes are "subcognitive": They are the basic operations of the brain, corresponding to the basic noncognitive operations of a computer, only much more complex. They are unconscious, exactly as Lashley observed. But this is no surprise, since many of our biological functions are unconscious. The hypothesis of the unconscious, with its posit of unconscious *representations*, does not concern these.

The above is not yet a "connectionist model of consciousness," but it does make the identity hypothesis less hopeless. A full defense of the identity hypothesis would consist in a thorough review of every empirical finding that ever suggested the existence of unconscious representations. Presently, we will need to settle for a quick look at the two cases raised by Lashley, vision and language production. These are surely cognitive enough!

Vision has been the subject of lively research within connectionism and allied studies of computational neuroscience, generating many papers, several books, and even a few patents (Kienker, Sejnowski, Hinton, and Schumacher 1986; Churchland and Sejnowski 1989; Arbib and Hanson 1987; Grossberg 1988; Faggin and Lynch 1989; Grossberg and Mingolia 1989). Networks are succeeding at mimicking several aspects of human vision, from the capacities of "early vision," like the separation of figure from ground, to the achievements of full-fledged perception, like the recognition of faces or handwritten characters. The various simulated neural nets engaged in these tasks are all cousins of NETtalk, differing in size and in some organizational details, but no different in kind. Just as NETtalk leaps from words to phonemes via a process of complex but immediate cognition, so do these.

None of these networks, however, simulate the whole of the visual process. They suggest, in fact, a confirmation of the standard computational model of vision, a hierarchical progression from retinal patterns through what Marr (1982) called the "primal sketch," assembled of edges and gradients, on up to a three-dimensional model of a world of meaningful objects. At each stage in the hierarchy we find representations, and the various networks just mentioned simulate isolated transitions in the hierarchy, rather than the whole process.

Does this provide evidence for the cognitive unconscious? It would, if the various representations of low-level vision were unconscious. But they are not. I think Lashley's earlier characterization is worth rehearsing:

Look at a complicated scene. It consists of a number of objects standing out against an indistinct background: desks, chairs, faces. Each consists of a number of lesser sensations combined in the object, but there is no experience of putting them together. (1956, 4)

Lashley's "lesser sensations" include, I suggest, exactly the low-level visual representations: edges, figural boundaries, and the like.[4] These are as much a part of our conscious perception of any scene as the high-level awareness of the names and meanings of things. Our awareness of them is fleeting and vague, but real and easily intensified with a shift of attention.[5] But, as

Lashley observes, there is no experience of putting them together. That is the job of the hardware, and falls outside of the circle of consciousness. It is an unconscious process, but not a process involving unconscious representations.

Linguistic productivity is also a hot topic for connectionists (McClelland and Rumelhart 1986; Rumelhart and McClelland 1987). Indeed, this is the research area where connectionists fight pitched battles with proponents of classical computational models (Fodor and Pylyshyn 1988; Smolensky, this volume). At present, there are debates raging over the abilities or networks to embody structured representations, to generate recursive and iterative structures, and otherwise capture the features of human language. In one example, Rumelhart and McClelland created a simulated network of 920 units designed to transform verbs from the present to the past tense. As with NETtalk, Rumelhart and McClelland's network was not initially programmed to perform this task, but began with random connections between units, and a learning procedure like that employed with NETtalk led to a gradual adjustment of weights in the network, ultimately achieving good success rates with English verbs. Interestingly, the learning curve displayed by the network closely mirrored the curve for children learning the same task. At first, the network learns each verb as a separate case, treating both regular and irregular verbs a unique instances. Then, with the introduction of many new verbs, including many regular verbs, the network overgeneralizes, adding -ed to everything, producing past-tense forms like "gived" or "gaved" for "gave." Finally, the network sorts out the distinction between the regular verbs and the many special cases, and achieves a high overall level of performance. At no stage is anything like a rule for past tense production introduced. Again, nothing representational intervenes between the present tense and the past. The hardware makes the leap, unmediated by any cognitive program. Again, this network imitates only a fragment of our linguistic competence. But nonetheless it suggests how the hardware of the brain might explain Lashley's observation that

When we think in words, the thoughts come in grammatical form with subject, verb, object, and modifying clauses falling into place without our having the slightest perception of how the sentence structure is produced.

As above, the suggestion is that there is nothing representational involved in this process. Something is happening, and we don't know what it is--but I've tried to make it more plausible that the something in question is not itself cognitive, and hence not unconscious cognition featuring unconscious representations. Or, to switch from Dylan to Hamlet, the rest is silence. What is not silent is representation. The subcognitive biological processes deliver many representations--exactly as many, I propose, as there are states of awareness.

IV. SOME CONSEQUENCES

Near the end of *Dr. Jekyll and Mr. Hyde*, Robert Louis Stevenson reveals the journal of Dr. Jekyll and his tale of addiction and transformation. Jekyll, writing about himself in the third person, reports on the moral distance between himself and Mr. Hyde:

Henry Jekyll stood at times aghast before the acts of Edward Hyde; but the situation was apart from ordinary laws, and insidiously relaxed the grasp of conscience. It was Hyde, after all, and Hyde alone, that was guilty. Jekyll was no worse; he woke again to his good qualities seemingly unimpaired; he would even make haste, where it was possible, to undo the evil done be Hyde. And thus his conscience slumbered. (p. 87)

Dr. Jekyll's attitude toward Mr. Hyde is not unlike the popular attitude toward the unconscious: it is the other within. Primarily following a popularized awareness of Freud, it is commonplace for people (my students, for example) to believe in a Mr. Hyde within them, clamoring for release but simultaneously beyond their understanding and control. For this reason, perhaps, modern readers find the parable of Dr. Jekyll immediately comprehendible, and more or less buy into Dr. Jekyll's own understanding of his case: an uncontrollable demon lives within him, but the demon is not him; hence, he is not responsible or even able to understand the demon's acts.

But Stevenson makes it very clear that this interpretation of the relation of Jekyll to Hyde is an error and that Jekyll is living in profound bad faith. The psychotropic effects of the famous drug are about the same as a few beers; its main influence is to change Jekyll's appearance, offering him a disguise so complete that even he is deceived. He may feel detached, but Stevenson emphasizes that Jekyll initiates and thoroughly enjoys everything he does as Hyde. It was Jekyll, after all, and Jekyll alone, that was guilty.

The analogy between Hyde and the unconscious is extreme; Jekyll is an extreme character. But some morals may be drawn nonetheless. One is that the belief that our actions spring from unconscious causes does tend to forestall efforts at reflective self-understanding. Such self-understanding, I imagine, takes practice and care. Without practice, we could lose the ability to reflect upon our aims and motives. Thus, the belief that we are largely unconscious creatures could have the self-confirming effect of rendering us obscure to ourselves.

A second effect of the hypothesis of the unconscious is more directly related to contemporary cognitive science. The hypothesis of the unconscious is a corollary of a more general assumption that a representation is one kind of thing, a state of awareness another. According to cognitive science, it may be that representations are sometimes correlated with states of awareness. But that correlation doesn't matter for the explanation of behavior, because from the cognitive point of view representations are doing *all* of the explanatory work. To put the same point in other words, the cognitive explanation of our behavior is entirely constructed from outside the behaving individual. It is an objective description, in the third person, and our subjective first-person contribution is irrelevant. The ultimate effect, then, of the detachment of representation and consciousness (together with the belief in the efficacy of representation) is that the understanding of our actions is possible only from outside, as Jekyll pretended to understand Hyde, and not from within, as he should have understood himself. What self-knowledge we may achieve will not be reflective (or only accidentally so), but rather achieved only by considering ourselves as one object among many others, viewed at a distance. Cognitive science, in short, treats us *as if* we were unconscious--not just partly unconscious, but wholly unconscious, all of the time.

The identity hypothesis unites consciousness and representation, and begins to resolves the quandaries of cognitive science over the concept of consciousness. The hypothesis knits the subjective and the objective. Under the hypothesis, cognitive models of behavior are also predictors of experience, and experience is a reliable indicator of cognition. The anxieties expressed at the outset by Dennett evaporate, and it may turn out that like representation, consciousness is everywhere, lighting now on these closing words, returning to that pang of thirst, now quite acute, savoring a thoroughly rehearsed plan to allay it, and leaping to conclusions--representations--everywhere.

NOTES

[1]   Identifying consciousness with representation leads immediately to the question of the nature of representation in psychology, an issue explored at length in Simple Minds (1989). The present argument doesn't depend on a particular theory of representation, provided that representation is understood broadly enough to serve the variety of functions of human cognition. Specifically, representation should not be limited to linguistic representation.

[2]   Often the distinction between primary and reflective awareness is sharpened by crediting reflective knowledge to a special process known as introspection. What sort of process might this be? One view is that introspection is a special kind of inner sense, analogous to our ordinary perception of the outside world but directed at ourselves (e.g., Armstrong 1968, Humphrey 1987). If this is so, then introspective awareness really is just primary awareness with a special sort of object.   Accordingly, the problem of primary awareness truly is the primary problem. Solve it, and introspection can be treated as a (very) special case. By the same token, the announcement that introspection is the perception of oneself does nothing to solve the problem of consciousness!   Even if introspection is self-perception, one still wonders what it means to perceive anything at all, including oneself.

A second view of introspection treats it as a species of reflection, distinct only in its object (e.g., Garfield 1989).   Introspective judgments, in this view, are the conclusions of complex reasoning about ourselves over time, the relativity of our perceptions, the variance in our situations, and so forth.   If this is so, then the first proposal about the nature of reflective consciousness is largely correct.   Inferential complexity is its mark, and to call such reflective reasoning introspective is only to give the same process a slightly more restrictive label—complex reasoning about ourselves.   In sum,   introspection is either a species of (inferentially straightforward) primary awareness, or a species of (inferentially sophisticated) reflective awareness.   For the limited aims of this paper, this analysis licenses us to restrict our gaze to the continuum of primary-to-reflective awareness.   (The limits of the paper also rule out a discussion of the notorious notion of qualia. As Ende (1983) says, "this is another story and shall be told another time.")

[3]   Reflective states of awareness also exhibit a multiplicity of content: If a representation R causes another representation R', then both R and R' can be causally active at the same time; by the identity theory, both are states of awareness.   This conforms to our phenomenal experience: You can see that you have rubbers bands, photographs, etc. and at the same time see that you have no stamps.   The primary awareness and reflective awareness are simultaneously parts of a complex state of consciousness.

[4]   As foreshadowed in the previous note, we are simultaneously conscious of both the low level "lesser sensations" and the high level percepts.

[5]   The identity theory may also offer a model of attention: Perhaps attention is an increase in reflective (i.e., inferential) processing. After a quick glance at my face, you're aware of its shape (as a primary state of awareness) and become aware of (reflectively) that the face before you is mine. But you can launch other reflections from the primary awareness of the shape of my face, noting other features or aspects of the shape. Attention to a stimulus, in short, might be reflection in the presence of the stimulus.

REFERENCES

Arbib, M. and Hanson, A.: 1987, *Vision, Brain, and Cooperative Computation*, Bradford Books/MIT Press, Cambridge, MA.

Armstrong, D. M.: 1968, *A Materialist Theory of the Mind*, Routledge and Kegan Paul, London.

Churchland, P. S., and Sejnowski, T.: 1989, 'Neural Representation and Neural Computation', in L. Nadel, L. Cooper, P. Culicover, and R. Harnish, (eds.), *Neural Connections, Mental Computation*, Bradford Books/MIT Press, Cambridge, MA.

Dennett, D.: 1978, 'Artificial Intelligence as Philosophy and as Psychology', in *Brainstorms*, Bradford Books/MIT Press, Cambridge, MA.

Dennett, D.: 1987, 'Consciousness', in R. Gregory, (ed.), *Oxford Companion to the Mind*, Oxford University Press.

Ende, M.: 1983, *The Neverending Story*, Doubleday, New York.

Faggin, F. and Lynch, G.: 1989, 'Brain Learning and Recognition Emulation Circuitry and Method of Recognizing Events', United States Patent Number 4,802,103.

Fodor, J.: 1975, *The Language of Thought*, Crowell, New York.

Fodor, J.: 1981, *RePresentations*, Bradford Books/MIT Press, Cambridge, MA.

Fodor, J. and Pylyshyn, Z.: 1988, 'Connectionism and Cognitive Architecture: A Critical Analysis', in S. Pinker and J. Mehler, (eds.), *Connections and Symbols*, Bradford Books/MIT Press, Cambridge, MA.

Garfield, J.: 1989, 'The Myth of Jones and the Mirror of Nature: Reflections on Introspection', *Philosophy and Phenomenological Research* 1(1),1-26.

Grossberg, S. (ed.): 1988, *Neural Networks and Natural Intelligence*, Bradford Books/MIT Press, Cambridge, MA.

Grossberg, S. and Mingolia, E.: 1989, 'Neural Networks for Machine Vision', United States Patent Number 4,803,736.

Horgan, T. and Tienson, J.: 1989, 'Representation Without Rules', *Philosophical Topics* 15.

Humphrey, N.: 1987, *The Uses of Consciousness*, American Museum of Natural History, New York.

Jackendoff, R.: 1989, *Consciousness and the Computational Mind*, Bradford Books/MIT Press, Cambridge, MA.

Kienker, P., Sejnowski, T., Hinton, G., and Schumacher, L.: 1986, 'Separating Figure from Ground with a Parallel Network', *Perception* 15, 197-216.

Lashley, K.: 1956, 'Cerebral Organization and Behavior', in H. Solomon, S. Cobb, and W. Penfield, (eds.), *The Brain and Human Behavior*, Williams and Wilkins, Baltimore.

Lloyd, D.: 1989, *Simple Minds*, Bradford Books/MIT Press, Cambridge, MA.

Marr, D.: 1982, *Vision*, Freeman, San Francisco

McClelland, J. and Rumelhart, D.: 1986, *Parallel Distributed Processing, Volume II: Psychological and Biological Models*, Bradford Books/MIT Press, Cambridge, MA.

McClelland, J., Rumelhart, D., and Hinton, G. E.: 1986, 'The Appeal of Parallel Distributed Processing', in D. Rumelhart and J. McClelland, (eds.), *Parallel Distributed Processing. Volume I: Foundations*, Bradford Books/MIT Press, Cambridge, MA.

Nadel, L., Cooper, L. A., Harnish, R. M., and Culicover, P.: 1989, 'Connections and Computation', in L. Nadel, L. Cooper, P. Culicover, and R. Harnish, (eds.), *Neural Connections, Mental Computation*, Bradford Books/MIT Press, Cambridge, MA.

Rumelhart, D. and McClelland, J.: 1987, 'Learning the Past Tenses of English Verbs: Implicit Rules or Parallel Distributed Processing', in B. MacWhinney, (ed.), *Mechanisms of Language Acquisition*, Lawrence Erlbaum Associates, Hillsdale, NJ.

Sejnowski, T. and Rosenberg, C.: 1987, 'Parallel Networks that Learn to Pronounce English Text', *Complex Systems*, 1, 145-168.

Department of Philosophy
Trinity College
Hartford, CT 06106

INDEX OF NAMES

INDEX OF SUBJECTS

STUDIES IN COGNITIVE SYSTEMS

Series Editor: James H. Fetzer, *University of Minnesota, Duluth*

KLUWER ACADEMIC PUBLISHERS – DORDRECHT / BOSTON / LONDON